ArtScroll Mishnah Series®

*A rabbinic commentary to the Six Orders of the Mishnah*

Rabbi Nosson Scherman / Rabbi Meir Zlotowitz

*General Editors*

A PROJECT OF THE

# Mesorah Heritage Foundation

THE COMMENTARY HAS BEEN NAMED **YAD AVRAHAM**
AS AN EVERLASTING MEMORIAL AND SOURCE OF MERIT
FOR THE *NESHAMAH* OF
אברהם יוסף ע״ה בן הר״ר אליעזר הכהן גליק נ״י
**AVRAHAM YOSEF GLICK** ע״ה
WHOSE LIFE WAS CUT SHORT ON 3 TEVES, 5735

*Published by*
Mesorah Publications, ltd

# the mishnah

**ARTSCROLL MISHNAH SERIES** / A NEW TRANSLATION WITH A COMMENTARY **YAD AVRAHAM** ANTHOLOGIZED FROM TALMUDIC SOURCES AND CLASSIC COMMENTATORS.

INCLUDES THE COMPLETE HEBREW TEXT OF THE COMMENTARY OF **RAV OVADIAH BERTINORO**

FIRST EDITION
*First Impression . . . January 1989*

REVISED EDITION
*First Impression . . . February 2008*
*Second Impression . . . January 2011*

*Published and Distributed by*
**MESORAH PUBLICATIONS, Ltd.**
Brooklyn, New York 11232

*Distributed in Europe by*
**LEHMANNS**
Unit E, Viking Business Park
Rolling Mill Road
Jarrow, Tyne & Wear NE32 3DP
England

*Distributed in Australia & New Zealand by*
**GOLDS WORLD OF JUDAICA**
3-13 William Street
Balaclava, Melbourne 3183
Victoria Australia

*Distributed in Israel by*
**SIFRIATI / A. GITLER — BOOKS**
6 Hayarkon Street
Bnei Brak 51127

*Distributed in South Africa by*
**KOLLEL BOOKSHOP**
Ivy Common 105 William Road
Norwood 2192, Johannesburg, South Africa

---

**THE ARTSCROLL MISHNAH SERIES®**
**SEDER KODASHIM Vol. I(b); *MENACHOS***


*4401 Second Avenue / Brooklyn, N.Y. 11232 / (718) 921-9000 / www.artscroll.com*

---



ISBN 10: 0-89906-303-9
ISBN 13: 978-0-89906-303-4

*Typography by Compuscribe at* ArtScroll Studios, Ltd.
*4401 Second Avenue / Brooklyn, NY 11232 / (718) 921-9000*

Printed in the United States of America by Noble Book Press
Bound by Sefercraft Inc., Quality Bookbinders, Brooklyn, N.Y.

## ☙ Seder Kodashim Vol. I (b):

## מסכת מנחות
## Tractate Menachos

*The Publishers are grateful to*

YAD AVRAHAM INSTITUTE

*and the*

MESORAH HERITAGE FOUNDATION

*for their efforts in the publication of the*

ARTSCROLL MISHNAH SERIES

לֹא נֶאֱמַר נֶפֶשׁ בְּכָל קָרְבְּנוֹת נְדָבָה אֶלָּא בְמִנְחָה . . .
אָמַר הַקָּבָּ״ה מַעֲלֶה אֲנִי עָלָיו כְּאִילוּ הִקְרִיב נַפְשׁוֹ.

*The word "soul" is not said regarding any voluntary offering except for the minchah . . . The Holy One Blessed is He said, "I regard it as if he had offered his soul to Me* (*Menachos* 104b).

*This volume is dedicated to the memory of*

**שמעון בן משה עמוס ע״ה**

**Simon Amos**

January 26, 1972 / י׳ שבט תשל״ב

*Simon Amos made his soul an*
*offering to the One Above.*
*All his life he longed for the privilege of living in Zion.*
*When he moved from Morocco to his cherished goal,*
*he kept alive the ideals that brought him there:*
*faith in his Maker*
*and love of his fellow Jew,*
*truth and kindness and good nature.*
*He brought goodness to his Land,*
*and his Land gave holiness to him.*

**תנצב״ה**

# PATRONS OF THE MISHNAH

With generosity, vision, and devotion to the perpetuation of Torah study, the following patrons have dedicated individual volumes of the Mishnah.

## SEDER ZERAIM

BERACHOS:

In memory of

**ר׳ אברהם יוסף ז״ל ב״ר אליעזר הכהן ודבורה נ״י**

**Avraham Yosef Glick ז״ל**

PEAH:

In memory of

**הגאון הרב ר׳ אהרן ב״ר מאיר יעקב זצ״ל**

**Rabbi Aron Zlotowitz זצ״ל**

**והרבנית פרומא בת ר׳ חיים צבי ע״ה**

**Rebbetzin Fruma Zlotowitz ע״ה**

DEMAI:

**Chesky and Sheindy Paneth and family**

In memory of their parents

ר׳ אברהם מרדכי בן ר׳ שרגא פייוועל ז״ל – Avrohom Mordechai Mendlowitz ז״ל

ר׳ יעקב חיים בן ר׳ יחזקאל ז״ל – Yaakov Chaim Paneth ז״ל

and in memory of his brother

ר׳ משולם בן ר׳ יעקב חיים ז״ל – Meshulam Paneth ז״ל

**Moshe and Esther Beinhorn and family**

In memory of their grandparents

ר׳ ישראל מרדכי ב״ר חיים צבי הי״ד וזוג׳ פעסיל ב״ר משה הי״ד

ר׳ משה ב״ר שלום יוסף הי״ד וזוג׳ איידיל ב״ר יהודה אריה ע״ה

ר׳ יחיאל מיכל ב״ר אברהם זאב הי״ד וזוג׳ שיינדל ב״ר יוסף הי״ד

ר׳ יצחק ב״ר משה הי״ד וזוג׳ לאה גיטל ב״ר חיים עזרא הי״ד

KILAYIM:

**Mr. and Mrs. Louis Glick**

In memory of

יעקב מאיר חיים בן אפרים אליעזר הכהן ז״ל – Jerome Schottenstein ז״ל

SHEVIIS:

In memory of

**ר׳ אריה לייב בן שמואל יוסף ז״ל**

**Aryeh Leib Pluchenik ז״ל**

TERUMOS:

**Benzi and Esther Dunner**

In memory of their grandparents

ר׳ אורי יהודה ב״ר אברהם אריה ז״ל וזוג׳ מרת רבקה בת שרה ע״ה

# PATRONS OF THE MISHNAH

MAASROS, MAASER SHENI:

**Barry and Sipora Buls and Family**

In memory of our parents

אברהם בן מרדכי ז״ל   חיה שיינדל בת חיים צבי ע״ה

Abraham and Jeanette Buls ע״ה

אלטר חיים משולם בן יעקב ז״ל   אסתר בת ראובן ע״ה

Meshulam and Esther Kluger ע״ה

and in memory of our grandparents

מרדכי בן אברהם יצחק ז״ל וזוג׳ רבקה בת אברהם ע״ה – בולס

חיים צבי בן דוד ז״ל וזוג׳ פיגא בת יצחק ע״ה – מאשקאוויטש

יעקב ז״ל הי״ד וזוג׳ טאבא ע״ה הי״ד – קלוגר

ראובן ז״ל הי״ד וזוג׳ פיגא בת יחזקאל נתן ע״ה הי״ד – שעכטר־בירנבוים

CHALLAH, ORLAH, BIKKURIM:

**Yossi and Linda Segel   Danny and Shani Segel   and families**

In memory of their father

ר׳ ברוך בן ר׳ יוסף הלוי ז״ל – Baruch Segel ז״ל

**Chesky and Sheindy Paneth and family**

In memory of their parents

ר׳ אברהם מרדכי בן ר׳ שרגא פייוועל ז״ל – Avrohom Mordechai Mendlowitz ז״ל

ר׳ יעקב חיים בן ר׳ יחזקאל ז״ל – Yaakov Chaim Paneth ז״ל

and in memory of his brother

ר׳ משולם בן ר׳ יעקב חיים ז״ל – Meshulam Paneth ז״ל

**Moshe and Esther Beinhorn and family**

In memory of their uncle

ר׳ אברהם זאב בן ר׳ יחיאל מיכל ז״ל – Avrohom Beinhorn ז״ל

## SEDER MOED

SHABBOS:

**Mr. and Mrs. Philip Amin**

**Mr. and Mrs. Lee R. Furman**

In memory of their son and brother

קלמן בן ר׳ פסח ז״ל – Kalman Amin ז״ל

ERUVIN:

**Mr. and Mrs. Lawrence M. Rosenberg**

In honor of their parents

ר׳ גרשון בן ר׳ יהודה ומרת שרה שיינא בת דוב בערל עמו״ש

Judge and Mrs. Gustave Rosenberg עמו״ש

and in memory of their brother and sister

אברהם דוד ודבורה חאשא חוה בני ר׳ גרשון

# PATRONS OF THE MISHNAH

BEITZAH:

**Mr. and Mrs. Herman Wouk**

In memory of their בכור and ילד שעשועים

אברהם יצחק ע״ה בן חיים אביעזר זעליג נ״י

PESACHIM:

**Mr. and Mrs. Leonard A. Kestenbaum**

In memory of their father ר׳ דוד ב״ר אליהו זצ״ל – David Kestenbaum זצ״ל

SHEKALIM:

In memory of **ר׳ יוסף דוד ב״ר משה גאלדוואררם זללה״ה**

ROSH HASHANAH, YOMA, SUCCAH:

**ר׳ יוסף שמעון בן חיים ע״ה – 1st Lt. Joseph Simon Bravin ע״ה**

TAANIS, MEGILLAH, MOED KATAN, CHAGIGAH:

In memory of

**מו״ר הרה״ג ר׳ גדליה הלוי שארר זצ״ל**

**HaGaon HaRav Gedalia Halevi Schorr זצ״ל**

## SEDER NASHIM

YEVAMOS:

**David and Rochelle Hirsch**

In memory of their father Mr. Henry Hirsch ז״ל

KESUBOS:

In memory of

**מרת בילא בת ר׳ צבי מאיר ע״ה – Mrs. Bertha Steinmetz ע״ה**

NEDARIM:

**The Knoll Family** (Israel and Venezuela)

In memory of their parents

ר׳ צבי הירש בן ר׳ שרגא פייוול ע״ה

ומרת פעסיא דבורה בת ר׳ יעקב דוד ע״ה

NAZIR:

In memory of

**יוטא ע״ה בת ר׳ יקותיאל יהודה לאי״ט – Yitty Leibel ע״ה**

SOTAH:

In honor of the

**Fifth Avenue Synagogue**

GITTIN, KIDDUSHIN:

**Bruce and Ruth Rappaport**

In memory of his parents

ר׳ יששכר ב״ר יעקב ז״ל

ומרת בלומא שושנה בת ר׳ ברוך ע״ה

# PATRONS OF THE MISHNAH

## SEDER NEZIKIN

BAVA KAMMA:

In memory of

**הרב שמעון ב״ר נחמיה הלוי ז״ל**

**Rabbi Shimon Zweig ז״ל**

BAVA METZIA:

**The Steinmetz family**

In memory of their parents

ר׳ שמעון ב״ר שאול יהודה ז״ל

וזוגתו בילא בת ר׳ צבי מאיר ע״ה

BAVA BASRA:

In memory of

**ר׳ יצחק מאיר ב״ר משה ז״ל – Mr. Irving Bunim ז״ל**

SANHEDRIN:

**The Zweig and Steinmetz families**

In memory of

**סימא בת ר׳ שמעון ע״ה – Sima Rabinowitz ע״ה**

MAKKOS, SHEVUOS:

In memory of

**יהושע יצחק ז״ל בן אברהם מאיר נ״י – Joshua Waitman ז״ל**

EDUYOS:

**Mr. and Mrs. Woli and**
**Chaja Stern** (Saõ Paulo, Brazil)

In honor of their children

Jacques and Ariane Stern  Jaime and Ariela Landau

Michael and Annete Kierszenbaum

AVODAH ZARAH, HORAYOS:

In memory of our Rebbe

**מור״ר שרגא פייבל בן ר׳ משה זצ״ל**

**Reb Shraga Feivel Mendlowitz זצ״ל**

AVOS:

**Mr. Louis Glick  Mr. and Mrs. Sidney Glick**

**Mr. and Mrs. Mortimer Sklarin**

In memory of their beloved mother

מרת רבקה בת ר׳ משה גליק ע״ה – Mrs. Regina Glick ע״ה

**Mr. Louis Glick  Shimon and Mina Glick and family**

**Shimon and Esti Pluchenik and family**

In memory of their beloved wife, mother and grandmother

מרת דבורה בת ר׳ שמעון גליק ע״ה – Mrs. Doris Glick ע״ה

# PATRONS OF THE MISHNAH

## SEDER KODASHIM

ZEVACHIM:

**Mr. and Mrs. Richard Hirsch**

In memory of their son

הילד אליעזר ז״ל בן יהודה זליג שיחי׳ — Lawrence A. Hirsch ז״ל

MENACHOS:

In memory of

**שמעון בן משה עמוס ז״ל – Simon Amos ז״ל**

CHULLIN:

**The Steinmetz and Barouch families**

In memory of

רבקה עטיה בת ר׳ שמעון ע״ה — Ruth Barouch ע״ה

BECHOROS:

**Yad Avraham Institute**

In honor of

Bruce and Ruth Rappaport

ARACHIN:

In memory of

**גילה מסעודה ע״ה בת ר׳ יעקב נ״י**

**Gillah Amoch ע״ה**

**דפנה ע״ה בת ר׳ יעקב נ״י**

**Amy Amoch ע״ה**

KEREISOS:

In memory of

**ר׳ דוד ז״ל בן ר׳ שמעון נ״י – David Litman ז״ל**

TEMURAH, MEILAH:

Baruch and Susie Singer and Yitzchak Ahron

Rabbi Eli Hersh and Rivky Singer

Rabbi Nussie and Ruchy Singer

Yossie and Surie Singer

Sruly Singer and Leah

In honor of

**Rebbetzin Bluma Singer שתחי׳**

In memory of

**הרה״ג ר׳ יצחק אהרן** בן הרה״ג ר׳ אליהו זינגער זצ״ל

נפ׳ י״ג טבת תשס״א

הרה״ג ר׳ אליהו בן הרה״ג ר׳ שמעון זינגער זצ״ל
וזוגתו הרבנית רייזל בת הרה״ח ר׳ יששכר דוב ע״ה

הרה״צ ר׳ ישראל אריה ליב האלפערן בן הרה״צ ר׳ ברוך מסאקאליוזקא זצ״ל
וזוגתו הרבנית שבע בת הרה״ג ר׳ אריה ליבוש ע״ה

## PATRONS OF THE MISHNAH

TAMID, MIDDOS, KINNIM:

**Hashi and Miriam Herzka Moishe and Channie Stern**
**Avi and Freidi Waldman Benzi and Esti Dunner**
**Dovid and Didi Stern Avrumi and Esti Stern**
In honor of our dear parents
**William and Shoshana Stern שיחי׳**
London, England

### SEDER TOHOROS

KEILIM I-II:

**Leslie and Shira Westreich**
**Adam and Dayna – Joshua Rayna and Dina**
In memory of
**Larry Westreich – אריה לייב ב״ר יהושע ז״ל**
and in memory of our parents and grandparents
**הרב יהושע בן מו״ר הרב הגאון יוסף יאסקא ז״ל**
**גיטל בת זאב וואלף ע״ה**

OHOLOS:

In memory of
**הרב יהושע בן מו״ר הרב הגאון יוסף יאסקא ז״ל**
**Rabbi Yehoshua Westreich ז״ל**
and
**Gerda Westreich – גיטל בת זאב וואלף ע״ה**

NEGAIM:

**Moshe and Esther Beinhorn and family**
In memory of
יוסף דוד ז״ל בן יצחק אייזיק
Yosef Dovid Beinhorn ז״ל

PARAH:

**Moshe and Esther Beinhorn and family**
In memory of their uncles and aunts
אברהם צבי, חוה, רחל, חיים עזרא, אריה לייביש,
ישראל ברוך, שמואל דוד, ומשה הי״ד, והילד שלמה ע״ה
children of
יצחק בן משה שטיינבערגער ז״ל וזוג׳ לאה גיטל בת חיים עזרא ע״ה הי״ד

**Chesky and Sheindy Paneth and family**
In memory of their grandparents
הרב יחזקאל ב״ר יעקב חיים פאנעטה ז״ל הי״ד וזוג׳ רחל לאה בת ר׳ אשר לעמל ע״ה
הרב חיים יהודה ב״ר משולם ווייס ז״ל וזוג׳ שרה רחל בת ר׳ נתן קארפל ע״ה
הרב שרגא פייוועל ב״ר משה מענדלאוויטש זצ״ל וזוג׳ בלומא רחל בת ר׳ שמעון הלוי ע״ה
ר׳ ישכר בעריש ב״ר אברהם הלוי לאמפערט ז״ל וזוג׳ גיטל פערל בת ר׳ בצלאל ע״ה

# Patrons of the Mishnah

MIKVAOS:

**Mr. and Mrs. Louis Glick**

In memory of his father

ר׳ אברהם יוסף בן ר׳ יהושע העשיל הכהן ז״ל

Abraham Joseph Glick ז״ל

NIDDAH:

**Moshe and Esther Beinhorn and family**

In memory of his beloved mother

טילא בת ר׳ יצחק ע״ה

Mrs. Tilli Beinhorn ע״ה

נפ׳ כ״ו טבת תשס״ח

MACHSHIRIN, ZAVIM:

**David and Joan Tepper and family**

In memory of their parents

ר׳ מנחם מענדל ב׳׳ר יעקב ז׳׳ל ומרת מינדל בת ר׳ אריה ליב ע״ה

Milton and Minnie Tepper ז״ל

ר׳ ראובן ב״ר נחמיה ז״ל ומרת עטיל בת ר׳ ישראל נתן נטע ע״ה

Rubin and Etta Gralla ז״ל

TEVUL YOM, YADAYIM, UKTZIN:

**Barry and Tova Kohn and family**

In memory of their beloved brother

הרב מנחם מנדל בן ר׳ יוסף יצחק אייזיק זצ״ל

HaRav Menachem Kohn זצ״ל

נפ׳ כ״ז מנחם אב תשס״ו

And in memory of their fathers, and grandfathers

ר׳ יוסף יצחק אייזיק ב״ר בן ציון ז״ל, נפ׳ י׳ שבט תשנ״ח — Josef Kohn ז״ל

ר׳ בנימין אלכסנדר ב״ר דוד ז״ל, נפ׳ ל׳ שבט תשס״א — Benjamin Wiederman ז״ל

and יבל׳׳ח in honor of their mothers and grandmothers שתחיי לאוי״ט

Helene Kohn Sylvia Wiederman

**הדרן עלך ששה סדרי משנה**

# הסכמה

RABBI MOSES FEINSTEIN
455 F. D. R. DRIVE
NEW YORK, N. Y. 10002

OREGON 7-1222

משה פיינשטיין
ר״מ תפארת ירושלים
בנוא יארק

בע״ה

הנה ידידי הרב הגאון ר׳ אברהם יוסף ראזענבערג שליט״א אשר היה מתלמידי החשובים ביותר וגם הרביץ תורה בכמה ישיבות ואצלינו בישיבתנו בסטעטן איילאנד, ובזמן האחרון הוא מתעסק בתרגום ספרי קדש ללשון אנגלית המדוברת ומובנת לבני מדינה זו, וכבר איתמחי גברא בענין תרגום לאנגלית וכעת תרגם משניות לשפת אנגלית וגם לקוטים מדברי רבותינו מפרשי משניות על כל משנה ומשנה בערך, והוא לתועלת גדול להרבה אינשי ממדינה זו שלא התרגלו מילדותם ללמוד המשנה וגם יש הרבה שבעזר השי״ת התקרבו לתורה ויראת שמים כשכבר נתגדלו ורוצים ללמוד שיוכלו ללמוד משניות בנקל בשפה המורגלת להם, שהוא ממזכי הרבים בלמוד משניות וזכותו גדול. ואני מברכו שיצליחהו השי״ת בחבורו זה. וגם אני מברך את חברת ארטסקרול אשר תחת הנהלת הרב הנכבד ידידי מוהר״ר מאיר יעקב בן ידידי הרב הגאון ר׳ אהרן שליט״א זלאטאוויץ אשר הוציאו כבר הרבה חבורים חשובים לזכות את הרבים וכעת הם מוציאים לאור את המשניות הנ״ל.

ועל זה באתי על החתום בז׳ אדר תשל״ט בנוא יארק.

נאום משה פיינשטיין

# מכתב ברכה


יעקב קמנצקי

RABBI J. KAMENECKI

38 SADDLE RIVER ROAD

MONSEY, NEW YORK 10952


בע"ה

יום ה' ערב חג השבועות תשל"ס, פה מאנסי.

כבוד הרכני איש החסד שוע ונדיב מוקיר רבנן מר אלעזר נ"י גליק שלו' וברכת כל טוב.

מה מאד שמחתי בהודעי כי כבודו רכש לעצמו הזכות שייקרא ע"ש בנו המנוח הפירוש מבואר על כל ששת סדרי משנה ע"י "ארטסקראל" והנה חברה זו יצאה לה מוניטין בפירושה על תנ"ך, והנה נקוה שכשם שהצליחה בתורה שבכתב כן תצליח בתורה שבע"פ. ובהיות שאותיות "משנה" הן כאותיות "נשמה" לפיכך טוב עשה בכוונתו לעשות זאת לעילוי נשמת בנו המנוח אברהם יוסף ע"ה, ומאד מתאים השם "יד אברהם" לזה הפירוש, כדמצינו במקרא (ש"ב י"ח) כי אמר אין לי בן בעבור הזכיר שמי וגו'. ואין לך דבר גדול מזה להפיץ ידיעת תורה שבע"פ בקרב אחינו שאינם רגילים בלשון הקדש. וד' הטוב יהי' בעזרו ויוכל לברך על המוגמר. וירוה רוב נחת מכל אשר אתו כנפש מברכו.

יעקב קמנצקי

# מכתב ברכה

YESHIVAT TELSHE
Kiryat Telshe Stone
Jerusalem, Israel

ישיבת טלז
קרית טלז־סטון
ירושלים

בע״ה — ד׳ בהעלותך — לבני א״י — תשל״ט — פה קרית טלז, באה״ק

מע״כ ידידי האהובים הרב ר׳ מאיר והרב ר׳ נתן, נר״ו, שלום וברכה נצח!

אחדשה״ט באהבה ויקר,

לשמחה רבה היא לי להודע שהרחבתם גבול עבודתכם בקדש לתורה שבע״פ, בהוצאת המשנה בתרגום וביאור באנגלית, וראשית עבודתכם במס׳ מגילה.

אני תקוה שתשימו לב שיצאו הדברים מתוקנים מנקודת ההלכה, וחזקה עליכם שתוציאו דבר נאה ומתוקן.

בפנותכם לתורה שבע״פ יפתח אופק חדש בתורת ה׳ לאלה שקשה עליהם ללמוד הדברים במקורם, ואלה שכבר נתעשרו מעבודתכם במגילת אסתר יכנסו עתה לטרקלין חדש וישמשו להם הדברים דחף ללימוד המשנה, וגדול יהי׳ שכרכם.

יהא ה׳ בעזרכם בהוספת טבעת חדשה באותה שלשלת זהב של הפצת תורת ה׳ להמוני עם לקרב לב ישראל לאבינו שבשמים בתורה ואמונה טהורה.

אוהבכם מלונ״ח,
מרדכי

# מכתב ברכה

RABBI SHNEUR KOTLER
BETH MEDRASH GOVOHA
LAKEWOOD, N. J.

בס״ד

שניאור קוטלר
בית מדרש גבוה
לייקוואוד, נ. דז.

בשורת התרחבות עבודתם הגדולה של סגל חבורת ,,ארטסקרול״, המעתיקים ומפרשים, לתחומי התושבע״פ, לשים אלה המשפטים לפני הציבור כשלחן ערוך ומוכן לאכול לפני האדם [ל׳ רש״י], ולשימה בפיהם – לפתוח אוצרות בשנות בצורת ולהשמיעם בכל לשון שהם שומעים – מבשרת צבא רב לתורה ולימודה [ע׳ תהלים ס״ח י״ב בתרגום יונתן], והיא מאותות ההתעוררות ללימוד התורה, וזאת התעודה על התנוצצות קיום ההבטחה ,,כי לא תשכח מפי זרעו״. אשרי הזוכים להיות בין שלוחי ההשגחה לקיומה וביצועה.

יה״ר כי תצליח מלאכת שמים בידם, ויזכו ללמוד וללמד ולשמור מסורת הקבלה כי בהרקת המים החיים מכלי אל כלי תשתמר חיותם, יעמוד טעמם בם וריחם לא נמר. [וע׳ משאחז״ל בכ״מ ושמרתם זו משנה – וע׳ חי׳ מרן רי״ז הלוי עה״ת בפ׳ ואתחנן]. ותהי׳ משנתם שלמה וברורה, ישמחו בעבודתם חברים ותלמידים, ,,ישוטטו רבים ותרבה הדעת״, עד יקויים ,,אז אהפוך אל העמים שפה ברורה וגו׳ ״ [צפני׳ ג׳ ט׳, ע׳ פי׳ אבן עזרא ומצודת דוד שם].

ונזכה כולנו לראות בהתכנסות הגליות בזכות המשניות, כל׳ חז״ל עפ״י הכתוב ,,גם כי יתנו בגוים עתה אקבצם״, בגאולה השלמה בב״א.

הכו״ח לכבוד התורה, יום ו׳ עש״ק לס׳ ,,ויוצא פרח ויצץ ציץ ויגמול שקדים״, ד׳ תמוז התשל״ט

יוסף חיים שניאור קוטלר
בלאאמו״ר הגר״א זצוק״ל

# מכתב ברכה

ב״ה

**ישיבה דפילאדעלפיא**

ב״ה

לכבוד ידידי וידיד ישיבתנו, מהראשונים לכל דבר שבקדושה

הרבני הנדיב המפורסם ר׳ אליעזר הכהן גליק נ״י

אחדש״ה באהבה

בשורה טובה שמעתי שכב׳ מצא את המקום המתאים לעשות יד ושם להנציח זכרו של בנו **אברהם יוסף ע״ה** שנקטף בנעוריו. ,,ונתתי להם בביתי ובחומתי יד ושם״. אין לו להקב״ה אלא ד׳ אמות של הלכה בלבד. א״כ זהו בית ד׳ לימוד תורה שבע״פ וזהו המקום לעשות יד ושם לנשמת בנו ע״ה.

נר ד׳ נשמת אדם אמר הקב״ה נרי בידך ונרך בידי. נר מצוה ותורה אור, תורה זהו הנר של הקב״ה וכששומרים נר של הקב״ה שעל ידי הפירוש ,,**יד אברהם**״ בשפה הלועזית יתרבה ויתפשט לימוד ושקידת התורה בבתי ישראל. ד׳ ישמור נשמת אדם.

בנו אברהם יוסף ע״ה נתברך בהמדה שבו נכללות כל המדות, לב טוב והיה אהוב לחבריו. בלמדו בישיבתנו היה לו הרצון לעלות במעלות התורה וכשעלה לארצנו הקדושה היתה מבוקשו להמשיך בלמודיו. ביקוש זה ימצא מלואו על ידי הרבים המבקשים דבר ד׳, שהפירוש ,,**יד אברהם**״ יהא מפתח להם לים התלמוד.

התורה נקראת ,,אש דת״ ונמשלה לאש ויש לה הכח לפעפע ברזל לקצוץ כוחות האדם, הניצוץ שהאיר בך רבנו הרב שרגא פייוועל מנדלויץ זצ״ל שמרת עליו, ועשה חיל. עכשיו אתה מסייע להאיר נצוצות בנשמות בני ישראל שיעשה חיל ויהא לאור גדול.

תקותי עזה שכל התלמידי חכמים שנדבה רוחם להוציא לפועל מלאכה ענקית זו לפרש המשניות כולה, יצא עבודתם ברוב פאר והדר ויכונו לאמיתה של תורה ויתקדש ויתרבה שם שמים על ידי מלאכה זו.

יתברך כב׳ וב״ב לראות ולרוות נחת רוח מצאצאיו.

הכו״ח לכבוד התורה ותומכיה עש״ק במדבר תשל״ט

אלי׳ שוויי

# מכתב ברכה

דוד קאהן

ביהמ״ד גבול יעבץ
ברוקלין, נוא יארק

בס״ד כ״ה למטמונים תשל״ט

כבוד רחימא דנפשאי, עושה ומעשה
ר׳ אלעזר הכהן גליק נטריה רחמנא ופרקיה

שמוע שמעתי שכבר תקעת כפיך לתמוך במפעל האדיר של חברת ארטסקרול – הידוע בכל קצווי תבל ע״י עבודתה הכבירה בהפצת תורה – לתרגם ולבאר ששה סדרי משנה באנגלית. כוונתך להנציח זכר בנך הנחמד אברהם יוסף ז״ל שנקטף באבו בזמן שעלה לארץ הקודש בתקופת התרוממות הנפש ושאיפה לקדושה, ולמטרה זו יכונה הפירוש בשם ,,**יד אברהם**״; וגם האיר ה׳ רוחך לגרום עילוי לנשמתו הטהורה שעי״ז יתרבה לימוד התורה שניתנה בשבעים לשון, על ידי כלי מפואר זה.

מכיון שהנני מכיר היטיב שני הצדדים, אוכל לומר לדבק טוב, והנני תקוה שיצליח המפעל הלזה לתת יד ושם וזכות לנשמת אברהם יוסף ז״ל. חזקה על חברת ארטסקרול שתוציא דבר נאה מתוקן ומתקבל מתחת ידה להגדיל תורה ולהאדירה.

והנני מברך אותך שתמצא נוחם לנפשך, שהאבא זוכה לברא, ותשבע נחת – אתה עם רעיתך תחיה – מכל צאצאיכם היקרים אכי״ר

ידידך עז
דוד קאהן

# Preface

אָמַר ר׳ יוֹחָנָן: לֹא כָּרַת הקב״ה בְּרִית עִם יִשְׂרָאֵל אֶלָּא עַל־תּוֹרָה שֶׁבְּעַל
פֶּה שֶׁנֶּאֱמַר: ,,כִּי עַל־פִּי הַדְּבָרִים הָאֵלֶּה כָּרַתִּי אִתְּךָ בְּרִית . . .״

*R' Yochanan said: The Holy One, Blessed is He, sealed a covenant with Israel only because of the Oral Torah, as it is said [Exodus 34:27]: For according to these words have I sealed a covenant with you . . . (Gittin 60b).*

*With gratitude to* Hashem Yisbarach *we present the Jewish public with* Menachos, *the second tractate in* Seder Kodashim. *The ArtScroll Mishnah Series is now half done,* baruch Hashem, *and work is proceeding on the remaining three* Sedarim. *All of this is thanks to the vision and commitment of* MR. AND MRS. LOUIS GLICK. *In their quiet, self-effacing way, they have been a major force for the propagation of Torah knowledge and the enhancement of Jewish life for a generation. The commentary to the mishnayos bears the name* YAD AVRAHAM, *in memory of their son* AVRAHAM YOSEF GLICK ע״ה. *An appreciation of the* niftar *will appear in Tractate Berachos. May this dissemination of the Mishnah in his memory be a source of merit for his soul.* תנצב״ה.

*By dedicating the ArtScroll Mishnah Series, the Glicks have added a new dimension to their tradition of service. The many study groups in synagogues, schools, and offices throughout the English-speaking world are the most eloquent testimony to the fact that thousands of people thirst for Torah learning presented in a challenging, comprehensive, and comprehensible manner.*

*We are proud and grateful that such venerable luminaries as* MARAN HAGAON HARAV YAAKOV KAMINETZKI זצ״ל *and* להבל״ח MARAN HAGAON HARAV MORDECHAI GIFTER שליט״א *have declared that this series should be translated into Hebrew.* Baruch Hashem, *it has stimulated readers to echo the words of King David:* גַּל־עֵינַי וְאַבִּיטָה נִפְלָאוֹת מִתּוֹרָתֶךָ, *Uncover my eyes that I may see wonders of Your Torah* (Psalms 119:18).

*May we inject two words of caution:*

*First, although the Mishnah, by definition, is a compendium of laws, the final halachah does not necessarily follow the Mishnah. The development of halachah proceeds through the Gemara, commentators, codifiers, responsa, and the acknowledged* poskim. *Even when our commentary cites the* Shulchan Aruch, *the intention is to sharpen the reader's understanding of the*

*Mishnah, but not to be a basis for actual practice. In short, this work is meant as a first step in the study of our recorded Oral Law — no more.*

*Second, as we have stressed in our other books, the ArtScroll commentary is not meant as a substitute for the study of the sources. While this commentary, like others in the various series, will be immensely useful even to accomplished scholars and will often bring to light ideas and sources they may have overlooked, we strongly urge those who can, to study the classic* sefarim *in the original. It has been said that every droplet of ink coming from* Rashi's *pen is worthy of seven days' contemplation. Despite the exceptional caliber of our authors, none of us pretends to replace the study of the greatest minds in Jewish history.*

*This volume was written by* RABBI MATIS ROBERTS, *mashgiach of Yeshiva Shaar HaTorah, who has contributed several fine volumes to the ArtScroll Mishnah Series. His manuscript was edited by* RABBI NAFTOLI KEMPLER, *of Yeshiva Torah Temimah, and* RABBI YEHEZKEL DANZIGER, *editor-in-chief of the Mishnah Series, whose work is well known from earlier volumes. Also contributing to this volume were* RABBI HERSH GOLDWURM, *whose encyclopedic knowledge was invaluable, andwho wrote the two appendices that appear at the end of this book; and* RABBI HILLEL DANZIGER, *who has joined our staff as a mishnayos editor.* MICHAEL HOREN'S *beautiful drawings add an extra dimension to this work.*

*We are also grateful to the staff of Mesorah Publications:* REB SHEAH BRANDER, *who remains the leader in bringing beauty of presentation to Torah literature;* RABBI AVIE GOLD, YOSEF GESSER, RABBI SHIMON GOLDING, YOSAIF TIMINSKY, MICHAEL ZIVITZ, MENACHEM BROGNA, LEA FREIER, SHEILA TENNENBAUM, MRS. ESTHER FEIERSTEIN, MRS. MENUCHA SILVER, MRS. SARA MALINE, ZISSI GLATZER, BASSIE GOLDSTEIN, MRS. FAYGIE WEINBAUM, MRS. JUDI DICK, *and* FAGIE ZLOTOWITZ.

*Finally, our gratitude goes to* RABBI DAVID FEINSTEIN שליט״א *and* RABBI DAVID COHEN שליט״א, *whose concern, interest, and guidance throughout the history of the ArtScroll Series have been essential to its success.*

*Rabbi Nosson Scherman / Rabbi Meir Zlotowitz*

י״ח שבט תשמ״ט / *January 24, 1989*
*Brooklyn, New York*

## ◆§ Note to revised edition

*We would like to acknowledge the contribution of the following individuals who worked on this revised edition, each in their own area of expertise: Rabbi Moshe Rosenblum, Rabbi Moishe Deutsch, Rabbi Yechezkel Sochaczewski, Rabbi Yitzchok Herzberg, Mrs. Faygie Weinbaum, Mrs. Chumie Lipschitz, and Miss Sury Reinhold.*

## ◆§ מסכת מנחות

## ◆§ Tractate Menachos

*Translation and anthologized commentary by*

Rabbi Matis Roberts

*Edited by*

Rabbi Naftoli Kempler

Rabbi Yehezkel Danziger

וְנֶ֗פֶשׁ כִּֽי־תַקְרִ֞יב קׇרְבַּ֤ן מִנְחָה֙ לַֽיהֹוָ֔ה סֹ֖לֶת יִהְיֶ֣ה קׇרְבָּנ֑וֹ
וְיָצַ֤ק עָלֶ֙יהָ֙ שֶׁ֔מֶן וְנָתַ֥ן עָלֶ֖יהָ לְבֹנָֽה׃ וֶֽהֱבִיאָ֗הּ אֶל־בְּנֵ֣י
אַהֲרֹן֮ הַכֹּהֲנִים֒ וְקָמַ֨ץ מִשָּׁ֜ם מְלֹ֣א קֻמְצ֗וֹ מִסׇּלְתָּהּ֙
וּמִשַּׁמְנָ֔הּ עַ֖ל כׇּל־לְבֹנָתָ֑הּ וְהִקְטִ֨יר הַכֹּהֵ֜ן אֶת־אַזְכָּרָתָהּ֙
הַמִּזְבֵּ֔חָה אִשֵּׁ֛ה רֵ֥יחַ נִיחֹ֖חַ לַֽיהֹוָֽה׃ וְהַנּוֹתֶ֙רֶת֙ מִן־
הַמִּנְחָ֔ה לְאַהֲרֹ֖ן וּלְבָנָ֑יו קֹ֥דֶשׁ קׇֽדָשִׁ֖ים מֵאִשֵּׁ֥י יְהֹוָֽה׃ וְכִ֥י
תַקְרִ֛ב קׇרְבַּ֥ן מִנְחָ֖ה מַאֲפֵ֣ה תַנּ֑וּר סֹ֣לֶת חַלּ֤וֹת מַצֹּת֙
בְּלוּלֹ֣ת בַּשֶּׁ֔מֶן וּרְקִיקֵ֥י מַצּ֖וֹת מְשֻׁחִ֥ים בַּשָּֽׁמֶן׃ וְאִם־
מִנְחָ֥ה עַל־הַֽמַּחֲבַ֖ת קׇרְבָּנֶ֑ךָ סֹ֛לֶת בְּלוּלָ֥ה בַשֶּׁ֖מֶן מַצָּ֥ה
תִהְיֶֽה׃ פָּת֤וֹת אֹתָהּ֙ פִּתִּ֔ים וְיָצַקְתָּ֥ עָלֶ֖יהָ שָׁ֑מֶן מִנְחָ֖ה
הִֽוא׃ וְאִם־מִנְחַ֥ת מַרְחֶ֖שֶׁת קׇרְבָּנֶ֑ךָ סֹ֥לֶת בַּשֶּׁ֖מֶן תֵּעָשֶֽׂה׃
וְהֵבֵאתָ֣ אֶת הַמִּנְחָ֗ה אֲשֶׁ֥ר יֵעָשֶׂ֛ה מֵאֵ֖לֶּה לַֽיהֹוָ֑ה
וְהִקְרִיבָהּ֙ אֶל־הַכֹּהֵ֔ן וְהִגִּישָׁ֖הּ אֶל־הַמִּזְבֵּֽחַ׃ וְהֵרִ֨ים
הַכֹּהֵ֤ן מִן־הַמִּנְחָה֙ אֶת־אַזְכָּ֣רָתָ֔הּ וְהִקְטִ֖יר הַמִּזְבֵּ֑חָה
אִשֵּׁ֛ה רֵ֥יחַ נִיחֹ֖חַ לַֽיהֹוָֽה׃ וְהַנּוֹתֶ֙רֶת֙ מִן־הַמִּנְחָ֔ה
לְאַהֲרֹ֖ן וּלְבָנָ֑יו קֹ֥דֶשׁ קׇֽדָשִׁ֖ים מֵאִשֵּׁ֥י יְהֹוָֽה׃ כׇּל־הַמִּנְחָ֗ה
אֲשֶׁ֤ר תַּקְרִ֙יבוּ֙ לַֽיהֹוָ֔ה לֹ֥א תֵעָשֶׂ֖ה חָמֵ֑ץ כִּ֤י כׇל־שְׂאֹר֙
וְכׇל־דְּבַ֔שׁ לֹֽא־תַקְטִ֥ירוּ מִמֶּ֛נּוּ אִשֶּׁ֖ה לַֽיהֹוָֽה׃ קׇרְבַּ֥ן
רֵאשִׁ֛ית תַּקְרִ֥יבוּ אֹתָ֖ם לַֽיהֹוָ֑ה וְאֶל־הַמִּזְבֵּ֥חַ לֹא־יַעֲל֖וּ
לְרֵ֥יחַ נִיחֹֽחַ׃ וְכׇל־קׇרְבַּ֣ן מִנְחָתְךָ֮ בַּמֶּ֣לַח תִּמְלָח֒ וְלֹ֣א
תַשְׁבִּ֗ית מֶ֚לַח בְּרִ֣ית אֱלֹהֶ֔יךָ מֵעַ֖ל מִנְחָתֶ֑ךָ עַ֥ל
כׇּל־קׇרְבָּנְךָ֖ תַּקְרִ֥יב מֶֽלַח׃ וְאִם־תַּקְרִ֛יב מִנְחַ֥ת בִּכּוּרִ֖ים
לַֽיהֹוָ֑ה אָבִ֞יב קָל֤וּי בָּאֵשׁ֙ גֶּ֣רֶשׂ כַּרְמֶ֔ל תַּקְרִ֕יב אֵ֖ת מִנְחַ֥ת
בִּכּוּרֶֽיךָ׃ וְנָתַתָּ֤ עָלֶ֙יהָ֙ שֶׁ֔מֶן וְשַׂמְתָּ֥ עָלֶ֖יהָ לְבֹנָ֑ה מִנְחָ֖ה
הִֽוא׃ וְהִקְטִ֨יר הַכֹּהֵ֜ן אֶת־אַזְכָּרָתָ֗הּ מִגִּרְשָׂהּ֙ וּמִשַּׁמְנָ֔הּ
עַ֖ל כׇּל־לְבֹנָתָ֑הּ אִשֶּׁ֖ה לַֽיהֹוָֽה׃

Leviticus 2:1-16

*When a person offers a minchah-offering to* HASHEM, *his offering shall be of fine flour; he shall pour oil upon it and place frankincense upon it. He shall bring it to the sons of Aaron, the Kohanim; he shall take from there his full kometz from it, from its fine flour and from its oil, as well as all its frankincense; and the Kohen shall burn its remembrance upon the Altar— it is a fire-offering, a pleasing aroma to* HASHEM. *The remainder of the minchah-offering is for Aaron and his sons; it is most holy, from the fire-offerings of* HASHEM. *When you offer a minchah-offering that is baked in an oven, it shall be of fine flour: unleavened loaves mixed with oil, or unleavened wafers smeared with oil. If your offering is a minchah-offering on a griddle, it shall be made of fine flour mixed with oil, it shall be unleavened. You shall break it into pieces and pour oil upon it — it is a minchah-offering. If your offering is a minchah-offering in a pan, it shall be made of fine flour with oil. You shall bring the minchah-offering that will be prepared from these and present it to* HASHEM; *you shall bring it to the Kohen who shall bring it near the Altar. The Kohen shall take from the minchah-offering its remembrance portion and burn it on the Altar — a fire-offering, a satisfying aroma to* HASHEM. *The remainder of the minchah-offering is for Aaron and his sons; it is most holy, from the fire-offerings of* HASHEM. *Any minchah-offering that you offer to* HASHEM *may not be prepared leavened, for you shall not burn [upon the Altar] any leavening or fruit-honey as a fire-offering to* HASHEM. *You shall offer them as a first-fruit offering to* HASHEM, *but they may not go up upon the Altar for a pleasing aroma. You shall salt your every minchah-offering with salt; you may not discontinue the salt of your God's covenant from upon your minchah-offering — on your every offering shall you offer salt. When you bring a minchah-offering of the first grain to* HASHEM: *from ripe ears, parched over fire, ground from plump kernels, shall you offer the minchah-offering of your first grain. You shall put oil upon it and place frankincense upon it — it is a minchah-offering. The Kohen shall burn [upon the Altar] its remembrance portion — from its flour and its oil, as well as its frankincense — it is a fire-offering to* HASHEM.

וְזֹ֥את תּוֹרַ֖ת הַמִּנְחָ֑ה הַקְרֵ֨ב אֹתָ֤הּ בְּנֵֽי־אַהֲרֹן֙ לִפְנֵ֣י
יהוָ֔ה אֶל־פְּנֵ֖י הַמִּזְבֵּֽחַ׃ וְהֵרִ֨ים מִמֶּ֜נּוּ בְּקֻמְצ֗וֹ מִסֹּ֤לֶת
הַמִּנְחָה֙ וּמִשַּׁמְנָ֔הּ וְאֵת֙ כָּל־הַלְּבֹנָ֔ה אֲשֶׁ֖ר עַל־
הַמִּנְחָ֑ה וְהִקְטִ֣יר הַמִּזְבֵּ֗חַ רֵ֧יחַ נִיחֹ֛חַ אַזְכָּרָתָ֖הּ לַיהוָֽה׃
וְהַנּוֹתֶ֣רֶת מִמֶּ֔נָּה יֹאכְל֖וּ אַהֲרֹ֣ן וּבָנָ֑יו מַצּ֤וֹת תֵּֽאָכֵל֙
בְּמָק֣וֹם קָדֹ֔שׁ בַּחֲצַ֥ר אֹֽהֶל־מוֹעֵ֖ד יֹאכְלֽוּהָ׃ לֹ֤א תֵאָפֶה֙
חָמֵ֔ץ חֶלְקָ֛ם נָתַ֥תִּי אֹתָ֖הּ מֵאִשָּׁ֑י קֹ֤דֶשׁ קָֽדָשִׁים֙ הִ֔וא
כַּֽחַטָּ֖את וְכָאָשָֽׁם׃ כָּל־זָכָ֞ר בִּבְנֵ֤י אַהֲרֹן֙ יֹֽאכְלֶ֔נָּה
חָק־עוֹלָם֙ לְדֹרֹ֣תֵיכֶ֔ם מֵאִשֵּׁ֖י יהוָ֑ה כֹּ֛ל אֲשֶׁר־יִגַּ֥ע בָּהֶ֖ם
יִקְדָּֽשׁ׃ וַיְדַבֵּ֥ר יהוָ֖ה אֶל־מֹשֶׁ֥ה לֵּאמֹֽר׃ זֶ֡ה קָרְבַּן֩ אַהֲרֹ֨ן
וּבָנָ֜יו אֲשֶׁר־יַקְרִ֣יבוּ לַֽיהוָ֗ה בְּיוֹם֙ הִמָּשַׁ֣ח אֹת֔וֹ עֲשִׂירִ֨ת
הָאֵפָ֥ה סֹ֛לֶת מִנְחָ֖ה תָּמִ֑יד מַחֲצִיתָ֣הּ בַּבֹּ֔קֶר וּמַחֲצִיתָ֖הּ
בָּעָֽרֶב׃ עַל־מַחֲבַ֗ת בַּשֶּׁ֛מֶן תֵּעָשֶׂ֖ה מֻרְבֶּ֣כֶת תְּבִיאֶ֑נָּה
תֻּפִינֵי֙ מִנְחַ֣ת פִּתִּ֔ים תַּקְרִ֥יב רֵֽיחַ־נִיחֹ֖חַ לַיהוָֽה׃
וְהַכֹּהֵ֨ן הַמָּשִׁ֧יחַ תַּחְתָּ֛יו מִבָּנָ֖יו יַעֲשֶׂ֣ה אֹתָ֑הּ חָק־עוֹלָ֕ם
לַיהוָ֖ה כָּלִ֥יל תָּקְטָֽר׃ וְכָל־מִנְחַ֥ת כֹּהֵ֛ן כָּלִ֥יל תִּהְיֶ֖ה לֹ֥א
תֵאָכֵֽל׃

Leviticus 6:7-16

*This is the teaching of the minchah-offering: The sons of Aaron shall bring it near before* HASHEM, *to the front of the Altar. He shall lift a portion from it in his kometz, from the fine flour of the minchah-offering and from its oil, and all of the frankincense that is on the minchah-offering; and he shall burn it upon the Altar for a pleasing aroma — that is its remembrance before* HASHEM. *What remains of it Aaron and his sons shall eat; it shall be eaten in the form of unleavened bread in a holy place; in the Courtyard of the Tent of the Meeting shall they eat it. It may not be baked as leavened bread, I have presented it as their portion from My fire-offerings; it is among the most holy offerings, like the chatas-offering and the asham-offering. Every male of the children of Aaron may eat it as an eternal portion for your generations from the fire-offerings of* HASHEM; *whatever touches them acquires holiness.* HASHEM *spoke to Moses saying: This is the offering of Aaron and his sons, which they are to offer to* HASHEM *on the day one of them is inducted: a tenth-ephah of fine flour as a continual minchah-offering; half of it in the morning and half in the afternoon. It should be prepared on a pan with oil, after having been scalded are you to bring it; a repeatedly baked minchah-offering, broken into pieces are you to offer it, as a pleasing aroma to* HASHEM. *The Kohen from among his sons who is anointed in his place shall perform it; it is an eternal requirement for* HASHEM; *it is to be burned in its entirety. Every minchah-offering of a Kohen shall be burnt in its entirety; it shall not be eaten.*

# General Introduction to Menachos

Tractate *Menachos*, the second volume of *Seder Kodashim*, deals with the laws of the flour-offering. This is a Temple offering whose prime ingredient is flour in either its raw form or as a baked or fried cake. Such an offering is known as a מִנְחָה, *minchah*[1] [pl. *menachos*].

Like its companion tractate, *Zevachim*, Tractate *Menachos* discusses a variety of offerings with a commonality of ritual. In many respects, *Menachos* parallels *Zevachim* (see especially Chapters 1 and 2), and in some instances even completes discussions relevant to the earlier tractate (see, for example, mishnahs 9:7,8 and much of Chapter 13). The most essential features of the sacrificial service of the flour offering have close counterparts in the animal sacrifice. In order to avoid unnecessary duplications, therefore, the following introduction will assume that the reader is already familiar with the basic laws of sacrifices, especially those relevant to animal offerings. These have been extensively outlined in the General Introduction to *Zevachim*.

## I. Comparison to Animal Offerings

### A: Similarities

As noted in the General Introduction to *Zevachim*, an offering is not, as a rule, burnt in its entirety on the Altar. Rather, a part of the offering is removed by a special procedure to be placed on the Altar, and this validates the entire offering and permits the remainder for consumption. In the case of the animal sacrifice, it is the blood which is the critical substance; its application to the wall of the Altar or its horns (depending on the type of offering) permits the burning of the sacrificial parts and the consumption of the remaining meat. In the case of the *minchah*, it is a small part of the flour and oil of the *minchah*-offering which is removed by the *Kohen* and burnt on the Altar. The burning of this portion validates the *minchah* and permits

1. The origin of the word מִנְחָה, *minchah*, is somewhat unclear. *Radak* (*Shorashim*) traces it to the root מנח, which would mean something *placed* or *set down*. This may be in the sense of something presented, since in addition to its sacrificial connotation, we find the word מִנְחָה used in Scripture in the sense of a gift (see *Genesis* 43:11, 25; see also *R' Hirsch* to *Lev.* 2:1). The afternoon prayer is known by this name because the time for its recital is the period of the day appropriate for the concluding offering of the day — the *minchah* which accompanies the afternoon *tamid*-offering (*Radak* ibid.).

its remainder for consumption. [In addition, most *minchah*-offerings are sprinkled with a substance known as *levonah* (frankincense); this too must be burnt on the Altar in order to validate the *minchah*-offering and permit its remainder.][1]

Furthermore, just as four essential actions — known as *avodos* — make up the sacrificial procedure for the animal sacrifice, so too there are four essential *avodos* which make up the offering procedure of the *minchah*. This will be elaborated below (section V).

Another point of similarity is the rule unique to the laws of *Kodashim* — that while all the commanded procedures are required (and not optional), they are not all essential to the validity of the offering; i.e., if they are omitted, the offering may still be valid. [See General Introduction to *Zevachim*, Section VII, B.] As with the animal sacrifices, the four *avodos* of its sacrificial procedure are all essential [מְעַכְּבִין]; i.e., the offering cannot be valid without them.

## B: Differences

There are, however, some basic differences between the animal sacrifice and its *minchah* counterpart. First, the animal sacrifice has three elements: the blood, whose application to the Altar is critical to the validity of the offering; the sacrificial parts (*emurin*), a combination of fats and internal organs which are burnt on the Altar (but whose burning is not critical to the validity of the sacrifice); and the meat of the sacrifice which is eaten by the *Kohanim* and/or the owner. The *minchah*, on the other hand, has no more than two components: parts that are burnt on the Altar [the small portion of flour (and oil) removed from the *minchah*, along with the *levonah*], and the remainder which is eaten by the *Kohanim*. All parts of the *minchah* designated for burning must be burnt for the *minchah* to be valid.

Another salient difference is that unlike the animal offering, the *minchah* requires an entire set of preliminary procedures to prepare the *minchah* for its actual offering. These procedures vary from *minchah* to *minchah*, as will be described below.

The discussions in this tractate fall under two categories. The opening chapters of the tractate (Ch. 1-4) focus on the *avodah* (sacrificial service) of the *minchah*. This is many ways an extension of the discussions of *Zevachim*. The second part of the tractate offers a discussion of the different types of *minchah*-offerings and a comparison of their preparatory steps. In addition, Chapters 3 and 4 digress to include a wide-ranging discussion of the details of the laws of numerous *mitzvos*, most notably *mezuzah*, *tefillin*, and *tzitzis*. These are only touched on in the mishnah but are dealt with at length in the *Gemara*.

---

1. There are also some *minchah*-offerings, however, which are completely burnt on the Altar, as will be explained. The comparison to animal offerings obviously does not apply to them.

# II. The Minchah's Ingredients

The majority of *minchah*-offerings contain three ingredients: flour, oil, and *levonah* (frankincense).

## A: Flour

A *minchah* must contain a minimum of one עִשָּׂרוֹן, *issaron* (one-tenth of an *ephah*), of high-grade wheat flour. An *issaron* is equal to 43.2 egg volumes [or between 86 and 153 ounces, depending on the various opinions for converting Rabbinic measures into contemporary ones]. This flour is refined until only the finest part of the kernel remains, and from this, the flour is made for the *minchah*. This type of flour is known as סֹלֶת, *soless* or *fine flour* (see mishnah 6:5-7 and comm. there).

Some *minchah*-offerings, such as the *minchas nesachim* (see below), contain two or three *issaron* of flour (*Numbers* 15:4-9), and a voluntary *minchah* may contain up to sixty *issaron* of flour (mishnah 12:4).

## B: Oil

A *minchah* generally contains one *log* (six egg volumes, or between 12 and 21.25 ounces) of olive oil, while a *minchas nesachim* contains either two or three *logs* of oil per *issaron* of flour, depending on the type of offering (see *Numbers* 15:4-9).

The amount of oil added to a voluntary *minchah* containing more than one *issaron* is the subject of a dispute in mishnah 9:3. According to the majority opinion, it requires one *log* per *issaron*.

## C: Frankincense

Most *menachos* also contain a measure of לְבוֹנָה [*levonah*], *frankincense*.[1] This is not mixed into the *minchah* (it is in fact inedible) but placed on top of it. The amount of *levonah* required is a *kometz* — the amount that fits into the middle three fingers of the hand when they are folded over the palm. [This is elaborated in greater detail in the comm. to 1:2.]

In addition to the ingredients mentioned above, water is added to the *menachos* which are baked or fried in order to make a dough (mishnah 5:2). There are also two *menachos* (the *minchas omer* and *minchah* of the *sotah*) which are made of barley flour and two *menachos* (the sinner's *minchah* and the *sotah's minchah*) which require no oil or *levonah*.

1. The Scriptural term לְבוֹנָה, *levonah*, is generally translated as frankincense. This is a resinous substance deriving from the sap of certain trees. This hardens into granules, which are burnt as incense. Whether the trees identified as the sources of frankincense are indeed identical to the ones from which *levonah* was taken is difficult to determine. However, *Aruch HaShulchan HeAsid* 19:8 cites from the *siddur* of *Shelah* that *levonah* indeed comes from the sap of a tree. See also *Tiferes Yisrael* in his *Chomer BaKodesh* (introduction to *Seder Kodashim*) 2:67. The commentary will refer to this simply as *levonah*.

# III. Categories of Minchah

There are two categories of *minchah*-offerings: voluntary *menachos* — those which are brought as the result of a personal vow; and obligatory *menachos* — offerings that are incumbent on either the individual or the community for any of a variety of reasons.

## A: מִנְחַת נְדָבָה, the Voluntary Minchah-offerings

The Torah lists five types of voluntary *minchah*-offerings:

(1) the מִנְחַת סֹלֶת, *minchas soless* (*fine flour*), which is offered in its raw, flour state;

(2) the מִנְחַת מַחֲבַת, *minchas machavas*, which is offered after it has been fried on a griddle;

(3) the מִנְחַת מַרְחֶשֶׁת, *minchas marcheshes*, which is offered after having been fried in a pan (see mishnah 5:8); and

(4,5) the מִנְחַת מַאֲפֵה תַנּוּר, *oven-baked minchah*. This latter type of *minchah* is baked directly in an oven, and it comes in two varieties: חַלּוֹת, *challos*, loaves baked with oil; and רְקִיקִין, *rekikin*, wafers baked without oil, but on which oil is later smeared (see mishnah 5:9).[1]

The designation of the type of *minchah*-offering to be offered generally takes place at the time of the initial pledge. The person declares what type of *minchah* he will bring by saying, "I take upon myself to bring a *minchas soless*," for example. Later he sets aside flour to fulfill his pledge by stating, "This is for my vow." He may also do this all in one stage by declaring, "This [*issaron* of flour] is for a *minchas soless*."

Should he simply pledge a *minchah*, without specifying which type, by declaring, "I take upon myself to bring a *minchah*," there is a dispute among the *Tannaim* whether he must bring a *minchas soless* or whether he is later free to designate whatever type of *minchah* he chooses (mishnah 13:1).

## B: מִנְחַת חוֹבָה, the Obligatory Minchah-offerings

In addition to voluntary *menachos*, the Torah also requires *minchah*-offerings of both the congregation and the individual on certain occasions:

### 1) מִנְחַת חוֹטֵא, sinner's minchah-offering

This is the *minchah* prescribed by the Torah (*Lev.* 5:11) for someone who has transgressed a prohibition which obligates him to bring a *chatas* for atonement, but who is too poor to afford the usual animal offering or its bird substitute. Not all *chatas* situations are amenable to this type of substitution; it is restricted to the specific prohibitions mentioned in *Leviticus* 5:1-14. [This *minchah* constitutes the lower end of the קָרְבָּן עוֹלֶה וְיוֹרֵד, *variable chatas-offering*.] It consists of wheat flour but has no oil or *levonah*.

---

1. The commentaries use the acronym סְחַרְרְחַר as a mnemonic for the five varieties of *menachos*: סֹלֶת, חַלּוֹת, רְקִיקִין, מַחֲבַת, מַרְחֶשֶׁת (*Tif. Yis.*. Introduction to *Seder Kodashim*).

### 2) מִנְחַת קְנָאוֹת, jealousy minchah

This is the *minchah* brought as part of the process connected with testing the *sotah* [married woman suspected of adultery] under the special circumstances described in the Torah (*Numbers* Ch. 5) and in the first three chapters of tractate *Sotah*. It is made from barley and likewise has no oil or *levonah*.

### 3) מִנְחַת חֲבִיתִּין, minchas chavitin

This is a *minchah* brought each day by the *Kohen Gadol*. It consists of one *issaron* of fine wheat flour kneaded and baked into twelve loaves. The *chavitin*-offering is brought in halves: six loaves in the morning and six loaves in the afternoon (*Ravad*); or according to others, twelve half-loaves in the morning and twelve half-loaves in the afternoon (*Rambam*) (*Lev.* 6:12-15; see mishnah 6:5 and comm. there).

### 4) מִנְחַת חִינוּךְ, inaugural minchah.

This is a *minchah* brought by every *Kohen* on the day he is initiated into the Temple service. Its procedure is identical to the *chavitin* (*Lev.* ibid.), except that it is not offered in halves but all at once (*Rambam, Maaseh HaKorbanos* 13:4).

As with all *menachos* brought by a *Kohen*, these two offerings are burnt on the Altar in their entirety.

### 5) מִנְחַת נְסָכִים [minchas nesachim], minchah of libations.

This is a *minchah* which is brought to accompany any animal *olah*- or *shelamim*-offering, whether voluntary or obligatory (such as the *mussaf* brought on the Sabbath and Festivals). The size of the *minchah* varies according to the animal of the offering — three *issaron* of flour and six *log* of oil for a bull, two *issaron* and four *log* for a ram, and one *issaron* with three *log* of oil for a lamb. It is also accompanied by a libation [*nesech*] of wine; the amount of wine per animal equals the amount of oil. In addition, the *chatas*- and *asham*-offering of the *metzora* also require *nesachim* (*Lev.* 14:10,20; mishnah 9:6; *Numbers* 15:1ff).

### 6) מִנְחַת הָעוֹמֶר, omer minchah

This is the communal *minchah* brought on the second day of Pesach (16th of Nissan). It is brought from barley harvested and milled in a special manner and it permits the consumption of the year's new crop of grain (*Lev.* 2:14-17; 23:9-14, mishnah 10:1ff).

## C: Additional Minchah-type Offerings

The *minchah*-offerings discussed to this point are all flour-offerings of which a part of the flour or prepared loaf is actually offered on the Altar. Our tractate also devotes considerable attention to four other baked items which figure in the sacrificial service, but of which no part actually comes to the Altar.

### 1) לֶחֶם הַפָּנִים, lechem hapanim

The Torah decrees that twelve loaves be baked each week and placed on the *shulchan*, the golden table which stands in the *Kodesh* (Holy) of the Temple Sanctuary. These twelve unleavened loaves of bread are accompanied on the *shulchan* by two spoons full of *levonah*. Each Sabbath day the breads and *levonah* are removed and replaced. The outgoing *levonah* is burnt on the Altar and the breads are eaten by the *Kohanim* (*Lev.* 23:10; mishnah 11:4ff).

### 2) שְׁתֵּי הַלֶּחֶם, shtei halechem

On the Festival of Shavuos, there is an offering of two communal *shelamim* lambs; these are accompanied by two loaves of leavened bread. Although these loaves do not undergo *kemitzah* and no part of them is brought on the Altar [indeed, it is forbidden to offer anything leavened (*chametz*) on the Altar], they are considered a sanctified offering because the Torah requires the *shtei halechem* (two loaves) to be "waved" together with the two lambs. [The rite of waving is known as תְּנוּפָה, *tenufah* (see mishnah 5:6).] This establishes a link between the *avodah* of the lambs and the status of the loaves. As a result the loaves cannot be eaten by the *Kohanim* until the blood *avodah* of the lambs is complete, and invalidations affecting the lambs carry over to the loaves as well (see mishnah 2:3; *Gem.* 46b,47a).

### 3) לַחְמֵי תוֹדָה, todah breads

The Torah requires that a *todah* (thanksgiving-offering) be accompanied by four varieties of bread consisting of ten loaves each. Here too no part of the loaves is offered on the Altar. Rather, the *todah* is slaughtered and offered, thereby permitting the loaves for consumption. One loaf of each variety is given to the *Kohen*, and the remaining loaves are eaten by the owner of the *todah*. Since the loaves become permitted through the offering of the *todah*, a link is established between them, which affects them in many ways. See mishnah 2:3 and Chapter 7 at length.

### 4) לַחְמֵי נָזִיר, nazir's loaves

When a *nazir* concludes his term of abstinence (from wine, hair-cutting, and contamination to the *tumah* of the dead), he must offer three animal sacrifices. Along with these, he must bring two types of breads: *challos* and *rekikin*. One loaf of each kind is waved with the thigh of the *nazir's* ram and then belongs to the *Kohen*. The remaining nine loaves of each variety are eaten by the *nazir* (*Lev.* 6:13ff; see mishnah 7:2).

## IV. The Preliminary Steps

Before the offering of a *minchah* can begin, its ingredients must be mixed and prepared, and it must undergo certain rites preliminary to its *avodah*.

### A: Preparing the Minchah

The different types of *menachos* are prepared in different ways. However,

the steps by which the oil and flour are mixed is the same for most *minchah*-offerings.

### 1) Consecration and measurement

One begins the process by verbally consecrating the ingredients to be used and measuring out the required amount of fine wheat flour and olive oil. There were measuring vessels in the Temple for measuring the flour and the oil precisely (mishnah 9:1) — too much or too little disqualifies the offering (mishnah 1:3, 3:5).

### 2) Mixing the oil and flour

A small amount of oil is poured into a vessel;[1] this is called מַתַּן שֶׁמֶן בִּכְלִי, *placing the oil in a vessel*; the flour is then added to the vessel. More oil is then poured on top of the flour, and the entire *minchah* is mixed together; this second application of oil, together with the mixing, is referred to by the mishnah (3:2) as בְּלִילָה, *mixing*. The mixture is then placed in a *kli shareis* (sacred Temple vessel).[2]

### 3) Processing the minchah

At this point the procedure for the *minchas soless* [fine flour *minchah*] and the fried and baked *menachos* diverges.

**(a) מִנְחַת סֹלֶת, minchas soless [minchah of fine flour]**

The *minchas soless* now receives its third application of oil: יְצִיקָה, *pouring*. All the oil that remains of its *log* is poured on top of the flour, and it is now ready for the addition of the *levonah* (see below).

**(b) מַחֲבַת, machavas, and מַרְחֶשֶׁת, marcheshes**

After the flour has received its second application of oil and been mixed with it in the manner described above, it is kneaded with lukewarm water,[3] but caution must be exercised that the dough should not become *chametz* [leavened] (mishnah 5:2). The oil is then mixed with the dough and fried[4] in either a *machavas* or a *marcheshes*. The *machavas* is a flat griddle which allows most of the oil to burn off, thereby creating a somewhat harder product. The *marcheshes* is a deeper pan which retains more of the oil, and whose product is therefore softer (see mishnah, 5:8).

The fried cake is then broken into pieces [this is known as פְּתִיתָה, *fragmenting*] and placed in a *kli shareis*, and the rest of the *minchah's* oil is then poured onto the pieces in fulfillment of the יְצִיקָה, *pouring*, requirement.

---

1. This follows the opinion of *Rashi*. According to *Rambam*, the oven-baked *challos* and *rekikin* did not have this step; all their oil is added in the בְּלִילָה stage; see comm. to mishnah 6:3.

2. This follows the opinion of *Rambam* (*Maaseh HaKorbanos* 13:5). Others are of the opinion that the oil and flour were initially placed and mixed in a *kli shareis* (*Tosafos* 9a, s.v. ריש לקיש; see *Kesef Mishneh*).

3. This follows the view of *Rambam* (*Maaseh HaKorbanos* 13:6). However, *Rashi* (74b, s.v. קודם לעשייתן) states that it was kneaded with water *before* the second application of oil. The oil is then added to the dough and mixed with it.

4. See footnote to the end of mishnah 5:8.

**(c) מַאֲפֵה תַנּוּר, Oven-Baked Minchah**

The *minchah*-offerings that are baked in an oven come in two forms: *challos*, loaves, and *rekikin*, wafers. Unlike the earlier *minchah*-offerings, these do not have a third application of oil. For the *challos*, the remaining oil is added at the time of the בְּלִילָה (*mixing*), prior to the baking. The *rekikin* are baked only with water and their oil is smeared on after the baking (*Rambam, Maaseh HaKorbanos* 13:8). This is called מְשִׁיחָה, *smearing*, and it replaces the בְּלִילָה, *mixing*, procedure (see mishnah 6:3).[2] These too are broken into pieces [פְּתִיתָה].

All these fried and baked *menachos* are baked in ten loaves (per *issaron* of flour) before being broken into pieces, except for the *chavitin* which is made into twelve (mishnah 6:5).

**(d) Obligatory Minchah-Offering**

The obligatory minchah-offerings are offered in their unbaked state. Thus, their procedure conforms to the *minchas soless*. The exception to this is the מִנְחַת חוֹטֵא, *sinner's minchah*, and the מִנְחַת קְנָאוֹת, *jealousy minchah*, which are offered without oil. Another exception is the *chavitin* of *Kohen Gadol*, which is dropped into boiling water after being mixed with oil, then kneaded and baked slightly, after which it is fried on a griddle (*Rambam, Maaseh HaKorbanos* 13:2,3; see *Mishneh LaMelech*).

### 4) Levonah

The *minchah* is now ready for its preliminary rites. At this point a *kometz* of *levonah* is placed on top of the *minchah*. The exceptions to this are the *minchas nesachim* (which contains oil but not *levonah*) and the *sinner's minchah* (which contains neither oil nor *levonah*) (mishnah 5:3).

## B: Preliminary Rites

The preparation of the *minchah* thus far does not require the involvement of a *Kohen*. The *minchah* mixture is now brought to the *Kohen* and undergoes the following:

### 1) תְּנוּפָה [tenufah], waving

This is a rite not required for most *menachos*. The only two full-fledged *minchah*-offerings requiring waving are the *minchah* of the *omer* and the *jealousy minchah* of the *sotah*. The *Kohen* takes the *minchah* (in the latter case, together with the *sotah*) and waves it to and fro, and up and down. Although required, this rite is not essential, and if the *Kohen* failed to perform it, the *minchah* is nonetheless valid. The two loaves which accompany the communal *shelamim* lambs [*shtei halechem*] also require waving (see mishnah 5:5,6).

1. According to *Rashi* and *Tosafos*, the oven-baked *minchah*-offerings did have the initial placement of oil in the vessel before the flour was added. According to *Rambam*, however, no oil was added to the vessel prior to the flour; rather, all the oil was added in the mixing or the smearing respectively. See *Mishneh LaMelech, Maaseh HaKorbanos* 13:8 and comm. to mishnah 6:3.

### 2) הַגָּשָׁה [hagashah], bringing near to the Altar

The *Kohen* takes the *minchah* and touches the vessel to the southwest corner of the outer Altar (mishnah 5:5; *Zevachim* 6:2). Nothing more is done in this rite other than to bring it near to the Altar. The *minchah* may now be removed from the immediate vicinity of the Altar. This rite is also not essential to the *minchah's* validity.

The *minchah* is now ready for its *avodah* to begin. Preparetory to this, the *levonah* is pushed to one side of the *kli shareis* in order to allow for the removal of the *kometz* of flour (and oil) without the admixture of even one grain of *levonah* (see below).

# V. The Avodah

## A: Minchah-offerings Which Undergo Kemitzah

The sacrificial service of an offering is known as its *avodah*. As already mentioned, there is a parallel between the *avodah* of the animal sacrifices and those of the *minchah*. Just as an animal offering has four essential *avodos* — viz., (1) שְׁחִיטָה, *slaughtering;* (2) קַבָּלָה, *receiving the blood;* (3) הוֹלָכָה, *conveying it to the Altar;* (4) זְרִיקָה, *throwing the blood on the Altar* — so too most *minchah*-offerings undergo four corresponding *avodos*. These are:

(1) קְמִיצָה [*kemitzah*], *removing the small portion of flour to be burnt on the Altar;*

(2) נְתִינָה בִּכְלִי שָׁרֵת, *placing the portion removed in a sanctified Temple vessel* (known as a *kli shareis*);

(3) הוֹלָכָה, *conveying it to the Altar;*

(4) הַקְטָרָה, *burning it on the Altar.*

The first *avodah* — the act of removal — is referred to as קְמִיצָה, *kemitzah.* The *Kohen* bends the three middle fingers of his right hand over his palm to form a cavity and then fills this cavity with the flour (or baked pieces) of the *minchah* and removes it from the *minchah*. The portion removed is known as the קֹמֶץ, *kometz*, and what remains is referred to as שִׁירַיִם, *remainder*. Removing the *kometz* from the flour corresponds to the slaughter of the animal in that it separates the essential Altar part from the body of the offering. Placing the *kometz* in the *kli shareis* corresponds to receiving the animal's blood in a *kli shareis* [both these acts serve to further sanctify the substance for its special role on the Altar]; transporting the *kometz* to the Altar and (and burning it there) is equivalent to conveying the blood to the Altar; and burning the *kometz* on the Altar corresponds to applying the blood to the side of the Altar. [These correlations have legal significance, as will be seen in Chapters 1 and 2.]

As mentioned above, the *levonah* (frankincense) also plays an essential role in the *minchah's* offering. After the *kemitzah* of the flour and the placement of the *kometz* in a *kli shareis*, the *levonah* is gathered up from on top of the *minchah* and added to the *kometz;* the two are thus conveyed to the Altar and

burnt together (*Sotah* 14b, *Rambam, Maaseh HaKorbanos* 13:12).[1] Before being placed on the Altar, the *kometz* is salted.

### B: Minchah-offerings Burnt Entirely

There are three types of *minchah*-offerings which are burnt in their entirety on the Altar. These are the daily *chavitin*-offering of the *Kohen Gadol*, the *minchas nesachim* which accompanies the *olah*- and *shelamim*-sacrifices, and any *minchah* brought by a *Kohen* (mishnah 6:2). No *kemitzah* takes place for these offerings; they are carried directly to the Altar, salted, and placed there for burning.

### C: The Remainder

Those *minchah*-offerings which have only their *kometz* burnt on the Altar have their remaining part eaten after the *kometz* has been burnt. This remaining part is known as שִׁירַיִם, *the remainder*. The *minchah* is considered in the category of קָדְשֵׁי קָדָשִׁים, *most holy offerings*, and can therefore be eaten only by *Kohanim*, and in the Temple Courtyard [cf. *Zevachim* 5:3,5].

## VI. נְסָכִים, Wine Offerings

Another type of offering which figures prominently in this volume is the wine *nesech* [libation]. This consists of a minimum of three *logs* of wine (mishnah 13:5). The wine is brought to the Altar in a *kli shareis* and poured into one of the two specially placed silver bowls [סְפָלִים] attached to the top of the Altar at its southwest corner. These bowls were punctured and the wine drained from them into a pipe leading to a deep cavity beneath the Altar. These cavities were known as שִׁיתִין, *shissin*. (See *Succah* 4:9, 48a,b; *Rashi* and *Tosafos* there).[2]

There are two types of wine offerings. The first is an obligatory offering to accompany an *olah*- or *shelamim*-offering. In this context it comes together with a *minchah*-offering [*minchas nesachim*] at a rate of six *logs* for a bull or cow, four for a ram, and three for a sheep. The second is as a voluntary offering. In such a case, a minimum of three *logs* is required.

❦ ❦ ❦

The details of the preparation of the various types of *minchah*-offerings are involved and subject to much debate. Aside from the classic commentaries

1. However, this view of the sequence may not be universally accepted; this will be discussed in the preface to mishnah 2:1 in a footnote, and in the comm. to mishnah 2:5. There is also a question as to which *avodah* the gathering of the *levonah* should be assigned, or indeed whether it constitutes an *avodah* at all. This too will be discussed in mishnah 2:5.

2. Others explain that wine dripped onto the Altar top and drained from there through a pipe in the Altar's top to the cavity beneath the Altar (*Rashi, Succah* 48b; *Rav* to *Succah* 4:9).

cited in this volume, several valuable works on the sacrificial service make a wealth of information available to the interested reader. Of special interest are עבודת הקרבנות and מבואי הקדשים in Hebrew. A recently published English booklet called *Korban Minchah* (M'chon Harbotzas Torah, Baltimore 1987) offers a pictorial guide to the *minchah* service, as well as many valuable footnotes.

# פרק ראשון ⁂
# Chapter One

Tractate *Menachos* deals with the rules of flour-offerings in all their various forms. [A flour-offering is known as a *minchah*; the plural of this is *menachos*.] Since all types of offerings share many features and rules, it is not surprising that some sections of this tractate parallel the discussions found in Tractate *Zevachim* in regard to animal offerings. In line with this, *Menachos* follows the format established in *Zevachim* by first delineating the factors that invalidate an offering.

The essence of any sacrificial offering is the placement of a part or all of its substance on the Altar. It is this which validates the offering and achieves atonement for its owner (thereby discharging his obligation), and permits the remainder of the offering (if any) for consumption. In the case of animal offerings, the atoning substance is the animal's blood (see General Introduction to *Zevachim*). In the case of *menachos*, the critical substance is the flour of the offering along with its frankincense.

In order to validate an offering, the portion of its substance used for atonement must be removed according to a carefully defined procedure. The procedures associated with removing and placing this part of the offering on the Altar are known as עֲבוֹדוֹת, *avodos* [singular: עֲבוֹדָה, *avodah*; this term may also be used to refer to sacrificial procedures in general]. Of these *avodos*, many are critical to the offering's validity [מְעַכְּבִין], and the failure to perform them invalidates the offering; there are others, however, which are commanded by the Torah but their omission does not prevent the offering's acceptance [אֵינָן מְעַכְּבִין].

*Minchah*-offerings follow this pattern as well. Most *menachos* are not burnt in their entirety on the Altar, and their validation therefore depends on removing a small portion of them to burn on the Altar. The portion removed is known as the *kometz* and the act of removal as *kemitzah*. The *avodos* which are critical to the validity of these *menachos* are the ones beginning with *kemitzah*. There are four critical *avodos*: (a) *kemitzah* (removing the *kometz* of flour), (b) placing the *kometz* in a sacred vessel [known as a *kli shareis*], (c) conveying the *kometz* to the Altar, (d) burning the *kometz* on the Altar (see General Introduction).[1]

For the *minchah* to be valid, these four *avodos* must be properly performed. At the same time, since these four are the only critical *avodos* of the *minchah*-offering, improper intentions invalidate the *minchah*-offering only when they are expressed during one of these four *avodos*, as mishnah 1 will teach.

---

1. This is in contrast to animal offerings, in which burning the sacrificial parts is not considered a critical *avodah*. Burning the *kometz* of a *minchah* corresponds to throwing the blood of the animal offering (*Gem.* 13b).

[א] **כָּל** הַמְּנָחוֹת שֶׁנִּקְמְצוּ שֶׁלֹּא לִשְׁמָן כְּשֵׁרוֹת, אֶלָּא שֶׁלֹּא עָלוּ לַבְּעָלִים מִשּׁוּם חוֹבָה;

**ר׳ עובדיה מברטנורא**

**פרק ראשון – כל המנחות. (א) כל המנחות שנקמצו שלא לשמן.** כגון שהתנדב מנחת מרחשת והביאה, וקמצה הכהן לשם מחבת: **בשרות.** ומקטיר הקומץ ושיריה נאכלים, שקמיצת המנחה במקום שחיטת הקרבן עומדת, וכשם שכל הזבחים שנשחטו שלא לשמן כשרים כדילפינן מקרא בריש מסכת זבחים (דף ב,א), הכי נמי כל המנחות שנקמצו שלא לשמן כשרות: **אלא שלא עלו לבעלים לשם חובה.** הוה מצי למתני ולא עלו לבעלים לשם חובה, והא דקתני אלא, דמשמע

**יד אברהם**

# 1.

The validity of an offering depends not only on the correct performance of its *avodah* [sacrificial service], but also on the intent of the person performing the *avodah*. One of the intents relevant to the validity of an offering is מַחֲשֶׁבֶת לִשְׁמָהּ, *intent for the designated purpose* of the offering; i.e., that the *avodah* be intended for the type of offering for which this sacrifice was originally designated. In the case of an animal offering this means that the *avodah* of an *olah*, for example, must be performed for the sake of an *olah* and not for a *shelamim*. In the case of a *minchah*-offering it means that the type of *minchah* known as a מִנְחַת מַחֲבַת, *minchas machavas*, be offered for this designation, and not as a מִנְחַת מַרְחֶשֶׁת, *minchas marcheshes*. [These terms will be defined in the commentary to this mishnah.]

Nevertheless, except for the exceptions listed in this mishnah (and *Zevachim* 1:1), an offering which is made for the sake of a designation different than its own remains valid; it is affected only to the extent that it does not fulfill the owner's obligation to bring this offering, as this mishnah will explain.

The rule given in this mishnah does not mean that the *Kohen* making the offering must actively intend it for its designation. Rather, as demonstrated by the *Gemara* in *Zevachim* (2b), סְתָמָא לִשְׁמָהּ קָאֵי, *the absence of intent is treated as intent for the designated purpose.* This means that if the *Kohen* performs any of the *avodos* without specifying for what type of offering it be, the offering is valid and fulfills the owner's obligation. An offering is affected by improper intent only when the person performing the *avodah* intends it for a designation different from its own. [See comm. at the end of this mishnah.]

כָּל הַמְּנָחוֹת שֶׁנִּקְמְצוּ — *All minchah-offerings whose kemitzah was performed*

[*Kemitzah* — the act of removing the *kometz* from the *minchah* — is the first of the four essential *avodos* of a *minchah's* offering (*Lev*. 2:2). The *Kohen* bends the middle three fingers of his right hand over his palm to form a hollow. The flour that fills this hollow is then removed from the *minchah* to form the *kometz* that is eventually burn on the Altar (see comm. at the end of mishnah 2 for a more detailed discussion).]

שֶׁלֹּא לִשְׁמָן — *for [the sake of] a designation other than their own*

The Torah defines various types of *minchah*-offerings. Whenever a person dedicates a *minchah*, he verbally designates which type of offering he means his offering to be. The *min-*

1
1

**1.** All *minchah*-offerings whose *kemitz*ah was performed for [the sake of] a designation other than their own are valid, but they are not credited to the owner as fulfillment of [his] obligation;

YAD AVRAHAM

*chah* is then supposed to be offered in accord with its designation, not a different one. The mishnah now defines the rule for a *minchah* offered not for its own designation, but for a different one. For example, the *kemitzah* of a מִנְחַת מַרְחֶשֶׁת, *minchas marcheshes*, was performed with the intent that it be for a מִנְחַת מַחֲבַת, *minchas machavas* (*Rav*).[1] [Both the *marcheshes* and *machavas* are *menachos* which are baked *before* their *kemitzah* (and then broken into small pieces). The *marcheshes* is prepared in a frying pan, while the *machavas* is fried on a flat griddle. The difference in preparation makes for a different consistency once the *minchah* is baked; see mishnah 5:8 for further explanation.]

The same is true if he offers a *minchah* with the intent that it serve as an animal sacrifice (*Zevach Todah*, s.v. שלא לשמן; see *Gem.* 2b).

The rule about to be stated by the mishnah also applies to an improper intent expressed during any of the other three essential procedures of the *minchah's* offering. The mishnah specifies *kemitzah* only because it is the first of these *avodos* (*Tos.*).[2]

Whether the mishnah means that the intent was expressed mentally or verbally is the subject of dispute among *Rishonim*. There is also a question whether the mishnah's ruling applies only to a deliberate misintention or even to an improper intention resulting from a mistake regarding the type of *minchah* being offered. Both these issues will be dealt with in the comm. at the end of this mishnah.

כְּשֵׁרוֹת, אֶלָּא שֶׁלֹּא עָלוּ לַבְּעָלִים מִשּׁוּם חוֹבָה; — *are valid, but they are not credited to the owner as fulfillment of [his] obligation;*

[The *minchah* is not disqualified by this improper intention. Therefore, the offering of the *minchah* continues, the *kometz* is burnt on the Altar, and the remainder of the *minchah* is eaten by the *Kohen*, as with any *minchah*-offering.] However, the owner's vow [or obligation] to bring a *minchah* is

1. [It is not entirely clear what it means that he offers a *machavas* for the sake of a *marcheshes*. By the time *kemitzah* is performed, the *minchah* has already been baked and it has therefore become either a *machavas* or a *marcheshes*. Any intention to alter the designation under these conditions would seem to be meaningless (see *Gem.* 2b).

It may be that this means that the *Kohen* offers the *marcheshes* to fulfill a previous obligation for a *machavas*. (The *Gemara* 3a in fact discusses such a case.) Another possibility is that the intent is to obtain for the owner of the offering the atonement inherent in the other type of offering. However, it is not clearly specified that different types of *menachos* achieve different types of atonement (although this may be implicit in the Torah's provision of different types of *minchah*-offerings).]

2. However, improper intention during the *avodos* of תְּנוּפָה [*tenufah*], *waving*, and הַגָּשָׁה, *bringing* the *minchah*-offering *close* to the Altar (see 5:5), both of which are performed prior to *kemitzah*, does not effect the validity of the *minchah* (*Tos.* 2a, s.v. כל המנחות). [Although their performance requires a *Kohen*, they are not essential *avodos* — i.e., their omission does not disqualify the offering.]

# חוּץ מִמִּנְחַת חוֹטֵא וּמִנְחַת קְנָאוֹת. מִנְחַת חוֹטֵא וּמִנְחַת קְנָאוֹת שֶׁקְּמָצָן שֶׁלֹּא לִשְׁמָן,

## ר׳ עובדיה מברטנורא

דכל דינה כמנחות כשרות אלא דבר זה, לאשמועינן דאסור לשנויי בה שינוי אחר, שאם עבר וקמצה שלא לשמה אסור לתת הקומץ בכלי שרת שלא לשמה: **שלא עלו לבעלים לשם חובתו.** ולא יצא ידי נדרו, וצריך להביא מנחה אחרת לשם מרחשת: **חוץ ממנחת חוטא.** כגון מנחה הבאה על טומאת מקדש וקדשיו, אם לא תשיג ידו לשתי תורים: **ומנחת קנאות.** של סוטה. שאם קמצן שלא לשמן, כגון לשם נדבה, או נתן בכלי שרת את הקומץ שלא לשמו, או הלך או הקטיר שלא לשמו, או חישב באחת מן העבודות הללו הריני עובד לשמן ושלא לשמן, אלו מנחות פסולות ואין שיריהן נאכלים. וטעמא הוי משום דמנחת חוטא חטאת קרייה רחמנא, ובחטאת כתיב (ויקרא יד,לג־לד) ושחט אותה לחטאת ולקח מדם החטאת, שתהא שחיטה ולקיחה, דהיינו קבלת הדם, לשם חטאת, ומנחת קנאות הואיל וכתיב בה עון, דכתיב (במדבר ה,טו) מנחת זכרון מזכרת עון, כחטאת שויוה רבנן. ומנחת העומר, אף על גב דלאו מנחת חוטא היא ולאו מנחת קנאות היא, קמצה שלא לשמה פסולה [מהקטיר], ואין שיריה נאכלים, הואיל ובאה להתיר החדש ולא התירה. וכל המנחות שנקמצו שלא לשמן כשרות דתנן במתניתין, דוקא במנחות שאין להם זמן קבוע איירי, ולא במנחת העומר שקבע לה זמן:

## יד אברהם

not fulfilled with this sacrifice, and he must bring another one (*Rav*).

This principle is derived in *Zevachim* (4a,b) by Scriptural exegesis from a combination of several verses stated in regard to the *shelamim*-offering. It is extended by exegetical analogy to include all other types of offerings, including *menachos* (*Tos* 2a, s.v. כל המנחות).

Although the offering remains valid and may be burnt on the Altar, it is nevertheless forbidden to offer any offering with improper intent. One who professes an incorrect intention during the critical *avodos* transgresses the negative commandment (*Lev.* 7:18): ... לֹא יֵחָשֵׁב, which is construed by the *Gemara* (*Zevachim* 29b) to mean, *he may not intend [a wrong intent]* (*Rambam, Pesulei HaMukdashin* 18:1,2; see *Mishneh LaMelech* there who notes that *Ramban* and *Rashi* cite a different verse as the source).

Moreover, from the mishnah's addition of the word אֶלָּא, *but*, [when the mishnah could simply have said וְלֹא, *and they are not credited, etc.*] the *Gemara* (2a) deduces that *only* in this way do they differ from properly brought offerings, but they are considered completely valid offerings in all other respects. Consequently, the *Kohen* must continue to perform the other *avodos* with the proper intention, i.e., for the original designation of this *minchah*.

The *Gemara* (2b) cites the opinion of the *Tanna* R' Shimon, who disputes the ruling of this mishnah and states that when a *minchah* of one type is offered as a different type of *minchah*, it remains fully valid. R' Shimon contends that since each type of *minchah* is of a different consistency as a result of its distinct method of preparation or its ingredients (see Ch. 5), the type of designation for which it is being offered is self-evident and a contrary intention cannot have any effect. In his view, the disqualification derived by the *Gemara* for incorrect designation applies only to animal offerings, since there is nothing in their *avodah* that contradicts the improper intention. The halachah, however, follows the view of the mishnah (*Rambam, Pesulei HaMukdashin* 15:2).[1]

1. See *Gem.* 2b where R' Ashi offers a way of reconciling R' Shimon's view with that of our mishnah.

1
1

except for the sinner's *minchah*-offering and the jealousy *minchah*-offering. [If] one performed the *kemitzah* of the sinner's *minchah*-offering or the jealousy *minchah*-offering for [the sake of] a designation other than their own,

YAD AVRAHAM

חוּץ מִמִּנְחַת חוֹטֵא — *except for the sinner's minchah-offering*

This refers to the *minchah*-offering brought for certain transgressions in place of a *chatas* (sin-offering) by one who cannot afford to bring the prescribed lamb or two birds for atonement. An example of this is the *chatas*-offering of one who entered the Temple or ate sacred food while *tamei* [ritually contaminated] (*Rav*). Such an offering is known as a קָרְבָּן עוֹלֶה וְיוֹרֵד, *variable chatas*, because the nature of the offering varies according to the means of the sinner. The other instances of this class of offerings are the other transgressions described in *Lev.* 5:1-10.

וּמִנְחַת קְנָאוֹת. — *and the jealousy minchah-offering.*

[This refers to the *minchah*-offering brought by a *sotah*, a woman suspected by her husband of infidelity. Under the circumstances described in *Numbers* Chapter 5 (see also *Sotah* Ch. 1), the wife is brought to the Temple to undergo a ritual of examination which includes this offering.]

If either the sinner's *minchah* or the jealousy *minchah* is offered for a designation other than its own, the *minchah* is completely invalidated and its offering must cease. Both of these are considered by the Torah as sin-offerings and they are therefore treated the same as the *chatas* (the animal offering which is brought to atone for sins involving *kares*). As taught by the mishnah in *Zevachim* 1:1, the *chatas* is completely invalidated by being offered for the wrong designation (*Rav*, *Rambam Comm.* from *Gem.* 4a).

Another exception to the rule stated in the mishnah is the מִנְחַת הָעוֹמֶר, *omer-minchah*, which is the *minchah* brought each year on the second day of Pesach to permit the new grain from that year's crops to be eaten (see *Lev.* 23:9ff; see below, Ch. 10). This, too, is completely invalid if not brought for its own sake. The *omer*-offering is not brought for atonement but to permit the consumption of the new grain. Since it cannot fulfill this function when brought with the wrong intent, it is automatically devoid of any validity at all. The reason it is not listed in the mishnah is because the mishnah is discussing only offerings which have no fixed time for their offering (*Rav*, *Rambam Comm.* from *Gem.* 4a).

This, however, is the subject of a dispute in the *Gemara*. *Rambam* in his Code (*Pesulei HaMukdashin* 14:3) accepts the opposing view (*Gem.* 5b), that since this offering is an unusual type of *minchah* (consisting of barley flour rather than the usual wheat flour, as well as other differences; see *Rashi*), the laws invalidating an offering because of improper intentions during its *avodah* cannot be said to apply to it (see also *Likkutei Halachos* 2b; *Zevach Todah* ad loc.).

מִנְחַת חוֹטֵא וּמִנְחַת קְנָאוֹת שֶׁקְּמָצָן שֶׁלֹּא לִשְׁמָן, — *[If] one performed the kemitzah of the sinner's minchah-offering or the jealousy minchah-offering for [the sake of] a designation other than their own,*

[The mishnah will now list different combinations of proper and improper

מנחות
א/א

נָתַן בִּכְלִי, וְהָלַךְ, וְהִקְטִיר, שֶׁלֹּא לִשְׁמָן, אוֹ לִשְׁמָן וְשֶׁלֹּא לִשְׁמָן, אוֹ שֶׁלֹּא לִשְׁמָן וְלִשְׁמָן — פְּסוּלוֹת.

כֵּיצַד לִשְׁמָן וְשֶׁלֹּא לִשְׁמָן? לְשֵׁם מִנְחַת חוֹטֵא וּלְשֵׁם מִנְחַת נְדָבָה. אוֹ

---

**יד אברהם**

intentions which invalidate the sinner's *minchah* and jealousy *minchah*. The mishnah defines this rule in terms of these two because it concerns their total invalidation; the same principle, however, applies to other types of *menachos* in regard to crediting them toward the fulfillment of the owner's obligation (see *Rav* to *Zevachim* 1:4).]

The first case listed is one in which he made the *kemitzah* for the sake of another designation; for example, for the sake of a voluntary *minchah* (*Tif. Yis.*).

נָתַן בִּכְלִי, וְהָלַךְ, וְהִקְטִיר, שֶׁלֹּא לִשְׁמָן, — *[or] he placed [them] in a vessel, or carried [them], or burnt [them] on the Altar for a designation other than their own,*

[Or, after removing the *kometz* properly, he placed it in a *kli shareis* (sacred vessel), the second *avodah* in a *minchah's* offering, for the sake of a different designation. Or he carried the *kometz* to the Altar, or placed it on the fire of the Altar with the improper intent. The improper designation of any of these four acts which comprise the essential *avodos* of a *minchah*-offering invalidates the *minchah*.] These four *avodos* parallel the four essential *avodos* of an animal sacrifice: the slaughtering, receiving of the blood, carrying of the blood to the Altar, and throwing it on the Altar (*Tos.* 2a, s.v. כל הזבחים, from *Gem.* 13b).

אוֹ לִשְׁמָן וְשֶׁלֹּא לִשְׁמָן, — *or for their own designation and a designation other than their own,*

He performed any of these four *avodos* with the intention that it be for the sake of that *minchah's* designation as well as for the sake of a different designation (*Rav*). Or, he had the proper intention while performing one of the *avodos* and an improper intention during another (*Tif. Yis.*). [The combination of intentions invalidates the same as an intention for the wrong designation, as the mishnah will state below.]

The same ruling appears in *Zevachim* 1:4 and *Pesachim* 5:2 in connection with animal offerings. In *Pesachim*, the *Gemara* (59b, 60b) notes R' Meir's principle (*Temurah* 5:4) that when two contradictory thoughts are included in one statement, the first is considered definitive and the second one is disregarded [תְּפוֹס לָשׁוֹן רִאשׁוֹן]. According to this view, if the *Kohen* intended the *minchah* for two different designations during one *avodah*, the second designation would be disregarded and the *avodah* would be considered to have been performed exclusively for the sake of the first designation. Thus in our case, in which the first intention was for the proper designation, the *minchah* would remain valid. The *Gemara* therefore says that if the mishnah's ruling is to be understood as consistent with R' Meir's opinion, it must refer to a case in which the two intentions were expressed during two separate *avodos;* for example, with the *kemitzah* being performed for the sake of the proper

1 [or] he placed [them] in a vessel, or carried [them],
1 or burnt [them] on the Altar for a designation other than their own, or for their own designation and a designation other than their own, or for a designation other than their own as well as their own designation — they are invalid.

What is [an example of] "for their own designation and a designation other than their own"? For the sake of a sinner's *minchah*-offering and for the sake of a voluntary *minchah*-offering. [What



designation, and the burning of the *kometz* for a different designation.[1]

However, R' Yose (ibid.) disputes R' Meir's principle and rules that when a statement contains two contradictory clauses, both are accepted as legally binding [אַף בִּגְמַר דְּבָרָיו אָדָם נִתְפָּס]. According to his view, our mishnah refers even to a case in which both intentions were expressed during the same *avodah*. [*Rav*, in explaining the mishnah to refer to two intentions in one *avodah*, obviously follows R' Yose's view, which is the one accepted as halachah (*Rambam, Hil. Temurah* 2:4; see *Tos. Yom Tov* to *Pesachim* 5:2 and *Yad Avraham* comm. there and *Zevachim* 1:4).]

או שֶׁלֹּא לִשְׁמָן וְלִשְׁמָן — פְּסוּלוֹת. — *or for a designation other than their own as well as their own designation — they are invalid.*

[In this case his first intention was for the sake of a different designation and his second was for its correct designation.] The mishnah teaches that we do not define his act by his final intention alone (*Rav*), but take into account his initial intention as well (*Rashi*).

כֵּיצַד לִשְׁמָן וְשֶׁלֹּא לִשְׁמָן? לְשֵׁם מִנְחַת חוֹטֵא וּלְשֵׁם מִנְחַת נְדָבָה. — *What is [an example of] "for their own designation and a designation other than their own"? For the sake of a sinner's minchah-offering and for the sake of a voluntary minchah-offering.*

[I.e., the *Kohen* performed one of the

1. The *Gemara* (*Pesachim* 60a) points out, however, that this part of the mishnah cannot simply be referring to two separate *avodos*, since that would merely be a restatement of the ruling that improper designation of even one *avodah* out of four suffices to invalidate. The *Gemara* therefore elaborates that according to R' Meir, the mishnah refers to a case in which the two intentions *concerned* two separate *avodos* but were *expressed* during a single *avodah*. In the context of *menachos* an example of this would be a case in which he removed the *kometz* for the sake of the proper designation, but with the additional intention of burning it for a different designation. This additional intention takes effect because of the principle of מְחַשְּׁבִין מֵעֲבוֹדָה לַעֲבוֹדָה, *intentions expressed during one avodah about another avodah are effective*. Nevertheless, the intention concerning the second *avodah* is viewed as having been expressed during that later *avodah* (burning the *kometz*), so that the two *avodos* are each viewed as being offered for a different designation. Consequently, even R' Meir concurs that both must be taken into account, and the *minchah* is therefore invalidated.

שֶׁלֹּא לִשְׁמָן וְלִשְׁמָן? לְשֵׁם מִנְחַת נְדָבָה וּלְשֵׁם מִנְחַת חוֹטֵא.

[ב] **אַחַת** מִנְחַת חוֹטֵא, וְאַחַת כָּל הַמְּנָחוֹת

ר׳ עובדיה מברטנורא

**או שלא לשמן ולשמן.** דלא תימא לשמן ושלא לשמן הוא דפסולה, דתפוס לשון אחרון, אבל שלא לשמן ולשמן כשרות, קא משמע לן:

יד אברהם

four *avodos* of the sinner's *minchah*-offering with the intention that it be for that designation and also for the sake of a voluntary offering.]

אוֹ שֶׁלֹּא לִשְׁמָן וְלִשְׁמָן? לְשֵׁם מִנְחַת נְדָבָה וּלְשֵׁם מִנְחַת חוֹטֵא. — *[What is an example of] "for a designation other than their own as well as their own designation"? For the sake of a voluntary minchah-offering as well as for the sake of a sinner's minchah-offering.*

[The *Kohen* first intended the *avodah* to be for a voluntary offering and then intended that it be for its own designation.]

The *Tanna's* illustration of the rule about combined intentions would seem to be unnecessary, since the rule itself is straightforward and does not require explanation. Perhaps the *Tanna* wishes to emphasize that even two such *minchah*-offerings, which are comparable in all ways except that the sinner's *minchah*-offering is not mixed with oil and frankincense, can still invalidate each other by being offered one for the sake of the other (*Tif. Yis.*).

The mishnah has to this point defined the invalidation for intending a *minchah* for the wrong designation. The same laws apply if the *Kohen* performed the *avodah* with the intent that it be for the sake of a person other than the owner of the offering (*Tos.* 2a, s.v. שלא לשמן).

There is a dispute among the *Rishonim* concerning the definition of מַחֲשָׁבָה, *intent*, in the context of this mishnah. According to *Rashi* and *Tosafos*, the mishnah means by this that the *Kohen* stated his improper intention verbally (*Rashi* 2a, s.v. כל המנחות; *Tos., Zevachim* 4b, s.v. מחשבה and *Bava Metzia* 43b s.v. מחשבה). Thus, a *minchah* would not be invalidated if the *Kohen* merely intended the offering for another designation without actually saying so.

However, *Rambam's* opinion seems to be that even if he does not express his intention verbally, the thought itself is sufficient to affect the sacrifice in the manner described (*Rambam, Hil. Pesulei HaMukdashin* 13:1, 15:1; see *Mishneh LaMelech* 13:1).

There is also a dispute recorded in the *Gemara* (49a) whether intent for the wrong designation affects the offering only if it was deliberate or even if it was inadvertent. *Rambam* (*Pesulei HaMukdashin* 15:1) rules that the improper intent takes effect only if it was deliberate. Therefore, if the *Kohen* mistakenly thought that the *minchah* he was offering was a *machavas* when in fact it was a *marcheshes*, the offering is not disqualified in any way.

Others dispute this ruling, and maintain that even an inadvertent intention is included in the ruling of the mishnah (*Or Zarua, Hil. Pesach* 232; see *Zevach Todah* 2a, s.v. ודוקא).

1 is an example of] "for a designation other than
2 their own as well as their own designation"? For the sake of a voluntary *minchah*-offering as well as for the sake of a sinner's *minchah*-offering.

**2.** The sinner's *minchah*-offering, as well as any other *minchah*-offering, whose

### YAD AVRAHAM

In the preface to this mishnah we noted the *Gemara's* statement that סְתָמָא לִשְׁמָא קָאֵי, *the absence of intent is treated as intent for the designated purpose.* There are two approaches to understanding this rule among the more recent commentators. One view is that there is indeed a requirement that an offering's *avodah* be dedicated to the purpose for which the offering was designated. Nevertheless, express intent is not necessary because it is implicit in the very nature of the offering that it is being offered for its designation. Thus, unless there is a contrary intent, the absence of intent is treated as equivalent to intent for the offering's designation (see *Kovetz Shiurim* of *R' Elchanan Wasserman* v.2, pp.41-43).

Another approach assumes that an offering's designation is essentially inviolate and does not require any active dedication during its sacrificial service. However, as we have seen in this mishnah, when an offering is made for both a correct and incorrect designation, the improper intention also takes effect and disqualifies the offering by its presence. By the same token, whenever an offering is made for the sake of an incorrect designation, the incorrect designation takes effect alongside the offering's proper, natural designation and thereby invalidates the offering (*Chidushei HaGriz,* to *Zevachim* 2 and to *Hil. Pesulei HaMukdashin* 4; see further, *Kehilas Yaakov* Ch. 2; and *Yad Avraham* comm. to *Zevachim*, end of mishnah 1:1).

## 2.

The following mishnah lists the qualifications and prerequisites for performing *kemitzah*, and the proper method for performing it. The mishnah will also present a dispute whether those who are unfit to perform *kemitzah* totally invalidate an offering by doing so, or whether it is only their *avodah* that is invalid, not the *minchah* as a whole. Thus, the *kometz* can be replaced in the *minchah* and a new *kemitzah* can be performed by an eligible *Kohen.*

אַחַת מִנְחַת חוֹטֵא, וְאַחַת כָּל הַמְּנָחוֹת, — *The sinner's minchah-offering, as well as any other minchah-offering,*

Although the rule which is about to be stated applies to all *menachos* whose *kometz* is taken, the sinner's *minchah* is specified in deference to the opinion of R' Shimon, who explains that the reason a sinner's *minchah* does not require oil or *levonah* (frankincense) is because the Torah considers it inappropriate for him to bring an elegant offering. One might consequently have thought that its status is inferior, and that those who are disqualified from performing *kemitzah* for other *menachos* would still be qualified to do so for this one. The mishnah therefore informs us that even such an offering must be made by one who is valid for other offerings (*Gem.* 6a).

# שֶׁקְּמָצָן זָר, אוֹנֵן, טְבוּל יוֹם, מְחֻסַּר בְּגָדִים, מְחֻסַּר כִּפּוּרִים, שֶׁלֹּא רְחוּץ יָדַיִם וְרַגְלַיִם, עָרֵל,

**ר׳ עובדיה מברטנורא**

(ב) **זר ואונן וטבול יום כו׳.** כלהו מפורשים בפרק שני דזבחים (משנה א), ומוכחינן להו מקראי דעבודתן פסולה: **ערל.** כהן שמתו אחיו מחמת מילה:

**יד אברהם**

שֶׁקְּמָצָן זָר, — *whose kemitzah was performed by a non-Kohen,*

A non-*Kohen* cannot perform the *avodah* of any offering [with the exception of slaughtering an animal offering (*Gem.* 19a; *Zevachim* 3:1)], as derived by the *Gemara* (*Zevachim* 15b). A non-*Kohen* is defined as anyone who is not a descendant of Aaron in the male line (*Rambam, Bias HaMikdash* 9:1).

אוֹנֵן, — *[or] an onein,*

One who lost any of the close relatives for whom he is obligated to mourn [i.e., his father, mother, brother, sister, son, daughter or spouse] is classified as an *onein* on the day of the death. At that time, he is forbidden to eat from sacrifices, and if he is a *Kohen*, he is forbidden to perform the *avodah*.[1] If he does perform one of the *avodos* of an offering, he invalidates it (*Rav* to *Zevachim* 2:1).

טְבוּל יוֹם, — [*or*] *a tevul yom* (lit., *one who immersed that day*),

One who becomes *tamei* [ritually contaminated] is forbidden to perform the *avodah*, eat *kodashim* [sacrificial foods], or even enter the Temple until he purifies himself by immersing in a *mikveh*. Even then, he must wait until sunset of that day before his purity is complete (*Lev*. 11:24). From the time he immerses until sunset, he is classified a *tevul yom* [literally, *one who immersed that day*]. At this point, he is considered *tahor* (purified) only in regard to non-holy substances (*chullin*), but he retains a residue of his earlier *tumah*. In this reduced state of *tumah*, he is still prohibited to eat *kodashim* (*Lev*. 22:7), and certainly to perform the *avodah* [or even to enter the Temple Courtyard] (*Rav* to *Zevachim* 3:1).

מְחֻסַּר בְּגָדִים, — [*or*] *who lacks vestments,*

The Torah specifies four articles of clothing which must be worn by a regular *Kohen*, and eight which must be worn by the *Kohen Gadol* [High Priest] (*Exodus* 28). When describing the procedure by which the *Kohanim* were first initiated by Moshe into their Temple role, the Torah concludes the passage describing the donning of their priestly garments (*Ex*. 29:9) with the statement: וְהָיְתָה לָהֶם כְּהֻנָּה לְחֻקַּת עוֹלָם, *and the priesthood will be to them for an everlasting decree.* From this the *Gemara* derives that their ability to function as *Kohanim* [in regard to performing the

1. On the Biblical level, the mourner is considered an *onein* only the day of the death. Rabbinically, however, he is considered an *onein* on the night which follows, and until nightfall of the day of the burial [if the burial is not on the same day as the death] (*Rambam, Bias HaMikdash* 2:9-10). Thus, during the later period he is Rabbinically forbidden to eat from the sacrifices or perform the *avodah* (ibid.). The *Gemara* (99b-100b) also records the view of one *Tanna* that the latter period of *aninus* is also Biblically forbidden.

1 *kemitzah* was performed by a non-*Kohen*, [or] an
2 *onein*, [or] a *tevul yom*, [or] who lacks vestments, [or]
who lacks atonement, [or] whose hands and feet have
not been washed, [or] who is uncircumcised,

YAD AVRAHAM

*avodah*] is only when their vestments are upon them [בִּזְמַן שֶׁבִּגְדֵיהֶם עֲלֵיהֶם כְּהֻנָּתָם עֲלֵיהֶם]. Without them, they have no more right to perform the *avodah* than a non-*Kohen*, and they therefore disqualify any *avodah* which they perform (*Zevachim* 17b).

By the same token, a *Kohen* who wears extra garments, or has something separating his garments from his skin, is also disqualified from performing the *avodah* (*Rav* to *Zevachim* 2:1 from *Gem.* there).

מְחֻסַּר כִּפּוּרִים, — [*or*] *who lacks atonement,*

Certain types of *tumah*-contaminations (namely, *zav, zavah, metzora,* and a woman who has given birth; see glossary) require that the person bring a sacrifice to complete the purification process (*Kereisos* 2:1). In all of these cases, the person must first undergo a prescribed waiting period, immerse in a *mikveh*, and await sunset, but it is not until the day after the immersion that he may offer the sacrifices which complete his purification (see *Lev.* 12:15). Accordingly, such a person's purification takes place in three stages. The immersion removes the *tumah* as far as *chullin* (non-holy substances) is concerned, nightfall restores *taharah* (purity) in regard to *terumah*,[1] but the person still remains *tamei* in regard to the Temple and *kodashim* until his sacrifices are offered (*Rav* to *Zevachim* 2:1).

שֶׁלֹּא רְחוּץ יָדַיִם וְרַגְלַיִם, — [*or*] *whose hands and feet have not been washed,*

The Torah dictates that the *Kohanim* wash their hands and feet with water from a special tank located in the Temple Courtyard before performing the sacrificial service (*Ex.* 30:18ff). [This tank is known as the כִּיּוֹר, *kiyor*.] The Torah (ibid. v.21) uses the same language to refer to this law as it does to describe the law of the priestly vestments — חֻקַּת עוֹלָם, *an everlasting decree* (see above). From this the *Gemara* (*Zevachim* 17b-18a) derives [through the hermeneutic principle of גְּזֵירָה שָׁוָה] that just as one is essential to the fitness of the *Kohen* performing the *avodah*, so is the other (*Rav*, ad loc.).

עָרֵל, —[*or*] *who is uncircumcised,*

This is derived by the *Gemara* (*Zevachim* 22b) from a verse in *Ezekiel* (44:9), which, in connection with the sacrificial service, compares the uncircumcised man to a non-Jew, implying that the former is as disqualified from performing the *avodah* as the latter.

*Rav* and *Rashi* are of the opinion that the disqualification extends even to a *Kohen* who has a legitimate reason not to circumcise — i.e., one whose older brothers died as a result of circumcision. Even though it is not permitted to circumcise

1. *Terumah* is the portion of the crop (of *Eretz Yisrael*) which must be separated from the produce and given to a *Kohen*. It may be eaten only by *Kohanim* (and members of their household) who are *tahor*. A *tevul yom* is considered *tamei* in this respect, but not a מְחֻסַּר כִּפּוּרִים, *person who lacks atonement.*

טָמֵא, יוֹשֵׁב, עוֹמֵד עַל גַּבֵּי כֵלִים, עַל גַּבֵּי בְהֵמָה, עַל גַּבֵּי רַגְלֵי חֲבֵרוֹ — פָּסַל. קָמַץ בַּשְּׂמֹאל, פָּסַל. בֶּן בְּתֵירָא אוֹמֵר: יַחֲזִיר

ר׳ עובדיה מברטנורא

**יושב.** דבעינן לעמוד לשרת. **על גבי כלים כו׳.** דבעינן שלא יהיה דבר חוצץ בינו ובין הרצפה: **בן בתירא אומר יחזיר.** הקומץ לתוך המנחה ויחזור ויקמוץ בימין. והוא הדין לכל הנך פסולים דחשיב במתניתין, סבירא ליה לבן בתירא שאם עבר אחד מהן וקמץ, יחזיר הקומץ למקומו ויחזור כהן כשר ויקמוץ. ואין הלכה כבן בתירא:

יד אברהם

such a person for fear that he too may perish, he is nevertheless disqualified from performing the *avodah* if he is a *Kohen*.

*Rabbeinu Tam*, however, contends that only one who was uncircumcised in violation of the commandment is disqualified; one who is permissibly uncircumcised is considered a victim of circumstances and his validity for the *avodah* is not affected (*Tos.* to *Zevachim* 22b, s.v. ערל, and *Chagigah* 4b, s.v. דמרבה).

טָמֵא, — [*or*] *who is tamei,*

[A person who is *tamei* is prohibited from performing the *avodah* (see above, s.v. טבול יום).]

Although there is really no need for the mishnah to list this case — since the mishnah has already stated that even a *tevul yom* who has immersed to purify himself from *tumah* cannot perform the *avodah* for the remainder of that day — the mishnah mentions it because it forms part of a common mishnaic grouping with the one *who is uncircumcised* [see, for example, *Yevamos* 7:1] (*Shitah Mekubetzes* #12).

One who is *tamei* also renders that which he touches *tamei*. It would therefore seem obvious that the *minchah* can no longer be brought, quite apart from the invalidity of the *kemitzah*, because the *minchah* has become *tamei* by its contact with the person. The novelty of the mishnah's ruling, however, is in the case of one who is *tamei* because he came in contact with a dead *sheretz*. Since he is not an *av hatumah* (source of *tumah*) but only a *rishon* (first level of acquired *tumah*), the person can only transmit his *tumah* to a foodstuff but not to a utensil. Moreover, he affects only that portion of the *minchah's* flour which he actually touches. Therefore, if not for the fact that his *kemitzah* invalidates the offering because he is disqualified from performing the *avodah*, it would still be possible to use the remainder of the flour which he did not touch to make a new offering (*Rashba*).[1]

יוֹשֵׁב, — [*or* ] *who is sitting,*

The *Kohen* must perform the Temple service standing, as stated in the verse (*Deut.* 18:5): כִּי בוֹ בָּחַר ה׳ אֱלֹהֶיךָ ... לַעֲמֹד לְשָׁרֵת, *for him [*the *Kohen] has Hashem chosen ... to stand and to serve* (*Rav* from *Zevachim* 23b).

עוֹמֵד עַל גַּבֵּי כֵלִים, — *[or] standing upon utensils,*

The *Kohen* must be standing on the floor of the Courtyard when he does the *avodah*, with nothing interposing [חוֹצֵץ] between his bare feet and the floor (*Rav*). This is derived in the *Gemara* (*Zevachim* 24a) by analogy with the *Kohen's* vestments. Both the vestments and the floor sanctify the

1. Had the *Kohen* been an *av hatumah*, however, he would transmit *tumah* to the bowl in which the flour is held, and the bowl would in turn transmit its acquired *tumah* to all the flour within it.

1 [or] who is *tamei*, [or] who is sitting, [or] stand-
2 ing upon utensils, [or] an animal, [or] on his
colleague's feet — is invalid. [If] one performed *kemitzah* with the left hand, he has invalidated [it]. Ben Beseira says: He should replace [it]

## YAD AVRAHAM

*Kohen* so that he may perform the *avodah* (since he cannot perform it without being dressed in the vestments, nor can he do it anywhere else but in the Temple Courtyard). Therefore, just as nothing may interpose between the *Kohen* and his vestments while he is performing the *avodah* (see *Zevachim* 20a), so too nothing is permitted to come between the *Kohen* and the floor upon which he stands (*Tos.* to *Zevachim* 24a, s.v. הואיל; *Shitah Mekubetzes* there #6; see *Rashi* ad loc. for an alternative explanation).

עַל גַּבֵּי בְהֵמָה, עַל גַּבֵּי רַגְלֵי חֲבֵרוֹ — [*or*] *an animal, [or] on his colleague's feet* —

Even the flesh of an animal or another human being is considered an interposition between the *Kohen* and the floor (*Shitah Mekubetzes* 6a # 13), despite the general principle that something is not considered an interposition to something else of its own kind [מִין בְּמִינוֹ אֵינוֹ חוֹצֵץ; see *Succah* 37b et al.] (*Zevachim* 24a).

For a discussion of why this principle is not in fact applied here, see *Tosafos* to *Zevachim* 110a, s.v. מין, *Succah* 37a s.v. כי; *Ramban, Hil. Bechoros* Vilna ed. p. 31; see also *Teshuvos Avnei Nezer, Yoreh Deah* 266.

פָּסַל. — *is invalid* (lit., *he has invalidated it*).

[The *avodah* is invalid, and the offering is thereby disqualified completely and must be replaced.]

The list in this mishnah is not complete. One who has drunk wine just prior to doing the *avodah* or allowed his hair to grow [beyond the permitted length] also invalidates the offering (*Tos.*; cf. *Zevach Todah*).

קָמַץ בִּשְׂמֹאל, פָּסַל. — *[If] one performed kemitzah with the left hand, he has invalidated [it].*

[*Kemitzah*, like all *avodos*, must be performed with the right hand. This is derived in the case of *kemitzah* in the following manner: The Torah states, concerning the offering of a *metzora* [a person afflicted with certain kinds of skin discolorations that render him *tamei*] (*Lev.* 14:15): וְלָקַח הַכֹּהֵן מִלֹּג הַשָּׁמֶן וְיָצַק עַל כַּף הַכֹּהֵן הַשְּׂמָאלִית, *And the Kohen shall take from the log of oil and he shall pour it on the left palm of the Kohen.* Since the specification of the left palm is mentioned again in the next verse, its seemingly redundant usage in this verse is understood to indicate that *only* in these cases in which the Torah specifies the use of the left palm is the left palm valid for the sacrificial service; otherwise, the right palm must be used. Accordingly, the verse concerning a *minchah* (*Lev.* 9:17): וַיַּקְרֵב אֶת הַמִּנְחָה וַיְמַלֵּא כַפּוֹ מִמֶּנָּה, *and he brought forward the minchah and he filled his palm with it*, is understood to refer specifically to the right hand (*Gem.* 9b).

בֶּן בְּתֵירָא אוֹמֵר: יַחֲזִיר — *Ben Beseira says: He should replace [it]*

He should return the *kometz* of flour to the pan containing the remainder of the offering (*Rav*) [thereby restoring it to its full measure].

# וְיַחֲזֹר וְיִקְמֹץ בְּיָמִין.

# קָמַץ, וְעָלָה בְיָדוֹ צְרוֹר, אוֹ גַרְגִּיר מֶלַח, אוֹ קֹרֶט שֶׁל לְבוֹנָה, פָּסַל. מִפְּנֵי שֶׁאָמְרוּ:

**ר' עובדיה מברטנורא**

**עלה בידו צרור.** נמלא קומץ חסר מקום הצרור: **או גרגיר מלח או קורט של לבונה.** דקודם קמילה בורר כל הלבונה לצד אחד וקומץ ואחר כך מלקט [אותה] ונותנה עם הקומץ ושורף הכל, ואם נזדמן בתוך הקומץ גרגיר מלח או קורט של לבונה, הרי הקומץ חסר כדי מקום הקורט:

**יד אברהם**

וְיַחֲזֹר וְיִקְמֹץ בְּיָמִין. — *and perform kemitzah again with the right hand.*

[According to Ben Beseira, neither the *kometz* nor the *minchah* as a whole becomes invalidated by a left-handed *kemitzah*.] Rather, since *kemitzah* cannot be performed with the left hand, a left-handed *kemitzah* is not considered an *avodah* at all, and it does not invalidate (*Gem.* 6b, as explained by *Keren Orah*). In effect, it is treated as though someone merely removed some flour from the *minchah* prior to *kemitzah*, which certainly does not invalidate the measure of the *minchah* (*Chazon Ish* 21:4). Consequently, the *kometz* should be returned to the pan (to complete the measure of the *minchah*) and a new and proper *kemitzah* should be performed.

Although Ben Beseira expresses his dissent only in the case of a *kemitzah* performed with the left hand, he in fact dissents in all of the instances cited previously in this mishnah and allows the *kometz* to be replaced whenever the *kemitzah* was performed by a disqualified person (*Rav* from *Gem.* 6b). He derives this from the verse (*Lev.* 2:2): וְקָמַץ מִשָּׁם, *and he shall perform kemitzah from there,* which he interprets to mean from the place where he had previously performed *kemitzah*, thereby establishing the principle that a second *kemitzah* is possible [after an initial invalid one] (*Gem.* ibid.).

According to the *Tanna Kamma*, however, a left-handed *kemitzah*, or the *kemitzah* of a disqualified person, is considered an *avodah* — albeit an invalid one — and it therefore invalidates the *minchah*. This precludes the repetition of the *avodah* (*Keren Orah*).

Since Ben Beseira allows the *kometz* to be replaced in all the earlier cases of this mishnah, the rule for the left-handed *kemitzah* should have been included with them as part of that long list. The reason it is listed separately is because there would be reason to believe that even according to Ben Beseira *kemitzah* with the left hand invalidates the *minchah* so that it cannot be reused. This is because the left hand is valid for *avodah* in one instance — viz., on Yom Kippur, when the *Kohen Gadol* carries the spoon containing the incense into the Holy of Holies with his left hand (*Rashi* to 6b, s.v. ביה"כ). One might therefore have thought that a left-handed *kemitzah* cannot be ignored, but must be recognized as an invalid *avodah*, which thereby invalidates the entire offering. To preclude this error the mishnah lists this case — and Ben Beseira's dissent — separately (*Tos.* 6a, s.v. בן בתירא).

If the *Kohen* placed the improperly taken *kometz* in a *kli shareis* (sacred vessel) to carry it to the Altar — and thus further sanctified it for the next stages of the offering — there is a dispute in the *Gemara* (6b) whether the offering would still be salvageable according to Ben Beseira. According to one view, after this sanctification the invalid *kemitzah* can no longer be viewed

1 and perform *kemitzah* again with the right hand.
2 [If] he performed *kemitzah*, and a pebble came into his hand, or a grain of salt, or a particle of frankincense, he has invalidated [it]. Because they said:

### YAD AVRAHAM

as irrelevant and the *kometz* can no longer be replaced. See *Chazon Ish* 21:4 for an explanation of this position.

**קָמַץ, וְעָלָה בְיָדוֹ צְרוֹר,** — *[If] he performed kemitzah, and a pebble came into his hand,*

In removing the *kometz*, a pebble became mixed in with the flour, so that the *kometz* falls short of the amount of flour it should contain by the volume of the pebble (*Rav*).

**אוֹ גַרְגִּיר מֶלַח,** — *or a grain of salt,*

Or, instead of a pebble, the *kometz* was found to contain a grain of salt. Although salt is added to a *kometz* on the Altar before it is burnt, the *kometz* itself must contain a full measure of flour. Therefore, a *kometz* containing a grain of salt is considered as deficient as one containing a pebble (*Rav; Rashi* to mishnah and to *Gem.* 11a, s.v. מלח).

**אוֹ קֹרֶט שֶׁל לְבוֹנָה,** — *or a particle of frankincense,*

The same is true for a piece of *levonah* (frankincense) that was scooped up with the *kometz*. Although *levonah* is a part of almost every *minchah* and is placed on top of the flour of the offering, it is moved to one side just before *kemitzah* so as not to be included in the *kometz*. Only afterward is it gathered up and burnt together with the *kometz* on the Altar. Therefore, if it is found in the *kometz*, the *kometz* is considered deficient (*Rav, Rashi* from *Gem*. 11a).

Accordingly, the mishnah could have stated that the inclusion of a particle of *levonah* makes the *kometz* deficient and it would have been obvious that salt and a pebble do so as well. However, the mishnah listed these cases in ascending order [לֹא זוֹ אַף זוֹ, a standard procedure in Mishnah] (*Rashi* to *Gem.* 11a, s.v. מלח).

**פָּסַל.** — *he has invalidated [it].*

The Torah (*Lev.* 2:2) requires the removal of a *full kometz* [מְלֹא קֻמְצוֹ]; thus, a deficient *kometz* is not valid (see *Rashi* ibid.; *Zevach Todah*), and its *kemitzah* invalidates the *minchah*.

Actually, even if the pebble were found in the remainder of of the *minchah*, the *minchah* should be invalid, since it would then be evident that the offering lacked the necessary amount of flour at the time of its *kemitzah* (see mishnah 3:5). However, it is rare for a *minchah* to be that carefully measured that it contains only the exact minimum amount of flour required. Thus, it can generally be assumed that even after deducting for the pebble, the *minchah* still contains the requisite amount of flour and the presence of the pebble in the remainder would thus not affect the validity of the offering itself (*Tos*. 10b, s.v. קמץ).[1]

1. A *minchah* cannot be composed of any amount of flour. As mishnah 12:3 will teach, even a voluntary *minchah*, whose upper limit is not defined by the Torah but is left to the discretion of the donor, must be donated in multiples of an *issaron*. Increments of less than a full *issaron* invalidate the *minchah* (*Gem.* 76b). Accordingly, *Tosafos'* remark that *menachos* generally contain a bit more flour than the exact amount required presents a problem. *Chazon Ish* (21:13) explains that since real measurements cannot be expected to be made with perfect mathematical precision, the law requiring multiples of an *issaron*

**מנחות**
**א/ב**

# הַקֹּמֶץ הַיָּתֵר וְהֶחָסֵר פָּסוּל.

אֵיזֶה הוּא הַיָּתֵר? שֶׁקְּמָצוֹ מְבֹרָץ. וְחָסֵר? שֶׁקְּמָצוֹ בְּרָאשֵׁי אֶצְבְּעוֹתָיו. כֵּיצַד הוּא עוֹשֶׂה? פּוֹשֵׁט אֶת אֶצְבְּעוֹתָיו עַל פַּס יָדוֹ.

### ר׳ עובדיה מברטנורא

**מבורץ.** מלא וגדוש: **שקמצו בראשי אצבעותיו.** שלא פשטן על כל פס ידו: **פושט את אצבעותיו על פס ידו.** מכניס צדי אצבעותיו בקמח ומכניס הקמח לתוך ידו, ומוחק באצבע קטנה שלא יצא הקמח חוץ לקמיצה, ומוחק בגודל שלא יצא הקמח חוץ לאצבע, וזה היה צריך לעשות במנחת מחבת ומרחשת דמעשיהן אפויין ולאחר אפייתן פותתן וקומץ, ואי אפשר לפותתן דקות כל כך שלא יהיו יוצאות חוץ לקומץ, הלכך מוחק בגודל מלמעלה ובאצבע קטנה מלמטה, וזו היתה מעבודות קשות שבמקדש, דבקושי גדול יכול להשוות שלא יהא לא חסר ולא יתר. ורמב״ם כתב, שנדחו דברי האומר שזו עבודה קשה שבמקדש, והוא מפרש וקומץ כדקמצי אינשי האמור בגמרא [דף יא,א], דהיינו שממלא כפו ממנו כדרך שבני אדם ממלאים ידיהם ממה שלוקחים בידם. ואני אומר, שאין פירוש כדקמצי אינשי אלא שמכניס צדי אצבעותיו בקמח ומכניס הקמח בצדי אצבעותיו לתוך ידו, אבל אינו נוטל קמח אלא מלא שלש אצבעותיו על פס ידו ולא יותר, וכדי שלא יהיה מבורץ ומצבץ ויוצא, מוחק מלמטה באצבע [קטנה] ומלמעלה בגודל, ולא נדחו כלל דברי האומר שזו עבודה קשה מעבודות קשות שבמקדש, ושיטת הגמרא כדברי, וכן פירשוה כל רבותי:

### יד אברהם

Seemingly, the *kemitzah* of a deficient *kometz* should not invalidate the *minchah* according to Ben Beseira, and the *Kohen* should be able to replace the deficient *kometz* and perform another *kemitzah*. If so, however, the mishnah should not have presented this ruling anonymously but should have stated that Ben Beseira dissents in this case as well.

*Tosafos* suggest that the anonymous *Tanna* of the mishnah may be indicating by this that the opinion of Ben Beseira is not accepted as the halachah. However, *Tosafos* also speculate that even Ben Beseira agrees with this ruling, because the *kemitzah* in this case included invalid ingredients rather than just being performed improperly (*Tos.* 10b, s.v. קמץ; cf. *Tos. Yom. Tov; Tos. R' Akiva*).

**— מִפְּנֵי שֶׁאָמְרוּ: הַקֹּמֶץ הַיָּתֵר וְהֶחָסֵר פָּסוּל.** *Because they said: The kometz which is excessive or deficient is invalid.*

[The previous ruling is an instance of the general law that a *kometz* can be neither larger nor smaller than it should be.]

There would seem to be yet another reason why these offerings should be invalid. Since a foreign article — namely, the pebble or grain of salt or *levonah* — separates between the flour and the *Kohen's* hand, or between the particles of the flour itself, it constitutes a חֲצִיצָה, *interposition*, which invalidates. However, the mishnah is discussing a situation in which the pebble, salt or *levonah* was found at the edge of the *kometz* — near the thumb or little finger, where it does not constitute an interposition — and it is therefore invalid only because the *kometz* is not full (*Gem.* 11a; *Rashi* ibid.).

contains a measure of leeway. The amount by which such measurements generally deviate from the mathematical amount is acceptable up to the point where the deviation becomes noticeable (see *Tos.* 23a, s.v. הוא). The amount displaced by a grain of salt is within this allowable deviation.

1 The *kometz* which is excessive or deficient is invalid.
2 Which is excessive ? [One in which] he removed a heaped *kometz*. [Which is] deficient? [One in which] he performed *kemitzah* with his fingertips. How does he do [it]? He extends his fingers over the palm of his hand.

YAD AVRAHAM

.אֵיזֶה הוּא הַיָּתֵר? שֶׁקְּמָצוֹ מְבֹרָץ — *Which is excessive? [One in which] he removed a heaped kometz.*

That is, a *kometz* which overflows the cavity formed by his middle three fingers (*Rav, Rashi* 6a) [extending beyond his index or ring finger]. *Rashi* offers a second explanation, that מְבֹרָץ refers to a case in which excess flour comes between his fingertips and his palm.

?וְחָסֵר — *[Which is] deficient?*

Although the cases discussed by our mishnah are all examples of a deficient *kometz*, the mishnah wishes to cite an example which parallels the one given for the excessive *kometz* (*Tos*. 6a, s.v. חסר).

.שֶׁקְּמָצוֹ בְּרָאשֵׁי אֶצְבְּעוֹתָיו — *[One in which] he performed kemitzah with his fingertips.*

I.e., he did not extend his fingers over the entire palm of his hand [but merely curled them over] (*Rav, Rashi* 6a, 11a, s.v. בראשי אצבעותיו).

.כֵּיצַד הוּא עוֹשֶׂה? פּוֹשֵׁט אֶת אֶצְבְּעוֹתָיו עַל פַּס יָדוֹ — *How does he do [it]? He extends his fingers over the palm of his hand.*

He bends the three middle fingers [of his right hand] until the fingertips reach the palm of his hand (*Gem*. 11a), thereby forming a pocket. He then places his hand in the flour and pushes into it, forcing flour to enter the cavity between his fingers and palm, and fill it. Any excess flour which overflows the cavity is then brushed off with the little finger and thumb.

This is the procedure as described by *Tiferes Yisrael*. The *Chafetz Chaim* in his *Toras HaKodashim* [notes to his *Likkutei Halachos*] (11a, #3) describes the procedure somewhat differently: The *Kohen* forced the side of his *open* palm into the flour and then closed the middle three fingers over the palm to form the *kometz*, which he then removed from the *minchah*. [The language of *Rav*, however, indicates that he too understood the procedure to follow *Tiferes Yisrael's* description of it.]

This is the procedure for a מִנְחַת סוֹלֶת, *fine flour minchah*, that is, a *minchah* whose offering (*kemitzah* and burning) takes place while it is still flour. There are other types of *menachos* which must first be made into a form of bread before their *kemitzah* can take place, such as the *machavas* [a *minchah* prepared on a griddle] and the *marcheshes* [a *minchah* prepared in a deep pan] (see *Lev*. 2:5ff and mishnah 5:8 below). These are baked prior to *kemitzah* in their respective vessels and are then broken into pieces (see mishnah 6:4) and placed in a *kli shareis*. Their *kemitzah* consists of scooping up some of these pieces in the manner described above for the flour *minchah*. However, the procedure for ensuring that the pieces would exactly fill his closed hand without overflowing or leaving any empty space is extremely difficult for

[ג] **רִבָּה** שַׁמְנָהּ, וְחִסֵּר שַׁמְנָהּ, חִסֵּר לְבוֹנָתָהּ — פְּסוּלָה.

**ר' עובדיה מברטנורא**

(ג) **ריבה שמנה.** ששיעור השמן לוג לכל עשרון, ואם ריבה, שנתן שני לוגין או יותר לעשרון דחזו לשתי מנחות, פסל: **חסר שמנה.** פחות מלוג שמן לעשרון סולת: **חיסר לבונתה.** שלא נתן בה אלא קורט אחד של לבונה, אבל אם יש בה שני קרטין כשרה, דכתיב (ויקרא ו,ח) את כל הלבונה אשר על המנחה, כל, משמע אפילו קורט אחד, דכל משמע כל דהוא, כדכתיב (מלכים־ב ד,ב) אין לשפחתך כל בבית, את, לרבות עוד קורט אחד, הרי שנים. ואילו רבה לבונתה לא קתני, דלא פסל אלא כשרבה יותר על שני קומצים דאז רבה יותר מדאי:

**יד אברהם**

these types of *menachos*, since these pieces have a certain size to them which does not necessarily fit the hollow of his hand precisely. In these cases, the *Kohen* has to carefully rub off the excess from the sides of the *kometz* with his thumb and little finger (*Rav* from *Gem*. ibid.).

*Rambam* rules that he closes all of his fingers over his palm, not just three. He seems to have understood that the conclusion of the *Gemara* rejects the view that only the three middle fingers were used (*Rambam, Maaseh HaKorbanos* 13:13; see *Kesef Mishneh* ad loc., and *Rav*).

If the *Kohen* removed the *kometz* by digging his fingers into the flour and then closing them over his palm, or by running the back of his hand along the surface of the flour until a sufficient amount had accumulated in his hand from around the sides, it is uncertain whether the *kemitzah* is valid (*Gem*. 11a).

## 3.

רִבָּה שַׁמְנָהּ, — *[If] he increased its oil,*

[The standard voluntary *minchah* consists of an *issaron* (tenth of an *ephah*)[1] of flour or a multiple thereof.] The amount of oil which must be mixed with such a *minchah* is one *log* of oil for every *issaron* of flour (*Rav* from mishnah 9:3). If the *Kohen* preparing the *minchah* increased the amount of oil beyond what was required, the *minchah* is invalid.

The mishnah speaks of a case in which the extra oil had also been consecrated and designated for this particular *minchah*, as evidenced by the mishnah's use of the phrase *its oil*. Nevertheless, the addition of extra oil invalidates the *minchah*, but only if at least two full *logs* of oil have been mixed into the *minchah* — an amount sufficient for two offerings (*Rav; Rambam* from *Gem.* 11a). Anything less than that is considered part of the basic measure of oil, which includes any amount from one to two *logs* (*Zevach Todah*). But if he added oil which had been designated for another offering, or oil which had not been consecrated for use in offerings (*chullin*), even a small amount invalidates the offering (*Rambam, Pesulei HaMukdashin* 11:8,9 from *Gem.* ibid., as explained by *Tos. R' Akiva Eiger*).[2]

However, the opinion of *Rashi* is that

1. A *log* is a liquid measure equal to the volume of six eggs. An *ephah* is seventy-two times that amount, or four hundred and thirty-two eggs. Thus, a tenth of an *ephah* is the equivalent of forty-three and one-fifth eggs (*Rashi* to *Ex.* 16:36).

2. *Tos. Yom Tov* assumes that *Rambam* does not distinguish between its own properly

**3.** [I]f] he increased its oil, or reduced its oil, [or] he reduced its frankincense — it is invalid.

**YAD AVRAHAM**

additional oil of any kind invalidates (see *Rashi* 11a, s.v. ב׳ לוגין; as explained by *Kesef Mishneh, Hil. Pesulei HaMukdashin* 11:9; *Tos. Yom Tov; Keren Orah*). This is because oil which is designated for the offering beyond the required measure does not become consecrated, and it is thus the same as any other non-consecrated oil which is added to a *minchah* (*Rashba* to 11b, s.v. ומ״מ). According to this view, the novelty of the mishnah's ruling is that a *minchah* can be invalidated *even* by oil designated for its use if too much is added [and certainly by the addition of other kinds of oil] (*Tos. Yom Tov*).

וְחִסֵּר שַׁמְנָהּ, — *or reduced its oil,*

He used less than a *log* of oil for an *issaron* of flour (*Rav*). From the word (*Lev.* 6:8) מִשַּׁמְנָהּ, *from its oil*, the *Gemara* (9b) derives that if it is lacking even some of its prescribed measure, the offering is invalid (*Rashi*).

— חִסֵּר לְבוֹנָתָהּ — *[or] he reduced its frankincense —*

The Torah requires most *menachos* to contain a measure of an incense known as *levonah*, frankincense (*Lev.* 2:1).

A *minchah* should properly contain a full *kometz* of frankincense (*Gem.* 11b). However, if he used as little as two grains, the offering is valid. The invalidation mentioned here for using a reduced amount of *levonah* refers to a case in which he placed only one grain of *levonah* on the *minchah*-offering.

The validity of just two grains is derived from the verse (*Lev.* 6:8): וְאֵת כָּל הַלְּבֹנָה אֲשֶׁר עַל הַמִּנְחָה, *and any of the frankincense which is upon the minchah*. The word כָּל [usually rendered as *all*] is translated to mean *any*, implying that even one grain is sufficient. From the additional word אֵת used in this verse we see an indication that at least one more grain is necessary (*Rav* from *Gem.* 11b).

This follows the view of R' Yehudah. However, the *Gemara* cites two other opinions in this matter. R' Shimon holds that the offering is valid if just one grain is burnt, while R' Meir contends that anything less than a full *kometz* of *levonah* at the time of burning is invalid (ibid.). *Rashi* (11b, s.v. רבי מאיר) interprets the mishnah in accordance with the opinion of R' Meir, since it does not cite a specific *Tanna* [and an anonymous mishnah is generally assumed to express the opinion of R' Meir]. However, *Rav*, as well as *Rambam* (*Hil. Pesulei HaMukdashin* 11:8), interpret the mishnah in accordance with the view of R' Yehudah. Possibly, their source is the fact that the mishnah (below) does not mention the burning of an olive's volume of frankincense as it does that of oil — thereby indicating that burning an olive's volume is not essential (*Tos. R' Akiva;* see below, s.v. או להקטיר לבונתה בחוץ).

*Rav* indicates that the *minchah* is valid even if he originally placed only two grains of frankincense on it. However, the *Gemara* (11b) seems to state clearly that in order for the *minchah* to be valid, it must initially contain an entire *kometz* of frankincense. The leniency of the *Tannaim* mentioned above is only in regard to the amount which must remain at the time the *levonah* is burnt on the Altar, for which as little as two grains suffice to validate the *minchah* according to R' Yehudah (*Tos. R' Akiva Eiger*).

*Sfas Emes*, though, notes that *Rambam*, in his formulation of this law (*Pesulei*

designated oil and other oil but requires a full extra *log* to invalidate in all cases. This seems to be the view of *Kesef Mishneh* as well. See further, fn. at the end of mishnah 3:2.

*HaMukdashin* 11:8), neglects to mention that the *minchah* must initially possess a full *kometz* of *levonah* to be valid, indicating that he too is of the opinion that just two grains suffice even initially. Accordingly, *Sfas Emes* suggests that *Rav* and *Rambam* understood the *Gemara's* statement that a *minchah* initially requires a full *kometz* of *levonah* to mean that this is the proper procedure for the *minchah*, but the *minchah* is in fact valid even if it contained no more than two grains from the very beginning.

.פְּסוּלָה — *it is invalid.*

[Any of these changes in composition invalidate the offering.]

In contrast to the mishnah's formulation of the rule for oil, the mishnah does not state that if he increased the amount of *levonah* in the *minchah* the offering is invalid. The reason is that an excess of *levonah* invalidates only if he used at least two *kematzin* (pl. of *kometz*), a very great increase over the proper measure of two grains (*Rav; Rashi* to 11b, s.v. שהפריש לה שני קמצים; see *Tos. Yom Tov, Rashash*).

Others contend that if he added two *kematzin* the offering is valid, since either *kometz* can legitimately serve as the *levonah* for this offering. According to them, a *minchah* is invalidated only if he added more than one *kometz* of *levonah* but less than two, because the extra measure is not sufficient for this function (*Tos.* 11b, s.v. כגון; *Rashba*).

[A *minchah* must also contain the correct amount of flour (which is always an *issaron* or some multiple of it). Less than an *issaron* invalidates (mishnah 3:5), as does more than an *issaron* (or a multiple of it) (*Gem.* 76b).]

## פִּגּוּל, Piggul

In mishnah 1 we learned that an offering can be invalidated by an improper intent during any one of its four essential *avodos*. The intention dealt with in that mishnah is for the incorrect sacrificial designation [or owner]. This mishnah will teach that there are two more improper intentions that invalidate an offering: the intention to consume the offering past its proper time and the intention to consume it outside its designated area. However, in contrast to the disqualification that results from making an offering for the wrong designation [or owner], which in most cases affects only the owner's fulfillment of his obligation but not the validity of the offering itself, the improper intentions defined in this mishnah invalidate the offering completely.

(a) מַחֲשֶׁבֶת חוּץ לִזְמַנּוֹ, *intent for beyond its time*

The Torah states in regard to the *shelamim*-offering (*Lev.* 7:18): וְאִם הֵאָכֹל יֵאָכֵל מִבְּשַׂר זֶבַח שְׁלָמָיו בַּיּוֹם הַשְּׁלִישִׁי לֹא יֵרָצֶה הַמַּקְרִיב אֹתוֹ לֹא יֵחָשֵׁב לוֹ פִּגּוּל יִהְיֶה וְהַנֶּפֶשׁ הָאֹכֶלֶת מִמֶּנּוּ עֲוֹנָהּ תִּשָּׂא, *And if some of the meat of his shelamim-offering should be eaten on the third day* [after the offering's slaughter — i.e., beyond its allotted time], *it shall not be accepted; he who offers it, it shall not count for him, it is an abomination; and the soul that eats from it shall bear its sin.* The *Gemara* (*Zevachim* 29a) notes that the verse cannot be referring to an offering actually eaten on the third day, because it is impossible that a properly made offering should be retroactively invalidated by a transgression committed two days later! It therefore concludes that the Torah must be discussing an "eating" which takes place at the time of the offering itself — namely, an intention on the part of the person performing one of the essential *avodos* of the sacrifice to eat it beyond the time permitted for its

eating.[1] Such an intent during the *avodah* invalidates the offering immediately [without regard to whether it is actually eaten on the third day or not].

An offering invalidated because of time-intent is known as פִּגּוּל, *piggul*, literally *an abomination*, after the word used for it in this verse. In the terminology of the mishnah this type of intent is referred to as מַחֲשֶׁבֶת חוּץ לִזְמַנּוֹ, *intent for beyond its time*. The meat of an offering which has become *piggul* is forbidden and its consumption [at anytime] is subject to the punishment of *kares* — Divinely decreed excision.

(b) מַחֲשֶׁבֶת חוּץ לִמְקוֹמוֹ, *intent for outside its place*

In addition to invalidating a sacrifice offered with the intention that it be eaten beyond its time [*piggul*], the Torah also invalidates any sacrifice offered with the intention that it be eaten outside its prescribed area [מַחֲשֶׁבֶת חוּץ לִמְקוֹמוֹ, *intent for outside its place*]. Here too, the disqualification takes effect immediately, even if the offering is never removed from its proper confines. However, in contrast to the time-related disqualification of *piggul*, the meat of an offering invalidated for reasons of place-intent is not subject to the penalty of *kares*. An offering disqualified due to this type of intent is not referred to as *piggul*, but simply as פָּסוּל, *invalid*.[2]

(c) אֲכִילָה, *consumption*

In the context of these two invalidations, the term *eating* or *consumption* is understood to have a double meaning: (a) consumption by people; (b) consumption by the Altar. Thus, whether he intended to eat the meat of the offering past the time given for its eating, or burn its sacrificial parts (*emurin*) on the Altar past the time allotted for this, the offering is rendered *piggul* and subject to *kares*. Similarly, whether he intended to eat the meat of the offering outside the place designated for its eating, or burn its sacrificial parts on an Altar outside the area designated for this, the offering is rendered invalid.

As stated in the preface to mishnah 1, the laws of *minchah*-offerings are derived exegetically from those of animal sacrifices. Therefore, these principles stated in connection with animal offerings apply to *menachos* as well, as the mishnah will now set forth.

1. *Toras Kohanim* (ad loc.) arrives at this conclusion from the segment of the verse which says that *he who offers it, it shall not count for him*, indicating that the passage is discussing an invalidation which occurs during the process of offering the sacrifice, and not afterward when it is eaten.

2. This disqualification is derived from a later verse (*Lev.* 19:7) in which the Torah seemingly repeats the *piggul* invalidation: וְאִם הֵאָכֹל יֵאָכֵל בַּיּוֹם הַשְּׁלִישִׁי פִּגּוּל הוּא לֹא יֵרָצֶה, *And if it should be eaten on the third day, it is piggul; it shall not be accepted.* Since this principle has already been stated in the earlier passage (*Lev.* 7:18), this later verse is understood to refer to one who offered the sacrifice with the intention of violating its terms in another [yet similar] manner, i.e., by intending to consume its meat outside its prescribed area. However, the *kares* penalty for eating the meat of the invalidated offering is stated only in the earlier verse, and that verse states: וְהַנֶּפֶשׁ הָאֹכֶלֶת מִמֶּנּוּ, *and the soul that eats from "it"* is punished with *kares*. The word *it* is understoood to be a limitation — i.e., the Torah limits the *kares* penalty to the case of that verse, which concerns one who intends to consume it after its permitted time, not one who intends to eat it outside its prescribed place (*Toras Kohanim* loc. cit.).

מנחות א/ג

**הַקּוֹמֵץ אֶת הַמִּנְחָה לֶאֱכוֹל שְׁיָרֶיהָ בַּחוּץ, אוֹ כְּזַיִת מִשְּׁיָרֶיהָ בַּחוּץ; לְהַקְטִיר קֻמְצָהּ בַּחוּץ, אוֹ כְּזַיִת מִקֻּמְצָהּ בַּחוּץ; אוֹ לְהַקְטִיר לְבוֹנָתָהּ בַּחוּץ –**

**ר׳ עובדיה מברטנורא**

**לאבול שיריה בחוץ.** חוץ לעזרה: **או להקטיר קומצה בחוץ.** דמחשבה פוסלת בין שחשב על אכילת אדם בין שחשב על אכילת מזבח, דכתיב (ויקרא ז,יח) ואם האכל יאכל, בשתי אכילות הכתוב מדבר, אחת לאכילת אדם ואחת לאכילת מזבח, וההוא קרא במחשבה מיירי דכתיב (שם) המקריב אותו לא יחשב, בשעת הקרבה הוא נפגל ואינו נפגל ביום השלישי, אלמא במחשבה מיירי שחשב עליו לאכלו ביום השלישי:

**יד אברהם**

הַקּוֹמֵץ אֶת הַמִּנְחָה — *[If] one performed kemitzah on a minchah-offering*

Here too *kemitzah* is used as an example, as it was in the first mishnah, because it is the first of the *minchah's* essential *avodos*. However, the ruling given applies to all four of its essential *avodos* [as stated below] (*Tif. Yis.*).

לֶאֱכוֹל שְׁיָרֶיהָ בַּחוּץ, — *[intending] to eat its remainder outside,*

[When *kemitzah* is performed on a *minchah*, only a small percentage of the flour is removed. The much larger part of the offering which remains is referred to as שִׁירַיִם, *the remainder*. This part is eaten by the *Kohanim* after the *kometz* has been burnt on the Altar.]

In the case under discussion, the *Kohen* bringing the *minchah*-offering intended, while performing *kemitzah*, to eat the remainder of the *minchah* outside the Temple Courtyard [עֲזָרָה]. Since a *minchah* must be eaten within the Courtyard, his intent was to eat it outside its assigned area (*Rav*). [All offerings classified as קָדְשֵׁי קָדָשִׁים, *most-holy offerings*, must be eaten within the Temple Courtyard (*Zevachim* 5:1), and *menachos* are included in this category (*Lev.* 2:3).]

אוֹ כְּזַיִת מִשְּׁיָרֶיהָ בַּחוּץ; — *or an olive's volume of its remainder outside;*

[A *kezayis* is the minimum amount of food whose consumption is legally considered an act of *eating* in regard to the laws of the Torah that deal with eating. That is, wherever the Torah requires that something be eaten (e.g., *matzah* on *Pesach*), or stipulates a punishment for something that should not be eaten (e.g., lashes for eating non-kosher food), a minimum of a *kezayis* — the volume of an olive — must be consumed before the obligation is fulfilled or the punishment is incurred.[1] Since the Torah defines *piggul* and the related place-invalidation as the intent to *eat* part of the offering beyond its time or outside its place, this intent to eat cannot invalidate the *minchah* unless it too concerns at least a *kezayis* of the offering.]

לְהַקְטִיר קֻמְצָהּ בַּחוּץ, — *[or] to burn its kometz outside,*

1. Although the punishment of *malkus* (lashes) is not incurred for eating less than a *kezayis* of the prohibited food, it is nevertheless forbidden to eat even the smallest amount of it (*Yoma* 74a).

1 [If] one performed *kemitzah* on a *minchah*-
3 offering [intending] to eat its remainder outside, or
an olive's volume of its remainder outside; [or] to
burn its *kometz* outside, or an olive's volume of its
*kometz* outside; or to burn its frankincense outside —

### YAD AVRAHAM

[Or, rather than intending to eat the *kometz* outside the Courtyard, the *Kohen* intended at the time of *kemitzah* that he would burn the *kometz* on an Altar outside the Temple's Courtyard.]

The verses which teach the invalidation of an offering because of the intention to violate the rules of the sacrifice use the idiom הָאָכֹל יֵאָכֵל, which is translated as *if it should be eaten*, but which literally means *if it should be eaten, should be eaten.* This repetition, so to speak, of the phrase *should be eaten* is taken exegetically to teach that the verse refers to two types of consumption: the eating of the meat by people, and the consumption of the blood and sacrificial parts by the Altar (*Rav* from *Toras Kohanim* loc. cit.; see *Zevachim* 2:2). Since *menachos* are analogous to animal sacrifices in these matters, we derive that an invalid intention concerning the burning of the *kometz* is treated in the same manner as an invalid intention concerning the application of the blood of an animal sacrifice (*Rav*).

או כְּזַיִת מִקֻּמְצָהּ בַּחוּץ; — *or an olive's volume of its kometz outside;*

Just as the intent to eat must concern a *kezayis* of the *kometz* before it can invalidate, so too an improper intent in regard to burning must concern at least a *kezayis* to invalidate. Since the invalidation for intending to burn on an Altar outside the proper place is derived from the repetition of words in the phrase הָאָכֹל יֵאָכֵל, *if it should be eaten*, as explained above, the intent-to-burn invalidation must conform to the same requirements as those that govern intent to eat — namely, it must concern at least a *kezayis* of the offering (*Rav* from *Gem.* 17b).

או לְהַקְטִיר לְבוֹנָתָהּ בַּחוּץ — — *or to burn its frankincense outside —*

[After the *minchah* has its *kometz* removed for burning on the Altar, its *levonah* (frankincense) is collected from atop the *minchah* and also burnt on the Altar.] Whereas the burning of the *kometz* is considered analogous to the application of an animal offering's blood to the Altar, the burning of the *levonah* corresponds to the burning of the sacrificial parts of the animal sacrifice. Therefore, the intent to burn its *levonah* outside the Courtyard invalidates the same as the intent to burn the sacrificial parts of an animal offering outside the Courtyard (*Rav*).

The mishnah does not qualify this by stating that he intended to burn at least an olive's volume of the *levonah* outside the Temple Courtyard, because it follows the opinion of those who maintain that even if only one grain of the frankincense is burnt the offering is valid [and thus an intention concerning that quantity is sufficient to invalidate the *minchah*] (*Rashi* 11b, s.v. פסול; see above, s.v. חסר לבונתה; cf. *Shitah Mekubetzes* ibid. 4).

פָּסוּל, וְאֵין בּוֹ כָּרֵת. לֶאֱכוֹל שְׁיָרֶיהָ לְמָחָר, אוֹ כְזַיִת מִשְּׁיָרֶיהָ לְמָחָר; לְהַקְטִיר קֻמְצָהּ לְמָחָר, אוֹ כְזַיִת מִקֻּמְצָהּ לְמָחָר; אוֹ לְהַקְטִיר לְבוֹנָתָהּ לְמָחָר – פִּגּוּל, וְחַיָּבִין עָלָיו כָּרֵת. זֶה הַכְּלָל: כָּל הַקּוֹמֵץ, וְהַנּוֹתֵן בִּכְלִי, וְהַמְהַלֵּךְ, וְהַמַּקְטִיר, לֶאֱכוֹל דָּבָר שֶׁדַּרְכּוֹ לֶאֱכוֹל,

ר' עובדיה מברטנורא

**פסולה.** דמחשבת חוץ למקומו פוסלת בקמילת המנחה כמו שפוסלת בשחיטת הזבח, ומה שפוסל בזבח בשחיטה בקבלת הדם בהולכה בזריקת הדם, פוסל המנחה בקמילה בנתינה בכלי שרת בהולכה בהקטרת הקומץ ולבונה, ארבעה כנגד ארבעה, והקומץ והלבונה עלמן חשובים גבי מנחה כמו הדם והאמורים אלל הזבח. ושירי מנחה הנאכלים, כבשר הזבח הנאכל. ובפרק שני דזבחים (משנה ג) מפורשים כל הני פסולי, והתם (דף כח,א) ילפינן להו כולהו מקראי: **לאכול דבר שדרכו לאכול.** כגון שירים:

יד אברהם

פָּסוּל, — *it is invalid,*

In all the above cases, the intention at the time of *kemitzah* to eat or burn the *minchah's* components outside the Courtyard invalidates the *minchah*, just as a similar intention expressed at the time of slaughtering invalidates an animal sacrifice (*Rav*).

וְאֵין בּוֹ כָּרֵת. — *but it carries no [penalty of] kares.*

[Intent to consume outside the proper place renders an offering only invalid, not *piggul*. Thus, no *kares* is attached to the *minchah's* subsequent consumption, as explained in the preface.]

לֶאֱכוֹל שְׁיָרֶיהָ לְמָחָר, אוֹ כְזַיִת מִשְּׁיָרֶיהָ לְמָחָר; — *[If he did so intending] to eat its remainder tomorrow, or an olive's volume of its remainder tomorrow;*

[The next set of cases deals with improper time-intent rather than place-intent.] The *Kohen* performed the *kemitzah* with the intention of eating the remainder of the *minchah* on the day following its *kemitzah*. Accordingly, he has intended to eat it beyond its allotted time, since a *minchah* may be eaten for only one day and night [i.e., the day of its *kemitzah* and the night which follows], but not the following day (*Rashi* from *Zevachim* 6:1). [Here, too, the intent must concern a minimum of a *kezayis* in order to take effect.]

The time span for the consumption of the *minchah's* remainder is learned from the Torah's comparison of the *minchah* to the *chatas* and *asham* [*Lev.* 6:10] (*Rashi*), whose meat is eaten for only a day and a night (*Tos. Yom Tov* from *Zevachim* 5:3; 5:5).

לְהַקְטִיר קֻמְצָהּ לְמָחָר, אוֹ כְזַיִת מִקֻּמְצָהּ לְמָחָר; אוֹ לְהַקְטִיר לְבוֹנָתָהּ לְמָחָר – — *[or] to burn its kometz [on the Altar] tomorrow, or an olive's volume of its kometz tomorrow; or to burn its frankincense [on the Altar] tomorrow —*

The *kometz* and *levonah* must be burnt on the Altar before sunset of the day on which they are removed from the *minchah* (*Gem.* 20b, 26b; *Megillah* 2:5, 20b). Thus, in the context of the intention to burn the *kometz* or *levonah*

1 it is invalid, but it carries no [penalty of] *kares*.
3 [If he did so intending] to eat its remainder to-
morrow, or an olive's volume of its remainder tomorrow; [or] to burn its *kometz* [on the Altar] tomorrow, or an olive's volume of its *kometz* tomorrow; or to burn its frankincense [on the Altar] tomorrow — it is *piggul*, and one is liable to *kares* over it. This is the rule: Anyone who performs *kemitzah*, or places [the *kometz*] in a vessel, or conveys [it], or burns [it on the Altar], [intending] to eat something which is meant to be eaten,

### YAD AVRAHAM

the word *tomorrow* is defined as any time past sundown of the day of the offering (*Gem.* 20b, *Rashi* s.v. דם נפסל).[1]

פִּגּוּל, וְחַיָּבִין עָלָיו כָּרֵת. — *it is piggul, and one is liable to kares over it.*

[The offering is invalidated as *piggul* (see preface), and one who eats from its meat is subject to the punishment of *kares*.]

This is derived from the Torah's use of the phrase וְהַנֶּפֶשׁ הָאֹכֶלֶת מִמֶּנּוּ עֲוֹנָהּ תִּשָּׂא, *and the soul that eats from it shall bear its sin*, concerning the punishment for *piggul* (*Lev.* 7:18). This same phrase is used as well in reference to נוֹתָר, *nossar* [leftover sacrifices], which may also not be eaten (ibid. 19:8). Just as the punishment for the latter is *kares* (ibid.), so is that of the former (*Rashi* from *Kereisos* 5a).

זֶה הַכְּלָל: כָּל הַקּוֹמֵץ, וְהַנּוֹתֵן בִּכְלִי, וְהַמְהַלֵּךְ, וְהַמַּקְטִיר, — *This is the rule: Anyone who performs kemitzah, or places [the kometz] in a vessel, or conveys [it], or burns [it on the Altar],*

[Following *kemitzah*, the *Kohen* places the *kometz* in a כְּלִי שָׁרֵת, *kli shareis*, a sacred vessel, to sanctify it. He then carries it to the Altar, and places it on the fire to burn.] These four acts are the four *avodos* of the *minchah*, paralleling the four blood *avodos* of the animal sacrifice — slaughtering, receiving the blood, carrying the blood to the Altar, and applying it there (*Rav, Rashi*). Just as these invalid intentions disqualify the offering if they occur during the performance of the four essential *avodos* of the animal offering (see *Toras Kohanim* loc. cit.), so too they invalidate a *minchah*-offering during the four essential *avodos* of the *minchah* (*Rambam Comm*).

לֶאֱכוֹל דָּבָר שֶׁדַּרְכּוֹ לֶאֱכוֹל, — *[intending] to eat something which is meant to be eaten,*

In order for an intent concerning the time or place of eating to take effect, the intent must concern a part of the offering which is meant to be eaten — viz., the remainder of the *minchah* (*Rav*).

1. There is some question whether sundown in this context is to be taken literally or whether it is the equivalent of nightfall. See *Tosafos* to *Zevachim* 56a, s.v.מנין; *Shaagas Aryeh* Ch. 17; this issue has been discussed at length in the *Yad Avraham* comm. to *Zevachim* 2:2.

מנחות א/ג

וּלְהַקְטִיר דָּבָר שֶׁדַּרְכּוֹ לְהַקְטִיר – חוּץ לִמְקוֹמוֹ, פָּסוּל וְאֵין בּוֹ כָּרֵת; חוּץ לִזְמַנּוֹ, פִּגּוּל, וְחַיָּבִין עָלָיו כָּרֵת – וּבִלְבַד שֶׁיִּקְרַב הַמַּתִּיר כְּמִצְוָתוֹ. כֵּיצַד קָרַב הַמַּתִּיר כְּמִצְוָתוֹ? קָמַץ בִּשְׁתִיקָה

ר' עובדיה מברטנורא

**דבר שדרכו להקטיר.** כגון הקומץ, אבל אם חשב לאכול הקומץ או להקטיר השירים חוץ לזמנו, לא פסל, דבטלה דעתו אצל כל אדם: **ובלבד שיקרב המתיר.** הקומץ כהלכתו כאילו היה כשר, שלא יהא שם שום פסול אלא הפגול בלבד, אבל אם יש בו פסול אחר, אינו חשוב יותר פגול ואין בו כרת: **קמץ בשתיקה.** שלא חשב שום מחשבת פסול בשעת קמילה:

יד אברהם

וּלְהַקְטִיר דָּבָר שֶׁדַּרְכּוֹ לְהַקְטִיר — *or to burn [on the Altar] something which is meant to be burnt [on the Altar]* —

[Similarly, the intent to burn upon the Altar outside its permitted time or place is only significant if it concerns something that should be burnt upon the Altar, i.e., the *kometz*.]

חוּץ לִמְקוֹמוֹ, פָּסוּל וְאֵין בּוֹ כָּרֵת; חוּץ לִזְמַנּוֹ, פִּגּוּל, וְחַיָּבִין עָלָיו כָּרֵת — *[if the intent was for] outside its area, it is invalid but carries no [penalty of] kares; [if it was for] beyond its time, it is piggul, and one is liable to kares over it* —

Only the intent to consume the offering in its proper fashion can invalidate it as either *piggul* or as a general invalidation. However, if he intended to eat the *kometz* [which should be burnt upon the Altar], or to burn the remainder [which should be eaten, and not burnt on the Altar] outside its allotted time or place, it does not invalidate the offering, because his intention is considered incongruous (*Rav*).

וּבִלְבַד שֶׁיִּקְרַב הַמַּתִּיר כְּמִצְוָתוֹ. — *provided that the part which makes it permissible is offered as required.*

[The term מַתִּיר, *mattir*, refers to the part of the offering which renders the remainder of it permissible for consumption.] In the case of the *minchah* this would be its *kometz* (*Rav*).

Although the intention to eat the *minchah's* remainder or to burn its *kometz* past its time renders it *piggul*, the invalidation takes effect only once all four *avodos* of the *minchah* have been completed. The *Gemara* (*Zevachim* 28b) draws from this a correlation between the validation of a proper offering and the establishment of the *piggul* disqualification — כְּהַרְצָאַת כָּשֵׁר כַּךְ הַרְצָאַת פָּסוּל, *the manner in which a valid offering is rendered acceptable is the same manner by which the invalid one is accepted* [i.e., established as *piggul*]. This means that the part of the *minchah* whose offering would ordinarily permit the remainder to be eaten — its *kometz* — must be properly offered free of any invalidation other than *piggul* before the *piggul* invalidation can take effect. However, if any disqualification other than *piggul* is present, so that even had the *minchah* not been subjected to *piggul* intent it would still never have become permissible, the *piggul* invalidation does not take effect (*Rav*). [Therefore,

1
3

or to burn [on the Altar] something which is meant to be burnt [on the Altar] — [if the intent was for] outside its area, it is invalid but it carries no [penalty of] *kares*; [if it was for] beyond its time, it is *piggul*, and one is liable to *kares* over it — provided that the part which makes it permissible is offered as required.

In what manner is the part which makes it permissible [considered to have been] offered as required? [If] he performed *kemitzah* in silence



although the offering remains invalid because of its non-*piggul* disqualification, the *kares* penalty, which is unique to *piggul*, does not apply to its meat.]

This is derived (*Gem.* 16b) from the Scriptural use of the words לֹא יֵרָצֶה, *it shall not be accepted,* to describe the invalidation of *piggul* (*Lev.* 19:7). The word יֵרָצֶה, *shall be accepted,* is the very term used to describe the validity of a valid offering (ibid. 22:27). From this we derive that the two are analogous: that just as a valid offering must be brought without disqualification in order to be accepted, so too a *piggul* offering must be offered without any further disqualification before the law of *piggul* can take effect (*Rashi*).

The *kometz* is the *mattir* of the *minchah*, and its offering on the Altar is therefore the criterion for determining the establishment of *piggul* in a *minchah*. In the case of an animal offering, the blood is the *mattir*, and it must be applied to the wall of the Altar without any disqualification in order for the *piggul* classification to take effect (see *Zevachim* 2:2-4).

?כֵּיצַד קָרַב הַמַּתִּיר כְּמִצְוָתוֹ — *In what manner is the part which makes it permissible* [*considered to have been*] *offered as required?*

[The mishnah will now define which combinations of proper and improper intentions prevent an offering from becoming *piggul*.]

It is unclear why this elaboration is necessary here, as well as twice in *Zevachim* [2:4; 6:7] (*Tos.* to *Zevachim* 65b, s.v. כיצד).

קָמַץ בִּשְׁתִיקָה — [*If*] *he performed kemitzah in silence*

That is, he did not have any invalidating intention during the *kemitzah* (*Rav*). This could mean that he had no specific intention at all [since an offering brought in such a manner is valid (see comm. at the end of mishnah 1)], or that he specifically intended it for the proper time (*Tif. Yis.*).

According to the view of *Rashi* and *Tosafos* that improper intentions invalidate only when they are verbalized (see comm. at the end of mishnah 1), the term *silence* is meant literally — i.e., he said nothing at the time of the *kemitzah*. His unspoken thoughts at this moment are of no consequence. However, according to *Rambam's* view that even unarticulated thoughts suffice to invalidate, the word *silence* is used here in a borrowed sense and must be understood to mean the absence of any improper thought.

וְנָתַן בִּכְלִי, וְהָלַךְ, וְהִקְטִיר חוּץ לִזְמַנּוֹ; אוֹ שֶׁקָּמַץ חוּץ לִזְמַנּוֹ, וְנָתַן בִּכְלִי, וְהָלַךְ, וְהִקְטִיר בִּשְׁתִיקָה; אוֹ שֶׁקָּמַץ, וְנָתַן בִּכְלִי, וְהָלַךְ, וְהִקְטִיר חוּץ לִזְמַנּוֹ — זֶה הוּא שֶׁקָּרַב הַמַּתִּיר כְּמִצְוָתוֹ.

[ד] **כֵּיצַד** לֹא קָרַב הַמַּתִּיר כְּמִצְוָתוֹ? קָמַץ חוּץ לִמְקוֹמוֹ, וְנָתַן בִּכְלִי, וְהָלַךְ, וְהִקְטִיר חוּץ לִזְמַנּוֹ; אוֹ שֶׁקָּמַץ

**ר׳ עובדיה מברטנורא**

**ונתן בכלי והלך והקטיר חוץ לזמנו.** כלומר, שבשלשת עבודות הללו חשב על השירים לאכלן חוץ לזמנו: (ד) **קמץ חוץ למקומו.** חשב בשעת קמילה לאכול השירים חוץ לעזרה: **נתן בבלי הלך והקטיר חוץ לזמנו.** ובאחת משלשת עבודות הללו חשב על השירים לאכלן חוץ לזמנו:

**יד אברהם**

אוֹ שֶׁקָּמַץ, וְנָתַן בִּכְלִי, וְהָלַךְ, וְהִקְטִיר חוּץ — לִזְמַנּוֹ — *or he performed kemitzah, placed [the kometz] in a vessel, conveyed [it], and burnt [it on the Altar for] beyond its time* —

I.e., he performed all four of the essential *avodos* with the intention of eating the remainder or burning the *kometz* beyond the allotted time (*Tif. Yis.*).

זֶה הוּא שֶׁקָּרַב הַמַּתִּיר כְּמִצְוָתוֹ. — *these are [the cases in which] the part which makes it permissible has been offered as required.*

[In all of these cases, the *avodah* proceeded to the burning of the *kometz* without any improper intention other than *piggul*, thereby satisfying the requirement that the *mattir* — the part which makes it permissible — *be offered as required.* Therefore, the invalidation of *piggul* takes effect and imposes the penalty of *kares* on one who eats the meat, as explained above. The following mishnah will delineate which cases are excluded by this rule.]

— וְנָתַן בִּכְלִי, וְהָלַךְ, וְהִקְטִיר חוּץ לִזְמַנּוֹ; *but placed [the kometz] in a vessel, conveyed [it], or burnt [it on the Altar for] beyond its time;*

After removing the *kometz* without *piggul* intent, he performed one of the remaining three *avodos* of the *minchah* — placing the *kometz* in a *kli shareis* (sacred vessel), conveying it to the Altar, or burning it on the Altar — with the intention of eating the remainder of the *minchah* after the permitted time (*Rav, Tos. Yom Tov*).

אוֹ שֶׁקָּמַץ חוּץ לִזְמַנּוֹ, וְנָתַן בִּכְלִי, וְהָלַךְ, וְהִקְטִיר בִּשְׁתִיקָה; — *or he performed kemitzah [with intent for] beyond its time, but placed [the kometz] in a vessel, conveyed [it], and burnt [it on the Altar] in silence;*

[He had the intention, at the time of *kemitzah*, to eat the remainder or burn the *kometz* past its time, but he performed the other three *avodos* with no improper intention.]

1
4
but placed [the *kometz*] in a vessel, conveyed [it], or burnt [it on the Altar for] beyond its time; or he performed *kemitzah* [with intent for] beyond its time, but placed [the *kometz*] in a vessel, conveyed [it], and burnt [it on the Altar] in silence; or he performed *kemitzah*, placed [the *kometz*] in a vessel, conveyed [it], and burnt [it on the Altar for] beyond its time — these are [the cases in which] the part which makes it permissible has been offered as required.

**4.** In what manner is the part which makes it permissible not [considered to have been] offered as required? [If] he performed *kemitzah* [with intent for] outside its area, but he placed [the *kometz*] in a vessel, conveyed [it], or burnt [it on the Altar for] beyond its time; or he performed *kemitzah*

YAD AVRAHAM

4.

כֵּיצַד לֹא קָרַב הַמַּתִּיר כְּמִצְוָתוֹ? — *In what manner is the part which makes it permissible not [considered to have been] offered as required?*

[The mishnah will now illustrate the types of combined intents which prevent the *piggul* invalidation from taking effect despite the intent for *piggul*. Although in these cases the offering is in any case invalidated because of the second disqualifying intent, the more severe *piggul* classification — with its associated *kares* penalty — does not take effect.]

קָמַץ חוּץ לִמְקוֹמוֹ, — *[If] he performed kemitzah [with intent for] outside its area,*

He intended, at the time of *kemitzah*, to eat the remainder of the *minchah* outside the Temple Courtyard (*Rav*).

וְנָתַן בִּכְלִי, וְהָלַךְ, וְהִקְטִיר חוּץ לִזְמַנּוֹ; — *but he placed [the kometz] in a vessel, conveyed [it], or burnt [it on the Altar for] beyond its time;*

After performing *kemitzah* with intent to eat the remainder outside the *minchah's* area, he performed one of the remaining three *avodos* with the intention to eat the remainder past its time (*Rav*). [Thus, the improper time-intent, which should render this *minchah* as *piggul*, followed a non-*piggul* invalidating intent.]

חוּץ לִזְמַנּוֹ, וְנָתַן בִּכְלִי, וְהָלַךְ, וְהִקְטִיר חוּץ לִמְקוֹמוֹ; אוֹ שֶׁקָּמַץ, וְנָתַן בִּכְלִי, וְהָלַךְ, וְהִקְטִיר חוּץ לִמְקוֹמוֹ; מִנְחַת חוֹטֵא וּמִנְחַת קְנָאוֹת שֶׁקְּמָצָן שֶׁלֹּא לִשְׁמָן, וְנָתַן בִּכְלִי, וְהָלַךְ, וְהִקְטִיר חוּץ לִזְמַנָּן; אוֹ שֶׁקָּמַץ חוּץ לִזְמַנָּן, וְנָתַן בִּכְלִי, וְהָלַךְ, וְהִקְטִיר שֶׁלֹּא לִשְׁמָן; אוֹ שֶׁקָּמַץ, וְנָתַן בִּכְלִי, וְהָלַךְ, וְהִקְטִיר שֶׁלֹּא לִשְׁמָן — זֶה הוּא שֶׁלֹּא קָרַב הַמַּתִּיר כְּמִצְוָתוֹ.

**ר׳ עובדיה מברטנורא**

**מנחת חוטא וקנאות.** יש בהן עוד פסול אחר המוליאן מידי פגול, כגון שלא לשמן, דאמרינן בריש פרקין (משנה א) דפסולות אם קמצן שלא לשמן, ושלשת שאר העבודות חשב עליהן חוץ לזמנן, או אפילו הראשונה חוץ לזמנה והשאר שלא לשמן, [הוציאו] מידי פגול: **או שקמץ או נתן בכלי או הוליך או הקטיר שלא לשמן.** כלומר אי זו מאלו שעשה שלא לשמן והשאר על מנת לאכול שירים חוץ לזמנו לא קרב המתיר כמצותו ואין בשירים כרת:

**יד אברהם**

אוֹ שֶׁקָּמַץ חוּץ לִזְמַנּוֹ, וְנָתַן בִּכְלִי, וְהָלַךְ, וְהִקְטִיר חוּץ לִמְקוֹמוֹ; — *or he performed kemitzah [for] beyond its time, but he placed [the kometz] in a vessel, conveyed [it], and burnt [it] outside its place;*

He performed all [or any] of the latter three *avodos* with the intention of eating the remainder outside the Courtyard (*Tif. Yis.*). [Thus, the *piggul*-intent preceded the non-*piggul* invalidating intent. Nevertheless, the subsequent non-*piggul* invalidation blocks the *piggul* from taking effect, as the mishnah will teach below.]

אוֹ שֶׁקָּמַץ, וְנָתַן בִּכְלִי, וְהָלַךְ, וְהִקְטִיר חוּץ לִמְקוֹמוֹ; — *or he performed kemitzah, placed [the kometz] in a vessel, conveyed [it], or burnt [it for] outside its area;*

He performed any of these with an improper intention concerning place and did the others with an improper intention concerning time (*Tif. Yis.*).

מִנְחַת חוֹטֵא וּמִנְחַת קְנָאוֹת שֶׁקְּמָצָן שֶׁלֹּא לִשְׁמָן, —[*or*] *the sinner's minchah-offering or jealousy minchah-offering whose kemitzah he performed for a designation other than its own,*

These *menachos* are unique in that they are rendered invalid even if they are offered for the sake of a different type of *minchah* or a different owner, as explained in mishnah 1 (*Rav*). [Thus, if a *minchah* of this type had its *kemitzah* performed for the sake of another designation, it is immediately invalidated.]

וְנָתַן בִּכְלִי, וְהָלַךְ, וְהִקְטִיר חוּץ לִזְמַנָּן; — *and placed [the kometz] in a vessel, conveyed [it], and burnt [it on the Altar for] beyond its time;*

After performing the *kemitzah* for the wrong designation, he performed

[for] beyond its time, but he placed [the *kometz*] in a vessel, conveyed [it], and burnt [it] outside its place; or he performed *kemitzah,* placed [the *kometz*] in a vessel, conveyed [it], or burnt [it for] outside its area; [or] the sinner's *minchah*-offering or jealousy *minchah*-offering whose *kemitzah* he performed for a designation other than its own, and placed [the *kometz*] in a vessel, conveyed [it], and burnt [it on the Altar for] beyond its time; [or] he performed *kemitzah* [for] beyond its time, and placed [the *kometz*] in a vessel, conveyed [it], and burnt [it on the Altar] for a designation other than its own; or he performed *kemitzah*, placed [the *kometz*] in a vessel, conveyed [it], and burnt [it on the Altar] for a designation other than its own; these are [cases in which] the part which makes it permissible was not offered as required.

YAD AVRAHAM

the latter three *avodos* with the *piggul*-intention of eating or burning the *minchah* beyond its time (*Rav*).[1] [Thus, the *piggul*-intention follows another invalidating intention.]

אוֹ שֶׁקָּמַץ חוּץ לִזְמַנּוֹ, וְנָתַן בִּכְלִי, וְהָלַךְ, וְהִקְטִיר שֶׁלֹּא לִשְׁמָן; — *[or] he performed kemitzah [for] beyond its time, and placed [the kometz] in a vessel, conveyed [it], and burnt [it on the Altar] for a designation other than its own;*

[In this case the *piggul*-intent occurred during the *kemitzah* and was followed by the non-*piggul* invalidating intent.]

אוֹ שֶׁקָּמַץ, וְנָתַן בִּכְלִי, וְהָלַךְ, וְהִקְטִיר שֶׁלֹּא לִשְׁמָן — *or he performed kemitzah, placed [the kometz] in a vessel, conveyed [it], and burnt [it on the Altar] for a designation other than its own;*

He performed any of the four *avodos* for the wrong designation, and the others with the intention to eat the offering after the permitted time (*Rav*).

זֶה הוּא שֶׁלֹּא קָרַב הַמַּתִּיר כְּמִצְוָתוֹ. — *these are [cases in which] the part which makes it permissible was not offered as required.*

[All the above-mentioned cases are examples of the *mattir* — the part of the *minchah* whose offering would permit the remainder of the *minchah* to be eaten in a non-*piggul* setting —

1. [It is unclear why *Rav* changes his interpretation from the previous series of cases, in which he interpreted the mishnah to mean that the *Kohen* performed any one of the services listed with an improper intention concerning time, but not that he did so with all of them.]

# לֶאֱכוֹל כְּזַיִת בַּחוּץ וּכְזַיִת לְמָחָר; כְּזַיִת לְמָחָר וּכְזַיִת בַּחוּץ; כַּחֲצִי זַיִת בַּחוּץ וְכַחֲצִי זַיִת לְמָחָר; כַּחֲצִי זַיִת לְמָחָר וְכַחֲצִי זַיִת בַּחוּץ — פָּסוּל, וְאֵין בּוֹ כָּרֵת. אָמַר רַבִּי יְהוּדָה: זֶה הַכְּלָל: אִם מַחֲשֶׁבֶת הַזְּמַן קָדְמָה לְמַחֲשֶׁבֶת הַמָּקוֹם, פִּגּוּל וְחַיָּבִים עָלָיו כָּרֵת; וְאִם מַחֲשֶׁבֶת הַמָּקוֹם קָדְמָה לְמַחֲשֶׁבֶת הַזְּמַן, פָּסוּל, וְאֵין בּוֹ כָּרֵת.

### ר׳ עובדיה מברטנורא

**כזית בחוץ כזית למחר.** חשב באחת מן העבודות שתי מחשבות חוץ לזמנו וחוץ למקומו. ועד השתא איירינן [בשתי] עבודות שחשב באחת חוץ לזמנו ובאחרת חוץ למקומו, ועכשיו מיירי שחשב בשתיהן בעבודה אחת, ולרבי יהודה אילטריך, דלא תימא בשתי עבודות הוא דפליג רבי יהודה דבתר קמייתא אזלינן אבל בחדא עבודה מודה, קא משמע לן: **בזית למחר וכזית בחוץ.** אף על פי שחשב תחלה לחוץ לזמנו, הואיל ושניה מידי כרת: **אמר רבי יהודה זה הכלל כו׳.** רבי יהודה פליג אתנא קמא בין בעבודה אחת בין בשתי עבודות. ואין הלכה כרבי יהודה:

### יד אברהם

not being offered properly. In all of them, the *kometz* was invalidated for reasons other than *piggul*, and the *piggul* invalidation consequently does not take effect.]

Furthermore, it makes no difference whether the non-*piggul* invalidation preceded the *piggul*-intent or followed it. In either case, the *kometz* was invalidated before it was burnt on the Altar, and the *piggul* classification is therefore prevented from taking effect, as the mishnah has made clear by its various illustrations (*Rav*).

לֶאֱכוֹל כְּזַיִת בַּחוּץ וּכְזַיִת לְמָחָר; — [*If he intended*] *to eat an olive's volume outside and an olive's volume tomorrow;*

In contrast to the previous cases, in which the different intentions were expressed during two different *avodos*, in the cases which follow the two improper intentions — one concerning place and one concerning time — were expressed during the same *avodah*. The novelty of this ruling is in regard to R' Yehudah's dissenting opinion, as will be explained below (*Rav*).

[The mishnah speaks of his intention in regard to a *kezayis* (olive's volume) of the offering, because this is the minimum amount which an improper intention must concern in order to take effect, as we learned in mishnah 3 (s.v. או כזית משיריה).]

כְּזַיִת לְמָחָר וּכְזַיִת בַּחוּץ; — [*or*] *an olive's volume tomorrow and an olive's volume outside;*

Here again the mishnah teaches that although the improper intention concerning time was expressed before that of place, the latter intention nevertheless prevents the *piggul* invalidation from taking effect in the *minchah* (ibid.).

כַּחֲצִי זַיִת בַּחוּץ וְכַחֲצִי זַיִת לְמָחָר; כַּחֲצִי זַיִת לְמָחָר וְכַחֲצִי זַיִת בַּחוּץ — — [*or*] *half an olive's volume outside and half an olive's volume tomorrow;* [*or*] *half an*

1
4 [If he intended] to eat an olive's volume outside and an olive's volume tomorrow; [or] an olive's volume tomorrow and an olive's volume outside; [or] half an olive's volume outside and half an olive's volume tomorrow; [or] half an olive's volume tomorrow and half an olive's volume outside — it is invalid, but it carries no *kares* [penalty]. Said R' Yehudah: This is the rule: If the intent of time preceded the intent of place, [it is] *piggul* and one is liable to *kares* over it; but if the intent of the place preceded the intent of time, it is invalid, but carries no *kares* [penalty].

YAD AVRAHAM

*olive's volume tomorrow and half an olive's volume outside —*

In this last set of cases, the two intentions each concern only half a *kezayis*, so that it is only by considering the two of them in combination that we have an improper intention concerning the minimum necessary to invalidate (*Gem.* 12b).

.פָּסוּל, וְאֵין בּוֹ כָּרֵת — *it is invalid, but it carries no kares [penalty].*

[In the first two cases, the presence of the improper place-intent prevents the *piggul* invalidation from taking effect. This suffices to invalidate the offering, but without any *kares* penalty attaching to it. In the last two cases, the *piggul*-intention itself is insufficient, since it concerned only half a *kezayis*, less than the minimum necessary to invalidate.

Nevertheless, the offering is invalid. This is because both the time intention and the place intention are invalidating intentions of the same sort, notwithstanding the fact that the former carries the additional penalty of *kares*, while the latter does not. The two half-*kezayis* intentions therefore combine to form a single invalidating intention directed at a full *kezayis*.]

אָמַר רַבִּי יְהוּדָה: זֶה הַכְּלָל: אִם מַחֲשֶׁבֶת הַזְּמַן קָדְמָה לְמַחֲשֶׁבֶת הַמָּקוֹם, פִּגּוּל וְחַיָּבִים עָלָיו כָּרֵת; וְאִם מַחֲשֶׁבֶת הַמָּקוֹם קָדְמָה לְמַחֲשֶׁבֶת הַזְּמַן, פָּסוּל, וְאֵין בּוֹ כָּרֵת. — *Said R' Yehudah: This is the rule: If the intent of time preceded the intent of place, [it is] piggul and one is liable to kares over it; but if the intent of place preceded the intent of time, it is invalid, but carries no kares [penalty].*

[R' Yehudah maintains that once the *piggul*-intent has been expressed, it cannot be rendered ineffective by a subsequent improper intention. Only if the non-*piggul* invalidation precedes the *piggul* intention does the presence of the other disqualification prevent the *piggul* from taking effect.][1]

R' Yehudah maintains his position

1. R' Yehudah concurs with the ruling in the previous mishnah that *piggul* takes effect only once the *mattir* has been offered as required. Nevertheless, once the *kometz* has been

וַחֲכָמִים אוֹמְרִים: זֶה וָזֶה פָּסוּל וְאֵין בּוֹ כָּרֵת. לֶאֱכוֹל כַּחֲצִי זַיִת וּלְהַקְטִיר כַּחֲצִי זַיִת, כָּשֵׁר — שֶׁאֵין אֲכִילָה וְהַקְטָרָה מִצְטָרְפִין.

**יד אברהם**

whether the two intentions were expressed during the same *avodah* or during two separate *avodos* (*Rav*). Even within the span of one *avodah*, the first thought expressed is the one which takes effect in regard to the offering (*Rav* to *Zevachim* 2:5).

This explanation follows the interpretation of R' Yochanan in *Zevachim* (29b). According to this view, the mishnah states the cases in which the two improper intentions occur during a single *avodah* to highlight R' Yehudah's position: that even when the non-*piggul* invalidation occurs together with the *piggul*-intention in a single *avodah*, the *piggul*-intention still takes effect, according to R' Yehudah, if it occurs first. The *Gemara* (ibid.) also cites the interpretation of the *Amora* Ilpha who maintains that even R' Yehudah agrees that the precedence of the *piggul*-intent is not decisive when both are expressed during a single *avodah* (see *Gemara* there; for the explanation of the mishnah according to Ilpha, see *Yad Avraham* comm. to *Zevachim* 2:5).

וַחֲכָמִים אוֹמְרִים: זֶה וָזֶה פָּסוּל וְאֵין בּוֹ כָּרֵת. — *However, the Sages say: In either case it is invalid* (lit., *this and this are invalid*), *but it carries no kares* [*penalty*].

This is actually the opinion already stated by the first *Tanna*. The mish-

offered, the occurrence of the *piggul*-intent first in the sequence of the *avodos* gives it precedence over the non-*piggul*-intent in determining which of the two invalidations takes effect (*Keren Orah* to *Zevachim* 29b).

1 However, the Sages say: In either case it is invalid,
4 but it carries no *kares* [penalty]. [If he intended] to eat half an olive's volume and to burn half an olive's volume [on the Altar], it is valid — because eating and Altar-burning cannot be combined.



nah reiterates this position to indicate that it is the prevailing one (*Tos.* 12a, s.v. וחכ״א). The halachah follows this opinion (*Rav, Rambam, Pesulei HaMukdashin* 16:1,2).

לֶאֱכוֹל כַּחֲצִי זַיִת וּלְהַקְטִיר כַּחֲצִי זַיִת, כָּשֵׁר — שֶׁאֵין אֲכִילָה וְהַקְטָרָה מִצְטָרְפִין. — [*If he intended*] *to eat half an olive's volume and to burn half an olive's volume* [*on the Altar*], *it is valid — because eating and Altar-burning cannot be combined.*

The intent to eat [the remainder] and the intent to burn [the *kometz*] on the Altar cannot combine to form one invalidating intent. Thus, even if both intentions were for the same invalidation — either to eat half a *kezayis* and burn half a *kezayis* outside the permitted area, or to eat half a *kezayis* and burn half a *kezayis* on the Altar past the designated time — they cannot combine to invalidate, due to the dissimilarity of the intended acts. Since each half-*kezayis* intent lacks the power to invalidate on its own, the offering remains completely valid (*Rav, Rashi* to *Zevachim* 2:5).

[In the previous segment of the mishnah we learned that two disqualifying intentions each concerning just half a *kezayis* can invalidate an offering because they combine to form a single disqualifying intention directed at a full *kezayis*. There, however, the mishnah was referring to a case in which the time- and place-intents both concerned the same manner of consumption — either eating or burning on the Altar.]

### פרק שני

## Chapter Two

Chapter Two continues the delineation of the laws of *piggul* as they apply to *menachos.* The chapter deals with offerings consisting of two sacrificial components, or two offerings that are paired with each other (generally a flour offering which is associated with an animal offering), and how the two interact in regard to *piggul*.

[א] **הַקּוֹמֵץ** אֶת הַמִּנְחָה לֶאֱכוֹל שְׁיָרֶיהָ אוֹ לְהַקְטִיר קֻמְצָהּ לְמָחָר — מוֹדֶה רַבִּי יוֹסֵי בָּזֶה שֶׁהוּא פִּגּוּל וְחַיָּבִין עָלָיו כָּרֵת. לְהַקְטִיר לְבוֹנָתָהּ לְמָחָר — רַבִּי יוֹסֵי אוֹמֵר: פָּסוּל, וְאֵין בּוֹ כָּרֵת; וַחֲכָמִים אוֹמְרִים:

**ר׳ עובדיה מברטנורא**

**פרק שני – הקומץ את המנחה. (א) הקומץ את המנחה. מודה רבי יוסי שהוא פגול.** מפום דבעי למתני סיפא להקטיר לבונתה למחר רבי יוסי אומר פסול ואין בו כרת, מהו דתימא טעמא דרבי יוסי משום דסבר אין מפגלין בחצי מתיר, כלומר שאם חשב לעבוד למחר עבודת חצי מתיר לא פיגל, והך לבונה חצי מתיר הוא, דבין הקטרת קומץ ולבונה מתירים השירים, ואפילו רישא כי חשב בהקטרת קומץ עבודת חצי מתיר היא ופליג רבי יוסי, קא משמע לן דבהא מודה, דטעמא לאו משום הכי הוא, אלא משום דאין מתיר מפגל את המתיר:

**יד אברהם**

## 1.

The first mishnah analyzes the relationship between a *minchah*-offering's *kometz* and its *levonah* (frankincense) in regard to *piggul*. When a *minchah* is offered, it must contain a measure of *levonah* (the amount of a *kometz*). The *levonah* is placed on top of the *minchah* but is not taken together with the flour during *kemitzah*. Rather, it is pushed to one side before *kemitzah*, so that a *kometz* of flour can be removed without containing any grains of *levonah*. After the removal of the *kometz* of flour and its placement in a *kli shareis*, the *levonah* is gathered up and added to the *kometz* of flour in the *kli shareis* and the two are then burnt together on the Altar (*Rambam, Maaseh HaKorbanos* 13:12).[1]

A *minchah's* offering is not valid unless its *levonah* is also burnt (mishnah 3:5). Thus, an intent concerning the time of its burning should also be capable of effecting *piggul*. The following mishnah will discuss whether a *piggul*-intent during the *kemitzah* of the flour which is directed toward the burning of the *levonah* can indeed effect *piggul*.

הַקּוֹמֵץ אֶת הַמִּנְחָה לֶאֱכוֹל שְׁיָרֶיהָ אוֹ לְהַקְטִיר קֻמְצָהּ לְמָחָר — *[If] one performs kemitzah on a minchah-offering [intending] to eat its remainder or to burn its kometz tomorrow —*

[The *Kohen* bringing the offering

1. This is the sequence given by *Rambam*. It comes from the *Tosefta* (*Menachos* 1:10) and is cited by the *Gemara* in *Sotah* 14b. However, *Rashi* here (14b, s.v. ליקוט לבונה) seems to state that the *levonah* is gathered up after the *kometz* is burnt on the Altar and that the two are in fact not burnt together (*Mishneh LaMelech* to *Maaseh HaKorbanos* 13:12). Moreover, in yet another departure from the procedure described by the *Gemara* in *Sotah*, *Rashi* states here (16b, s.v. הילוך דמתן כלי) that the *levonah* need not be placed in a *kli shareis* for sanctification after it is removed from the flour [but it may be taken as is to the Altar for burning]. *Sfas Emes* (to 13b) suggests that *Rashi* may have understood from various indications in our *Gemara* here that the *Gemara* of *Menachos* assumes a different sequence than the *Gemara* of *Sotah* for the offering of the *kometz* and *levonah*.

2
1

1. [If] one performs *kemitzah* on a *minchah*-offering [intending] to eat its remainder or to burn its *kometz* tomorrow — R' Yose agrees in this case that it is *piggul* and that one is liable to *kares* over it. [If his intention was] to burn its frankincense tomorrow — R' Yose says: It is invalid, but it carries no *kares* [penalty]; but the Sages say:

### YAD AVRAHAM

intended, at the time of *kemitzah*, to delay eating the remainder of the *minchah* or burning its *kometz* on the Altar until the next day.]

מוֹדֶה רַבִּי יוֹסֵי בָזֶה שֶׁהוּא פִגּוּל וְחַיָּבִין עָלָיו כָּרֵת. — *R' Yose agrees in this case that it is piggul and that one is liable to kares over it.*

[The *minchah* is rendered *piggul* by either of these intentions and its consumption is now punishable by *kares*.] This is actually a typical case of *piggul* in a *minchah*-offering (as stated in mishnah 1:3), and R' Yose's concurrence with this ruling is explicated only because of his dissent in the very similar case which follows (*Rav* from *Gem.* 13a).

לְהַקְטִיר לְבוֹנָתָהּ לְמָחָר — — *[If his intention was] to burn its frankincense tomorrow —*

[If, while performing *kemitzah* on the flour, he intended to postpone burning the *levonah* of the *minchah* until the next day ...]

רַבִּי יוֹסֵי אוֹמֵר: פָּסוּל, וְאֵין בּוֹ כָּרֵת; — *R' Yose says: It is invalid, but it carries no kares [penalty];*

[The *minchah* is invalidated by this intention, but it does not become *piggul* and hence is not subject to the *kares* penalty.]

An offering's components can be divided into two categories: parts which permit — known as *mattirim* (sing., *mattir* — and parts which become permitted [either for eating or for burning on the Altar]. As explained in mishnah 1:3, the *mattir* in the case of a *minchah* is the part of the offering whose burning on the Altar permits the remainder of the offering to be eaten. Both the *kometz* and the *levonah* are considered the *mattirim* of the *minchah* (*Rashi* 13b, s.v. אומר היה ר' יוסי), because the *minchah* may not be eaten until both have been burnt on the Altar (see mishnah 3:5). In the opinion of R' Yose, when an offering has two *mattirim*, an intention expressed concerning one *mattir* while performing the *avodah* of the other *mattir* cannot render the offering *piggul* [אֵין מַתִּיר מְפַגֵּל מַתִּיר]. Therefore, if while performing the *kemitzah* of the flour, the *Kohen* intended to burn the *levonah* tomorrow, he does not render the *minchah*-offering *piggul* (*Rav* from *Gem.* 13b).

Nevertheless, the offering is invalidated by Rabbinic law to safeguard against the case in which he intends to burn the *kometz* itself tomorrow (*Gem.* 14b). [Performing the *kemitzah* of the flour while intending to burn the *kometz* tomorrow would render the *minchah*-offering *piggul* even according to R' Yose, since the intention and the act would then both involve the same *mattir*: the *kometz* of flour.]

פִּגּוּל וְחַיָּבִין עָלָיו כָּרֵת. אָמְרוּ לוֹ: מַה שָׁנָה זוֹ מִן
הַזֶּבַח? אָמַר לָהֶם: שֶׁהַזֶּבַח – דָּמוֹ, וּבְשָׂרוֹ,
וְאֵמוּרָיו אֶחָד, וּלְבוֹנָה אֵינָהּ מִן הַמִּנְחָה.

---

### ר' עובדיה מברטנורא

**מַה שָׁנָה זוֹ מִן הַזֶּבַח.** שֶׁהַשּׁוֹחֲטוֹ עַל מְנָת לְהַקְטִיר אֵמוּרִים לְמָחָר, פִּגּוּל: **אֵינָהּ מִן הַמִּנְחָה.** אֵינָהּ
מִמִּין הַמִּנְחָה כְּמוֹ הַקּוֹמֶץ, וְאַף עַל פִּי שֶׁהוּא מִמַּתִּירֵי הַמִּנְחָה, דְּקָסְבַר רַבִּי יוֹסֵי שָׁאֵין מַתִּיר מְפַגֵּל
אֶת הַמַּתִּיר, שָׁאֵין עֲבוֹדַת מַתִּיר זֶה שָׁהוּא קוֹמֶץ מוֹעֶלֶת לְפַגֵּל מַתִּיר הָאַחֵר שֶׁהִיא הַלְּבוֹנָה בְּמַחֲשָׁבָה
שֶׁהוּא מְחַשֵּׁב עַל הַלְּבוֹנָה בַּעֲבוֹדַת הַקּוֹמֶץ, וְרַבָּנָן אָמְרֵי לֵיהּ, כִּי אָמְרִינָן דְּאֵין מַתִּיר מְפַגֵּל אֶת
הַמַּתִּיר, הֵיכָא דְּלָא אֶקְבְּעוּ בְּחַד מָנָא, כְּגוֹן שְׁנֵי כְבָשֵׂי עֲצֶרֶת דִּשְׁנֵיהֶם מַתִּירִים אֶת הַלֶּחֶם, וְאִם שָׁחַט
אֶחָד מֵהֶם עַל מְנָת לֶאֱכוֹל אֶת חֲבֵירוֹ לְמָחָר, שְׁנֵיהֶם כְּשֵׁרִים, אֲבָל הֵיכָא דְּאֶקְבְּעוּ בְּחַד מָנָא, כְּגוֹן
קוֹמֶץ וּלְבוֹנָה שֶׁשְּׁנֵיהֶם בִּכְלִי אֶחָד, מוֹעֶלֶת מַחֲשֶׁבֶת מַתִּיר זֶה לְפַגֵּל מַתִּיר אַחֵר. וַהֲלָכָה כַּחֲכָמִים:

---

### יד אברהם

— וַחֲכָמִים אוֹמְרִים: פִּגּוּל וְחַיָּבִין עָלָיו כָּרֵת.
but the Sages say: [It is] piggul and
one is liable to kares over it.

[The Sages dispute R' Yose's ruling
and consider an intention during the
kemitzah of the flour about the burning of the levonah an effective piggul-
intention. One is therefore liable to
kares for eating the remainder of this
minchah.]

The Sages do not reject the principle
that piggul-intent during the avodah
of one mattir concerning another mattir cannot bring about a state of piggul.
Their ruling in mishnah 5 makes it
clear that indeed they too follow this
rule, as will be explained there. However, they restrict its application to instances in which the two mattirim are
independent bodies, such as the two
lambs of mishnah 5. In the case of this
mishnah they contend that since the
flour and levonah are both together in
the same vessel prior to kemitzah, the

vessel joins them into one legal entity
which is treated as a single body. Within a single sacrificial body, the Sages
rule that piggul-intent concerning any
part of it is effective in bringing about
piggul on the whole (Rav from Gem.
13b, Rashi).

— אָמְרוּ לוֹ: מַה שָׁנָה זוֹ מִן הַזֶּבַח? They
said to him: How is this different
from an animal sacrifice?

[An animal sacrifice also has two
parts offered on the Altar — its blood,
which is applied to the walls of the
Altar; and its emurin (sacrificial parts),
which are burnt on the Altar.] If the
animal is slaughtered with the intention of burning its emurin the next
day, it is rendered piggul, as stated
(without dispute) in Zevachim, mishnah 2:2 (Rav, Rashi), even though
the slaughter and the application of
the blood are two different mattirim
(Tif. Yis.).[1] Therefore, a minchah
too should be rendered piggul by the

---

1. [This cannot mean simply that two avodos are treated as the equivalent of two mattirim, since that would apply just as well to kemitzah and burning the kometz of the
minchah, and there would be no need for the Sages to prove their point from animal
offerings. Rather, the point would seem to be that the slaughter is considered primarily
a mattir of the blood, in that it sanctifies it for the remainder of its avodah (see Rashi 14b,
s.v. בשעת שחיטה; Tos. 14b, s.v. שחיטה וזריקה). Burning the emurin, on the other hand, is

2
1 [It is] *piggul* and one is liable to *kares* over it. They said to him: How is this different from an animal sacrifice? He said to them: Because [with] an animal sacrifice the blood, meat, and sacrificial parts are one, whereas the frankincense is not from the *minchah*-offering.

**YAD AVRAHAM**

intention during the *kemitzah* of the flour to burn the *levonah* past its time.

*Shitah Mekubetzes* (13a #4) explains the analogy to refer to the application of the animal offering's blood to the Altar and the burning of its *emurin* (rather than its slaughter). Both of these *avodos* are considered *mattirim* of the offering's meat for consumption, inasmuch as the meat does not become permitted for eating until the blood is thrown against the Altar wall, nor may it be eaten before the *emurin* are burnt as long as they are in existence and still fit for burning (see *Pesachim* 59b).[1] Thus, throwing the blood with the intention of burning the *emurin* the next day is tantamount to performing the *avodah* of one *mattir* with *piggul*-intent concerning another *mattir*.

**אָמַר לָהֶם: שֶׁהַזֶּבַח — דָּמוֹ, וּבְשָׂרוֹ, וְאֵמוּרָיו אֶחָד,** — *He said to them: Because [with] an animal sacrifice the blood, meat, and sacrificial parts are one,*

R' Yose responds that the relationship of an animal offering's blood, meat, and *emurin* is much closer than that of the *kometz* and *levonah* within the *minchah*. All the components of an animal offering are treated as one sacrifice, in which the blood serves as the *mattir* [not only of the meat but also] of the *emurin* themselves. [That is, the application of the blood not only permits the meat to be eaten, it also permits the *emurin* to be burnt on the Altar.] Accordingly, the *emurin* are not viewed as an independent *mattir*, and even R' Yose therefore accepts that a *piggul*-intent expressed during the *avodah* of the blood concerning the *emurin* is effective (*Rashi* 13b, s.v. אינה בעיכוב מנחה; *Meleches Shlomo; Tif. Yis.*). [His rule comes into play only in cases in which the two *mattirim* do not directly affect each other and their only relationship is that they both serve as *mattirim* of the same offering.]

**וּלְבוֹנָה אֵינָהּ מִן הַמִּנְחָה.** — *whereas the frankincense is not from the minchah-offering.*

[The relationship of the *kometz* of a

a *mattir* of the meat for eating, insofar that as long as the *emurin* are in existence and fit for burning, the meat may not be eaten until they have been burnt.]

1. Nevertheless, there is a difference in this respect between the function served by applying the blood of the sacrifice to the Altar and burning its *emurin*. The meat of the offering can never become permitted for eating unless the blood is applied. Burning the *emurin*, however, is not critical to permitting the consumption of the meat; if the *emurin* become disqualified or lost, the meat may be eaten even though the *emurin* will never be burnt (*Pesachim* 59b).

[However, though the mishnah compares the burning of the *levonah* to the burning of the *emurin*, the analogy does not hold true in this last respect. A *minchah's* remainder can never become permitted for consumption without its *levonah* being burnt on the Altar.]

[ב] **שָׁחַט** שְׁנֵי כְבָשִׂים לֶאֱכוֹל אַחַת מִן הַחַלּוֹת לְמָחָר; הִקְטִיר שְׁנֵי

ר׳ עובדיה מברטנורא

(ב) **שחט שני כבשים.** של עלרת, דכתיב בהו (ויקרא כג,יט) שני כבשים בני שנה לזבח שלמים, ואותן כבשים מתירין ומקדשין לשתי הלחם, שאין הלחם קדוש אלא בשחיטת שני כבשים, הואיל והוזקקו עמו בתנופה. ושאר כבשים של עלרת דמוספים ניגהו: **לאכול אחת מן החלות למחר.** וזמן אכילת החלות אינו אלא ליום ולילה, כדין מנחה, שנאמר בה (שם ו,י) כחטאת וכאשם:

יד אברהם

*minchah* to its *levonah* is not one in which a single *mattir* serves to permit all the components in the offering.] The *levonah* is not considered part of the main body of the *minchah* in the same way as the remainder of the *minchah*. This can be seen from the fact that the burning of the *levonah* may even precede the burning of the *kometz*,[1] whereas the *minchah's* remainder may not be eaten until after the *kometz* is burnt (*Gem.* ad loc.; cf. *Rav, Tos. Chadashim*). Since the *levonah* is not directly affected by the *kemitzah*, it is considered an independent *mattir*. Therefore, it is subject to the principle that an intention concerning one *mattir* which is expressed during the *avodah* of another *mattir* does not render the offering *piggul* (*Rashi* ad loc.).

The Sages, however, maintain that the fact that the *minchah* and the *levonah* reside together in one vessel before *kemitzah* suffices to combine them into one unit, so that an improper intention during one concerning the other renders the *minchah*-offering *piggul*, as explained above (*Rav* from *Gem.* ibid.). Only in cases in which the two *mattirim* are completely separate bodies (such as the two lambs of mishnah 5; see comm. there) do the Sages accept the rule that cross-*mattir* intentions cannot effect *piggul* (*Rav*).

The halachah follows the opinion of the Sages (*Rav; Rambam, Hil. Pesulei HaMukdashin* 14:10; see *Zevach Todah*, s.v. להקטיר לבונתה).

## 2.

The next three mishnayos deal with the *piggul* rules of sanctified substances (generally *menachos* of some type) which are not in themselves offered on the Altar, but which require the offering of some associated sacrifice to permit them for consumption. Since the *avodah* performed on the substance which is placed on the Altar acts to permit the non-Altar substance as well, the intent to eat the non-Altar item past its time is considered a *piggul*-intent. These mishnayos will define to what extent such linkage effects *piggul*.

The first two of these cases to be discussed are the שְׁתֵּי הַלֶּחֶם, *shtei halechem*, and the לֶחֶם הַפָּנִים, *lechem hapanim*. The *shtei halechem* are the two loaves that the Torah (*Lev.* 23:15ff) dictates be brought on Shavuos together with two lambs for a communal *shelamim*-offering (see preface to mishnah 4:2, and 11:1). No part of these two loaves is offered on the Altar; rather, they are waved

1. Although the *levonah* may be burnt before the *kometz* is burnt, it should not be burnt before the *kemitzah* of the flour (*Tos.* to 14a and *Zevachim* 43a s.v. והלבונה).

2 2. [If] he slaughtered [the] two lambs [intending] to
2 eat one of the loaves tomorrow; [or] he burnt



together with the two lambs in the rite known as *tenufah* (mishnah 5:6) and are then eaten by the *Kohanim* after the two *shelamim* lambs have been offered.

The *lechem hapanim* are twelve loaves that are placed each Shabbos on the *shulchan*, the golden table which stands in the קוֹדֶשׁ, *Holy*, in the Sanctuary of the Temple (*Lev.* 24:5ff). These are placed on the *shulchan* in two arrangements of six loaves each. Together with the loaves, two spoons full of *levonah* are placed on the *shulchan*, one for each rack of loaves. The following Shabbos, the loaves and spoons are removed and replaced by a new arrangement. The outgoing *levonah* is burnt on the Altar, and the old loaves are then eaten by the *Kohanim* (see mishnah 11:5ff).

שָׁחַט שְׁנֵי כְבָשִׂים — *[If] he slaughtered [the] two lambs*

[The two loaves of the *shtei halechem* are not offered upon the Altar; their sanctification and permission to be eaten derives entirely from the *avodah* done to the two *shelamim* lambs that accompany them. The slaughter of the lambs sanctifies them and the application of their blood to the Altar permits the *shtei halechem* to be eaten.]

Actually, the Torah describes a total of thirteen animals to be brought as offerings on Shavuos along with the two loaves of the *shtei halechem* (*Lev.* 23:17-19). The others, though, are *olos* and *chataos*, not *shelamim* (*Rav, Rambam Comm.*), and they are not associated with the *shtei halechem* in any sacrificial procedure. The Torah, however, requires (ibid. v.20) that the two *shelamim* lambs be waved together with the two loaves of the *shtei halechem* in the procedure known as *tenufah* (waving; see comm. to 3:2). This indicates that the Torah considers the two *shelamim* lambs integral parts of the *shtei halechem* offering and not just additional offerings (*Rav, Rambam Comm., Rashi* from *Gem.* 46b).[1]

לֶאֱכוֹל אַחַת מִן הַחַלּוֹת לְמָחָר; — *[intending] to eat one of the loaves tomorrow;*

The time allotted for eating these loaves is a day and a night [the day on which the lambs are offered and the night which follows], the same as for a regular *minchah* (*Rav*). [Therefore, the intention to eat them afterward constitutes an intention of *piggul*. Since the offering of the lambs serves as the *avodah* of the *shtei halechem*, a *piggul*-intention expressed during the slaughter of the lambs in regard to the consumption of the two loaves can render the offering *piggul*.]

1. *Rav* refers to the additional *olos* as part of the *mussaf*-offering. The *Gem.* (45b), however, quotes a *Baraisa* in which R' Akiva clearly distinguishes between the *mussaf*-offerings mentioned in *Numbers* 28:27 and the additional *olos* and *chataos* that accompany the *shtei halechem* (mentioned in *Leviticus*). *Rashi* and *Rambam* in their comm. here indeed do not refer to these as part of the *mussaf* (*Rashash* ). [However, *Shitah Mekubetzes* to 13b #20 cites a manuscript edition of *Rashi* which states the same as *Rav*, and from which *Rav* was obviously quoting.]

*Kesef Mishneh* to *Temidin U'Mussafin* 8:1 is of the opinion that R' Akiva's view on this point is disputed by the other *Tanna* in that *Baraisa* who, it seems, holds that the seven lambs mentioned in *Leviticus* are identical with the seven lambs mentioned in *Numbers* as part of the *mussaf* (see *Sfas Emes* to *Gem.* 45b).

מנחות ב/ב

בָזִיכִין לֶאֱכוֹל אֶחָד מִן הַסְּדָרִים לְמָחָר – רַבִּי יוֹסֵי אוֹמֵר: אוֹתָהּ הַחַלָּה וְאוֹתוֹ הַסֵּדֶר שֶׁחִשֵּׁב עָלָיו פִּגּוּל, וְחַיָּבִין עָלָיו כָּרֵת; וְהַשֵּׁנִי פָּסוּל וְאֵין בּוֹ כָּרֵת. וַחֲכָמִים אוֹמְרִים: זֶה וְזֶה פִּגּוּל, וְחַיָּבִין עָלָיו כָּרֵת.

### ר' עובדיה מברטנורא

**הקטיר שתי בזיכין.** לשתי מערכות של לחם הפנים, כדכתיב (ויקרא כד,ו) ושמת אותם שתים מערכות, והיתה על כל מערכת כף אחת שיש בו לבונה, כדכתיב (שם שם,ז) ונתת על המערכת לבונה זכה, ושתי הכפות הללו שבהם נתונה הלבונה נקראים שני בזיכים, והלבונה נקטרת כדכתיב (שם) והיתה ללחם לאזכרה, והלחם נאכל, וזמן אכילתו כל אותו שבת שמסירים אותו מן השלחן בלבד, ואם בשעה שהקטיר שני בזיכים של לבונה חשב על אחת מן המערכות של לחם לאכלו למחר, כלומר שלא בזמנו: **אותה חלה.** של שתי הלחם של עצרת: **ואותו הסדר.** של לחם הפנים: **זה וזה פגול.** שכולן נחשבים גוף אחד:

### יד אברהם

הִקְטִיר שְׁנֵי בָזִיכִין — *[or] he burnt the two spoonfuls [of frankincense]*

[The loaves of the *lechem hapanim* are not offered on the Altar. Rather, their *avodah* consists of burning the two spoonfuls of *levonah*, and it is this which permits the loaves to be eaten by the *Kohanim*. Thus, a *piggul*-intention expressed during the burning of the *levonah* concerning the consumption of the loaves is a *piggul*-intention.]

– לֶאֱכוֹל אֶחָד מִן הַסְּדָרִים לְמָחָר — *[intending] to eat one of the arrangements tomorrow* —

The loaves of the *lechem hapanim* may be eaten only on the Shabbos on which they are removed from the *shulchan* [golden table] (*Rav*) and the night which follows (*Tos. Yom Tov*; see mishnah 11:7). [Therefore, the intention to eat them the following day is a *piggul*-intention.]

*Rambam* in his *Comm.* cites the verse: בְּיוֹם הַשַּׁבָּת בְּיוֹם הַשַּׁבָּת, *on the Sabbath day, on the Sabbath day* (*Lev.* 24:8), as the Biblical source for the law that the *lechem hapanim* is eaten for only a day [and a night]. *Tos. Yom Tov* is somewhat puzzled by this, since that verse refers to arranging the *lechem hapanim*, not to eating them. He therefore suggests as an alternative the fact that the passage refers to the loaves as קֹדֶשׁ קָדָשִׁים, *most holy* (v. 9), indicating that they have the same status as other *most holy* offerings which must all be eaten within a day and night (see *Zevachim* 5:3ff).

רַבִּי יוֹסֵי אוֹמֵר: אוֹתָהּ הַחַלָּה וְאוֹתוֹ הַסֵּדֶר שֶׁחִשֵּׁב עָלָיו פִּגּוּל, וְחַיָּבִין עָלָיו כָּרֵת; — *R' Yose says: That loaf or that arrangement about which he [expressed his] intention is piggul, and one is liable to kares over it;*

The one loaf of the *shtei halechem*, or the one arrangement of *lechem hapanim*, that he intended to eat past its time becomes *piggul* (*Rav*). [Since he expressed a *piggul*-intention during the *avodah* which would ordinarily serve to permit this loaf or arrangement of loaves, it is rendered *piggul* even though the *avodah* was performed on the associated offering and not on the loaf itself.]

וְהַשֵּׁנִי פָּסוּל וְאֵין בּוֹ כָּרֵת. — *and the second one is invalid but carries no [penalty of] kares.*

[The loaf of the *shtei halechem* and the arrangement of the *lechem hapa-*

2 the two spoonfuls [of frankincense intending] to eat
2 one of the arrangements tomorrow — R' Yose says: That loaf or that arrangement about which he [expressed his] intention is *piggul,* and one is liable to *kares* over it; and the second one is invalid but carries no [penalty of] *kares.* But the Sages say: Both are *piggul,* and one is liable to *kares* over them.

**YAD AVRAHAM**

*nim* about which he did not intend *piggul* are not rendered *piggul* despite the *piggul*-invalidation of their companions. Nevertheless, they are invalidated even according to R' Yose, apparently by Rabbinic decree (see commentary to mishnah 1, s.v. רבי יוסי אומר).]

Although one who intends to eat even one *kezayis* of a *minchah* or animal sacrifice past its time renders the entire offering *piggul* (and not just that one *kezayis*), that is because the entire *minchah* or animal offering is considered a single unit [in the case of a *minchah*, by virtue of the vessel in which it is brought]. The two loaves of the *shtei halechem* and the two arrangements of *lechem hapanim*, however, are each considered separate entities, according to R' Yose (*Tif. Yis.*).

The *Gemara* (13b) cites another statement, which it attributes to R' Yose, that if his *piggul*-intention consisted of an intention to eat half a *kezayis* of each loaf past its time, they combine to form an intention concerning a full *kezayis*, and the entire offering is rendered *piggul* as a result. [As we learned in mishnah 1:3, an intention must concern at least one *kezayis* in order to bring about a state of *piggul*.] It is thus apparent that, even according to R' Yose, the two loaves can be considered as two parts of one unit. The *Gemara* (14b) explains R' Yose's opinion to be based on Scriptural indications that the Torah views the two loaves as a single unit in certain circumstances, but also as separate entities in other circumstances. This, according to R' Yose, teaches that if he treated them separately in his intent, they are viewed separately; but if his intent joined them together, they are dealt with as one unit. Thus, if he intended *piggul* in regard to only one of the loaves or arrangements, he has separated them in his mind and only that one unit is affected. However, if he intended *piggul* for half a *kezayis* of each of them, he has joined them in his mind, and they are therefore treated as a single entity, which results in the *piggul* taking effect.

וַחֲכָמִים אוֹמְרִים: זֶה וָזֶה פִּגּוּל, וְחַיָּבִין עָלָיו כָּרֵת. — *But the Sages say: Both* (lit., *this one and that one*) *are piggul, and one is liable to kares over them.*

The Sages contend that both loaves of the *shtei halechem*, as well as both arrangements of *lechem hapanim*, are treated as one unit (*Rav*) [and thus the *piggul* which takes effect concerning the one takes effect concerning the other as well].

The mishnah has discussed a case in which the *piggul*-intention concerned an entire arrangement of *lechem hapanim* loaves, when in fact the same could have been said had the intention concerned just one of the arrangement's six loaves. This was done in order to emphasize that even in a case in which his intention concerned a full arrangement of loaves, it is still the opinion of R' Yose that the other arrangement does not become *piggul*. However, according to the Sages, even if his intention concerned just one loaf — or even one

נִטְמֵאת אַחַת מִן הַחַלּוֹת אוֹ אֶחָד מִן הַסְּדָרִים – רַבִּי יְהוּדָה אוֹמֵר: שְׁנֵיהֶם יֵצְאוּ לְבֵית הַשְּׂרֵפָה, שֶׁאֵין קָרְבַּן צִבּוּר חָלוּק. וַחֲכָמִים אוֹמְרִים: הַטָּמֵא בְּטֻמְאָתוֹ, וְהַטָּהוֹר יֵאָכֵל.

**ר׳ עובדיה מברטנורא**

**נטמאת אחת מן החלות.** דוקא בנטמאת אחת משתי הלחם קודם זריקת דם הכבשים, או אחד מן הסדרים קודם הקטרת הבזיכים, הוא דאפליגו רבי יהודה ורבנן, אבל אם נטמא לאחר זריקת הדם או לאחר הקטרת הבזיכים, דברי הכל הטמא בטומאתו והטהור יאכל: **שאין קרבן צבור חלוק.** בגמרא (דף טו,א) מסיק דלא מקרא ולא מסברא אמרה רבי יהודה למלתיה, אלא תלמוד ערוך בידו, וכך היה מקובל מרבותיו שאין קרבן צבור חלוק, ואם נפסל אציו נפסל כולו:

**יד אברהם**

*kezayis* of one loaf (see *Zevach Todah*) — both arrangements become *piggul* (*Tos.* 13b, s.v. לאכול אחד מן הסדרים). The same applies to the *shtei halechem* (*Zevach Todah;* see 1:3).

נִטְמֵאת אַחַת מִן הַחַלּוֹת אוֹ אֶחָד מִן הַסְּדָרִים — *[If] one of the loaves or one of the arrangements became tamei* —

[Any sanctified offering substance becomes disqualified by becoming *tamei* (ritually contaminated). Thus, if the *shtei halechem* loaves or *lechem hapanim* arrangements came in contact with some *tumah*-transmitting object and thereby became *tamei*, they are invalidated and, like any other invalidated sacrificial matter, they must be burned away from the Altar. The mishnah now considers what to do if only one of the two *shtei halechem* loaves or *lechem hapanim* arrangements became *tamei*. Unquestionably, that one loaf or arrangement must be destroyed; however, the mishnah will record a difference of opinion whether the invalidation of the one (by reason of *tumah*) automatically invalidates its companion as well.]

This discussion concerns only a case in which the *tumah*-contamination occurs before the blood of the lambs is applied to the Altar, or in the case of the *lechem hapanim* arrangements, before the *levonah* is burnt. Once the blood has been applied or the *levonah* burnt, the offering has been completed and all agree that only the one which was rendered *tamei* is affected while the other remains valid (*Rav, Rambam Comm.* from *Gem.* 14b, *Rashi*). [Once the procedures which validate an offering have been completed, there is no longer any relationship between the different components of the offering unless they are physically connected. Thus, even the dismembered limbs of an animal offering are not affected by each other's disqualifications once the offering's blood has been applied to the Altar. All the more so, then, that once the sacrificial procedure for the *shtei halechem* and *lechem hapanim* has been concluded, they are viewed as separate units which cannot be affected by each other's invalidations.]

רַבִּי יְהוּדָה אוֹמֵר: שְׁנֵיהֶם יֵצְאוּ לְבֵית הַשְּׂרֵפָה, — *R' Yehudah says: They should both go out to the place of burning,*

[The second loaf or arrangement of loaves becomes invalidated by default (although only the first is actually

2
2 [If] one of the loaves or one of the arrangements became *tamei* — R' Yehudah says: They should both go out to the place of burning, because a communal offering is not divisible; but the Sages say: The one which is *tamei* [remains] in its [state of] *tumah*, but the one which is *tahor* is eaten.

### YAD AVRAHAM

*tamei*), because one of them cannot be valid without the other (see below). Therefore, both must be burned away from the Altar at the *place of burning.*]

There were two places known as בֵּית הַשְּׂרֵפָה, *the place of burning*. One was located in the Temple Courtyard [to the east of the Altar, according to *Sifra, Lev.* 1:16] and the other outside the Courtyard on the Temple Mount. [This latter one was known as the בִּירָה, *birah*; see *Zevachim* 104b; *Rambam, Maaseh HaKorbanos* 7:4.] The mishnah in *Shekalim* (8:6,7) records a major Tannaitic dispute about which invalidations are burned at which site. *Rambam* (loc. cit.) accepts as halachah the view of R' Akiva there, according to which these invalidated loaves would be burned at the Courtyard site (see further, *Yad Avraham* comm. to *Zevachim* 12:6, s.v. נשרפין בבית הבירה).]

.שֶׁאֵין קָרְבַּן צִבּוּר חָלוּק — *because a communal offering is not divisible;*

An offering which is made on behalf of the entire nation, such as the *shtei halechem* or the *lechem hapanim*, must be treated as a single unit. Thus, if it cannot all be accepted as an offering (because part of it has become *tamei*), none of it is valid (*Rashi* 14b).

The *Gemara* states that R' Yehudah did not offer any derivation for his rule about the indivisibility of communal offerings; rather it was the tradition he had received from his teachers, that an offering of the congregation is indivisible, and if a portion of it is rendered unfit the entire offering becomes invalidated (*Rav* from *Gem.* 15a).

.וַחֲכָמִים אוֹמְרִים: הַטָּמֵא בְּטֻמְאָתוֹ, וְהַטָּהוֹר יֵאָכֵל — *but the Sages say: The one which is tamei [remains] in its [state of] tumah, but the one which is tahor is eaten.*

[The Sages do not accept R' Yehudah's tradition but rule that the invalidation of one of the paired offerings (for reasons other than *piggul*) does not automatically invalidate its companion. Therefore, the one loaf or arrangement of loaves which became *tamei* is disqualified, but the remaining one should be eaten.]

The halachah follows the view of the Sages (*Rav; Rambam Comm., Hil. Temidin U'Mussafin* 5:16).

Although both arrangements of the *lechem hapanim* and both loaves of the *shtei halechem*-offering have become invalidated according to R' Yehudah, and at least one of them according to the Sages, the *levonah* of the *lechem hapanim* or the blood of the accompanying lambs is still offered on the Altar (*Zevach Todah*).

Both aspects of this ruling require amplification. The case in which some of the breads of the *lechem hapanim* became *tamei* would seem to be akin to the case in which some of them were lost or destroyed. The *Gemara* (8a, 9b) states that if a part of the *lechem hapanim* was lost before the breads were removed from the *shulchan*, the *levonah* is not burnt on the Altar and everything is invalid. If, however, the loss occurred after the removal, or at least after

[ג] **הַתּוֹדָה** מְפַגֶּלֶת אֶת הַלֶּחֶם, וְהַלֶּחֶם אֵינוֹ מְפַגֵּל אֶת הַתּוֹדָה. כֵּיצַד? הַשּׁוֹחֵט אֶת הַתּוֹדָה לֶאֱכוֹל מִמֶּנָּה לְמָחָר, הִיא וְהַלֶּחֶם מְפֻגָּלִין. לֶאֱכוֹל מִן

### ר׳ עובדיה מברטנורא

(ג) **התודה מפגלת את הלחם.** שהלחם בא בשביל התודה והוא טפל לה, ואין התודה טפילה ללחם, וכן שני כבשים של עצרת, שתי הלחם הבאים עמהם הם טפלים לכבשים ואין הכבשים טפלים ללחם, והעיקר מפגל הטפילה ואין הטפילה מפגל העיקר, ואי אשמועינן תנא האי דינא בתודה ולא אשמועינן בכבשים של עצרת, הוה אמינא התם הוא דכי מפגל לחם לא מפגלא תודה משום דלא הוזקקו בתנופה עם החלות, אבל כבשים דהוזקקו בתנופה עם החלות, דכתיב (ויקרא כג,כ) והניף הכהן אותם על הלחם, אימא כי מפגל לחם לפגלו נמי כבשים, ואי תנא כבשים, הוה אמינא התם כי מפגלי כבשים מפגל לחם משום דהוזקקו זה עם זה בתנופה, אבל תודה דלא הוזקקו, אימא כי מפגל בתודה לא מפגלי בחלות, צריכא:

### יד אברהם

the time for removal had arrived (even if the removal had not actually taken place), the spoonfuls of *levonah* are burnt on the Altar. Nevertheless, the breads that remain are *not* eaten. [This is the same rule as for a *minchah* of which part of its remainder became lost or *tamei* after the *kemitzah* but before the burning of the *kometz* (see *Gem.* 9a,b).]

Accordingly, even if we were to assume that our mishnah refers to a case in which the one arrangement of *lechem hapanim* that became *tamei* was contaminated after the time had come to remove it — so that it is permitted to burn the spoonfuls of *levonah* — the uncontaminated arrangement should still not become permitted for eating (even according to the Sages).

*Zevach Todah* responds that we must conclude from this that the invalidation resulting from *tumah* is not the equivalent of being lost, but that since all the *lechem hapanim* is in fact present at the time the spoonfuls of *levonah* are burnt on the Altar, the burning permits the arrangement that did not become *tamei* (see further in his comments to *Gem.* 26a, s.v. ומסיק הג׳ בסוף).

In the case of the *tumah*-contamination of one of the *shtei halechem's* loaves, the reason there is no impediment to completing the offering of the *shelamim* lambs, or to eating the still-uncontaminated loaf (according to the Sages), would seem to be the ruling stated in the mishnah 4:3, that the presence of the loaves is not crucial to the offering of the lambs, and even if the loaves are destroyed or lost the two lambs should be offered. However, the *Gemara* (46a) states that once the lambs have been slaughtered, the *shtei halechem* become bound to them, and if either is now lost, the others are also invalidated (*Rashi* ibid.; see comm. at the end of mishnah 4:3). Since our mishnah presumably refers to a case in which the loaf became *tamei* even after the slaughter of the lambs, how can the mishnah validate the offering of the lambs? (See *Shitah Mekubetzes* 15a #1.) It would seem that here too a distinction must be made between a case in which the loaf was lost and one in which it become contaminated with *tumah* (as differentiated by *Zevach Todah* above in regard to the *lechem hapanim*).[1]

1. *Chazon Ish* (32:32) approaches these problems on the basis of רִצּוּי צִיץ, *the acceptance effected by the tzitz* for *tumah*-contaminated offerings. An exposition of his resolution, however, is beyond the scope of this work.

2
3

3. The *todah*-offering renders the bread *piggul*, but the bread does not render the *todah*-offering *piggul*. How so? [If] one slaughters the *todah*-offering [intending] to eat from it tomorrow, [both] it and the bread become *piggul*. [However, if

YAD AVRAHAM

### 3.

A *todah* [thanksgiving-offering] is a type of *shelamim* [peace offering] which is brought voluntarily to express one's gratitude to *Hashem* for having been delivered from a dangerous situation, specifically, those dangers mentioned in *Psalm* 107 — travel across the sea or desert, imprisonment, or illness (*Rashi* to *Lev*. 7:12, from *Berachos* 54b). One who vows to bring a *todah* must bring an animal (sheep, goat or cattle) accompanied by forty loaves, ten each of four different types (see mishnah 7:1). These are eaten along with the sacrifice (*Lev*. loc. cit.).

No part of these loaves is offered on the Altar. Rather, they are sanctified by the slaughter of the animal and become permitted for eating with the application of its blood to the Altar (see below, mishnah 7:3). Their relationship in regard to *piggul* is the subject of this mishnah.

הַתּוֹדָה מְפַגֶּלֶת אֶת הַלֶּחֶם, וְהַלֶּחֶם אֵינוֹ מְפַגֵּל אֶת הַתּוֹדָה. — *The todah-offering renders the bread piggul, but the bread does not render the todah-offering piggul.*

[The term *todah* is used in this context to refer specifically to the animal offering, and not to the breads which accompany it.

If one expresses intentions of *piggul* concerning the *todah* while performing its *avodah*, thereby rendering the offering *piggul*, the breads which accompany the *todah*-offering also become *piggul*. However, if he expresses a *piggul*-intention concerning the breads while performing the *avodah* of the *todah*, only the loaves become *piggul* but not the *todah*, as the mishnah will elaborate below.] This is because the loaves are not a primary offering, but are subsidiary to the animal sacrifice (*Rav* from *Gem*. 15a). Their subsidiary role is evident from the fact that they have no *avodah* of their own, and it is only the slaughter of the animal that sanctifies them (*Rashi* 15a, s.v. לחם גלל תודה). Only the primary portion of a paired offering can cause other portions to become *piggul* (*Rav*) [whereas the subsidiary component can only render itself *piggul*].

[In Mishnaic usage, the word לֶחֶם, *bread*, does not necessarily refer to leavened bread or *chametz*, but may refer to *matzah* (unleavened bread) as well. Thus, the mishnah refers to the loaves of the *todah* as *breads*, even though only ten of them were baked as *chametz* while the other thirty were baked as different types of *matzah*. The same is true of the *lechem hapanim*, of which none were permitted to be *chametz*.]

כֵּיצַד? הַשּׁוֹחֵט אֶת הַתּוֹדָה לֶאֱכוֹל מִמֶּנָּה לְמָחָר, הִיא וְהַלֶּחֶם מְפֻגָּלִין. — *How so? [If] one slaughters the todah-offering [intending] to eat from it tomorrow, [both] it and the bread become piggul.*

[If he intended at the time he

הַלֶּחֶם לְמָחָר, הַלֶּחֶם מְפֻגָּל, וְהַתּוֹדָה אֵינָהּ מְפֻגֶּלֶת.

הַכְּבָשִׂים מְפַגְּלִין אֶת הַלֶּחֶם, וְהַלֶּחֶם אֵינוֹ מְפַגֵּל אֶת הַכְּבָשִׂים. כֵּיצַד? הַשּׁוֹחֵט אֶת הַכְּבָשִׂים לֶאֱכוֹל מֵהֶן לְמָחָר, הֵם וְהַלֶּחֶם מְפֻגָּלִין. לֶאֱכוֹל מִן הַלֶּחֶם לְמָחָר, הַלֶּחֶם מְפֻגָּל, וְהַכְּבָשִׂים אֵינָן מְפֻגָּלִין.

---

**יד אברהם**

slaughtered the animal to eat its meat after the allotted time, which is one day and one night (*Zevachim* 5:6), both the meat and the bread become *piggul*, and anyone who eats from them is subject to the punishment of *kares*.]

The same is true if he intended to throw the blood on the Altar past the permitted time, or to burn its sacrificial parts after the allotted time (*Rambam, Hil. Pesulei HaMukdashin* 17:7). All of these intentions are accounted *piggul* (see *Zevachim* 2:2).

לֶאֱכוֹל מִן הַלֶּחֶם לְמָחָר, הַלֶּחֶם מְפֻגָּל, וְהַתּוֹדָה אֵינָהּ מְפֻגֶּלֶת. — [*However, if he intended*] *to eat from the bread tomorrow, the bread becomes piggul, but the todah-offering does not become piggul.*

[If he intended at the time he slaughtered the animal to eat just the bread after the day and night allotted for the *todah*, only the bread becomes *piggul*, not the meat of the *todah*.] Therefore, eating the meat is not punishable by *kares* (*Rashi*).

*Rashi's* wording seems to imply that though the offering does not become *piggul* it is nevertheless invalid (*Keren Orah; Sfas Emes*). However, *Rambam* (*Comm.*) states that the intention concerning the bread has no effect whatsoever on the meat of the offering. This seems to be the implication of his ruling in *Hil. Pesulei HaMukdashin* (17:7) as well. *Rashi's* source is unclear (*Keren Orah;* but see *Sfas Emes*; his view will be elaborated further in a footnote to mishnah 7:3, s.v. שחטה שלא לשמה).

הַכְּבָשִׂים מְפַגְּלִין אֶת הַלֶּחֶם, וְהַלֶּחֶם אֵינוֹ מְפַגֵּל אֶת הַכְּבָשִׂים. — *The lambs render the bread piggul, but the bread does not render the lambs piggul.*

The same rule of *piggul* given for the *todah* applies as well to the *shtei halechem* loaves which accompany the two lambs brought on Shavuos. The breads of the *shtei halechem* are subsidiary to the lambs. Consequently, *piggul*-intent toward the lambs affects the loaves as well, but *piggul*-intent concerning the loaves affects only the loaves and not the lambs, as the mishnah will now elaborate (*Rav*).

[The second part of this ruling is already evident from the dispute between R' Yose and the Sages in the previous mishnah. The mishnah here refers to a case in which the *piggul*-intent was directed toward both loaves; thus, even R' Yose agrees that both are rendered *piggul*.]

כֵּיצַד? הַשּׁוֹחֵט אֶת הַכְּבָשִׂים לֶאֱכוֹל מֵהֶן לְמָחָר, הֵם וְהַלֶּחֶם מְפֻגָּלִין. — *How so?* [*If*] *one slaughters the lambs* [*intending*] *to eat from them tomorrow,* [*both*] *they and the bread become piggul.*

[Since the bread is subsidiary to the lambs, a *piggul*-intent directed at the lambs renders even the bread *piggul*.]

לֶאֱכוֹל מִן הַלֶּחֶם לְמָחָר, הַלֶּחֶם מְפֻגָּל, וְהַכְּבָשִׂים אֵינָן מְפֻגָּלִין. — [*However, if*

2 he intended] to eat from the bread tomorrow, the
3 bread becomes *piggul*, but the *todah*-offering
does not become *piggul*.

The lambs render the bread *piggul*, but the bread does not render the lambs *piggul*. How so? [If] one slaughters the lambs [intending] to eat from them tomorrow, [both] they and the bread become *piggul*. [However, if he intended] to eat from the bread tomorrow, the bread becomes *piggul*, but the lambs do not become *piggul*.

YAD AVRAHAM

*he intended] to eat from the bread tomorrow, the bread becomes piggul, but the lambs do not become piggul.*

[If the *piggul*-intent is directed at the bread of the *shtei halechem*, only the breads become *piggul* but not the lambs. Since these two breads are a subsidiary part of the offering, their *piggul* cannot extend to the primary part of the offering — the two *shelamim* lambs.]

This ruling is quite obviously a restatement of the one given above for the *todah*-offering and its associated bread. Nevertheless, it was necessary for the mishnah to cite both of these rulings for the following reason: If it were to state it only in regard to the *todah* and its associated breads, we might have mistakenly assumed that the relationship between the *shelamim* lambs of Shavuos and the *shtei halechem* is stronger than that between the *todah* and its bread, so that a *piggul*-intent directed at the loaves *can* cause the *shelamim* lambs to become *piggul*. This is because the *shtei halechem* loaves are waved together with the two lambs in the ritual of *tenufah* (see comm. to mishnah 2, s.v. שחט שני כבשים), which is not the case with the *todah's* breads. On the other hand, were the mishnah to cite only the case of the *shelamim* lambs and *shtei halechem*-offering of Shavuos, one might have thought that only in such a case does the *piggul*-intention concerning the sacrifice affect the loaves as well, because of their being waved together. However, the *todah* loaves would not become *piggul* even when the sacrifice does. To preclude either of these errors, the mishnah states both rulings explicitly (*Rav* from *Gem.* 15a).

4.

Every *olah*- and *shelamim*-offering must be accompanied by a libation of wine called a נֶסֶךְ, *nesech* [pl., *nesachim*], as well as a *minchah*-offering (mishnah 9:6; *Rambam, Maaseh HaKorbanos* 2:2). These two are considered supplements to the animal offering, and their *piggul* relationship to the sacrifice is therefore somewhat analogous to those described in the previous two mishnayos.

However, in contrast to the breads of the *todah* and *shtei halechem*-offerings, the *minchah* and wine that accompany the *olah* and *shelamim* are not eaten but are rather offered in their entirety on the Altar. The *minchah* is completely burnt (mishnah 6:2; *Rambam, Maaseh HaKorbanos* 2:1), and the wine is poured out on the southwest corner of the Altar (*Zevachim* 6:2; *Rambam* loc. cit.;

[ד] **הַזֶּבַח** מְפַגֵּל אֶת הַנְּסָכִין, מִשֶּׁקָּדְשׁוּ בִכְלִי; דִּבְרֵי רַבִּי מֵאִיר. וְהַנְּסָכִין

ר׳ עובדיה מברטנורא

(ד) **הזבח מפגל את הנסכים.** והשותה מהן ענוש כרת: **משקדשו בכלי.** לאחר שנתנו אותם בכלי שרת, שהכלי מקדשן קדושת עולם, דשוב אין להם פדיון: **דברי רבי מאיר.** דרבי מאיר סבר שנסכים מתפגלים, לפי שהדם של הזבח הוא שמכשיר ומתיר אותן למזבח, והואיל ויש להן מתיר, מתפגלים במחשבת חוץ לזמנו, וחכמים פליגי עליה בפרק בית שמאי במסכת זבחים [מד,א] ואמרי שהנסכים אין להם מתיר, לפיכך אין מתפגלין. ואין הלכה כרבי מאיר:

יד אברהם

see comm. to mishnah 6:2, 12:5). Thus, the *avodah* of the animal offering does not serve to permit the wine and *minchah* for consumption. Nor is that *avodah* necessary to permit the wine and *minchah* to be offered on the Altar, since there is no requirement for them even to be brought on the same day as the sacrifice, as will be explained in the commentary. This gives rise to a dispute whether a *piggul* intent directed at the sacrifice carries over to the *minchah* and wine.

הַזֶּבַח מְפַגֵּל אֶת הַנְּסָכִין, — *The sacrifice renders the libations piggul,*

[According to this *Tanna*, the wine of the libation is considered a subsidiary part of the *sacrifice* [the *olah* or *shelamim*-offering], and a *piggul*-intent directed at the animal offering consequently renders the wine of the libation *piggul* as well.] Therefore, one who drinks from this wine is subject to the punishment of *kares* (*Rav; Rashi*).

*Rav* and *Rashi* apparently interpret the word נְסָכִים, *nesachim*, to refer specifically to the wine component of this supplemental offering. [We have followed this view in translating the word as *libations*.] However, *Rambam* states that the term נְסָכִים, *nesachim*, refers to the wine libation and the *minchah* collectively. [The term נֶסֶךְ, *nesech*, literally means *pour* and obviously refers to the libation which is poured on the Altar. In this context, however, it is *Rambam's* opinion that the plural form is used to refer to the combined supplemental offering of the *minchah* of flour and the libation of wine. ] The *minchah* by itself is referred to as the מִנְחַת נְסָכִים, *minchas nesachim* [the *minchah* of the *nesachim* supplement] (*Rambam, Maaseh HaKorbanos* 2:1). Thus, according to *Rambam*, the mishnah's case here refers to both the wine and the *minchah*.

Even according to *Rav* and *Rashi*, the laws stated in this mishnah pertain to the *minchah* as well as to the libations; however, in their view the mishnah refers explicitly only to the wine (see *Tos. Yom Tov* here and in *Zevachim* 4:3, s.v. ומנחת נסכים).

מִשֶּׁקָּדְשׁוּ בִכְלִי; — *once they have been consecrated in a vessel;*

[The *piggul*-intent expressed during the slaughter of the sacrifice causes the wine and flour of its *nesachim* to become *piggul* as well only if they have already been sanctified in a *kli shareis* before the sacrifice is slaughtered. If they have not yet been sanctified, they do not become *piggul* (even when they are later consecrated).]

[Before any *minchah* and wine libation may be offered, the flour and wine must each be sanctified for offering by being placed in a *kli shareis*, i.e., a consecrated utensil designated for use in the *avodah* of the Temple.] Once they have been placed in the *kli shareis*, they become permanently sanctified and can no longer be redeemed [from that state] (*Rav* from

2 **4.** **T**he sacrifice renders the libations *piggul*, once
4 they have been consecrated in a vessel; [these are] the words of R' Meir. But the libations

### YAD AVRAHAM

mishnah 12:1). Therefore, at that point they are eligible to being rendered *piggul* by the slaughter of the sacrifice.

[However, if the *olah* or *shelamim* is slaughtered before the flour and wine have been sanctified in a *kli shareis*, the slaughter of the sacrifice cannot affect them. Since these substances have not yet been fixed as offerings and may still be redeemed (see mishnah 12:1), they are not yet subject to sacrificial invalidations, nor can they yet be considered a part of the animal sacrifice. Thus, even this *Tanna* agrees that they do not become *piggul*.][1]

It is clear that, according to this *Tanna*, the wine and flour become fixed to this sacrifice with its slaughter, and can no longer be reassigned to another offering. Were this not the case, *piggul* could not take effect on these *nesachim* even after they were consecrated, since they are not necessarily subsidiary to this sacrifice (*Gem.* 15b).

.דִּבְרֵי רַבִּי מֵאִיר — *[these are] the words of R' Meir.*

R' Meir maintains that the procedures performed with the blood of the sacrifice render the *nesachim* [libations] fit to be poured on the Altar [and the *minchah* fit to be burnt on it]. They are therefore susceptible to being rendered *piggul* by those *avodos* (*Rav*), the same as anything which is rendered fit for the Altar through another offering's procedures (*Rashi* from *Yoma* 60a).

Since the mishnah attributes this ruling to R' Meir rather than stating it anonymously, it is implicit that others disagree. The Sages (whose opinion is recorded in *Zevachim* 4:3) contend that the *nesachim* are not susceptible to *piggul* at all (*Rav* from *Gem.* 15b),[2] because the *avodah* of the *olah* or *shelamim* sacrifice which they accompany plays no role in their offering (*Rashi*). This may be seen from the fact that the *nesachim* need not be brought on the same day as the animal sacrifice, but may be brought even several days later (*Rav* from *Gem.*). In such a case, it is clearly not the *avodah* of the sacrifice which is rendering the *nesachim* fit for the Altar (*Gem.* 15b). Rather, they must be considered offerings in their own right [whose own *avodah* fulfills all their sacrificial requirements], and not a subsidiary of the animal offering (*Rashi* 15b, s.v. ונסכיו). Therefore, contend the Sages, even when the *nesachim* are brought together with the *olah* or *shelamim*, it is not the *avodah* of the sacrifice which is rendering them fit for their offering on the Altar (*Rav*).

R' Meir accepts that the *nesachim* can be brought even several days after the sacrifice, and he agrees that in such a case the *nesachim* will not be

1. Obviously, the wine and flour do not become *piggul* even if they are subsequently sanctified as offerings, because a *piggul*-intent can take effect only at the time of an *avodah*.

2. This reasoning suffices to explain why they cannot be rendered *piggul* through the sacrifice. In fact, however, they cannot be rendered *piggul* even by their own offering because they are offered in their entirety on the Altar, and only a part of the offering which becomes permitted by another part can become *piggul* (see *Zevachim* 4:3).

# אֵינָן מְפַגְּלִין אֶת הַזֶּבַח. כֵּיצַד? הַשּׁוֹחֵט אֶת הַזֶּבַח לֶאֱכוֹל מִמֶּנּוּ לְמָחָר, הוּא וּנְסָכָיו מְפֻגָּלִין. לְהַקְרִיב מִן הַנְּסָכִין לְמָחָר, הַנְּסָכִין מְפֻגָּלִין, וְהַזֶּבַח אֵינוֹ מְפֻגָּל.

---

**יד אברהם**

rendered *piggul* by the sacrifice offered days earlier. However, he contends that when the *nesachim* are brought together with the sacrifice, the sacrifice permits them to be offered on the Altar (*Rav* from *Gem.* 15b), because the *nesachim* accompanying an animal sacrifice may not be offered before the sacrifice itself (see *Sfas Emes*).

In the opinion of the Sages, this regulation is merely akin to a time constraint, but there is no inherent interaction between the sacrifice and the *nesachim* in regard to permitting the latter's offering (*Chazon Ish* 14:1).

וְהַנְּסָכִין אֵינָן מְפַגְּלִין אֶת הַזֶּבַח. — *But the libations do not render the sacrifice piggul.*

[The libations are considered subsidiary to the sacrifice and their *piggul* can therefore not affect the main part of the offering (even according to R' Meir), as we have learned previously in connection with the breads of the *shtei halechem* and *todah*-offerings (see mishnahs 3,4).]

כֵּיצַד? הַשּׁוֹחֵט אֶת הַזֶּבַח לֶאֱכוֹל מִמֶּנּוּ לְמָחָר, הוּא וּנְסָכָיו מְפֻגָּלִין. — *How so? [If] one slaughters the sacrifice [intending] to eat from it tomorrow, [both] it and its libations become piggul.*

[The mishnah now illustrates R' Meir's ruling. If one slaughtered an *olah* or *shelamim* intending to eat it past its time, he renders both the animal and its *nesachim* to be *piggul*.

Since the primary sacrifice was made *piggul*, the supplementary parts of the offering — the wine libation and *minchah* — follow suit (see mishnah 3).]

The same law applies if he intended to burn the sacrificial parts of the *shelamim* or the limbs of the *olah* after the allotted time for burning these on the Altar. The mishnah cites the case of eating to emphasize that, although his intention concerned eating, it nevertheless affects the libations, which are not eaten but are offered on the Altar (*Tif. Yis.*).

[The use of the word *tomorrow* in this mishnah to denote a *piggul*-intention is not true for all offerings requiring libations. The *shelamim* of an individual may be eaten for two days and one night and an intention to eat it *tomorrow* is therefore not *piggul*. For this type of offering the mishnah must mean that he intended to eat from the sacrifice after its allotted time of two days.]

לְהַקְרִיב מִן הַנְּסָכִין לְמָחָר, הַנְּסָכִין מְפֻגָּלִין, וְהַזֶּבַח אֵינוֹ מְפֻגָּל. — *[However, if he intended] to offer the libations tomorrow, the libations become piggul, but the sacrifice does not become piggul.*

[Since the *piggul*-intent was directed at the subsidiary part of the offering, only that part becomes *piggul*, as explained in the previous mishnayos.

According to the Sages, however, the libations are not considered subsidiary to the animal offering, and thus they do not become *piggul* under any circumstances, as explained above.] The halachah is in accordance with the opinion of the Sages (*Rav; Rambam, Hil. Pesulei HaMukdashin* 18:8; *Likkutei Halachos*).

2 do not render the sacrifice *piggul.* How so? [If] one
4 slaughters the sacrifice [intending] to eat from it tomorrow, [both] it and its libations become *piggul.* [However, if he intended] to offer the libations tomorrow, the libations become *piggul,* but the sacrifice does not become *piggul.*

### YAD AVRAHAM

We have followed to this point *Rav's* explanation, that the point of dispute between R' Meir and the Sages is whether or not the *nesachim* are considered a subsidiary offering of the animal sacrifice. This would seem to be the view of *Rambam* as well, as may be deduced from his rulings in this matter (*Tos. Yom Tov* to mishnah 7:4; *Keren Orah*), and as stated by him in his *Comm.* to *Zevachim* 4:3.

However, as noted in the previous section, the *Gemara* states that in order for the *piggul* of the sacrifice to take effect in the *nesachim*, the *nesachim* must also be irrevocably bound to this particular sacrifice. The *Gemara* states that R' Meir accepts the view that *nesachim* become permanently fixed to the sacrifice for which they were designated with the slaughter of that sacrifice, and they can no longer be shifted to serve as the *nesachim* of a different sacrifice. From the *Gemara's* statement that this is R' Meir's view, *Tosafos* (15b, s.v. אפשר) deduce that the Sages do not accept this proposition. *Tosafos* therefore explain that the root of the dispute between R' Meir and the Sages is precisely this issue — whether the slaughter of the sacrifice fixes the *nesachim* to this particular sacrifice so that they can no longer be reassigned to another sacrifice. The Sages do not accept that the *nesachim* become bound, and as a result rule that they do not become *piggul* along with the animal sacrifice.[1]

## 5.

There are two components of a *minchah*-offering which must be burnt on the Altar to render the remainder permissible for consumption — the *kometz* of its flour and the *levonah* (frankincense). These are known as its *mattirim* (permitting substances), as we learned in mishnah 1. The following mishnah will discuss whether a *piggul* intention expressed during the *avodah* of just one of these two *mattirim* suffices to render the *minchah*-offering *piggul*. This discussion is not limited to the *minchah*-offering, but applies to all cases in which a *piggul* intent is expressed during the *avodah* of "half a *mattir,*" i.e., one part of a two-part *mattir.*

1. It follows from this that the Sages may well accept R' Meir's contention that the sacrifice permits the offering of the *nesachim*, but they consider this insufficient to render them *piggul* because the *nesachim* may still be switched to a different sacrifice (*Keren Orah*; cf. *Chazon Ish* 14:1). According to *Rav's* explanation, though, the reverse is true: The Sages can accept that the *nesachim* become permanently bound to the sacrifice at the time of its slaughter, but they reject the notion that the sacrifice in any way permits the offering of the *nesachim*.

In a second explanation, *Tosafos* also consider the possibility that in the case of a valid offering the Sages accept the principle that the animal's slaughter binds its *nesachim* to it. They dispute R' Meir only because in this case the offering is invalid, and its slaughter, therefore, does not have the power to bind the *nesachim* to it. See further, comm. to mishnah 7:4, s.v. נסכים שקדשו בכלי.

[ה] **פִּגֵּל** בַּקֹּמֶץ וְלֹא בַלְּבוֹנָה; בַּלְּבוֹנָה וְלֹא בַקֹּמֶץ — רַבִּי מֵאִיר אוֹמֵר: פִּגּוּל, וְחַיָּבִים עָלָיו כָּרֵת; וַחֲכָמִים אוֹמְרִים: אֵין בּוֹ כָּרֵת עַד שֶׁיְּפַגֵּל אֶת כָּל הַמַּתִּיר.

### ר׳ עובדיה מברטנורא

(ה) **פיגל בקומץ.** בהקטרת הקומץ חשב על השירים לאכלן שלא בזמנן: **עד שיפגל בכל המתיר.** והקטרת אחד מהן חצי מתיר הוא, דאיכא נמי הקטרת חבירו, שאין שירי המנחה מותרים באכילה לכהן עד שיקטירו הקומץ והלבונה:

### יד אברהם

פִּגֵּל בַּקֹּמֶץ וְלֹא בַלְּבוֹנָה; בַּלְּבוֹנָה וְלֹא בַקֹּמֶץ — — [*If*] *he intended piggul with the kometz but not with the frankincense;* [*or*] *with the frankincense but not with the kometz —*

When burning the *kometz* on the Altar, he intended to eat the remainder of the *minchah* after its allotted time; however, he did not intend anything improper while burning the *levonah* (*Rav; Rashi*). [Or, he expressed the *piggul*-intention while burning the *levonah* but not while burning the *kometz*.] Since both the *minchah* and the *levonah* must be burnt on the Altar for the *minchah* to be valid, he has expressed his *piggul*-intention during only half the *avodah* of הַקְטָרָה, *burning on the Altar.*

*Rambam* explains the mishnah to be discussing a case in which the half-*mattir piggul*-intention was expressed during the first of the *minchah's* essential *avodos* — *kemitzah* — rather than during burning, which is the last; i.e., he intended *piggul* either while removing the *kometz* or while gathering up of the *levonah* from the *minchah* (*Rambam Comm.; Hil. Pesulei HaMukdashin* 16:7). The implications of this, and the reason why *Rav* and *Rashi* avoid this explanation, will be discussed below.

רַבִּי מֵאִיר אוֹמֵר: פִּגּוּל, וְחַיָּבִים עָלָיו כָּרֵת; — *R' Meir says: It is piggul and one is liable to kares over it;*

[It is R' Meir's opinion that the *minchah* becomes *piggul* even though the *piggul* intention was expressed during the *avodah* of only one of its two *mattirim*.] Or as the *Gemara* (14a) puts it, מְפַגְּלִין בַּחֲצִי מַתִּיר, *one can bring about piggul [even] with [the avodah of] half the [total] mattir* (see *Rashi* 14a, s.v. ולאפוקי מדר״מ).

וַחֲכָמִים אוֹמְרִים: אֵין בּוֹ כָּרֵת עַד שֶׁיְּפַגֵּל אֶת כָּל הַמַּתִּיר. — *but the Sages say: There is no kares for it unless he intends piggul with all that renders it permissible.*

The Sages reject R' Meir's view and rule that אֵין מְפַגְּלִין בַּחֲצִי מַתִּיר, *one cannot bring about piggul with [the avodah of] half the mattir* (permitting substance, the part of the offering which renders the remainder permissible). Since the remainder of the *minchah* does not become permitted for eating until both the *kometz* and the *levonah* have been burnt on the Altar, it is clear that each one by itself is only part of the total *mattir*. Therefore, the offering cannot be rendered *piggul* by the intention expressed while burning just the *kometz* or just the *levonah* (*Rav*).

Although the Sages dispute the *piggul* classification and the *kares* penalty associated with it, they agree that the *minchah* is nevertheless invalidated by the half-*mattir* intention (*Gem.* 14b;

**5.** [If] he intended *piggul* with the *kometz* but not with the frankincense; [or] with the frankincense but not with the *kometz* — R' Meir says: It is *piggul* and one is liable to *kares* over it; but the Sages say: There is no *kares* for it unless he intends *piggul* with all that renders it permissible.

### YAD AVRAHAM

*Rambam, Pesulei HaMukdashin* 16:7). This is by Rabbinic decree, because there are offerings whose entire *mattir* consists of just a *kometz* of flour or just *levonah*. These would become *piggul* during the burning of either the *kometz* or the *levonah* respectively. Accordingly, the Sages invalidated even a *minchah* with both these *mattirim* when *piggul* was intended during just one of them (*Gem.* 14b; see below).

Examples of such offerings are the sinner's *minchah* [מִנְחַת חוֹטֵא] and jealousy *minchah* [מִנְחַת קְנָאוֹת; see comm. to mishnah 1:1], which do not contain *levonah*, and whose entire *mattir* is just the *kometz* of flour. Thus, an improper intention during the burning of their *kometz* renders them *piggul* even according to the Sages. Similarly, the loaves of the *lechem hapanim* become permitted through the offering of the two spoonfuls of *levonah* that are placed on the *shulchan* with them (see comm. to mishnah 2); thus, these loaves become *piggul* through an intention expressed during the burning of just their *levonah* (*Gem.*).

This ruling of this mishnah would seem to contradict the ruling stated at the very beginning of mishnah 1, that a *piggul*-intention expressed during *kemitzah* suffices to render the offering *piggul*.

*Rashi* (14a, s.v. לאפוקי מדר״מ) resolves this by explaining that the *kemitzah* of the flour has no counterpart in the offering of the *levonah*. [Although the *levonah* must be gathered up from on top the *minchah's* flour before being brought to the Altar, this is not considered an *avodah* (presumably because there is no formal procedure attached to its removal as there is with the *kemitzah* of the flour).][1] Consequently, at the stage of *avodah* represented by *kemitzah*, there is considered to be only one *mattir* — the *kometz* — and a *piggul* intent during the *kemitzah* can therefore render the offering *piggul*.[2] For this reason *Rashi*

1. Although the *Gemara* (13b) states that the gathering of the *levonah* must be done by a *Kohen* and its performance by a non-*Kohen* invalidates the *minchah*, this is because the gathering of the *levonah* is considered an aspect of the *avodah* of הוֹלָכָה, *conveying to the Altar* (see fn. below). *Rashi* further states (16b, s.v. הילוך דמתן כלי) that, upon being gathered up from the *minchah*, the *levonah* does not even require sanctification in a *kli shareis* before being burnt on the Altar. This is yet a further indication that the removal of the *levonah* from the *minchah* is not classified as an *avodah* equivalent to the *kemitzah* of the flour. Although the *Gemara* in *Sotah* (14b) cites the *Tosefta* that the *levonah* was placed in the *kli shareis* together with the *kometz*, *Sfas Emes* points out that *Rashi* apparently understood that the *Gemara* in *Menachos* differs with the *Tosefta* in regard to the procedure for offering the *minchah* (see *Sfas Emes* at the beginning of this chapter, and footnote to mishnah 1).

2. The fact that his *piggul*-intention during the *kemitzah* was directed at burning only the *kometz* and not the *levonah* is irrelevant; the rule that the *avodah* of half a *mattir* cannot

מוֹדִים חֲכָמִים לְרַבִּי מֵאִיר בְּמִנְחַת חוֹטֵא וּבְמִנְחַת קְנָאוֹת, שֶׁאִם פִּגֵּל בַּקֹּמֶץ, שֶׁהוּא פִּגּוּל וְחַיָּבִין עָלָיו כָּרֵת, שֶׁהַקֹּמֶץ הוּא הַמַּתִּיר.

שָׁחַט אֶחָד מִן הַכְּבָשִׂים לֶאֱכוֹל שְׁתֵּי חַלּוֹת לְמָחָר, הִקְטִיר אֶחָד מִן הַבָּזִיכִים לֶאֱכוֹל שְׁנֵי

### ר׳ עובדיה מברטנורא

**במנחת חוטא ובמנחת קנאות.** שאין בהן לבונה, והקומץ לבדו הוא המתיר: **שחט אחד מן הכבשים.** של כבשי עצרת. ואין הלחם מותר אלא אחר שישחטו שניהן: **הקטיר אחד מן הבזיכין.** והרי אין מתיר הלחם אלא הקטרת שניהם:

### יד אברהם

explains that our mishnah, which considers the *kometz* to be just half a *mattir*, cannot be discussing the *avodah* of *kemitzah* but must rather be referring to the *avodah* of הַקְטָרָה, burning on the Altar. Since both the *kometz* and the *levonah* must be burnt on the Altar, each is only a partial *mattir* in regard to the *avodah* of burning.

However, as noted above, *Rambam* (*Comm.* and *Pesulei HaMukdashin* 16:7) explains the mishnah to be dealing with a case in which the *piggul*-intention is expressed during the *avodah* of *kemitzah* rather than during the *avodah* of burning. That is, the *Kohen* intended *piggul* either while removing the *kometz* of flour or removing the *levonah* from the *minchah*. According to *Rambam*, gathering up the *levonah* is also considered an *avodah*, and the *kemitzah* of the flour by itself is therefore the *avodah* of only half a *mattir*.[1] For this reason, an intention of *piggul* during just one of these two procedures is subject to the dispute between R' Meir and the

cause *piggul* refers only to the *avodah* in which the improper intention is expressed, not to the *avodah* at which the intention is directed (*Rashi* ibid.).

1. There is some question as to which category of *avodah* the gathering up of the *levonah* should be assigned. The *Gemara* (13b) seems to say that it should be considered a form of הוֹלָכָה (*conveying*, since there is no way to burn the *levonah* on the Altar without first removing it from the *minchah* (see *Mishneh LaMelech* to *Pesulei HaMukdashin* 11:1). [*Rashi*, however, seems to have understood that according to the *Gemara's* conclusion gathering the *levonah* is not part of any *avodah*. The reason it invalidates the *minchah* when done by a non-*Kohen* is because an act of *holachah* (conveying) is performed by him when he hands over the *levonah* he collected to the *Kohen* for burning. (See *Rashi* 13b, s.v. משום הולכה.)]

This statement of the *Gemara*, however, presents great difficulties according to *Rambam*, since the gathering of the *levonah* should then not be considered a co-*mattir* of the *kemitzah*. *Chazon Ish* 22:12 postulates that although the removal of the *levonah* is classified as *holachah* for technical reasons, since it parallels *kemitzah* in the order of the *avodah* it is considered part of the same *mattir* as *kemitzah*.

*Keren Orah* asserts that *Rambam's* view is that gathering the *levonah* is a counterpart of the *avodah* of *kemitzah*. He suggests that *Rambam* may have understood that there is a dispute in this matter between the *Gemara* here (which states that gathering the *levonah* comes under the category of *holachah* (conveying) and the *Tosefta* cited in *Sotah* 14b, which indicates that is an *avodah* in its own right analogous to *kemitzah* (cf. *Sfas Emes* cited in fn. above). *Rambam* rules according to the *Tosefta*.

2
5 The Sages concur with R' Meir concerning the sinner's *minchah*-offering and the jealousy *minchah*-offering, that if he intended *piggul* with the *kometz*, it is *piggul* and one is liable to *kares* over it, since the *kometz* is that which renders it permissible.

[If] he slaughtered one of the lambs [intending] to eat [the] two loaves tomorrow, [or] he burnt one of the spoonfuls [of frankincense intending] to eat [the] two

**YAD AVRAHAM**

Sages. Accordingly, the statement made in mishnah 1, that a *piggul*-intention during *kemitzah* renders the *minchah*-offering *piggul*, is true only according to the opinion of R' Meir (*Tos. Yom Tov* to mishnah 1; *Zevach Todah* ibid.; cf. *Birchas HaZevach, Tzon Kodashim*).

*Keren Orah*, however, suggests that the phrase *one who performs kemitzah* in the opening ruling of mishnah 1 may in fact be referring to both the *kemitzah* and the lifting of the *levonah*. The mishnah employs this terminology as a form of shorthand for the first *avodah* of the *minchah*.

מוֹדִים חֲכָמִים לְרַבִּי מֵאִיר בְּמִנְחַת חוֹטֵא וּבְמִנְחַת קְנָאוֹת, שֶׁאִם פִּגֵּל בַּקֹּמֶץ, שֶׁהוּא פִּגּוּל וְחַיָּבִין עָלָיו כָּרֵת, שֶׁהַקֹּמֶץ הוּא הַמַּתִּיר. — *The Sages concur with R' Meir concerning the sinner's minchah-offering and the jealousy minchah-offering, that if he intended piggul with the kometz, it is piggul and one is liable to kares over it, since the kometz is that which renders it permissible.*

Since these *menachos* do not contain any *levonah*, their only *mattir* is their *kometz*; therefore, *piggul* intent while burning the *kometz* renders the *minchah*-offering *piggul* (*Rav*).

This statement is obvious, since no other *mattir* exists in these cases. However, we previously learned that although the Sages do not accept that *piggul* can be effected by half a *mattir*, they do agree that the *minchah* is invalidated by such an intention on the Rabbinic level. The mishnah mentions the concurrence of the Sages in this case to indicate that the reason the Sages invalidated the *minchah* Rabbinically in the previous case is because of its similarity to this one (*Gem.* 14b; see above s.v. וחכמים אומרים).

שָׁחַט אֶחָד מִן הַכְּבָשִׂים לֶאֱכוֹל שְׁתֵּי חַלּוֹת לְמָחָר, — *[If] he slaughtered one of the lambs [intending] to eat [the] two loaves tomorrow,*

As we learned in mishnah 2, the two loaves of the *shtei halechem*-offering brought on Shavuos do not become permitted for eating until both lambs of the accompanying offering have been offered (*Rav*). For this reason, if he slaughtered the lambs with the intention of eating the loaves past their time, he renders them *piggul*, as taught in mishnah 2. [That mishnah, however, referred to a case in which both lambs were slaughtered with *piggul*-intent. This mishnah discusses what the law is if he intended *piggul* while slaughtering just one of the lambs.]

הִקְטִיר אֶחָד מִן הַבָּזִיכִים לֶאֱכוֹל שְׁנֵי סְדָרִים לְמָחָר — — [*or*] *he burnt one of the spoonfuls* [*of frankincense intending*] *to eat* [*the*] *two arrangements tomorrow* —

The *lechem hapanim* loaves are not permitted for eating until both spoonfuls of *levonah* that join them on the

סְדָרִים לְמָחָר — רַבִּי מֵאִיר אוֹמֵר: פִּגּוּל וְחַיָּבִים עָלָיו כָּרֵת; וַחֲכָמִים אוֹמְרִים: אֵין פִּגּוּל עַד שֶׁיְּפַגֵּל אֶת כָּל הַמַּתִּיר.

שָׁחַט אֶחָד מִן הַכְּבָשִׂים לֶאֱכוֹל מִמֶּנּוּ לְמָחָר, הוּא פִּגּוּל וַחֲבֵרוֹ כָּשֵׁר. לֶאֱכוֹל מֵחֲבֵרוֹ לְמָחָר, שְׁנֵיהֶם כְּשֵׁרִים.

**ר׳ עובדיה מברטנורא**

**רבי מאיר אומר פגול.** דסבר חלי מתיר נמי מפגל. ואין הלכה כרבי מאיר:

**יד אברהם**

*shulchan* have been burnt on the Altar. Accordingly, an intention of *piggul* expressed during the burning of these spoonfuls renders the loaves *piggul*, as explained in mishnah 2. [The mishnah now defines the law for a *piggul*-intention expressed while burning just one of them.]

רַבִּי מֵאִיר אוֹמֵר: פִּגּוּל וְחַיָּבִים עָלָיו כָּרֵת; — *R' Meir says: It is piggul and one is liable to kares over it;*

[The one lamb is half the *mattir* of the *shtei halechem*, as is the one spoonful for the *lechem hapanim*.] Since R' Meir's opinion is that one can render an offering *piggul* with the intention he expresses while performing only part of the *mattir*, these offerings are rendered *piggul* (*Rav*).

וַחֲכָמִים אוֹמְרִים: אֵין פִּגּוּל עַד שֶׁיְּפַגֵּל אֶת כָּל הַמַּתִּיר. — *but the Sages say: There is no piggul unless he intends piggul with all that renders it permissible.*

[The Sages follow their previously stated position that an offering cannot be rendered *piggul* by an intention expressed during the *avodah* of only half the *mattir*. Therefore, the loaves of the *shtei halechem* and *lechem hapanim* do not become *piggul*.] Nevertheless, they are (Rabbinically) invalidated because of their similarity to the case in which the intention was expressed during the slaughter of both lambs or the burning of both spoonfuls of *levonah* (*Gem.* 14b).

The halachah follows the view of the Sages (*Rambam, Pesulei HaMukdashin* 17:14).

שָׁחַט אֶחָד מִן הַכְּבָשִׂים לֶאֱכוֹל מִמֶּנּוּ לְמָחָר, הוּא פִּגּוּל וַחֲבֵרוֹ כָּשֵׁר. — [*If*] *he slaughtered one of the lambs* [*intending*] *to eat from it tomorrow, it is piggul but its companion is valid.*

[In this case, he slaughtered one of the lambs intending to eat from it past its time. Since he intended *piggul* toward this lamb, it becomes *piggul*. However, it does not invalidate the second lamb because each is a separate

2
5 arrangements tomorrow — R' Meir says: It is *piggul* and one is liable to *kares* over it; but the Sages say: There is no *piggul* unless he intends *piggul* with all that renders it permissible.

[If] he slaughtered one of the lambs [intending] to eat from it tomorrow, it is *piggul* but its companion is valid. [However, if he intended] to eat from its companion tomorrow, they are both valid.

YAD AVRAHAM

offering.] Although the two lambs function as the joint *mattirim* of the *shtei halechem* [and are to this extent both parts of the larger, overall offering], invalidation of one *mattir* cannot cause another *mattir* to become *piggul* unless they become merged into a single sacrificial unit, as described in mishnah 1 (*Tif. Yis.*). See below.

The ruling that the one lamb becomes *piggul* is true even according to the accepted view that *piggul* cannot be brought about by an intention expressed during the *avodah* of only half a *mattir*. This is because the *avodah* of the lambs serves a double function: It permits the *shtei halechem*, but it also permits the lambs themselves. Although the mishnah has stated above that each lamb is considered just half a *mattir*, this is so only when it is viewed relative to the *shtei halechem*, which require the offering of both lambs to become permitted. Relative to the permissibility of each lamb itself, however, its own *avodah* is its complete *mattir*. Therefore, as far as rendering the lamb *piggul*, its own *avodah* suffices to render it *piggul* according to all opinions (*Keren Orah; Sfas Emes*). Although it is evident from mishnah 3:6 that neither of the lambs may be eaten until both have been offered, that is not because they are joint *mattirim* for each other. Rather, it is due to a procedural regulation concerning the obligation to offer the two lambs on Shavuos that both must be offered in order for either to be valid (*Sfas Emes*).

לֶאֱכוֹל מֵחֲבֵרוֹ לְמָחָר, שְׁנֵיהֶם כְּשֵׁרִים. — *[However, if he intended] to eat from its companion tomorrow, they are both valid.*

A *piggul*-intent directed from one *mattir* to another has no validity whatsoever, as we learned in mishnah 1 (*Tif. Yis.*). Although in regard to the *kometz* and *levonah* discussed there the Sages ruled that it *does* render the offering *piggul*, that is only because the two *mattirim* have been joined into a single sacrificial unit by their presence in the same *kli shareis*. Where there is no combination of the two *mattirim*, the Sages also accept the principle that a *piggul*-intent directed from one *mattir* to another does not bring about *piggul* (*Rav* to mishnah 1). Therefore, both lambs remain completely valid (*Rambam, Maaseh HaKorbanos* 17:17).

# פרק שלישי
# Chapter Three

[א] **הַקּוֹמֵץ** אֶת הַמִּנְחָה לֶאֱכוֹל דָּבָר שֶׁאֵין דַּרְכּוֹ לֶאֱכוֹל, לְהַקְטִיר דָּבָר שֶׁאֵין דַּרְכּוֹ לְהַקְטִיר — כָּשֵׁר. רַבִּי אֱלִיעֶזֶר פּוֹסֵל.

**ר׳ עובדיה מברטנורא**

**פרק שלישי – הקומץ רבה. (א) הקומץ את המנחה לאכול.** חוץ לזמנו: **דבר שאין דרכו לאכול.** כגון הקומץ והלבונה: **ולהקטיר.** חוץ לזמנו: **דבר שאין דרכו להקטיר.** השיריים, שדרכן לאכול ואין דרכן להקטיר: **כשר.** דאין זו חשובה מחשבה, דבטלה דעתו אצל כל אדם: **רבי אליעזר פוסל.** דכתיב (ויקרא ז,יח) ואם האכל יאכל מבשר זבח שלמיו, בשתי אכילות הכתוב מדבר, אחת אכילת אדם ואחת אכילת מזבח, לומר לך, כשם שפוסלת אכילת אדם לאדם כגון שירים אם חשב עליהם לאדם לאכלם חוץ לזמנו, ואכילת מזבח למזבח כגון קומץ אם חשב עליו להקטירו שלא בזמנו, כך פוסלת מחשבת אכילת אדם כגון שירים אם חשב עליהם למזבח להקטירן חוץ לזמנן, מדאפקינהו רחמנא לתרווייהו בלשון אכילה, שמע מינה כי הדדי נינהו, ומחשבים מזו לזו. ורבנן סברי, להכי אפקה רחמנא להקטרה בלשון אכילה, לומר לך, מה אכילה בכזית אף מחשבת הקטרה בכזית, ולעולם אכילה כאורחיה משמע, קומץ למזבח ושירים לאדם. והלכה כחכמים:

**יד אברהם**

## 1.

It has already been explained (mishnah 1:3) that the *kometz* is to the remainder of the *minchah* what the blood is to the animal sacrifice. Thus, if *kemitzah* is performed with the intention to burn the *kometz* or eat the remainder beyond the allotted time, it is *piggul.* If the intention is to burn or eat outside the assigned place, the offering is invalidated [although it is not *piggul* and there is no *kares* penalty for eating it]. Our mishnah discusses types of wrong intentions that do not fall under the *piggul* category. This mishnah parallels mishnah 3:3 in *Zevachim* which details the exceptions to the *piggul* rule in the context of animal sacrifices.

הַקּוֹמֵץ אֶת הַמִּנְחָה לֶאֱכוֹל דָּבָר שֶׁאֵין דַּרְכּוֹ לֶאֱכוֹל, — *[If] one performs kemitzah on a minchah-offering [intending] to eat something which is not meant to be eaten,*

He performed the *kemitzah* with the intention of eating from it after the allotted time has passed. This intention would ordinarily render the *minchah*-offering *piggul.* In this case, however, he intended to eat something such as the *kometz* or the *levonah*, which are meant to be burnt on the Altar rather than eaten (*Rav*).

לְהַקְטִיר דָּבָר שֶׁאֵין דַּרְכּוֹ לְהַקְטִיר — *[or] to burn [upon the Altar] something which is not meant to be burnt —*

Or he intended to burn the remainder of the *minchah* on the Altar after the allotted time. This is the reverse of the previous case, inasmuch as he intended to burn on the Altar something which is meant to be eaten (*Rav*).

כָּשֵׁר. — *it is valid.*

Such intentions do not invalidate the offering. Since eating that which is supposed to be burnt or burning that which is to be eaten would be highly unusual, the intention to do them is considered incongruous and cannot invalidate the offering (*Rav*).

3
1

**1.** [If] one performs *kemitzah* on a *minchah*-offering [intending] to eat something which is not meant to be eaten, [or] to burn [upon the Altar] something which is not meant to be burnt — it is valid. R' Eliezer invalidates [it].

### YAD AVRAHAM

Actually, this ruling is implicit in the ruling of mishnah 1:3 which specifies that *piggul* applies only to an intention to eat that which is meant to be eaten or to burn on the Altar that which is meant to be burnt there. The mishnah reiterates it here, however, in order to record the dissenting view of R' Eliezer (*Tos.* 17a, s.v. הקומץ).

The mishnah's ruling also applies to the intention to eat or burn something on an Altar outside the Temple Courtyard. Although this would ordinarily render the *minchah* invalid, if the intention reverses the proper procedure, the *minchah* is not invalidated (*Tos.* 17b, s.v. אמר).

רַבִּי אֱלִיעֶזֶר פּוֹסֵל. — *R' Eliezer invalidates [it].*

[R' Eliezer considers the intentions to eat and burn on the Altar completely interchangeable, even where they are inappropriate.] As noted in the commentary to 1:3 (s.v. להקטיר קמצה בחוץ), the Torah (*Lev.* 7:18) uses the phrase וְאִם הֵאָכֹל יֵאָכֵל, *and if it should be eaten*, to describe the improper intention of *piggul*. This constitutes a double usage of the verb אָכֹל, *to eat*. From this the Sages deduced that the verse defining the law of *piggul* refers to both an intention concerning human consumption [of the portion of the offering which may be eaten (אֲכִילַת אָדָם)] and the Altar's consumption [of that which is meant to be burnt (אֲכִילַת מִזְבֵּחַ)]. According to R' Eliezer this juxtaposition teaches that the two forms of consumption are interchangeable; an intention to apply one form of consumption to something which actually requires the other is effective in bringing about a state of *piggul* (*Rav* from *Gem.* 17a).

Actually, this only suffices to explain why the intention to eat that which is ordinarily burnt has significance, since the consumption of the Altar is also referred to as *eating*. It does not explain why an intention to burn that which is supposed to be eaten is also considered effective. *Tosafos* (17a, s.v. מדאפקינהו) explain that since the reference to the consumption of the Altar is made in connection with the part of the sacrifice which is to be eaten [מִבְּשַׂר זֶבַח הַשְּׁלָמִים, *the meat of the shelamim-offering*], we conclude that the consumption of the Altar may be considered *eating* even for that which is normally subject to human consumption.

The first *Tanna*, however, disagrees with R' Eliezer's interpretation of the Torah's double usage of the term *eating*. He maintains that the Torah refers to the consumption on the Altar as "eating" only to teach us that both the intentions of eating and burning on the Altar must concern a certain minimum to be considered legally effective intentions. Throughout Torah law, the term *eat* refers to the consumption of at least a *kezayis* of food — i.e., the volume of an olive. Since the Torah defines the law of *piggul* in terms of eating, the intention to eat a part of the offering past its permitted time must concern at least a *kezayis* of the offering's meat or flour to be effective. And since the Torah also refers to the Altar's consumption as *eating*, we derive that so too the intention to burn

לֶאֱכוֹל דָּבָר שֶׁדַּרְכּוֹ לֶאֱכוֹל, לְהַקְטִיר דָּבָר שֶׁדַּרְכּוֹ לְהַקְטִיר — פָּחוֹת מִכַּזַּיִת — כָּשֵׁר. לֶאֱכוֹל כַּחֲצִי זַיִת וּלְהַקְטִיר כַּחֲצִי זַיִת — כָּשֵׁר, שֶׁאֵין אֲכִילָה וְהַקְטָרָה מִצְטָרְפִין.

**יד אברהם**

a sacrificial part of the offering must be directed at a minimum of a *kezayis* of it before it can bring about *piggul* (*Rav* from *Gem.* 17b).

The halachah follows the view of the *Tanna Kamma* (*Rav; Rambam, Pesulei HaMukdashin* 14:8).

There are two opinions in the *Gemara* concerning R' Eliezer's view. The opinion followed by the commentary to this point is that R' Eliezer considers it *piggul* on a Biblical level, as derived from the verse הֵאָכֹל יֵאָכֵל. Accordingly, the mishnah should actually have stated, ר׳ אֱלִיעֶזֶר מְפַגֵּל, *R' Eliezer considers it piggul*, rather than *invalidates*, which might indicate just a Rabbinic invalidation. The reason the term פּוֹסֵל, *invalidates*, is used is because this ruling also includes the invalidation for an intent to eat or burn outside its designated place, for which the term *considers it piggul* would be inappropriate (*Tos. Yom Tov; Tos.* 17b; see *Tos.* 18a, s.v. אלא).

According to another opinion in the *Gemara*, however, R' Eliezer's invalidation is indeed only Rabbinic in nature. [According to this view, R' Eliezer invalidates an offering made with an intent to burn that which is to be eaten or vice versa as a safeguard against an instance in which the intent concerns eating or burning something which is appropriate.] Accordingly, the mishnah uses the word פּוֹסֵל, *invalidates*, to denote a Rabbinic invalidation (*Tos. Yom Tov* ibid.).

לֶאֱכוֹל דָּבָר שֶׁדַּרְכּוֹ לֶאֱכוֹל, לְהַקְטִיר דָּבָר שֶׁדַּרְכּוֹ לְהַקְטִיר — פָּחוֹת מִכַּזַּיִת — כָּשֵׁר. — *[If his intent was] to eat something which is meant to be eaten, [or] to burn [upon the Altar] something which is meant to be burnt — but less than an olive's volume — it is valid.*

[If he intended to eat or burn after the allotted time less than a *kezayis* it has no invalidating effect whatsoever, because eating or burning less than this amount is of no significance (see 1:3). The same is true if he intended to eat or burn less than a *kezayis* outside the designated place.]

לֶאֱכוֹל כַּחֲצִי זַיִת וּלְהַקְטִיר כַּחֲצִי זַיִת — כָּשֵׁר, שֶׁאֵין אֲכִילָה וְהַקְטָרָה מִצְטָרְפִין. — *[If his intent was] to eat something half an olive's volume and to burn half an olive's volume — it is valid, for eating and Altar-burning are not combined.*

Even though his combined intent concerned consuming a *kezayis* of the *minchah* beyond its time, it is not *piggul*, because the intent was an amalgam of two uncombinable intentions. To effect *piggul*, the intent must be about either eating a full *kezayis* or burning a full *kezayis*.

Actually this was already stated verbatim by the mishnah at the end of the first chapter (1:4). Nonetheless, it is repeated here to indicate that it holds true even according to R' Eliezer, who maintains that an intention to burn that which is ordinarily eaten, or vice versa, also invalidates the offering. According to his view it follows that if one intended to eat half a *kezayis* of the *kometz* and half a *kezayis* of the remainder, it *does* invalidate the *minchah*, because the intent to eat the *kometz* is an effective *piggul*-intention. One might therefore have thought that even an intent to burn half a *kezayis* and eat half a *kezayis* of the remainder should be Rabbinically invalidated because of its similarity to the above case (*Shitah Mekubetzes* 17a, #10).

3 [If his intent was] to eat something which is
1 meant to be eaten, [or] to burn [upon the Altar] something which is meant to be burnt — but less than an olive's volume — it is valid. [If his intent was] to eat something half an olive's volume and to burn half an olive's volume — it is valid, for eating and Altar-burning are not combined.

**YAD AVRAHAM**

According to the view that R' Eliezer invalidates an intent to eat that which is to be burnt as a result of Rabbinic decree, one can explain that the mishnah teaches that even R' Eliezer agrees that they did not enact a similar decree to invalidate an intention concerning half a *kezayis* (*Tos. Yom Tov* from *Rashi*).

## 2.

The following mishnah defines which steps of the *minchah's* process are essential to its validity. The procedure for offering is described at length in the General Introduction. What follows here is a brief description of the standard procedure for preparing a *minchah* prior to its *avodah* [i.e., *kemitzah*]:

מַתַּן שֶׁמֶן — *placing oil in the vessel* in which the *minchah is* prepared. Almost all *menachos* must contain a measure of olive oil; some of this required measure is poured into the vessel before the flour is added.

בְּלִילָה — *mixing*. The required amount of flour is placed in the vessel, more oil is added on top of it, and it is mixed together. The mixture is then placed in a *kli shareis* (sacred vessel).

יְצִיקָה — *pouring*. The remaining oil is poured on top of the mixture, in the *kli shareis*. The *levonah* (frankincense) is added at this point.

הַגָּשָׁה — *bringing near*. The vessel containing the *minchah* is brought by the *Kohen* to the southwest corner of the Altar [see 5:5].

The above is the procedure for the מִנְחַת סֹלֶת, *fine flour minchah*. There are several types of *menachos* which are fried or baked before the *avodah* commences. These are the *machavas* and *marcheshes* (mishnah 5:8), as well as the oven-baked *menachos* — the *challos* and *rekikin* (mishnah 5:9, 6:3). These *menachos* follow the same routine as the flour *minchah* described above, except that after the בְּלִילָה, *mixing*, the batter is kneaded with warm water and then either fried on a griddle or in a pan, or baked in an oven. There is no יְצִיקָה, *pouring*, with the oven-baked *menachos*, all their oil is added earlier (mishnah 6:3).

Following the frying or baking, these *menachos* undergo פְּתִיתָה, *fragmentation*, in which the *minchah* is broken up into small pieces to prepare it for the *kemitzah* (see 6:4).

Some *menachos* also require תְּנוּפָה, *waving*, a special rite in which the *minchah* is waved in all directions prior to הַגָּשָׁה, *bringing it close* to the Altar. This applies to the *omer*-offering and the מִנְחַת קְנָאוֹת, *jealousy minchah*, brought by the *sotah* [suspected adulteress] (see mishnah 5:5,6).

[ב] **לֹא** יָצַק, לֹא בָלַל, לֹא פָתַת; לֹא מָלַח,

— ר' עובדיה מברטנורא —

(ב) **לא יצק.** סדר המנחה, בתחלה נותן שמן בכלי, ואחר כך נותן את הסלת, ואחר כך חוזר ויוצק שמן ובולל, והכי מפרש בפרק [אלו] המנחות נקמצות [עה,א]. לא יצק ולא בלל כשר, כגון שנתן כל השמן שבלוג במתן ראשון [שהוא קודם] לעשייתה, דאי חיסר שמנה, אמרינן בפרק קמא [דף יא,א] שהיא פסולה. ובגמרא בפרקין (דף יח,א) מוכח דיציקה מעכבת, ומפרש לא יצק, לא יצק כהן אלא זר, דמקמיצה ואילך מצות כהונה, אבל יציקה ובלילה כשרים בזר. ולא בלל דקתני, על כרחך לא בלל כלל, דבלילה ודאי אינה מעכבת, ומתניתין הכי קאמר, לא יצק כהן אלא זר, או לא בלל כלל, כשר: **לא פתת.** [כדכתיב] (ויקרא ב,ו) פתות אותה פתים, אף על גב דבמנחת מחבת בלבד כתיב, הוא הדין לכל המנחות הנאפות תחלה, כגון מחבת ומרחשת ומאפה, מצוה לפותתן כולן ואחר כך קומץ, וזה אם לא פתת אלא כדי קמילה, כשר: **לא מלח.** כל המנחה כולה, אלא הקומץ. דאילו מליחת הקומץ מעכבת היא:

יד אברהם

לֹא יָצַק, — *[If] he did not pour,*

That is, the *Kohen* did not pour the oil on top of the mixed *minchah*. [In this and all the cases which follow in this list, the *minchah* is valid, as will be stated below.]

The mishnah cannot be understood simply — that the *minchah* is valid even if the oil is not poured on at all — because it is clear from the Torah's repetition of this requirement (*Lev.* 2:1,6) that יְצִיקָה, *pouring*, is necessary to the validity of a *minchah*. Consequently, the mishnah must be understood to mean that it was poured on by a non-*Kohen* instead of a *Kohen* (*Rav* from *Gem.* 18a).

Although the oil was poured by a non-*Kohen*, the *minchah* is nonetheless valid. The services of a *Kohen* are required only from the procedure of *kemitzah* and onward, as derived from the verse (*Lev.* 2:2): וֶהֱבִיאָהּ אֶל בְּנֵי אַהֲרֹן הַכֹּהֲנִים וְקָמַץ..., *And he shall bring it to the sons of Aaron, the Kohanim, and he will perform kemitzah* ... (*Gem.* 18b). The implication here is that the preparation of the *minchah* had been completed before it comes to the *Kohen* (*Zevach Todah*). Since the pouring of the oil is mentioned before the *kemitzah*, we conclude that it does not require a *Kohen* (*Rashi* to *Lev.* ad loc.).

The mishnah's usage of the phrase *it is valid* would seem to imply that it is valid only expost facto [בְּדִיעֲבַד]. Actually, however, there is no requirement whatsoever for a *Kohen* to perform this service. The mishnah chooses this phraseology — rather than saying that a non-*Kohen* may pour — only in order to be consistent with the wording of the remainder of the cases, which are indeed valid only expost facto (*Zevach Todah*).

The mishnah is disputed by R' Shimon, who maintains that if the oil is poured by a non-*Kohen* it invalidates the *minchah* (*Gem.* 18b).

לֹא בָלַל, — *[or] he did not mix,*

If the oil and flour in the utensil were not mixed together [as in the regular procedure, when oil is added to the flour after it is placed in the vessel], the *minchah* is nevertheless valid (*Rav* from *Gem.* ibid.).

It is important to note that the *minchah* cannot be missing any oil; the mishnah speaks of a case in which the required amount of oil was poured into the vessel in the initial application of the oil, before the flour was added. If, however, the *minchah* was in fact missing any of the required amount of oil, the *minchah* is invalid, as stated in mishnah 1:3 (*Rav; Rashi*).

2. [If] he did not pour, [or] he did not mix, [or] he did not break [it] into pieces; [or] he did not salt,



While a *minchah* is valid even if it was not mixed, it must be *able* to be mixed. Thus, if the flour and oil were placed in a utensil in a manner which made mixing impossible — e.g., the amount of flour was too large to allow for a proper mixing — the *minchah* is invalidated. For this reason, the maximum amount of flour that can be brought in one vessel is sixty *issaron* [see mishnah 12:4] (*Gem.* 18b).

Ordinarily, there is a rule that any requirement repeated by the Torah in regard to the sacrificial service is essential — i.e., the failure to fulfill it invalidates the offering. The *mitzvah* of בְּלִילָה, *mixing*, however, is not considered essential to the validity of the *minchah* even though it is repeated many times in the Torah. This is because the *mitzvah* of mixing is never stated as a command — *you shall mix* — but rather as a description: סֹלֶת בְּלוּלָה בַשֶּׁמֶן, *flour mixed in oil.* Therefore, the actual mixing is not considered necessary for the validity of the offering. However, since the Torah does describe the offering as being mixed, it is assumed that the *minchah* must be at least capable of being mixed (*Tos.* ibid., s.v. ואמר).

**לֹא פָתַת; — *[or] he did not break [it] into pieces;***

With the exception of the מִנְחַת סֹלֶת, *fine flour minchah*, all *menachos* are baked prior to *kemitzah* (see *Lev.* 2:4-10). The *minchah* must then be broken into smaller pieces before the *kemitzah* is performed. This is derived from the verse (ibid. 6): פָּתוֹת אֹתָהּ פִּתִּים וְיָצַקְתָּ עָלֶיהָ שָׁמֶן, *break it into pieces and pour oil upon it.* The mishnah teaches that if he did not break the *minchah* into pieces as small as required (see below, s.v. או שפתתן פתים מרובות), but into larger pieces, the *minchah* is valid, provided the sizes of the pieces are small enough to allow for a *kemitzah* (*Rav; Rashi*).

The implication of *Rashi's* and *Rav's* explanation is that a minimal amount of breaking is essential to the validity of the *minchah:* It must at least be broken into pieces small enough for *kemitzah.* If, however, the *minchah* was not broken at all, it would be invalid. *Tosafos Yom Tov* challenges this assumption and notes that *Rambam* (*Maaseh HaKorbanos* 13:1) does not require any breaking at all for the *minchah* to be valid.

Others explain that *Rav* and *Rashi* agree with *Rambam.* The entire *minchah* can remain intact, but one piece must be broken off to facilitate the *kemitzah* act [see above, mishnah 1:2] (*Mahariach; Rashash; Sfas Emes*).

**לֹא מָלַח, — *[or] he did not salt,***

That is, he did not salt the entire offering, just the *kometz.* [A *minchah,* like all offerings, must be salted (*Lev.* 2:13).] However, if he neglected to salt even the *kometz,* the *minchah* is not valid (*Rav*). This is derived from the verse (*Lev.* 2:13): וְכָל קָרְבַּן מִנְחָתְךָ בַּמֶּלַח תִּמְלָח, *And every one of your minchah-offerings you shall salt with salt* — i.e., the part of the *minchah* that is offered on the Altar [the *kometz*] requires salting, but not the entire *minchah* (*Tos. Yom Tov* from *Gem.* 20a).

The implication of this interpretation of the mishnah is that the entire offering should be salted but it remains valid even if only the *kometz* was salted. *R' Akiva Eiger* takes strong issue with this implication, citing Rav's opinion in the *Gemara* (20a) that it is not necessary to salt any of the *minchah* besides the *kometz.*[1] *R' Akiva*

1. See *Sfas Emes* 6a, s.v. או גרגיר מלח who defends *Rav's* view.

לֹא הֵנִיף, לֹא הִגִּישׁ; אוֹ שֶׁפִּתְּתָן פִּתִּים מְרֻבּוֹת, וְלֹא מְשָׁחָן – כְּשֵׁרוֹת.

**ר׳ עובדיה מברטנורא**

**לא הניף.** במנחת חוטא ומנחת קנאות דטעונות תנופה: **לא הגיש.** כדכתיב (שם שם,ח) והגישה אל המזבח, שהכהן מוליכה אצל המזבח ומגישה בקרן דרומית מערבית כנגד חודה של קרן: **פתיתים מרובות.** גדולות יותר מהדין שמפורש בהן מנחת ישראל כופל אחת לשנים ושנים לארבע ומבדיל. ואיצטריך לאשמועינן פתיתים גדולות ואף על גב דאשמועינן דאי לא פתת כשרה, דסלקא דעתך אמינא דהתם הוא דליכא תורת חלות עליהן, אבל הכא דלאו תורת חלות איכא ולאו פתיתים איכא, אימא לא, קא משמע לן: **ולא משחן.** הרקיקים הטעונים משיחה, כדכתיב (שמות כט,ב) ורקיקי מצות משוחים בשמן, אחר אפייתן מושחן וחוזר ומושחן עד שיכלה כל השמן שבלוג:

**יד אברהם**

*Eiger* therefore explains that the mishnah's statement refers to the salting of the *kometz.* According to this interpretation, our mishnah states that although the *kometz* should be salted, it is valid even if it was not (*Tos. R' Akiva Eiger*). Accordingly, our mishnah's view is disputed by a *Baraisa* cited by the *Gemara* (20a) which states that if the *kometz* was not salted, the *minchah* is invalid. *Rambam* (*Isurei Mizbe'ach* 5:12) rules in accord with the *Baraisa* (see *Kesef Mishneh* ad loc.).

According to another explanation, the mishnah means that if the salting is performed by a non-*Kohen* it is valid (*Rambam Comm.* from *Gem.* 20a; see *Zevach Todah* ibid., s.v. ואפילו).

In view of the rule cited previously (s.v. לא יצק), that all procedures of the *minchah* from *kemitzah* and forward require the services of a *Kohen,* why is salting the *kometz* valid if it is performed by a non-*Kohen? Sfas Emes* answers that the above-mentioned rule applies only to those steps of the *minchah* mentioned after *kemitzah* in the Torah's basic description of the *minchah*-offering, i.e., after the verse וְקָמַץ, *and [the Kohen] shall remove a kometz.* The *mitzvah* of salting, however, is mentioned in a different section (ibid. 2:13) and thus does not require a *Kohen* even though its performance follows the *kemitzah.* [A basis for this reasoning can be found in *Ramban's* commentary to *Lev.* 1:2.]

לֹא הֵנִיף, — *[or] he did not wave,*

The *omer*-offering brought on the second day of Pesach, and the *jealousy minchah* brought for a *sotah* (see mishnah 1:1), undergo a procedure called תְּנוּפָה, *tenufah.*[1] This requires the *Kohen* to take the *minchah* and wave it to and fro and then up and down (see mishnah 5:5,6). [In the case of the jealousy *minchah*, the woman also places her hand on the *minchah* and waves it together with the *Kohen* (*Sotah* 3:1).] However, if *tenufah* is not performed, the *minchah* is valid nonetheless (*Tif. Yis.*).

In mentioning the *tenufah* after salting, the mishnah is apparently not adhering to the precise order of the procedures, as the *tenufah* took place *before* the salting (*Tos.* 18a, s.v. לא מלח). However, according to *Rav's* interpretation, that the salting discussed in the mishnah refers to salting the entire of-

1. [*Rav* mentions the מִנְחַת חוֹטֵא, *sinner's minchah* (see 1:1), as an example of a *minchah* that must be waved. This must be a misprint since it is clear from mishnah 5:5 that this is not the halachah. The text should be emended to read *the minchah of the omer*. The same error appears in the text of *Rashi* (18a, s.v. ולא פתת) and was emended in the standard (Vilna) edition of the *Gemara*.]

3 [or] he did not wave, [or] he did not bring [it] near;
2 or [if] he broke them into large pieces, or he did
not anoint them — they are valid.



fering, this procedure may very well have taken place before the waving (*Rashash*).[1]

;לֹא הִגִּישׁ — *[or] he did not bring [it] near;*

He did not perform the act of carrying the *minchah* close to the southwestern corner of the Altar before performing its *kemitzah* (*Rav;* see preface).

,אוֹ שֶׁפְּתָתָן פִּתִּים מְרֻבּוֹת — *or [if] he broke them into large pieces,*

The *menachos* which are baked prior to *kemitzah* must be broken into pieces before the *kemitzah* can take place. The procedure for doing so is to take each of the *minchah's* loaves and fold into halves, and those halves into quarters, with this process continuing until all the pieces end up the size of an olive (6:4; see comm. there, s.v. וכלן כזיתים). However, if he left larger pieces, i.e., pieces larger than an olive's size, the *minchah* is nevertheless valid (*Rav* from *Gem.* 18b).

Although the mishnah has already stated that if one did not break up the *minchah* at all it is valid, it is nonetheless necessary to mention that if he left a *minchah* fragmented into large pieces it is also valid. The reason for this is that, in a sense, an unbroken *minchah* might be considered better than one broken into large pieces. The Torah (*Lev.* 2:4,6) describes a *minchah* either as חַלּוֹת, *loaves*, or as פִּתִּים, *pieces*. One might, therefore, have supposed that a *minchah* broken into too large pieces is invalid because it is considered neither חַלָּה, *loaf* (as it is not whole), nor פִּתִּים, *pieces* (as the pieces are too large). Therefore, the mishnah teaches that even larger pieces qualify as fragments of a *minchah* (ibid.).

Another interpretation of the mishnah is that he broke it into more — rather than larger — pieces. Although each of the more numerous pieces would naturally be smaller than prescribed, the *minchah* remains valid (*Gem.* ibid.).

— וְלֹא מְשָׁחָן — *or he did not anoint them —*

One type of oven-baked *minchah* is that of רְקִיקִין, *rekikin* [wafers] (*Lev.* 2:4). These were baked and then smeared with oil afterward. This procedure, known as מְשִׁיחָה, *anointing*, replaces the second application of oil common to most other types of *menachos* (see mishnah 6:3). Our mishnah teaches that if the oil was not applied to the *minchah* after its baking, it is nevertheless valid (*Rav*).

The mishnah cannot mean that no oil was applied to the *rekikin*, since the *minchah* would then be invalid for lacking its required amount of oil (see mishnah 1:3). Rather, the mishnah must mean that the oil was all added prior to the *rekikin's* baking, so that none was left for smearing them afterward.

This explanation seems straightforward enough according to the view of *Rashi* (74b) and *Tosafos* (75a) in their commentaries to mishnah 6:3 that the *rekikin* are baked with oil just as all other *menachos*,

1. *Tif. Yis.* presents a different order to the mishnah. In brief, the *Tanna* first mentions יְצִיקָה, *pouring oil*; בְּלִילָה, *mixing*; פְּתִיתָה, *breaking into pieces*; and מְלִיחָה, *salting*, in order of their appearance in the Torah. These are given as one set because they do not require a *Kohen*. תְּנוּפָה, *tenufah*, and הַגָּשָׁה, bringing the *minchah* near to the Altar, are mentioned later because they should be performed by a *Kohen* and are valid only after the fact with a non-*Kohen*.

מנחות
ג/ב

נִתְעָרֵב קֻמְצָהּ בְּקֹמֶץ חֲבֶרְתָּהּ, בְּמִנְחַת כֹּהֲנִים, בְּמִנְחַת כֹּהֵן הַמָּשִׁיחַ, בְּמִנְחַת נְסָכִין – כְּשֵׁרָה. רַבִּי יְהוּדָה אוֹמֵר: בְּמִנְחַת כֹּהֵן הַמָּשִׁיחַ וּבְמִנְחַת נְסָכִין פְּסוּלָה, שֶׁזּוֹ בְּלִילָתָהּ עָבָה, וְזוֹ בְּלִילָתָהּ רַכָּה,

ר׳ עובדיה מברטנורא

**במנחת כהנים כשרה.** שכולן כליל כמוהו: **במנחת כהן המשיח ובמנחת נסכים פסולה.** לפי שהקומץ דמנחת ישראל בלילתו עבה, לוג אחד שמן לעשרון סלת, ומנחת נסכים ושל כהן משיח בלילתן רכה, שלשה לוגים לעשרון, כדכתיב במנחת נסכים (במדבר טו,ד) [עשרון] בלול ברביעית ההין שמן, ובמנחת כהן המשיח הוא אומר (ויקרא ו,יג) סולת מנחה תמיד, הרי היא לך כמנחת התמיד שהיא עשרון סלת בלול ברביעית ההין:

יד אברהם

that each of the previously described *menachos* is valid (*Meleches Shlomo*).

נִתְעָרֵב קֻמְצָהּ בְּקֹמֶץ חֲבֶרְתָּהּ, — *[If] its kometz mixed with the kometz of another,*

[The *kematzim* of two *menachos* were mixed together and cannot be separated.]

בְּמִנְחַת כֹּהֲנִים, — *[or] with the minchah-offering of Kohanim,*

[Alternatively, the *kometz* of one *minchah* was mixed with a *Kohen's minchah*.] The *minchah* of a *Kohen* is distinguished by the requirement that the entire *minchah* be burnt on the Altar (*Rav* from *Lev.* 6:16).

בְּמִנְחַת כֹּהֵן הַמָּשִׁיחַ, — *[or] with the minchah-offering of the Anointed Kohen,*

The *Anointed Kohen* — i.e., the *Kohen Gadol* — is required to offer a *minchah* each day, half in the morning and half in the afternoon. This *minchah* is known as the מִנְחַת חֲבִתִּין, *minchas chavitin*, and it too is burnt in its entirety on the Altar (ibid. v. 15; see mishnah 4:8).

בְּמִנְחַת נְסָכִין — *[or] with the minchah of the libations* —

These are the *menachos* which, with the second application of oil for בְּלִילָה, *mixing*, being omitted before baking and replaced by מְשִׁיחָה, *anointing*, after baking. Accordingly, the only application of oil completely omitted from the *rekikin* (as taught in mishnah 6:3) is the customary final application — יְצִיקָה, *pouring*. Since the initial application of oil to the empty vessel applies to *rekikin* as well, it is possible for all the oil to have been added at this point, so that it is possible for the *minchah* not to be missing any of its required amount of oil and yet not to undergo *anointing*. However, *Rambam's* view seems to be that these were baked without oil at all, and only after the baking was oil smeared on them through *anointing* (see *Lechem Mishneh* and *Mishneh LaMelech* to *Maaseh HaKorbanos* 13:5; *Keren Orah* to 74b). Thus, there is no place for the oil to have been added, unless we conjecture that the mishnah means that he deviated from the procedure for *rekikin* and added the oil to the dough before baking them (see *Zevach Todah*, who concluded that the matter needs further study).

כְּשֵׁרוֹת. — *they are valid.*

[These departures from the prescribed procedures for *menachos* do not invalidate them, for the reasons previously explained.]

Other versions of the mishnah use the singular term כְּשֵׁרָה, *it is valid*, indicating

3
2 [If] its *kometz* mixed with the *kometz* of another, [or] with the *minchah*-offering of *Kohanim*, [or] with the *minchah*-offering of the Anointed *Kohen*, [or] with the *minchah*-offering of the libations — it is valid. R' Yehudah says: In the case of the *minchah*-offering of the Anointed *Kohen* and the *minchah*-offering of libations it is invalid, because this [one's] mixture is thicker, and this one's mixture is thinner,



along with libations of wine [*nesachim*], accompany *olah*- and *shelamim*-offerings (see preface to 2:4). They too are totally burnt (*Rambam, Hil. Maaseh HaKorbanos* 2:1).

.כְּשֵׁרָה — *it is valid.*

Since the *kometz* mixed with other items that are burnt on the Altar, the entire mixture can be burnt on the Altar. Thus, the *minchah* is valid (*Tif. Yis.*).

The *kometz* is not nullified by the larger volume of the *minchah* with which it is mixed [and thereby deprived of its character as the *kometz* of its *minchah*], because this *Tanna* maintains that substances which are offered on the Altar do not nullify one another [אֵין עוֹלִין מְבַטְּלִין זֶה אֶת זֶה] (*Tos. Yom Tov* from *Gem.* 22b; see below s.v. והן).

רַבִּי יְהוּדָה אוֹמֵר: בְּמִנְחַת כֹּהֵן הַמָּשִׁיחַ וּבְמִנְחַת נְסָכִין פְּסוּלָה, — *R' Yehudah says: In the case of the minchah-offering of the Anointed Kohen and the minchah-offering of libations it is invalid,*

R' Yehudah disagrees with the *Tanna Kamma* in the latter two cases, in which the *kometz* was mixed with the *minchah* of the *Kohen Gadol* or with the *minchah* of libations. The basis for his disagreement is the difference in the consistency of the two types of *minchah* that were mixed up, as the mishnah proceeds to explain.

According to some commentators, it is just the *kometz* (and, by default, its *minchah*) that becomes invalidated (*Rav; Tos. Yom Tov*); others contend that both offerings are invalidated (*Rashi; Tos.*). This will be explained below. The mishnah's use of the singular פְּסוּלָה, *it is invalid*, is not conclusive, as it can be interpreted to mean *each* of the *menachos* is invalid (*Rashi*).

שֶׁזּוֹ בְּלִילָתָהּ עָבָה, — *because this [one's] mixture is thicker,*

The *kometz's* dough is thicker because a regular *minchah* consists of one *log* of oil per *issaron* of flour, a relatively small proportion of oil to flour (*Rav;* see mishnah 9:3; *Rashi, Lev.* 2:1, s.v. סלת).

וְזוֹ בְּלִילָתָהּ רַכָּה, — *and this one's mixture is thinner,*

The *minchah* of the *Kohen Gadol* consists of three *logs* of oil for an *issaron* of flour (*Rav*).

[This is derived from the Torah's phrase (*Lev.* 6:13): סֹלֶת מִנְחָה תָּמִיד, *fine flour for a minchah, constantly,* which is understood exegetically to be comparing this offering to the מִנְחַת תָּמִיד, the *minchah* which is brought with the daily offering. Just as the *minchah* of the daily *tamid*-offering (which

# וְהֵן בּוֹלְעוֹת זוֹ מִזּוֹ.

— ר' עובדיה מברטנורא —

**והן בולעות זו מזו.** הקומץ בולע ממנחת נסכים וממנחת כהן משיח, ורבה שמנן של מנחות הללו על הקומץ ומבטלות ליה, והוי מנחה שלא הוקטר קומצה ופסולה הנקמצת. אבל מנחת נסכים כשרה ולא הוי כרבה שמנה, כיון שלא מדעת עירבו, השמן שבולעתו בטל לגבה וכמאן דליתיה. ואין הלכה כרבי יהודה:

**יד אברהם**

is a lamb) consists of an *issaron* of flour and a fourth of a *hin* — i.e., three *logs* — of oil, so too does the *chavitin* of the *Kohen Gadol* (*Num.* 28:5) (*Rav* from *Gem.* 51a).]

Similarly, the libation *minchah* [*minchas nesachim*] contains three *logs* of oil per *issaron* of flour [for a lamb offering] (*Rav*), and two *logs* for a ram and bull (*Tos. Yom Tov*). The oil to flour ratio of the *minchah* of libations is specified in the Torah (*Num.* 15). [Since these *menachos* contain double or triple the amount of oil that a regular *minchah* contains, the consistency of their dough is much lighter.]

וְהֵן בּוֹלְעוֹת זוֹ מִזּוֹ. — *and they absorb from each other.*

Since there is more oil in the *minchas nesachim* [libations] or the *minchah* of the *Kohen* than in an ordinary *minchah*, the flour of the *kometz* of the ordinary *minchah* absorbs oil from the other *minchah* and [a portion of it] becomes nullified by the greater quantity of oil absorbed. As a result, the *kometz* flour loses its legal standing and is for all practical purposes considered to be non-existent. The ordinary *minchah* from which the *kometz* was taken is thus invalidated as a *minchah* whose *kometz* was not [completely] burnt on the Altar (*Rav*).

[This is based on the principle of בִּטּוּל בְּרוֹב, *nullification in the majority*, a well-known Talmudic principle whereby a smaller quantity which is mixed with a larger quantity (in a manner that it is no longer detectable) is nullified and legally considered non-existent.]

The other *minchah*, however, being the majority component of this mixture, is obviously not nullified and remains valid (*Rav; Rashi* original manuscript, as cited by *Shitah Mekubetzes* 22a #22).

The Rabbis [i.e., the first *Tanna* of the mishnah], however, hold that both *menachos* are valid. Their view is based on the principle that עוֹלִין אֵין מְבַטְּלִין זוֹ אֶת זוֹ, *substances which are offered on the Altar do not nullify each other*[1] (*Gem.* 22b) and therefore there

1. At issue is the interpretation of a verse in the Torah concerning the *avodah* of the *Kohen Gadol* on Yom Kippur. The Torah states (*Lev.* 16:18): וְלָקַח מִדַּם הַפָּר וּמִדַּם הַשָּׂעִיר, *and he shall take from the blood of the bull and of the blood of the he-goat [together]* (and perform the *zerikah* on the Altar). By repeatedly referring to this mixture as *the blood of the bull and the blood of the goat*, the Torah indicates that the rule of בִּטּוּל, *nullification*, is not in effect. If it were, the amount of the bull's blood, which is far greater than the goat's blood, would nullify it, and the latter would no longer be considered a distinct legal entity.

The Rabbis understand this to be teaching that עוֹלִין אֵין מְבַטְּלִין זוֹ אֶת זוֹ, *substances which are offered on the Altar do not nullify each other*. Thus the lesser amount of goat's blood is not nullified by the greater amount of bull's blood. R' Yehudah, for his part, derives from the above-mentioned verse his principle that מִין בְּמִינוֹ לֹא בָּטֵל, *like*

is no concern that the *kometz* can be nullified by the *minchas nesachim* or the *minchah* of the *Kohen Gadol* since both are to be burnt on the Altar (*Rambam Comm.; Tos. R' Akiva Eiger*).

We have explained the mishnah to this point according to *Rav*, who is supported by *Tos. Yom Tov*. However, *Rashi* (22a, s.v. הן) and *Tosafos* contend that *both* offerings are invalidated. In their opinion, the *kometz* is invalidated not because it becomes nullified by the absorption, but simply because its oil content is increased by the absorption from the other, more oil-laden, *minchah*. This invalidates it because of the rule taught in mishnah 1:3 that *if he increased its oil it is invalid.*[1] The other *minchah* is invalidated because as a result of the absorption by the *kometz*, its own oil is decreased and as that mishnah (ibid.) states, *if he decreased its oil it is invalid.* Although the oil is still physically present, it becomes nullified in the *kometz* and ceases to have any legal existence; it is therefore considered "missing" (*Rashi* 23a; *Tos. R' Akiva*).

However, according to the Rabbis' view that עוֹלִין אֵין מְבַטְּלִין זוֹ אֶת זוֹ, *substances which are offered on the Altar do not nullify each other*, all components of the mixture retain their legal standing, and the oil of each *minchah* is thus attributed to its own offering. Consequently, neither *minchah* is considered to contain the wrong quantity of oil. Only according to R' Yehudah, whose opinion it is that even items offered on the Altar are governed by the regular rules of nullifications, is there a problem of wrong quantity of oil for each *minchah*. Since the flour of the *kometz* nullifies the oil it absorbs,[2] it prevents it from being considered part of the *minchah* to which it actually belongs (*Tos. R' Akiva Eiger*, in resolution of questions raised by *Tos. Yom Tov*).[3]

*substances do not nullify each other*. Thus, the goat's blood does not become nullified by the bull's blood because both are the same kind of substances: blood (*Gem.* 22a; see *Zevachim* 8:6).

1. *Tos. Yom Tov* questions this explanation on the basis that the invalidation of *increased oil* is only if he added an extra *log*. The amount of oil absorbed by the *kometz*, however, cannot be that great and it is therefore not enough to invalidate (*Tif. Yis.*). *Keren Orah* and *Chazon Ish* (29:3) answer that a minimum of an extra *log* is necessary to invalidate applies only to extra oil sanctified for this particular *minchah*. Oil designated for another *minchah* invalidates even in a small amount (*Rambam, Pesulei HaMukdashin* 11:8). Since the extra oil absorbed by the *kometz* comes from a different *minchah*, the *kometz* can be invalidated by any amount of it. [*Tos. Yom Tov*, however, is consistent with his view in mishnah 1:3 that excess oil never invalidates unless there is an extra *log*. See comm. and fn. to mishnah 1:3 above, s.v רבה שמנה.]

2. *Shitah Mekubetzes* points out that although the oil is nullified by the flour which absorbs it, this does not render it legally non-existent — or else it would not be considered as too much oil in the *kometz*. It is negated only to the extent that it can no longer be viewed as part of its own *minchah* but rather as part of the *kometz* which absorbed it (see *Shitah Mekubetzes* #17).

3. The *Gemara* (22b-23a) questions R' Yehudah's invalidation on the basis of R' Yehudah's own well-known principle that מִין בְּמִינוֹ אֵינוֹ בָטֵל, *like substances do not nullify each other* (see *Zevachim* 8:6). Accordingly, the oil of the *minchah* which becomes absorbed by the *kometz* should be prevented from becoming nullified by the presence of the *kometz's*

[ג] **שְׁתֵּי** מְנָחוֹת שֶׁלֹּא נִקְמְצוּ וְנִתְעָרְבוּ זוֹ בְּזוֹ – אִם יָכוֹל לִקְמוֹץ מִזּוֹ בִּפְנֵי עַצְמָהּ וּמִזּוֹ בִּפְנֵי עַצְמָהּ, כְּשֵׁרוֹת; וְאִם לָאו, פְּסוּלוֹת.

הַקֹּמֶץ שֶׁנִּתְעָרֵב בְּמִנְחָה שֶׁלֹּא נִקְמְצָה,

ר׳ עובדיה מברטנורא

(ג) **אם יכול לקמצן מזו בפני עצמה ומזו בפני עצמה.** שנפלה זו בלד זה של כלי וזו בלד זה ונשאר מהן כדי קומץ שלא נתערב, כשרות, ואם לאו, פסולות, דאמר בתורת כהנים מסלתה ולא מסולת

יד אברהם

3.

שְׁתֵּי מְנָחוֹת שֶׁלֹּא נִקְמְצוּ — *[If] two minchah-offerings in which kemitzah had not been performed*

[I.e., they both are the types of *menachos* which require *kemitzah*, but it had not yet been done.]

וְנִתְעָרְבוּ זוֹ בְּזוֹ — *mixed together* —

They fell into the same *kli shareis*, one next to the other and partially overlapping (*Tif. Yis.*).

אִם יָכוֹל לִקְמוֹץ מִזּוֹ בִּפְנֵי עַצְמָהּ וּמִזּוֹ בִּפְנֵי עַצְמָהּ, כְּשֵׁרוֹת; — *if it is possible to perform kemitzah in each by itself, they are valid;*

If enough flour which had not become mixed together remains to allow for *kemitzah* to be performed in each of them separately, the *Kohen* may perform *kemitzah* in the identifiable part of each of them and thereby validate both *menachos* (*Rav*).

וְאִם לָאו, פְּסוּלוֹת. — *if not, they are invalid.*

[If the flour of the two *menachos* mixed together to such an extent that not even a *kometz* of flour from each *minchah* remains clearly identifiable, both *menachos* are invalid. In order for a *kemitzah* to validate a *minchah*, the *kometz* removed must be made up entirely of flour from that *minchah*. Once the two *menachos* have been completely mixed, it becomes impossible to know whether each *kometz* is made up of flour from one *minchah* or both. Consequently, both *menachos* are invalid.]

This is derived from the verse (*Lev.* 2:2): וְקָמַץ מִשָּׁם מְלֹא קֻמְצוֹ מִסָּלְתָּהּ, *and he shall take from there his full kometz from its flour*, which indicates that the entire *kometz* must consist of *its flour*

own oil (see *Shitah Mekubetzes* 22b #3). The *Gemara* (23b) explains that R' Yehudah's principle does not apply in cases in which an unlike kind is also present to nullify. Since the flour of the *kometz* is greater than the oil absorbed from the second *minchah*, we *discount the like kind* [i.e., the oil of the *kometz*] *as if it were not present, and the unlike kind overwhelms it* [the absorbed substance] *and nullifies it* [סַלֵּק אֶת מִינוֹ כְּמוֹ שֶׁאֵינוֹ, וְשֶׁאֵינוֹ מִינוֹ רָבָה עָלָיו וּמְבַטְּלוֹ].

Although R' Yehudah's view is not accepted as halachah — which follows the principle that מִין בְּמִינוֹ בָטֵל, *a substance which mixes in a like kind does become nullified* — his rule concerning ... סַלֵּק, *discount* ... has application even according to the halachically accepted view. See *Yoreh Deah* 98:2.

3 **3.** [If] two *minchah*-offerings in which *kemitzah*
3 had not been performed mixed together — if it is possible to perform *kemitzah* in each by itself, they are valid; if not, they are invalid.

[If] a *kometz* mixed with a *minchah*-offering in which *kemitzah* had not been performed,

**YAD AVRAHAM**

and not that of another *minchah* (*Rav* from *Toras Kohanim* ad loc.).[1]

Even if there is enough unmixed flour to make it possible to perform *kemitzah* for one of the *menachos* but not the other, both are still invalid. In order for a *kometz* to be offered on the Altar, it must have the capacity to permit the remainder of its *minchah* for consumption. In this case, even if he were to perform the *kemitzah* on the one *minchah*, its remainder could still not be eaten because it remains mixed together with the other, unpermitted *minchah*. Therefore, the *kometz* would not be valid for burning. This is analogous to a *minchah* whose remainder became *tamei* before its *kometz* had been burnt on the Altar, about which the *Gemara* (26a) rules that the *kometz* may not be brought to the Altar (*Zevach Todah;* see mishnah 4).

הַקֹּמֶץ שֶׁנִּתְעָרֵב בְּמִנְחָה שֶׁלֹּא נִקְמְצָה, לֹא יַקְטִיר. — *[If] a kometz mixed with a minchah-offering in which kemitzah had not been performed, it is not burnt [on the Altar].*

If the *kometz* from one *minchah* mixed with another *minchah* which still requires *kemitzah*, nothing of this mixture may be offered on the Altar. One cannot simply remove two *kematzin* for burning, since there is no way of knowing that each consists only of a full *kometz* and not a mixture of the original *kometz* and part of the *minchah* into which it fell. At the same time, we cannot just burn the entire mixture together [thus assuring that the *kometz* of the first is burnt and thereby validating at least that *minchah*], because there is no obligation to burn any part of a *minchah* other than its *kometz* (*Rav; Rashi*).

From these comments it would appear that there is no prohibition on burning the mixture; it is merely not a *mitzvah*. Indeed, *Shitah Mekubetzes* (23a #7) assumes that if one wishes to burn the mixture he may do so. Many commentators, however, find this puzzling. If, indeed, there is no prohibition on burning a *minchah* which has not had its *kometz* removed, why should the entire mixture not be burnt to assure that at least the *kometz* of the first *minchah* is not wasted (*Sfas Emes; Zevach Todah Chidushei HaGriz*)? Some commentators explain that burning the whole mixture

1. The mishnah in *Zevachim* (8:9) states that if the blood of two sacrifices became mixed and the mixture was applied to the Altar, both sacrifices are valid. This does not compare to our situation. In the case of animal sacrifices, it is necessary for only a drop of blood from each offering to reach the Altar in order to validate them, and we may safely assume that at least one drop from each animal's blood is present in the mixture applied to the Altar. However, each *minchah* is valid only if an entire *kometz* of its flour is removed in one *kemitzah*; this is something which can never be known when two *menachos* are mixed (*Tif. Yis.*).

# לֹא יַקְטִיר. וְאִם הִקְטִיר, זוֹ שֶׁנִּקְמְצָה עָלְתָה לַבְּעָלִים, וְזוֹ שֶׁלֹּא נִקְמְצָה לֹא עָלְתָה לַבְּעָלִים.
# נִתְעָרֵב קֻמְצָהּ בִּשְׁיָרֶיהָ, אוֹ בִשְׁיָרֶיהָ שֶׁל חֲבֶרְתָּהּ, לֹא יַקְטִיר; וְאִם הִקְטִיר, עָלְתָה לַבְּעָלִים.

## ר׳ עובדיה מברטנורא

חברתה: **לא יקטיר.** ואפילו כל המעורבת, דאין הקטרה מצוה אלא בקומץ, ומקמץ נמי לא קמין שני קומצים דילמא בכל קומץ יש מזה שנתערב וליכא קומץ שלם מחד מנחה: **ואם הקטיר.** כל המעורבת, היא לא עלתה לבעלים, דהא לא נקמצה, ואין מנחת נדבה כיתרת בלא קמיצה: **נתערב קומצה בשיריה.** לא יקטיר את כולה משום דהשירים אסורים להקטיר, דכתיב (ויקרא ב,יא) לא תקטירו ממנו אשה לה׳, כל שממנו לאישים הרי הוא בבל תקטירו:

## יד אברהם

would appear as if he had added to the *kometz*, and it is therefore Rabbinically prohibited to do so (*Zevach Todah*). Others conclude from this that there is a restriction against performing unnecessary burnings on the Altar (*Mikdash David* 25:1).[1]

וְאִם הִקְטִיר, זוֹ שֶׁנִּקְמְצָה עָלְתָה לַבְּעָלִים, — *But if he burnt [it], the one in which kemitzah had been performed is credited to the owner,*

If he burnt the entire mixture on the Altar, the *minchah* whose *kometz* had been taken is valid because its *kometz* was in fact offered on the Altar (*Rav*).

וְזוֹ שֶׁלֹּא נִקְמְצָה לֹא עָלְתָה לַבְּעָלִים. — *and the one in which kemitzah had not been performed is not credited to the owner.*

A voluntary *minchah* cannot be offered in its entirety without *kemitzah* (*Rav*). Although the *minchah* of a *Kohen* is totally burnt on the Altar (*Lev.* 6:16), and thus does not require *kemitzah*, a non-*Kohen* does not have the option of offering his *minchah* in this manner (*Zevach Todah*).

נִתְעָרֵב קֻמְצָהּ בִּשְׁיָרֶיהָ, אוֹ בִשְׁיָרֶיהָ שֶׁל חֲבֶרְתָּהּ, — *[If] its kometz mixed with its remainder, or with the remainder of another [minchah-offering],*

[The *kometz* was mixed either with its own remainder or with the remainder of another *minchah* whose *kometz* had previously been taken. Thus, the part which should be burnt on the Altar (the *kometz*) is mixed together with a part that should be eaten (the remainder).]

לֹא יַקְטִיר; — *he should not burn [it on the Altar];*

He may not burn the mixture, because the remainder of a *minchah* may not be burnt on the Altar. This is derived from the verse (*Lev.* 2:11): לֹא תַקְטִירוּ מִמֶּנּוּ אִשֶּׁה לַה׳, *You shall not burn from it to HASHEM*, which is exegetically understood to mean כָּל שֶׁמִּמֶּנּוּ לָאִישִׁים, *any offering from which a part has been designated to be burnt on the Altar fire* [e.g., the *kometz*], *do not burn* [the remainder on the Altar]. Accordingly, if a *minchah* has had its *kometz* removed, its remainder is prohibited from being burnt on the Altar (*Rav; Rashi*).

This prohibition clearly does not apply

1. See *Sfas Emes*, who suggests that the restriction against burning the mixture may actually be Biblical.

3 it is not burnt [on the Altar]. But if he burnt [it], the
3 one in which *kemitzah* had been performed is credited to the owner, and the one in which *kemitzah* had not been performed is not credited to the owner.

[If] its *kometz* mixed with its remainder, or with the remainder of another [*minchah*-offering], he should not burn [it on the Altar]; but if he did burn [it], it is credited to the owner.

### YAD AVRAHAM

in the previous case in which the *kometz* was mixed with a *minchah* from which the *kometz* had not yet been taken. As long as the *kemitzah* has not been performed, the rest of the *minchah* has not yet been identified as the שִׁירַיִם, *remainder* (*Shitah Mekubetzes*). [Thus, in the opinion of some, that mixture *may* be burnt on the Altar, though there is no obligation to do so; see comm. above s.v. הַקּוֹמֵץ.]

וְאִם הִקְטִיר, עָלְתָה לַבְּעָלִים. — *but if he did burn [it], it is credited to the owner.*

[Although he has transgressed the Torah's prohibition against burning the remainder, once the mixture has been burnt the *kometz* has been offered, and he need not bring another *minchah*.]

**◆§ צִיץ מְרַצֶּה, the tzitz effects acceptance**

Among the special garments worn by the *Kohen Gadol* is the צִיץ, *tzitz*, a golden plate with the words קֹדֶשׁ לַה', *Holy unto* H*ASHEM*, inscribed onto it. Two fingers in width, the *tzitz* is worn by the *Kohen Gadol* on his forehead (*Ex.* 28:36-38).

The *tzitz* is invested by the Torah with the power to effect acceptance (or atonement) for an offering that becomes *tamei*. If the blood of a sacrifice or the *kometz* of a *minchah* become *tamei*, they are disqualified from the Altar. If they are improperly offered on the Altar, therefore, the offering should be invalid. However, the presence of the *tzitz*[1] effects an acceptance for the *tumah*-contaminated sacrifice to the extent that it is considered valid, after the fact, if it was offered in violation of the ban on doing so. This is derived from the verse in the Torah which says concerning the *tzitz* (ibid. v. 38): וְהָיָה עַל מֵצַח אַהֲרֹן וְנָשָׂא אַהֲרֹן אֶת עֲוֹן הַקֳּדָשִׁים אֲשֶׁר יַקְדִּישׁוּ בְּנֵי יִשְׂרָאֵל לְכָל מַתְּנֹת קָדְשֵׁיהֶם וְהָיָה עַל מִצְחוֹ תָּמִיד לְרָצוֹן לָהֶם לִפְנֵי ה', *And it shall be on the forehead of Aaron, and Aaron shall bear the sin of those sanctified objects which the Children of Israel shall sanctify for all their sanctified gifts; and it shall be on his forehead constantly for acceptance for them before* H*ASHEM*. "Bearing the sin of sanctified objects" is understood to mean that the *tzitz* affords atonement for the sin of an offering brought in a state of *tumah* (*Toras Kohanim* to *Lev.* 1:4; *Gem.* 25a). [See further in *Pesachim* 7:7 and *Yad Avraham* comm. there.]

1. There is a Tannaitic dispute whether the *tzitz* must be worn to effect this atonement or its mere existence is sufficient to accomplish this. See *Yoma* 7b and *Pesachim* 77b.

מנחות
ג/ג

נִטְמָא הַקֹּמֶץ וְהִקְרִיבוֹ, הַצִּיץ מְרַצֶּה; יָצָא וְהִקְרִיבוֹ, אֵין הַצִּיץ מְרַצֶּה; שֶׁהַצִּיץ מְרַצֶּה עַל הַטָּמֵא, וְאֵינוֹ מְרַצֶּה עַל הַיּוֹצֵא.

### ר׳ עובדיה מברטנורא

**נטמא הקומץ והקריבו הציץ מרצה.** דכתיב (שמות כח,לח) ונשא אהרן את עון הקדשים, אינו נושא אלא עון טומאה, שיש בה לד קל שהותרה מכללה בלבור, דכתיב בתמיד (במדבר כח,ב) במועדו, ואפילו בטומאה: **ואינו מרצה על היוצא.** ואף על גב דיש בו נמי לד קל שהותר מכללו בבמה, שנאסר יוצא במשכן והותר בבמה שבנוב וגבעון שלא היו שם קלעים, אף על פי כן אין הציץ מרצה ביוצא, דכתיב (שמות כח,לח) לרצון להם לפני ה׳, עון דלפני ה׳ אין, עון דיוצא לא:

### יד אברהם

נִטְמָא הַקֹּמֶץ וְהִקְרִיבוֹ, הַצִּיץ מְרַצֶּה; — *[If] the kometz became tamei and he offered it, the tzitz effects acceptance;*

The *kometz*, like all sacrificial matter, becomes disqualified by becoming contaminated with *tumah*; thus it cannot be burnt on the Altar. However, the rule for *tumah*-contaminated offerings is that if they should be offered on the Altar despite their disqualification, the *tzitz* effects an acceptance for them (after the fact) and the owners need not bring another one. Thus, the mishnah teaches that if the *kometz* became *tamei* but was offered anyway, it has been accepted and the owner has discharged his obligation to bring a *minchah* (*Tif. Yis.*). The remainder of the *minchah* is eaten (*Toras HaKodashim).*

This applies whether the *kometz* was rendered *tamei* deliberately or inadvertently, as long as the one who offered it on the Altar was unaware of the *tumah* at the time he placed it on the Altar. If the *Kohen* offered the *kometz* knowing that it was *tamei,* the remainder may not be eaten by Rabbinic decree (*Toras HaKodashim* from *Gem.* 25b; see *Likkutei Halachos* ibid.).

יָצָא וְהִקְרִיבוֹ, אֵין הַצִּיץ מְרַצֶּה; — *[if] it went out and he offered it, the tzitz does not effect acceptance;*

[If the *kometz* is removed from the Temple Courtyard, it is also invalidated. For this invalidation, however, the *tzitz* is ineffective and the offering can no longer be offered.]

שֶׁהַצִּיץ מְרַצֶּה עַל הַטָּמֵא, — *for the tzitz effects acceptance for that which is tamei,*

Concerning the ability of the *tzitz* to effect acceptance for invalidations, the Torah states simply: וְנָשָׂא אַהֲרֹן אֶת עֲוֹן הַקֳּדָשִׁים, *and Aaron will bear the sin of the sanctified objects.* The Torah does not specify, however, exactly which invalidation is meant. Since the Torah is not explicit, we apply this leniency only to an invalidation toward which we see the Torah applied other leniencies. In regard to the *tumah* disqualifications, we find that the Torah was lenient with it and made it acceptable under certain circumstances — viz., a קָרְבַּן צִבּוּר, *communal offering,* which is offered even in a state of *tumah,* if necessary [see

3
3 [If] the *kometz* became *tamei* and he offered it, the *tzitz* effects acceptance; [if] it went out and he offered it, the *tzitz* does not effect acceptance; for the *tzitz* effects acceptance for that which is *tamei*, but not for that which went out.



*Pesachim* 7:4] (*Rav* from *Gem.* 25a).

The requirement that the invalidation in question be one with such a leniency is alluded to in the wording of the verse concerning the *tzitz*, which says לְרָצוֹן לָהֶם, *for acceptance for them* — indicating that the *tzitz* is effective for something which is *accepted for them*, i.e., something valid in other circumstances (*Tos.* ad loc., s.v. הא אינו, cited by *Tos. Yom Tov*).

וְאֵינוֹ מְרַצֶּה עַל הַיּוֹצֵא. — *but not for that which went out.*

[As explained above, the invalidation for being taken out of the confines of the Temple Courtyard is something which is unaffected by the *tzitz*.]

Actually this invalidation, too, has the leniency of being acceptable elsewhere — in the instance of a sacrifice offered on a בָּמָה [*bamah*], private altar [during the historical periods in which they were permitted (see *Zevachim* 14:4)]. Since a *bamah* could be erected anywhere, it has no enclosed courtyard to limit the space where its offerings may be taken; thus, the invalidation of יוֹצֵא, *that which is taken out*, does not apply to offerings. Nonetheless, this exception is not sufficient grounds to include the invalidation of offerings which left the Courtyard in the category of invalidations for which the *tzitz* effects atonement. The *tzitz* is effective only for an invalidation which has acceptability in the Temple, as it says (loc. cit.): לְרָצוֹן לָהֶם לִפְנֵי ה׳, *for acceptance before* HASHEM — and the phrase לִפְנֵי ה׳, *before* HASHEM, alludes to the Temple area (*Rav*, *Rashi* from *Gem.* 25a; cf. *Tos. Yom Tov*).

## 4.

The *Gemara* in *Pesachim* (77a) cites a *Baraisa* which records a dispute between R′ Yehoshua and R′ Eliezer concerning an animal sacrifice whose meat was lost or became *tamei* before the application of its blood to the Altar [*zerikah*]. R′ Yehoshua maintains that אִם אֵין בָּשָׂר אֵין דָּם, *if there is no meat there is no blood*, i.e., the blood of such a sacrifice can no longer be applied to the Altar, since there is no meat left for it to permit. Consequently, the sacrifice is invalid. He derives this from the verse (*Deut.* 12:27): וְעָשִׂיתָ עֹלֹתֶיךָ הַבָּשָׂר וְהַדָּם, *and you shall prepare your olah-offering, the meat and the blood*, which indicates that the blood and the meat are integral components of the sacrifice and thus are dependent on each other. R′ Eliezer disputes this contention and maintains that דָּם אַף עַל פִּי שֶׁאֵין בָּשָׂר, *[there is] blood although there is no meat*, i.e., the *avodah* of the blood may be performed even if there is no edible part of the sacrifice left to permit. Hence, the sacrifice is valid. The following mishnah applies this dispute to the laws of *menachos*.

[ד] **נִטְמְאוּ** שְׁיָרֶיהָ, נִשְׂרְפוּ שְׁיָרֶיהָ, אָבְדוּ שְׁיָרֶיהָ — כְּמִדַּת רַבִּי אֱלִיעֶזֶר, כְּשֵׁרָה; וּכְמִדַּת רַבִּי יְהוֹשֻׁעַ, פְּסוּלָה. שֶׁלֹּא בִכְלִי שָׁרֵת, פְּסוּלָה. רַבִּי שִׁמְעוֹן מַכְשִׁיר.

**ר׳ עובדיה מברטנורא**

(ד) **כמדת רבי אליעזר כשרה.** על דעתו של רבי אליעזר דאמר בפרק כיצד צולין (מסכת פסחים עז,א) דם אף על פי שאין בשר, הכי נמי קומץ אף על פי שאין שירים כשר להקטיר קומץ: **כמדת רבי יהושע.** דאמר אם אין בשר אין דם, הכי נמי פסול להקריב הקומץ, והוא שלא נשתייר דבר מן השירים שלא נטמא. והלכה כרבי יהושע: **שלא בבלי שרת.** שלא קידש הקומץ בכלי שרת. אבל בתחלת המנחה כולי עלמא לא פליגי דבעי כלי, כדאמרינן בפרק שתי הלחם (יא,ד): **ורבי שמעון מכשיר.** טעמא דרבי שמעון מפרש בגמרא (כו,א), משום דאמר קרא (ויקרא ו,י) קדש קדשים היא כחטאת וכאשם, ומדאקיש רחמנא מנחה לחטאת דעבודתו במתנה באצבע ממש, שמע מינה דקומץ המנחה נמי אם רצה עובדה בידו בלא כלי, ובלבד שיעבוד בידו הימנית, דומיא דחטאת שנאמר בו אצבע, דכתיב ביה (שם ד,כה) ולקח הכהן מדם החטאת באצבעו, וכל מקום שנאמר אצבע וכהונה אינו אלא ימין. ואין הלכה כרבי שמעון:

**יד אברהם**

נִטְמְאוּ שְׁיָרֶיהָ, נִשְׂרְפוּ שְׁיָרֶיהָ, אָבְדוּ שְׁיָרֶיהָ — *If its remainder became tamei, burnt, or lost* —

[That which remains of a *minchah* after its *kometz* has been taken is the *minchah*-offering's equivalent of an animal offering's meat. It becomes permissible for consumption with the burning of the *kometz* in the same manner that the sacrifice's meat becomes permissible for consumption with the application of the animal's blood to the Altar. Thus, if the *minchah's* remainder becomes *tamei* (and thus unfit to be eaten), or it is destroyed or lost before the *kometz* is burnt on the Altar, the situation is the same as when an animal sacrifice's meat becomes *tamei*, lost or destroyed before the *zerikah* of the blood.]

כְּמִדַּת רַבִּי אֱלִיעֶזֶר, כְּשֵׁרָה; — *according to the rule of R' Eliezer, it is valid;*

Just as he permits performing the *zerikah* with the blood of an animal sacrifice despite the loss of its meat, so too he would validate the offering of the *kometz* despite the loss of the *minchah's* remainder (*Rav*).

וּכְמִדַּת רַבִּי יְהוֹשֻׁעַ, פְּסוּלָה. — *but according to the rule of R' Yehoshua, it is invalid.*

Just as R' Yehoshua rules that there can be no offering of blood unless the meat of the animal is intact and fit for consumption, so too he would not permit the offering of the *kometz* if the remainder is not available to be eaten (*Rav*).

However, R' Yehoshua agrees that not all the remainder must be available to be eaten in order for the *minchah* to be valid. If as little as a *kezayis* (olive's volume) of the remainder of the *minchah* is still present and *tahor*, the *kometz* may be offered (*Gem.* 26a).[1] In such a case, however, the remainder

1. There is actually a dispute between R' Yochanan and Reish Lakish on this matter (*Gem.* 9a). In the view of Reish Lakish: שִׁירַיִם שֶׁחָסְרוּ בֵּין קְמִיצָה לְהַקְטָרָה אֵין מַקְטִיר קֹמֶץ עֲלֵיהֶן, *a*

3
4

**4.** If its remainder became *tamei*, burnt, or lost — according to the rule of R' Eliezer, it is valid; but according to the rule of R' Yehoshua, it is invalid. [If it was] not [placed] in a sacred vessel, it is invalid. R' Shimon validates [it].

YAD AVRAHAM

may not be eaten, because the *Gemara* derives exegetically that in order for the remainder of the *minchah* to be eaten, it must be completely intact at the time the *kometz* is offered (*Tos. R' Akiva Eiger* from *Gem.* 9b).[1]

The use of the word פְּסוּלָה, *invalid* [rather than לֹא יַקְטִיר, *he should not burn it on the Altar*,] indicates an expost facto (בְּדִיעֲבַד) invalidation. Nevertheless, the *Gemara* (*Pesachim* 78b) concludes that in a case in which the remainder became *tamei*, but the *kometz* was offered anyway, R' Yehoshua agrees that the *minchah* is valid expost facto. The mishnah's use of the term *invalid* is precise, however, in regard to the cases in which the remainder was lost or destroyed. In such a case, even if the *kometz* was offered it is not valid (*Tos. R' Akiva, Likkutei Halachos* from *Pesachim* 78b).

שֶׁלֹּא בִּכְלִי שָׁרֵת, פְּסוּלָה. — *[If it was] not [placed] in a sacred vessel, it is invalid.*

As described previously (see General Introduction), the *minchah* procedure involves placing all the ingredients of the *minchah* in a *kli shareis* (sacred vessel) to sanctify them before proceeding to *kemitzah*. After the *kometz* is removed, it is placed into a second *kli shareis* [for further sanctification]. The *kometz* is taken in this *kli shareis* to the Altar and burnt. Our mishnah teaches that if the *kometz* was not placed in a *kli shareis* after it was separated from the remainder of the *minchah*, it is invalid (*Rav*). [As noted several times, placing the *kometz* in a *kli shareis* is one of the four critical *avodos* of a *minchah's* offering.]

רַבִּי שִׁמְעוֹן מַכְשִׁיר. — *R' Shimon validates [it].*

The Torah states (*Lev.* 6:10) concerning a *minchah:* קֹדֶשׁ קָדָשִׁים הוּא כַּחַטָּאת וְכָאָשָׁם, *it is most holy, like a chatas-offering and like an asham-offering.* R' Shimon interprets the Torah's comparison of the *minchah* to the *chatas* to mean that the *kometz* can be offered by hand. Just as the *chatas'* blood is applied to the Altar by hand, with the *Kohen* daubing it on the horn of the Altar with the finger of his right

*remainder which became deficient between the kemitzah and the [time of its] burning does not [warrant] having the kometz burnt on its account.* The interpretation followed in this commentary is that of R' Yochanan, that the *kometz* is burnt as long as at least a *kezayis* of the remainder remains.

1. The exegesis cited by the *Gemara* to support this ruling would seem to indicate that the exclusion applies only to cases in which the portion of the remainder which is missing was lost or burnt; if it was intact but *tamei*, however, the uncontaminated part would be permissible to eat because the entire remainder is, in fact, physically intact (see 2:2). *Rambam*, however, states that in all of these cases the remainder is forbidden (*Hil. Pesulei HaMukdashin* 11:20). [Nevertheless, in regard to the *lechem hapanim* (*panim* bread), he rules that the *tumah* of one does not affect the others (*Temidin U'Mussafin* 5:16). His opinion on the matter is therefore unclear (*Zevach Todah*).]

הִקְטִיר קֻמְצָהּ פַּעֲמַיִם, כְּשֵׁרָה.

[ה] **הַקֹּמֶץ** – מִעוּטוֹ מְעַכֵּב אֶת רֻבּוֹ.

ר׳ עובדיה מברטנורא

**הקטיר קומצה פעמים.** חלי קומץ בפעם אחת וחלי קומץ בפעם אחרת. ודוקא נקט פעמים ותו לא, דאין קומץ פחות משני זיתים וכי פליג ליה לשתי פעמים נמצא שאין הקטרה בפחות מכזית, ולפיכך כשרה, אבל אם חלקה לשלש או לארבע פעמים, דעביד להו הקטרה פחותה מכזית, פסולה: **(ה) מעוטו מעכב את רובו.** שאם חסר כל שהוא פסול, דאמר רחמנא (ויקרא ב,ב) מלא קומצו:

יד אברהם

hand, so too if the *Kohen* desires, he may offer the *kometz* of the *minchah* by hand instead of in a *kli shareis* (*Rav* from *Gem.* 26a). Thus, the *kometz* need not be placed in a *kli shareis* at all (*Gem.* 26b).

R' Shimon does agree, however, that the entire *minchah* must be placed in a *kli shareis* prior to the *kemitzah* (*Rav, Rashi* from *Gem.* 26a, 96a).

*Rambam (Comm.)*, however, indicates that according to R' Shimon no *kli shareis* is necessary for the *minchah* process at all. In his opinion, R' Shimon's comparison is to the *emurin* (sacrificial parts) of the *chatas* (rather than the blood), which are offered without any vessel at all (see *Sfas Emes*).

הִקְטִיר קֻמְצָהּ פַּעֲמַיִם, כְּשֵׁרָה. — *[If] he burnt its kometz twice, it is valid.*

If he divided the *kometz* and offered it by halves it is valid, as each of the halves is in itself a *kezayis* (olive's volume). A *kometz* cannot be divided into more than two parts, though, because as a rule the volume of a *kometz* (determined by the size of the *Kohen's* hand) is approximately two *kezaysim*. Less than half would mean that the amount being burnt each time would not meet the minimum requirement for burning on the Altar — a *kezayis* — violating the principle that אֵין הַקְטָרָה פְּחוּתָה מִכְּזַיִת, *there is no [valid] burning on the Altar of less than a kezayis* (*Rav* from *Gem.* 26a).

There is another opinion in the *Gemara* (loc. cit.) according to which the *kometz* can be offered in more than two segments because *burning is valid even with less than a kezayis* [at one time]. The halachah, however, follows the opinion cited by *Rav* that *burning is not valid with less than a kezayis*. Therefore, even though the *kometz* may be burnt in parts, each part must contain at least a *kezayis* (*Rambam, Hil. Pesulei HaMukdashin* 11:15 as explained by *Kesef Mishneh*).

*Sfas Emes* postulates that this invalidation applies only in the case cited by *Rav*, that the *kometz* was divided into three or more equal segments, because then none of the segments contains a *kezayis*. If, however, *one* of the parts was a *kezayis*, the offering of the *kometz* would be valid even if the remainder of the *kometz* was offered in less than *kezayis*-sized parts. In this manner, the *kometz* could be offered in more than two segments. *Kesef Mishneh* (loc. cit.), however, seems to indicate that each part burnt must contain a *kezayis*.

## 5.

The next mishnah is the first of a series of wide-ranging discussions on the subject of מְעַכְּבִין זו אֶת זו, multipart *mitzvos* whose facets *are all essential to [the validity of] one another*.[1]

1. The word מְעַכֵּב literally means *to obstruct* or *to hold back*. Our translation throughout

3 [If] he burnt its *kometz* twice, it is valid.

5 **5.** The *kometz* — its smaller part is essential to [the validity of] its larger part.

### YAD AVRAHAM

The Torah's commandments fall under two general categories: Those which are לְמִצְוָה, *commanded*, i.e., obligatory but not critical to the validity of the entire *mitzvah;* and those that are לְעִכּוּבָא, *essential* to the validity of the *mitzvah* as a whole. For example: The Torah commands that after the blood of a sacrifice has been properly applied to the Altar, the שִׁירַיִם, *remainder*, of the blood be poured on the base of the Altar (*Zevachim* 5:1ff). This is itself an obligatory act but it is not critical to the validity of the sacrifice. Thus, if there was no remaining blood, or if that which remained was not poured on the base of the Altar, it is not מְעַכֵּב [*essential to*] the validity of the sacrifice (ibid.). There are many other *mitzvos*, by contrast, in which each of the components is essential. For instance, the four fringes of the *tzitzis* are interdependent, and the absence or invalidation of one automatically invalidates the other three. Thus, if one cannot make all four of the *tzitzis* properly, there is no point in making any of them at all. The four, therefore, are said to be מְעַכְּבוֹת זו אֶת זו, *essential to the validity of one another.*

Generally speaking, any requirement spelled out in the Torah is considered critical (*Tos.* to *Gittin* 4b, et al. see *Tos., Pesachim* 11a). Regarding the laws of *Kodashim*,[1] however, a requirement must be repeated twice to be considered essential to the validity of the *mitzvah*; a requirement stated once is considered obligatory but not essential. In addition, the Torah indicates essentiality by the use of certain key words or phrases such as כָּכָה, *thus*; חוקה, *a statute;* זאת, *the following*; and others (*Gem.*).

The following mishnayos offer a detailed listing of those parts of *mitzvos* which are essential to the validity of the overall *mitzvah*, and those which are not, beginning with the burning on the Altar of the *kometz*, the topic of our chapter.

הַקֹּמֶץ – מִעוּטוֹ מְעַכֵּב אֶת רֻבּוֹ. — *The kometz — its smaller part is essential to [the validity of] its larger part.*

I.e., if even a small part of the *kometz* is missing, the rest of it is invalidated from being offered on the Altar (*Rav*). This is derived from the Torah's repeated use of the phrase מְלֹא קֻמְצוֹ, *his full kometz* (*Lev.* 2:2, ibid. 5:12). In line with the principle of שְׁנָה עָלָיו הַכָּתוּב לְעַכֵּב, *the Torah repeated it to indicate that it is essential*, the repetition of the phrase *full kometz* indicates that the entire *kometz* is necessary for the validity of the *minchah* (*Gem.* 27a; see comm. to mishnah 1, s.v. לא יצק).

reflects the intention of the phrase rather than its literal meaning. In mishnah 4:4, however, the explanation is closer to the literal meaning of obstruction, as explained there.

1. The rule that the repetition of a requirement [or a key word] is needed to indicate essentiality with regard to the laws of *Kodashim* is abundantly clear from the *Gemara* throughout *Zevachim* (see for example, 4b, 5a; *Menachos* 19a et al.). The Scriptural source for this principle (unique to *Kodashim*) is not, however, clear; see *Keren Orah* to *Zevachim* 4b, end of s.v. ועוד כתב שם.

מנחות
ג/ה

הָעִשָּׂרוֹן – מִעוּטוֹ מְעַכֵּב אֶת רֻבּוֹ. הַיַּיִן – מִעוּטוֹ מְעַכֵּב אֶת רֻבּוֹ. הַשֶּׁמֶן – מִעוּטוֹ מְעַכֵּב אֶת רֻבּוֹ. הַסֹּלֶת וְהַשֶּׁמֶן מְעַכְּבִין זֶה אֶת זֶה. הַקֹּמֶץ וְהַלְּבוֹנָה מְעַכְּבִין זֶה אֶת זֶה.

**ר' עובדיה מברטנורא**

**העשרון.** מנחה שהיא פחותה מעשרון אפילו כל שהוא פסולה: **היין.** חצי ההין לפר, ושלישית ההין לאיל, ורביעית ההין לכבש, וכן השמן, בין למנחת נסכים שהוא כשיעור היין, בין למנחת נדבה שהוא לוג אחד שמן: **הסולת והשמן.** של מנחה: **מעכבים זה את זה.** דכתיב (שם ב,טז) מגרשה ומשמנה: **הקומץ והלבונה מעכבים זה את זה.** דכתיב (שם ו,ח) והרים ממנו בקמצו וגו' על כל לבונתה:

**יד אברהם**

הָעִשָּׂרוֹן — *[For] the issaron* —

[An *issaron* (tenth of an *ephah*) is the minimum quantity of flour necessary for a *minchah* (see 9:3).]

מִעוּטוֹ מְעַכֵּב אֶת רֻבּוֹ. — *its smaller part is essential to [the validity of] its larger part.*

[If even the slightest amount is missing from the required measure, the *minchah* is not valid.] This is derived from the word מִסָּלְתָּהּ, *from its flour* (*Gem.* loc. cit.), in which the suffix ה — meaning *its* — is extra, indicating that its entire measure of flour is necessary (*Rashi*, ad loc.).

If the mishnah were following the order of the *minchah* process, it would have mentioned the invalidation of the *issaron* —the necessary quantity of flour — before the invalidation of the *kometz* — which is the part removed from the flour. Instead, the mishnah cites the requirement for the *kometz* prior to that of the entire *minchah*, because it is a continuation of the previous mishnah's discussion dealing with the *kometz* (*Tif. Yis.*).

הַיַּיִן — *[For] wine* —

This refers to the libations of wine which accompany *olah*- and *shelamim*-sacrifices (as well as certain others; see preface to 2:4). These consist of one half of a *hin* for a bull, one third of a *hin* for a ram, and one fourth of a *hin* for a lamb [a *hin* equals twelve *logs*] (*Rav* from *Num.* 15).

מִעוּטוֹ מְעַכֵּב אֶת רֻבּוֹ. — *its smaller part is essential to [the validity of] its larger part.*

If even a small part of the prescribed amount is missing, the libations are invalid. This is derived from the verse (*Num.* v. 11): כָּכָה יֵעָשֶׂה לַשּׁוֹר הָאֶחָד . . ., *so shall be done for one ox, etc.* The phrase כָּכָה, *thus,* is a phrase indicating essentiality, which in our case means that each of the prescribed amounts is critical to the validity of the libations (*Gem.* loc. cit.; *Rashi* ibid.).

הַשֶּׁמֶן — *[For] oil* —

The mishnah refers to the quantity of both the oil which accompanies a *minchas nesachim* (*minchah* of libations), for which the prescribed amount parallels the amount of the wine (*Num.* ibid.), as well as the oil for a voluntary *minchah*, for which the prescribed amount is one *log* (see comm. to 2:3, s.v. שזו בלילתה עבה).

3
5 [For] the *issaron* — its smaller part is essential to [the validity of] its larger part. [For] wine — its smaller part is essential to [the validity of] its larger part. [For] oil — its smaller part is essential to [the validity of] its larger part. The flour and the oil are essential to [the validity of] each other. The *kometz* and the frankincense are essential to [the validity of] each other.

**YAD AVRAHAM**

מִעוּטוֹ מְעַכֵּב אֶת רֻבּוֹ. — *its smaller part is essential to [the validity of] its larger part.*

[If anything less than the prescribed amount is offered, it is invalid.] The verse כָּכָה, *thus,* cited above in regard to the wine, refers to the oil of *minchas nesachim* as well. In regard to the oil of a voluntary *minchah,* the Torah (*Lev.* 2:2) says וּמִשַּׁמְנָהּ, *and from its oil,* to indicate that the entire prescribed measure of oil is necessary (*Gem.* loc. cit.).

The *Tanna* lists each of these separately, rather than simply stating: [*For*] *the kometz, issaron, wine, and oil, their smaller parts, etc*., because each of these is derived from a separate verse (*Tif. Yis.*).

הַסֹּלֶת וְהַשֶּׁמֶן מְעַכְּבִין זֶה אֶת זֶה. — *The flour and the oil are essential to [the validity of] each other.*

The mishnah refers to the two ingredients of a *minchah* (*Rav*), teaching that both are necessary for the *minchah* to be valid (*Tif. Yis.*). This is derived from that which the Torah states (*Lev.* 2:2): מִסָּלְתָּהּ וּמִשַּׁמְנָהּ, *from its flour and from its oil,* and repeats again by stating (ibid. v. 16), מִגִּרְשָׂהּ וּמִשַּׁמְנָהּ, *from its meal and from its oil,* thus indicating that the presence of both ingredients is necessary for the validity of the offering (*Gem.* 27a).

הַקֹּמֶץ וְהַלְּבוֹנָה — *The kometz and the frankincense*

These are the parts of the *minchah* which are offered on the Altar (see 1:1).

מְעַכְּבִין זֶה אֶת זֶה. — *are essential to [the validity of] each other.*

The Torah states (*Lev.* 2:2): וְקָמַץ מִשָּׁם מְלֹא קֻמְצוֹ מִסָּלְתָּהּ וּמִשַּׁמְנָהּ עַל כָּל לְבוֹנָתָהּ, *and he shall take a kometz from there from its flour and its oil in addition to its frankincense,* and again (ibid. 6:8): וְהֵרִים מִמֶּנּוּ בְּקֻמְצוֹ מִסֹּלֶת הַמִּנְחָה וּמִשַּׁמְנָהּ וְאֵת כָּל הַלְּבֹנָה אֲשֶׁר עַל הַמִּנְחָה, *And he shall lift from it with his kometz from the flour of the minchah and its oil, and all the frankincense which is on the minchah.* The repeated references to the *kometz* and the *levonah* indicate that both are required for the offering of either one to be valid (*Gem.* loc. cit.).

## 6.

The previous mishnah listed the parts of a *minchah* which are essential to the validity of the whole. The following mishnah continues the delineation in the context of the laws of other sacrifices.

[ו] **שְׁנֵי** שְׂעִירֵי יוֹם הַכִּפּוּרִים מְעַכְּבִין זֶה אֶת זֶה. שְׁנֵי כִבְשֵׂי עֲצֶרֶת מְעַכְּבִין זֶה אֶת זֶה. שְׁתֵּי חַלּוֹת מְעַכְּבוֹת זוֹ אֶת זוֹ. שְׁנֵי סְדָרִים מְעַכְּבִין זֶה אֶת זֶה. שְׁנֵי בָזִיכִין מְעַכְּבִין זֶה אֶת זֶה. הַסְּדָרִים וְהַבָּזִיכִין מְעַכְּבִין זֶה אֶת זֶה. שְׁנֵי מִינִים שֶׁבְּנָזִיר,

ר׳ עובדיה מברטנורא

(ו) **שני שעירי יום הכיפורים.** השעיר אשר עלה עליו הגורל לה׳, והשעיר המשתלח לעזאזל: **שני כבשי עצרת.** שני כבשי שלמים שבאים חובה על שתי הלחם: **שתי חלות.** שתי הלחם של עצרת: **ושני סדרים.** שתי מערכות של לחם הפנים, שש חלות לכל מערכת: **שני בזיכין.** שתי כפות שבהן הלבונה, ונתונים על שתי המערכות: **הסדרים והבזיכין מעכבין זה את זה.** שאם אין מערכות של לחם על השלחן, לא יתן בו את הבזיכים של לבונה, ואם אין בזיכים, לא יתן את הלחם: **שני מינים שבנזיר.** חלות מצות, ורקיקי מצות:

יד אברהם

שְׁנֵי שְׂעִירֵי הַכִּפּוּרִים — *The two he-goats of Yom Kippur*

The *avodah* of Yom Kippur calls for two identical goats to be brought to the Temple. Lots are cast to designate one to be sacrificed "for *Hashem*" and the other to be sent "to Azazel," i.e., to be killed by being thrown off a cliff in the desert (*Rav* from *Lev.* 16:5-8; see *Yoma* 6:1ff).

מְעַכְּבִין זֶה אֶת זֶה. — *are essential to [the validity of] each other.*

Both he-goats are halachically interdependent; the loss of one disqualifies the other. This is derived from the verse (*Lev.* 16:34) with which the Torah describes the entire service of Yom Kippur: וְהָיְתָה זֹּאת לָכֶם לְחֻקַּת עוֹלָם, *And this shall be to you for an everlasting decree.* The word חֹק, *decree,* is understood to emphasize essentiality, indicating that the *avodah* must be performed as stated in order to be valid (*Tos. Yom Tov* from *Gem.* 27a).

שְׁנֵי כִבְשֵׂי עֲצֶרֶת — *The two lambs of Shavuos*

The reference is to the sacrifice of the two lambs which were brought as *shelamim*-offerings along with the שְׁתֵּי הַלֶּחֶם *[shtei halechem], the two loaves of bread* which constituted the communal offering of Shavuos (*Rav* from *Lev.* 23:19; see preface to 2:2).

מְעַכְּבִין זֶה אֶת זֶה. — *are essential to [the validity of] each other.*

A disqualification in one of the lambs invalidates the other as well. This is derived from the verse (loc. cit., v. 20): קֹדֶשׁ יִהְיוּ לַה׳ לַכֹּהֵן, *they shall be sanctified unto Hashem, for the Kohen* (*Tos. Yom Tov*). The word יִהְיוּ is a derivative of הֲוָיָה, *being,* which denotes that it is imperative that it be done in the prescribed manner (*Gem.* loc. cit.).

שְׁתֵּי חַלּוֹת מְעַכְּבִין זוֹ אֶת זוֹ. — *The two loaves are essential to [the validity of] each other.*

The two loaves of Shavuos [also referred to as the *shtei halechem*, two breads] (*Rav*) must both be brought for either to be valid.

The interdependence of the *shtei*

3 **6.** The two he-goats of Yom Kippur are essen-
6 tial to [the validity of] each other. The two lambs of Shavuos are essential to [the validity of] each other. The two loaves are essential to [the validity of] each other. The two arrangements are essential to [the validity of] each other. The two spoonfuls [of frankincense] are essential to [the validity of] each other. The arrangements and the spoonfuls [of frankincense] are essential to [the validity of] each other. The two kinds [of breads] of the *nazir,*

**YAD AVRAHAM**

*halechem* is derived from the verse cited above (*Gem.* 27a).

שְׁנֵי סְדָרִים — *The two arrangements*

The Torah commands that twelve loaves be placed each week on the *shulchan*, the golden table which stands in the Sanctuary of the Temple. These twelve loaves are known collectively as the לֶחֶם הַפָּנִים [*lechem hapanim*], *panim* breads. These are arranged on the *shulchan* in two stacks of six each (*Rav;* see preface to 2:2).

מְעַכְּבִין זֶה אֶת זֶה. — *are essential to [the validity of] each other.*

This is derived from the verse (*Lev.* 24:9) which describes the *panim* bread: מֵאִשֵּׁי ה׳ חָק עוֹלָם, *from the fire-offerings to* HASHEM, *an eternal decree.* The term חק, *decree,* is always interpreted to mean עִכּוּבָא, *essentiality,* as if to say the Torah's requirement is a חק and not subject to omission (*Tos. Yom Tov*).

שְׁנֵי בָזִיכִין — *The two spoonfuls [of frankincense]*

The בָּזִיכִין are spoons of frankincense (*levonah*) which were placed on the *shulchan* in the Temple along with the two arrangements of *lechem hapanim*. The *levonah* was the part burnt on the Altar to permit the consumption of the *lechem hapanim* loaves (*Rav;* see preface to 2:2).

מְעַכְּבִין זֶה אֶת זֶה. — *are essential to [the validity of] each other.*

Like the *lechem hapanim* themselves, two spoonfuls of *levonah* are interdependent. This is derived from the same verse as the arrangements themselves — חָק עוֹלָם, *an everlasting decree* (*Tos. Yom Tov* from *Gem.* 27a).

הַסְּדָרִים וְהַבָּזִיכִין מְעַכְּבִין זֶה אֶת זֶה. — *The arrangements and the spoonfuls [of frankincense] are essential to [the validity of] each other.*

Neither may be placed on the *shulchan* without the other (*Rav*). Neither may the *lechem hapanim* be eaten by the *Kohanim* nor the *levonah* offered on the Altar in the absence of the other member of the pair (*Tif. Yis.*). This too is derived from the verse cited above (*Gem.* 27a).

שְׁנֵי מִינִים שֶׁבַּנָּזִיר, — *The two kinds [of breads] of the nazir,*

[A *nazir* is a person who undertakes a vow for a specified period of time that enjoins him from drinking wine

שְׁלֹשָׁה שֶׁבַּפָּרָה, אַרְבָּעָה שֶׁבַּתּוֹדָה, אַרְבָּעָה שֶׁבַּלּוּלָב, אַרְבָּעָה שֶׁבַּמְּצֹרָע – מְעַכְּבִין

ר׳ עובדיה מברטנורא

**ושלשה שבפרה אדומה.** עץ ארז, ואזוב, ושני תולעת: **ארבעה שבתודה.** ארבעה מינים של לחם שמביאים על שלמי תודה, חלות מצות, ורקיקי מצות, וסולת מורבכת, וחלות לחם חמץ: **ארבעה שבלולב.** לולב, ואתרוג, הדס, וערבה, אם נוטל ארבעתן בכל היום כולו אף על פי שנוטל אחד מהן בשחרית ואחד בין הערבים, יצא, דקיימא לן לולב אין צריך אגד, אבל אם חסר אחד מן המינים ונטל כל השלשה, לא קיים מצוה כלל: **ארבעה שבמצורע.** עץ ארז, ואזוב, ושני תולעת, והצפור החיה:

יד אברהם

or consuming grape products, cutting his hair, or coming into contact with a corpse. At the end of this period, the *nazir* undergoes a concluding ritual which involves cutting his hair and offering sacrifices (see *Numbers* 6:1-21; General Introduction to ArtScroll *Nazir* p. 7).] As part of his offering, the *nazir* must bring two types of breads to accompany his sacrifice (see *Num.* 6:15ff; mishnah 7:2).

These loaves are essential to each other, as derived from the words (ibid. v. 21), כֵּן יַעֲשֶׂה, *so shall he do*, which is an emphasis indicating essentiality (*Gem.* loc. cit., *Rashi* ibid.).

שְׁלֹשָׁה שֶׁבַּפָּרָה, — *the three [ingredients added to] the [red] cow,*

The Torah's purification process for the *tumah* brought about by contact with a human corpse calls for sprinkling the contaminated person or object with מֵי חַטָּאת, *purification water*. This consists of the ashes of a *parah adumah*, a completely red cow that has been slaughtered and burned according to a special procedure. The ashes are then dissolved in a receptacle containing spring water, and the solution is sprinkled on the *tamei* person.

While the *parah* is being burnt, the Torah calls for the addition of three items to the fire: cedar wood, hyssop, and a strip of red wool (*Num.* 19:1ff; see *Parah* 3:1 for details of the procedure) (*Rav; Tif. Yis.*). Each of these items is essential to the validity of the *parah* ashes. The necessity of each one of them to the validity of the rest of the process is derived from the opening verse in the section of *parah* (*Num.* 19:1): זֹאת חֻקַּת הַתּוֹרָה, *This is the decree of the Torah* (*Rashi* ad loc.). As explained previously, the word חק connotes essentiality.

אַרְבָּעָה שֶׁבַּתּוֹדָה, — *the four [kinds of bread] of the todah-offering,*

The *todah* is a special *shelamim*, which is brought to express gratitude to *Hashem* for deliverance from a dangerous situation (such as a dangerous illness, a perilous sea voyage, desert crossing or release from captivity). It is accompanied by four varieties of loaves (*Rav;* see preface to 2:3). Our mishnah states that all four types are necessary for the validity of the breads. This is because the *todah* is compared to that of the *nazir*, in the verse (*Lev.* 7:13): עַל זֶבַח תּוֹדַת שְׁלָמָיו, *in addition to the sacrifice of his todah-shelamim-offering* — the extra word *shelamim* being understood to refer to that of the *nazir* (*Gem.* loc. cit.).

אַרְבָּעָה שֶׁבַּלּוּלָב, — *the four [species] of the lulav,*

I.e., the four species which are taken with the *lulav* on Succos: the *lulav*,

3 the three [ingredients added to] the [red] cow,
6 the four [kinds of bread] of the *todah*-offering,
the four [species] of the *lulav*, and the four [ingre-
dients] of the *metzora's* purification are essential

### YAD AVRAHAM

*esrog, hadas,* and *aravah*[1] (*Rav*).

The mishnah teaches that the four species of the *lulav* are essential to one another, i.e., the absence or invalidation of one of them prevents the fulfillment of the *mitzvah* of the others (*Rav*). This is derived from the verse (*Lev.* 23:40): וּלְקַחְתֶּם, *and you shall take,* which is interpreted to denote לְקִיחָה תַּמָּה, *a complete taking,* i.e., a taking of all the species together (*Gem.* loc. cit.).

However, there is a dispute in the *Gemara* (27a) whether one can fulfill his obligation with the four species by taking them individually at separate times of the day or whether all four must be taken together at one time. The halachah follows the first view (*Shulchan Aruch, Orach Chaim* 651:12).

The commentary follows the view of *Halachos Gedolos* (cited by *Tos.* 27a, s.v. לא שנו; *Succah* 34b s.v. שתהא) that four species of the *lulav* are really separate *mitzvos* that are interdependent. There is no absolute requirement that they be taken as a unit, although it is preferable as a הִדּוּר מִצְוָה, *adornment of the mitzvah.* Accordingly, if a person took his *lulav* and *esrog* and afterward discovered that his *aravah,* for example, was missing or invalid, he would merely have to take the *aravah* again but not the *lulav* and other species. [According to some, he would make the blessing אֲשֶׁר קִדְּשָׁנוּ בְּמִצְוֹתָיו וְצִוָּנוּ עַל נְטִילַת עֲרָבָה (*Magen Avraham* 591:25; cf. *Rabbenu Tam* cited by *Tos.* ibid.).]

Others contend that the four species can be taken separately only if all of them were in front of him at the time of the taking. If, however, one of the species was missing, the *mitzvah* cannot be performed, even if the missing one was eventually taken (*Keren Orah; Sfas Emes*).

— אַרְבָּעָה שֶׁבַּמְּצֹרָע — *and the four [ingredients] of the metzora's purification*

The purification process of the *metzora* [a person afflicted with certain types of skin discolorations which the Torah defines as sources of *tumah*; often translated as *leper*] calls for the use of cedar wood, hyssop, a strip of red wool, and a pair of birds [see *Lev.* 14:1ff] (*Rav* from *Lev.* 14:4). All these ingredients are essential, as derived from the verse (ibid. v. 2): זֹאת תִּהְיֶה

1. The mention of the species of the *lulav* appears incongruous in this mishnah, which seems to deal only with items that pertain to the Temple service. Seemingly, its place should have been in the next mishnah which discusses general *mitzvos* (see *Rashash* to mishnah 7). [However, we do find that the taking of the four species is, in some respects, compared to the Temple service because, like sacrifices, they effect רִצּוּי, *acceptance* (see *Succah* 38a). The acceptance quality of the *lulav* species also has some halachic ramifications in regard to the invalidation of a מִצְוָה הַבָּאָה בַּעֲבֵירָה, *mitzvah which is accomplished through the transgression of a prohibition.* According to some opinions, this concept applies only to *mitzvos* which are done for רִצּוּי, *acceptance* — i.e., to evoke a favorable response from the Almighty — such as blessings and the Temple service. Nevertheless, the *Gemara* applies it to the taking of the *lulav* (see *Succah* 3:1, 30a) because it, too, effects an acceptance (see *Ritva* to *Succah* 9a; *Tos. Rabbeinu Shimshon* to *Pesachim* 35b). Perhaps it is for this reason that it is included in the mishnah's discussion of invalidation concerning the Temple service.]

מנחות
ג/ו

זֶה אֶת זֶה. שֶׁבַע הַזָּיוֹת שֶׁבַּפָּרָה מְעַכְּבוֹת זוֹ אֶת זוֹ. שֶׁבַע הַזָּיוֹת שֶׁל בֵּין הַבַּדִּים, וְשֶׁעַל הַפָּרוֹכֶת, וְשֶׁעַל מִזְבַּח הַזָּהָב מְעַכְּבוֹת זוֹ אֶת זוֹ.

### ר׳ עובדיה מברטנורא

**שבע הזיות שבפרה אדומה.** דכתיב (במדבר יט,ד) והזה אל נוכח פני אוהל מועד מדמה שבע פעמים: **שבע הזיות של בין הבדים.** ביום הכיפורים, דכתיב (ויקרא יז,יד) ולפני הכפורת יזה שבע פעמים: **ושעל הפרוכת ושעל מזבח הזהב.** ביום הכיפורים, ובפר כהן משיח, ובפר העלם דבר של צבור, ושעירי עבודה זרה. שכל אלו טעונים הזיה על הפרוכת ועל מזבח הזהב כמו שמפורש בפרשת ויקרא ובאחרי מות. ושעירי עבודה זרה מרבינן להו מקרא דכתיב (שם ד,כ) ועשה לפר כאשר עשה לפר החטאת, לפר, זה פר כהן משיח, החטאת, אלו שעירי עבודה זרה. וארבע מתנות שעל ארבע קרנות שעל מזבח הזהב נמי מעכבות זו את זו, אף על פי שלא הוזכרו במשנה: (ז) **שבעה קני מנורה.** כדכתיב (שמות כה,לב) וששה קנים יוצאים מצדיה, והקנה

### יד אברהם

תּוֹרַת הַמְּצֹרָע, *This shall be the law of the metzora*. [The word תִּהְיֶה, *shall be*, is interpreted as an imperative, i.e., it shall be only in the prescribed manner.] (*Gem.* 27a).

מְעַכְּבִין זֶה אֶת זֶה. — *are essential to [the validity of] one another.*

[In each of these groups, the absence or invalidity of any of the items stands in the way of the validity of the others, as explained above.]

שֶׁבַע הַזָּיוֹת שֶׁבַּפָּרָה מְעַכְּבוֹת זוֹ אֶת זוֹ. — *The seven sprinklings of the [red] cow are essential to [the validity of] one another.*

The Torah's purification process for one who is *tamei* from contact with the dead requires the use of the ashes of the *parah adumah* as explained above. Before burning the *parah adumah* — which was done at a site outside Jerusalem — the *Kohen* had to take some of its blood and sprinkle it seven times toward the Temple, as described in the verse (*Num.* 19:4): וְהִזָּה אֶל נֹכַח פְּנֵי אֹהֶל מוֹעֵד מִדָּמָהּ שֶׁבַע פְּעָמִים, *and he shall sprinkle from its blood toward the face of the Ohel Moed seven times* (*Rav*). These seven sprinklings are all essential, as derived from the word חֻקַּת, *decree*, used in the passage [v. 2] (*Gem.* 27a).

שֶׁבַע הַזָּיוֹת שֶׁל בֵּין הַבַּדִּים, — *The seven sprinklings between the poles,*

Certain offerings had their blood sprinkled inside the Sanctuary itself [as opposed to having it applied on the outer Altar, as is done for most sacrifices]. This is prescribed for the bull and the goat brought on Yom Kippur; the special *chatas* of the *Kohen Gadol;* the *par he'elam davar* (bull for communal oversight); and the he-goat brought for a communal transgression of the sin of idolatry (see *Zevachim* 5:1,2 and *Yad Avraham* comm. ad loc.).

In the Yom Kippur service, the blood of the bull and he-goat is first sprinkled in the קֹדֶשׁ הַקֳּדָשִׁים, *Holy of Holies,* while the *Kohen Gadol*

3
6

to [the validity of] one another. The seven sprinklings of the [red] cow are essential to [the validity of] one another. The seven sprinklings between the poles, and on the Curtain, and on the Golden Altar are essential to [the validity of] one another.

YAD AVRAHAM

faces the Ark stationed between the poles (which extend from the Ark). He sprinkles the blood one time in an upward motion and seven times in a downward motion (*Rav*). Each of these sprinklings is critical to the validity of the others, as derived from the word חֹק, *decree*, which is used in reference to the Yom Kippur service (*Gem.* 27a).

וְשֶׁעַל הַפָּרוֹכֶת, וְשֶׁעַל מִזְבַּח הַזָּהָב — *and on the Curtain, and on the Golden Altar*

After the blood of each of these two Yom Kippur offerings is sprinkled between the poles of the Ark, it is also sprinkled on the פָּרוֹכֶת, *Curtain*, that divides between the Holy of Holies and the rest of the Sanctuary [קֹדֶשׁ]. Here too, each requires one sprinkling upward and seven downward. Afterward, the blood of the bull and the goat is mixed together, and the mixture is applied to all four corners of the Golden Altar in the Sanctuary and then sprinkled seven times atop it (*Lev.* 16). [See ArtScroll *Yoma* 5:1-5 for a lengthy description of this procedure.] Each of these seven sprinklings is critical to the validity of the others. Similarly, there are seven sprinklings performed with the blood of the *chatas* of the *Kohen Gadol* and the *par he'elam davar* brought for a communal transgression, and the he-goat brought for communal idolatry. These too are sprinkled on the Curtain and on the Golden Altar (*Rav;* see preface).

The fact that the sprinklings of the Yom Kippur service are essential to each other's validity is derived from the word חֹק, as cited above. The essentiality of all the sprinklings of the latter three is derived from the verse (*Lev.* 4:20): וְעָשָׂה לַפָּר כַּאֲשֶׁר עָשָׂה לְפַר הַחַטָּאת כֵּן יַעֲשֶׂה לוֹ, *And he shall do to the bull* [of the *chatas* for communal oversight] *as he did to the bull of the chatas* [of the *Kohen Gadol*], *so shall he do to it*. The repetition of this exhortation (see *Torah Temimah* ad loc.) indicates that it must be fulfilled as stated in order to be valid (*Gem.* loc. cit.).

מְעַכְּבוֹת זוֹ אֶת זוֹ. — *are essential to [the validity of] one another.*

[All of the sprinklings in each group must be performed in order for the others to be valid, as explained above.]

It should be noted that following the Mishnaic form of תָּנָא וְשִׁיֵּיר, *he taught and omitted*, the mishnah's list is not all inclusive. Omissions from this mishnah include the הַזָּאוֹת שֶׁבַּמְּצוֹרָע, *sprinklings of the metzora*, and the sacrifices of Succos, in which each component is also essential to the whole process (*Tos.* 27a, s.v. ארבעה).

[ז] **שִׁבְעָה** קְנֵי מְנוֹרָה מְעַכְּבִין זֶה אֶת זֶה. שִׁבְעָה נֵרוֹתֶיהָ מְעַכְּבִין זֶה אֶת זֶה. שְׁתֵּי פָרָשִׁיּוֹת שֶׁבַּמְּזוּזָה מְעַכְּבוֹת זוֹ אֶת זוֹ, וַאֲפִילוּ כְּתָב אֶחָד מְעַכְּבָן. אַרְבַּע פָּרָשִׁיּוֹת שֶׁבַּתְּפִלִּין

**ר׳ עובדיה מברטנורא**

האמצעי, הרי שבעה קני מנורה: **שתי פרשיות שבמזוזה.** שמע, והיה אם שמוע: **ואפילו כתב אחד מעכבן.** אפילו אות אחת שהיא דבוקה לחברתה ואינה מוקפת גויל כהלכתה, פוסל במזוזה ובתפילין ובספר תורה: **ארבע פרשיות שבתפילין.** קדש, והיה כי יביאך, שמע, והיה אם שמוע, מעכבות זו את זו, בין בתפלה של ראש שכותבין כל פרשה ופרשה בקלף בפני עצמו, בין בתפלה של יד שכל ארבעתן כתובים בקלף אחד:

**יד אברהם**

## 7.

Having discussed those aspects of the *avodah* which are essential to each other, the mishnah now proceeds to discuss this principle in connection with other *mitzvos*.

שִׁבְעָה קְנֵי מְנוֹרָה — *The seven branches of the menorah*

The *menorah* in the Temple was a seven-branched candelabrum — a center branch and the six branches extending from it (*Rav* from *Ex.* 25:32).

מְעַכְּבִין זֶה אֶת זֶה. — *are essential to [the validity of] one another.*

I.e., the absence of any one of the branches invalidates the whole *menorah*. This is derived from the verse (*Ex.* 25:36): כַּפְתֹּרֵיהֶם וּקְנֹתָם מִמֶּנָּה יִהְיוּ, *and their buttons and branches shall be from it*. The word יִהְיוּ, *shall be*, indicates that it must be made in the prescribed way to be valid (*Gem.* 28a; *Rashi*).

שִׁבְעָה נֵרוֹתֶיהָ — *Its seven lamps*

The lamps were the receptacles which were placed at the top of each branch to hold the oil and wicks (*Rashi*).

מְעַכְּבִין זֶה אֶת זֶה. — *are essential to [the validity of] one another.*

This too is derived from the verse quoted above.

The mishnah indicates that only the branches and the lamps of the *menorah* are essential but not the ornamental designs which the Torah describes for the *menorah*, i.e., גְּבִעִים, *cups;* כַּפְתּוֹרִים, *buttons*; and פְּרָחִים, *flowers* (see *Ex.* 25:31ff). This is puzzling because the phrase יִהְיוּ, *shall be*, from which the essentiality of all the branches is derived, is used by the Torah in connection with all the details of the *menorah*. Why then are only the branches and the lamps considered essential? Perhaps the answer lies in the fact that the *menorah* is valid even if it is not made of gold, as derived by the *Gemara* (28a). The ornaments, by contrast, are required to be of gold. It follows then, that a *menorah* of a metal other than gold has no ornaments. Thus, we conclude that the ornaments are not absolutely essential [even for a gold *menorah*] (*Tos.* 28a, as explained by *Tos. Yom Tov.*).

שְׁתֵּי פָּרָשִׁיּוֹת שֶׁבַּמְּזוּזָה — *The two [Scriptural] passages which are in a mezuzah*

The *mezuzah* consists of two passages: the passage of שְׁמַע יִשְׂרָאֵל, *Shema Yisrael* (*Deut.* 6:4), and the passage beginning: וְהָיָה אִם שָׁמֹעַ, *And it shall be, if*

3 **7.** The seven branches of the *menorah* are essen-
7 tial to [the validity of] one another. Its seven lamps are essential to [the validity of] one another. The two [Scriptural] passages which are in a *mezuzah* are essential to [the validity of] each other, and even the writing of one [letter] is essential to them. The four passages which are in *tefillin*

### YAD AVRAHAM

*you will listen* (ibid. 11:13) [which is read together with the former] (*Rav*).

מְעַכְּבוֹת זוֹ אֶת זוֹ, — *are essential to [the validity of] each other,*

[A *mezuzah* with just one of these passages is not valid.]

וַאֲפִילוּ כְּתָב אֶחָד מְעַכְּבָן. — *and even the writing of one [letter] is essential to them.*

The mishnah does not mean simply that the *mezuzah* is invalid if it is missing one letter; that is self-understood. Rather, the mishnah means that if even one letter is attached to another, so that it is not surrounded by blank parchment, the *mezuzah* is invalid (*Rav* from *Gem.* 29a).

This is derived from the word (loc. cit. v. 20) וּכְתַבְתָּם, *and you shall write them,* which is interpreted to denote כְּתִיבָה תַּמָּה, *a perfect writing,* which means that each letter must be perfectly formed and surrounded by clear parchment[1] (*Rashi*).

The mishnah's choice of the phrase כְּתָב אֶחָד, literally, *one writing,* rather than אוֹת אַחַת, *one letter,* accounts for the *Gemara's* explanation that the letter itself is not missing or even misformed, but simply not מֻקָּף גְּוִיל, *surrounded by blank parchment.* This is not a deficiency in the shape of the letter but rather in its *writing,* thus the mishnah's phrase: *[even] one writing* is essential to the validity of the *mezuzah* (*Chidushei HaGriz*). Indeed, there is a view among some authorities that it is invalid only if the letter was not מֻקָּף גְּוִיל at the time of the writing; if the situation came about after the writing, e.g., a hole was made in the parchment of a written *mezuzah* adjacent to a letter, the *mezuzah* is valid (*Beis Yosef, Orach Chaim* 32); *Orach Chaim* 32:16).

אַרְבַּע פָּרָשִׁיּוֹת שֶׁבַּתְּפִלִּין — *The four passages which are in tefillin*

The four *parshiyos* (passages) of *tefillin* consist of the two passages included in the *mezuzah* (see above), plus the passages beginning קַדֶּשׁ לִי כָל בְּכוֹר, *sanctify to Me every firstborn* (*Ex.* 13:1), and the ensuing passage

1. This requirement is called מֻקָּף גְּוִיל, *surrounded by [blank] parchment.* There is a question whether this applies only if two letters are touching or even if the letter is itself not surrounded by blank parchment, for example, if the last letter of the *mezuzah* was written at the bottom of the parchment, leaving no blank parchment, or if a hole punctured the parchment next to a letter (*Beis Yosef, Orach Chaim* 32). One opinion holds that the requirement for blank parchment is a definition of a properly shaped letter. Thus, if any letter was not completely surrounded by blank parchment, it is invalid, even if it is not touching any other letter. The other opinion holds that the Torah merely requires that the *writing* be תַּמָּה, *perfect,* i.e., that two letters should not run together. If, however, it is a single letter that is not surrounded by blank parchment there is no invalidation (see *Beis Halevi al HaTorah* at the end).

# מְעַכְּבוֹת זוֹ אֶת זוֹ, וַאֲפִילוּ כְּתָב אֶחָד מְעַכְּבָן. אַרְבַּע צִיצִיּוֹת מְעַכְּבוֹת זוֹ אֶת זוֹ, שֶׁאַרְבַּעְתָּן מִצְוָה אַחַת. רַבִּי יִשְׁמָעֵאל אוֹמֵר: אַרְבַּעְתָּן אַרְבַּע מִצְוֹת.

ר׳ עובדיה מברטנורא

**ארבעתן ארבע מצות.** ואין מעכבות זו את זו. ואין הלכה כרבי ישמעאל:

יד אברהם

(v. 11) beginning וְהָיָה כִּי יְבִאֲךָ ה׳, *And it shall be when* HASHEM *will bring you* (*Rav*).[1] Each of these passages includes a reference to either the *tefillin* placed on the arm or that placed on the head (*Rashi*) and they are therefore all included in the *tefillin* (*Shitah Mekubetzes* 27 #11).

מְעַכְּבוֹת זוֹ אֶת זוֹ, — *are essential to [the validity of] one another,*

All four passages are essential for the *tefillin,* both in the *tefillah* of the head, in which each *parshah* is written on a separate parchment [and placed in separate compartments],[2] and in the *tefillah* for the arm, in which all four *parshiyos* are written on one parchment (*Rav*). This is derived from the word וְהָיוּ, *and they shall be,* in the phrase וְהָיוּ לְטוֹטָפוֹת בֵּין עֵינֶיךָ (*Rashi;* see above concerning the seven branches of the *menorah*).

וַאֲפִילוּ כְּתָב אֶחָד מְעַכְּבָן. — *and even the writing of one [letter] is essential to them.*

[If even one letter is not properly written the *tefillin* are invalidated, as explained above concerning the *mezuzah.*]

The same ruling applies to a *Sefer Torah* (*Rav*), as the phrase וּכְתַבְתָּם, *and you shall write them* (see above, s.v. ואפלו כתב אחד, concerning *mezuzah*), refers to a *Sefer Torah* as well (*Beis Yosef,* to *Yoreh Deah* 274; *Tos. Yom Tov*).

אַרְבַּע צִיצִיּוֹת מְעַכְּבוֹת זוֹ אֶת זוֹ, — *The four fringes of the tzitzis are essential to the validity of one another,*

1. *Tefillin* consists of two components: בָּתִּים [*batim*], lit., *houses*, the thick black leather casings specially prepared as prescribed by halachah; and פָּרָשִׁיּוֹת [*parshiyos*], the four passages of the Torah written on small parchment and inserted into the *batim.* The *tefillah shel rosh* (of the head) is formed into four compartments and a parchment containing one of the four *parshiyos* is inserted into each compartment. The *tefillah shel yad* (of the hand) has just one compartment, into which is inserted one parchment with all four *parshiyos* written on it.

2. According to *Rashi* and *Rambam*, the order in which the passages of the *tefillin* are placed in the four compartments of the *tefillah shel rosh* is the order in which they appear in the Torah: קַדֶּשׁ לִי; וְהָיָה כִּי יְבִאֲךָ; שְׁמַע יִשְׂרָאֵל; וְהָיָה אִם שָׁמֹעַ. According to *Rabbeinu Tam* the order is: קַדֶּשׁ לִי; וְהָיָה כִּי יְבִאֲךָ; וְהָיָה אִם שָׁמֹעַ; שְׁמַע יִשְׂרָאֵל (see *Orach Chaim* 34).

3 are essential to [the validity of] one another, and
7 even the writing of one [letter] is essential to them. The four fringes of the *tzitzis* are essential to the validity of one another, as they are all four one *mitzvah*. R' Yishmael says: The four of them are four *mitzvos*.

### YAD AVRAHAM

[*Tzitzis* must be placed on all four corners of a garment in order for the *mitzvah* to be fulfilled (*Deut.* 22:12). Each of these corners must have *tzitzis* in order for the *tzitzis* on any of them to be valid.]

שֶׁאַרְבַּעְתָּן מִצְוָה אַחַת. — *as they are all four one mitzvah.*

[The *tzitzis* of the four corners comprise one *mitzvah*, rather than being considered a separate obligation for each corner.]

רַבִּי יִשְׁמָעֵאל אוֹמֵר: אַרְבַּעְתָּן אַרְבַּע מִצְוֹת. — *R' Yishmael says: The four of them are four mitzvos.*

He contends that each corner carries a separate obligation for *tzitzis*, and they are not essential to one another[1] (*Rav*).

The *Gemara* questions the difference between the first *Tanna* and R' Yishmael. Since both obviously agree that all four corners require *tzitzis*, what practical difference does it make whether all four are one *mitzvah* or four *mitzvos*? The *Gemara* replies that one difference is concerning a garment of five corners. According to the first *Tanna*, every garment has an obligation for four *tzitzis*, which are considered one unit. Thus, a five-cornered garment would require only four *tzitzis*. According to R' Yishmael, each corner is a separate *mitzvah* and therefore a five-cornered garment would require five *tzitzis*.

Another difference discussed by the *Gemara* concerns wearing a *tallis* on *Shabbos* while walking from one domain to the next. If the *tzitzis* do not fulfill the *mitzvah*, they are considered an extra appendage and wearing the garment from one domain to the next is forbidden under the *melachah* category of *carrying*. Thus, wearing a *tallis* with less than four *tzitzis* depends on the dispute between the first *Tanna* and R' Yishmael: According to the first *Tanna*, since there is no *mitzvah* with less than four *tzitzis*, the *tallis* cannot be worn from one domain to the next. According to R' Yishmael, each corner is a separate *mitzvah*, so that the *tallis* may be worn even if it has less than four *tzitzis*.

The halachah follows the opinion of the first *Tanna* (*Rav; Orach Chaim* 13).

1. *Chidushei HaRashba* disagrees with *Rav* and offers a novel interpretation of R' Yishmael's view according to which R' Yishmael agrees that all four *tzitzis* are essential to one another. He contends only that all four *tzitzis* are separate *mitzvos*, but not that one *tzitzis* is valid without the other. Accordingly, even in R' Yishmael's view less than four *tzitzis* do not fully fulfill the *mitzvah*. In the view of the first *Tanna*, by contrast, all four *tzitzis* are components of one *mitzvah*.

## פרק רביעי ◆§

# Chapter Four

Having listed in the previous chapter the *mitzvos* whose individual components are essential to the validity of the others, the mishnah now turns its attention to those *mitzvos* whose individual components are not essential to the validity of the others.

מנחות ד/א

# [א] הַתְּכֵלֶת אֵינָהּ מְעַכֶּבֶת אֶת הַלָּבָן, וְהַלָּבָן אֵינוֹ מְעַכֵּב אֶת הַתְּכֵלֶת. תְּפִלָּה שֶׁל יָד אֵינָהּ מְעַכֶּבֶת שֶׁל רֹאשׁ,

ר׳ עובדיה מברטנורא

**פרק רביעי – התכלת. (א) התכלת אינה מעכבת את הלבן.** אף על גב דמצוה לתת שני חוטין של תכלת ושני חוטין של לבן, או חוט אחד של תכלת ושלשה חוטים של לבן, אפילו הכי אין זה מעכב את זה, ואם נתן ארבעתן של תכלת או ארבעתן של לבן, יצא: **תפלה של יד אינה מעכבת של ראש.** רמב״ם כתב, דוקא שתיהן מצויין אצלו, אבל אם אין מצויה אצלו אלא אחת מהן, לא יניח האחת עד שימצא האחרת, גזרינן שמא יטעה ויסמוך על אחת תמיד. וזה דלא כהלכתא, דמאן דאמר הכי בגמרא [מנחות מד, א] הדר ביה מכח מה שהקשו לו, ואלא מאן דלית ליה תרתי מצות חדא מצוה נמי לא לעביד, בתמיה. והלכה, בין שתיהן מצויין אצלו בין שאין מצויין אצלו אינן מעכבות זו את זו, וכן הורו כל רבותי הלכה למעשה:

יד אברהם

## 1.

The first mishnah begins with the *mitzvah* of *tzitzis,* the last *mitzvah* mentioned in the previous mishnah. The Torah (*Numbers* 15:38) commands: וְעָשׂוּ לָהֶם צִיצִת עַל כַּנְפֵי בִגְדֵיהֶם לְדֹרֹתָם וְנָתְנוּ עַל צִיצִת הַכָּנָף פְּתִיל תְּכֵלֶת, *And they shall make for themselves tzitzis on the corners of their garments for their generations, and they shall place on the tzitzis of the corner a thread of blue wool.* This teaches that *tzitzis* consist of both white thread and blue thread.[1] In total, four *tzitzis* threads are inserted at each of the garment's four corners and folded over so that there are eight strands hanging down at each corner. The four threads can be derived from a second verse stated in regard to *tzitzis* (*Deut.* 22:12): גְּדִלִים תַּעֲשֶׂה לָּךְ — *you shall make for yourself twisted threads.* Since to *twist threads* requires at least two threads, and the plural form גְּדִלִים indicates that at least two of these strands are necessary for *tzitzis,* we conclude that *tzitzis* are comprised of four threads (*Gem.* 39b).

According to most authorities, the *mitzvah* consists of two white threads and two blue on each corner [which are then folded and tied to form eight threads] (*Rashi; Tos.*). According to another view, the division is three white threads and one half-white and half-blue [so that after folding and tying them there are seven white and one blue] (*Rambam, Hil. Tzitzis* 1;6), while a third view holds that the *mitzvah* requires three white threads and one blue [making for six white and two blue after they are folded] (*Ravad* ad loc.).

The specifics of the laws of *tzitzis, tefillin,* and *mezuzos* and their manufacturer are not discussed in the Mishnah. This is probably due to the fact they were so much a part of universal and daily practice at the time of the Mishnah's writing that it was considered unnecessary to incorporate in the Mishnah the

1. תְּכֵלֶת means wool dyed blue. The blue dye is only valid if processed in a specific manner, the art of which is unknown to us today. Hence our *tzitzis* consist of only the white wool which is not dyed [which is a valid way of performing the *mitzvah*, as will be stated in the mishnah] (*Rambam Comm.;* cf. *Hil. Tzitzis* Ch. 2; see Appendix I).

4 **1.** The blue thread is not essential to [the validity of]
1 the white thread, and the white is not essential to [the validity of] the blue. The *tefillah* of the hand is not essential to [the validity of] that of the head,

### YAD AVRAHAM

detailed laws, which were common knowledge. Similarly the Mishnah never sets forth the specifics of the text of daily prayers, because due to their universal practice their laws were well known *(Rambam Comm.)*.

הַתְּכֵלֶת אֵינָהּ מְעַכֶּבֶת אֶת הַלָּבָן, וְהַלָּבָן אֵינוֹ מְעַכֵּב אֶת הַתְּכֵלֶת. — *The blue thread is not essential to* [*the validity of*] *the white thread, and the white is not essential to* [*the validity of*] *the blue.*

If one had only white threads or only blue available he can make the *tzitzis* with four threads of the one color and it is valid *(Rav; Rashi)*.

Using only two of the one color is not sufficient because the *mitzvah* of *tzitzis* requires four threads (*Tos. Yom Tov* from *Tos.*, see prefatory remarks; cf. *Rambam, Hil. Tzitzis* 1:1,4 and *Kesef Mishneh* ad loc.).

Accordingly, the independence of the components of *tzitzis* is not the same type of independence as that stated in the mishnah below in regard to the components of *tefillin*. When the mishnah states below that the *tefillin* of the head and the *tefillin* of the hand are not dependent on each other, what is meant is that each one is valid by itself. Concerning *tzitzis*, however, what is meant is that all four threads can be of one color, not that the *mitzvah* is valid with only the two white threads or the two blue ones. The reason for this difference is that the two *tefillin* are essentially two separate *mitzvos* and thus a *mitzvah* can be performed with one alone. The four threads of *tzitzis*, by contrast, comprise one *mitzvah*, and when worn together, the blue and white threads comprise two parts of one whole (*Levush Techeiles* cited by *Meleches Shlomo;* see *Rambam* loc. cit. 1:5).

The *Gemara* 38a cites the dissenting view of Rabbi (R' Yehudah HaNasi), that neither of the two types of thread is valid without the other. Although the *Gemara* offers interpretations to reconcile our mishnah with this view, the halachah follows the simple meaning of the mishnah that the white threads and blue threads are not dependent on each other (*Rambam, Hil. Tzitzis* 1:4; see also *Orach Chaim* 13:2).[1]

תְּפִלָּה שֶׁל יָד אֵינָהּ מְעַכֶּבֶת שֶׁל רֹאשׁ, — *The tefillah of the hand is not essential to [the validity of] that of the head,*

[I.e., in the absence of the hand *tefillah* one may wear the head *tefillah* alone and fulfill that *mitzvah*.]

Conventionally, *tefillin* are worn as a set, with the *tefillah*[2] of the hand

1. *Baal HaMaor* (to *Shabbos* 25b) records with approval a view that the halachah follows Rabbi's opinion and the white threads are *not* valid without the blue. The way we make *tzitzis* today, using only white threads, does not fulfill the *mitzvah* of *tzitzis*. Accordingly, it would be prohibited for us to wear a *tallis* on Shabbos in a public domain under the *melachah* category of carrying. Since the *mitzvah* remains unfulfilled without the blue threads, the *tzitzis* constitute an unnecessary appendage. This opinion, however, is not accepted as halachah (see *Beis Yosef, Orach Chaim* 13; *Pri Megadim,* Introduction to *Hil. Tzitzis*).

2. The word תְּפִלָּה is singular for תְּפִלִּין, which is the *Targum's* translation of the word לְטוֹטָפֹת in the Torah (*Ex.* 13:16, *Deut.* 6:8; 11:18). Some explain that it comes from the root

וְשֶׁל רֹאשׁ אֵינָהּ מְעַכֶּבֶת שֶׁל יָד. הַסֹּלֶת וְהַשֶּׁמֶן אֵינָם מְעַכְּבִין אֶת הַיַּיִן, וְלֹא הַיַּיִן מְעַכְּבָן. הַמַּתָּנוֹת שֶׁעַל מִזְבֵּחַ הַחִיצוֹן אֵינָן מְעַכְּבוֹת זוֹ אֶת זוֹ.

**ר׳ עובדיה מברטנורא**

**הסולת והשמן.** של מנחת נסכים, אין מעכבין את היין של נסכים, שאם הביאו את היין בלא סולת ושמן מנסכו: **והמתנות של מזבח החיצון.** כגון ארבע מתנות של חטאת. אין מעכבות זו את זו, שאם לא נתן אלא אחת כפר, דכתיב (דברים יב,כז) ודם זבחיך ישפך, שפיכה אחת משמע:

**יד אברהם**

preceding that of the head. In actuality, however, each of the *tefillin* is a separate *mitzvah* and is counted as such by the codifiers of the *mitzvos* (*Rambam, Sefer HaMitzvos, mitzvah* 12 and 13; *Chinuch, mitzvah* 421 and 422). What our mishnah teaches is that wearing both *tefillin* is not critical to the fulfillment of each *mitzvah;* if either of the *tefillin* is worn without the other, its *mitzvah* is fulfilled.

Ordinarily, the *tefillin* of the head should not be worn without those of the hand. This is derived from the verse (*Deut.* 6:8): וְהָיוּ לְטֹטָפֹת בֵּין עֵינֶיךָ, *and they shall be for tefillin* (plural) *between your eyes,* which is interpreted by the *Gemara* (36a) to teach that כָּל זְמַן שֶׁהֵם בֵּין עֵינֶיךָ יִהְיוּ שְׁנַיִם, *whenever you wear them between your eyes* [i.e., on the head above the area that is between your eyes] *they should be two* [i.e., one should then be wearing both *tefillin*]. Consequently, the head *tefillin* should always be accompanied and preceded by the hand *tefillin.* However, our mishnah refers to a case in which one does not have both *tefillin* or, because of an emergency, he cannot wear both. Under such circumstances the restriction against wearing the head *tefillin* alone is not in force (*Rosh*).

What *berachah* is made when only the head *tefillin* are donned? This depends on the procedure ordinarily followed when both *tefillin* are worn.

In the view of *Rashi* (36a) and *Rambam,* only one *berachah* [לְהָנִיחַ תְּפִלִּין] is made when donning both *tefillin* together. Accordingly, when donning just the head *tefillin,* only one *berachah* is made [in this case עַל מִצְוַת תְּפִלִּין]. This is the view of the *Shulchan Aruch* (*Orach Chaim* 25:9, 26:2) and *Arizal,* followed by Sephardim and many chassidic groups.

The Ashkenazic custom follows *Rama* (*Orach Chaim* 25:9) who rules in accordance with the view of *Tosafos* and *Rosh* that when donning both *tefillin*, one makes the *berachah* לְהָנִיחַ תְּפִלִּין on the hand *tefillin* and another *berachah* — עַל מִצְוַת תְּפִלִּין — on the head *tefillin.* Thus, the head *tefillin* are actually preceded by two *berachos*: The לְהָנִיחַ תְּפִלִּין made before donning the hand *tefillin* [but which includes also the *mitzvah*

פלל, *to confront* (as the word וַיְפַלֵּל [*Psalms* 106:30] is interpreted in *Sanhedrin* 44a), because with our *tefillin* we *confront* the world with our proclamation of *Hashem's* presence among us. This is based on the Torah's statement (*Deut.* 28:10): וְרָאוּ כָּל עַמֵּי הָאָרֶץ כִּי שֵׁם ה׳ נִקְרָא עָלֶיךָ, *And all the nations of the land shall see that the Name of HASHEM is called upon you* — which the *Gemara* (35b) interprets to refer to *tefillin* of the head (*Tos.* to 34b, s.v. לטוטפת; cf. *Tur, Orach Chaim* 25; *Tif. Yis.*). In common usage, the plural form *tefillin* is used even when referring to only one *tefillah*.

Alternatively, the root of the word תְּפִלִּין is פלל, *to think* (as in רְאֹה פָנֶיךָ לֹא פִלָּלְתִּי, *I would not have thought to see your face* [*Gen.* 48:11]). The connection to *tefillin* is that *tefillin* require thought and concentration, as evidenced by the halachah that while wearing *tefillin* one is enjoined from הֶיסֵּחַ הַדַּעַת, *distracting thoughts* (*Rashash*).

and that of the head is not essential to [the validity of] that of the hand. The flour and the oil are not essential to the wine, nor is the wine essential to them. The blood applications on the outer Altar are not essential to [the validity of] one another.



of the head *tefillin* to follow] and the עַל מִצְוַת תְּפִלִּין made immediately before the head *tefillin* are donned. Accordingly, when wearing just the head *tefillin*, both these *berachos* are recited — לְהָנִיחַ תְּפִלִּין and עַל מִצְוַת תְּפִלִּין (*Rama, Orach Chaim* 26:2).

וְשֶׁל רֹאשׁ אֵינָהּ מְעַכֶּבֶת שֶׁל יָד. — *and that of the head is not essential to [the validity of] that of the hand.*

I.e., conversely, one can, if need be, wear the *tefillin* of the hand without wearing that of the head.

*Rambam (Comm.)* explains that one may wear one of the pair of *tefillin* only if the other one is at least available to him; that is, he has both of the pair but due to circumstances can put on only one of them. If he has only one of the pair, however, he should not wear that one alone, because we fear that he may erroneously conclude that one of the *tefillin* is sufficient and become lax about performing the *mitzvah* in its entirety. This reasoning is found in the *Gemara* (44a) but is rejected there. Therefore, the final halachah is that one should wear one of the *tefillin*, even if its counterpart is unavailable to him *(Rav)*.

Indeed, *Rambam's* ruling in *Mishneh Torah* (*Hil. Tefillin* 4:4) concurs with the *Gemara's* conclusion, and is at variance with his view in his *Commentary. Kesef Mishneh* (ad loc.) concludes that *Rambam's* words in his *Commentary* must therefore be ascribed to an erring student, rather than to *Rambam* himself (see Kafich edition of *Commentary*, footnote 7).

הַסֹּלֶת וְהַשֶּׁמֶן אֵינָם מְעַכְּבִין אֶת הַיַּיִן, וְלֹא הַיַּיִן מְעַכְּבָן. — *The flour and the oil are not essential to the wine, nor is the wine essential to them.*

As described earlier in this tractate (2:4), the libations which accompany a sacrifice consist of a *minchah*-offering and wine *nesech* [libation] which was poured out on the southwest corner of the Altar. Our mishnah teaches that the *minchah* and wine libation are not essential to each other, and if one did not have the flour and oil to make the *minchah* and poured only the wine — or vice versa — the offering he has made is nevertheless valid *(Rav)*. This applies both to the *minchas nesachim* brought together with an animal sacrifice as well as to one donated as an independent offering (*Zevach Todah*).

The mishnah's statement applies only to the relationship of the flour and oil of the *minchah* to the wine of the *nesech* and vice versa. The implication, however, is that the oil and flour of the *minchah* itself *are* essential to each other. This is derived from the ruling stated previously (3:5) concerning the voluntary *minchah (Tos.)*.

הַמַּתָּנוֹת שֶׁעַל מִזְבֵּחַ הַחִיצוֹן אֵינָן מְעַכְּבוֹת זוֹ אֶת זוֹ. — *The blood applications on the outer Altar are not essential to [the validity of] one another.*

Many animal sacrifices call for the blood of the offering to be thrown on the Altar more than once. For example, a *chatas*-offering must have its blood applied to each of the four horns of the Altar. Nevertheless, all offerings are valid even if their blood is applied to the Altar only once. This is derived from the verse (*Deut.* 12:27): וְדַם זְבָחֶיךָ יִשָּׁפֵךְ עַל מִזְבַּח ה', *and the blood of your sacrifices shall be poured on the Altar of* *HASHEM*, which indicates that even

[ב] **הַפָּרִים,** וְהָאֵילִים, וְהַכְּבָשִׂים אֵינָן מְעַכְּבִין זֶה אֶת זֶה. רַבִּי שִׁמְעוֹן אוֹמֵר: אִם הָיוּ לָהֶם פָּרִים מְרֻבִּים וְלֹא הָיוּ לָהֶם נְסָכִים, יָבִיאוּ פַּר אֶחָד וּנְסָכָיו, וְלֹא יִקְרְבוּ כֻלָּן בְּלֹא נְסָכִין.

**ר' עובדיה מברטנורא**

(ב) **הפרים והאילים והכבשים.** הנך דכתיבי בפרשת אמור אל הכהנים (ויקרא כג,יח) והקרבתם על הלחם שבעת כבשים תמימים בני שנה ופר בן בקר אחד ואילים שנים, הבאים עם שתי הלחם של עצרת, אינם מעכבים הפרים שנים ואיל אחד ושבעה כבשים של מוספים של עצרת הכתובים בפרשת פנחס, שאין [שני] פרים של מוספים מעכבין הפר של שתי הלחם, ולא הפר של שתי הלחם מעכב שני פרים של מוספים, וכן שני אילים של שתי הלחם אין מעכבין האיל אחד של מוספים, ולא איל אחד של מוספים מעכב שני האילים של שתי הלחם, וכן הכבשים אין מעכבין אלו את אלו: **רבי שמעון אומר אם היו להם פרים מרובין.** כלומר, דמים כדי לקנות פרים כדי צרכן, ולא היו להם דמים לקנות נסכים, יביאו פר אחד ונסכיו, ומפיק לה מקרא דכתיב (יחזקאל מו,ז) ואיפה לפר ואיפה לאיל יעשה מנחה ולכבשים כאשר תשיג ידו, וכי מדת פרים ואילים אחת היא, והלא מנחת פרים שלשה עשרון ומנחת אילים שני עשרון, אלא להודיעך שמוטב להביא פר אחד איל אחד עם איפתו, מדה הראויה לו, מלהביא פרים מרובים ואילים מרובים בלא מנחתם. ואין הלכה כרבי שמעון:

**יד אברהם**

one pouring is sufficient (*Rav* from *Gem.* 44b).

This applies not only to the *chatas*-offering but to any of the numerous offerings that require more than one "throwing" on the Altar, as described in *Zevachim* Ch. 5 *(Tif. Yis.)*. *Rav* singles out *chatas* as an example only because it is actually the subject of a dispute between Beis Shammai and Beis Hillel (*Zevachim* 4:1). Beis Shammai contend that two of the required blood applications of a *chatas* are essential; Beis Hillel hold that even when offering a *chatas*, one blood application is sufficient. Our mishnah's statement that *all* blood offerings on the outer Altar are not essential to one another indicates that it follows the view of Beis Hillel (*Mahariach*).

## 2.

The following mishnah discusses the status of the sacrifices brought on the Festival of Shavuos.

The sacrifices of Shavuos fall into two categories. One is the Festival *mussaf*, which is identical to the *mussaf* for Pesach and for Rosh Chodesh: *olah*-offerings of two bulls, one ram, and seven lambs, and a *chatas*-offering of one goat. These offerings are listed in the Torah in its section on *mussaf*-offerings [*Numbers* 28:26-31]. The other offerings are brought in conjunction with the *shtei halechem*, the special offering of the *two loaves* brought on that day (see preface to 2:2). These offerings, mentioned in the Torah's section on Festivals (*Leviticus* 23:15-22), consist of *olah*-offerings of one bull, two rams, and seven lambs; a *chatas*-offering of one goat, and two lambs for a *shelamim*-offering. In total, then, on Shavuos there were twenty *olah*-offerings brought (three bulls, three rams, and fourteen lambs); two goats for *chatas*-offerings; and two

4
2

**2.** The bulls, the rams, and the lambs are not essential to one another's [validity]. R' Shimon says: If they had many bulls but no libations, they should bring one bull with its libations rather than offering all of them without libations.

### YAD AVRAHAM

lambs as *shelamim*-offerings (*Rambam, Temidin U'Mussafin* 8:1).[1]

The mishnah discusses the relationship between the two categories of Shavuos offerings: the *mussaf* and those sacrifices brought in conjunction with the two loaves of the *shtei halechem*.

הַפָּרִים, וְהָאֵילִים, וְהַכְּבָשִׂים אֵינָן מְעַכְּבִין זֶה אֶת זֶה. — *The bulls, the rams, and the lambs are not essential to one another's [validity].*

I.e., the animal sacrifices brought together with the *shtei halechem* and the animals brought for the *mussaf*-offering are not essential to each other. Thus, even if one did not bring the bull with the *shtei halechem*, he may still offer the bulls of the *mussaf*, and vice versa. The same applies to the other animals of the two varieties of sacrifices: the two rams of the *shtei halechem* offering are not essential to the ram of the *mussaf* and vice versa; nor are the seven lambs of the *shtei halechem* and the seven of the *mussaf* interdependent (*Rav* from *Gem.* 45a).

While the mishnah discusses only the two varieties of sacrifices, the same law applies to the various animals of the *mussaf* itself. The two bulls of the *mussaf* are not essential to each other, nor are the seven lambs [and certainly the bulls are not essential to the lambs or the ram and vice versa] (*Tos. Yom Tov* from *Gem.* ibid.).

The *olah*-sacrifices accompanying the *shtei halechem* [i.e., the bull, two rams, and seven lambs], however, are all necessary if any of them is to be valid, as derived from the verse (loc. cit. v. 18): יִהְיוּ עוֹלָה לַה׳, *they shall be an olah-offering for HASHEM* (*Tos. Yom Tov* from *Gem.* ibid.; *Rashi* ad loc.). According to *Rambam Comm.* this means only that the two rams are necessary to each other's validity, as are the seven lambs to one another. The lambs, however, may be brought even in the absence of the rams or the bull, or vice versa (*Tos. Yom Tov*).

Others maintain that this derivation refers only to the rams of the *shtei halechem* offering, but the other accompanying offerings are not essential to each other (*Kesef Mishneh* to *Hil. Temidin U'Mussafin* 8:17).

רַבִּי שִׁמְעוֹן אוֹמֵר: אִם הָיוּ לָהֶם פָּרִים מְרֻבִּים וְלֹא הָיוּ לָהֶם נְסָכִים, יָבִיאוּ פַּר אֶחָד וּנְסָכָיו, וְלֹא יִקְרְבוּ כֻּלָּן בְּלֹא נְסָכִין. — *R' Shimon says: If they had many bulls but no libations, they should bring one bull with its libations rather than offering all of them without libations.*

If there was sufficient money to purchase all of the necessary bulls, but not the ingredients for the *nesachim* as well, it is preferable to offer one bull

1. This view is stated explicitly by R' Akiva in a *Baraisa* cited by the *Gem.* (45b). It seems to be the understanding of *Kesef Mishnah* (loc. cit.) that the other *Tanna* mentioned in that *Baraisa* — R' Tarfon — disputes this and considers the seven lambs mentioned in *Lev.* 23:18 as *olos* to be brought with the *shtei halechem* as identical with the seven *olah* lambs mentioned in *Numbers* as part of the *mussaf* of Shavuos (see also *Sfas Emes*). In any case, *Rambam* (loc. cit.) rules according to the opinion of R' Akiva.

מנחות
ד/ג

[ג] **הַפָּר**, וְהָאֵילִים, וְהַכְּבָשִׂים, וְהַשָּׂעִיר אֵינָן מְעַכְּבִין אֶת הַלֶּחֶם, וְלֹא הַלֶּחֶם מְעַכְּבָן. הַלֶּחֶם מְעַכֵּב אֶת הַכְּבָשִׂים, וְהַכְּבָשִׂים אֵינָן מְעַכְּבִין אֶת הַלֶּחֶם; דִּבְרֵי רַבִּי עֲקִיבָא.

**ר׳ עובדיה מברטנורא**

(ג) **הפר** [**והאיל**] **והכבשים והשעיר.** הבאים בגלל הלחם. וכלן עולות, חוץ מן השעיר שהוא חטאת: **אין מעכבין את הלחם.** שאם הביאו שתי הלחם של עצרת בלא הקרבנות הללו, [מקודשין]: **הלחם מעכב את הכבשים.** הנך כבשים הן שני כבשים דשלמים שהוזקקו לתנופה עם הלחם: **והכבשים אין מעכבים את הלחם.** שאם לא נמצאו כבשים, מביאים שתי הלחם והן קדושים כאילו הביאום עם הכבשים:

**יד אברהם**

properly with its *nesachim* rather than bringing all of the bulls for the sacrifices of that day without their libations (*Rav*).

R' Shimon derives this in the following manner: A verse in *Ezekiel* (46:7) states: וְאֵיפָה לַפָּר וְאֵיפָה לָאַיִל יַעֲשֶׂה מִנְחָה, *and one ephah for a bull and an ephah for the ram he will make a minchah.* The *Gemara* points out that this statement presents difficulties, because the measurement of flour brought as a *minchah* with a bull is not equal to that which is brought with a ram. [A bull requires three *essronim* of flour and a ram only two *(Rashi)*.] Rather, the verse teaches that it is preferable to bring one bull or one ram with its *minchah* [of libations] than to bring all of them without the *minchah.* [I.e., the verse does not mean to compare the two *menachos* in their measurements but only to indicate that in both cases it is preferable to bring part of the sacrifice with its *nesachim* than the entire sacrifice without it (*Rav* from *Gem.* 45a).]

The halachah does not follow the view of R' Shimon *(Rav; Rambam Comm.)* but rather that of *Sifri* (to *Deut.* 25:14), which interprets this verse in a different manner (*Tos. Yom Tov* from *Tos.*).

## 3.

Continuing the discussion of the aspects of the offerings of Shavuos which are necessary for the validity of the others, the mishnah now focuses on the sacrifices which accompany the *shtei halechem* which is referred to here simply as לֶחֶם, *bread.* As described previously, the two loaves brought on Shavuos are accompanied by an *olah*-offering of one bull, two rams, and seven lambs; a *chatas*-offering of one goat and a *shelamim*-offering of two lambs. Of these sacrifices, the *shelamim* lambs are more closely linked to the *shtei halechem*-offering inasmuch as there is a requirement for them to be waved together with the loaves in the rite known as *tenufah* (see comm. to mishnah 3:2).

The law of the *sthei halechem* is stated by the Torah in *Leviticus* (23:15-22), while the *mussaf*-offerings of Shavuos are listed together with the *mussafim*

4
3

**3.** The bull, the rams, the lambs, and the goat are not essential to the [validity of the] bread, nor is the bread essential to their [validity]. The bread is essential to the [validity of the] lambs, but the lambs are not essential to the [validity of the] bread; [these are] the words of R' Akiva.

**YAD AVRAHAM**

of all the other Festivals in *Numbers* (28:26-31). Accordingly, the mishnah here refers to the *shtei halechem*-offering and all the sacrifices associated with it as *that which is stated in the Book of Leviticus,* in contrast to the two bulls, one ram, and seven lambs of the *mussaf*-offering which is referred to as *that which is stated in the Book of Numbers.*

הַפָּר, וְהָאֵילִים, וְהַכְּבָשִׂים, וְהַשָּׂעִיר — *The bull, the rams, the lambs, and the goat*

These sacrifices accompany the *shtei halechem.* All of these are *olah*-offerings except for the goat, which is a *chatas*-offering *(Rav).*

אֵינָן מְעַכְּבִין אֶת הַלֶּחֶם, וְלֹא הַלֶּחֶם מְעַכְּבָן. — *are not essential to the* [*validity of the*] *bread, nor is the bread essential to their* [*validity*].

If the two loaves of the *shtei halechem* were brought without these *olah*-offerings, they are nevertheless consecrated [and if the animal sacrifices are offered without the *shtei halechem,* they too are valid] (*Rav*).

הַלֶּחֶם מְעַכֵּב אֶת הַכְּבָשִׂים, — *The bread is essential to the [validity of the] lambs,*

This refers to the two lambs which were brought as *shelamim* and were waved together with the loaves of the *shtei halechem* (*Rav;* see preface to mishnah). These could not be offered without the two loaves, as derived from the verse (*Lev.* 23:20) קֹדֶשׁ יִהְיוּ לַה׳ לַכֹּהֵן, *they shall be consecrated unto* H*ASHEM*, *to the Kohen.* This refers to the loaves, which are sanctified to H*ASHEM* and are given to the *Kohen* [to eat] (*Gem.* 45b). The word יִהְיוּ — *they shall be* — which indicates that the subject of the word is necessary for the validity of the entire offering (see comm. to 3:6, s.v. מְעַכְּבִין זֶה אֶת זֶה) refers to the loaves (*Rashi*).

וְהַכְּבָשִׂים אֵינָן מְעַכְּבִין אֶת הַלֶּחֶם; דִּבְרֵי רַבִּי עֲקִיבָא. — *but the lambs are not essential to the [validity of the] bread; [these are] the words of R' Akiva.*

Even if there are no lambs available, the loaves of the *shtei halechem* can be offered, and they are sanctified just as if they were brought with the lambs *(Rav).*

*Rambam* (*Comm.*) indicates that the loaves of the *shtei halechem* may be eaten in the absence of the lambs. While this is true according to Biblical law, there is a Rabbinic ordinance against eating the loaves under these circumstances, for fear that people will erroneously conclude that the loaves can be eaten without offering the lambs even when the lambs are present (*Gem.* 46b; *Rambam, Temidin U'Mussafin* 8:16; see *Sfas Emes*).

R' Akiva agrees that when the lambs and loaves are brought together, the primary offering is that of the lambs, and the loaves then require the offering of the lambs before becoming permitted for consumption

אָמַר שִׁמְעוֹן בֶּן נַנָּס: לֹא כִי; אֶלָּא הַכְּבָשִׂים מְעַכְּבִין אֶת הַלֶּחֶם וְהַלֶּחֶם אֵינוֹ מְעַכֵּב אֶת הַכְּבָשִׂים. שֶׁכֵּן מָצִינוּ כְּשֶׁהָיוּ יִשְׂרָאֵל בַּמִּדְבָּר אַרְבָּעִים שָׁנָה קָרְבוּ כְבָשִׂים בְּלֹא לֶחֶם; אַף כָּאן יִקָּרְבוּ כְבָשִׂים בְּלֹא לֶחֶם. אָמַר רַבִּי שִׁמְעוֹן: הֲלָכָה כְּדִבְרֵי בֶן נַנָּס, אֲבָל אֵין הַטַּעַם כִּדְבָרָיו. שֶׁכָּל הָאָמוּר בְּחוּמַּשׁ הַפְּקוּדִים קָרַב בַּמִּדְבָּר,

ר׳ עובדיה מברטנורא

**קרבו כבשים בלא לחם.** שהרי לא היה להם לחם במדבר אלא המן: **הלכה כדברי בן ננס.** דכבשים מעכבים את הלחם, אבל אין הטעם כדבריו, דהוא אומר במדבר קרבו כבשים דשלמים, ולא היא, שכל האמור בחומש הפקודים, בספר במדבר, כגון קרבנות מוספים האמורים בפרשת פנחס, קרבו במדבר, וכל האמור בתורת כהנים, דהיינו בספר ויקרא, לא קרבו במדבר. והנך כבשים האמורים באמור אל הכהנים כגון הנך שבעה כבשים ופר ואילים דעולה דעל הלחם ושני כבשים דשלמים, לא קרבו במדבר:

יד אברהם

written in it — refers to the lambs, as the phrase לַה׳ לַכֹּהֵן refers to an offering which is partially offered to HASHEM and partially given to the *Kohen*. Since the bread is given only to the *Kohen*, with no part of it being burnt on the Altar, the verse must refer to the lambs alone (*Gem.* 45b).

שֶׁכֵּן מָצִינוּ כְּשֶׁהָיוּ יִשְׂרָאֵל בַּמִּדְבָּר אַרְבָּעִים שָׁנָה קָרְבוּ כְבָשִׂים בְּלֹא לֶחֶם; — *For we find that when Israel was in the Wilderness for forty years, the lambs were offered without bread;*

The Shavuos offerings in the

(*Tos. Yom Tov*).[1] His dispute is only that it is possible for the loaves to be offered even if no lambs are available. [See further, comm. at end of this mishnah.]

אָמַר שִׁמְעוֹן בֶּן נַנָּס: לֹא כִי; אֶלָּא הַכְּבָשִׂים מְעַכְּבִין אֶת הַלֶּחֶם וְהַלֶּחֶם אֵינוֹ מְעַכֵּב אֶת הַכְּבָשִׂים. — *Said Shimon ben Nannas: Not so; rather the lambs are essential to the [validity of the] bread, while the bread is not essential to the [validity of the] lambs.*

He contends that the verse mentioned above — and the word יִהְיוּ

1. Accordingly, R' Akiva's view is consistent with the anonymous ruling of mishnah 2:3, that the loaves of the *shtei halechem* are subsidiary to the two lambs in regard to the laws of *piggul* (see comm. there). Although it might be argued that the mishnah there follows the view of Shimon ben Nannas who disputes R' Akiva (see below), it is evident from *Ramban's* rulings that he considers that mishnah to be consistent with R' Akiva's view. In *Hil. Temidin U'Mussafin* (8:15) he rules in accord with R' Akiva, that the lambs are not essential to the validity of the *shtei halechem*. Yet in *Hil. Pesulei HaMukdashin* 17:8 he rules in accord with mishnah 2:3, that the *shtei halechem* are rendered *piggul* through the two lambs, but not vice versa. Obviously, then, *Rambam* understood that even R' Akiva agrees that when the lambs are present, the *shtei halechem* are subsidiary to them, and the lambs are considered the *mattir* of the loaves (*Tos. Yom Tov*).

4 Said Shimon ben Nannas: Not so; rather the lambs
3 are essential to the [validity of the] bread while the bread is not essential to the [validity of the] lambs. For we find that when Israel was in the Wilderness for forty years, the lambs were offered without bread; therefore, now too the lambs can be offered without bread. Said R' Shimon: The halachah follows the words of Ben Nannas, but not for his reason. For whatever is mentioned in the *Book of Numbers* was offered in the Wilderness,

**YAD AVRAHAM**

Wilderness were not accompanied by *shtei halechem*, since they had no bread then, only manna *(Rav; Rashi,* as cited by *Tos.; Rambam Comm.)*.

Others reject this explanation because it is clear from the *Gemara* (95a) that the *lechem hapanim* and the *minchah* of the *omer* [both of which are made of grain] *were* offered in the Wilderness (*Tos.* 45b; s.v. קרבו). Moreover, it is quite explicit in the Scriptural description of the erection of the *Mishkan* (*Exodus* 40:23) that *lechem hapanim* bread was placed on the *shulchan* (*Keren Orah*; see *Sfas Emes*).

Another explanation is that the loaves of the *shtei halechem* must be brought from produce of the Land of Israel [which was obviously not available in the Wilderness] (*Rashi* from *Gem.* 83b). In a similar vein, *Tos.* submit that the reason that the *shtei halechem* were not brought in the Wilderness is based on a derivation from Scripture that the *shtei halechem* were to be brought only after entry into Eretz Yisrael.

אַף כָּאן יִקְרְבוּ כְבָשִׂים בְּלֹא לֶחֶם. — *therefore, now too the lambs can be offered without bread.*

[Since the two lambs offering was valid in the Wilderness even without the *shtei halechem,* it follows that even in Temple times the same should hold true.]

Actually Ben Nannas derives his opinion from the verse לַה׳ לַכֹּהֵן cited above. He cites the example of the Jews in the Wilderness simply to prove the correctness of his interpretation of that verse (*Shitah Mekubetzes* #7).

אָמַר רַבִּי שִׁמְעוֹן: — *Said R' Shimon:*

[This refers to R' Shimon bar Yochai, not Shimon ben Nannas. Whenever R' Shimon is mentioned without further identification, the reference is to R' Shimon bar Yochai.]

הֲלָכָה כְּדִבְרֵי בֶן נַנָּס, אֲבָל אֵין הַטַּעַם כִּדְבָרָיו. — *The halachah follows the words of Ben Nannas, but not for his reason.*

It is true that the lambs are essential to the loaves, and not vice versa, as Ben Nannas maintains, but, according to R' Shimon, for a different reason. The explanation offered by Ben Nannas — that the lambs were offered in the Wilderness without the loaves — is incorrect because in the Wilderness no part of the sacrifice was offered *(Rav)*.

שֶׁכָּל הָאָמוּר בְּחוּמַשׁ הַפְּקוּדִים קָרֵב בַּמִּדְבָּר, — *For whatever is mentioned in the Book of Numbers* (lit., *countings*) *was offered in the Wilderness,*

Those sacrifices mentioned in the Book of *Numbers* [*Bamidbar*], such as

וְכָל הָאָמוּר בְּתוֹרַת כֹּהֲנִים לֹא קָרַב בַּמִּדְבָּר; מִשֶּׁבָּאוּ לָאָרֶץ, קָרְבוּ אֵלּוּ וָאֵלּוּ. וּמִפְּנֵי מָה אֲנִי אוֹמֵר יִקְרְבוּ כְבָשִׂים בְּלֹא לֶחֶם? שֶׁהַכְּבָשִׂים מַתִּירִין אֶת עַצְמָן בְּלֹא לֶחֶם, לֶחֶם בְּלֹא כְבָשִׂים אֵין לִי מִי יַתִּירֶנּוּ.

ר׳ עובדיה מברטנורא

**לחם בלא כבשים אין לו מי יתירנו.** שאין הלחם מותר באכילה לכהנים עד שיקרבו כבשים.

יד אברהם

Thus, the offerings which accompany the *shtei halechem,* which are listed in *Leviticus,* were not offered at all in the Wilderness *(Rav).* [Accordingly, the assumption of Ben Nannas that the sacrifices were brought without the loaves is incorrect.] Although no verse is cited to support this statement, the Sages had an Oral Tradition that this was the case (*Rambam Comm.*).[1]

*Tiferes Yisrael* points out that *Rambam's* citation of an Oral Tradition seems unnecessary, as the entire passage in *Leviticus* describing the various Festival offerings begins with the phrase כִּי תָבֹאוּ אֶל הָאָרֶץ, *When you shall come into the Land* [indicating that the obligation for these offerings begins only after entering the Land of Israel]. [Apparently, *Rambam* understands the mishnah to refer to *all* offerings cited in *Leviticus,* not only those mentioned in this passage, although it is clear that some offerings mentioned only in *Leviticus,* such as those of the Yom Kippur service, were brought even in the Desert (see *Sfas Emes*).]

מִשֶּׁבָּאוּ לָאָרֶץ, קָרְבוּ אֵלּוּ וָאֵלּוּ. — *once they came to the Land [of Israel], both these and those were offered.*

[As soon as they left the Wilderness the *mussaf*-offerings described in Ch. 28, were offered in the Wilderness (*Rav*).

The Sages refer to *Chumash Bamidbar* as חוּמַשׁ הַפְּקוּדִים, *the Book of Countings* (or *Numbers*). [The name used today — בַּמִּדְבָּר, *Bamidbar,* which derives from the key word found in the opening verse of the Book — is of relatively recent vintage.] The reason for this is apparently that this Book begins with a counting of the Jewish people. *Netziv* elaborates that the whole narrative of *Bamidbar* is set against the backdrop of two countings; the opening census which took place in the second year of the Jewish exodus from Egypt (Chapters 1-4), and the closing census (Ch. 26) which took place at the end of the forty years' wandering in the Wilderness. See *Haamek Davar's* introduction to *Bamidbar.*

וְכָל הָאָמוּר בְּתוֹרַת כֹּהֲנִים — *and whatever is mentioned in Leviticus*

I.e., the Festival sacrifices mentioned in the Book of *Leviticus* [or *Vayikra,* which is called *Toras Kohanim* because it deals to a large extent with areas of law vital to *Kohanim*] (*Rav*).

לֹא קָרַב בַּמִּדְבָּר; — *was not offered in the Wilderness;*

1. *Sfas Emes* notes that this may help resolve the question of why there is no mention of the *shtei halechem* or the *omer* in the *mussaf* prayer. Since the *shtei halechem* and the *omer* were included in the offerings mentioned in *Leviticus*, they were not brought in the Wilderness. Accordingly, they have the status of *mitzvos* which apply only in Eretz Yisrael and are not incumbent in the Diaspora. The *mussaf,* by contrast, was brought in the Wilderness and is thus incumbent on Jews everywhere. This obligation is fulfilled through the *mussaf* prayer.

4
3
and whatever is mentioned in *Leviticus* was not offered in the Wilderness; once they came to the Land [of Israel], both these and those were offered. Why [then] do I say that lambs may be offered without bread? Because the lambs render themselves permissible without bread, [but the] bread without the lambs has nothing to render it permissible.

YAD AVRAHAM

and entered the Land of Israel, both the lambs and the loaves of the *shtei halechem* were offered. Thus, there was never a time when only the lambs were offered, as Ben Nannas contends.]

וּמִפְּנֵי מָה אֲנִי אוֹמֵר יִקְרְבוּ כְבָשִׂים בְּלֹא לֶחֶם? — *Why [then] do I say that lambs may be offered without bread?*

[Having refuted Ben Nannas' reasoning, R' Shimon must now explain why he agrees with his ruling that the bread is not essential to the lambs.]

שֶׁהַכְּבָשִׂים מַתִּירִין אֶת עַצְמָן בְּלֹא לֶחֶם, — *Because the lambs render themselves permissible without bread,*

The lambs are permitted [i.e., their אֵמוּרִין, *sacrificial parts*, become fit for burning on the Altar and their meat fit to be eaten] as soon as they are slaughtered *(Rabbeinu Gershom)*.

לֶחֶם בְּלֹא כְבָשִׂים אֵין לִי מִי יַתִּירֶנּוּ. — *[but the] bread without the lambs has nothing to render it permissible.*

No part of the bread itself is offered on the Altar; it does not become permitted to the *Kohanim* until the lambs are offered on the Altar *(Rav)*. [It is axiomatic to R' Shimon that, having been consecrated, the loaves of the *shtei halechem* cannot become permitted for eating unless some *avodah* is performed on the Altar to permit them. The only *avodah* related to the *ashtei halechem* which can do so is the offering of the two lambs, which indeed permits them even according to R' Akiva when they are present, as explained above. Therefore, R' Shimon argues, the *shtei halechem* can never be valid without the lambs (see *Sfas Emes* to the mishnah).]

Some authorities maintain that the halachah follows the view of R' Shimon (*Rav; Ravad* to *Hil. Temidin U'Mussafin* 8:15) because he and Ben Nannas form a majority opinion against that of R' Akiva (*Kesef Mishneh* ibid.). Others contend that the halachah nevertheless follows the view of R' Akiva (*Rambam* ibid.; cf. *Kesef Mishneh* ad loc.; *Zevach Todah*). [This view is also presented in a later mishnah (6:2) as undisputed, another indication that the halachah follows this opinion (*Tos. Yom Tov; Bircas HaZevach* to 74b).]

As noted in the comm. above, this mishnah deals with the question of whether the *shelamim* lambs may be offered even when there are no loaves available for the *shtei halechem* and vice versa. The *Gemara* (46a) states, however, that if the loaves were present at the time the lambs were slaughtered, the lambs and loaves become bound to each other and the loss of one of them [prior to the completion of the *avodah*] will now invalidate the others (*Rambam, Temidim U'Mussafin* 8:15).[1] See comm. at end of mishnah 2:2.

1. The *Gem.* also considers the possibility that the binding takes place even earlier, at the

[ד] **הַתְּמִידִין** אֵינָן מְעַכְּבִין אֶת הַמּוּסָפִים; וְלֹא הַמּוּסָפִים מְעַכְּבִין אֶת הַתְּמִידִים; וְלֹא הַמּוּסָפִים מְעַכְּבִין זֶה אֶת זֶה. לֹא הִקְרִיבוּ כֶבֶשׂ בַּבֹּקֶר, יַקְרִיבוּ בֵּין הָעַרְבָּיִם.

ר׳ עובדיה מברטנורא

והלכה כרבי שמעון: (ד) **התמידים אינן מעכבין את המוספים.** בגמרא (מט,ב) מפרש, דלענין קדימה קאמר דאין מעכבין זה את זה, דאי בעי תמידין מקריב ברישא ואי בעי מוספין מקריב ברישא, ואף על גב דכתיב (ויקרא ו,ה) וערך עליה העולה, ומשמע העולה דהיינו עולת תמיד תהא ראשונה לכל הקרבנות, אין זה אלא למצוה בעלמא אבל לא לעכב:

יד אברהם

## 4.

The following mishnah deals with the תָּמִיד, *tamid*-offering, and the קְטוֹרֶת [*ketores*], *incense*-offering, both of which were brought twice daily, once in the morning and once in the afternoon. The *tamid* is a communal *olah*-offering, and it should be the first sacrifice of the day brought on the Altar. Likewise, no sacrifice should be brought after the afternoon *tamid*. This is derived by the *Gemara* in *Pesachim* (58a) from the Torah's description of the *tamid*-offering (*Leviticus* 6:5). The daily incense is offered on the מִזְבַּח הַזָּהָב, *the Golden Altar*, which stands inside the Sanctuary of the Temple in the קֹדֶשׁ, *Holy* [in contrast to the Altar used for all other sacrifices which is located in the Courtyard].

הַתְּמִידִין אֵינָן מְעַכְּבִין אֶת הַמּוּסָפִים; — *The tamid-offerings are not essential to the [validity of the] mussaf-offerings;*

If a *mussaf* was offered prior to the *tamid*, the former is valid and the latter may still be offered (*Tif. Yis.* from *Gem.*).

Although the Torah requires that the *tamid* be the first sacrifice offered each day on the Altar, failure to comply with this regulation does not invalidate either of the offerings (*Rav* from *Gem.* 49a,b).

If one were to follow the pattern of the previous mishnayos, the simple interpretation of the mishnah would be that the *tamid* and the *mussaf* are not essential to each other; i.e., the absence of the *tamid* does not effect the validity of the *mussaf* or vice versa. Indeed, this interpretation is advanced by *Rabbenu Gershom*. The *Gemara*, however, does not offer this interpretation, apparently because it is considered self-evident. There is no reason to suppose that the *tamid* and the *mussaf* should be linked since they are two separate offerings. The *Gemara*, therefore, interprets the mishnah in the sense of precedence — i.e., the *precedence* of the *tamid* does not affect the *mussaf* — although this interpretation is inconsistent with the phrase אֵין מְעַכְּבִין as used in the previous mishnayos (*Keren Orah* to *Gem.* 49a s.v. אמר ליה).

וְלֹא הַמּוּסָפִים מְעַכְּבִין אֶת הַתְּמִידִים; — *nor are the mussaf-offerings essential to the [validity of the] tamid-offerings;*

The precedence of the *mussaf* is not essential to the validity of the after-

time the lambs and loaves are waved together in *tenufah* (see mishnah 5:6). *Rambam* (*Temidin U'Mussafin* 8:15) cites this as halachah (see *Ravad* and commentators there).

**4.** The *tamid*-offerings are not essential to the [validity of the] *mussaf*-offerings; nor are the *mussaf*-offerings essential to the [validity of the] *tamid*-offerings; nor are the *mussaf*-offerings essential to each other's [validity].

[If] they did not offer a lamb in the morning, they should [nonetheless] offer [one] in the afternoon.



noon *tamid*. The mishnah teaches that if the *tamid* was brought prior to the *mussaf*, the latter may nevertheless be offered (*Shitah Mekubetzes* §12) and the former is also valid (*Tif. Yis.*; cf. *Keren Orah*).

וְלֹא הַמּוּסָפִים מְעַכְּבִין זֶה אֶת זֶה. — *nor are the mussaf-offerings essential to each other's [validity].*

The *mussaf*-offerings consist of both *olah*-offerings and *chatas*-offerings. Generally, when these two types of sacrifices are brought together, the rule is that the *chatas* must precede the *olah* (*Zevachim* 10:2,4; *Pesachim* 59a). However, if they violated that rule, and offered the *olah*-offerings first, the *mussaf* is still valid. Similarly, if there are two *mussaf* sacrifices to be brought — e.g., it is Shabbos as well as Rosh Chodesh — the order of precedence is determined by frequency; thus, the Shabbos *mussaf* is brought prior to the Rosh Chodesh *mussaf*. Nevertheless, if the order was reversed, the sacrifices are valid (*Tif. Yis.*).

Here, too, the mishnah might have lent itself to an interpretation that if some of the *mussaf*-sacrifices are unavailable, the others may nevertheless be offered. However, this would not be an absolute rule, as the *mussaf*-sacrifices of Succos *are* necessary for the validity of one another. Thus, the mishnah must be explained in the sense that order of precedence of the *mussaf* is not essential (*Tos. Yom Tov* from *Gem.* 44b).

לֹא הִקְרִיבוּ כֶבֶשׂ בַּבֹּקֶר, יַקְרִיבוּ בֵּין הָעַרְבַּיִם. — *[If] they did not offer a lamb in the morning, they should [nonetheless] offer [one] in the afternoon.*

I.e., if the lamb of the morning *tamid* was not brought, the afternoon *tamid* is brought regardless (*Tif. Yis.*).

From indications later in this mishnah, the *Gemara* (50a) deduces that there is a clause missing from the mishnah at this point. The text of this segment of the mishnah should read as follows: [*If*] *they did not offer the morning tamid, they may not offer the tamid of the afternoon. When is this stated? Before the Altar was dedicated* [i.e., at the time the morning *tamid* was omitted, the Altar had not yet been dedicated for use, but it was then dedicated in time for the afternoon *tamid*]. *However, if the Altar was dedicated, they should offer that of the afternoon.* [I.e., if the Altar was fit for use in the morning but the *tamid* was omitted for some reason, the afternoon *tamid* is offered.]

In discussing the offerings which were brought at the time of the dedication of the Altar, the Torah states (*Ex.* 29:39): אֶת הַכֶּבֶשׂ הָאֶחָד תַּעֲשֶׂה בַבֹּקֶר וְאֵת הַכֶּבֶשׂ הַשֵּׁנִי תַּעֲשֶׂה בֵּין הָעַרְבָּיִם, *the one lamb you shall make in the morning and the second lamb you shall make in the afternoon.* The *Gemara* takes this as an indication that on the

מנחות
ד/ד

אָמַר רַבִּי שִׁמְעוֹן: אֵימָתַי? בִּזְמַן שֶׁהָיוּ אֲנוּסִין אוֹ שׁוֹגְגִין. אֲבָל אִם הָיוּ מְזִידִין וְלֹא הִקְרִיבוּ כֶּבֶשׂ בַּבֹּקֶר, לֹא יַקְרִיבוּ בֵּין הָעַרְבָּיִם.

לֹא הִקְטִירוּ קְטֹרֶת בַּבֹּקֶר, יַקְטִירוּ בֵּין הָעַרְבָּיִם.

### ר׳ עובדיה מברטנורא

**אמר רבי שמעון אימתי כו'.** בגמרא (נ,א) מפרש דמתניתין חסורי מחסרא והכי קתני, לא הקריבו כבש בבקר לא יקריבו בין הערבים, במה דברים אמורים שלא נתחנך המזבח, אבל נתחנך המזבח יקריבו בין הערבים, אמר רבי שמעון אימתי בזמן שהיו אנוסים או שוגגים, אבל אם מזידים לא הקריבו כבש בבקר, לא יקריבו בין הערבים, והכי פירושו, לא הקריבו התמיד של שחר לא יקריבו התמיד של בין הערבים, דהכי מדרש קרא, אם את הכבש אחד תעשה בבקר (שמות כט,לט), הוכשר שני ליקרב בין הערבים, ואי לא, לא, במה דברים אמורים שלא נתחנך מזבח, דהאי קרא בחנוך כתיב בפרשת ואתה תצוה, דכתיב לעיל מיניה (שם שם,לח) וזה אשר תעשה על המזבח, אבל נתחנך מזבח, שכבר הקריב עליו קרבנות, אפילו לא הקריב תמיד של שחר יקריב תמיד של בין הערבים, דכתיב בפרשת פנחס (במדבר כח,ד) ואת הכבש השני תעשה בין הערבים כמנחת הבקר וכנסכו, ובההוא קרא לא כתיב את הכבש האחד תעשה בבקר, ותניא בספרי האי קרא למה נאמר, והלא נאמר למעלה בפרשה ואת הכבש השני תעשה כו', לפי שנאמר עמו את הכבש אחד תעשה בבקר, הרי שלא הקריבו של שחר שומע אני שלא יקריבו של בין הערבים, תלמוד לומר קרא בתרא ואת הכבש השני, מגיד לך שאם לא הקריב של שחר יקריב של בין הערבים, אבל אם מזידים כו' לא יקריבו בין הערבים, אותן המזידים, אבל כהנים אחרים יכולים להקריב: **לא הקטירו קטרת בבקר יקטירו בין הערבים.** דקטרת לא שכיחא בחד גברא שיקטיר קטרת פעמים רבות כמו בעולה, כדאמרינן ביומא (כו, א) שלא שנה בה אדם מעולם מפני שהיא מעשרת דכתיב (דברים לג,י) ישימו קטורה באפך וסמיך ליה ברך ה' חילו, הלכך לא קנסינן להו, שמתוך שהיא חביבה עליהם לא פשעי בה ואינו מצוי שיניחו אותה מזידין. ואין הלכה כרבי שמעון בשתיהן:

### יד אברהם

day that the Altar was consecrated, the afternoon *tamid* could not be brought unless it was preceded by the morning *tamid*. In a later passage (*Num.* 28:8), when discussing the permanent institution of the *tamid*-offerings, the Torah repeats the statement cited above and then adds — apparently superfluously — וְאֵת הַכֶּבֶשׂ הַשֵּׁנִי תַּעֲשֶׂה בֵּין הָעַרְבָּיִם, *And the second lamb you shall make in the afternoon,* indicating that the afternoon *tamid* may be brought independent of the morning *tamid*. From this we conclude that in the normal procedure, the afternoon *tamid* is to be brought whether or not that of the morning was offered (*Rav* from *Gem.* 50a).[1]

1. Although the identical phrase also appears in the passage in *Exodus*, it is nonetheless not interpreted in the same manner. Rather, the *Gemara* (*Yoma* 34a) derives from it that the afternoon *tamid* is similar to that of the morning in that the *ketores* [incense] must precede the *nesachim* [libations]. Once that has been established concerning the offerings of the dedication of the Altar, it is understood that the same applies to all *tamid*-offerings, and the repetition of this verse in *Numbers* is thus unnecessary. It is therefore understood to teach that under ordinary circumstances the omission of the morning *tamid* does not affect the afternoon one (*Tzon Kodashim;* cf. *Tos. Yom Tov; Bircas HaZevach*).

Said R' Shimon: When? When they acted under constraint or unwittingly. However, if they [acted] intentionally and did not offer the lamb in the morning, they may not offer [one] in the afternoon.

[If] they did not burn the incense in the morning, they burn [it] in the afternoon.

YAD AVRAHAM

אָמַר רַבִּי שִׁמְעוֹן: אֵימָתַי? — *Said R' Shimon: When?*

When does it hold true that the afternoon *tamid* may be offered even if the morning sacrifice was not [except for the day on which the Altar has been dedicated] (*Tif. Yis.*)?

בִּזְמַן שֶׁהָיוּ אֲנוּסִין או שׁוֹגְגִין. — *When they acted under constraint or unwittingly.*

[If the *Kohanim* failed to bring the morning *tamid* by error or due to circumstances beyond their control, they may bring the afternoon *tamid*.]

אֲבָל אִם הָיוּ מְזִידִין וְלֹא הִקְרִיבוּ כֶבֶשׂ בַּבֹּקֶר, לֹא יַקְרִיבוּ בֵּין הָעַרְבָּיִם. — *However, if they [acted] intentionally and did not offer the lamb in the morning, they may not offer [one] in the afternoon.*

If the *Kohanim* deliberately neglected to bring the morning *tamid*, those *Kohanim* may not offer the afternoon *tamid* [as a penalty]. The *tamid* is, however, offered by other *Kohanim* (*Rav* from *Gem.* 50a).

Since, as a rule, the afternoon *tamid* was brought by the same *Kohanim* who offered that of the morning, the phrase *they may not offer [one] in the afternoon* can be understood to refer to those specific *Kohanim* rather than to the *tamid* itself (*Tif. Yis.* from *Yoma* 26a).

The halachah does not follow this statement of R' Shimon (*Rav; Rambam Comm., Hil. Temidin U'Mussafin* 1:12).

לֹא הִקְטִירוּ קְטֹרֶת בַּבֹּקֶר, יַקְטִירוּ בֵּין הָעַרְבָּיִם. — *[If] they did not burn the incense in the morning, they burn [it] in the afternoon.*

[This segment of the mishnah is not a continuation of R' Shimon's statement, but an independent statement made by the first *Tanna*.]

Whereas it was stated previously that before the Altar was dedicated, the absence of the morning *tamid* prevents the afternoon *tamid* from being offered, the same is not true of the *ketores* [incense]. In the event that the morning *ketores* was not brought, the afternoon *ketores* was brought regardless. In this *Tanna's* view, only the afternoon portion of the incense is offered under these circumstances (*Tif. Yis.*).

The *Brisker Rav* (R' Y. Z. Soloveitchik) points out in his commentary to *Chumash* (*Ex.* 29) that there is one slight difference in the phraseology. In the *Exodus* passage, the Torah states: אֶת הַכֶּבֶשׂ הָאֶחָד, *the one lamb*, while in *Numbers* the verse reads: אֶת הַכֶּבֶשׂ אֶחָד, *one lamb*, without the definite article. Since in the daily procedure, the afternoon *tamid* is independent of that of the morning it is referred to simply as *one lamb*, i.e., not the first of a pair. In the passage regarding the dedication of the Altar, however, the morning *tamid* is described as *the one*, i.e., the first of the pair, since the morning and afternoon *tamid* were then interdependent.

# אָמַר רַבִּי שִׁמְעוֹן: וְכֻלָּהּ הָיְתָה קְרֵבָה בֵּין הָעַרְבַּיִם. שֶׁאֵין מְחַנְּכִין אֶת מִזְבַּח הַזָּהָב אֶלָּא בִקְטֹרֶת הַסַּמִּים; וְלֹא מִזְבַּח הָעוֹלָה אֶלָּא בְתָמִיד שֶׁל שַׁחַר;

### ר׳ עובדיה מברטנורא

**שאין מחנכים את מזבח הזהב אלא בקטרת הסמים.** של בין הערבים, דכתיב (שמות ל,ז) בבקר בהטיבו את הנרות יקטירנה, כלומר כשמדשן את המנורה מן האפר שיש שם מהדלקת הנרות, ואי לאו דעבד הדלקה באורתא מאי בעי למתקן בצפרא, אלמא חנוך המנורה בין הערבים, וכיון דמנורה נתחנכה בערב, קטרת נמי נתחנכה בערב, דכתיב (שם שם,ח) ובהעלות אהרן את הנרות בין הערבים יקטירנה:

### יד אברהם

אָמַר רַבִּי שִׁמְעוֹן: וְכֻלָּהּ הָיְתָה קְרֵבָה בֵּין הָעַרְבַּיִם. — *Said R' Shimon: All of it was offered in the afternoon.*

R' Shimon agrees with the first *Tanna* that the failure to bring the morning *ketores* would not prevent the afternoon portion from being offered even on the day of the Altar's dedication. He disagrees with him, however, concerning the amount that should be brought that afternoon. In R' Shimon's opinion, if the morning incense was not offered, both portions are offered in the afternoon. In his view, the entire incense was actually one unit which was divided into two parts [and thus, in order to fulfill the *mitzvah*, the whole unit must be brought] (*Tos.* 50a, s.v. בד״א).

Unlike the case of the morning *tamid* that was neglected, in which, in R' Shimon's view, the negligent *Kohanim* are penalized and not allowed to bring the afteroon *tamid*, the *ketores* may be brought by the same *Kohen* who failed to bring it in the morning. This is because the privilege of burning the incense was not usually given to the same *Kohen* twice, since its merit brought wealth to those who offered it (*Yoma* 26a). As a result, all the *Kohanim* were anxious to make the offering, and the Temple officers were therefore careful to give every *Kohen* an opportunity to do so. Therefore, the Rabbis found it unnecessary to penalize the *Kohen* who neglected to bring the *ketores*, because it was unlikely that he would receive the opportunity in any case (*Rav* from *Gem.* 50a; *Tif. Yis.*; cf. *Rashi*; *Tos.*).

Apparently, the first *Tanna* holds that the morning and afternoon incense offerings are in reality two separate *mitzvos*. Thus, when fulfilling the *mitzvah* of the afternoon incense, the regular amount is used. This seems to parallel a difference of opinion among the *Rishonim* regarding the *mitzvah* of the incense: According to *Rambam* (*Sefer HaMitzvos, mitzvah* 39), the morning and afternoon incense are reckoned as one *mitzvah;* however, *Ramban* (summary at the end of *Sefer Hamitzvos*) counts them as two (see *Mishnah LaMelech, Klei HaMikdash* 2:8). The dispute between R' Shimon and the first *Tanna* whether the entire daily measure of *ketores* is brought or just that of the afternoon hinges on the same question: According to R' Shimon, it is one *mitzvah;* according to the first *Tanna* it is two *(Keren Orah).* For a discussion of R' Shimon's view from a different perspective, see *Chidushei HaGriz* to *Rambam* loc. cit.

The halachah follows the view of the first *Tanna*, that only the afternoon portion of the *ketores* is brought *(Rav; Rambam Comm.).*

שֶׁאֵין מְחַנְּכִין אֶת מִזְבַּח הַזָּהָב אֶלָּא בִקְטֹרֶת הַסַּמִּים; — *For the Golden Altar was*

4 Said R' Shimon: All of it was offered in the
4 afternoon. For the Golden Altar was dedicated only with the [burning of the] incense; and the *Olah* Altar only with the *tamid* of the morning;



*dedicated only with the* [*burning of the*] *incense;*

The mishnah now explains the basic distinction made by the first *Tanna,* namely, that the omission of the morning incense even prior to the dedication of the Altar does not prevent the afternoon *ketores* from being brought, whereas the omission of the morning *tamid* on the day of the Altar's dedication does prevent the afternoon *tamid* from being offered (*Tif. Yis.*).

The Golden Altar upon which incense is burnt became dedicated and fit for use with the offering of the afternoon incense. This is derived in the following manner: The Torah writes (*Ex.* 30:7): וְהִקְטִיר עָלָיו אַהֲרֹן קְטֹרֶת סַמִּים בַּבֹּקֶר בַּבֹּקֶר בְּהֵיטִיבוֹ אֶת הַנֵּרֹת יַקְטִירֶנָּה. *And Aaron shall burn incense on it* [the Golden Altar], *each morning, when he cleans out the lamps he shall burn it* (the incense). By mentioning the need for the הַטָבַת הַנֵּרֹת, *cleaning the menorah's lamps,* at the time of the morning incense, the Torah makes it clear that prior to the lighting of the *menorah* in the morning, there had been a previous lighting the preceding afternoon [necessitating that the *menorah* be cleaned]. Evidently, then, the dedication of the *menorah* called for the first lighting to take place in the afternoon. The following verse then states: וּבְהַעֲלֹת אַהֲרֹן אֶת הַנֵּרֹת בֵּין הָעַרְבַּיִם יַקְטִירֶנָּה, *And Aaron shall burn it* [the incense] *when he lights the lamps in the afternoon,* thus comparing the lighting of the *menorah* to the burning of the incense. Therefore, just as the first lighting of the *menorah* had to take place in the afternoon, so too the first burning of the incense had to take place in the afternoon (*Rav* from *Gem.* 50a).

[It follows from this that since the burning of the incense dedicates the Golden Altar, and the first incense-burning takes place in the afternoon, that the Torah clearly permits burning the afternoon incense even though the Altar had not yet been dedicated that morning.]

The mishnah uses the term חִנּוּךְ — which literally means *training* — in reference to the dedication of the utensils of the Temple, because it refers to that which the vessels become "accustomed" to their functions through usage (*Rambam Comm.*).

וְלֹא מִזְבַּח הָעוֹלָה אֶלָּא בְתָמִיד שֶׁל שַׁחַר; — *and the Olah Altar only with the tamid of the morning;*

[The Altar in the Temple Courtyard upon which all the sacrifices are burnt is known as the מִזְבַּח הָעוֹלָה, *Olah Altar*. It was dedicated by its use in offering the morning *tamid.* Therefore, the morning *tamid* could not be omitted prior to the Altar's dedication, because without it the Altar was not yet fit for the offering of sacrifices. The incense, however, could be brought in the afternoon, even if it was neglected in the morning, because it was not the morning incense which dedicated the Golden Altar for this function but the afternoon one.]

וְלֹא אֶת הַשֻּׁלְחָן אֶלָּא בְלֶחֶם הַפָּנִים בַּשַּׁבָּת; וְלֹא אֶת הַמְּנוֹרָה אֶלָּא בְשִׁבְעָה נֵרוֹתֶיהָ בֵּין הָעַרְבָּיִם.

[ה] **חֲבִתֵּי** כֹּהֵן גָּדוֹל לֹא הָיוּ בָאוֹת חֲצָיִים; אֶלָּא מֵבִיא עִשָּׂרוֹן שָׁלֵם וְחוֹצֵהוּ, וּמַקְרִיב מֶחֱצָה בַּבֹּקֶר וּמֶחֱצָה בֵּין הָעַרְבָּיִם. וְכֹהֵן שֶׁהִקְרִיב מֶחֱצָה בְּשַׁחֲרִית וּמֵת,

**ר׳ עובדיה מברטנורא**

(ה) **חביתי כהן גדול.** מנחת כהן גדול שמביא בכל יום, ועל שם דכתיב בה (ויקרא ו,יד) על מחבת בשמן תעשה, משום הכי קרי לה חביתין: **לא היו באין חצאין.** שלא יביא מביתו חצי עשרון בבקר וחצי עשרון בערב:

**יד אברהם**

וְלֹא אֶת הַשֻּׁלְחָן אֶלָּא בְלֶחֶם הַפָּנִים בַּשַּׁבָּת; — *and the shulchan only with the lechem hapanim on the Sabbath;*

[The *shulchan* could only be inaugurated by arranging the *lechem hapanim* (see 2:2) on it on Shabbos.] In addition, the *lechem hapanim* itself could only be sanctified by being placed on the *shulchan* on Shabbos; if it was placed there during the week it has no effect (*Gem.* 50a).

וְלֹא אֶת הַמְּנוֹרָה אֶלָּא בְשִׁבְעָה נֵרוֹתֶיהָ בֵּין הָעַרְבָּיִם. — *and the menorah only with its seven lamps in the afternoon.*

[The *menorah* was dedicated for its function with the lighting of its lamps in the afternoon, as explained above.]

## 5.

The following mishnah discusses the special *minchah* brought by the *Kohen Gadol* each day, called the מִנְחַת חֲבִיתִּין, *minchas chavitin*, because it is prepared on a מַחֲבַת, *griddle* (*Rav*).

As described in the Torah (*Lev.* 6:13), the daily *chavitin* consist of an *issaron* of flour [and three *log* of oil]. This is donated by the *Kohen Gadol* himself. The *chavitin* are baked into twelve loaves (mishnah 6:5) and offered half in the morning and half in the afternoon (*Lev.* ibid.).

Continuing the theme of the previous discussions, the mishnah focuses on the relationships of the two halves of the *minchas chavitin*.

חֲבִתֵּי כֹּהֵן גָּדוֹל לֹא הָיוּ בָאוֹת חֲצָיִים; — *The chavitin of the Kohen Gadol were not brought by halves;*

Although the *chavitin* are offered by halves, they must come from a full *issaron* (*Gem.* 50b). The *Kohen Gadol* cannot bring just half an *issaron* of flour to the Temple in the morning and another half in the evening. Rather, he must [verbally consecrate] and bring to the Temple a full *issaron* in the morning and then divide it (*Rav* from *Gem.* 50b).

4 and the *shulchan* only with the *lechem hapa-*
5 *nim* on the Sabbath; and the *menorah* only with its seven lamps in the afternoon.

**5.** The *chavitin* of the *Kohen Gadol* were not brought by halves; rather, he brings a full *issaron* and divides it, and offers half in the morning and half in the afternoon. [If] a *Kohen* offered half in the morning and died,

### YAD AVRAHAM

אֶלָּא מֵבִיא עִשָּׂרוֹן שָׁלֵם וְחוֹצֵהוּ, וּמַקְרִיב מֶחֱצָה בַבֹּקֶר וּמֶחֱצָה בֵּין הָעַרְבַּיִם. — *rather, he brings a full issaron and divides it, and offers half in the morning and half in the afternoon.*

The *Kohen Gadol* must [consecrate and] bring to the Temple the entire *issaron* of flour in the morning and then offer half in the morning and half in the afternoon. The verse dealing with the *chavitin* states: מַחֲצִיתָהּ בַּבֹּקֶר וּמַחֲצִיתָהּ בָּעָרֶב, *half of it in the morning and half of it in the evening*. By phrasing it as *half of it* rather than simply *half*, the Torah indicates that each time the *chavitin* is brought, it must be as half of a whole (*Gem.* 50b; *Rashi* cited by *Tos. Yom Tov*).

Like all offerings, the ingredients of a *minchah*-offering must receive verbal consecration [קִדּוּשַׁת פֶּה], i.e., they must be verbally dedicated as an offering by the person donating the *minchah*. The minimum amount of flour that can be consecrated is an *issaron* (see mishnah 12:3); as our mishnah teaches, this is true even of the *chavitin* of the *Kohen Gadol*. However, in addition to verbal consecration, a *minchah* must also undergo קִדּוּשׁ כְּלִי, sanctification in a *kli shareis* [sacred vessel] before its *avodah* can begin. The *Gemara* (7b,8a) records a dispute between the *Amoraim* R' Elazar and R' Yochanan whether the *chavitin* can be sanctified in a *kli shareis* half an *issaron* at a time, or whether the entire *issaron* must be sanctified at once in order to take effect (*Rashi* 7b).[1] *Rambam* (*Maaseh HaKorbanos* 13:2) accepts as the halachah the opinion of R' Yochanan, that it *cannot* be sanctified half an *issaron* at a time.

There is disagreement between the commentators regarding how the *chavitin* were divided: *Rambam (Maaseh HaKorbanos* 13:4) maintains that all twelve loaves were baked together and each loaf was then split, with twelve half-loaves being offered in the morning and the other twelve half-loaves in the afternoon. *Ravad* (ibid.) contends that six whole loaves were offered in the morning and six in the afternoon. Furthermore, it seems that in this view there is no need to bake all twelve in the morning; rather, the six loaves of the afternoon offering may be baked in the afternoon just prior to their offering (see *Kesef Mishneh* and *Mishneh LaMelech* ad loc.). *Keren Orah* deduces that this is *Rashi's* view as well (cf. *Mikdash David* 8:4).

1. *Tosafos* (7b, s.v. ואם איתא) consider the further possibility that according to R' Elazar not only *chavitin*, but all *menachos*, may receive their sanctification in a *kli shareis* half an *issaron* at a time (cf. *Keren Orah*).

וּמִנּוּ כֹּהֵן אַחֵר תַּחְתָּיו, לֹא יָבִיא חֲצִי עִשָּׂרוֹן מִבֵּיתוֹ, וְלֹא חֲצִי עֶשְׂרוֹנוֹ שֶׁל רִאשׁוֹן; אֶלָּא מֵבִיא עִשָּׂרוֹן שָׁלֵם וְחוֹצֵהוּ, וּמַקְרִיב מֶחֱצָה וּמֶחֱצָה אָבֵד. נִמְצְאוּ שְׁנֵי חֲצָיִים קְרֵבִין וּשְׁנֵי חֲצָיִים אוֹבְדִין. לֹא מִנּוּ כֹּהֵן אַחֵר, מִשֶּׁל מִי הָיְתָה קְרֵבָה? רַבִּי שִׁמְעוֹן אוֹמֵר: מִשֶּׁל צִבּוּר.

### ר׳ עובדיה מברטנורא

**ולא חצי עשרונו של ראשון.** שנשאר מן העשרון שלם שהביא הראשון שמת ולא קרב אלא חציו: **ושני חציין אובדים.** חצי עשרונו של ראשון שמת, וחצי עשרונו של זה שעמד: **משל צבור.** דכתיב (שם ו,טו) חק עולם, חק זה יהא משל עולם, כלומר משל צבור מתרומת הלשכה:

### יד אברהם

וְכֹהֵן שֶׁהִקְרִיב מֶחֱצָה בְּשַׁחֲרִית וּמֵת, וּמִנּוּ כֹּהֵן אַחֵר תַּחְתָּיו, לֹא יָבִיא חֲצִי עִשָּׂרוֹן מִבֵּיתוֹ, — *[If] a Kohen offered half in the morning and died, and they appointed another Kohen in his place, he should not bring half an issaron of his own* (lit., *from his house*),

If the *Kohen Gadol* dies after the first half of his *chavitin* has been offered in the morning, and a replacement is appointed in time for the second half to be offered in the afternoon, he may not simply provide another half an *issaron.* This would not comply with the requirement for the *chavitin* to be half of a whole *issaron* (*Gem.* 50b).

וְלֹא חֲצִי עֶשְׂרוֹנוֹ שֶׁל רִאשׁוֹן; — *nor the half of the first one's issaron;*

He may also not simply offer the remaining half of his predecessor's *minchah* (*Rav*). This is derived from the phrase וּמַחֲצִיתָהּ בָּעֶרֶב, *and half of it in the evening.* The conjunction *and* indicates that the two halves must be similar: Just as the first half was the donation of the *Kohen Gadol* who offers it and could not be from anyone else, so too the second half must belong to the offering *Kohen Gadol* and no one else (*Rashi* ad loc.; *Malbim* to *Sifra* 6:44).

אֶלָּא מֵבִיא עִשָּׂרוֹן שָׁלֵם וְחוֹצֵהוּ, וּמַקְרִיב מֶחֱצָה וּמֶחֱצָה אָבֵד. — *rather, he brings a full issaron and divides it in half, and he offers half, and half is destroyed.*

[He must consecrate a full *issaron* of flour for the *minchah*, of which half is brought for the afternoon *chavitin.* The other half cannot be used and it is therefore left standing to become invalidated by remaining overnight [לִינָה] (see *Zevachim* 56a), after which it is burned away from the Altar [as are all offerings left over past their time] (*Gem.* 50b).

נִמְצְאוּ שְׁנֵי חֲצָיִים קְרֵבִין — *Thus, two halves are offered*

[In the situation in which the *Kohen Gadol* died after his morning *chavitin* were brought and a new *Kohen Gadol* was appointed in enough time to bring the afternoon *chavitin,* it turns out that two halves of two *essronim* are offered — the half which the first *Kohen* brought in the morning and the half which the second brings in the afternoon.]

וּשְׁנֵי חֲצָיִים אוֹבְדִין. — *and two halves are destroyed.*

The two unused halves remaining

4 and they appointed another *Kohen* in his place, he
5 should not bring half an *issaron* of his own, nor the half of the first one's *issaron*; rather, he brings a full *issaron* and divides it in half, and he offers half, and half is destroyed. Thus, two halves are offered and two halves are destroyed. [If] they did not appoint another *Kohen*, from whom was it brought? R' Shimon says: From the public.

YAD AVRAHAM

from each *issaron* — namely, the half left over from the *minchah* of the first *Kohen Gadol* and the half remaining from the second *Kohen Gadol's* offering — are not offered but are invalidated by being left overnight and then burned *(Tif. Yis.)*.

[The rule for disqualified offerings is that, כָּל שֶׁפְּסוּלוֹ בְּגוּפוֹ יִשָּׂרֵף מִיָּד; בְּדָם וּבִבְעָלִים תְּעֻבַּר צוּרָתָן וְיוֹצְאִין לְבֵית הַשְּׂרֵפָה, *whatever is disqualified by reason of itself* (e.g., *tumah* or leaving the Courtyard) *may be burnt immediately; but if it is disqualified through its blood or through its owner, it must be left until its form becomes marred* (i.e., overnight), *and then go out to the place of burning* (*Pesachim* 34b; see *Yad Avraham* comm. to *Zevachim* 8:4). Since the unused halves of the *chavitin*-offering are not inherently disqualified but merely unusable because the owner is dead or not in need of it, they must be left overnight before being burned. The place of burning for such an offering would be the one located in the Courtyard (comm. ibid.).]

לֹא מִנּוּ כֹהֵן אַחֵר, מִשֶּׁל מִי הָיְתָה קְרֵבָה? — *[If] they did not appoint another Kohen, from whom was it brought?*

[Although under ordinary circumstances the *chavitin* are considered the personal offering of the *Kohen Gadol*, if there is no *Kohen Gadol*, the *chavitin* are offered nonetheless. This is derived from Scripture, as will be explained below. The question the mishnah will now discuss is whose obligation it is to pay for the *chavitin* in the event of the death of the *Kohen Gadol*: the public or the heirs of the deceased *Kohen Gadol*.]

*Rambam (Temidin U'Mussafin* 3:22) cites this segment of the mishnah as a continuation of the previous case; i.e., in the event that the *Kohen Gadol* died after bringing the morning *chavitin* and no other *Kohen Gadol* was appointed by the afternoon, whose responsibility is it to bring the afternoon *chavitin?* However, the same responsibility to maintain the *chavitin*-offering continues until a new *Kohen Gadol* is appointed (*Zevach Todah;* see below).

רַבִּי שִׁמְעוֹן אוֹמֵר: מִשֶּׁל צִבּוּר. — *R' Shimon says: From the public.*

In the passage discussing the *minchas chavitin* it is written (v. 15): וְהַכֹּהֵן הַמָּשִׁיחַ תַּחְתָּיו מִבָּנָיו יַעֲשֶׂה אֹתָהּ חָק עוֹלָם לַה׳ כָּלִיל תָּקְטָר, *And the Kohen who is anointed in his place* [i.e., in Aaron's place] *from his sons shall make it; an everlasting decree before HASHEM, it shall be totally burnt.* R' Shimon interprets the word חָק עוֹלָם to mean *a decree for the "world"* — i.e., the public (*Gem.*) — indicating that, if there is no *Kohen Gadol*, the public must provide the *minchas chavitin* from the Temple treasury (*Rav*).

רַבִּי יְהוּדָה אוֹמֵר: מִשֶּׁל יוֹרְשִׁים. וּשְׁלֵמָה הָיְתָה קְרֵבָה.

ר׳ עובדיה מברטנורא

**רבי יהודה אומר משל יורשים.** דכתיב (שם שם,טו) והכהן המשיח תחתיו מבניו, והכי משמע, והכהן המשיח שמת, תחתיו אחד מבניו יעשה אותה: **ושלימה היתה קריבה.** כל זמן שהיא באה משל צבור לרבי שמעון או משל יורשים לרבי יהודה, שלימה היתה קריבה, עשרון שלם ולא חצי עשרון. רבי שמעון מפיק ליה מכליל תקטר (שם), שלא יקטירוה לחצאים אלא כולה כשהיא באה משל צבור, ורבי יהודה מפיק לה מדכתיב (שם) מבניו יעשה אותה, כשאחד מבניו מקריב לאחר שמת אביו דהיינו היורשים, יעשה אותה ולא חציה. והלכה כרבי יהודה שמשל יורשים היא באה:

יד אברהם

רַבִּי יְהוּדָה אוֹמֵר: מִשֶּׁל יוֹרְשִׁים. — *R' Yehudah says: From the heirs.*

He exegetically interprets the first half of the verse as follows: *If the Kohen who is anointed* [dies], *from his sons* [i.e., one of his sons] *shall make it* (*Rav*).

וּשְׁלֵמָה הָיְתָה קְרֵבָה. — *And it was offered whole.*

When offered in the absence of a *Kohen Gadol*, the *minchas chavitin* is offered as a whole *issaron* [rather than the usual half *issaron* at a time] (*Rav*). [Thus in the event that the *Kohen Gadol* died after bringing the half *issaron* for the morning *chavitin* and no other *Kohen Gadol* was appointed, the afternoon *chavitin* consists of a full *issaron*.] If the situation continues, a full *issaron* is brought every morning and every afternoon until a new *Kohen Gadol* is appointed (*Gem.* 52a).

According to R' Shimon [who holds that in the absence of a *Kohen Gadol* the *chavitin* are brought by the public], this is derived from the words

4
5 R' Yehudah says: From the heirs. And it was offered whole.



כָּלִיל תָּקְטָר, *it shall be totally burnt,* which he interprets to mean that a *whole issaron* is burnt. According to R' Yehudah [who places the obligatigon on the heirs of the deceased *Kohen Gadol*], it is derived from the phrase מִבָּנָיו יַעֲשֶׂה אֹתָהּ, *one of his sons shall make it* — i.e., *it* and not half of it (*Rav* from *Gem.* 51b).

The halachah follows the view of R' Yehudah, that it is brought by the heirs (*Rav; Rambam, Temidin U'Mussafin* 3:22).

The commentaries point out an apparent contradiction in *Rambam's* rulings. While *Rambam* rules like R' Yehudah that it is the heirs of the deceased *Kohen Gadol* who have the responsibility for supplying the *chavitin* until the *Kohen Gadol* is replaced, elsewhere he indicates that it is the public's obligation. He rules (*Hil. Shekalim* 4:4) that if the *Kohen Gadol* dies, the *minchas chavitin* is brought from the treasury of the Temple.

Some commentators explain that *Rambam's* ruling that the heirs bring the *chavitin* is the formulation of the *Scriptural* halachah; the Rabbis, however, decreed that the public provide the funds for the *chavitin* lest the heirs of the *Kohen Gadol* be remiss in their obligation. Indeed, there is support for such a view in the *Gemara* (51b) and this is the opinion of R' Yose in *Shekalim* [7:7,8] (*Lechem Mishneh, Temidin U'Mussafin* 3:22).

*Zevach Todah* suggests that *Rambam's* ruling that it is incumbent upon the heirs to bring the *chavitin* applies only on the day that the *Kohen Gadol* dies, leaving the afternoon *chavitin* unoffered. If the situation of having no *Kohen Gadol* persists for a longer period, then it is the public's obligation to insure that the *chavitin* be brought, as we fear the heirs will be too lax in the performance of this task. Careful reading of the *Rambam's* text makes this explanation quite plausible.

## פרק חמישי

# Chapter Five

Chapter Five deals with some of the basic laws and regulations governing the preparation of the *minchah*-offering. Certain procedures apply only to some types of *menachos* and not to others. This chapter delineates which procedures apply to which *menachos*.

[א] **כָּל** הַמְּנָחוֹת בָּאוֹת מַצָּה חוּץ מֵחָמֵץ שֶׁבַּתּוֹדָה וּשְׁתֵּי הַלֶּחֶם, שֶׁהֵן בָּאוֹת חָמֵץ. רַבִּי מֵאִיר אוֹמֵר: שְׂאוֹר בּוֹדֶה לָהֶן מִתּוֹכָן וּמְחַמְּצָן. רַבִּי יְהוּדָה אוֹמֵר: אַף הִיא אֵינָהּ מִן

### ר׳ עובדיה מברטנורא

**פרק חמישי – כל המנחות. (א) כל המנחות באות מצה חוץ מחמץ שבתודה.** דכתיב (ויקרא ז,יג) על חלות לחם חמץ: **ושתי הלחם.** דכתיב (שם כג,יז) חמץ תאפינה: **שאור היה בודה להן מתוכן.** מתוך עשרון דתודה ושתי הלחם היה מוציא שאור, שהיה לש מן הסולת מעט לאחר שנמדד וטומנו בסלת ומתחמץ מאליו וממנו מחמץ השאר, שממקום אחר לא היה יכול להביא שלא תהא מנחה יתירה: **היא אינה מן המובחר.** שאינה מחמצת יפה, לפי שאין לה שאור מחומץ יפה:

### יד אברהם

## 1.

כָּל הַמְּנָחוֹת בָּאוֹת מַצָּה — *All minchah-offerings are brought as matzah*

In its discussion of the general laws of *menachos*, the Torah states מַצּוֹת תֵּאָכֵל, *it should be eaten as matzah* [unleavened bread][1] (*Lev.* 6:9). Although this is not explicitly mentioned in connection with every single *minchah*, it is derived exegetically that any offering which falls under the *minchah* category is bound by the same requirement. In addition to the positive requirement that a *minchah* be of unleavened dough there is also a negative precept: לֹא תֵאָפֶה חָמֵץ, *it should not be baked leavened*, which applies to all *menachos* (*Gem.* 53a).

חוּץ מֵחָמֵץ שֶׁבַּתּוֹדָה — *except for the leavened [bread] of the todah-offering*

The *todah*-offering is accompanied by four varieties of bread, of ten loaves each (*Lev.* 7:12; see below 6:5). One of these varieties is specified to be leavened, as it says, עַל חַלֹּת לֶחֶם חָמֵץ, *in addition to loaves of leavened bread* [ibid. 7:13] (*Rashi*).

וּשְׁתֵּי הַלֶּחֶם, שֶׁהֵן בָּאוֹת חָמֵץ. — *and the shtei halechem, which are brought leavened.*

The *shtei halechem* are the two loaves brought on Shavuos (*Tif. Yis.*; see preface to 2:2). These are also brought as leavened bread, as stated explicitly in the Torah (*Lev.* 23:17): חָמֵץ תֵּאָפֶינָה, *they are to be baked leavened* (ibid.). [Neither of these, however, is offered on the Altar.]

*Tosafos* question the *Tanna's* selection of the *shtei halechem* or the *todah* loaves as exceptions to the rule of *menachos*, inasmuch as neither are ever called a *minchah* by the Torah. Furthermore, the *todah* loaves are explicitly excluded from the *minchah* category by the *Gemara* (46b). Perhaps the *Tanna* includes the *shtei halechem* in the *minchah* category because the Torah in one instance refers to them as a מִנְחָה חֲדָשָׁה, *new minchah* (*Lev.* 23:16). The *todah* loaves, too, are considered a *minchah* because, in ways, their laws are

1. It is apparent from numerous sources that unleavened bread is not necessarily the crisp *matzah* that is familiar to us. In the times of the Talmud it was baked in a more breadlike manner, resembling pita (see mishnah 6:3; *Pesachim* 7a; *Mishneh Berurah* 46:12 et al.). As long as it is not allowed to become leavened, it is considered *matzah*.

5
1 **1.** All *minchah*-offerings are brought as *matzah* except for the leavened [bread] of the *todah*-offering and the *shtei halechem*, which are brought leavened. R' Meir says: He abstracts sourdough for them from within themselves and leavens them. R' Yehudah says: This, too, is not

**YAD AVRAHAM**

compared to those of the *shtei halechem* (*Rashba;* cf. *Tos. Yom Tov* cited in comm. to mishnah 3, s.v. לחם הפנים).

*Sfas Emes* (59a, s.v. במשנה) suggests that actually all baked offerings are considered forms of *menachos*. The *Gemara's* exclusion of the *todah* from the *minchah* category refers to the classification of the offering as a whole, in which the loaves of the *todah* are only secondary to the animal offerings which constitute the major part of the offering. See comm. to mishnah 3 below, s.v. לחם הפנים.

רַבִּי מֵאִיר אוֹמֵר: שְׂאוֹר בּוֹדֵה לָהֶן מִתּוֹכָן וּמְחַמְּצָן. — *R' Meir says: He abstracts sourdough for them from within themselves and leavens them.*

Ordinarily, leavened bread is made by adding some sourdough (dough already thoroughly leavened) to the freshly made batter to hasten the leavening process. When baking the leavened loaves of the *todah* and *shtei halechem*, however, this method is problematical, because dough brought from elsewhere and mixed into the flour of the *minchah* would increase the measure of the *minchah*, and thereby invalidate it. Therefore, he should remove a bit of flour from the *issaron* required for each of these loaves (see 6:5; 7:1), mix it with water, bury it in the flour, and allow it to leaven. This can then be used to leaven the rest of the flour of the *minchah* (*Rav; Rashi*).[1]

רַבִּי יְהוּדָה אוֹמֵר: אַף הִיא אֵינָהּ מִן הַמֻּבְחָר. — *R' Yehudah says: This, too, is not preferred.*

The bit of leavened dough made from the *minchah* flour will not leaven the remainder of the flour well because it itself is not yet thoroughly leavened (*Rav*).[2]

1. *Tiferes Yisrael* (*Boaz*) asks why R' Meir does not simply advise adding water to all the flour and letting it stand until the entire dough becomes leavened. This would not create an overabundant *minchah*, since nothing extra would be added to the mixture. To resolve this, *Tif. Yis.* offers a novel approach. He suggests that this solution is not given because dough must stand for several days after it is mixed with water to become properly leavened. This cannot be done in the case of a *minchah* because once the *minchah* is kneaded in the *kli shareis* used for making dough in the Temple, it becomes sanctified and consequently invalidated if left overnight. Therefore, R' Meir suggests taking a small measure of the flour and mixing it with water. [This could seemingly be done without using a sanctified mixing vessel.] This small amount can be prepared several days in advance so that it has an opportunity to become more leavened. [This would necessitate measuring out the entire *issaron* several days earlier, but this does not pose a problem because the measures used for dry substances were not sanctified and thus would not sanctify the flour; see mishnah 9:5.] This better-leavened dough could then be added to the *minchah* as it is prepared (*Tif. Yis.*; see *Tif. Yaakov* who points out several difficulties with this approach).

2. *Tif. Yis.*, following his explanation of R' Meir, explains that R' Yehudah does not accept

הַמְּבֻחָר. אֶלָּא מֵבִיא אֶת הַשְּׂאוֹר, וְנוֹתֵן לְתוֹךְ הַמִּדָּה, וּמְמַלֵּא אֶת הַמִּדָּה. אָמְרוּ לוֹ: אַף הִיא הָיְתָה חֲסֵרָה אוֹ יְתֵרָה.

[ב] **כָּל** הַמְּנָחוֹת נִלּוֹשׁוֹת בְּפוֹשְׁרִין, וּמְשַׁמְּרָן שֶׁלֹּא יַחֲמִיצוּ. וְאִם הֶחֱמִיצוּ שְׁיָרֶיהָ,

### ר׳ עובדיה מברטנורא

**אלא מביא שאור.** שמחומץ יפה מתוך ביתו, ונותן לתוך העשרון, ומוסיף וממלאהו סלת: **אף היא היתה חסרה או יתירה.** כגון אם השאור עבה ומגובל בקושי עם מעט מים, אינו מחזיק נפח גדול כאילו היה קמח ונמצא העשרון יותר, לפי שאם לא היה שאור מגובל היה נפחו גדול מעכשיו, ואם אינו מגובל יפה שנתן בו מים הרבה, נמצא נפחו גדול משאילו היה קמח ונמצא עשרון חסר, שאם לא בשביל המים לא יהיה מלא. והלכה כרבי יהודה:

### יד אברהם

אֶלָּא מֵבִיא אֶת הַשְּׂאוֹר, וְנוֹתֵן לְתוֹךְ הַמִּדָּה, וּמְמַלֵּא אֶת הַמִּדָּה. — *Rather, he brings sourdough, places it within the measure, and then fills the measure.*

He brings a bit of thoroughly leavened dough of his own and places it in the measuring vessel before he measures the *issaron* of flour, and then fills the remainder of the vessel with the flour for the *minchah* (*Rav*). [In this manner, the sourdough becomes sanctified as part of the *issaron* of the *minchah* together with the flour.]

אָמְרוּ לוֹ: — *They said to him:*

R' Meir [or those who agreed with him (*Keren Orah* 53b, s.v. גמרא)] argued that R' Yehudah's method of using sourdough as part of the measured *issaron* still leaves the following problem.

אַף הִיא הָיְתָה חֲסֵרָה אוֹ יְתֵרָה. — *This, too, would be deficient or excessive.*

Using a bit of sourdough as part of the *issaron* would result in a situation in which the *minchah* contains either a smaller or larger volume than required. The *issaron* requirement for a *minchah* refers to the volume of flour which must be used. Adding a piece of sourdough to the flour before the *issaron* is measured distorts this measurement. If the sourdough originally contained just a little water, the sourdough will actually be denser and have a smaller volume than the original volume of flour. Thus, filling the measuring vessel on top of it will result in the use of somewhat more than an *issaron* of flour. By the same token, if a larger amount of water was used, the sourdough will take up more space than the original volume of flour and the resulting measurement will be short of a true *issaron* (*Rav; Rashi*).

R Yehudah, however, maintains

R' Meir's suggestion of making sourdough from flour which has previously been measured for the *minchah* and then set it aside to become leavened for a few days, because a person will not want to wait that long for fear that something may happen to invalidate the remainder of the measured flour that he consecrated for the *minchah*. Thus, he will probably try to hurry the process and use dough which was not permitted to stand long enough. This will not leaven thoroughly, as explained above (ibid.).

5
2

preferred. Rather, he brings sourdough, places it within the measure, and then fills the measure. They said to him: This, too, would be deficient or excessive.

**2.** All *minchah*-offerings are kneaded with lukewarm water, and one guards them from becoming leavened. If its remainder became leavened,

YAD AVRAHAM

that the requirement for an *issaron* does not refer to the measure of flour but to the actual contents of the *issaron* measuring vessel at the time the measurement is made. Thus, there is no question of the sourdough distorting the measurement, because whatever the *issaron* vessel holds after the sourdough has been added will be considered a valid *issaron* (*Tos.* to 54a, s.v. ת״ש; *Rambam, Hil. Maaseh HaKorbanos* 9:18; see *Lechem Mishneh* ad loc.; cf. *Tif. Yis.*).

Alternatively, R' Yehudah agrees that the *issaron* requirement refers to the flour. He solves the problem of the correct measure by first measuring the amount of flour required to produce the sourdough and then simply adding the amount required to make a full *issaron*. R' Meir rejects this solution out of fear that he may forget to measure the flour and use finished, but unmeasured, sourdough instead (*Tif. Yis.*; see *Shitah Mekubetzes* to 53b #7).

The halachah follows the opinion of R' Yehudah (*Rav; Rambam* loc. cit).

There is another view that disputes this (*Rambam Comm.*). Since the mishnah states the dissenting view in the plural form, it indicates that it is to be considered the majority opinion (*Keren Orah* to *Gem.* 53b).

2.

כָּל הַמְּנָחוֹת — *All minchah*-offerings

I.e., all *menachos* that are baked before their *kemitzah* (see General Introduction). The מִנְחַת סֹלֶת, *fine flour minchah*, is not included in this category, as it is processed as flour (*Rambam Comm.; Sfas Emes*).

נִלוֹשׁוֹת בְּפוֹשְׁרִין, — *are kneaded with lukewarm water,*

To make a proper dough, the flour must be mixed with water. Thus, lukewarm water (which makes a better dough) is added to the flour (*Tos.* 57a, s.v. מִנְחַת). Although the Torah does not explicitly state this requirement, it is self-evident (*Chazon Ish* 35:1).

From *Rashi* (74b, *msc.* s.v. קודם לעשייתן; see also *Tos.* 67b, s.v. יצק) it emerges that the *minchah* is mixed with water *before* oil is applied to the flour and mixed with it [בְּלִילָה; see preface to mishnah 3:2]. Thus, the oil is added to and mixed with the dough, not the flour.

However, *Rambam* (*Maaseh HaKorbanos* 13:6) states that the oil was added and mixed with the flour first, and only then was lukewarm water added and kneaded with the flour to form a dough (see *Mikdash David* Ch. 8).

וּמְשַׁמְּרָן שֶׁלֹּא יַחֲמִיצוּ. — *and one guards them from becoming leavened.*

[The *Kohen* who prepares the *minchah* must therefore take care that it does not become leavened, since *menachos* offered on the Altar may not be leavened, as the mishnah will state below. The leavened doughs discussed

# עוֹבֵר בְּלֹא תַעֲשֶׂה; שֶׁנֶּאֱמַר: „כָּל־הַמִּנְחָה אֲשֶׁר תַּקְרִיבוּ לַה׳ לֹא תֵעָשֶׂה חָמֵץ״. וְחַיָּבִים עַל לִישָׁתָהּ, וְעַל עֲרִיכָתָהּ, וְעַל אֲפִיָּתָהּ.

**ר׳ עובדיה מברטנורא**

(ב) **שנאמר כל המנחה אשר תקריבו לה׳ לא תעשה חמץ.** ארישא קאי דקתני ומשתמרות שלא יחמיצו, וקודם קמיצה משתעי. ושיריה ילפינן מקרא אחרינא דכתיב (ויקרא ו,י) לא תאפה חמץ חלקם, אף חלקם של כהנים שהם שירי המנחה שנשארו מן הקומץ, אף זו לא תאפה חמץ. ובחמוץ דוקא הוזהרו על השירים, אבל מותר ללוש אותם בדבש ולטגנן בו: **עריכתה.** שמתעסק בה בידים אחר לישה. וחייבין על כל אחת ואחת, לפי שנאמר לא תעשה חמץ, יכול לא יהא חייב אלא אחת, תלמוד לומר לא תאפה, אפיה בכלל היתה ולמה יצאת, להקיש אליה, מה אפייה מיוחדת שהיא מעשה יחידי וחייבין עליה בפני עצמה, אף אני אביא לישה ועריכתה וכל מעשה יחידי שבה, לאתויי קיטוף שהוא מעשה יחידי וחייבין עליה בפני עצמה. וקטוף הוא שמחליק פניה במים, ואף על גב דלא מחזי כל כך מעשה:

**יד אברהם**

in the previous mishnah are the *shtei halechem* and *todah* loaves. These are eaten in their entirety, with no part of them being offered on the Altar.]

In the preparation of *matzah* for Pesach, by contrast, it is forbidden to use lukewarm water because the dough may leaven too rapidly, and one cannot rely on properly guarding it against rising. In dealing with *menachos*, this is permitted because the *Kohanim* in the Temple were very zealous in fulfilling their Torah duties and could be relied upon to guard carefully against leavening (*Pesachim* 36a; *Rambam, Hil. Maaseh HaKorbanos* 12:21).

Apparently, in preparing the *minchah*, the use of lukewarm water is not only permitted but preferred. Although this increases the chance of leavening the dough, which is not permitted for *menachos* brought on the Altar, this is done because lukewarm water bakes a better loaf (*Tif. Yis.*). Others explain that since the Torah prescribes a *mitzvah* of שִׁימּוּר, *guarding* against the dough becoming leavened, the Torah indicates creating circumstances which call for caution, i.e., using water that ordinarily leavens rapidly and making the effort to see that it does not (*Zevach Todah*; see *Pesachim* 40a).

**וְאִם הֶחֱמִיצוּ שְׁיָרֶיהָ, עוֹבֵר בְּלֹא תַעֲשֶׂה; — *If its remainder became leavened, he transgresses a prohibition;***

[It is not only forbidden to offer any *chametz* (leavened flour) on the Altar (*Lev.* 2:11), and thus to allow a *minchah* to become *chametz*, but it is even forbidden to allow the remainder of the *minchah* (which is eaten by the *Kohanim*, not offered on the Altar) to become leavened.] One who does so transgresses a Torah prohibition, as derived from the verse (*Lev.* 6:10): לֹא תֵאָפֶה חָמֵץ חֶלְקָם נָתַתִּי מֵאִשָּׁי, *It shall not be baked leavened; their portion I have given to them from my fire-offering.* The verse is exegetically interpreted to read לֹא תֵאָפֶה חָמֵץ חֶלְקָם, *It shall not be baked leavened, their portion* — even the portion of the *Kohanim* must not be leavened (*Rav* from *Gem.* 55a).

Although the mishnah's first statement refers to all *menachos* except the fine flour *minchah*, the above statement regarding the remainder of the *minchah* becoming leavened refers *only* to the fine flour *minchah*. All other *menachos* are baked before *kemitzah* when there is as yet no distinction between the *kometz* and the remainder. Thus, when their *kometz* is removed

5 he transgresses a prohibition; as it is written (*Lev.*
2 2:11): *Any minchah-offering which you shall offer to* HASHEM *shall not be made leavened.* And they are liable for its kneading, its arrangement, and for its baking.

### YAD AVRAHAM

their remainder is already in a baked state, and something already baked (without having become leavened) can no longer become leavened (*Sfas Emes*). Only in the case of a *minchas soless* (fine flour *minchah*), whose *kometz* is removed while it is still flour, can the remainder still be susceptible to becoming *chametz*. This explains the mishnah's change from the plural form (*all menachos*) to the singular (*if "its" remainder became leavened*), for only the remainder of the fine flour *minchah* is now under discussion (*Keren Orah*).

שֶׁנֶּאֱמַר: ,,כָּל הַמִּנְחָה אֲשֶׁר תַּקְרִיבוּ לַה' לֹא תֵעָשֶׂה חָמֵץ". — *as it is written (Lev.* 2:11): *"Any minchah-offering which you shall offer to* HASHEM *shall not be made leavened."*

This verse is cited to support the law implicit in the mishnah's earlier statement, that there is an obligation to guard the dough from leavening even prior to *kemitzah* (*Rav; Rashi*). [It cannot be understood to apply to the prohibition against allowing the remainder to become leavened, since this verse deals with the entire *minchah* prior to *kemitzah*, not to that which remains afterward.]

וַחַיָּבִים — *And they are liable*

[Those who prepare a leavened *minchah* are punished by *malkus* (lashes) if they intentionally place sourdough on it and cause it to leaven during its preparation.]

Although leavening is a natural process and not something made by a person, the fact that one sets the process into motion is enough to make him responsible for the result. This is similar to cooking on the Sabbath. Although all one did was set the pot on the fire, he is liable for the cooking which results (*Gem.* 56b, 57a).

עַל לִישָׁתָהּ, — *for its kneading,*

לִישָׁה, *kneading*, consists of creating a dough by adding water to the flour and mixing it to form a mass (*Tif. Yis.*).

וְעַל עֲרִיכָתָהּ, — *its arrangement,*

*Arrangement* refers to the process of shaping the dough into loaves after the kneading, and smearing it with liquid (*Rav; Tif. Yis.*).

וְעַל אֲפִיָּתָהּ. — *and for its baking.*

In addition to the verse quoted in the mishnah, the Torah also expresses the prohibition against allowing a *minchah* to leaven with the words (*Lev.* 6:10) לֹא תֵאָפֶה חָמֵץ, *it shall not be baked leavened.* Although the act of baking was included in the general term לֹא תֵעָשֶׂה חָמֵץ, *it shall not be made leavened*, it is specified as a separate prohibition, to teach that each step in the baking process is prohibited separately (*Rav* from *Gem.* 55b).[1]

1. This is based on one of the thirteen hermeneutic principles: כָּל דָּבָר שֶׁהָיָה בִּכְלָל וְיָצָא מִן הַכְּלָל . . . לְלַמֵּד עַל הַכְּלָל כֻּלּוֹ יָצָא, *anything which was included in a group and then specified* [for a halachah] . . . *was specified to teach* [the halachah] *regarding the entire group*. I.e., baking is but one step in the process of making the *minchah*. Since it was singled out for mention in the prohibition against leavening, it teaches that each step of the *minchah* process is also judged separately (*Gem.* ibid.).

# [ג] **יֵשׁ** טְעוּנוֹת שֶׁמֶן וּלְבוֹנָה; שֶׁמֶן וְלֹא לְבוֹנָה; לְבוֹנָה וְלֹא שֶׁמֶן; לֹא שֶׁמֶן וְלֹא לְבוֹנָה. וְאֵלּוּ טְעוּנוֹת שֶׁמֶן וּלְבוֹנָה: מִנְחַת הַסֹּלֶת, וְהַמַּחֲבַת, וְהַמַּרְחֶשֶׁת, וְהַחַלּוֹת, וְהָרְקִיקִין, מִנְחַת כֹּהֲנִים, וּמִנְחַת כֹּהֵן מָשִׁיחַ,

**ר׳ עובדיה מברטנורא**

(ג) **מנחת סלת.** המתנדב מנחה סתם, מביא סולת ושמן ולבונה ובוללה וקומלה כמו שהיא קודם אפייה. ובדידה כתיב שמן ולבונה, וכל הני אחריני גמרי ממנחת סולת דכתיב בה (ויקרא ב,א) נפש, דמשמע דכל מנחת יחיד טעונה שמן ולבונה: **והחלות והרקיקין.** למנחת מאפה תנור קרי החלות והרקיקין, דאי בעי חלות מייתי ואי בעי רקיקין מייתי: **ומנחת כהנים.** כהן שהתנדב אחת מחמשת מנחות הללו: **מנחת כהן משיח.** מנחת חביתין:

**יד אברהם**

Since there is a separate prohibition to perform any of these steps in the baking process, someone who leavens the *minchah* when kneading it, and who then arranges it, and bakes it is liable for each of these three acts. The *Gemara* (56b) refers to this as the principle of מְחַמֵּץ אַחַר מְחַמֵּץ, *leavening after leavening* [i.e., assisting in the production of a leavened *minchah* (*Rashi* 56b, s.v. הכל מודים)]. Since the Torah prohibits each step of the process it is clear that even though it had already been leavened at the time of kneading, he is liable *again* for the arranging and the baking (*Gem.* 55b). The reason for this would seem to be that each step of the baking process is capable of increasing the degree of the leavening (*Chasam Sofer* to *Shabbos* 131a). However, if one causes an otherwise invalid *minchah* (i.e., one that is *tamei*) to become leavened, he is not liable for this prohibition; the Torah prohibits only the leavening of a valid *minchah* (*Gem.* 57a).

## 3.

יֵשׁ טְעוּנוֹת שֶׁמֶן וּלְבוֹנָה; שֶׁמֶן וְלֹא לְבוֹנָה; לְבוֹנָה וְלֹא שֶׁמֶן; לֹא שֶׁמֶן וְלֹא לְבוֹנָה. — *There are [minchah-offerings] that require oil and frankincense; oil but not frankincense; frankincense but not oil; neither oil nor frankincense.*

[In addition to flour, the two basic ingredients of a *minchah* are oil and *levonah*. However, not every *minchah* requires both these additional ingredients; some require one or the other of the two, and some require neither.]

וְאֵלּוּ טְעוּנוֹת שֶׁמֶן וּלְבוֹנָה: מִנְחַת הַסֹּלֶת, — *The following require oil and frankincense: The minchah-offering of fine flour,*

Someone who vows to offer a *minchah*, without specifying which type, brings the מִנְחַת סֹלֶת, *minchah of fine flour*. This *minchah* consists of an *issaron* of fine grade flour; it is mixed with oil, and frankincense is added. Its *kometz* is separated in its unbaked form [and the *levonah* is then removed and added to the *kometz* for burning] (*Rav; Rashi;* see *Lev.* 2:2ff; above mishnah 3:2).

*Rashash* questions this generalization, pointing out that it is actually only the disputed view of R' Yehudah in a later mishnah (13:1); the halachah follows the

**3.** There are [*minchah*-offerings] that require oil and frankincense; oil but not frankincense; frankincense but not oil; neither oil nor frankincense. The following require oil and frankincense: The *minchah*-offering of fine flour, the *machavas* [*minchah*-offering], the *marcheshes* [*minchah*-offering], the *challos*, the *rekikin*, the *minchah*-offering of *Kohanim*, the *minchah*-offering of the Anointed *Kohen*,



view that one who does not specify the type of *minchah* intended may bring any of the five types of voluntary *menachos* (*Rav* ibid.; *Rambam, Hil. Maaseh HaKorbanos* 17:5). It is therefore unclear why *Rav* and *Rashi* assume that this mishnah follows R' Yehudah's opinion (see *Mishneh LaMelech*).

וְהַמַּחֲבַת, וְהַמַּרְחֶשֶׁת, — *the machavas [minchah-offering], the marcheshes [minchah-offering],*

[The *machavas* and *marcheshes* are *menachos* which are fried in their oil (*Rashi* to *Lev.* 2:5). The *machavas* is made on a griddle and the *marcheshes* in a deep pan, as explained in mishnah 8.] These voluntary *menachos* are baked prior to *kemitzah* (see *Lev.* 2:5-10).

וְהַחַלּוֹת, וְהָרְקִיקִין, — *the challos, the rekikin,*

Another category of voluntary *minchah* is the מִנְחַת מַאֲפֵה תַנּוּר, *the oven-baked minchah*, baked directly in an oven without any pan or griddle (below, mishnah 9). This may be brought in either of two forms: *challos*, loaves, which are mixed with oil, and *rekikin*, wafers, which are only smeared with oil (*Lev.* 2:4, *Rashi* ad loc.; see further in mishnah 6:3). [Since neither of these standard translations completely reflects the meanings of these names, the commentary will refer to them simply as *challos* and *rekikin*.]

Although in the passage about *menachos* in the Torah, this category precedes those previously stated, the *Tanna* lists the others first because they are similar to the *minchas soless* (fine flour) — which was listed first in the mishnah — in the manner in which they are mixed with oil (*Tif. Yis.*; see 6:3).

מִנְחַת כֹּהֲנִים, — *the minchah-offering of Kohanim,*

This refers to any of these voluntary *menachos* when it is brought by a *Kohen* (*Rav*). [The *menachos* of *Kohanim* are considered a distinct category because they are totally burnt on the Altar, as opposed to those of non-*Kohanim*, in which only the *kometz* is burnt on the Altar, and the remainder is eaten by *Kohanim* (see commentary to mishnah 5, s.v. רבי שמעון אומר).]

וּמִנְחַת כֹּהֵן מָשִׁיחַ, — *the minchah-offering of the Anointed Kohen,*

[The term *Anointed Kohen* refers to the *Kohen Gadol*.] Thus, the Anointed *Kohen's minchah* refers to the daily *minchas chavitin* of the *Kohen Gadol* (*Rav*; see 4:5).

מנחות
ה/ג

וּמִנְחַת גּוֹיִם, וּמִנְחַת נָשִׁים, וּמִנְחַת הָעֹמֶר. מִנְחַת נְסָכִין טְעוּנָה שֶׁמֶן וְאֵין טְעוּנָה לְבוֹנָה. לֶחֶם הַפָּנִים טָעוּן לְבוֹנָה וְאֵין טָעוּן שֶׁמֶן. שְׁתֵּי הַלֶּחֶם, מִנְחַת חוֹטֵא, וּמִנְחַת קְנָאוֹת, לֹא שֶׁמֶן וְלֹא לְבוֹנָה.

**ר׳ עובדיה מברטנורא**

**גוי.** מתנדב מנחה, כדילפינן מאיש איש (שם כב,יח), מלמד שהנכרים מביאין נדרים ונדבות כישראל: **ומנחת נשים.** אשה שהתנדבה מנחה: **ומנחת נסכים.** לא בעי לבונה, דשמן נאמר בה ולא לבונה: **ולחם הפנים.** כתיב ביה (ויקרא כד,ז) ונתת על המערכת לבונה זכה, ולא כתיב ביה שמן: **שתי החלות.** של עצרת, לא הוזכר בהן לא שמן ולא לבונה: **מנחת חוטא ומנחת קנאות.** בהדיא כתיב בהו (שם ה,יא) לא ישים עליה שמן ולא יתן עליה לבונה:

**יד אברהם**

וּמִנְחַת גּוֹיִם, — *the minchah-offering of gentiles,*

A gentile may offer sacrifices, including a *minchah,* in the Temple, as derived from the extra word אִישׁ in the verse (*Lev.* 22:18): אִישׁ אִישׁ מִבֵּית יִשְׂרָאֵל וּמִן הַגֵּר בְּיִשְׂרָאֵל אֲשֶׁר יַקְרִיב קָרְבָּנוֹ, *Any man* [lit., *a man, a man*] *from the house of Israel or from the proselytes in Israel who will offer his offering* (*Rav* from *Gem.* 73b).

This represents the view of R' Yose HaGlili. However, R' Akiva states that a gentile may offer only an *olah* and no other offering (*Gem.* 73b). *Rambam* rules that the halachah follows R' Akiva and thus a gentile cannot offer a *minchah* (*Rambam Comm.*, ed. Kafich, see note 10 there; *Hil. Maaseh HaKorbanos* 3:2).

וּמִנְחַת נָשִׁים, — *the minchah-offering of women,*

I.e., a *minchah* brought by a woman (*Rav*).

It is puzzling that the mishnah finds it necessary to mention that a woman's *minchah* requires oil and *levonah*. Why would one suppose that a woman's *minchah* is in any way different than a man's? (*Chidushei HaGriz*). [Perhaps since a woman's *minchah* differs from that of a man in regard to the ritual of *tenufah* (see mishnah 5), one might have thought that it differs in regard to other laws as well.]

The requirement for oil and *levonah* is mentioned by the Torah in connection with the *minchas soless* (*Lev.* 2:1) [the first *minchah* listed in the Torah]. From the word נֶפֶשׁ , *an individual* [lit., *soul*], with which the Torah opens this passage, we learn that this requirement is shared by all *menachos* of an individual [which is the common denominator of all the *menachos* cited until this point] (*Rav; Rashi* from *Gemara* 59a).

וּמִנְחַת הָעֹמֶר. — *and the minchah-offering of the omer.*

This is a communal *minchah*-offering brought on the sixteenth of Nissan [the second day of Pesach] from the new crop of barley (see *Lev.* 2:14ff; ibid. 23:10,11). The requirement for oil and *levonah* for this *minchah* is stated explicitly in the Torah (ibid. 2:15) (*Rashi; Tos. Yom Tov*).

מִנְחַת נְסָכִין טְעוּנָה שֶׁמֶן וְאֵין טְעוּנָה לְבוֹנָה. — *The minchah-offering of libations requires oil but not frankincense.*

The *minchas nesachim* is the *minchah* brought together with a wine libation (*nesech*) to accompany *olah* and *shelamim* sacrifices (*Tif. Yis.;* see

5
3

the *minchah*-offering of gentiles, the *minchah*-offering of women, and the *minchah*-offering of the *omer*. The *minchah*-offering of libations requires oil but not frankincense. The *lechem hapanim* requires frankincense but not oil. The *shtei halechem*, the sinner's *minchah*-offering, and the jealousy *minchah*-offering [require] neither oil nor frankincense.



preface to 2:4). It requires no *levonah* because the passage concerning the *minchas nesachim* (*Num.* 15) makes no mention of *levonah* as it does for oil (*Rav*). The *Gemara* also cites Biblical exegesis to indicate that a *minchas nesachim* is excluded from the requirement of *levonah* (see *Gem.* 59a).

לֶחֶם הַפָּנִים טָעוּן לְבוֹנָה וְאֵין טָעוּן שֶׁמֶן. — *The lechem hapanim requires frankincense but not oil.*

Two spoonfuls of *levonah* are placed on the *shulchan* in the Temple alongside the *lechem hapanim* [see preface to mishnah 2:2], as stated explicitly in the Torah (*Lev.* 24:7). Oil, however, is not mentioned in regard to this *minchah* (*Rav*). The *Gemara* (59a) cites Biblical exegesis to support this exclusion as well.

Actually, the *lechem hapanim* is never specifically referred to as a *minchah* by the Torah. However, from their inclusion in the mishnah's listing of *menachos* it is apparent that this offering is regarded as such. *Rashi*, too, in his commentary to *Lev.* (24:9) refers to the *lechem hapanim* as a *minchah* [generalizing that any grain offering is called a *minchah*] (*Tos. Yom Tov; Tos.* 55a, s.v. כל; *Ramban* to *Lev.* loc. cit.; *Rishon LeTzion*; see *Sfas Emes* cited above, comm. to mishnah 1, s.v. ושתי הלחם).

שְׁתֵּי הַלֶּחֶם, — *The shtei halechem,*

I.e., the two loaves brought on Shavuos (*Rav;* see comm. to mishnah 2:2). In stating the obligation to add oil and *levonah* to the *minchas omer*, the Torah (*Lev.* 2:15) adds the words מִנְחָה הִוא, *it is a minchah*, from which the *Gemara* derives that *it* (i.e., the *omer*) requires oil and frankincense but the *shtei halechem* do not (*Gem.* 59a).

מִנְחַת חוֹטֵא, — *the sinner's minchah-offering,*

This is a *minchah* brought as a *chatas*-offering by a sinner who is destitute, for the transgression of entering the Temple grounds or eating consecrated food while in a state of *tumah* (*Tif. Yis.;* see comm. to mishnah 1:1).

וּמִנְחַת קְנָאוֹת, — *and the jealousy minchah-offering,*

The *minchah* brought as part of the special test of a *sotah* [suspected adulteress] (*Tif. Yis.;* see comm. to mishnah 1:1).

לֹא שֶׁמֶן וְלֹא לְבוֹנָה. — *[require] neither oil nor frankincense.*

These last three *menachos* do not include either oil or *levonah*. Concerning the last two of these *menachos* the Torah explicitly states: לֹא יָשִׂים עָלֶיהָ שֶׁמֶן וְלֹא יִתֵּן עָלֶיהָ לְבֹנָה, *he is not to put oil on it nor place frankincense on it* [*Lev.* 5:11; see *Numbers* 5:15] (*Rav*).

In both these instances, the Torah gives as the reason the fact that these *menachos* come as a result of sin (ibid.) and it is therefore improper that they should be elegant offerings (*Rashi, Lev.* 5:11 from *Gem.* 6a).

[ד] **וְחַיָּב** עַל הַשֶּׁמֶן בִּפְנֵי עַצְמוֹ, וְעַל הַלְּבוֹנָה בִּפְנֵי עַצְמָהּ. נָתַן עָלֶיהָ שֶׁמֶן, פְּסָלָהּ. לְבוֹנָה, יִלְקְטֶנָּה. נָתַן שֶׁמֶן עַל שְׁיָרֶיהָ, אֵינוֹ עוֹבֵר בְּלֹא תַעֲשֶׂה. נָתַן כְּלִי עַל גַּבֵּי כְלִי, לֹא פְסָלָהּ.

ר׳ עובדיה מברטנורא

(ד) **וחייב על השמן.** אם נתנו על מנחת חוטא או על מנחת קנאות: **נתן כלי.** שיש בו שמן, על גבי כלי של מנחת חוטא: **לא פסלה.** ולא אמרינן הרי עבר על מה שכתוב בתורה (ויקרא

יד אברהם

## 4.

This mishnah is a continuation of the previous one, which concludes with the prohibition of adding oil or frankincense to the sinner's *minchah* and the jealousy *minchah*.

וְחַיָּב — *He is liable*

[He is punished by *malkus* (lashes) for transgressing the prohibition against adding oil and frankincense to either the *sinner's minchah* or *the jealousy minchah.*]

עַל הַשֶּׁמֶן בִּפְנֵי עַצְמוֹ — *for the oil by itself*

If he placed just the oil on one of these two *menachos* he is liable for lashes (*Rav; Rashi*).

*Rambam* (*Maaseh HaKorbanos* 12:8) indicates that he must actually offer the *minchah* to be liable for adding the oil [or the frankincense], an opinion apparently not shared by most other commentators. *Rambam* agrees, however, that the *minchah* is invalidated merely by adding the oil (*Zevach Todah*).

וְעַל הַלְּבוֹנָה בִּפְנֵי עַצְמָהּ. — *and on the frankincense by itself.*

Adding *levonah* to these *menachos* is a transgression independent of the injunction against adding oil. Since it is a separate action, it makes him liable for lashes even if he did not add oil (*Zevach Todah*).

There is a dispute among the *Rishonim* whether one who puts both oil and frankincense on these *menachos* is liable for both or only for the oil. According to *Rashi* (60a) he is liable for both and that is the very point of the mishnah: If one adds both oil and *levonah* to these *menachos* he is liable to two sets of lashes. Although the *minchah* was already invalidated when he added the oil (as explained below), he is nevertheless liable for adding the *levonah*. This is comparable to the prohibition against leavening a *minchah* (mishnah 2). Although the *minchah* becomes invalidated the moment it becomes leavened, each additional act which contributes to the leavening constitutes a separate and additional liability (see comm. to mishnah 2, s.v. ולאפיתה).

*Rabbeinu Tam* (*Tos.* 60a, s.v. יכול), however, maintains that if one added both oil and *levonah* to these *menachos* he is liable only for the oil, because once he adds the oil the *minchah* is invalidated [and therefore no longer subject to the bans regulating the processing of a *minchah*]. Accordingly our mishnah really means that one is liable *either* for the oil *or* for the frankincense. One can incur both liabilities only by transgressing with two separate *menachos* [or by adding oil and *levonah* simultaneously to one *minchah*] (*Zevach Todah*).

נָתַן עָלֶיהָ שֶׁמֶן, פְּסָלָהּ. — *[If] he placed oil upon it, he has invalidated it.*

[If someone transgressed the above prohibition and placed oil on either

5 **4. H**e is liable for the oil by itself and on the
4 frankincense by itself. [If] he placed oil upon it, he has invalidated it. [If he added] frankincense, he should remove it. [If] he placed oil on its remainder, he does not transgress a prohibition. [If] he placed a vessel upon a vessel, he does not invalidate it.



the sinner's *minchah* or the jealousy *minchah*, it is invalidated. However, this applies only if he placed the oil on at least a *kezayis* (the volume of an olive) of the *minchah* (*Gem.* 59b).

There is an unresolved question in the *Gemara* whether any amount of oil placed on that *kezayis* of the *minchah* invalidates it, or whether at least a *kezayis* of oil is necessary to invalidate. Therefore, if he put in less than a *kezayis*, it is invalidated due to the doubt (*Rambam, Hil. Pesulei HaMukdashin* 11:12).

לְבוֹנָה, יִלְקְטֶנָּה. — *[If he added] frankincense, he should remove it.*

[I.e., if he added only *levonah*, the *minchah* is not invalidated. He merely has to remove the *levonah* before he offers the *minchah* on the Altar.]

The *Gemara* shows by means of Biblical exegesis that although neither oil nor *levonah* may be added to the sinner's *minchah* [and jealousy *minchah*], the *minchah* is invalidated by this addition in only one of the two cases. Since the oil cannot be completely removed from the *minchah* once it has been added, and the *levonah* can, the *Gemara* concludes that the invalidation refers to the case of oil, not to the case of *levonah* (*Gem.* 59b). It follows from this that as long as the *levonah* has *not* been removed, the *minchah* is not fit to be offered (*Gem.* ibid; see *Rambam, Hil. Pesulei HaMukdashin* 11:10 and *Kesef Mishneh*).

Only a *kezayis* or more of *levonah* invalidates the offering. However, it does not matter whether or not the portion of the *minchah* upon which it was placed consists of a *kezayis* or less (*Gem.* 59b; *Rambam, Pesulei HaMukdashin* 11:13).

נָתַן שֶׁמֶן עַל שְׁיָרֶיהָ, אֵינוֹ עוֹבֵר בְּלֹא תַעֲשֶׂה. — *[If] he placed oil on its remainder, he does not transgress a prohibition.*

This is derived from the words (loc. cit.): לֹא יָשִׂים עָלֶיהָ שֶׁמֶן, *he shall not place upon it oil* — עָלֶיהָ, *upon it* [the full *minchah*], but not upon its remainder (*Toras Kohanim*). [Assumedly, the same would apply to the *levonah*.]

Despite the mishnah's wording which indicates that he merely *does not transgress*, it seems apparent from the wording of *Toras Kohanim* that adding oil to the remainder is perfectly permissible. The mishnah may have used this phrase simply out of consistency with the first portion of the mishnah, which reads *he is liable* (*Zevach Todah;* cf. *Sfas Emes*).

נָתַן כְּלִי עַל גַּבֵּי כְלִי, — *[If] he placed a vessel upon a vessel,*

I.e., he placed a vessel containing oil [or *levonah* (*Tos. Yom Tov*)] upon the vessel containing the *sinner's minchah* [or the *jealousy minchah* (ibid.)] (*Rav; Rashi*).

The same would be true if he placed the vessel of oil directly on the flour of the *minchah* (*Zevach Todah*), as long as he did not mix the oil into the flour (*Rambam Comm.*).

לֹא פְּסָלָהּ. — *he does not invalidate it.*

He does not transgress the Torah's

[ה] **יֵשׁ** טְעוּנוֹת הַגָּשָׁה וְאֵינָן טְעוּנוֹת תְּנוּפָה; תְּנוּפָה וְלֹא הַגָּשָׁה; הַגָּשָׁה וּתְנוּפָה; לֹא תְנוּפָה וְלֹא הַגָּשָׁה. אֵלּוּ טְעוּנוֹת הַגָּשָׁה וְאֵינָן טְעוּנוֹת תְּנוּפָה: מִנְחַת הַסֹּלֶת, וְהַמַּחֲבַת, וְהַמַּרְחֶשֶׁת, וְהַחַלּוֹת, וְהָרְקִיקִין, מִנְחַת כֹּהֲנִים, מִנְחַת כֹּהֵן מָשִׁיחַ,

**ר' עובדיה מברטנורא**

ה,יא) שלא ישים עליה שמן, שלא הזהירה תורה אלא שלא יתן השמן לתוך הסולת או לתוך הקמח: (ה) **טעונות הגשה.** בחודה של קרן דרומית מערבית, כדכתיב (ויקרא ב,ח) והגישה אל המזבח: **והחלות והרקיקין.** מנחת מאפה תנור: **מנחת כהנים.** שהיא כולה כליל:

**יד אברהם**

injunction that states, *And do not place on it oil,* because that refers only to actually adding oil to the flour [not merely *placing* it in a vessel on the *minchah*][1] (*Rav*).

The mishnah's last phrase, *he does not invalidate it,* in contrast with the previous phrase, *he does not transgress,* would seem to indicate that though he does not invalidate the *minchah* by putting a vessel of oil on top of it, it is nevertheless forbidden. *Rambam* (*Maaseh HaKorbanos* 12:8) states clearly, however, that he neither invalidates nor transgresses by placing the oil or the *minchah* in a vessel. The reason for the mishnah's change of language therefore remains unclear (*Lechem Mishneh* ad loc.; cf. *Rashash*).

## 5.

The following two mishnayos provide a discussion of the procedures of הַגָּשָׁה, *hagashah* (bringing near), and תְּנוּפָה, *tenufah* (waving).

*Hagashah*, which translates as *bringing near*, is a procedure performed on the *minchah* prior to *kemitzah.* It involves taking the *kli shareis* containing the entire *minchah* and *bringing it near*, i.e., touching it, to the southwestern corner of the Altar (*Zevachim* 6:2; see comm. there). This requirement is derived from the verse stated in connection with the *minchas machavas* [griddle *minchah*] (*Lev.* 2:8): וְהֵבֵאתָ אֶת הַמִּנְחָה אֲשֶׁר יֵעָשֶׂה מֵאֵלֶּה לַה׳, וְהִקְרִיבָהּ אֶל הַכֹּהֵן וְהִגִּישָׁהּ אֶל הַמִּזְבֵּחַ, *And you shall bring the minchah-offering which will be made from these to HASHEM, and he shall bring it to the Kohen, and he shall bring it close to the Altar.* Nothing is actually done at this point to the *minchah* itself; it is merely brought to the corner of the Altar.

The procedure of *tenufah*, waving, will be described in the following mishnah.

1. *Rashash* suggests a novel interpretation of the mishnah's seemingly unusual phrase *in a vessel on top of a vessel* [which apparently is not interpreted literally but means simply that he placed the oil in a vessel on top of the *minchah,* as explained]. He construes the wording in the sense of *either or;* i.e., *if he places the oil* either *in a vessel* or *on a vessel* (meaning not on the *minchah* but rather on the vessel of the *minchah*), it is not invalid. *Rashash* concedes, however, that *Rambam Comm.* does not seem to support this interpretation.

5
5 **5.** There are [*minchah*-offerings] that require bringing near but do not require waving; waving but not bringing near; bringing near and waving; neither waving nor bringing near. The following require bringing near but do not require waving: the *minchah*-offering of fine flour, the *machavas*, the *marcheshes*, the *challos*, the *rekikin*, the *minchah*-offering of *Kohanim*, the *minchah*-offering of the Anointed *Kohen*,

### YAD AVRAHAM

יֵשׁ טְעוּנוֹת הַגָּשָׁה וְאֵינָן טְעוּנוֹת תְּנוּפָה; — *There are [minchah-offerings] that require bringing near but do not require waving;*

Some *menachos* require the procedure of *hagashah*, i.e., bringing the offering to the southwestern corner of the Altar (*Rav*), but do not require the procedure of *tenufah*, which involves "waving" the offering in the manner prescribed in the next mishnah.

תְּנוּפָה וְלֹא הַגָּשָׁה; הַגָּשָׁה וּתְנוּפָה; לֹא תְנוּפָה וְלֹא הַגָּשָׁה. — *waving but not bringing near; bringing near and waving; neither waving nor bringing near.*

[I.e., some offerings require one of the above-mentioned procedures, some both and some neither.]

אֵלּוּ טְעוּנוֹת הַגָּשָׁה וְאֵינָן טְעוּנוֹת תְּנוּפָה: — *The following require bringing near but do not require waving:*

In contrast to mishnah 3, which first mentions the offerings which require both items mentioned there [the oil and the *levonah*], this mishnah begins by first mentioning those which require only one of the items under discussion — *hagashah*. This is because the *Tanna* wishes to begin with the laws of the voluntary *menachos*, just as he did in the previous mishnah (*Ri Migash*, cited by *Meleches Shlomo;* cf. *Tif. Yis.* #28).

מִנְחַת הַסֹּלֶת, וְהַמַּחֲבַת, וְהַמַּרְחֶשֶׁת, וְהַחַלּוֹת, וְהָרְקִיקִין, — *the minchah-offering of fine flour, the machavas, the marcheshes, the challos, the rekikin,*

All these require *hagashah*, i.e., must be brought to the corner of the Altar before their *kemitzah*. Although the verse requiring *hagashah* is stated specifically only in connection with the *minchas machavas*, the phrase אֲשֶׁר יֵעָשֶׂה מֵאֵלֶּה, *which will be made from these*, indicates that all the *menachos* under discussion in that passage, i.e., the *menachos* listed here, are included (*Tos.* 60a, s.v. מנחת חוטא). [The *tenufah* rite, however, is not stated in regard to these *menachos* and there is no indication that they require it.]

מִנְחַת כֹּהֲנִים, מִנְחַת כֹּהֵן מָשִׁיחַ, — *the minchah-offering of Kohanim, the minchah-offering of the Anointed Kohen,*

[They are included in the *hagashah* requirement by virtue of the verse (*Lev.* 6:7): זֹאת תּוֹרַת הַמִּנְחָה הַקְרֵב אֹתָהּ בְּנֵי אַהֲרֹן לִפְנֵי ה׳ אֶל פְּנֵי הַמִּזְבֵּחַ, *This is the law of the minchah-offering: The children of Aharon must bring it close before* HASHEM *to the face of the Altar* (see below; s.v. רבי שמעון אומר).]

מִנְחַת גּוֹיִם, מִנְחַת נָשִׁים, מִנְחַת חוֹטֵא. רַבִּי שִׁמְעוֹן אוֹמֵר: מִנְחַת כֹּהֲנִים, מִנְחַת כֹּהֵן מָשִׁיחַ אֵין בָּהֶן הַגָּשָׁה, מִפְּנֵי שֶׁאֵין בָּהֶן קְמִיצָה; וְכָל שֶׁאֵין בָּהֶן קְמִיצָה אֵין בָּהֶן הַגָּשָׁה.

[ו] **אֵלּוּ** טְעוּנִין תְּנוּפָה וְאֵין טְעוּנִין הַגָּשָׁה: לֹג שֶׁמֶן שֶׁל מְצֹרָע וַאֲשָׁמוֹ, וְהַבִּכּוּרִים כְּדִבְרֵי רַבִּי אֱלִיעֶזֶר בֶּן יַעֲקֹב,

ר׳ עובדיה מברטנורא

**וכל שאין בהם קמיצה.** להתיר השירים מן המנחה לכהנים, אין בהן הגשה. ואין הלכה כרבי שמעון: (ו) **לוג ואשם מצורע.** כתיב בהו (שם יד,יב) והניף: **והבכורים כדברי רבי אליעזר בן יעקב.** גרסינן. כלומר, דשמעינן ליה בעלמא דאמר בכורים טעונים תנופה והלכה כמותו:

יד אברהם

מִנְחַת גּוֹיִם, מִנְחַת נָשִׁים, — *the minchah-offering of gentiles, the minchah-offering of women,*

[A gentile or a woman who brings any of the voluntary *menachos* listed above must also have his/her *minchah* brought close to the Altar (see comm. to mishnah 3).]

מִנְחַת חוֹטֵא. — *[and] the sinner's minchah-offering.*

The *hagashah* requirement for this type of *minchah* is derived by Biblical exegesis; see *Gem.* 60a.

רַבִּי שִׁמְעוֹן אוֹמֵר: מִנְחַת כֹּהֲנִים, מִנְחַת כֹּהֵן מָשִׁיחַ אֵין בָּהֶן הַגָּשָׁה, מִפְּנֵי שֶׁאֵין בָּהֶן קְמִיצָה; וְכָל שֶׁאֵין בָּהֶן קְמִיצָה אֵין בָּהֶן הַגָּשָׁה. — *R' Shimon says: The minchah-offering of Kohanim [and] the minchah-offering of the Anointed Kohen do not require being brought near, because they do not require kemitzah; and anything which does not require kemitzah does not require being brought near.*

Any *minchah* which does not undergo the *avodah* of *kemitzah* to render the remainder of the *minchah* permissible to *Kohanim* does not require the *hagashah* rite (*Rav*).

Through an exegesis of the words of the passage discussing the *hagashah* procedure, R' Shimon concludes that any *minchah* which does not have a remainder permitted to *Kohanim* is not included in the Torah's obligation for *hagashah* (see *Gemara* 61a).

According to the exegesis provided by the *Gemara*, the criterion for the *hagashah* requirement is not *kemitzah* per se; it is the permissibility of the remainder to *Kohanim*. Hence the sinner's *minchah* of a *Kohen* which, according to R' Shimon, requires *kemitzah* (see 6:1), still does not require *hagashah* [because the remainder cannot be eaten] (*Shitah Mekubetzes* 61a #11, cf. *Tos.*).[1]

1. *Rav's* description in our mishnah of *kemitzah* as *the act which renders the remainder permissible to the Kohanim* hardly seems necessary at this point in the tractate. However, in light of *Shitah's* explanation, it seems likely that *Rav* wished to emphasize that it is the permissibility to the *Kohanim* which is important to R' Shimon, not the *kemitzah* in itself.

5
6

the *minchah*-offering of gentiles, the *minchah*-offering of women, [and] the sinner's *minchah*-offering. R' Shimon says: The *minchah*-offering of *Kohanim* [and] the *minchah*-offering of the Anointed *Kohen* do not require being brought near, because they do not require *kemitzah*; and anything which does not require *kemitzah* does not require being brought near.

**6.** The following require waving but not bringing near: the *log* of oil of the *metzora* and his *asham*-offering, the *bikkurim* according to R' Eliezer ben Yaakov,

## YAD AVRAHAM

## 6.

אֵלּוּ טְעוּנִין תְּנוּפָה וְאֵין טְעוּנִין הַגָּשָׁה: — *The following require waving but not bringing near:*

[The following offerings must undergo *tenufah* (waving) prior to being offered on the Altar, but not *hagashah* (being brought near to the Altar).]

לֹג שֶׁמֶן שֶׁל מְצֹרָע — *the log of oil of the metzora*

This is the oil which a *metzora* brings as part of his purification process. [A *metzora* is a person afflicted with one of a variety of skin afflictions and discolorations which render him *tamei* (see *Lev.* Ch. 13); this is generally, but probably inaccurately, translated as *leper*.] The *Kohen* sprinkles the oil seven times toward the Sanctuary and then places some on the right thumb, large toe, and ear of the *metzora* (*Tif. Yis.* from *Lev.* Ch. 14).

וַאֲשָׁמוֹ, — *and his asham-offering,*

I.e., the *asham*-offering which is brought by the *metzora* as part of the purification process requires *tenufah* (*Lev.* 14:12). [No animal offering, however, requires *hagashah*, which is a procedure reserved only for *menachos*.]

וְהַבִּכּוּרִים כְּדִבְרֵי רַבִּי אֱלִיעֶזֶר בֶּן יַעֲקֹב, — *the bikkurim according to R' Eliezer ben Yaakov,*

*Bikkurim* are the first fruits of one's crops, which one must bring to the Temple. The owner reads a specified passage and presents the fruits to the *Kohen* (*Deut.* Ch. 26).

From the passage concerning *bikkurim*, R' Eliezer ben Yaakov derives exegetically that they are compared to a *shelamim*-offering and thus require *tenufah* [but not *hagashah*] (*Gem.* 61a).

Actually, there is another *Tanna* who arrives at the same conclusion from a different verse, but the mishnah chose to cite R' Eliezer because of the high esteem in which his words were regarded (*Gem.* 61b).

מנחות ה/ו

# וְאֵמוּרֵי שַׁלְמֵי יָחִיד וְחָזֶה וְשׁוֹק שֶׁלָּהֶן — אֶחָד אֲנָשִׁים וְאֶחָד נָשִׁים; בְּיִשְׂרָאֵל, אֲבָל לֹא בַאֲחֵרִים; וּשְׁתֵּי הַלֶּחֶם וּשְׁנֵי כִבְשֵׂי עֲצֶרֶת. כֵּיצַד הוּא עוֹשֶׂה?

### ר׳ עובדיה מברטנורא

**ואמורי שלמי יחיד וחזה ושוק שלהן.** בהדיא כתיב בהו (ויקרא י,טו) שוק התרומה וחזה התנופה על אשי החלבים יביאו להניף: **אחד שלמי אנשים ואחד שלמי נשים.** טעונים תנופה, בישראל אבל לא באחרים, מפרש בגמרא (סא,ב) דהכי קאמר, אחד אנשים ואחד נשים קרבנן טעון תנופה, ותנופה עצמה בישראל, אבל לא בידי נשים, דהכי תניא, בני ישראל מניפין ואין הגוים מניפין, בני ישראל מניפין ולא בנות ישראל מניפות: **שתי הלחם וכבשי שלמים של עצרת.** הבאים בגלל הלחם. כתיב בהו (שם כג,כ) והניף הכהן אותם על לחם הבכורים, ולא על ממש, אלא סמוך להם, כבשים בצד הלחם, כדברי רבי בברייתא. וכן הלכה:

### יד אברהם

וְאֵמוּרֵי שַׁלְמֵי יָחִיד — *the sacrificial parts of an individual's shelamim-offering*

The term אֵמוּרִין [*emurin*] refers to the sacrificial parts of an animal offering (*Tif. Yis.*). The requirement of *tenufah* for the *emurin* of a *shelamim-offering* is stated explicitly in *Lev.* 10:15.

— וְחָזֶה וְשׁוֹק שֶׁלָּהֶן — *and its breast and thigh [portions]* —

Although the meat of a *shelamim* is eaten by the owner of the offering, the Torah stipulates that the thigh and breast be given to the *Kohen* to eat (*Lev.* 7:30-34). Their waving is mandated explicitly in the Torah (*Lev.* 10:15).

In view of the fact that the breast and thigh of the communal *shelamim*-offering of Shavuos also require *tenufah*, as stated below (mishnah 7), it is unclear why the mishnah specifies only the *shelamim* of an individual. [Although the mishnah does state below that the *shelamim* of Shavuos require *tenufah* along with the *shtei halechem*, this would seem to refer to the *tenufah* performed on them while they are still alive, since the *tenufah* is mentioned as taking place together with the *shtei halechem*. As mishnah 7 will teach, the *shelamim* lambs of Shavuos undergo *tenufah* twice: once before they are slaughtered, and then again the breast and thigh after the slaughter.]

However, according to the view of *Rambam* (*Hil. Temidin Umussafin* 8:11), that the *tenufah* of the breast and thigh parts of the communal *shelamim* was also performed together with the *shtei halechem* loaves, it can be reasoned that both *tenufah* requirements for this offering are included in the mishnah's mention below of the *tenufah* requirement for the *shtei halechem and two lambs of Shavuos* (*Rashash*).[1] [However, it is not at all clear that *Rambam's* view on this matter is universally accepted. Indeed, the source for this ruling

1. The *Brisker Rav* (*R' Y.Z. Soloveitchik*) explains that there is a basic difference between the *tenufah of the* individual *shelamim* and that of the communal *shelamim* brought on Shavuos. The *tenufah* of the individual *shelamim* is a function of the sacrifice itself. The *tenufah* of the communal *shelamim*, on the other hand, is part of the Festival obligation to bring the *shtei halechem* (many of the differences in the *tenufah* of the two offerings can be explained in the light of this analytical distinction; see below). Thus, the mishnah omits the communal *shelamim* from the list of offerings that require *tenufah*, since only the *tenufah* that is the function of the offering is mentioned (*Chidushei HaGriz, Maaseh HaKorbanos* 9:3).

5
6 the sacrificial parts of an individual's *shelamim*-offering and its breast and thigh [portions] — both [of] men and [of] women; of [male] *Yisraelim,* but not of others; the *shtei halechem* and the two lambs of Shavuos. How does he do [it]?

YAD AVRAHAM

that the post-slaughter *tenufah* is also done together with the *shtei halechem* is not explicit. This will be discussed further in mishnah 7, s.v. ושחוטים.]

Alternatively, one can reason that the mishnah mentions the *shelamim*-offering of an individual because that is the source of the requirement for the other *shelamim*-offering as well, as explained by the *Gemara* (62a) (*Zevach Todah*).

אֶחָד אֲנָשִׁים וְאֶחָד נָשִׁים; — *both [of] men and [of] women;*

The *shelamim*-offerings of both men and women require *tenufah* (*Rav*).

בְּיִשְׂרָאֵל, אֲבָל לֹא בַאֲחֵרִים; — *of [male] Yisraelim, but not of others;*

I.e., although all the above-mentioned offerings require *tenufah*, the actual *tenufah* is performed only by male Jews, not by women or by gentiles (*Rav; Tif. Yis.* from *Gem.* 61b).

The process of *tenufah* requires the *Kohen* to place his hand under those of the owner of the offering and for them to wave it together. However, this applies only to the offering of a male *Yisrael;* that of a woman or of a gentile is waved solely by the *Kohen*. This is derived from the opening phrase of the Torah's passage describing *tenufah* (*Lev.* 7:29): דַּבֵּר אֶל בְּנֵי יִשְׂרָאֵל, *speak to the children* [lit., *sons*] *of Israel*, from which the *Gemara* deduces that it is done by *the sons of Israel* but not the daughters; *the sons of Israel* but not by gentiles (*Rav* from *Gem.* 61b according to *Rashi's* version; *Tif. Yis.*).

According to other versions of the *Gemara*, the offering of a gentile is not waved at all. The gentile's *shelamim*-offering is distinct in the fact that it is not eaten by its owner but entirely by *Kohanim*. Thus, it is distinguished by the absence of *tenufah* as well (*Tos.*, s.v. בשחיטה; *Shitah Mekubetzes* #2).[1]

וּשְׁתֵּי הַלֶּחֶם וּשְׁנֵי כִּבְשֵׂי עֲצֶרֶת. — *the shtei halechem and the two lambs of Shavuos.*

The *shtei halechem* loaves of Shavuos and the two *shelamim* lambs that accompany them as a sacrifice (see preface to mishnah 2:2, comm. to 4:2) require *tenufah*, as stated explicitly in the Torah (*Lev.* 23:20).

The loaves, however, are excluded from the *hagashah* procedure, as shown by the *Gemara* (60b; see comm. to mishnah 5, s.v. רבי שמעון אומר; *Shitah Mekubetzes* to 60a #3).

כֵּיצַד הוּא עוֹשֶׂה? — *How does he do [it]?*

[What is the process for waving the *shtei halechem* and two lambs?]

1. As noted above, there is a dispute (*Gem.* 73b, *Yevamos* 74a) whether a gentile can offer a *shelamim* altogether. However, all are in agreement that a gentile may not eat his *shelamim*-offering; it is eaten by Jews (*Shitah Mekubetzes* ibid.). Our mishnah's exclusion of a gentile from the *tenufah* apparently assumes that a gentile may bring a *shelamim*-offering. However, the halachah follows the view that a gentile may not bring a *shelamim*-offering, only an *olah*, so that the discussion of the *tenufah* is moot (*Tos.; Zevach Todah*).

נוֹתֵן שְׁתֵּי הַלֶּחֶם עַל גַּבֵּי שְׁנֵי כְבָשִׂים וּמַנִּיחַ שְׁתֵּי יָדָיו מִלְּמַטָּן. מוֹלִיךְ וּמֵבִיא; מַעֲלֶה וּמוֹרִיד; שֶׁנֶּאֱמַר: ,,אֲשֶׁר הוּנַף וַאֲשֶׁר הוּרָם". תְּנוּפָה הָיְתָה בַּמִּזְרָח וְהַגָּשָׁה בַּמַּעֲרָב, וּתְנוּפוֹת קוֹדְמוֹת לְהַגָּשׁוֹת. מִנְחַת הָעֹמֶר וּמִנְחַת קְנָאוֹת טְעוּנוֹת תְּנוּפָה וְהַגָּשָׁה.

### ר' עובדיה מברטנורא

**שנאמר.** [במלואים] (שמות כט,כז) אשר הונף ואשר הורם, ומהונף והורם דמלואים ילפינן אשר תנופות. תנופה, מוליך ומביא. תרומה, מעלה ומוריד: **תנופה היתה במזרח.** כלומר, אף במזרח של מזבח יכול להניף, וכל שכן במערבו דקרוב יותר להיכל: **ותנופות קודמות להגשות.** בתחלה מניף ואחר כך מגיש, ובמנחת העומר ובמנחת קנאות איירי דטעונות תנופה והגשה, וכתיב במנחת קנאות (במדבר ה,כה) והניף את המנחה לפני ה', והדר והקריב אותה אל המזבח:

### יד אברהם

נוֹתֵן שְׁתֵּי הַלֶּחֶם עַל גַּבֵּי שְׁנֵי כְבָשִׂים — *He puts the shtei halechem on top of the two lambs*

The *Gemara* explains that he actually places the loaves and [live] lambs next to — rather than on top of — each other (*Rav* from *Gem.* 62a).

וּמַנִּיחַ שְׁתֵּי יָדָיו מִלְּמַטָּן. מוֹלִיךְ וּמֵבִיא; — *and places his two hands beneath them. He extends and brings;*

With his hands beneath them, he waves them toward the east, the south, the west, and the north (*Tif. Yis.*).

מַעֲלֶה וּמוֹרִיד; — *raises and lowers;*

I.e., he also raises it upward and lowers it in a downward motion. The *Gemara* (62a) explains the significance of this procedure as follows. "He extends them to the four directions [to offer them] to the Master of all four directions [of the world]. He lifts and lowers them to the Master of heaven and earth." In an additional explanation provided by the *Gemara* (ibid.), he waves them to the four directions [as a supplication] to ward off harmful winds, and he lifts and lowers them to prevent damaging dew (*Gem.* 62a).

*Tosafos* (62a, s.v. כדי לעצור) suggest that according to this latter reason it may be that the elaborate *tenufah* described here was performed only in the case of the Shavuos offering [and not for the other offerings requiring *tenufah*], because it is on Shavuos that the Almighty decrees the fate of that year's fruits (*Rosh Hashanah* 16a) [which would be adversely affected by the harmful winds and dew].[1]

שֶׁנֶּאֱמַר: ,,אֲשֶׁר הוּנַף וַאֲשֶׁר הוּרָם". — *as it says (Ex. 29:27): "Which was waved and which was raised."*

This description of the *tenufah* procedure [written in connection with

1. The *Gemara* (*Succah* 37b) applies the motions of the *tenufah* to the *mitzvah* of *lulav*. This procedure is called נַעֲנוּעִים, *waving* (see *Tos.* 62a s.v. כדי and *Yad Avraham* comm. to *Succah* 3:9, footnote 1, for a detailed description of this rite). There is a custom that while saying the word אֶחָד in the daily *Shema Yisrael*, one moves one's head in the directions of *tenufah* to demonstrate *Hashem's* complete mastery of the world (*Orach Chaim* 61:6; see *Meiri, Succah* ad loc.).

5 He puts the *shtei halechem* on top of the two lambs
6 and places his two hands beneath them. He extends
and brings; raises and lowers; as it says (*Ex.* 29:27):
*Which was waved and which was raised.* Waving
was [done] in the east and bringing near in the
west, and the wavings precede bringing near. The
*minchah* of the *omer* and the jealousy *minchah*-
offering require waving and bringing near.

### YAD AVRAHAM

the מִלּוּאִים, *initiation rites*, of Aaron and his sons at the time of the inauguration of the *Mishkan* (Tabernacle)] indicates two aspects to the *tenufah*: a waving motion (in all four directions), and a raising and lowering motion.

The *tenufah* procedure for the other offerings is derived from the above Scriptural source (*Rav*).

תְּנוּפָה הָיְתָה בַּמִּזְרָח — *Waving was [done] in the east*

That is, *tenufah* could be performed for offerings even on the eastern side of the Altar and certainly on the western side, which is closer to the Sanctuary (*Rav; Rashi*).

*Rambam* (*Hil. Maaseh HaKorbanos* 9:6), however, interprets the mishnah to mean that *tenufah* could be done only on the eastern side of the Altar (see *Kesef Mishneh; Zevach Todah*).

וְהַגָּשָׁה בַּמַּעֲרָב, — *and bringing near in the west,*

The rite of *hagashah*, bringing the *minchah* near the Altar, requires that the offering be brought close to the southwest side of the Altar, as derived from the verse (*Lev.* 6:7): הַקְרֵב אֹתָהּ בְּנֵי אַהֲרֹן לִפְנֵי ה׳ אֶל פְּנֵי הַמִּזְבֵּחַ, *The sons of Aaron shall bring it near before HASHEM, to the front of the Altar*. The phrase *before HASHEM* refers to the western side, which faces the Holy of Holies in which the *Shechinah* is present. The words *to the front of the Altar* are understood to mean its southern side, where the ramp leading to the top of the Altar is located. To satisfy both these conditions, the offering is brought close to the southwestern corner of the Altar (*Gem.* 19a).

וּתְנוּפוֹת קוֹדְמוֹת לְהַגָּשׁוֹת. — *and the wavings precede bringing near.*

In the case of the *minchas omer* and the jealousy *minchah* — which require both *tenufah* and *hagashah* — *tenufah* is performed before *hagashah*. Concerning the jealousy *minchah*, the Torah states explicitly (*Num.* 5:25) that he must first perform the *tenufah* and then perform the *hagashah* (*Rav*). [The order of the procedures of the *omer minchah* is derived from that of the jealousy *minchah*.

מִנְחַת הָעֹמֶר וּמִנְחַת קְנָאוֹת טְעוּנוֹת תְּנוּפָה וְהַגָּשָׁה. — *The minchah of the omer and the jealousy minchah-offering require waving and bringing near.*

The *tenufah* requirement is stated explicitly in regard to the *omer* (*Lev.* 23:11), and the *hagashah* requirement is derived through Biblical exegesis (*Gem.* 60b). In the case of the jealousy *minchah*, the requirement for both procedures is stated explicitly (*Numbers* 5:25).

לֶחֶם הַפָּנִים וּמִנְחַת נְסָכִים, לֹא תְנוּפָה וְלֹא הַגָּשָׁה.

[ז] **רַבִּי** שִׁמְעוֹן אוֹמֵר: שְׁלֹשָׁה מִינִים טְעוּנִים שָׁלֹשׁ מִצְוֹת — שְׁתַּיִם בְּכָל אַחַת וְאַחַת, וְהַשְּׁלִישִׁית אֵין בָּהֶן. וְאֵלּוּ הֵן: זִבְחֵי שַׁלְמֵי יָחִיד, וְזִבְחֵי שַׁלְמֵי צִבּוּר, וַאֲשַׁם מְצֹרָע. זִבְחֵי שַׁלְמֵי יָחִיד טְעוּנִים סְמִיכָה חַיִּים וּתְנוּפָה שְׁחוּטִים — וְאֵין בָּהֶם תְּנוּפָה חַיִּים. זִבְחֵי שַׁלְמֵי צִבּוּר טְעוּנִים תְּנוּפָה חַיִּים

**ר׳ עובדיה מברטנורא**

(ז) **שלשה מינין.** שלמי יחיד, ושלמי צבור שהם כבשי עצרת, ואשם מצורע, שלשה מינים הללו טעונים בין שלשתן שלש מצות, סמיכה, תנופה חיים, תנופה שחוטים: **שתים.** מצות מן השלש יש בכל מין ומין, והשלישית אין בהם, דאין בכל מין אלא שתים: **שלמי יחיד.** כתיב בהו סמיכה בויקרא: **ותנופה שחוטים.** בחזה ושוק שלהן, בלו את אהרן: **שלמי צבור.** כתיב בהו תנופה חיים, והניף הכהן אותם (ויקרא כג,כ), דהיינו חיים, ותנופה שחוטים, בחזה ושוק שלהן, דילפי (מקדשי) [צ״ל משלמי] יחיד, אבל סמיכה לא בעו, דהלכתא גמירי לה דאין בכל קרבנות צבור אלא שתי סמיכות בלבד, סמיכה של שעיר המשתלח ושל פר העלם דבר של צבור:

**יד אברהם**

לֶחֶם הַפָּנִים וּמִנְחַת נְסָכִים, לֹא תְנוּפָה וְלֹא הַגָּשָׁה. — *[But] the lechem hapanim and the minchah-offering of libations [require] neither waving nor bringing near.*

They are excluded from *hagashah* by Biblical exegesis, as shown by the *Gemara* (60b). Neither do they require *tenufah*, because there is no Biblical reference to indicate such a requirement.

## 7.

The next mishnah compares the procedures of *tenufah* and *semichah*. *Semichah* is a procedure common to many animal sacrifices in which the owner places his hands on the animal's head and leans on it with his full weight.

*Tenufah* takes two forms: raising and waving an animal sacrifice while it is still alive, and doing the same to the slaughtered sacrifice. Thus, the mishnah actually discusses three procedures: *tenufah* on a living animal; *tenufah* on a slaughtered animal; and *semichah*.

Although the mishnah's rule is stated by R' Shimon it is not disputed by any *Tanna* (*Rambam Comm.*).

רַבִּי שִׁמְעוֹן אוֹמֵר: שְׁלֹשָׁה מִינִים טְעוּנִים שָׁלֹשׁ מִצְוֹת — *R' Shimon says: There are three types [of offerings], which [between them] require three procedures:*

The three types of offerings listed below require between them a total of three procedures (*Rav*) [besides the essential four *avodos* of an offering].

5
7 [But] the *lechem hapanim* and the *minchah*-offering of libations [require] neither waving nor bringing near.

**7.** R' Shimon says: There are three types [of offerings], which [between them] require three procedures: two for each one, but not the third. They are: the individual's *shelamim*-offerings, communal *shelamim*-offerings, and the *asham*-offering of the *metzora*. The individual's *shelamim*-offerings require leaning while living and waving when slaughtered — but they do not require waving while living. Communal *shelamim*-offerings require waving while living

YAD AVRAHAM

שְׁתַּיִם בְּכָל אַחַת וְאַחַת, וְהַשְּׁלִישִׁית אֵין בָּהֶן. — *two for each one, but not the third.*

Each of these three offerings requires two of the three procedures listed. None of them, however, requires all three (*Rav*).

וְאֵלּוּ הֵן: זִבְחֵי שַׁלְמֵי יָחִיד, וְזִבְחֵי שַׁלְמֵי צִבּוּר, וַאֲשַׁם מְצֹרָע. — *They are: the individual's shelamim-offerings, communal shelamim-offerings, and the asham-offering of the metzora.*

[The three types of offerings subject to this rule are the *shelamim* brought by an individual, the communal *shelamim*, and the *asham* brought by a *metzora* as part of his purification process (see comm. to mishnah 6, s.v. לוג שמן and s.v. ואשמו).]

The only instance of a communal *shelamim*-offering is that which is brought together with the *shtei halechem* on Shavuos (*Rav*).

זִבְחֵי שַׁלְמֵי יָחִיד טְעוּנִים סְמִיכָה חַיִּים — *The individual's shelamim-offerings require leaning while living*

*Semichah* (leaning) must be performed by the owner on his *shelamim*-offering prior to slaughter, as stated explicitly in the Torah (*Lev.* 3:2): וְסָמַךְ יָדוֹ עַל רֹאשׁ קָרְבָּנוֹ וּשְׁחָטוֹ, *and he shall lean his hand on the head of his offering and [then] slaughter it.*

וּתְנוּפָה שְׁחוּטִים — *and waving when slaughtered —*

The Torah requires the sacrificial parts and the breast and thigh parts of the *shelamim*-offering to be waved, as explained in the previous mishnah. This obviously takes place after the animal is slaughtered (*Tif. Yis.*).

וְאֵין בָּהֶם תְּנוּפָה חַיִּים. — *but they do not require waving while living.*

The verse which requires the *tenufah* of the Shavuos sacrifice while living (see below) states (*Lev.* 23:20): וְהֵנִיף הַכֹּהֵן אֹתָם, *And the Kohen shall wave them.* The word *them* is restrictive and is interpreted to exclude the individual's *shelamim*-offering (*Gem.* 62b).

זִבְחֵי שַׁלְמֵי צִבּוּר טְעוּנִים תְּנוּפָה חַיִּים — *Communal shelamim-offerings require waving while living*

The Torah states explicitly ... וְהֵנִיף אֹתָם, *he shall wave them* [the two

מנחות ה/ח

וּשְׁחוּטִים — וְאֵין בָּהֶן סְמִיכָה. וַאֲשַׁם מְצֹרָע טָעוּן סְמִיכָה וּתְנוּפָה חַי — וְאֵין בּוֹ תְּנוּפָה שָׁחוּט.

[ח] **הָאוֹמֵר:** הֲרֵי עָלַי בְּמַחֲבַת, לֹא יָבִיא בְּמַרְחֶשֶׁת. בְּמַרְחֶשֶׁת, לֹא יָבִיא

**ר' עובדיה מברטנורא**

**אשם מצורע.** כתיב ביה תנופה חי, כדכתיב (שם) והניף הכהן אותם, בפרשת זאת תהיה. וסמיכה, דאי אפשר לקרבן יחיד שלא יסמוך ידו על ראש קרבנו: **אבל לא תנופה שחוט.** דמיעט רחמנא גבי שלמי יחיד (ויקרא ז,ל) את החזה להניף אותו, אותו, למעוטי אשם של מצורע שאינו טעון תנופה שחוט:

**יד אברהם**

lambs brought with the *shtei halechem*], indicating that the lambs are waved in their entirety, i.e., prior to being slaughtered (*Rav* from *Lev.* 23:20; see *Rashi* ad loc.).

— וּשְׁחוּטִים — *and when slaughtered* —

The requirement for *tenufah* of the slaughtered sacrifice is derived from that of the individual's *shelamim*-offering (*Rav* from *Gem.* 62a). Thus, the *shelamim* lambs undergo *tenufah* twice: once before being slaughtered and again afterward.

There is a dispute among the *Tannaim* whether the *tenufah* done after the slaughter is performed with the entire carcass of the lambs — just like the *tenufah* performed on them while they were still alive, or whether only the breast and thigh parts are waved — like the individual's *shelamim*-offering from which this is derived.

*Rambam* (*Hil. Temidin U'Mussafin* 8:11) [as well as *Rav*] rules in accordance with the latter view, as indicated by the fact that he mentions only that the breast and thigh of the communal *shelamim* are waved after slaughter (*Rashash*). Others contend that in addition to the breast and thigh parts, the *emurin* are also waved, just as with the individual's *shelamim* (*Rabbeinu Gershom* to *Gem.* 62a).

*Rambam* (there) also mentions that the breast and thigh of the slaughtered communal *shelamim*-offering are waved together with the loaves of the *shtei halechem*. Although the derivation for *tenufah* cited above is only in regard to the *tenufah* which is done while the animal is still alive, since the *tenufah* which is performed after it has been slaughtered is derived from the *tenufah* of the living offering, it is presumed to have the same requirement (*Lechem Mishneh*).[1]

.וְאֵין בָּהֶן סְמִיכָה — *but they do not require leaning.*

This is known from an Oral Tradition received by Moshe at Sinai, that communal offerings do not require *semichah* (*Rav* from *Gem.* 62b), with

1. *Lechem Mishneh* assumes that *Rambam* requires that both *tenufos* of the lambs be performed together with the *shtei halechem* loaves. However, *Rambam* does not clearly say so, and the *Brisker Rav* (to *Maaseh HaKorbanos* 9:3, cited in the fn. to mishnah 6) argues that according to *Rambam* the loaves are waved only together with the slaughtered *shelamim*; the *tenufah* performed with the living animals is done without the loaves. This, he agrees, is disputed by *Rashi* (62a, s.v. בין ירכותיהן), who makes it clear that the *shtei halechem* loaves are waved with the living animals as well (see there at length).

5 and when slaughtered — but they do not require lean-
8 ing. The *asham*-offering of the *metzora* requires leaning and waving while living — but it does not require waving when slaughtered.

**8.** One who says, "I take upon myself [to bring] in a *machavas*," may not bring [it] in a *marcheshes*. [If he says,] "in a *marcheshes*," he may not bring [it]



the exception of two: the *par he'elem davar* [the bull brought for communal error], and the he-goat of *Azazel* [the scapegoat which is sent to be hurled from a cliff on Yom Kippur] (*Rashi*).

וַאֲשַׁם מְצֹרָע טָעוּן סְמִיכָה — *The asham-offering of the metzora requires leaning*

This is part of the general rule for all offerings by an individual (*Rav;* see 9:7).

וּתְנוּפָה חַי — — *and waving while living —*

Regarding this offering, the Torah states clearly (*Lev.* 14:12,13): וְהֵנִיף אֹתָם תְּנוּפָה לִפְנֵי ה׳ וְשָׁחַט ..., *and he shall wave it as a tenufah before* HASHEM, *and he shall slaughter ...*, indicating that the *tenufah* is done before the slaughtering (*Rav*).

וְאֵין בּוֹ תְּנוּפָה שָׁחוּט. — *but it does not require waving when slaughtered.*

This is deduced by Biblical exegesis from the Torah's statement concerning the *shelamim*-offering of an individual (*Lev.* 7:30): לְהָנִיף אֹתוֹ, *to wave it — it* and not the *asham*-offering of a *metzora* (*Rav* from *Gem.* 62b).

## 8.

The following mishnah discusses the distinctions between the *minchas machavas* and the *minchas marcheshes*. The *machavas* and the *marcheshes* were different utensils used to prepare the *minchah*. Precisely what distinguishes the *machavas* from the *marcheshes* is the subject of a dispute that follows.

הָאוֹמֵר: הֲרֵי עָלַי בְּמַחֲבַת, לֹא יָבִיא בְּמַרְחֶשֶׁת. — *One who says, "I take upon myself [to bring] in a machavas," may not bring [it] in a marcheshes.*

If someone specifically pledged to bring a *minchah* in a *machavas* (*Tif. Yis.*), he cannot fulfill his pledge by bringing a *minchah* prepared in a *marcheshes*.

בְּמַרְחֶשֶׁת, לֹא יָבִיא בְּמַחֲבַת. — *[If he says,] "in a marcheshes," he may not bring [it] in a machavas.*

[Conversely, if he pledged to bring a *minchah* made in a *marcheshes*, he cannot fulfill his pledge by bringing one prepared in a *machavas*.] Although these two *menachos* are in many respects identical, they are not interchangeable; it goes without saying that his pledge cannot be redeemed with an entirely different type of *minchah* (*Tif. Yis.*).

בְּמַחֲבַת. וּמַה בֵּין מַחֲבַת לְמַרְחֶשֶׁת? אֶלָּא שֶׁהַמַּרְחֶשֶׁת יֵשׁ לָהּ כִּסּוּי וְהַמַּחֲבַת אֵין לָהּ כִּסּוּי; דִּבְרֵי רַבִּי יוֹסֵי הַגְּלִילִי. רַבִּי חֲנַנְיָה בֶּן גַּמְלִיאֵל אוֹמֵר: מַרְחֶשֶׁת עֲמֻקָּה וּמַעֲשֶׂיהָ רוֹחֲשִׁים; וּמַחֲבַת צָפָה וּמַעֲשֶׂיהָ קָשִׁים.

## ר׳ עובדיה מברטנורא

(ח) **מרחשת עמוקה.** דכתיב (ויקרא ז,ט) וכל נעשה במרחשת, בתוכה משמע, אלמא יש לה תוך: **ומעשיה רוחשין.** שהשמן נע ונד בתוכה, לשון הרומש על הארץ, דמתרגמינן דרחיש. ויש שגורסין ומעשיה רכין, כלומר שעיסתה רכה: **ומחבת צפה.** דכתיב (שם) ועל מחבת, משמע עליה ולא בתוכה, אלמא אין לה תוך: **צפה.** שאינה עמוקה אלא שוליה צפין אצל אוגניה, כמו צף על פני המים: **ומעשיה קשים.** שהעיסה שמטגנים בה עיסתה קשה כדי שלא תשפך לחוץ, שהרי הכלי אין לו שפה:

## יד אברהם

וּמַה בֵּין מַחֲבַת לְמַרְחֶשֶׁת? אֶלָּא שֶׁהַמַּרְחֶשֶׁת יֵשׁ לָהּ כִּסּוּי וְהַמַּחֲבַת אֵין לָהּ כִּסּוּי; דִּבְרֵי רַבִּי יוֹסֵי הַגְּלִילִי. — *What is the difference between a machavas and a marcheshes? A marcheshes has a cover and a machavas does not have a cover; [these are] the words of R' Yose HaGlili.*

The tradition which R' Yose had received from his teachers (*Gem.* 63a) differentiated between the *machavas* and the *marcheshes* merely on the basis of the cover of the utensil: The *marcheshes* was a covered pan and the *machavas* was uncovered.[1]

The Torah uses slightly different wording for the *machavas* offering than for the *marcheshes*. The Torah states (*Lev.* 7:9): וְכָל נַעֲשָׂה בַמַּרְחֶשֶׁת וְעַל מַחֲבַת, *any [minchah] which is made in a marcheshes or on a machavas*, describing one as the *minchah* prepared *in* a *marcheshes* and the other as being prepared *on* a *machavas*. According to R' Yose HaGlili, the fact that the *marcheshes* was a covered pan accounts for the use of the preposition *in*, i.e., in a covered utensil; while in the case of the open *machavas* the preposition employed is *on*. The products of the *machavas* and the *marcheshes*, however, were of similar consistency (*Sfas Emes*).

רַבִּי חֲנַנְיָה בֶּן גַּמְלִיאֵל אוֹמֵר: מַרְחֶשֶׁת עֲמֻקָּה — *R' Chananyah ben Gamliel says: A marcheshes is deep*

As indicated by the verse (*Lev.* 7:9) which states: וְכָל נַעֲשָׂה בַמַּרְחֶשֶׁת, *anything made "in" a marcheshes*, indicating that it has the depth to contain something (*Rav* from *Gem.* ibid.). In contrast to R' Yose HaGlili, R' Chananyah ben Gamliel distinguishes between *machavas* and *marcheshes* on the basis of the shape of the utensil used to make it. *Marcheshes* is a utensil that has depth, i.e., a pan.

וּמַעֲשֶׂיהָ רוֹחֲשִׁים; — *and its products move around;*

The utensil used is deep and the oil collects in it. Therefore, the oil moves around in it (*Rav; Rashi* 63a), especially during the frying (*Tif. Yis.*).

Alternatively, *its products* [i.e., the dough baked in it] *quiver*, i.e., they

1. The term מַחֲבַת is thus related to the word חָבוּי, *hidden*, and חָפוּי, which means *covered*. The term is used in its reverse sense: with the cover removed [just as the phrase לְדַשֵּׁן אֶת הַמִּזְבֵּחַ means *to remove the ashes*] (*Tif. Yis.*).

in a *machavas*. What is the difference between a *machavas* and a *marcheshes*? A *marcheshes* has a cover and a *machavas* does not have a cover; [these are] the words of R' Yose HaGlili. R' Chananyah ben Gamliel says: A *marcheshes* is deep and its products move around; a *machavas* is flat and its products are hard.

**YAD AVRAHAM**

are spongy as a result of being saturated by the oil in which they are deep-fried (*Rashi* to *Lev.* 2:7).

Another version of the mishnah reads: וּמַעֲשֶׂיהָ רַכִּין, *and its product is soft* (*Rav*). I.e., its dough is prepared loosely [in a soft batter]. This is not the result of the use of a deep pan but rather the reverse: The use of such a batter is possible because the *marcheshes* has walls capable of retaining the soft batter as it bakes (*Rambam Comm.; Hil. Maaseh HaKorbanos* 13:7).

וּמַחֲבַת צָפָה — *a machavas is flat*

[I.e., a griddle,] as indicated in the verse (*Lev.* 7:9): וְעַל מַחֲבַת, *and "on" the machavas* (*Rav* from *Gem.*) [i.e., and not within it].

וּמַעֲשֶׂיהָ קָשִׁים. — *and its products are hard.*

Since the *machavas* is a flat griddle, with only a slight lip around it, its oil is burnt off during the baking. This causes the dough being baked upon it to become hard (*Rashi*).

Alternatively, since the *machavas* is a flat griddle, it cannot retain a soft batter as it bakes. Consequently, its dough must be prepared as a thick dough (*Rav; Rambam Comm., Hil. Maaseh HaKorbanos* 13:7). Thus, in *Rambam's* view, the difference between the final product of a *machavas* and that of a *marcheshes* is not the result of the type of vessel used, but rather the result of the way the dough is prepared in the first place (*Lechem Mishneh*).

The halachah follows the latter view in the mishnah (*Rambam*, loc. cit.), and it therefore does not matter whether the *minchah* is covered or not (*Likkutei Halachos*).[1]

1. [It is not explicitly stated whether the *machavas* and *marcheshes* were baked inside an oven or fried on top of a stove. Although the commentaries refer to them as אֲפוּיוֹת, *baked*, this term may be applied even to things made in a pan or griddle on top of a stove, as may be seen from *Yoreh Deah* 329:5. The halachic difference between baking and cooking (or frying) is whether the dough is "baked" by the heat of the pan or air, or whether this is accomplished through the hot liquid in which it sits (ibid. 2; *Shach* ad loc. 3; this is actually the subject of a dispute in *Yerushalmi*, cited by *Rash* in *Challah* 1:5). Thus, the halachah is that the blessing on eating a *minchah* is הַמּוֹצִיא לֶחֶם מִן הָאָרֶץ, as for bread (*Gem.* 75b). (However, see *Rash* to *Challah* 1:5 who questions whether this blessing applies to the *minchas machavas* and *marcheshes*, because they are fried in oil.)

From *Tosafos* (75b, s.v. חביצא) it is clear that these were fried; however, this too may mean inside an oven. The language of *Rashi* to *Lev.* 2:5 strongly indicates that these were fried on top of a fire (and not in an oven). A careful reading of the *Rash* cited above makes it clear that he too understood these two *menachos* to have been made on top of the fire.]

[ט] **הָאוֹמֵר:** הֲרֵי עָלַי בְּתַנּוּר, לֹא יָבִיא מַאֲפֵה כֻפָּח, וּמַאֲפֵה רְעָפִים, וּמַאֲפֵה יוֹרוֹת הָעַרְבִיִּים. רַבִּי יְהוּדָה אוֹמֵר: אִם רָצָה, יָבִיא מַאֲפֵה כֻפָּח. הֲרֵי עָלַי מִנְחַת מַאֲפֶה,

**ר׳ עובדיה מברטנורא**

(ט) **כופח.** מקום שפיתת קדרה אחת, ופעמים שמסיקים אותו ואופין בו עיסה: **רעפים.** טוול״ש בלע״ז, עשוין מחרס ומסיקין אותן בכבשן: **ויורות הערביין.** כמין גומא העשויה בקרקע וטוחה בטיט ומסיקין אש בתוכה עד שתתלבן ואופים בה עיסה: **אם רצה יביא מעשה כופח.** דכופח מין תנור הוא. ואין הלכה כרבי יהודה: **מנחת מאפה.** כתיבי בה חלות ורקיקים (ויקרא ב,ד):

**יד אברהם**

## 9.

Another category of *minchah* which an individual may bring voluntarily is the מִנְחָה מַאֲפֵה תַנּוּר, *oven-baked minchah.* In contrast with the *machavas* and *marcheshes* discussed in the previous mishnah, the oven-baked *minchah* is not baked in a utensil but in an oven. This *minchah* comes in two varieties: חַלּוֹת *[challos],* loaves, which are mixed with oil, and רְקִיקִין *[rekikin],* wafers, which are only smeared with oil after their baking (see *Lev.* 2:4). [The procedure for preparing these two types of *menachos* will be discussed in mishnah 6:3.]

הָאוֹמֵר: הֲרֵי עָלַי בְּתַנּוּר, לֹא יָבִיא מַאֲפֵה כֻפָּח, — *[If] one said, "I take upon myself [to bring] in an oven," he may not bring something baked in a small stove,*

If someone pledged to bring an oven-baked *minchah*, the connotation of his words does not include one which is baked in a כֻּפָּח, *a small stove*, which can hold only one pot at a time (*Rav; Rashi*).

[The stoves of those times were hollow containers, generally of earthenware with a hole on top upon which the pot was placed. The stove was filled with wood or coal (from a door on the side) and lit. The כֻּפָּח was a single-hole stove, with room for only one pot. (There was also a double-hole stove, known as a כִּירָה; see *Yad Avraham* comm. to *Shabbos* 3:1,2).] The stove could also be used for baking by placing dough inside the stove and pasting it to the upper wall of the stove's interior (*Rav*).

The תַּנּוּר, *oven*, was a similar type of vessel, and it could also be used for cooking (see *Shabbos* 3:2). However, it was large, and wider at the bottom than at the top, causing a greater amount of heat to be retained in the upper part. Thus, it was better suited to baking (*Rav* to *Shabbos* 3:2; see comm. there; see *Rashi* to *Shabbos* 117b, s.v. מרדה et al.).

וּמַאֲפֵה רְעָפִים, — *[nor] one baked on tiles,*

Nor may he bring a *minchah* baked upon tiles which were heated in a furnace (*Rav*).

וּמַאֲפֵה יוֹרוֹת הָעַרְבִיִּים. — *[nor] one baked in an Arabian cauldron.*

The Arabs used to dig a hole in the ground, coat it with lime, and then burn a fire within it until it whitened

9. [If] one said, "I take upon myself [to bring] in an oven," he may not bring something baked in a small stove, [nor] one baked on tiles, [nor] one baked in an Arabian cauldron. R' Yehudah says: If he wishes, he may bring that which is baked in a small stove. [If he said,] "I take upon myself [to bring] a baked *minchah*-offering,"

YAD AVRAHAM

from the heat. It would then be used for baking (*Rav*; see *Keilim* 5:10). [This, too, is precluded by the condition of such a pledge.]

The dough of a regular *minchah*-offering was kneaded and shaped within the Temple Courtyard (see comm. to mishnah 11:3). Since the alternative ovens mentioned here [certainly the last one] were not present in the Temple, our mishnah is obviously discussing a case in which the baking was done in ovens outside the Courtyard. It must be concluded, therefore, that the mishnah is discussing a case of someone who took the dough outside the Temple Courtyard to bake after it was kneaded. This, however, poses a problem. The Temple vessels used for preparing the dough were consecrated vessels (*klei shareis*) and they consequently sanctify the dough that is made in them. Accordingly, it should be forbidden to remove the dough from the Temple, and its removal should invalidate it!

However, whether something consecrated by a *kli shareis* is invalidated by being removed from the Courtyard is the subject of a dispute between *Rashi* and *Tosafos*. It is the opinion of *Tosafos* (9a, s.v. ריש לקיש; *Zevachim* 20b, s.v. יציאה, et al.) that although consecration by a *kli shareis* sanctifies a substance in regard to several invalidations (see *Me'ilah* 2:8), it does *not* extend to making it susceptible to the invalidation of leaving the Courtyard [יוֹצֵא]; only the beginning of the *avodah* [with *kemitzah* for a *minchah*, or slaughter in the case of an animal offering] imparts this level of sanctity. In the view of *Tosafos*, therefore, though it is improper to remove a *minchah* from the Temple once it has been consecrated, the mishnah may nevertheless be referring to such a case, since if one did so the offering is not invalidated.

Alternatively, it may be that the requirement for kneading and baking a *minchah* in the Temple is only a preference but not a halachic necessity. Thus, it is possible for a *minchah* to be baked outside the Temple and yet be valid (*Tif. Yis.*; cf. 9:2,4).

רַבִּי יְהוּדָה אוֹמֵר: אִם רָצָה, יָבִיא מַאֲפֵה כֻפָּח. — *R' Yehudah says: If he wishes, he may bring that which is baked in a small stove.*

In R' Yehudah's view, a כֻּפָּח, *stove*, is also considered a small oven by Torah standards (*Rav*) [and is thus included in the connotation of such a pledge]. R' Yehudah derives this from the Torah's repetition of the word תַּנּוּר, *oven* (*Lev.* 2:4 and 7:9), which, in his view, comes to include even a small stove in this category (*Gem.* 63a; *Rashi*).

The halachah follows the view of the first *Tanna* (*Rav; Rambam, Hil. Maaseh HaKorbanos* 17:1), and if one brought a *minchah* baked in such an oven instead of in a regular oven it is invalid (*Likkutei Halachos* from *Tosefta* 7:10).

הֲרֵי עָלַי מִנְחַת מַאֲפֵה, — *[If he said,] "I take upon myself [to bring] a baked minchah-offering,'*

[Someone pledged to bring a baked *minchah* — i.e., an oven-baked *minchah*.]

לֹא יָבִיא מֶחֱצָה חַלּוֹת וּמֶחֱצָה רְקִיקִין. רַבִּי שִׁמְעוֹן מַתִּיר מִפְּנֵי שֶׁהוּא קָרְבָּן אֶחָד.

ר׳ עובדיה מברטנורא

**לא יביא מחצה חלות.** דכל מנחות באות עשר, וזה לא יביא חמש חלות וחמש רקיקין, אלא או הכל חלות או הכל רקיקין (ויקרא ב,ד): **מפני שהוא קרבן אחד.** ששניהם כתובים במנחה אחת, הלכך יכול להביא מחלה ממין זה ומחלה ממין זה. ואין הלכה כרבי שמעון:

יד אברהם

לֹא יָבִיא מֶחֱצָה חַלּוֹת וּמֶחֱצָה רְקִיקִין — *he may not bring half as challas and half as rekikin.*

[As explained in the preface, the מַאֲפֵה תַנּוּר, *oven-baked minchah*, may be brought either as *challos*, loaves, or *rekikin*, wafers. The *minchah* is baked in ten loaves or wafers. Though he has a choice as to which variety to bring, his *minchah* must consist either entirely of *challos* or entirely of *rekikin*, but not a mixture of both (*Rav*).]

he may not bring half as *challos* and half as *rekikin*. R' Shimon permits [this] because it is one offering.

YAD AVRAHAM

The *Gemara* (63a,b) cites a dispute whether the *minchah* is actually invalid if he did bring a mixture.

רַבִּי שִׁמְעוֹן מַתִּיר מִפְּנֵי שֶׁהוּא קָרְבָּן אֶחָד. — *R' Shimon permits [this] because it is one offering.*

Since they are both included in one category of *minchah* in the Torah, they may be mixed together in one offering (*Rav* from *Gem.* 63b).

The halachah does not follow the view of R' Shimon (*Rav; Rambam Comm.*).

It is peculiar that *Rambam* does not explicitly rule on this dispute in his Code. Actually, he does make what may be considered an allusion that the halachah follows R' Yehudah (*Mishneh LaMelech, Maaseh HaKorbanos* 17:5). However, he does not indicate whether or not a *minchah* brought in this manner is invalid (ibid.; *Zevach Todah*).

## פרק ששי
## Chapter Six

The following chapter continues giving the details of the *minchah* process, beginning with *kemitzah,* the act of removing a portion of flour from the *minchah* to be burnt on the Altar.

[It should be noted that the order of the chapters in the Mishnayos texts does not correspond to those of the *Gemara*, as the tenth chapter of the Mishnayos text — *Rabbi Yishmael* — is printed in the *Gemara* as the sixth chapter. Hence, our chapter, which is the sixth in our text, is the seventh in the sequence as it appears in the *Gemara* (*Tif. Yis.*).]

מנחות ו/א

**[א] אֵלּוּ** מְנָחוֹת נִקְמָצוֹת, וּשְׁיָרֵיהֶן לַכֹּהֲנִים: מִנְחַת הַסֹּלֶת, וְהַמַּחֲבַת, וְהַמַּרְחֶשֶׁת, וְהַחַלּוֹת, וְהָרְקִיקִין, מִנְחַת גּוֹיִם, מִנְחַת נָשִׁים, מִנְחַת הָעֹמֶר, מִנְחַת חוֹטֵא, וּמִנְחַת קְנָאוֹת.

ר׳ עובדיה מברטנורא

**פרק שישי – אלו מנחות.** (א) אלו מנחות נקמצות. מנחת סולת נקמצת עיסה, ומנחת מחבת ומרחשת וחלות ורקיקים דהיינו מאפה, פותתן לאחר אפייתן, ובמנחת סלת כתיבה קמיצה בהדיא, ובאידך כתיב אזכרה, ואזכרה היינו קומץ: **מנחת גוים או נשים.** שהתנדבו אחת מאלו: **מנחת העומר.** אזכרה כתיב בה: **מנחת חוטא וקנאות.** כתיב בהו קמיצה:

יד אברהם

## 1.

אֵלּוּ מְנָחוֹת נִקְמָצוֹת, — *The following minchah-offerings require kemitzah,*

It has been stated numerous times in the course of this tractate that *kemitzah* is the first essential *avodah* of the *minchah's* offering. Yet the requirement for the *kemitzah* is not mentioned explicitly in the Torah in regard to every *minchah*. Many times the Torah mentions just אַזְכָּרָתָהּ, *its remembrance*, an ambiguous phrase. However, concerning the מִנְחַת סֹלֶת, *minchah of fine flour*, the Torah states (*Lev.* 2:2): וֶהֱבִיאָהּ אֶל בְּנֵי אַהֲרֹן הַכֹּהֲנִים וְקָמַץ מִשָּׁם מְלֹא קֻמְצוֹ מִסָּלְתָּהּ וּמִשַּׁמְנָהּ עַל כָּל לְבֹנָתָהּ וְהִקְטִיר הַכֹּהֵן אֶת אַזְכָּרָתָהּ הַמִּזְבֵּחָה ... רֵיחַ נִיחֹחַ לַה׳ — *And he shall bring it to the sons of Aaron, the Kohanim, and separate from there his full kometz from its flour and from its oil, in addition to all its frankincense; and the Kohen shall burn its remembrance on the Altar ... for a pleasing aroma to HASHEM.* From this verse, which explicitly describes the *kemitzah* act and concludes with reference to אַזְכָּרָתָהּ, *its remembrance*, we derive that whenever the Torah makes reference to אַזְכָּרָה, *a remembrance*, in connection with a *minchah*-offering, it means the *kometz*, thereby making it clear that these *menachos* require *kemitzah* (*Rashi Peirush*[1] from *Toras Kohanim*).

וּשְׁיָרֵיהֶן לַכֹּהֲנִים: — *and their remainders go to the Kohanim:*

That which remains of the *minchah* after the *kometz* has been removed is eaten by the *Kohanim* (see 1:2).

The mishnah now lists the *menachos* that require that a *kometz* be separated from them and offered on the Altar.

מִנְחַת הַסֹּלֶת, — *the minchah-offering of fine flour,*

1. In the following four chapters, the printed commentary attributed to *Rashi* seems in reality to be that of another unidentified commentator. What appears to be the authentic *Rashi* commentary was published by *R' Betzalel Ashkenazi* in his *Shitah Mekubetzes*; this was subsequently published in the glosses of the standard *Gemara* text under the heading of רש״י כת״י. Within these chapters, the *Rashi* manuscript published by the *Shitah* will be referred to as *Rashi ms*, while the commentary published as *Rashi* will be referred to as *Rashi Peirush*. [It should be noted, however, that some prominent commentators in their quotations of *Rashi* clearly refer to the *Peirush*.]

6
1

**1.** The following *minchah*-offerings require *kemitzah,* and their remainders go to the *Kohanim:* the *minchah*-offering of fine flour, the *machavas*, the *marcheshes*, the *challos*, the *rekikin,* the *minchah*-offering of gentiles, the *minchah*-offering of women, the *minchah*-offering of the *omer*, the sinner's *minchah*-offering, and the jealousy *minchah*-offering.

### YAD AVRAHAM

This requirement for *kemitzah* in a *minchas soless* [fine-flour *minchah*] is stated explicitly in the verse cited previously. The fact that the remainder is eaten by the *Kohanim* is stated in the following verse which says וְהַנּוֹתֶרֶת מִן הַמִּנְחָה לְאַהֲרֹן וּלְבָנָיו, *And that which remains of the minchah-offering [goes] to Aaron and his sons.*

וְהַמַּחֲבַת, וְהַמַּרְחֶשֶׁת, וְהַחַלּוֹת, וְהָרְקִיקִין, *— the machavas, the marcheshes, the challos, the rekikin,*

[These *menachos,* described in the previous chapter (3:8), are listed in the second chapter of *Leviticus* (2:5ff). At the conclusion of the section, the Torah says (*Lev.* 2:9,10): וְהֵרִים הַכֹּהֵן מִן הַמִּנְחָה אֶת אַזְכָּרָתָהּ וְהִקְטִיר הַמִּזְבֵּחָה . . . וְהַנּוֹתֶרֶת מִן־הַמִּנְחָה לְאַהֲרֹן וּלְבָנָיו, *And the Kohen shall lift from the minchah-offering its remembrance and burn it on the Altar . . . And the remainder of the minchah-offering goes to Aaron and his sons.* This is a reference to the *kemitzah,* as has been explained.]

מִנְחַת גּוֹיִם, *— the minchah-offering of gentiles,*

The idea that gentiles can bring *menachos* follows R' Yose HaGlili, who maintains that gentiles may offer even offerings that are eaten. R' Akiva, however, contends that a gentile may bring only an *olah* (*Gem.* 73b). The halachah follows the view of R' Akiva and thus a gentile cannot offer a *minchah* (*Rambam, Maaseh HaKorbanos* 3:2).

מִנְחַת נָשִׁים, *— the minchah-offering of women,*

I.e., any of the previously listed *menachos* which is offered by a woman (*Rav*). [Although there are details in which a woman's *minchah* differs from a man's *minchah* (see above 5:3), as far as *kemitzah* is concerned it is treated the same.]

מִנְחַת הָעֹמֶר, *— the minchah-offering of the omer,*

In regard to the *omer,* the Torah (*Lev.* 2:16) states: וְהִקְטִיר הַכֹּהֵן אֶת אַזְכָּרָתָהּ, *and the Kohen shall burn its remembrance* [which is a reference to the *kemitzah*] (*Rav*).

מִנְחַת חוֹטֵא, *— the sinner's minchah-offering,*

The Torah explicitly mentions *kemitzah* concerning this *minchah* (*Rav*), as stated (ibid. 5:12): וְקָמַץ הַכֹּהֵן מִמֶּנָּה מְלוֹא קֻמְצוֹ אֶת אַזְכָּרָתָהּ וְהִקְטִיר הַמִּזְבֵּחָה, *and the Kohen shall remove from it his full kometz, its remembrance, and he shall burn it on the Altar.*

וּמִנְחַת קְנָאוֹת. *— and the jealousy minchah-offering.*

Here, too, the Torah is explicit about the *kemitzah* (*Rav*), as stated (*Numbers* 5:26): וְקָמַץ הַכֹּהֵן מִן הַמִּנְחָה אֶת אַזְכָּרָתָהּ וְהִקְטִיר הַמִּזְבֵּחָה, *and the Kohen*

רַבִּי שִׁמְעוֹן אוֹמֵר: מִנְחַת חוֹטֵא שֶׁל כֹּהֲנִים נִקְמֶצֶת, וְהַקֹּמֶץ קָרֵב לְעַצְמוֹ וְהַשִּׁירַיִם קְרֵבִים לְעַצְמָן.

[ב] **מִנְחַת** כֹּהֲנִים, וּמִנְחַת כֹּהֵן מָשִׁיחַ, וּמִנְחַת נְסָכִים לַמִּזְבֵּחַ, וְאֵין בָּהֶם לַכֹּהֲנִים.

**ר' עובדיה מברטנורא**

**מנחת חוטא של כהנים נקמצת.** אף על גב דמנחת כהן נשרפת כלה כדכתיב (ויקרא ו, טז) וכל מנחת כהן כליל תהיה, מכל מקום בעיא קמיצה, והקומץ קרב לעצמו והשיריים קרבין לעצמן, אבל לתנא קמא אין מנחת כהן נקמצת, אלא נקטרת כמות שהיא, דסבר כל מנחה ששיריה נאכלים, נקמצת, ושאין שיריה נאכלים, אינה נקמצת. והלכה כתנא קמא:

**יד אברהם**

*shall remove from the minchah-offering its remembrance and burn [it] on the Altar.*

In the last three instances, the Torah mentions only the requirement of *kemitzah* but not the fact that the remainder is eaten by the *Kohanim*. However, the Torah (*Lev.* 6:9) states a generalization in regard to *menachos*: וְהַנּוֹתֶרֶת מִמֶּנָּה יֹאכְלוּ אַהֲרֹן וּבָנָיו, *and the remainder [of the minchah] Aaron and his sons shall eat.* From this we derive that, as a rule, *menachos* are eaten by the *Kohanim.* Even the unusual barley *menachos*, such as the *omer* and jealousy *minchah*, which cannot be included in this verse, also share the requirement to have their remainder eaten because it is considered self-evident that the entire purpose of *kemitzah* (according to the Sages of this mishnah) is to separate that which is offered on the Altar from that which is eaten (*Gem.* 72b, *Rashi* ibid.).

Obviously, R' Shimon, who in the subsequent segment of the mishnah rules that *kemitzah* is performed even on a *minchah* which is not eaten, does not subscribe to this reasoning. According to him, the *Gemara* (ibid.) offers other Scriptural sources for the fact that the remainders of *menachos* are eaten.

רַבִּי שִׁמְעוֹן אוֹמֵר: מִנְחַת חוֹטֵא שֶׁל כֹּהֲנִים נִקְמֶצֶת, — *R' Shimon says: The sinner's minchah-offering of Kohanim requires kemitzah,*

The entire *minchah* of a *Kohen* is burnt on the Altar, as stated explicitly in the Torah (*Lev.* 6:16): וְכָל מִנְחַת כֹּהֵן כָּלִיל תִּהְיֶה לֹא תֵאָכֵל, *any minchah of a Kohen shall be completely burnt; it shall not be eaten.* According to R' Shimon, however, the sinner's *minchah* of a *Kohen* requires *kemitzah* regardless (*Rav*). This is derived from the Torah's phrase describing the sinner's *minchah* (*Lev.* 5:13): וְהָיְתָה לַכֹּהֵן כַּמִּנְחָה, *and it shall be to the Kohen like the minchah-offering* — which R' Shimon interprets to mean that the sinner's *minchah* of the *Kohen* is similar to that of a non-*Kohen*. Just as the former requires *kemitzah*, so does that of the *Kohen* (*Gem.* 74a).

The Sages, for their part, apply this phrase to an entirely different issue (*Gem.* 73b), and thus contend that any *minchah* which is not eaten does not require *kemitzah* (see above *mishnah* 5:5, *Tif. Yis.*).

וְהַקֹּמֶץ קָרֵב לְעַצְמוֹ וְהַשִּׁירַיִם קְרֵבִים לְעַצְמָן. — *with the kometz being offered by itself and the remainder being offered by itself.*

Although R' Shimon contends that

6
2

R' Shimon says: The sinner's *minchah*-offering of *Kohanim* requires *kemitzah*, with the *kometz* being offered by itself and the remainder being offered by itself.

**2.** The *minchah*-offering of *Kohanim*, and the *minchah*-offering of the Anointed *Kohen*, and the libation *minchah*-offering belong to the Altar, and the *Kohanim* have no [share] in them.

**YAD AVRAHAM**

the Torah equates the sinner's *minchah* of a *Kohen* to that of a non-*Kohen*, the analogy is not all inclusive. Thus, we do not derive from it that the remainder of his sinner's *minchah* is eaten like the remainder of the non-*Kohen's minchah*, because the Torah focuses its comparison to a regular *minchah* on the *Kohen* himself, not on the burning of his *kometz* (*Gem.* 74a). From this R' Shimon deduces that the comparison is limited only to that which involves the *Kohen* — i.e., *kemitzah* — but not that which pertains to the Altar (*Rashi*).

The halachah follows the view of the first *Tanna*, that it is burnt without a *kometz* being removed first (*Rav; Rambam, Maaseh HaKorbanos* 12:9).

## 2.

Ordinarily, offerings are "shared" by the Altar and the *Kohanim*, i.e., part of the sacrifice is offered on the Altar while the remainder is eaten by the *Kohanim*. With an animal sacrifice, the Altar's share is the blood and *emurin* (sacrificial parts), with the remainder of the animal, or specific portions of it, going to the *Kohanim*. When dealing with a *minchah*, the *kometz* is the Altar's share while the remainder belongs to the *Kohanim*. The following mishnah illustrates exceptions to this pattern: offerings that are completely offered on the Altar leaving nothing to the *Kohanim*, and the opposite: offerings that are consumed exclusively by the *Kohanim*.

מִנְחַת כֹּהֲנִים, — *The minchah-offering of Kohanim,*

Any *minchah* brought by a *Kohen*, either as a voluntary offering or as an obligatory one (*Tif. Yis.*).

וּמִנְחַת כֹּהֵן מָשִׁיחַ, — *and the minchah-offering of the Anointed Kohen,*

That is, the *chavitin* of the *Kohen Gadol* [brought daily, see above 4:5] (*Tif. Yis.*).

וּמִנְחַת נְסָכִים — *and the libation minchah-offering*

The *minchah* which is part of the *nesachim* (libations) that accompany an animal sacrifice [see above, preface to mishnah 2:4] (*Tif. Yis.*).

לַמִּזְבֵּחַ, וְאֵין בָּהֶם לַכֹּהֲנִים. — *belong to the Altar, and the Kohanim have no [share] in them.*

These *menachos* have no remainder and are completely consumed by the Altar.

# בָּזֶה יָפֶה כֹּחַ הַמִּזְבֵּחַ מִכֹּחַ הַכֹּהֲנִים. שְׁתֵּי הַלֶּחֶם וְלֶחֶם הַפָּנִים לַכֹּהֲנִים, וְאֵין בָּהֶם לַמִּזְבֵּחַ. וּבָזֶה יָפֶה כֹּחַ הַכֹּהֲנִים מִכֹּחַ הַמִּזְבֵּחַ.

**ר' עובדיה מברטנורא**

(ב) **בזה יפה כח המזבח.** לא הוי צריך למיתני, דהא חזינן דבזה יפה כח המזבח ומלתא דפשיטא היא, אלא לאתויי המתנדב יין למזבח בלא קרבן, דלא תימא מזלפו על האישים על האש והוא נשרף וכלה ואין כח מזבח יפה בזה, קא משמע לן דלא, אלא מנסכו כשאר נסכים ויורד לשיתין, דהיינו כמין שני נקבים שהיו במזבח ויורדים למטה עד היסוד, כדי שיהיה כח המזבח יפה: **ובזה יפה כח הכהנים.** לאתויי שתי הלחם של עצרת אם הביאום בפני עצמן בלא כבשים, דלא תימא לשריפה עומדות ולא לאכילה כיון שלא קרבו כבשים שמתירים אותם, קא משמע לן דבזה יפה כח כהנים לעולם דלאכילה עומדות ולא לשריפה:

**יד אברהם**

The Torah (*Lev.* 6:16) explicitly requires that the *minchah* of *Kohanim* and the *minchah* of the Anointed *Kohen* [the daily *chavitin*] be completely burnt, as explained in the previous mishnah. Regarding the *minchas nesachim* [the libation *minchah*], we conclude from the fact that the Torah (*Num.* 15) makes no mention of *kemitzah* or consumption by the *Kohanim* that it too is completely burnt on the Altar.

The *Gemara* (74b) points out that these three *menachos* are the only offerings for which this statement can be made. No other offering belongs *completely* to the Altar. An *olah*, although completely consumed by the Altar, is not included in this category because its hide is awarded to the *Kohanim*. Similarly, the bird *olah* is not considered *wholly* consumed on the Altar, because its gullet and feathers are discarded. Even the wine libations on the Altar cannot be included in this category, because they are poured into special receptacles prepared for this purpose on top of the southwest corner of the Altar, from where the wine descends into the ground beneath the Altar (see below). Our mishnah refers only to items that are consumed by the fire of the Altar (see below).

.בָּזֶה יָפֶה כֹּחַ הַמִּזְבֵּחַ מִכֹּחַ הַכֹּהֲנִים — *In this, the right* (lit., *power*) *of the Altar is greater than the right of the Kohanim.*

This generalization is apparently redundant, as it is already sufficiently clear that in the above-mentioned cases the Altar's rights pre-empt those of the *Kohanim*. The *Gemara* (74b) explains that this last statement comes to exclude the offering of *nesachim*, since these are not burnt on the top of the Altar but rather poured into two perforated bowls attached to the top of the Altar at its southwest corner, from where the wine descended via pipes to a deep cavity beneath the Altar (*Succah* 4:9, *Rashi* 48b; see further *Yad Avraham* comm. there and below, mishnah 12:5). Accordingly, the mishnah's phrase emphasizes *"In this,* the right of the Altar is greater than that of the *Kohanim,"* but not in regard to the wine libations of the individual, which do not go on the Altar (*Rashi*).

*Rav* and *Rambam* (*Comm.*) explain this in just the opposite manner: The intention of this repetition is to *include* in the category of the Altar's share *nesachim* pledged by a private individual which consist of simply an appropriate amount of wine. By

6 In this, the right of the Altar is greater than the
2 right of the *Kohanim*. The *shtei halechem* and the *lechem hapanim* belong to the *Kohanim*, and the Altar has no share in them. In this, the right of the *Kohanim* is greater than the right of the Altar.



its otherwise unnecessary summation, our mishnah indicates that these wine libations, too, are *the right of the Altar*, i.e., they are poured through the bowls on the roof of the Altar in the manner of the *nesachim* that accompany an animal sacrifice, rather than being poured onto the flames of the Altar (*Rav; Rambam Comm.* from *Gem.* 74b).

This explanation is questioned by *Tos. Yom Tov.* On the contrary, if the libations of the individual are indeed classified as *the right of the Altar*, they should be consumed by the flames of the Altar, as are the *menachos* mentioned in the mishnah. Pouring them into the bowls and down to the ground beneath the Altar, on the other hand, should not be considered the regular share of the Altar, since there is nothing that is given to the flames of the Altar.

Apparently, *Rav* and *Rambam* make a distinction between solids and liquids in regard to the Altar's share. The sacrifice of animals and the burning of *menachos* on the Altar are considered the share of the Altar, because they are solids which are not immediately consumed. Liquids, however, are only considered as being given to the Altar if they are poured into the bowls of the Altar's roof.

*Rav* and *Rambam's* explanation, however, is not consistent with our version of the *Gemara* which states explicitly that the pouring of the wine into the bowls on the Altar's roof is *not* considered *the right of the Altar*, and that only items which are consumed by the Altar's fire fall under that category. Our version of the *Gemara*, then, can only be explained as above (*Mahariach*).

According to both these explanations, the *Gemara* here follows the opinion that the wine *nesachim* (libations) pledged by an individual are poured down specially prepared bowls on the Altar in the same fashion as the *nesachim* accompanying a sacrifice. This is not the opinion of Shmuel in the *Gemara* (*Zevachim* 91b), who says that the wine *nesachim* of the individual are spattered on the flames of the Altar itself, rather than poured into the bowls on the Altar. *Rambam's* ruling follows our *Gemara's* conclusion (see *Kesef Mishneh* ad loc.).

שְׁתֵּי הַלֶּחֶם וְלֶחֶם הַפָּנִים לַכֹּהֲנִים, וְאֵין בָּהֶם לַמִּזְבֵּחַ. — *The shtei halechem and the lechem hapanim belong to the Kohanim, and the Altar has no share in them.*

The *shtei halechem* offered on Shavuos are referred to by the Torah in one instance as *bikkurim* (*Lev.* 23:17), thereby indicating that they are eaten in their entirety by the *Kohanim*, just like actual *bikkurim* [the first fruits of one's produce which are brought to Jerusalem and given to the *Kohanim*] (*Gem.* 46b).

The *lechem hapanim* is explicitly designated for the *Kohanim* after its removal from the *shulchan* (*Lev.* 24:9).

וּבָזֶה יָפֶה כֹּחַ הַכֹּהֲנִים מִכֹּחַ הַמִּזְבֵּחַ. — *In this, the right of the Kohanim is greater than the right of the Altar.*

This seemingly superfluous generalization is intended to include in this category a situation in which the two communal *shelamim* lambs which normally accompany the *shtei halechem* (see mishnah 2:2) were not

[ג] **כָּל** הַמְּנָחוֹת הַנַּעֲשׂוֹת בִּכְלִי טְעוּנוֹת שָׁלֹשׁ מַתְּנוֹת שֶׁמֶן: יְצִיקָה, וּבְלִילָה, וּמַתַּן שֶׁמֶן בִּכְלִי קֹדֶם לַעֲשִׂיָּתָן. וְהַחַלּוֹת, בּוֹלְלָן; דִּבְרֵי רַבִּי.

### ר׳ עובדיה מברטנורא

(ג) **הנעשות בכלי.** כגון מנחת מרחשת ומחבת שהן נעשות בכלי, טעונות שלש מתנות שמן, למעוטי מנחת מאפה תנור שאינה טעונה יציקה: **ומתן שמן בכלי קודם לעשייתן.** תחלה נותן שמן בכלי שרת ונותן סולת עליו, דכתיב במנחת מרחשת (ויקרא ב, ז) סלת בשמן תעשה, כלומר תנתן, אלמא דטעונה מתן שמן קודם לעשייתה, ובמנחת מחבת כתיב בלילה ויציקה ולא כתיב בה מתן שמן בכלי תחלה, ובמרחשת כתיב מתן שמן ולא כתיב בה יציקה ובלילה, וגמרינן הך מהך, נאמר קרבנך במרחשת ונאמר קרבנך במחבת, וכיצד הוא עושה, נותן שמן תחלה בכלי שרת ונותן עליו את הסלת, [וחוזר] ונותן עליה שמן ובוללן, הרי מתן שמן בכלי ובלילה, ולשה במים, ואופה בתנור, ופותתה, ויוצק עליה שמן אחר פתיתה, וזו היא יציקה, הרי שלשתן, וקומץ, ומקטיר את הקומץ, והשאר נאכל לכהנים: **והחלות בוללן דברי רבי.** השתא מיירי במנחת מאפה תנור שהיא באה חלות או רקיקים, וכתיב בה (שם שם, ד) סולת חלות מצות בלולות בשמן, רבי סבר חלות בלולות כתיב, שבוללן כשהן חלות, ורבנן סברי סולת בלולות כתיב, מלמד שנבללת כשהיא סלת. והלכה כחכמים:

### יד אברהם

available and the *shtei halechem* had to be brought without this accompanying sacrifice. Although brought by themselves, the loaves nevertheless become permitted to the *Kohanim* and are not burnt (*Rav* from *Gem.* 74b).[1] This is in accordance with the view of R' Akiva (mishnah 4:3), who maintains that the lambs of the *shelamim* are not essential to the validity of the loaves. As the mishnah states there, Shimon ben Nannas and R' Shimon dispute this view (*Tos. Yom Tov; Bircas HaZevach*).

## 3.

כָּל הַמְּנָחוֹת הַנַּעֲשׂוֹת בִּכְלִי — *All minchah-offerings which are prepared in a vessel*

For example, the *minchas machavas* and *minchas marcheshes* which were prepared in their respective utensils [see 5:8] (*Rav*). The *minchas soless* and the *minchas omer* are also included in this category (*Tos.* 75a, s.v. מה להלן). Not included in this category are the oven-baked *menachos* [מַאֲפֵה תַנּוּר] (*Rav*). [These are baked in the oven without a utensil, and the mishnah deals with their procedure separately.]

טְעוּנוֹת שָׁלֹשׁ מַתְּנוֹת שֶׁמֶן: יְצִיקָה, וּבְלִילָה, וּמַתַּן שֶׁמֶן בִּכְלִי קֹדֶם לַעֲשִׂיָּתָן. — *require three applications of oil: pouring, mixing, and placing oil in the vessel prior to their preparation.*

When preparing these *menachos*, the required *log* of oil is not added all at once, but in three installments. These three applications are listed by the mishnah in reverse order. The first application — מַתַּן שֶׁמֶן בִּכְלִי, *the*

1. The *Gemara* (46b) notes that this is the subject of a dispute of *Tannaim* and that there is a view that when the loaves are brought without the accompanying *shelamim*, they are not eaten; rather they undergo *tenufah* and are then left to become disqualified overnight and are burnt the next day in the manner of other disqualified offerings.

6 **3.** All *minchah*-offerings which are prepared in
3 a vessel require three applications of oil:
pouring, mixing, and placing oil in the vessel
prior to their preparation. The *challos*, [however,]
one mixes them; [these are] the words of Rabbi.

YAD AVRAHAM

*placement of oil in the vessel* — is the first step in the *minchah's* preparation. Even before any flour is placed in it, a small amount of oil is placed in the *kli shareis*. The flour is then added to the vessel, followed by a second application of oil on top of it. This second application is part of the procedure known as בְּלִילָה, *mixing*, in which the oil and the flour are mixed together. This is followed by a third and final application of oil — יְצִיקָה, *pouring*. In the case of *menachos* which are baked (in a pan or griddle) prior to *kemitzah*, the mixture is kneaded with water after the second application of oil, baked, and broken into pieces; then the third measure of oil is poured onto those pieces (*Rav*). In the case of a *minchah* of fine flour, in which *kemitzah* is performed on the unbaked flour, the third application of oil is made directly to the flour (*Rambam, Maaseh HaKorbanos* 13:6).

Although the initial application of oil was obviously the first step, the mishnah lists the latter procedures before this one because they are stated first in the Torah (*Tif. Yis.*). The initial placement of oil is stated in connection with the *marcheshes* where the Torah states (*Lev.* 2:7): סֹלֶת בַּשֶּׁמֶן תֵּעָשֶׂה, *fine flour with oil shall it be made*. This indicates that the flour be placed in a vessel that already has oil in it. The latter two appear in connection with the *machavas*, as stated (ibid. vs. 5,6): סֹלֶת בְּלוּלָה בַשֶּׁמֶן ... פָּתוֹת אֹתָהּ פִּתִּים וְיָצַקְתָּ עָלֶיהָ שָׁמֶן, *fine flour mixed with oil ... break it into pieces and you shall pour upon it oil*. From the Torah's use of the word קָרְבָּנֶיךָ, *your offering*, concerning each of these offerings, the *Gemara* derives exegetically that all these *menachos* must undergo the same applications of oil (*Rav* from *Gem.* 74b). This rule is then extended to all *menachos* requiring oil, such as the *minchas soless* and the *omer minchah* (*Tos.* 75a, s.v. מה להלן).

In the view of *Tosafos* (9a, s.v. ריש לקיש), all three applications were performed in a *kli shareis*, as stated above. *Rambam* (loc. cit.) indicates that a *kli shareis* is required only for the last of the applications of oil (see *Kesef Mishneh, Lechem Mishneh* ibid.; cf. *Aruch HaShulchan HeAsid* 87:15).

However, oven-baked *menachos* — *challos* (loaves) and *rekikin* (wafers) — are excluded from יְצִיקָה, *pouring*. This is derived from the verse concerning the *minchas machavas* (*Lev.* 2:6): וְיָצַקְתָּ עָלֶיהָ שָׁמֶן, מִנְחָה הוּא, *You shall pour oil on it, it is a minchah-offering*. The otherwise redundant phrases *on it* and *it is a minchah-offering* indicate that the two oven-baked *menachos* — viz., the *challos* and the *rekikin* — are excluded from the third application of oil (*Gem.* 75a,b). However, the second application of oil — the בְּלִילָה, *mixing* — does apply to the oven-baked *menachos* as well. The mishnah now describes how the oil is added to these *menachos*.

וְהַחַלּוֹת, בּוֹלְלָן; דִּבְרֵי רַבִּי. — *The challos, [however,] one mixes them; [these are] the words of Rabbi.*

In the view of Rabbi (R' Yehudah HaNasi), the process for preparing the

וַחֲכָמִים אוֹמְרִים: סֹלֶת.
הַחַלּוֹת טְעוּנוֹת בְּלִילָה וְהָרְקִיקִים מְשׁוּחִים. כֵּיצַד מוֹשְׁחָן? כְּמִין כִּי. וּשְׁאָר הַשֶּׁמֶן נֶאֱכָל לַכֹּהֲנִים.

## ר' עובדיה מברטנורא

**חלות טעונות בלילה והרקיקים משוחים.** דכתיב (שם) חלות בלולות, ולא רקיקים בלולים, רקיקים משוחים, ולא חלות משוחות: **ביצד מושחן במין בי.** יונית, שהיא כמין ט' שלנו, כהפרשת גודל [של שמאל] מן האצבע [כזה C]:

## יד אברהם

*challos* of the oven-baked *minchah* calls for the procedure of *mixing* with oil to be performed *after* the flour has been baked into loaves (*Rav*). That is, they are mixed as *challos*, not as flour. Their procedure calls for the initial application of oil (before the addition of the flour) to take place as for all *menachos* (see below). but once the flour is added, it is immediately made into a dough (by being kneaded with water) and then baked into loaves. The loaves are then broken into pieces [פְּתִיתָה] and only then is the second application of oil made and the pieces mixed with the oil for the procedure of בְּלִילָה, *mixing* (*Gem.* 75a). This is derived from the verse (*Lev.* 2:4): סֹלֶת חַלּוֹת מַצֹּת בְּלוּלֹת בַּשֶּׁמֶן, *fine flour, loaves of matzos mixed with oil* — which indicates that they are mixed after being baked into loaves (*Rav* from *Gem.* 76a).

וַחֲכָמִים אוֹמְרִים: סֹלֶת. — *But the Sages say: [As] fine flour.*

They maintain that the phrase בְּלוּלָה בַשֶּׁמֶן, *mixed with oil,* refers back to the word סֹלֶת, *fine flour*; thus, the verse means that the oil and flour are mixed prior to baking (ibid.).

The translation of this part of the mishnah has followed *Rav* and *Ramban Comm.* According to *Rashi* (*Peirush* and *ms*), however, this should be translated: *And [as] loaves he mixes them.* In his view, the word חַלּוֹת, *loaves*, refers to all the baked and fried *menachos*, including the *machavas* and *marcheshes*. Thus, the dispute between Rabbi and the Sages concerns all baked or fried *menachos*. The Sages hold that the second application of oil is added to the flour whereas Rabbi holds that in all of these the baking is done first (*Rashi; Tos. Yom Tov;* see *Keren Orah; Sfas Emes*). [*Tos. Yom Tov* indicates that *Rav* and *Rambam* do not actually dispute this, but merely translate the word חַלּוֹת to refer to the *minchah* of that name, rather than the loaves of all baked *menachos*.]

The halachah follows the view of the Sages (*Rav; Rambam, Maaseh HaKorbanos* 13:8).

הַחַלּוֹת טְעוּנוֹת בְּלִילָה וְהָרְקִיקִים מְשׁוּחִים. — *The challos require mixing and the rekikin are anointed.*

The oven-baked *minchah* comes in two forms: *challos*, loaves, and *rekikin*, wafers. Each of these forms of the oven-baked *minchah* has its oil applied in a different way. The *challos* are "mixed" [in their unbaked state according to the Sages; or after their baking according to Rabbi, as above] and the *rekikin* are smeared, as described below (*Tos. Yom Tov; Tif. Yis.*).

6 But the Sages say: [As] fine flour.
3 The *challos* require mixing and the *rekikin* are anointed. How are they anointed? Like a *chi*. The remainder of the oil is eaten by the *Kohanim*.

YAD AVRAHAM

The contrast between the *challos* and the *rekikin* is indicated by the Torah (*Lev.* 2:4) which states: חַלּוֹת מַצֹּת בְּלוּלֹת בַּשֶּׁמֶן וּרְקִיקֵי מַצּוֹת מְשֻׁחִים בַּשָּׁמֶן, *loaves of matzah mixed with oil and wafers of matzah anointed with oil*, indicating that the *challos* [loaves] require only mixing while the *rekikin* [wafers] require only anointing (*Gem.* 76a).

[As mentioned previously, the oven-baked *menachos* differ from the others in the respect that they do not have a third application of oil; all their oil is added in the first two applications. *Challos* undergo בְּלִילָה, *mixing*, in the manner of all *menachos*, and in the *rekikin*, the second application — mixing — is replaced by מְשִׁיחָה, *anointing*.]

There is a question, however, if the oven-baked *menachos* shared with all other *menachos* the requirement for the first application of oil. According to *Tos.* (75a, s.v. מה להלן) that requirement applied to all *menachos* — *soless, machavas, marcheshes, challos,* and *rekikin*. *Rambam* (*Maaseh HaKorbanos* 13:8) indicates that oven-baked *menachos* require only the mixing or anointing but do not have any preliminary application of oil. Thus, the *rekikin*, which are anointed after their baking, are baked with only water (*Mishneh LaMelech*, loc. cit., cf. *Lechem Mishneh; Keren Orah*).

כֵּיצַד מוֹשְׁחָן? כְּמִין כִּי. — *How are they anointed? Like a chi.*

The oil was smeared on the *rekikin* in the shape of the Greek letter *chi*, which is shaped like an X (*Rambam, Hil. Klei HaMikdash* 1:9). Others contend that this refers to the Greek letter which resembles a Hebrew *tes* (*Rav; Rashi; Rabbeinu Gershom*). This is the lower case of the twentieth letter of the Greek alphabet (*Tos. Yom Tov*) [called upsilon; assumedly, it is referred to as כִּי because, being the twentieth letter, it is considered a parallel to the Hebrew *chof* whose numerical value is twenty].

Another view is that this refers to the eleventh letter in the Greek alphabet, *lambda*, which is shaped like an inverted "V" (*Aruch* כִּי; cited by *Tos.* 75a, s.v. כמין כי). [This too can be considered a parallel to the Hebrew letter *chof*, which is also the eleventh letter of the alphabet] (cf. *Tos.* loc. cit.; *Tif. Yis.* to *Zevachim* 10:8).

וּשְׁאָר הַשֶּׁמֶן נֶאֱכָל לַכֹּהֲנִים. — *The remainder of the oil is eaten by the Kohanim.*

[Not all the oil needs to be applied during the anointing. Whatever oil is left over after the *rekikin* have been anointed is eaten by the *Kohanim*.] This is the view of R' Shimon. The Sages, however, contend that he continues to anoint the wafers with oil until the entire *log* of oil is completely absorbed (*Gem.* 75a). *Rambam* (*Maaseh HaKorbanos* 13:9) rules in favor of the Sages (see *Kesef Mishneh, Lechem Mishneh* ad loc.).

[ד] **כָּל** הַמְּנָחוֹת הַנַּעֲשׂוֹת בִּכְלִי טְעוּנוֹת פְּתִיתָה. מִנְחַת יִשְׂרָאֵל, כּוֹפֵל אֶחָד לִשְׁנַיִם וּשְׁנַיִם לְאַרְבָּעָה, וּמַבְדִּיל. מִנְחַת כֹּהֲנִים, כּוֹפֵל אֶחָד לִשְׁנַיִם וּשְׁנַיִם לְאַרְבָּעָה, וְאֵינוֹ מַבְדִּיל.

ר׳ עובדיה מברטנורא

(ד) **כל המנחות הנעשות בבלי.** הכא לאו למעוטי מנחת מאפה תנור אתא, דכתיב (ויקרא ב, ו) פתות אותה פתים וגו׳ מנחה, לרבות כל המנחות לפתיתה, אלא למעוטי שתי הלחם ולחם הפנים שאין טעונים פתיתה: **כופל אחת לשתים.** דכתיב (שם) פתות אותה פתים, פתות היינו שנים, דכיון דנשבר היינו שתי חתיכות, פתים מרבינן שתהא החתיכה לשתי חתיכות דהיינו ארבעה, יכול יעשנה פרורים, תלמוד לומר אותה פתים, ולא פתיתיה לפתיתים. וכלן פתיתין כזיתים דסיפא דמתניתין לאו רבי שמעון קאמר ליה אלא דברי הכל היא, דלאחר שעשה פתיתין כזיתים, כופל כל זית לשנים ושנים לארבעה:

יד אברהם

## 4.

The following mishnah deals with the process of פְּתִיתָה, *fragmenting* or *breaking into pieces*. Once a *minchah* has been baked or fried, the final product must be broken into pieces before *kemitzah* can take place. This requirement is stated in the Torah in connection with the *minchas machavas* (*Lev.* 2:6): פָּתוֹת אֹתָהּ פִּתִּים, *break it into pieces*, but it applies to all the *menachos* which are baked or fried before their *kemitzah*, as the mishnah will state.

כָּל הַמְּנָחוֹת הַנַּעֲשׂוֹת בִּכְלִי — *All minchah-offerings which are prepared in a vessel*

The requirement of פְּתִיתָה, *breaking into pieces*, applies to all *menachos* prepared in a *kli shareis* [such as the *machavas* and *marcheshes*]. However, this term [unlike the identical phrase used in the previous mishnah] is not meant to exclude all those that are baked in an oven rather than a *kli shareis*, since the requirement clearly applies to the oven-baked *challos* and *rekikin* as well. The mishnah means to exclude only the *shtei halechem* of Shavuos and the *lechem hapanim* (*Rav*) [which are baked in an oven, not in a vessel] (*Rashi Peirush*). These are excluded by Biblical exegesis (*Tos. Yom Tov* from *Gem.* 75a). The mishnah's formula here is merely a rule of thumb, but the law is not actually dependent on whether it is prepared in a vessel or not (*Keren Orah*; cf. *Tif. Yis.*).

It would appear from this that even the *minchas soless*, the fine flour *minchah*, which is not baked prior to *kemitzah*, is included in the mishnah's subsequent requirement for פְּתִיתָה, *breaking into pieces* (*Shitah Mekubetzes* 75a #6). *Rashi* (comm. to *Lev.* 2:6), however, indicates that the requirement for פְּתִיתָה applies only to those *menachos* baked prior to *kemitzah*. This would exclude the *minchas soless* (*Mizrachi* ad loc.). According to the view cited below, that the *minchas soless* need never be baked at all (even prior to being eaten), it goes without saying that there is no requirement for פְּתִיתָה

6
4

4. **A**ll *minchah*-offerings which are prepared in a vessel require breaking into pieces. The *minchah*-offering of a *Yisrael* one folds in two and the two into four, and separates [them]. The *minchah*-offering of the *Kohanim* one folds in two and the two into four, and one does not separate them.

### YAD AVRAHAM

[which can only be done with baked items] (*Mishneh LaMelech, Maaseh HaKorbanos* 13:10).

.טְעוּנוֹת פְּתִיתָה — *require breaking into pieces.*

The Torah states concerning the *minchas machavas* [*minchah* prepared on a griddle] (*Lev.* 2:6): פָּתוֹת אֹתָהּ פִּתִּים, *break it into pieces,* which teaches that the *minchah* requires fragmentation into smaller pieces (פִּתִּים) prior to *kemitzah*, as described below (*Rashi,* as explained by *Zevach Todah,* cf. *Ravad* to *Toras Kohanim* ad loc.). This is extended by Biblical exegesis to the other baked *menachos,* with the exception of the *shtei halechem* and *lechem hapanim* (*Gem.* 75a).

מִנְחַת יִשְׂרָאֵל, כּוֹפֵל אֶחָד לִשְׁנַיִם וּשְׁנַיִם לְאַרְבָּעָה, — *The minchah-offering of a Yisrael, one folds in two and the two into four,*

The *minchah* is baked or fried into ten loaves [or cakes or wafers] as described below. Each of these loaves is then folded in half and then into quarters (*Rashi Peirush; Rambam, Maaseh HaKorbanos* 13:10). This is derived from the Torah's phrase פָּתוֹת אֹתָהּ פִּתִּים, *break it into fragments.* The word פָּתוֹת indicates breaking the pieces into two and the word פִּתִּים indicates another fragmentation (*Rav; Rambam Comm.*).

*Rav* explains the mishnah to mean that every *kezayis* of the *minchah* is first divided into two pieces and then into four. He apparently assumes that the *minchah* was first divided into olive-size pieces and then divided. This point is strongly contested by many commentators, who explain, as above, that each of the *minchah's* ten (or twelve) loaves is fragmented into four pieces (*Rashi Peirush; Rambam, Maaseh HaKorbanos* 13:10, cf. his *Comm.* (see *Keren Orah*).

.וּמַבְדִּיל — *and separates [them].*

The folded segments are then completely divided into quarters in order to allow for the *kemitzah* [which is impossible to do with an entire loaf] (*Rashi*).[1]

מִנְחַת כֹּהֲנִים, כּוֹפֵל אֶחָד לִשְׁנַיִם וּשְׁנַיִם לְאַרְבָּעָה, וְאֵינוֹ מַבְדִּיל. — *The minchah-offering of the Kohanim one folds in two and the two into four, and one does not separate them.*

Since the *minchah* of a *Kohen* is burnt in its entirety and requires no *kemitzah*, no separating is necessary (*Rashi;* see mishnah 2). The folding is therefore sufficient to fulfill the Torah's requirement for פְּתִיתָה (*Tif. Yis.; Zevach Todah*).

1. [It is apparent from this that though these *menachos* must be prevented from becoming *chametz* (mishnah 5:1), they were nevertheless soft and could be folded, not crisp and brittle as the matzos of today.]

# מִנְחַת כֹּהֵן הַמָּשִׁיחַ, לֹא הָיָה מְכַפְּלָהּ. רַבִּי שִׁמְעוֹן אוֹמֵר: מִנְחַת כֹּהֲנִים וּמִנְחַת כֹּהֵן מָשִׁיחַ אֵין בָּהֶם פְּתִיתָה, מִפְּנֵי שֶׁאֵין בָּהֶם קְמִיצָה; וְכָל שֶׁאֵין בָּהֶם קְמִיצָה אֵין בָּהֶם פְּתִיתָה. וְכֻלָּן כְּזֵיתִים.

מנחות ו/ה

[ה] **כָּל** הַמְּנָחוֹת טְעוּנוֹת שְׁלֹשׁ מֵאוֹת שִׁיפָה

### ר׳ עובדיה מברטנורא

**מכפלה.** לא היה מכפלה לארבעה, אלא לשנים, דלא כתיב בה אלא מנחת פתים, ולא פתות: **רבי שמעון אומר כו׳.** ואין הלכה כרבי שמעון: **(ה) שיפה.** שמשפשף החטה בין ידו לכלי כדי שתהא

### יד אברהם

מִנְחַת כֹּהֵן הַמָּשִׁיחַ, לֹא הָיָה מְכַפְּלָהּ — *The minchah-offering of the Anointed Kohen he did not fold.*

I.e., it was not folded into quarters; only into halves (*Rav* from *Gem.* 75b). The fact that the *Kohen Gadol's minchah* is folded less than other *menachos* is because the Torah describes his *minchah* (*Lev.* 6:14) simply as מִנְחַת פִּתִּים, *a minchah of pieces*, without the double statement פָּתוֹת אֹתָהּ פִּתִּים, *break it into pieces*, used in connection with the other *menachos* (*Rav; Rashi msc.*; cf. *Rashi Peirush*).

*Mishneh LaMelech* (*Maaseh HaKorbanos* 13:4) offers an explanation according to which there is actually no difference between the *minchah* of an ordinary *Kohen* and the *minchah* of the *Kohen Gadol;* see footnote below.

רַבִּי שִׁמְעוֹן אוֹמֵר: מִנְחַת כֹּהֲנִים וּמִנְחַת כֹּהֵן מָשִׁיחַ אֵין בָּהֶם פְּתִיתָה, — *R' Shimon says: The minchah-offering of the Kohanim and the minchah-offering of the Anointed Kohen are not broken into pieces,*

R' Shimon disagrees with the first *Tanna* regarding the requirement for פְּתִיתָה in the case of a *Kohen's* voluntary *minchah* and the Anointed *Kohen's* daily *minchah*. In his view these *menachos* do not require even the folding mentioned by the first *Tanna* (*Rashi Peirush; Tif. Yis.*).

מִפְּנֵי שֶׁאֵין בָּהֶם קְמִיצָה; וְכָל שֶׁאֵין בָּהֶם קְמִיצָה אֵין בָּהֶם פְּתִיתָה. — *since they do not require kemitzah; and whatever does not require kemitzah need not be broken into pieces.*

[I.e., according to R' Shimon, פְּתִיתָה is required as a preliminary step to *kemitzah*. Thus, those *menachos* that require no *kemitzah* require no פְּתִיתָה either.] [1]

1. R' Shimon's view regarding the Anointed *Kohen's* daily *minchah* [*minchas chavitin*] leads the commentators to grapple with a basic problem: How can R' Shimon exclude the daily *minchah* of the *Kohen Gadol* from the requirement for פְּתִיתָה when the verse (*Lev.* 6:14) explicitly describes this *minchah* as תֻּפִינֵי מִנְחַת פִּתִּים, *baked as a fragmented minchah*? (See *Rashi* ad loc.)

*Mizrachi* (ad loc.) concludes that R' Shimon disagrees only with the first *Tanna's* requirement to fold and refold the *minchah* of a *Kohen*. In his view, the necessity of folding the loaves into four is only to facilitate the *kemitzah*, and it is therefore unnecessary in the case of the *minchah* of a *Kohen*. R' Shimon agrees, however, that this *minchah* requires folding in two, as that is a separate *mitzvah*, independent of *kemitzah*. Thus,

The *minchah*-offering of the Anointed *Kohen* he did not fold. R' Shimon says: The *minchah*-offering of the *Kohanim* and the *minchah*-offering of the Anointed *Kohen* are not broken into pieces, since they do not require *kemitzah;* and whatever does not require *kemitzah* need not be broken into pieces. All of them are an olive's volume.

**5.** All *minchah*-offerings require three hundred

**YAD AVRAHAM**

וְכֻלָּן כְּזֵיתִים. — *All of them are an olive's volume.*

Some commentators explain this to be the statement of R' Shimon, who disagrees with the description of the breaking into pieces as the folding of the loaves into quarters. He maintains that the fragmenting process consists of folding and refolding the *minchah* until the pieces are reduced to the size of a *kezayis* (*Rashi ms; Rashba*).

Others contend that this statement is not a continuation of R' Shimon's view, but a new, anonymous ruling accepted even by the first *Tanna*. Thus, all agree that after folding the loaves in the manner described he continues to divide them until the pieces are the size of an olive, but not smaller (*Rashi Peirush; Rambam, Maaseh HaKorbanos* 13:10).

As noted above (s.v. מנחת ישראל), *Rav* explains this part of the mishnah to refer to the pieces *before* they were folded and refolded; i.e., the folding was done with pieces that were no bigger than a *kezayis* to begin with. This is disputed by most other commentators (see *Keren Orah*).

5.

כָּל הַמְּנָחוֹת טְעוּנוֹת שְׁלֹשׁ מֵאוֹת שִׁיפָּה — *All minchah-offerings require three hundred rubbings*

In order to facilitate removing the husks, the wheat is rubbed between the hands (*Rashi ms*), or between the hand and a utensil (*Rav*), before it is milled. Rubbing it in this manner and

even according to R' Shimon, the *minchas chavitin* is described as a מִנְחַת פִּתִּים, *fragmented minchah* (cf. *Korban Aharon* to *Toras Kohanim*).

*Mishneh LaMelech* (*Maaseh HaKorbanos* 13:4) expresses dissatisfaction with this explanation. He therefore suggests a resolution for this difficulty in light of *Rambam's* view (ad loc.) that the *minchas chavitin* which was to be brought *half in the morning and half in the afternoon* (*Lev.* 6:13) was actually brought as *half loaves*, i.e., all twelve of its loaves were baked in the morning and each was divided in half (see above mishnah 4:5). The Torah thus refers to this *minchah* as a מִנְחַת פִּתִּים, *a fragmented minchah*, because it was offered as twelve half-loaves. [This also explains the basis of the first *Tanna's* distinction between a regular *minchas Kohen*, which required folding into quarters, and the *minchas chavitin* which required only folding into two: Since the *minchas chavitin* was offered in the form of half loaves, folding each half loaf in two was the equivalent of folding each loaf into quarters.]

וַחֲמֵשׁ מֵאוֹת בְּעִיטָה; וְהַשִּׁיפָה וְהַבְּעִיטָה בַּחִטִּים. רַבִּי יוֹסֵי אוֹמֵר: [אַף] בַּבָּצֵק.

כָּל הַמְּנָחוֹת בָּאוֹת עֶשֶׂר עֶשֶׂר, חוּץ מִלֶּחֶם הַפָּנִים וַחֲבִתֵּי כֹהֵן גָּדוֹל, שֶׁהֵם בָּאוֹת שְׁתֵּים עֶשְׂרֵה; דִּבְרֵי רַבִּי יְהוּדָה. רַבִּי מֵאִיר אוֹמֵר: כֻּלָּן בָּאוֹת שְׁתֵּים עֶשְׂרֵה,

### ר׳ עובדיה מברטנורא

נוחה להסיר קליפתה: **בעיטה.** שבועט בעוטי אגרופו או בעוטי פס ידו. והיה שף אחת ובועט שתים, שף שתים ובועט שלש, וחוזר ועושה כסדר הזה עד שגומר חמש מאות בעיטות לשלש מאות שיפות: **הכי גרסינן רבי יוסי אומר בבצק.** כלומר, שיפה ובעיטה בבצק ולא בחטין. ואין הלכה כרבי יהודה: **עשר עשר חלות.** ומנחת סלת נמי אף על גב דקודם אפיה נקמצת, אפילו הכי עשר חלות היא באה: **לחם הפנים.** בהדיא כתיב ביה שתים עשרה חלות: **וחביתי כהן גדול.** נאמר בלחם הפנים חק עולם (ויקרא כד, ט), ונאמר בחביתי כהן גדול חק עולם (שם ו,טו), מה להלן שתים עשרה חלות, אף כאן שתים עשרה חלות, ומקריבין מהן שש חלות בבקר ושש חלות בערב:

### יד אברהם

then pounding it [see below] makes it easier to remove the husks from the kernels (*Tif. Yis.*).

The *Gemara* (76a) leaves unresolved the question of whether the three hundred rubbings means that it is rolled three hundred times back and three hundred times forth or a total of three hundred "rubbings," i.e., one hundred fifty back and one hundred and fifty forth.

וַחֲמֵשׁ מֵאוֹת בְּעִיטָה; — *and five hundred poundings;*

He pounds the wheat with his palm or fist (*Rav; Rashi ms*) or his foot (*Rambam Comm.*) five hundred times to loosen the husk (*Tif. Yis.*). The actual procedure was to roll the wheat once and pound it twice and then roll it twice and pound it three times. This procedure was repeated a hundred times, for a total of three hundred rubbings and five hundred poundings (*Rav* from *Gem.* 76a).

וְהַשִּׁיפָה וְהַבְּעִיטָה בַּחִטִּים. — *and the rubbings and poundings are to the wheat.*

I.e., it is the wheat that is rubbed and pounded in order to facilitate the removal of its husk (*Tif. Yis.*).

רַבִּי יוֹסֵי אוֹמֵר: [אַף] בַּבָּצֵק. — *R' Yose says: [Even] to the dough.*

The wording here is in line with the standard editions of the Mishnah. However, *Rav* (as well as other commentators) emends this to omit the word אַף, *even*. Thus, the proper version should read, *R' Yose says: To the dough.*

Only the dough is rubbed and pounded but not the wheat itself (*Rav* from *Gem.* ibid.). Thus, its function is not to facilitate the removal of the husk but to make for a more uniform dough (*Tif. Yis.*).

There is a version in *Tosefta* that reads: ר׳ יוֹסֵי אוֹמֵר: אַף בַּבָּצֵק — *R' Yose says: The dough also*, indicating that R' Yose agrees with the first *Tanna* that the rubbing and pounding procedure applies to the wheat but adds that the process is also performed on the dough. Accurate texts of *Tosefta*, however, concur with our version of the mishnah (*Tos. Yom Tov*, citing *Tosafos*).

6 rubbings and five hundred poundings; and the
5 rubbings and poundings are to the wheat. R′ Yose says: [Even] to the dough.

All *minchah*-offerings are brought in groups of ten [loaves], except for the *lechem hapanim* and the *chavitin* of the *Kohen Gadol*, which are brought in [groups of] twelve; [these are] the words of R′ Yehudah. R′ Meir says: They are all brought in groups of twelve [loaves],

**YAD AVRAHAM**

In yet another view, R′ Yose limits the pounding process to the dough, but agrees that the requirement for rubbing applies to the wheat as well (*Rambam Comm.*).

The halachah follows the view of the first *Tanna* (*Rav; Rambam, Isurei Mizbe'ach* 7:5).

**כָּל הַמְּנָחוֹת בָּאוֹת עֶשֶׂר עֶשֶׂר, —** *All minchah-offerings are brought in groups of ten [loaves],*

All *menachos* are fashioned into ten loaves for each *issaron* of flour (*Tif. Yis.*). This is derived from the Torah's requirement that the loaves of the *todah* offering be brought in groups of ten loaves (*Gem.* 76a; see mishnah 7:1).

Even the *minchas soless*, on which *kemitzah* is performed while it is still flour, must afterward be baked into ten loaves (*Rav; Rashi ms*). Even though its *avodah* has been completed, there is nevertheless a Biblical requirement that it be baked into ten loaves before being distributed to the *Kohanim*.

However, *Mishneh LaMelech* and *Lechem Mishneh* (*Maaseh HaKorbanos* 13:10; see also *Tos. Yom Tov*), in extensive analyses of this point, cite proofs from *Ramban* and *Rashi's* commentary to *Chumash* (*Lev.* 2:6) that the *minchas soless* did not have to be fashioned into ten loaves, nor even necessarily baked, for that matter.

**חוּץ מִלֶּחֶם הַפָּנִים וַחֲבִתֵּי כֹהֵן גָּדוֹל, שֶׁהֵם בָּאוֹת שְׁתֵּים עֶשְׂרֵה; דִּבְרֵי רַבִּי יְהוּדָה. —** *except for the lechem hapanim and the chavitin of the Kohen Gadol, which are brought in [groups of] twelve; [these are] the words of R′ Yehudah.*

Regarding the *lechem hapanim*, the Torah explicitly requires twelve loaves (*Lev.* 24:5), and the *Gemara* derives exegetically that this requirement applies to the *chavitin* as well (*Rav* from Gem. 76a).

**רַבִּי מֵאִיר אוֹמֵר: כֻּלָּן בָּאוֹת שְׁתֵּים עֶשְׂרֵה, —** *R′ Meir says: They are all brought in groups of twelve [loaves],*

In R′ Meir's view, all *menachos* are offered in twelve loaves, just as *lechem hapanim* and *chavitin*. He reasons that since *menachos* are considered קָדְשֵׁי קָדָשִׁים, *most-holy offerings* (because they are eaten only by *Kohanim* and only in the Temple Courtyard), they are more similar to the *lechem hapanim* and the *chavitin* than to the *todah* loaves, which rank only as *offerings of lesser holiness* [קָדָשִׁים קַלִּים]; see *Zevachim* 5:6. The first *Tanna*, however, considers it more plausible to derive the laws of *menachos* from the *todah* loaves because of their similarities to each other in numerous halachic details (*Gem.* ibid.).

חוּץ מֵחַלּוֹת תּוֹדָה וְהַנְּזִירוּת, שֶׁהֵן בָּאוֹת עֶשֶׂר עֶשֶׂר.

[ו] **הָעֹמֶר** הָיָה בָא עִשָּׂרוֹן מִשָּׁלֹשׁ סְאִין. שְׁתֵּי הַלֶּחֶם – שְׁנֵי עֶשְׂרוֹנִים מִשָּׁלֹשׁ סְאִין. לֶחֶם הַפָּנִים – עֶשְׂרִים וְאַרְבָּעָה עֶשְׂרוֹנִים מֵעֶשְׂרִים וְאַרְבַּע סְאִין.

### ר׳ עובדיה מברטנורא

**חוץ מחלות תודה שהן באות עשר.** כדבעינן למימר טעמא לקמן באידך פרקין (ז, א־ב). ואין הלכה כרבי מאיר: (ו) **העומר היה בא עשרון משלש סאין.** מנחת העומר שמביאין ממחרת הפסח היו קוצרין שלש סאין דהיינו איפה שעורים, וטוחנין אותו, [ומניפין] אותו בנפה שלש עשרה פעמים עד שמעמידים סלתו על עשרון שהיא עשירית האיפה. וטעמא דבעי עשרון של עומר שלש סאים של שעורים, כיון דמתבואה חדשה הוא ושל שעורים יש בהן סובין הרבה וסולת מועט ולא אתי עשרונו מובחר אלא משלש סאין: **שתי הלחם שתי עשרונים משלש סאין.** כיון דמחטים קאתו, אף על גב דמתבואה חדשה אתיין, דבעצרת תבואה של חטין חדשה היא, אפילו הכי שתי עשרונים מובחרים אתו משלש סאין: **לחם הפנים עשרים וארבעה עשרונים.** דהכי כתיב (ויקרא כד,ה) שתים עשרה חלות שני עשרונים יהיה החלה האחת: **מעשרים וארבע סאים.** כיון דמחטין אתו ומתבואה ישנה, נפיק עשרון מובחר מסאה:

### יד אברהם

חוּץ מֵחַלּוֹת תּוֹדָה וְהַנְּזִירוּת, שֶׁהֵן בָּאוֹת עֶשֶׂר עֶשֶׂר. — *except for the loaves of the todah-[offering] and the nazir's [offering], which are brought in groups of ten.*

[Both the *todah* loaves and the *nazir*-offering's loaves — i.e., the two types of loaves which a *nazir* brings upon completion of his vow — require twelve loaves, as derived below (*Rav* from *Gem.* 76a, see mishnah 7:1,2).

The halachah follows the view of the first *Tanna* (*Rav; Rambam, Maaseh HaKorbanos* 13:10).

## 6.

The following mishnah begins a discussion (which continues into the next chapter) of the actual measurements of the different *menachos*. An *ephah* consists of three *seah*. An *issaron*, which means literally a *tenth*, is one-tenth of an *ephah*.

הָעֹמֶר — *The omer-offering*

The *omer*-offering is the special communal *minchah* that is brought on the sixteenth of Nissan [the second day of Pesach] (*Tif. Yis.*) to permit consumption of the new crop of grain (*Lev.* 23:14; mishnah 10:6). Unlike almost all other *menachos*, the *omer*-offering is made of barley flour rather than wheat flour (*Sotah* 2:1).

6 except for the loaves of the *todah*-[offering]
6 and the *nazir's* [offering], which are brought in groups of ten.

**6.** The *omer*-offering consisted of one *issaron* [of flour] refined from three *seahs.* The *shtei halechem* [consisted of] two *essronim* [refined] from three *seahs.* The *lechem hapanim* [consisted of] twenty-four *essronim* [refined] from twenty-four *seahs.*

### YAD AVRAHAM

הָיָה בָא עִשָּׂרוֹן מִשָּׁלֹשׁ סְאִין. — *consisted of one issaron [of flour] refined* (lit., *which comes*) *from three seahs.*

The offering consisted of an *issaron* (tenth of an *ephah*) of fine flour, which was refined from three *seah* of barley. Three *seah* — or one *ephah* — of barley were harvested. This was ground, sifted, and resifted thirteen times (see mishnah 7) to yield one *issaron* of fine flour, which was then used for the *omer*-offering (*Rav*). It was necessary to use so much grain to produce this small amount of flour because the *minchah* of the *omer* was brought from fresh barley, which generally contains a large amount of chaff and requires a greater degree of sifting than does wheat (*Rav* from *Gem.* 76b).

שְׁתֵּי הַלֶּחֶם — שְׁנֵי עֶשְׂרוֹנִים מִשָּׁלֹשׁ סְאִין. — *The shtei halechem [consisted of] two essronim [refined] from three seahs.*

The *shtei halechem* are the *two loaves* brought on Shavuos. Each one must consist of one-tenth of an *ephah* of flour (*Lev.* 23:17). Since they were brought from fresh wheat, which has less chaff than does barley, three *seah* of grain are sufficient to provide two *essronim* of refined flour for the offering (*Rav* from *Gem.* ibid.).

לֶחֶם הַפָּנִים — עֶשְׂרִים וְאַרְבָּעָה עֶשְׂרוֹנִים — *The lechem hapanim [consisted of] twenty-four essronim*

[The total volume of flour in the weekly *lechem hapanim* is twenty-four *essronim,* as stated in the passage (*Lev.* 24:5): *twelve loaves, each loaf two essronim* (*Rav*).

מֵעֶשְׂרִים וְאַרְבַּע סְאִין. — *[refined] from twenty-four seahs.*

Older wheat yields a greater percentage of fine flour than fresh wheat. Since the *lechem hapanim* are made from old wheat, it is easier to refine an *issaron* of fine flour from it than it is from fresh wheat. Consequently, one *issaron* of fine flour can be produced from each *seah* of grain (*Rav* from *Gem.* 76b).

Although decreasing or increasing the measure of the *minchah* itself invalidates it, changing the measure of grain from which the offering is taken does not affect the validity (*Gem.* 76b).

[ז] **הָעֹמֶר** הָיָה מְנֻפֶּה בִּשְׁלֹשׁ עֶשְׂרֵה נָפָה, וּשְׁתֵּי הַלֶּחֶם בִּשְׁתֵּים עֶשְׂרֵה, וְלֶחֶם הַפָּנִים בְּאַחַת עֶשְׂרֵה. רַבִּי שִׁמְעוֹן אוֹמֵר: לֹא הָיָה לָהּ קִצְבָה; אֶלָּא סֹלֶת מְנֻפָּה כָּל צָרְכָּהּ הָיָה מֵבִיא, שֶׁנֶּאֱמַר: ,,וְלָקַחְתָּ סֹלֶת וְאָפִיתָ אֹתָהּ״ – עַד שֶׁתְּהֵא מְנֻפָּה כָּל צָרְכָּהּ.

**ר׳ עובדיה מברטנורא**

(ז) **היה מנופה בשלש עשרה נפה.** זו למעלה מזו. וכל זה למצוה אבל לא לעכב, שאם הביא עומר עשרון מארבע סאין או שהביאו משני סאין, לא פסל: **רבי שמעון אומר לא היה לה קצבה.** דאפילו לכתחלה לא נתנו חכמים קצבה מכמה סאין חטין או שעורין מביאין עומר ושתי הלחם ולחם הפנים, אלא רואין בסולת שתהא מנופה כל צרכה ודיו. ואין הלכה כרבי שמעון:

**יד אברהם**

## 7.

הָעֹמֶר הָיָה מְנֻפֶּה בִּשְׁלֹשׁ עֶשְׂרֵה נָפָה, — *The omer-offering was sifted through thirteen sieves,*

Thirteen sieves are placed one above the other (*Rav*), each one finer than the one above it. Thus, the flour first filtered through the coarsest sieve at the top and then through the one below it, etc.

In a *baraisa* cited by the *Gemara* (76b), there seems to be a dispute of *Tannaim* regarding the nature of the sifting process. According to the *Tanna Kamma*, only two sieves are used but the process is repeated thirteen times, thereby removing all dust and chaff from the flour, as well as sifting out the fine flour from the coarser flour with which it was mixed. What the mishnah means, then, is that the flour is *sifted thirteen times.* According to R' Shimon ben Elazar, thirteen separate sieves were used. This view is apparently favored by *Rav* and *Tos. Yom Tov*, as well as *Rambam Comm.* because the mishnah's words, בִּשְׁלֹשׁ עֶשְׂרֵה נָפָה, is more readily translated *through thirteen sieves* rather than *thirteen times*[1] (*Rashash; Zevach Todah;* cf. *Lechem Mishneh, Temidin U'Mussafin* 12:7).

וּשְׁתֵּי הַלֶּחֶם בִּשְׁתֵּים עֶשְׂרֵה, וְלֶחֶם הַפָּנִים בְּאַחַת עֶשְׂרֵה. — *the shtei halechem through twelve, and the lechem hapanim through eleven.*

Since the *omer* required the greatest amount of sifting and the *lechem hapanim* the least, as stated above (mishnah 6), the number of sieves required was set accordingly (*Rambam,*

1. This follows the interpretation of *Rashi Peirush*. However, *Rashi ms* explains that even this *Tanna* agrees that thirteen sieves were used but that they were used alternatingly, not sequentially. That is, first the finest sieve was used, followed by the coarsest. This was followed by the second finest, the second coarsest, the third finest, etc. In his view R' Shimon ben Elazar is merely amplifying the *Tanna Kamma's* statement.

6
7
**7.** The *omer*-offering was sifted through thirteen sieves, the *shtei halechem* through twelve, and the *lechem hapanim* through eleven. R' Shimon says: There was no set amount; rather he brought flour that was sifted as much as necessary, as it is stated (*Lev.* 24:5): *And you shall take fine flour and you shall bake it* — until it is sifted as much as necessary.

YAD AVRAHAM

*Temidin U'Mussafin* 8:4). However, if one did not follow this procedure, the *minchah* is nevertheless valid (*Rav; Rambam* ibid. 5). Only the measure of flour actually used in the offering is critical (*Zevach Todah;* see comm. to mishnah 6).

In the opinion of others, the varying number of sieves required for the *omer, shtei halechem,* and *lechem hapanim* is based on an oral halachah transmitted to Moshe at Sinai, rather than on the different nature of the grains used (*Rashi Peirush;* cf. *Tos. Yom Tov*). According to this opinion, it could be argued that the offering is not valid if sifted with less than the required number of sieves (*Tos. Yom Tov;* cf. *Zevach Todah*).

רַבִּי שִׁמְעוֹן אוֹמֵר: לֹא הָיָה לָהּ קִצְבָה; אֶלָּא סֹלֶת מְנֻפָּה כָּל צָרְכָּהּ הָיָה מֵבִיא, — *R' Shimon says: There was no set amount; rather he brought flour that was sifted as much as necessary,*

The Rabbis set no specific requirements for the amount of grain from which these *menachos* must be taken (*Rav*), nor for the amount of sieves required for the sifting (*Tif. Yis.;* cf. *Keren Orah*). As long as the required measure of grain is properly sifted it is fully acceptable for the offering (*Rav*).

Others explain R' Shimon to be in disagreement with only the last statement of the first *Tanna,* i.e., that the *lechem hapanim* must be sifted through eleven sieves. R' Shimon maintains that this is not necessary; as long as the flour is fully sifted it is acceptable (*Rashi msc.*).

שֶׁנֶּאֱמַר: „וְלָקַחְתָּ סֹלֶת וְאָפִיתָ אֹתָהּ" — עַד שֶׁתְּהֵא מְנֻפָּה כָּל צָרְכָּהּ. — *as it is stated* (*Lev.* 24:5): *"And you shall take fine flour and you shall bake it" — until it is sifted as much as necessary.*

The Torah statement *and you shall take fine flour* indicates that as long as it is fine flour when it is taken it is sufficient, regardless of how many times it was sifted (*Rashi ms;* cf. *Peirush*).

In all the above cases, the flour must be sifted to obtain סֹלֶת, *fine flour*. Indeed, this is the rule for all *menachos* other than the jealousy *minchah* of the *sotah* (see 2:1). The *soless* is that which remains *on top* of the last sieve; what falls through that sieve is considered flour dust, not fine flour (see *Avos* 5:15). However, the grains of *soless* are not used as is but are then taken and ground into a thin flour (*Rashi Peirush; Rashi* and *Machzor Vitri* to *Avos* 5:15; see *Aruch HaShulchan HeAsid* 116:5).

# פרק שביעי
# Chapter Seven

[א] **הַתּוֹדָה** הָיְתָה בָאָה חָמֵשׁ סְאִין יְרוּשַׁלְמִיּוֹת, שֶׁהֵן שֵׁשׁ מִדְבָּרִיּוֹת, שְׁתֵּי אֵיפוֹת; הָאֵיפָה שָׁלֹשׁ סְאִין, עֶשְׂרִים עִשָּׂרוֹן — עֲשָׂרָה לְחָמֵץ וַעֲשָׂרָה לְמַצָּה. עֲשָׂרָה לְחָמֵץ — עִשָּׂרוֹן לְחַלָּה. וַעֲשָׂרָה לַמַּצָּה —

**ר׳ עובדיה מברטנורא**

**פרק שביעי – התודה היתה. (א) התודה. חמש סאין ירושלמיות שהן שש מדבריות.** חמש סאין של ירושלים הן שש מאותן שהיו במדבר בימי משה, שהוסיפו על המדה שהיתה בימי משה שתות, דקיימא לן מוסיפין על המדות ואין מוסיפין יותר משתות, ואותו שתות הוא שתות מלבר: **שתי איפות.** כלומר, הנך שש סאין הם שתי איפות, שהם עשרים עשרון, שהרי בכל איפה עשרה עשרונות: **עשרה לחמץ.** עשרה עשרונים לעשר חלות חמץ שבתודה:

**יד אברהם**

## 1.

The *todah*-offering (see preface to 2:3) was accompanied by a total of forty loaves in four different varieties. These loaves consisted of three varieties of *matzah* [ten loaves each] and a fourth group of ten leavened loaves (*Lev.* 7:11ff).

הַתּוֹדָה הָיְתָה בָאָה חָמֵשׁ סְאִין יְרוּשַׁלְמִיּוֹת, שֶׁהֵן שֵׁשׁ מִדְבָּרִיּוֹת, — *The todah-offering consisted of* (lit., *would come from*) *five Jerusalem seahs, which are six Wilderness seahs,*

The total amount of flour required by the Torah for the forty loaves of the *todah*-offering is two *ephahs*, which comes to six *seahs*, as derived by the *Gemara* (77b). This, of course, refers to the *seah* measures in use at the time the Torah was given at Sinai. Subsequently, the Sages enlarged the *seah* measure by 20 percent [so that each original Biblical *seah* was now only ⅚ of its new counterpart].[1] This new measure came to be known as the *Jerusalem seah*, and it was the standard of measure used in [early] Mishnaic times.[2] Hence, five Jerusalem *seahs* are actually six Biblical *seahs* [or *Wilderness seahs*, because the Jews received the Torah in the Wilderness] (*Rav; Tif. Yis.*).

The authority of the Sages to increase Biblical measures is derived by the *Gemara* (77a) from a verse in *Ezekiel* (45:11). This is also the source for increasing the measure by one-sixth (*Rav*).

שְׁתֵּי אֵיפוֹת; הָאֵיפָה שָׁלֹשׁ סְאִין, — *[or]*

1. This calculation is referred to by the *Gemara* as a שְׁתוּת מִלְּבַר, *a sixth of the total* [lit. *a sixth from without*]. This means that for every five units of measure, a sixth equal measure was added, so that each of the original units is now a sixth of the total. In other words, the *seah* was actually increased by ⅕ of its former size. The converse of this calculation is called שְׁתוּת מִלְּגוֹ, *a sixth of itself* [lit. *a sixth from within*], which would mean dividing the measure into six parts and adding one of those sixths to the total (*Gem.* 77a; *Rashi* ibid.).

2. In the late Mishnaic period, the measures were again enlarged by a sixth in what came to be known as מִדּוֹת צִפּוֹרִיּוֹת, *Tzipporian measures*.

7 **1.** The *todah*-offering consisted of five Jerusa-
1 lem *seahs*, which are six Wilderness *seahs*,
[or] two *ephahs*; the *ephah* is three *seahs*, [or] twenty *issaron* — ten for leavened [loaves] and ten for *matzah*. Ten for the leavened [loaves] — one *issaron* per loaf. Ten for the *matzah* —



*two ephahs; the ephah is three seahs,*

[I.e., the six Wilderness *seahs* are the equivalent of two *ephahs*. The *ephah* is a common Biblical measure.]

עֶשְׂרִים עִשָּׂרוֹן – — *[or] twenty issaron* —

Each *ephah* consists of ten *essronim*. [The term עִשָּׂרוֹן, *issaron*, means a *tenth* and refers to a tenth of an *ephah*.] Thus, the two *ephahs* equal twenty *essronim* (*Rav*).

עֲשָׂרָה לְחָמֵץ וַעֲשָׂרָה לְמַצָּה. — *ten for leavened [loaves] and ten for matzah.*

The forty *todah* loaves are baked in four different varieties, each consisting of ten loaves. One variety was baked as *chametz* [leavened bread]. However, the two *ephahs* (or twenty *essronim* of flour which the Torah requires for the *todah* loaves are divided equally between the leavened loaves and the *matzah* loaves, notwithstanding the fact there were thirty unleavened loaves and only ten leavened loaves. [Thus, each *chametz* loaf is made of three times as much flour as its *matzah* counterpart.]

The equal division of flour between the leavened and unleavened loaves of the *todah* is derived from the verse (*Lev.* 7:13): עַל חַלֹּת לֶחֶם חָמֵץ, *in addition to leavened loaves of bread*. [This is stated after the Torah spells out the requirements for the three varieties of *matzah* in the previous verse.] This teaches us that the quantity of flour used for leavened bread should equal that of all three varieties of *matzah* [mentioned in the previous verse] (*Gem.* 77b; *Rashi* ad loc.).

עֲשָׂרָה לְחָמֵץ – עִשָּׂרוֹן לְחַלָּה. — *Ten for the leavened [loaves] — one issaron per loaf.*

Each of the ten loaves of the leavened bread is made from one *issaron* of flour (*Tif. Yis.*).

The Torah (*Num.* 18:11) requires that one loaf from each variety be given to a *Kohen* (see mishnah 2). The Torah refers to these four loaves as *terumah*. The *Gemara* (77b) derives from this that these loaves equal one-tenth of the total *minchah*, just as *terumah* consists of one-tenth of the grain [referring to the *terumah* which the *Levi* must give from the tithe given to them (*Rashi*)]. It is thus evident that ten loaves are required for each of the four varieties.

וַעֲשָׂרָה לַמַּצָּה – — *Ten for the matzah* —

[As mentioned above, the total flour used for the unleavened loaves equals that of the leavened ones. However, the distribution of the flour between the individual loaves is not the same. While the ten *essronim* of the leavened bread is separated into ten loaves, the same amount of flour for the unleavened part of the *todah* is divided into the *thirty* loaves of *matzah*, as the mishnah now explains.]

וּבַמַּצָּה שְׁלֹשָׁה מִינִין: חַלּוֹת, וּרְקִיקִים, וּרְבוּכָה; נִמְצְאוּ שְׁלֹשָׁה עֶשְׂרוֹנוֹת וּשְׁלִישׁ לְכָל מִין, שָׁלֹשׁ חַלּוֹת לְעִשָּׂרוֹן.

בְּמִדָּה יְרוּשַׁלְמִית, הָיוּ שְׁלֹשִׁים קַב: חֲמִשָּׁה עָשָׂר לֶחָמֵץ וַחֲמִשָּׁה עָשָׂר לַמַּצָּה. חֲמִשָּׁה עָשָׂר לֶחָמֵץ – קַב וָחֵצִי לְחַלָּה. וַחֲמִשָּׁה עָשָׂר לַמַּצָּה – וְהַמַּצָּה שְׁלֹשָׁה מִינִין: חַלּוֹת, וּרְקִיקִין, וּרְבוּכָה. נִמְצְאוּ חֲמֵשֶׁת קַבִּים לְכָל מִין; שְׁתֵּי חַלּוֹת לְקַב.

**ר' עובדיה מברטנורא**

**רבוכה.** חלוטה במים רותחין קרויה רבוכה. ורמב"ם פירש, רבוכה מרובה בשמן וקלויה בו, לפי שהיה בה שמן כנגד החלות והרקיקין: **נמצא שלשה עשרונות ושליש לכל מין ומין.** שבמצה: **שלשה חלות לעשרון.** דהוה להו עשר חלות לשלשה עשרונות ושליש: **במדה ירושלמית.** שלא היו בה עשרונות אלא קבים, הוי הנך חמש סאין שלשים קבין, שהסאה ששה קבים. ובגמרא בברייתא מייתי מגזרה שוה שכל מין ומין מארבעה מינים שבתודה היו בהם עשר חלות, ואמרו, נאמר כאן (ויקרא ז, יד) והקריב ממנו אחד מכל קרבן תרומה לה', ונאמר בתרומת מעשר (במדבר יח, כו) [ממנו] תרומה לה', מה להלן אחד מעשר אף כאן אחד מעשר. ולמדנו שמין אחד של חמץ היה עשרה עשרונים כנגד שלש מינים של מצה, מדכתיב (ויקרא ז, יג) על חלות לחם חמץ, אמרה תורה כנגד חמץ הבא מצה:

**יד אברהם**

וּבַמַּצָּה שְׁלֹשָׁה מִינִין: חַלּוֹת, וּרְקִיקִים, וּרְבוּכָה; — *and the matzah consists of three varieties: challos, rekikin, and revuchah;*

The *challos* [loaves] are mixed with oil and then baked, while the *rekikin* [wafers] are those upon which oil is smeared after they are baked [see above, mishnah 6:3]. The רְבוּכָה, *revuchah,* are loaves which contain an amount of oil equal to the other two types combined — one-fourth of a *log* (*Gem.* 89a) — and which are scalded in boiling water prior to being baked (*Rav; Rashi*). According to *Rambam* (*Maaseh HaKorbanos* 9:19), they were only partially baked after being scalded and were then fried in their oil.

נִמְצְאוּ שְׁלֹשָׁה עֶשְׂרוֹנוֹת וּשְׁלִישׁ לְכָל מִין, שָׁלֹשׁ חַלּוֹת לְעִשָּׂרוֹן. — *thus, [there are] three and one-third essronos for each variety, three loaves per issaron.*

[The one *ephah* — ten *essronos* — of flour allotted to the *matzah* loaves is divided equally among three different types of unleavened loaves, thus allowing three and one-third *essronos* for the ten loaves of each type. Thus, three loaves consist of one *issaron* of flour.]

The plural of *issaron* in Scripture is *essronim*. In mishnah, however, the plural *essronos* also appears. Our transliteration follows the particular form used in any given mishnah. It should also be noted that in Hebrew, items numbering more than

7 and the *matzah* consists of three varieties: *challos,*
1 *rekikin,* and *revuchah*; thus, [there are] three and one-third *essronos* for each variety, three loaves per *issaron.*

In the Jerusalem measure, there are thirty *kav*: fifteen for the leavened [loaves] and fifteen for the *matzah*. Fifteen for the leavened [loaves] — one and a half *kavs* per loaf. Fifteen for the *matzah* — and the *matzah* consists of three varieties: *challos, rekikin,* and *revuchah*. Thus, there are five *kavs* for each variety; two loaves per *kav.*

### YAD AVRAHAM

ten generally revert to the singular form; this too has been followed in the transliterations.

בְּמִדָּה יְרוּשַׁלְמִית, הָיוּ שְׁלֹשִׁים קַב: חֲמִשָּׁה עָשָׂר לֶחָמֵץ וַחֲמִשָּׁה עָשָׂר לַמַּצָּה. — *In the Jerusalem measure, there are thirty kav: fifteen for the leavened [loaves] and fifteen for the matzah.*

The Jerusalem measure no longer employed the *issaron.* Instead each new Jerusalem *seah* was divided into six *kav.* Thus, the five Jerusalem *seah* of the *todah*-offering totaled thirty *kav* (*Rav*). Since the total is divided equally between the *chametz* and *matzah* varieties, each category receives fifteen *kav* of flour.

חֲמִשָּׁה עָשָׂר לֶחָמֵץ – קַב וָחֵצִי לְחַלָּה. וַחֲמִשָּׁה עָשָׂר לַמַּצָּה – וְהַמַּצָּה שְׁלֹשָׁה מִינִין: חַלּוֹת, וּרְקִיקִין, וּרְבוּכָה. נִמְצְאוּ חֲמֵשֶׁת קַבִּים לְכָל מִין; שְׁתֵּי חַלּוֹת לְקַב. — *Fifteen for the leavened [loaves] — one and a half kavs per loaf. Fifteen for the matzah — and the matzah consists of three varieties: challos, rekikin, and revuchah. Thus, there are five kavs for each variety; two loaves per kav.*

[The amount of flour actually used in the *todah* loaves did not change, only the system of measures (*Shitah Mekubetzes*). The *Tanna* therefore goes through the same calculation for the Jerusalem measure that he made for the Biblical measure.

The entire offering consists of thirty *kavs* of flour; this is divided fifteen for the leavened loaves and fifteen for the unleavened ones. Since there are ten leavened loaves, each loaf consists of one and a half *kavs*. The thirty unleavened loaves are also made from fifteen *kavs*, thus allowing half a *kav* for each loaf.]

## 2.

In addition to the *todah*-offering, there are two other offerings which are accompanied by a variety of loaves. One was the מִלֻּאִים [*milluim*], *initiation-offerings,* which were brought when Aaron and his sons were inaugurated as *Kohanim*. The other is the offering brought by the *nazir* upon the completion of the term of his vow. The next mishnah details the manner in which these offerings differ from the *todah* loaves.

[ב] **הַמִּלֻּאִים** הָיוּ בָאִים כַּמַּצָּה שֶׁבַּתּוֹדָה: חַלּוֹת, וּרְקִיקִים, וּרְבוּכָה. הַנְּזִירוּת הָיְתָה בָאָה שְׁתֵּי יָדוֹת בְּמַצָּה שֶׁבַּתּוֹדָה: חַלּוֹת וּרְקִיקִים, וְאֵין בָּהּ רְבוּכָה; נִמְצָא עֲשָׂרָה קַבִּים יְרוּשַׁלְמִיּוֹת, שֶׁהֵן שִׁשָּׁה עֶשְׂרוֹנוֹת וְעַדְוַיִן. וּמִכֻּלָּן הָיָה נוֹטֵל אֶחָד מֵעֲשָׂרָה תְּרוּמָה, שֶׁנֶּאֱמַר: „וְהִקְרִיב מִמֶּנּוּ אֶחָד מִכָּל קָרְבָּן תְּרוּמָה לַה׳ ”.

**ר׳ עובדיה מברטנורא**

(ב) **המלואים.** שהיו בימי משה כשנתחנך אהרן ובניו לכהונה: **היו באים כמצה שבתודה חלות ורקיקים ורבוכה.** דכתיב במלואים (ויקרא ח, כו) ומסל המצות אשר לפני ה׳ לקח חלת מצה אחת וחלת לחם שמן אחת ורקיק אחד, חלת מצה אלו חלות, וחלת לחם שמן זו רבוכה דמוסיף בה שמן כנגד חלות ורקיקים, ורקיק זה רקיק: **נזירות.** לחמי נזיר, שנאמר (במדבר ו, טו) וסל מצות סלת חלות בלולות בשמן ורקיקי מצות משוחים בשמן, ורבוכה לא הוזכר שם: **שני ידות.** שני חלקים של מיני מצה שבתודה היו בנזירות, וכדמפרש ואזיל: **נמצאו.** לנזירות: **עשר קבין.** שהרי בשלשה מיני מצה שבתודה היו חמשה עשר קבין, והוי להו עשרה שני ידות של חמשה עשר: **שהן שש עשרונות ועדוין.** כלומר, ועוד שנוסף עליהן, שהרי היו שלשה עשרונים ושליש לכל מין כדאמרן לעיל (משנה א) גבי מצה שבתודה, נמצא לשני מינים שש עשרונות ושני שלישי עשרון, והיינו דקאמר שש עשרונות ועדוין: **ומכולן.** מכל ארבעה מינים שבתודה היו הכהנים נוטלים אחד מעשרה תרומה:

**יד אברהם**

הַמִּלֻּאִים — *The initiation-offerings*

When the *Mishkan* (Tabernacle) was first built in the Wilderness, and Aaron and his sons were inaugurated as *Kohanim,* they brought a series of offerings called *milluim,* which included a ram — referred to as the אֵיל הַמִּלֻּאִים, *ram of initiation* — and three different types of *menachos* (*Lev.* 8:22-28).

הָיוּ בָאִים כַּמַּצָּה שֶׁבַּתּוֹדָה: חַלּוֹת, וּרְקִיקִים, וּרְבוּכָה. — *were brought like the matzah of the todah-offering: challos, rekikin, and revuchah.*

The Torah (*Lev.* 8:26) states: וּמִסַּל הַמַּצּוֹת אֲשֶׁר לִפְנֵי ה׳ לָקַח חַלַּת מַצָּה אַחַת וְחַלַּת לֶחֶם שֶׁמֶן אַחַת וְרָקִיק אֶחָד, *and from the basket of matzos which is before HASHEM he took one matzah loaf, one oil bread loaf, and one wafer.* [These were waved by the *Kohen* together with the thigh and sacrificial parts of the *milluim* ram (ibid.).] The verse specifies three varieties of unleavened loaves: *matzah loaf*, which refers to the *challos;* the *"oil bread" loaf* which refers to the *revuchah* [due to its larger amount of oil — as much as the *challos* and *rekikin* combined]; and the *rekikin*, wafer (*Rav* from *Gem.* 78a). There is, however, no mention in the Torah of a leavened loaf; thus the *millium* is accompanied only by three unleavened loaves.

הַנְּזִירוּת הָיְתָה בָאָה שְׁתֵּי יָדוֹת בְּמַצָּה שֶׁבַּתּוֹדָה: — *That of the nazir consisted*

7
2
**2.** The initiation-offerings were brought like the *matzah* of the *todah*-offering: *challos, rekikin,* and *revuchah*. That of the *nazir* consisted of two parts of the *matzah* of the *todah*-offering: *challos* and *rekikin*, but it has no *revuchah;* thus, [it consists of] ten Jerusalem *kavs* which equal six *essronos* and [the] excess. From all of them he would take one-tenth for *terumah*, as it is stated (*Lev.* 7:14): *And he shall bring from it one from every offering as a terumah to* HASHEM.

**YAD AVRAHAM**

*of two parts of the matzah of the todah-offering:*

I.e., the loaves of the *nazir* offerings consisted of two of the three types of *matzah* loaves of the *todah*-offering, as explained below (*Rav*).

חַלּוֹת וּרְקִיקִים, וְאֵין בָּהּ רְבוּכָה; — *challos and rekikin, but it has no revuchah;*

In describing the loaves required of a *nazir* as part of his offering brought upon the completion of his vow, the Torah (*Num.* 6:15) describes only חַלֹּת בְּלוּלֹת בַּשֶּׁמֶן, *loaves mixed with oil* [the *challos* of our mishnah], and רְקִיקֵי מַצּוֹת מְשֻׁחִים בַּשָּׁמֶן, *matzah wafers smeared with oil* [the *rekikin* of our mishnah]. However, no *revuchah* or leavened loaves are mentioned (*Rav;* cf. *Gem.* 78a).

נִמְצָא עֲשָׂרָה קַבִּים יְרוּשַׁלְמִיּוֹת — *thus, [it consists of] ten Jerusalem kavs*

Since the three varieties of *matzah* for the *todah* require a total of fifteen *kavs* of flour (as stated before), and the *nazir's* loaves consist of two out of three parts of the *todah's* loaves, the two varieties brought by the *nazir* call for just ten *kavs* of flour (*Rav*).

שֶׁהֵן שִׁשָּׁה עֶשְׂרוֹנוֹת וְעַדְוַיִן. — *which equal six essronos and [the] excess.*

Since each variety of *todah* loaf consisted of three and a third *essronim* as measured by the Biblical (Wilderness) standard, this offering requires double that amount — which amounts to six and two-thirds *essronos*.

וְעַדְוַיִן is the plural of וְעוֹד, literally, *and some*. In this context, it refers to the extra fraction of an *issaron* (one-third) contained in each variety.

וּמִכֻּלָּן — *From all of them*

From each of the flour varieties included in the *todah* loaves (*Rav*) and each of the two varieties of the *nazir* loaves (*Tif. Yis.*).

הָיָה נוֹטֵל אֶחָד מֵעֲשָׂרָה תְּרוּמָה, שֶׁנֶּאֱמַר: „וְהִקְרִיב מִמֶּנּוּ אֶחָד מִכָּל קָרְבָּן תְּרוּמָה לַה׳ ״. — *he would take one-tenth for terumah, as it is stated* (*Lev.* 7:14): *"And he shall bring from it one from every offering as terumah to* HASHEM*."*

[The *Kohen* took one-tenth of the loaves as a *terumah*, literally, *separation* (something "lifted" from the main body of a thing).]

The word *terumah*, which the Torah uses to describe the part of the *todah* loaves to be given to the *Kohen*, teaches that it is compared to the תְּרוּמַת מַעֲשֵׂר, the *terumah of the tithe*, which is given by the *Leviim* to the *Kohanim*

מנחות
ז/ג

„אֶחָד" – שֶׁלֹּא יִטּוֹל פָּרוּס. „מִכָּל קָרְבָּן" – שֶׁיְּהוּ כָּל הַקָּרְבָּנוֹת שָׁוִין, וְשֶׁלֹּא יִטּוֹל מִקָּרְבָּן לַחֲבֵרוֹ. „לַכֹּהֵן הַזֹּרֵק אֶת דַּם הַשְּׁלָמִים לוֹ יִהְיֶה" – וְהַשְּׁאָר נֶאֱכָל לַבְּעָלִים.

[ג] **הַשּׁוֹחֵט** אֶת הַתּוֹדָה בִּפְנִים וְלַחְמָהּ חוּץ לַחוֹמָה, לֹא קָדַשׁ הַלֶּחֶם.

ר׳ עובדיה מברטנורא

**שלא יטול פרוס.** שבור וחתוך: **שיהיו כל הקרבנות שוין.** המינים יהיו שוין, עשרה חלות לכל מין: **שלא יטול תרומה מקרבן על חבירו.** שאם היה ממין זה חמשה וממין זה חמשה עשר, נמצא מפריש מזה על זה: (ג) **השוחט את התודה בפנים.** לפנים מן העזרה: **ולחמה חוץ לחומה.** בגמרא (עח, ב) מוקמינן לה חוץ לחומת בית פאגי. רבותי פירשו חוץ לחומה החיצונה

יד אברהם

from the *maaser* (tithe) they receive. Just as the *terumas maaser* given by the *Levi* is one-tenth of the total he receives from the *Yisrael* (as stated explicitly in the Torah), so too, the one loaf given to the *Kohen* from the *todah* loaves must represent one-tenth of the total number of its loaves (*Gem.* 77b).

In the *Gemara*, this portion of the mishnah precedes the previous half (*Meleches Shlomo*).

.אֶחָד" – שֶׁלֹּא יִטּוֹל פָּרוּס„ — *"One" — that he may not take [it] broken.*

The *Tanna* now expounds the verse just cited, which concludes with the words לַכֹּהֵן הַזֹּרֵק ... לוֹ יִהְיֶה, *to the Kohen who throws* ... [i.e., its blood on the Altar] *shall it belong.*

The word אֶחָד, *one,* in the verse has the connotation of wholeness, i.e., the loaf given to the *Kohen* must be whole and not broken. Thus, if one of the loaves breaks after the *zerikah* [throwing] of the blood of the *todah*, the *Kohen* must take a whole loaf for his *terumah*, rather than a broken one (*Tif. Yis.*).

The mishnah indicates that the only restriction against a broken loaf is that it cannot be given to the *Kohen*. The other loaves are valid even if they are not whole. This is true only for loaves broken *after* the *todah's* blood was applied to the Altar. However, if any loaf breaks before the offering is slaughtered, that loaf is invalidated. If the break occurred between the slaughter and the *zerikah*, all the loaves become invalidated (*Tif. Yis.*). In this case the *todah* itself remains valid [i.e., the blood of the *todah* may be applied to the Altar and its meat may be eaten], but the owner has not fulfilled his vow and must therefore offer another *todah* with forty new loaves (*Zevach Todah* from *Gem.* 46a).

— „מִכָּל קָרְבָּן" – שֶׁיְּהוּ כָּל הַקָּרְבָּנוֹת שָׁוִין, *"From every offering" — that all the offerings should be equal,*

Each of the four varieties of the *todah's* loaves must consist of the same number — ten loaves (*Rav;* cf. *Rashi Peirush, Sfas Emes*). [The term קָרְבָּן, *offering*, refers here to the individual varieties of loaves (*Rav*).]

.וְשֶׁלֹּא יִטּוֹל מִקָּרְבָּן לַחֲבֵרוֹ — *and that he may not take from one offering for another.*

[He may not take as *terumah* for one

7
3 *One* — that he may not take [it] broken. *From every offering* — that all the offerings should be equal, and that he may not take from one offering for another. *To the Kohen who throws the blood of the shelamim-offering shall it belong* — and the remainder is eaten by the owner.

**3.** [If] one slaughtered the *todah*-offering inside while its loaves were outside the wall, the bread is not sanctified. [If] he



variety a loaf from another variety.] The mishnah means to explain by this the reason for the previous statement. [Indeed, the text as it appears in the *Gemara* is שֶׁלֹּא יִטּוֹל, without the conjunction *and* (*Tos. Yom Tov*).] The loaves must be of an equal number because if he has only five of one type and fifteen of another, the loaf he brings from the five is actually the *terumah* for five of those of the other variety as well of those of its own, which is unacceptable (*Rav; Rashi ms*).

Others understand this last segment to be an independent statement: He may not give the *Kohen* two loaves from one variety and none from another (*Rashi Peirush*).

„לַכֹּהֵן הַזֹּרֵק אֶת דַּם הַשְּׁלָמִים לוֹ יִהְיֶה" — וְהַשְּׁאָר נֶאֱכָל לַבְּעָלִים. — *"To the Kohen who throws the blood of the shelamim-offering shall it belong" — and the remainder is eaten by the owner.*

[Only the one loaf must be given to the *Kohen;* the remaining nine loaves from each variety are eaten by the owner of the offering.]

## 3.

In the passage concerning the *todah* loaves the Torah states (*Lev.* 7:13): עַל חַלֹּת לֶחֶם חָמֵץ יַקְרִיב קָרְבָּנוֹ עַל זֶבַח תּוֹדַת שְׁלָמָיו, *With loaves of leavened bread shall he bring his offering, together with his todah shelamim-offering.* The words יַקְרִיב קָרְבָּנוֹ עַל זֶבַח תּוֹדַת, *he shall offer his offering together with his todah*, is taken by the *Gemara* to indicate that the loaves do not attain sacrificial sanctity until the *todah*-offering is slaughtered (*Gem.* 78b, cited by *Tos. Yom Tov*).

The *Gemara* records a dispute concerning the meaning of the word עַל, *in addition to,* in the above-cited verse. According to Reish Lakish, the term implies physical proximity; the loaves must be in the Temple Courtyard when the *todah*-offering is slaughtered in order to attain sanctity. In R' Yochanan's view, such immediate proximity is not required. It is clear, though, that there exists a certain interdependence between the loaves and the *todah*-offering. The following mishnah describes which invalidations of the offering affect the status of the loaves.

הַשּׁוֹחֵט אֶת הַתּוֹדָה בִּפְנִים וְלַחְמָהּ חוּץ לַחוֹמָה, לֹא קָדַשׁ הַלֶּחֶם. — *[If] one slaughtered the todah-offering inside while its loaves were outside the wall, the bread is not sanctified.*

The Torah describes the loaves as

**שְׁחָטָהּ עַד שֶׁלֹּא קָרְמוּ בַתַּנּוּר, וַאֲפִילוּ קָרְמוּ כֻּלָּן חוּץ מֵאֶחָד מֵהֶן, לֹא קָדַשׁ הַלֶּחֶם. שְׁחָטָהּ חוּץ לִזְמַנָּהּ וְחוּץ לִמְקוֹמָהּ, קָדַשׁ הַלֶּחֶם. שְׁחָטָהּ וְנִמְצֵאת טְרֵפָה, לֹא קָדַשׁ הַלֶּחֶם.**

**ר׳ עובדיה מברטנורא**

של ירושלים, [אבל חוץ לעזרה קדוש], ואף על גב דכתיב (ויקרא ז, יב) והקריב על זבח התודה חלות, דמשמע לכאורה שיהא הלחם אצלה בשעת זביחה, לא דרשינן על בסמוך. ורמב״ם גורס בית בגי, ומפרש שהוא מקום קרוב להר הבית אלא שהוא חוץ לחומת הר הבית ושם אופים המנחות, ועל שם כך היו קורים לו בית בגי, לשון פת בג המלך: **עד שלא קרמו בתנור.** לאו לחם נינהו אלא עיסה בעלמא: **שחטה.** על מנת לאכלה חוץ לזמנה, קדש הלחם ונפגל, על מנת לאכלה חוץ למקומה, קדש הלחם ונפסל, וטעמא דקדש הלחם, משום דפסולו בקדש, וקיימא לן כל שפסולו בקדש הקדש מקבלו: **שחטה ונמצאת טריפה לא קדש הלחם.** דפסולו קודם שחיטה הוא:

**יד אברהם**

being עַל זֶבַח תּוֹדַת שְׁלָמָיו, which literally translated would mean, *on the sacrifice of his todah shelamim.* This is taken to teach that they must be nearby it (see introduction to mishnah). Therefore, if the loaves were outside the wall while the *todah* was slaughtered inside the Temple Courtyard, the loaves do not attain any sanctity.

In the prevailing view of R' Yochanan in the *Gemara* (77b), the loaves become sanctified even if they are not within the Courtyard. When the mishnah states *outside the wall* it means that the loaves are outside an outer wall called the חוֹמַת בֵּית פָּאגֵי, *Beis Paggi wall* (*Rav* from *Gem.* 77b).

The exact location of the *Beis Paggi* wall is the subject of controversy. According to *Rashi* (*ms*) and *Rav,* it was the outer wall of Jerusalem; thus, as long as the loaves are anywhere in Jerusalem when the *todah* is slaughtered they become consecrated. Others contend that the *Beis Paggi* wall refers to the wall surrounding the Temple Mount (*Rashi Peirush*). *Rambam (Comm.)* explains the term to refer to the enclosed area outside the Temple Mount where the *menachos* were baked.

According to the view that the *Beis Paggi* wall is the wall around Jerusalem, it is not hard to understand why the bread is not sanctified if it was outside that wall; since the loaves of the *todah*-offering may not be eaten out of Jerusalem, they cannot attain sanctity there. However, according to the views that place the *Beis Paggi* wall inside Jerusalem, it is difficult to explain the invalidation of loaves which are beyond the *Beis Paggi*, since according to R' Yochanan there is no requirement for the loaves to be in the Courtyard near the offering. Apparently, even R' Yochanan, who does not interpret the word עַל to mean immediate proximity, nevertheless infers from it a degree of proximity (*Keren Orah*; cf. *Tos.*).

שְׁחָטָהּ עַד שֶׁלֹּא קָרְמוּ בַתַּנּוּר, — *[If] he slaughtered it before they became crusted in the oven,*

Until it becomes crusted, the dough does not have the status of bread (*Rav*) and cannot satisfy the Torah's requirement for *todah* loaves [לֶחֶם] (*Lev.* 7:12; *Gem.* 78b). [Thus, even if the loaves had already been kneaded, shaped, and placed in an oven to bake at the time the *todah*-offering was slaughtered, but they had not yet baked to the point of forming a crust,

7 slaughtered it before they became crusted in the
3 oven, or even if all were crusted except for one,
the bread is not sanctified. [If] he slaughtered it [for] beyond its time or [for] outside its place, the bread is sanctified. [If] he slaughtered it and it was found to be a *tereifah,* the bread is not sanctified.



they do not become consecrated with the slaughter of the sacrifice.]

וַאֲפִילוּ קָרְמוּ כֻלָּן חוּץ מֵאֶחָד מֵהֶן, לֹא קָדַשׁ הַלֶּחֶם. — *or even if all were crusted except for one, the bread is not sanctified.*

[In order for the *todah* loaves to become consecrated, all forty of them must be suitable for consecration.] Therefore, if any one of the loaves of the *todah* is still considered dough when the sacrifice is slaughtered, even those which have already crusted are not sanctified (*Tif. Yis.*). [Even though the flour was previously consecrated orally, the loaves require the further sanctification of the *todah's* slaughter to render them actual offerings. Thus, the loaves must be fit for their role at the time the *todah* is slaughtered, and if they are not, they never achieve offering status.]

שְׁחָטָהּ חוּץ לִזְמַנָּהּ וְחוּץ לִמְקוֹמָהּ, — *[If] he slaughtered it [for] beyond its time or [for] outside its place,*

He slaughtered the sacrifice with the intention of eating its meat after the allotted time [which renders it *piggul,* resulting in *kares* for one who eats it], or outside its allotted place [which creates a non-*kares* invalidation]. See mishnah 2:3.

קָדַשׁ הַלֶּחֶם. — *the bread is sanctified.*

The loaves are consecrated and are likewise *piggul* or invalidated (*Rav; Tif. Yis.*).

[*Piggul* is a state of sacrificial invalidation; therefore, in order for the *todah* loaves to become *piggul*, they must attain sacrificial sanctity. Thus, the mishnah teaches that they achieve this sanctification through the *piggul* offering.]

Although the *todah* itself is invalidated by its slaughter, the slaughter is still capable of sanctifying the loaves because *piggul* is פְּסוּלוֹ בַּקֹּדֶשׁ, *an invalidation in the Holy* (*Rav*); i.e., an invalidation which takes place in the Temple.[1] The rule for such things is that *any offering whose invalidation is in the Holy, the Holy accepts it* [*Zevachim* 7:5, 9:2] (*Rav*); i.e., such offerings are considered to possess a degree of validity despite their invalidation (as explained in *Zevachim*) and the *piggul*-slaughter of the *todah* therefore suffices to sanctify the loaves and render them *piggul* (and subject to the *kares* penalty for eating them).

שְׁחָטָהּ וְנִמְצֵאת טְרֵפָה, לֹא קָדַשׁ הַלֶּחֶם. — *[If] he slaughtered it and it was found to be a tereifah, the bread is not sanctified.*

If the animal was found to have been a *tereifah* — one with a terminal physical defect or damage, which

1. This is *Rashi's* interpretation of the rule. *Tosafos* and *Rambam* have somewhat different explanations (see *Yad Avraham* comm. to *Zevachim* 7:5, s.v. וזה הכלל). The essence of all these views is that the disqualifications which occur as part of a sanctified offering's *avodah* retain a degree of validity.

# שְׁחָטָהּ וְנִמְצֵאת בַּעֲלַת מוּם – רַבִּי אֱלִיעֶזֶר אוֹמֵר: קָדַשׁ; וַחֲכָמִים אוֹמְרִים: לֹא קָדַשׁ. שְׁחָטָהּ שֶׁלֹּא לִשְׁמָהּ – וְכֵן אֵיל הַמִּלּוּאִים,

ר׳ עובדיה מברטנורא

**שחטה ונמצאת בעלת מום רבי אליעזר אומר קדש.** בגמרא (עט, א) מוקי לה בדוקין שבעין, דבכי האי מומא סבר רבי אליעזר דאם עלו לא ירדו הואיל ואין מומן ניכר, הלכך קדש הלחם. ואין הלכה כרבי אליעזר: **שלא לשמה.** לא קדש הלחם, דכתיב (ויקרא ז, יג) על חלות לחם חמץ יקריב קרבנו על זבח תודת שלמיו, על זבח שנזבח לשם תודת שלמיו: **וכן איל המלואים.** לפי שהן היו תחלה לכל הקרבנות נקט איל המלואים, והוא הדין לאיל נזיר, דמלואים כקרבן יחיד הן חשובים:

יד אברהם

invalidates it for a sacrifice (as well as for general consumption) — the loaves are also invalidated, since this flaw was already in existence prior to the *todah's* slaughter (*Rav*).

— שְׁחָטָהּ וְנִמְצֵאת בַּעֲלַת מוּם — *[If] he slaughtered it and it was found to be blemished —*

The blemish referred to here is specifically the one known in the *Gemara* as דוּקִין שֶׁבָּעַיִן, *cataracts in the eye* (*Gem.* 79a), which is a defect which is not noticeable and thus of a less severe nature, as will be explained. Any obvious blemish, however, would completely invalidate the animal from being an offering and its loaves would then be in the same category as those of one found to be a *tereifah*. Thus, they would not become sanctified at all, as is the rule for any invalidation that was in place prior to the *todah's* slaughter (*Rav; Rashi*).

;רַבִּי אֱלִיעֶזֶר אוֹמֵר: קָדַשׁ — *R' Eliezer says: It is sanctified;*

R' Eliezer's view is based on the opinion of R' Akiva (*Zevachim* 9:3) that a blemish of this nature, since it is hardly discernible,[1] is in the category of invalidations which, if placed on the Altar, are not removed [אִם עָלוּ לֹא יֵרְדוּ].

As explained in mishnah 9:2 of *Zevachim*, there are many types of sacrificial invalidations which prevent an offering from being burnt on the Altar, but which nevertheless do not require that the offering be removed from the Altar if it was improperly placed on it. [In such cases, the invalid offering is left to be burnt on the Altar despite its invalidation.] The right to remain on the Altar serves as a yardstick for determining whether the *avodah* of that offering was at least partially valid despite the invalidation. If the invalidation was of the less severe kind which does *not* require removal from the Altar, it suffices to sanctify the loaves. It is the opinion of R' Akiva that an animal offering blemished by an eye cataract is allowed to remain on the Altar if it has

1. *Rav's* language indicates that the fact that the blemish is not discernible is the reason why it is not rejected expost facto from the Altar. In his comm. to the mishnah in *Zevachim* (9:3), *Rav* gives the fact that this blemish is not an invalidation for a bird offering (*Zevachim* 85b) as the reason for it falling under the category of invalidations which are not rejected from the Altar (*Tos. Yom Tov*).

7 [If] he slaughtered it and it was found to be
3 blemished — R' Eliezer says: It is sanctified; but the Sages say: It is not sanctified. [If] he slaughtered it for a designation other than its own — and so too the initiation ram,



been placed there (though it should not have been put there in the first place). Therefore, the slaughter of such a blemished *todah* animal sanctifies the *todah* loaves (*Rav* from *Gem.* 79a).

However, even R' Eliezer agrees in the case of the *tereifah* that its slaughter does not sanctify its loaves, since a *tereifah* must be removed from the Altar even if it was placed there [אִם עָלְתָה תֵּרֵד] (*Tif. Yis.*).

וַחֲכָמִים אוֹמְרִים: לֹא קָדַשׁ. — *but the Sages say: It is not sanctified.*

They maintain that R' Akiva's distinction between this blemish and a major blemish applies only to the animal itself but does not affect the status of the loaves [which remain unsanctified if the animal is blemished] (*Gem.* 79a).

However, *Rav's* language indicates that the opinion of the Sages here is based on the opinion of the Sages in *Zevachim* 9:3, that even animals with eye cataracts must be removed from the Altar. Some versions of the *Gemara* can indeed be reconciled with this explanation (*Tos. Yom Tov*).

— שְׁחָטָהּ שֶׁלֹּא לִשְׁמָהּ — *[If] he slaughtered it for a designation other than its own —*

[He slaughtered the *todah*-offering with the intent that it be for a different offering (see preface to 1:1). In such a case the loaves are not sanctified, as derived from the verse (*Lev.* 7:13): עַל חַלֹּת לֶחֶם חָמֵץ יַקְרִיב קָרְבָּנוֹ עַל זֶבַח תּוֹדַת שְׁלָמָיו, *With loaves of leavened bread shall he bring his offering together with his todah shelamim-offering* — i.e., together with an offering which was slaughtered with the specific purpose of a *todah* in mind (*Rav* from *Gem.* 78b).[1]

וְכֵן אֵיל הַמִּלּוּאִים, — *and so too the initiation ram,*

The *milluim* sacrifice was offered in the Wilderness when the *Kohanim* were first initiated into the Temple service (see previous mishnah). This offering must also be slaughtered with no disqualifying intent in order for its loaves to be sanctified. The laws of all loaves which accompany a sacrifice are derived one from another (*Tos. Yom Tov*). The same is true of the ram offering of the *nazir*. The mishnah cites the *milluim* offering because it was the first such offering to be mentioned in the Torah (*Rav* from *Gem.* 79a).

1. *Sfas Emes* questions the validity of a *todah* slaughtered for another designation. Since the loaves do not attain sanctity, as stated in this mishnah, it is essentially a *todah* without loaves. The absence of loaves at the very onset of the *todah* service is arguably an invalidation of the whole offering, as discussed by him at length.

This may serve to explain the implication of *Rashi's* commentary to mishnah 2:3, that even when just the loaves become *piggul* and not the *todah*, the offering is nevertheless disqualified (see *Sfas Emes* and comm. there, s.v. לאכול מן הלחם למחר). [However, from *Keren Orah* to mishnah 2:3 it is clear that he considers the offering valid even in the absence of the loaves.]

וְכֵן שְׁנֵי כִבְשֵׂי עֲצֶרֶת שֶׁשְּׁחָטָן שֶׁלֹּא לִשְׁמָן – לֹא קָדַשׁ הַלֶּחֶם.

[ד] **נְסָכִים** שֶׁקָּדְשׁוּ בִכְלִי וְנִמְצָא הַזֶּבַח פָּסוּל – אִם יֵשׁ שָׁם זֶבַח אַחֵר

ר׳ עובדיה מברטנורא

(ד) **נסכים שקדשו בכלי.** לאו דוקא בכלי, שאין נסכים מתקדשים ליפסל ביוצא ובלינה ואף על פי שקדשו בכלי, אלא בשחיטת הזבח, דכתיב זבח ונסכים, הנסכים תלוים בזבח: **ונמצא הזבח פסול.** שנפסל בזריקה, דאילו בשחיטה נפסל, לא קדשו נסכים:

יד אברהם

וְכֵן שְׁנֵי כִבְשֵׂי עֲצֶרֶת — *and so too the two lambs of Shavuos*

[The כִּבְשֵׂי עֲצֶרֶת, *lambs of the Shavuos* Festival, were accompanied by *shtei halechem, the two loaves*. The sanctity of these *shtei halechem*, too, was affected by the status of the animal sacrifice.]

Although in Chapter 4 (mishnah 3) R' Akiva maintains that the *shtei halechem* can be brought even without the lambs, he agrees that if they are brought together, the loaves become sanctified only with the slaughter of the lambs (*Likkutim*).

שֶׁשְּׁחָטָן שֶׁלֹּא לִשְׁמָן – לֹא קָדַשׁ הַלֶּחֶם. — *which one slaughtered for a designation other than their own — the bread is not sanctified.*

[In all of these cases, if the animal was slaughtered for a different type of offering, the accompanying loaves are not sanctified, just as in the case of the *todah*.]

## 4.

The ongoing discussion of the *todah* loaves and their relationship to the *todah*-offering is expanded in the following mishnah to include the relationship of *nesachim* — the *minchah* and wine libation that accompany a sacrifice — to the offerings which they accompany (see preface to 2:4). Specifically, the mishnah delineates what is to be done with the *nesachim* designated for a sacrifice once that sacrifice has been invalidated.

נְסָכִים שֶׁקָּדְשׁוּ בִכְלִי — *[If] libations were sanctified in a vessel*

[After the flour for the *minchah* and wine for the libation of a *nesachim* offering to accompany a sacrifice have been verbally designated, they must still be sanctified further in a *kli shareis* to attain physical sanctity, as do all *menachos* and libations (see comm. to mishnah 12:1). Therefore, before being sanctified in a *kli shareis* they are not susceptible to the sacrificial invalidations and problems discussed below.]

The *Gemara*, however, states that the *nesachim* are sanctified only with the slaughter of the offering which they accompany, not merely by being placed in a *kli shareis* [אֵין הַנְּסָכִים מִתְקַדְּשִׁים אֶלָּא בִּשְׁחִיטַת הַזֶּבַח]. Accordingly, the mishnah's statement that the *nesachim* were sanctified in a vessel must be understood as listing only one of the two conditions necessary for their sanctification, the other being the slaughter of the sacrifice (*Rav*, as explained by *Tos. Yom Tov*).

7 and so too the two lambs of Shavuos which one
4 slaughtered for a designation other than their own — the bread is not sanctified.

**4.** [If] libations were sanctified in a vessel and the sacrifice was found to be invalid — if there is another sacrifice present

**YAD AVRAHAM**

There is a dispute among the commentators concerning which aspect of the *nesachim's* sanctification is accomplished only by the slaughter of the sacrifice and to what extent simply being placed in the *kli shareis* sanctifies them. *Rav* states that until the sacrifice has been slaughtered, the *nesachim* do not even attain the basic sanctity which would make them subject to the disqualifications of לִינָה, *being left overnight*, and יוֹצֵא, *being taken out of the permitted place* [i.e., the Temple Courtyard]. *Rav's* interpretation follows the view of *Rashi* (*ms*, 79a).

*Tosafos* (79a, s.v. אין הנסכים) disagree, maintaining that the basic sanctification which subjects the *nesachim* to the disqualification of being left overnight[1] is effected by simply placing them in the *kli shareis*. The slaughter is necessary only to bind the *nesachim* to a specific sacrifice; as long as the sacrifice for which they have been designated has not been slaughtered, the *nesachim* may be transferred to another sacrifice without meeting any of the conditions described below. In the view of *Tosafos*, the sanctification referred to by the mishnah here has the purpose of making the *minchah* and wine the irrevocable companions of a specific sacrifice (*Tos. Yom Tov*).

[Clearly, even in the view of *Rav* and *Rashi*, without their having been sanctified first in a *kli shareis*, the slaughter of the sacrifice would not sanctify the wine and flour to be the *nesachim* of that sacrifice (*Tos. Yom Tov*).]

וְנִמְצָא הַזֶּבַח פָּסוּל — *and the sacrifice was found to be invalid —*

The sacrifice for which the *nesachim* were designated became invalidated during the *zerikah* [sprinkling of the blood] (*Rav* from *Gem.* 79a) — or at any point after the slaughter, such as the *kabbalah* (the receiving of the blood) and onward (*Tos. Yom Tov*).

However, if the invalidation occurred during the slaughter, the *nesachim* would not be sanctified at all (*Rav*). As explained above, it takes the slaughter of the sacrifice to sanctify the *nesachim*, and only a valid slaughter sanctifies (*Tos. Yom Tov*).

אִם יֵשׁ שָׁם זֶבַח אַחֵר — *if there is another sacrifice present*

If there is another sacrifice in the Temple for which no *nesachim* have yet been designated (*Rashi Peirush*).

1. In the view of *Tosafos* the *minchah* and wine brought as the *nesachim* companions of an animal sacrifice are treated no differently than any other *minchah*. However, it is the opinion of *Tosafos* (9a, s.v. ריש לקיש) that sanctification in a *kli shareis* does not subject any offering to the disqualification of יוֹצֵא, *being taken out* [of its permitted place], only to the disqualification of לִינָה, *being left overnight*. As noted in the comm. above, *Rashi* disputes this and rules that an ordinary offering becomes sanctified by a *kli shareis* even vis-a-vis the invalidation of being left overnight. *Nesachim* are an exception to this rule, according to *Rashi*, and do not become subject to either the invalidation of being left overnight or being removed from the Courtyard until the offering they accompany is slaughtered.

# יִקָּרְבוּ עִמּוֹ; וְאִם לָאו, יִפָּסְלוּ בְלִינָה.

ר׳ עובדיה מברטנורא

**אם יש שם זבח אחר יקרבו עמו.** בנסכים של צבור מוקמינן לה למתניתין, משום דלב בית דין מתנה עליהם, אם הוצרכו לזבח זה הוצרכו ואם לאו יהיו לזבח אחר, אבל בנסכים של יחיד אין כשרים לזבח אחר, ואפילו נסכים של צבור אין קרבים עם זבח אחר אלא אם כן היה אותו זבח זבוח כשנפסל הזבח הראשון, אבל אם לא היה זבוח בשעה שנפסל הזבח הראשון, אין קריבים עם הזבח האחר. ומתניתין חסורי מחסרא והכי קתני, [יקרבו עמו], במה דברים אמורים שהיה זבח זבוח באותה שעה, אבל אם לא היה זבח זבוח באותה שעה, נעשה כמו שנפסלו בלינה ופסולים. והכי מפרשא מתניתין בגמרא (עט, ב׳). וכל זמן שלא נתקדשו נסכים בכלי, אף על פי שנשחט הזבח, יכולים להקריב נסכים אפילו אחר כמה ימים, דקיימא לן מביא אדם קרבנו היום ונסכו אפילו אחר כמה ימים, בין נסכים של יחיד בין נסכים של צבור. וכן מצורע מביא אשמו היום ולוג שמן שלו לאחר כמה ימים:

יד אברהם

יִקָּרְבוּ עִמּוֹ; — *they are offered with it;*

[I.e., the *nesachim* may be transferred to the other sacrifice.]

As noted above, the mishnah refers to a case in which the sacrifice was slaughtered properly and became invalidated afterward. Thus, the *nesachim* have been sanctified. The *Gemara* (79b) concludes that once the *nesachim* have been sanctified by the sacrifice's slaughter, they should really become bound to that particular offering and not be transferable to another sacrifice. The reason they may be transferred when the sacrifice is invalidated is because of a general stipulation by the court in charge of the Temple that if the *nesachim* assigned to a sacrifice become unnecessary, they should be transferable to another sacrifice. This stipulation is viewed as being attached to the sanctification of the *nesachim* in the *kli shareis*; i.e., their sanctification is made conditional on their being needed. Therefore, if they are not needed [due to the sacrifices' invalidation], the sanctification is retroactively nullified (*Zevach Todah*).

This principle is referred to by the *Gemara* as לֵב בֵּית דִּין מַתְנֶה עֲלֵיהֶם, *the "mind" of the Court stipulates regarding them* [i.e., the will of the Court of the *Kohanim* who administer the performance of the communal offerings (*Rashi*)] (cf. *Shavuos* 11a and *Kesubos* 15b).

*Tosafos* (15b, s.v. אפשר לשנותן) state that it is self-evident that this principle applies only to קָרְבְּנוֹת צִבּוּר, *communal sacrifices*, since it is only over these offerings that the Court has jurisdiction. Accordingly, our mishnah refers only to communal sacrifices; *nesachim* brought for an individual's sacrifices cannot be redesignated once the sacrifice has been slaughtered (*Rav, Rashi ms*).

וְאִם לָאו, יִפָּסְלוּ בְלִינָה. — *if not, they become invalid by being left overnight.*

If the sacrifice is invalidated and there is no other sacrifice available to which to transfer the *nesachim*, they too become invalidated by being left overnight (*Rambam Comm.* ed. *Kafich*; see below).

Another version of this mishnah reads: וְאִם לָנוּ, יִפָּסְלוּ בְלִינָה, *if they were left overnight, they become invalid by being left overnight* (*Rashi msc.* 79a). If the *nesachim* could not be applied to any other sacrifice and end up being left overnight, they become invalidated (*Rashi*). [The novelty of this ruling would seem to be that the stipulation of the Court is not

7
4

they are offered with it; if not, they become invalid by being left overnight.

YAD AVRAHAM

invoked to nullify the sanctification of the *nesachim* unless they can be reassigned to another sacrifice that day. If they were not immediately reassigned, they remain sanctified and therefore become disqualified by being left overnight.]

The *Gemara* (79b) cites a *Baraisa* which states that our mishnah's permit to transfer the *nesachim* to another sacrifice applies only if the second sacrifice was already slaughtered at the time of the invalidation. Accordingly, the mishnah's text must be emended to read: ... יִקְרְבוּ עִמּוֹ. בַּמֶּה דְבָרִים אֲמוּרִים? שֶׁהָיָה זֶבַח זָבוּחַ בְּאוֹתָהּ שָׁעָה. אֲבָל אִם לֹא הָיָה זֶבַח זָבוּחַ בְּאוֹתָהּ שָׁעָה נַעֲשׂוּ כְּמוֹ שֶׁנִּפְסְלוּ בְּלִינָה וּפְסוּלִים — *... they should be offered with it. When is this said? When there was a sacrifice slaughtered at that time. However, if there was no sacrifice slaughtered at that time, they are considered as if they have been invalidated by being left overnight and are invalid* (*Rav; Rambam Comm.*).[1]

Seemingly, the stipulation of the Court can operate even if there is no other sacrifice already slaughtered at the time of the first sacrifice's invalidation. This should enable us to transfer the *nesachim* to a sacrifice slaughtered even later that day. The Rabbis, however, prohibited transfer in this case for fear that people seeing it might mistakenly assume that *nesachim* may be transferred from one sacrifice to another even when the first one has not been invalidated, and even when there is no stipulation in effect. This is not a concern when the second sacrifice has already been slaughtered at the time the first one is invalidated because people do not necessarily realize that a transfer is taking place. Rather they may assume that the *nesachim* now being applied to the second sacrifice was designated for it from the very beginning (*Rashi Peirush*).

In mishnah 2:4 we learned that in the opinion of R' Meir a *piggul* intention entertained while performing the *avodah* of a sacrifice renders its *nesachim piggul* as well. The *Gemara* there (15b) notes the dissenting view of the Sages who contend that the *nesachim* do not become *piggul* as a result of the *piggul* of the sacrifice. As the *Gemara* there explained this, it is the opinion of the Sages that the *nesachim* and sacrifice do not become bound to each other and that even after the sacrifice has been slaughtered the *nesachim* may still be transferred to another sacrifice. Therefore, the invalidation of the sacrifice does not affect the validity of the *nesachim*. In the opinion of R' Meir, though, the *nesachim* become bound to the sacrifice at the time of its slaughter and therefore become *piggul* with it.

According to this, the explanation of the mishnah cited above from the *Gemara*,

1. [The statement that "they are considered as if they have been invalidated by being left overnight and are invalid" requires some explanation. *Rambam* in his *Comm.* (see ed. Kafich) states that they must still be left overnight before being burned (cf. *Hil. Pesulei HaMukdashin* 12:6). Perhaps the intention is that though it should not really be necessary for these *nesachim* to become invalidated by being left overnight just because there is no other slaughtered sacrifice available at the moment — since it is possible that another one will be slaughtered later in the day and the *nesachim* can be applied to that one — the Rabbis nevertheless *treated* it as if it had already been invalidated by being left overnight to prevent it from being used (for the reason explained in the comm.). In actual practice, however, it will still have to be kept overnight to become Biblically disqualified before being burned. Ed.]

מנחות
ז/ד

וְלַד תּוֹדָה, וּתְמוּרָתָהּ, וְהַמַּפְרִישׁ תּוֹדָתוֹ וְאָבְדָה וְהִפְרִישׁ אַחֶרֶת תַּחְתֶּיהָ – אֵינָן טְעוּנִים לֶחֶם; שֶׁנֶּאֱמַר: „וְהִקְרִיב עַל זֶבַח הַתּוֹדָה" – הַתּוֹדָה טְעוּנָה לֶחֶם, לֹא וְלָדָהּ, וְלֹא חֲלִיפָתָהּ, וְלֹא תְמוּרָתָהּ טְעוּנִין לֶחֶם.

**ר' עובדיה מברטנורא**

**ולד תודה.** שהפריש תודה מעוברת וילדה: **וכן המפריש תודתו ואבדה והפריש אחרת תחתיה אינה טעונה לחם.** הראשונה, אם נמצאת לאחר הקרבת שניה, וכן שניה אם נמצאת הראשונה קודם הקרבתה והקריב ראשונה, שוב אין השניה טעונה לחם: **חליפתה.** היינו המפריש תודה ואבדה והפריש אחרת תחתיה: **תמורתה.** כגון שעומדת בעין ואומר זו תמורת זו, וכתיב (ויקרא כז, י) והיה הוא ותמורתו יהיה קדש:

**יד אברהם**

which is based on the principle that the *nesachim* become bound to the sacrifice at slaughter and become transferable in the case of an invalid offering only because of the stipulation of the Court, is true only according to R' Meir. According to the Sages, however, *nesachim* can always be transferred to another sacrifice, even in the case of an individual's offering (to which the Court's stipulation does not apply, as stated above), and even if the slaughtered sacrifice to which they were assigned was not invalidated at all! (*Tos.* 15b).

*Rambam*, however, rules in accordance with the Sages in regard to the *piggul* issue discussed in Chapter 2 (see *Pesulei HaMukdashin* 18:8), yet cites our mishnah in accordance with the interpretation of the *Gemara* (*Pesulei HaMukdashin* 12:6). Apparently, he maintains that the Sages agree to the basic principle that the *nesachim* are linked to their sacrifice and may not be transferred to another except through the stipulation of the Court. Nevertheless, the fact remains that the *nesachim* may be brought long after the sacrifice if they were not yet sanctified in a *kli shareis* when the sacrifice was slaughtered. Furthermore, in these circumstances they may even be transferred to a different sacrifice entirely. That is sufficient to disassociate them from their sacrifice to the extent that a *piggul* intention during the offering of the sacrifice does not invalidate the *nesachim* (*Tos. Yom Tov*).[1]

וְלַד תּוֹדָה, — *The offspring of a todah-offering,*

This refers to a case in which someone vowed to bring a *todah*, without designating any particular animal in the vow (*Gem.* 79b; see below). He then designated a pregnant animal for the *todah*-offering and it gave birth before being offered (*Rav*; cf. *Rashash*).

1. In a similar vein, *Keren Orah* (to *Gem.* 15b) suggests that *Rambam* understood that even the Sages agree with R' Meir that the *nesachim* become bound to the sacrifice at the time of its slaughter (and the *Gemara* does not mean to imply otherwise). The basis of their dispute is that since there is no obligation to bring the *nesachim* together with the sacrifice, the sacrifice cannot be considered the *mattir* of the *nesachim* and therefore cannot render it *piggul*. This appears to have been *Rav's* understanding of mishnah 2:4 as well, as has been explained in the comm. to that mishnah (s.v. דברי רבי מאיר and s.v. להקריב מן הנסכין). *Tosafos* (there) also offer a second explanation according to which the Sages can be reconciled with the rulings given here. This too has been explained in the comm. to mishnah 2:4 (see fn. to the end of that mishnah).

7 The offspring of a *todah*-offering, its *temurah*, or
4 one who set aside a *todah*-offering and it was lost and he set aside another in its place — do not require bread; as it is stated (*Lev.* 7:12): *And he shall offer with the sacrifice of the todah-offering* — the *todah*-offering requires bread, [but] neither its offspring, its replacement, nor its *temurah* require bread.

## YAD AVRAHAM

וּתְמוּרָתָהּ, — *its temurah,*

[*Temurah* refers to an instance in which one declared a substitute for a designated offering, saying, "Let this animal be the exchange of this one." Although this procedure is prohibited by Torah law (even if the second one is of a better quality than the first), and though the exchange cannot relieve the original offering of its sanctity, the Torah decrees that the substituted animal *also* becomes sanctified as a sacrifice (*Lev.* 27:10). Thus, if an exchange was made for a *todah*, the substituted animal is sanctified as the *temurah* of a *todah*, and it takes on the rules of the *todah*, except for the requirement of breads, as stated below (*Rambam, Hil. Temurah* 3:1).]

וְהַמַּפְרִישׁ תּוֹדָתוֹ וְאָבְדָה וְהִפְרִישׁ אַחֶרֶת תַּחְתֶּיהָ — *or one who set aside a todah-offering and it was lost and he set aside another in its place —*

If someone vowed to bring a *todah*-offering, and he then designated an animal for a *todah* and it was lost, he is required to replace the lost offering in order to fulfill his vow. In the case of this mishnah, the original was found after the replacement had already been sacrificed (*Rav*).

אֵינָן טְעוּנִים לֶחֶם; — *do not require bread;*

[Once the vow to bring a *todah* has been fulfilled with one of the animals, the *todah* animal which remains must also be sacrificed — whether it be the offspring, the *temurah*, or the original which had been lost and then rediscovered after its replacement has been sacrificed — but it is not accompanied by *todah* loaves.]

In the case of the lost *todah*, the same applies in reverse: If the original sacrifice was found and brought in fulfillment of the vow, it is brought with the loaves; its designated replacement is then brought without loaves (*Rav* from *Gemara* 80a).

*Rambam* (*Pesulei HaMukdashin* 12:8) has a different understanding of this *Gemara*. In his view, if the offspring is brought at the same time as the original sacrifice — or the *temurah* or replacement at the same time as the original — both offerings must be accompanied by loaves (see *Zevach Todah; Keren Orah*).

שֶׁנֶּאֱמַר: ,,וְהִקְרִיב עַל זֶבַח הַתּוֹדָה" — הַתּוֹדָה טְעוּנָה לֶחֶם, וְלֹא וְלָדָהּ, וְלֹא חֲלִיפָתָהּ, וְלֹא תְמוּרָתָהּ טְעוּנִין לֶחֶם. — *as it is stated* (*Lev.* 7:12): *"And he shall offer with the sacrifice of the todah-offering" — the todah-offering requires bread, [but] but neither its offspring, its replacement, nor its temurah require bread.*

This is the verse which defines the obligation of loaves for the *todah*. The Torah's use of the definite article — הַתּוֹדָה, *the todah-offering* — indicates that only the one being offered as the actual *todah* [i.e., in fulfillment of the

[ה] **הָאוֹמֵר:** „הֲרֵי עָלַי תּוֹדָה," יָבִיא הִיא וְלַחְמָהּ מִן הַחֻלִּין. תּוֹדָה מִן הַחֻלִּין וְלַחְמָהּ מִן הַמַּעֲשֵׂר, יָבִיא לַחְמָהּ מִן הַחֻלִּין. תּוֹדָה מִן הַמַּעֲשֵׂר וְלַחְמָהּ מִן הַחֻלִּין, יָבִיא.

**ר' עובדיה מברטנורא**

(ה) **יביא היא ולחמה מן החולין.** ולא מן המעשר, דכיון דאמר הרי עלי, הוי ליה דבר שבחובה, וכל דבר שבחובה אינו בא אלא מן החולין: **ואם אמר הרי עלי תודה מן החולין ולחמה מן המעשר יביא היא ולחמה מן החולין.** דלחם נגרר אחר תודה, וכיון דאמר הרי עלי תודה מן החולין, בעל כרחיה איחייב ליה בלחם, הלכך האי דמהדר ואמר לחמה מן המעשר לאו כלום הוא: **תודה מן המעשר ולחמה מן החולין יביא.** כלומר יביא כמו שנדר, ולאו חובה, דכל

**יד אברהם**

vow] requires loaves (*Tos. Yom Tov* from *Rambam Comm.* to *Temurah* 3:2).

The term *replacement* refers to the case cited above, in which one was lost and another was designated in its place (*Rav*). [In this case, whichever one is offered first is considered the primary *todah* and is the one which requires the loaves. The one which remains is not offered in fulfillment of the vow and it therefore is not accompanied by loaves.]

Voluntary offerings can be dedicated in one of two ways: (1) נֶדֶר, a *vow* by which one obligates himself to bring an offering, but without designating a specific animal at the time of the vow. This he does by stating, "I take upon myself to bring . . ." [הֲרֵי עָלַי . . .], specifying the type of offering he has in mind, but leaving it to a later time to designate an animal to be offered in fulfillment of his vow. (2) The second method is where he states at the outset, "Let this animal be a *todah*" (for example). This is known as a נְדָבָה, *donated offering*. One who vows a נְדָבָה, i.e., to bring a specific animal as an offering, has no obligation to bring a replacement if that animal is lost or invalidated (since the obligation is formulated in terms of the specific animal, not the person).

Accordingly, the ruling of the mishnah is stated for a נֶדֶר, *vow*. Since he has a personal obligation to supply a *todah*, if it is lost he must replace it. If the original is found after the replacement has been offered, it too must be offered, but it is no longer in fulfillment of the vow and it therefore does not require loaves. However, if he makes a נְדָבָה, donating a specific animal as his offering, he has no obligation to replace it if it is lost. Thus, if he does consecrate a replacement, he is in effect donating a new *todah*, and the replacement therefore requires loaves.

The offspring of such a donated *todah*, however, would not require loaves [since it is not actually a new *todah*]. It is tantamount to an offering brought with the money left over from that which had been designated for the purchase of a *todah*, which does not require loaves (*Gem.* 80a). The same is true of the *temurah* of a donated *todah* (*Keren Orah*).

[As noted above, *Rambam* has a different understanding of this matter, but an exposition of it is beyond the scope of this work. See *Keren Orah* and *Zevach Todah*.]

## 5.

The following two mishnayos are based on the principles of the law of *maaser sheni* (second tithe) and their applications to the *todah* and its loaves.

By Torah law, one must take a tenth of all his produce to Jerusalem and eat

**5.** One who says, "I take upon myself [to bring] a *todah*-offering," must bring it and its bread from that which is unconsecrated. [If he said,] "A *todah*-offering from that which is unconsecrated and its bread from *maaser*," he must bring its bread from that which is unconsecrated. [If he said,] "A *todah*-offering from *maaser* and its bread from that which is unconsecrated," let him bring [it].

### YAD AVRAHAM

it there. This is called מַעֲשֵׂר שֵׁנִי [*maaser sheni*], *the second tithe;* i.e., the tithe that is in addition to the one given to the *Levi.*

Although the produce of *maaser sheni* may be eaten only in Jerusalem, the Torah allows for the produce to be redeemed for money, which is taken to Jerusalem and spent in turn on food items that are eaten there. The money of *maaser sheni* may be used to purchase animals for voluntary *shelamim-offerings*, since these offerings are, in the end, eaten by their owners. However, one may not use this money to purchase sacrifices that he has an obligation to bring, even though he will eat them. The rule is that כָּל שֶׁבָּאָה חוֹבָה אֵינָהּ בָּאָה אֶלָּא מִן הַחֻלִּין, *whatever is brought as an obligation may be brought only from chullin* [unconsecrated matter], i.e., not from *maaser sheni* money. This principle will be elaborated in mishnah 6. The following mishnah discusses the laws of buying a *todah* or its loaves with *maaser sheni* money.

הָאוֹמֵר: "הֲרֵי עָלַי תּוֹדָה," יָבִיא הִיא וְלַחְמָהּ מִן הַחֻלִּין. — *One who says, "I take upon myself [to bring] a todah-offering," must bring it and its bread from that which is unconsecrated.*

If someone obligated himself to bring a *todah*, he may not purchase it with the money which he had consecrated by redeeming his *maaser sheni* with it. Since he has already accepted upon himself the obligation to bring such an offering, it is considered a mandatory sacrifice and it may therefore not be purchased with *maaser sheni* money (*Rav*).

תּוֹדָה מִן הַחֻלִּין וְלַחְמָהּ מִן הַמַּעֲשֵׂר, יָבִיא לַחְמָהּ מִן הַחֻלִּין. — *[If he said,] "A todah-offering from that which is unconsecrated and its bread from maaser," he must bring its bread from that which is unconsecrated.*

[In this case, he specified that the loaves of the *todah* be bought with *maaser sheni* money, but not the sacrifice itself.] Since he did not stipulate in his basic obligation of the *todah* that it be brought from *maaser* money, it becomes like a regular mandatory offering which must be brought from *chullin* (unconsecrated) funds. The obligation for loaves to accompany the sacrifice derives automatically from the basic obligation of the *todah;* therefore, these too must be brought from *chullin* funds (*Rav*).

תּוֹדָה מִן הַמַּעֲשֵׂר וְלַחְמָהּ מִן הַחֻלִּין, יָבִיא. — *[If he said,] "A todah-offering from maaser and its bread from that which is unconsecrated," let him bring [it].*

[If he expressly stipulated in his

הַתּוֹדָה, הִיא וְלַחְמָהּ מִן הַמַּעֲשֵׂר, יָבִיא. וְלֹא יָבִיא מֵחִטֵּי מַעֲשֵׂר שֵׁנִי, אֶלָּא מִמָּעוֹת מַעֲשֵׂר שֵׁנִי.

[ו] **מִנַּיִן** לָאוֹמֵר: „הֲרֵי עָלַי תּוֹדָה,״ לֹא יָבִיא אֶלָּא מִן הַחֻלִּין? שֶׁנֶּאֱמַר: „וְזָבַחְתָּ פֶּסַח לַה׳ אֱלֹהֶיךָ צֹאן וּבָקָר״. וַהֲלֹא אֵין פֶּסַח בָּא אֶלָּא מִן הַכְּבָשִׂים וּמִן הָעִזִּים? אִם כֵּן לָמָּה נֶאֱמַר „צֹאן וּבָקָר״? אֶלָּא לְהַקִּישׁ כָּל הַבָּא מִן הַבָּקָר וּמִן הַצֹּאן לַפֶּסַח.

### ר׳ עובדיה מברטנורא

שכן אם יביא שניהם מן החולין דשפיר עבד, אלא אם רצה להביא כמו שנדר יביא: **ולא יביא הלחם מחטי מעשר שני עצמו.** דלחם דומיא דשלמים בעינן, מה שלמים ממעות מעשר שני ולא ממעשר שני עצמו, אף לחם כן:

### יד אברהם

[If he stipulates that both the sacrifice and the loaves be brought from *maaser*, that too is valid.]

וְלֹא יָבִיא מֵחִטֵּי מַעֲשֵׂר שֵׁנִי, אֶלָּא מִמָּעוֹת מַעֲשֵׂר שֵׁנִי. — *However, he may not bring from wheat of maaser sheni, only from money of maaser sheni.*

[Even in this last case in which it is permitted to bring the flour out of *maaser sheni* money, permission applies only to purchase wheat from which to make flour with money used to redeem *maaser sheni*. However, one may not use the actual wheat of *maaser sheni* itself to make the flour.] This is because the permissibility of using *maaser sheni* for a *todah* is derived from the fact that it is acceptable for a *shelamim*. Therefore, just as the *shelamim* cannot be brought from the *maaser sheni* itself — as it involves only an animal and not produce — so too the *todah* cannot be brought from the *maaser sheni* itself (*Rav* from *Gem.* 81b-82a).

The *Gemara* (81b) cites a dispute as to initial commitment to bring a *todah* that it is to be bought with *maaser sheni* money, he may do so, despite the fact that he vowed to bring the loaves from *chullin* money. Since he is now voluntarily undertaking the obligation to bring a *todah* , he may pay for it out of *maaser* money, or stipulate that it be purchased from such funds. The fact that he committed himself to bring the loaves from *chullin* money cannot create an obligation to bring the *todah* itself from such funds.]

The phrase *let him bring it* means merely that he *may* pay for it out of the *maaser* funds; certainly if he brings from *chullin* money it is also valid (*Rav; Rashi; Tos., Rambam Comm.* from *Gem.* 81b).

[However, in his Codes (*Maaseh HaKorbanos* 16:16), *Rambam* implies that it is preferable that he bring it from *maaser* money in accordance with his vow.]

הַתּוֹדָה, הִיא וְלַחְמָהּ מִן הַמַּעֲשֵׂר, יָבִיא. — *"[Both] the todah-offering, and its bread from maaser," let him bring [it].*

7
6 "[Both] the *todah*-offering, and its bread from *maaser*," let him bring [it]. However, he may not bring from wheat of *maaser sheni*, only from money of *maaser sheni*.

**6.** From where is it [known] that one who says, "I take upon myself [to bring] a *todah*-offering," must bring from that which is unconsecrated? Because it is stated (*Deut.* 16:2): *And you shall sacrifice a pesach-offering to HASHEM your God, [from the] flocks and cattle.* But does not the *pesach*-offering come only from sheep or goats? If so, why does it say *flocks and cattle*? It is in order to compare all that comes from cattle and flocks to the *pesach*-offering.

### YAD AVRAHAM

whether grain which was originally bought with *maaser sheni* money for the purpose of being eaten in Jerusalem (in accordance with the laws of *maaser sheni*) may be subsequently used to provide the flour for the loaves of a *todah*. The halachah follows the majority view that this too is not permitted (*Zevach Todah*).

### 6.

מִנַּיִן לָאוֹמֵר: „הֲרֵי עָלַי תּוֹדָה," לֹא יָבִיא אֶלָּא מִן הַחֻלִּין? — *From where is it [known] that one who says, "I take upon myself [to bring] a todah-offering"* (lit., *a todah-offering is hereby upon me*), *must bring from that which is unconsecrated?*

[The mishnah now questions the source for the principle defined in the previous mishnah.]

שֶׁנֶּאֱמַר: „וְזָבַחְתָּ פֶּסַח לַה' אֱלֹהֶיךָ צֹאן וּבָקָר." וַהֲלֹא אֵין פֶּסַח בָּא אֶלָּא מִן הַכְּבָשִׂים וּמִן הָעִזִּים? — *Because it is stated* (*Deut.* 16:2): *"And you shall sacrifice a pesach-offering to HASHEM your God, [from the] flocks and cattle." But does not the pesach-offering come only from sheep or goats?*

[The Torah mentions flocks and cattle in reference to the *pesach* sacrifice, despite the fact that a *pesach*-offering can be brought only from lambs and kids and cannot be from cattle, as the Torah explicitly states (*Exodus* 12:5).]

[The term בָּקָר, *cattle*, refers specifically to the ox family. The term צֹאן in the Torah refers to both the sheep and goat families. It is translated here as flock to incorporate both these meanings.]

אִם כֵּן לָמָּה נֶאֱמַר „צֹאן וּבָקָר"? אֶלָּא לְהַקִּישׁ כָּל הַבָּא מִן הַבָּקָר וּמִן הַצֹּאן לַפֶּסַח. — *If so, why does it say "flocks and cattle"? It is in order to compare all that comes from cattle and flocks to the pesach-offering.*

[The purpose of the Torah's statement must be understood as comparing all other sacrifices of cattle, sheep, and goats to the *pesach*-offering, to teach the following principle:]

מָה הַפֶּסַח, שֶׁהוּא בָא בְּחוֹבָה, אֵינוֹ בָא אֶלָּא מִן הַחֻלִּין; אַף כָּל דָּבָר שֶׁהוּא בָא בְּחוֹבָה לֹא יָבוֹא אֶלָּא מִן הַחֻלִּין. לְפִיכָךְ הָאוֹמֵר: „הֲרֵי עָלַי תּוֹדָה," „הֲרֵי עָלַי שְׁלָמִים," הוֹאִיל וְהֵם בָּאִים חוֹבָה, לֹא יָבוֹאוּ אֶלָּא מִן הַחֻלִּין. וְהַנְּסָכִים בְּכָל מָקוֹם לֹא יָבוֹאוּ אֶלָּא מִן הַחֻלִּין.

ר' עובדיה מברטנורא

(ו) **מה פסח שהוא בא בחובה אינו בא אלא מן החולין.** דפסח מצרים לא בא אלא מן החולין, שעדיין לא היתה להם שום תבואת מעשר שני, שאין מעשר אלא משנכנסו לארץ, ומה פסח מצרים לא בא אלא מן החולין, אף פסח דורות אינו בא אלא מן החולין, שהרי הוא אומר (שמות יג, ה) ועבדת את העבודה הזאת בחדש הזה, שיהו כל עבודת החדש הזה כזה של מצרים: **אף כל דבר שבחובה נמי כו'.** לפיכך, האומר הרי עלי תודה או שלמים הואיל והן באים חובה דקאמר הרי עלי, לא יביא אלא מן החולין: **והנסכים.** אפילו אמר הרי עלי להביאם ממעשר, לא יביא אלא מן החולין, דכי שרא רחמנא לאתויי שלמים ממעשר הני מילי שלמים גופייהו דבני אכילה נינהו, אבל נסכים דכליל הם לא יביאו מן המעשר:

יד אברהם

מָה הַפֶּסַח, שֶׁהוּא בָא בְּחוֹבָה, אֵינוֹ בָא אֶלָּא מִן הַחֻלִּין; — *Just as the pesach-offering, which comes as an obligation, comes only from that which is unconsecrated;*

The original *pesach*-sacrifice offered in Egypt was perforce brought only from unconsecrated money, since the laws of *maaser sheni* did not go into effect until the Jewish nation entered the Land of Israel. Accordingly, we derive that all subsequent *pesach*-offerings must also be brought from *chullin* funds. This is based on the verse (*Exodus* see 13:5): וְעָבַדְתָּ אֶת הָעֲבוֹדָה הַזֹּאת בַּחֹדֶשׁ הַזֶּה, *And you shall [henceforth] perform this service in this month* — i.e., all the services for this month performed in subsequent generations shall be performed just like this [original] one (*Rav* from *Gem.* 82a).

אַף כָּל דָּבָר שֶׁהוּא בָא בְּחוֹבָה לֹא יָבוֹא אֶלָּא מִן הַחֻלִּין. — *so anything which comes as an obligation may be brought only from that which is unconsecrated.*

[By the verse's analogy of other offerings brought from cattle, sheep, and goats to the *pesach*-offering, we derive that all such offerings must be purchased out of *chullin* funds when they are obligatory offerings.]

7
6

Just as the *pesach*-offering, which comes as an obligation, comes only from that which is unconsecrated; so anything which comes as an obligation may be brought only from that which is unconsecrated. Therefore, if one says, "I take upon myself [to bring] a *todah*-offering"; [or] "I take upon myself [to bring] a *shelamim-offering*," since they come as an obligation, they may come only from that which is unconsecrated. However, libations in all cases come only from that which is unconsecrated.



It is unclear how this derivation is extended to include in this rule the *minchah* and loaves of a *todah* [which are not "flocks and cattle'] (*Tos.* 82a, s.v. להקיש).

לְפִיכָךְ הָאוֹמֵר: ,,הֲרֵי עָלַי תּוֹדָה," ,,הֲרֵי עָלַי שְׁלָמִים," הוֹאִיל וְהֵם בָּאִים חוֹבָה, לֹא יָבוֹאוּ אֶלָּא מִן הַחֻלִּין. — *Therefore, if one says, "I take upon myself [to bring] a todah-offering," [or] "I take upon myself [to bring] a shelamim-offering," since they come as an obligation, they may come only from that which is unconsecrated.*

Since he obligated himself personally to bring such an offering [rather than simply designating a specific animal to be consecrated for that type of offering], he has created for himself an obligation which cannot be discharged with consecrated funds. Thus, the animal he purchases as an offering to fulfill his vow must be paid for out of his *chullin* funds (*Rav*).

This statement is actually self-evident; it is stated only to contrast it to the following statement (*Rashi Peirush*).

וְהַנְּסָכִים בְּכָל מָקוֹם לֹא יָבוֹאוּ אֶלָּא מִן הַחֻלִּין. — *However, libations in all cases come only from that which is unconsecrated.*

Unlike the *todah* and the *shelamim*, which being voluntary offerings may be brought from *maaser sheni* money if so stipulated at the time of the vow, *nesachim* must always be purchased from unconsecrated funds (*Tif. Yis.*). Even if one stipulated at the time he pledged the *nesachim* that he be able to bring them from *maaser sheni* money, he may not do so. Since the *minchah* and wine libation which form the *nesachim* are entirely consumed by the Altar and not by the owner whatsoever, they are not similar to *shelamim* which, in certain circumstances, may be brought from the money of *maaser sheni* (*Rav; Rashi;* cf. *Tos.*). Alternatively, the Torah's language regarding *nesachim* indicates that they must be brought from wholly unconsecrated funds and not from *maaser sheni* (*Rambam Comm., Maaseh HaKorbanos* 17:7).

# פרק שמיני
# Chapter Eight

[א] **כָּל** קָרְבְּנוֹת הַצִּבּוּר וְהַיָּחִיד בָּאִים מִן הָאָרֶץ וּמִחוּצָה לָאָרֶץ, מִן הֶחָדָשׁ וּמִן הַיָּשָׁן, חוּץ מִן הָעֹמֶר וּשְׁתֵּי הַלֶּחֶם, שֶׁאֵינָן בָּאִים אֶלָּא מִן הֶחָדָשׁ וּמִן הָאָרֶץ. וְכֻלָּן אֵינָן בָּאִים אֶלָּא מִן הַמֻּבְחָר. וְאֵיזֶהוּ מֻבְחָר?

**ר' עובדיה מברטנורא**

**פרק שמיני – כל הקרבנות הצבור. (א) כל קרבנות. מן החדש ומן הישן.** במנחות קאמר: **שאינן באים אלא מן החדש.** בעומר כתיב (ויקרא כג, טז) מנחה חדשה, ובשתי הלחם כתיב (שמות לד, כב) בכורי קציר חטים: **ומן הארץ.** בעומר כתיב (ויקרא כג, י) כי תבואו אל הארץ [וגו'] וקצרתם את קצירה, ובשתי הלחם כתיב (שם שם, יז) ממושבותיכם תביאו לחם:

**יד אברהם**

## 1.

כָּל קָרְבְּנוֹת הַצִּבּוּר וְהַיָּחִיד בָּאִים מִן הָאָרֶץ וּמִחוּצָה לָאָרֶץ, — *All communal and individual offerings may come either from the Land [of Israel] or from outside the Land,*

I.e., the grain from which *menachos* are made need not necessarily be grown in the Holy Land (*Rashi; Rav*).

Although this statement can also be applied to animal sacrifices, the mishnah here is referring specifically to *menachos*. This is evident from the fact that it mentions only the exceptions to this rule as regards *menachos* [see below] but not as regards animal sacrifices, viz., the *maaser* (tithe) offering and the *bechor* (firstborn) offering, both of which are brought only from cattle of the Land of Israel (*Tos., Tos. Yom Tov*).

מִן הֶחָדָשׁ וּמִן הַיָּשָׁן, — *either from the new [crop] or from the old,*

This refers to *Menachos* (*Rav*) which may be brought from the "old" crop of previous years or from the "new" crop of the present year, as long as the *shtei halechem* of Shavuos, which render the new year's grain permissible for offerings in the Temple, have been brought (*Zevach Todah*).

חוּץ מִן הָעֹמֶר וּשְׁתֵּי הַלֶּחֶם, — *except for the omer and the shtei halechem,*

[I.e., the *omer*-offering, which is brought on the second day of Passover, and the *shtei halechem*, which are brought on Shavuos (see preface to 4:2).]

שֶׁאֵינָן בָּאִים אֶלָּא מִן הֶחָדָשׁ — *which may come only from the new [crop]*

[These two offerings must come from the new crop.] The Torah refers to the *omer* as רֵאשִׁית קְצִירְכֶם, *the first of your reaping* (*Lev.* 23:10), thereby indicating that it must come from the new harvest[1] (*Gem.* 83b; *Tos. Yom Tov*). The *shtei halechem* are referred to by the Torah (*Lev.* 23:16) as מִנְחָה חֲדָשָׁה, *a new minchah*, and as בִּכּוּרֵי

1. The source cited by *Rav* for the requirement to bring the *omer* from the new crop is problematic, as pointed out by *Tos. Yom Tov*.

8
1

1. All communal and individual offerings may come either from the Land [of Israel] or from outside the Land, either from the new [crop] or from the old, except for the *omer* and the *shtei halechem,* which may come only from the new [crop] and from the Land. All of them come only from choice [produce]. Which is choice?

**YAD AVRAHAM**

מַעֲשֶׂיךָ, *the bikkurim of your work* (*Ex.* 23:16) [i.e., the first fruit of the new crop]. Thus, they too must come from the new crop (*Rambam Comm.*).

There is a question whether these offerings are valid if they are brought from the old grain instead of the new. The *Gemara* cites a *Baraisa* which states that they are. However, our mishnah's use of the unequivocal phrase שֶׁאֵינָן בָּאִים אֶלָּא מִן הֶחָדָשׁ, *which come only from the new crop,* leads the *Gemara* to conclude that our mishnah disagrees (*Tos.* ibid.). *Rambam* (*Temidin Umussafin* 8:2) rules that the *shtei halechem* must be brought from the new grain, but that if there is none to be found it may be brought from the old. *Ravad* (ad loc.) regards the last statement as "a distortion of the halachah," apparently maintaining that the final halachah should follow our mishnah, rather than the *Baraisa.* The commentators offer various views as to whether *Rambam* indeed follows the opinion of the *Baraisa* against that of the mishnah as the basis for his ruling, or whether he is of the opinion that the mishnah did not disagree with the *Baraisa* regarding the *shtei halechem*[1] (see *Kesef Mishneh, Lechem Mishneh,* ad loc.).

.וּמִן הָאָרֶץ — *and from the Land.*

The passage concerning the *omer* begins with the words: *When you shall come to the Land which I am giving you* (*Lev.* 23:10). Concerning the *shtei halechem,* the Torah (ibid. v. 17) states: *from your settlements.* [Thus, these offerings must be brought from grain grown in Eretz Yisrael] (*Rav*).

.וְכֻלָּן אֵינָן בָּאִים אֶלָּא מִן הַמֻּבְחָר — *All of them come only from choice [produce].*

[All *menachos*, regardless of whether they are brought from the new crop or the old, must be made from grain of superior quality,] as it is stated [in reference to offerings] (*Deut.* 12:11): וְכֹל מִבְחַר נִדְרֵיכֶם, *and all the choice of your vows* (*Tosefta* 9:1).

This refers only to the majority of *menachos.* The *omer,* however, must be brought from the produce closest to Jerusalem [even if there is better grain in other localities] (*Tif. Yis.* from 10:2; see *Tiferes Yaakov*).

1. What complicates the issue further is that elsewhere (*Hil. Isurei Mizbe'ach* 6:15) *Rambam* cites the unequivocal statement of our mishnah that both the *omer* and the *shtei halechem* must be brought from the new grain of Eretz Yisrael in order to be valid. *Zevach Todah* therefore suggests that while *Rambam* follows the view of our mishnah that the *shtei halechem* are not valid from the old, that is only if there is new grain available; if there is no new grain to be found, even our mishnah agrees that it may be brought from the old.

מִכְמָס וּמְזוֹנִיחָה אַלְפָא לַסֹּלֶת. שְׁנִיָּה לָהֶם — חֲפָרַיִם בַּבִּקְעָה. כָּל הָאֲרָצוֹת הָיוּ כְשֵׁרוֹת, אֶלָּא מִכָּאן הָיוּ מְבִיאִים.

[ב] **אֵין** מְבִיאִין לֹא מִבֵּית הַזְּבָלִים, וְלֹא מִבֵּית הַשְּׁלָחִים, וְלֹא מִבֵּית הָאִילָן; וְאִם הֵבִיא, כָּשֵׁר. כֵּיצַד הוּא עוֹשֶׂה? נָרָהּ שָׁנָה רִאשׁוֹנָה,

### ר׳ עובדיה מברטנורא

**מכמס וזוניחה.** שמות של מקומות הן: **אלפא לסלת.** סלת שלהן ראשון ומובחר לכל הסלתות, כאל״ף זו שהיא ראשונה לכל האותיות: **אלפא.** זו אל״ף בלשון יוני: **שנייה להן.** קרובה סלתה להיות משובחת כסלת מכמס וזוניחה: **חפריים בבקעה.** שתי חפרים הן, אחת בהר ואחת בבקעה, ואותה שבבקעה היא שסלת שלה משובחת: **כל הארצות.** של ארץ ישראל היו כשרות, אלא שמכאן היו מביאים: **(ב) אין מביאין.** עומר ושתי הלחם: **לא מבית הזבלים.** משדה שצריכה לזבל, דשמא לא נזדבלה כל צרכה ונמצאו פירותיה כחושים, אי נמי, לפי שהזבל מבאיש ומפסיד טעם הפרי: **ולא מבית השלחים.** ארץ צמאה למים שפירותיה כחושין: **לא מבית האילן.** מתבואה שבין האילנות, שהאילנות הגדלים שם יונקים הקרקע ומכחישים הזרעים: **נרה.** חורש, לשון נירו לכם ניר (ירמיה ד, ג):

### יד אברהם

וְאֵיזֶהוּ מֻבְחָר? מִכְמָס וּמְזוֹנִיחָה אַלְפָא לַסֹּלֶת. — *Which is choice? Michmas and Mezonichah are the preferred areas for fine flour.*

[The preferred locales from which to select the grain for *menachos* were Michmas and Mezonichah.]

Alpha is the first letter of the Greek alphabet, thus signifying the first choice (*Rav; Rashi*).

Others explain the mishnah to be using the Semitic root אלף, *to learn*, to refer to places which are "learned," i.e., which habitually produce quality grain (*Rambam Comm.* to mishnah 3).

שְׁנִיָּה לָהֶם — חֲפָרַיִם בַּבִּקְעָה. — *Chafarayim in the valley is second to them.*

The fine flour produced in the region of Chafarayim is of a quality nearly as high as that of Michmas and Mezonichah (*Rav*).

There were two towns called Chafarayim, one in the highlands and one in the valley. The one in the valley produced very fine flour (*Rav*). This town is cited in *Joshua* (19:19) as being in the portion of the tribe of Issachar.

Other versions state עֲפָרַיִם, which is the town עֶפְרַיִן cited in *II Chronicles* (13:19). This version is borne out by the *Gemara* (85a), which cites עפרים in reference to the mishnah (*Meleches Shlomo*).

*Rashi* brings a third version, that the town cited in the mishnah is כפרים.

כָּל הָאֲרָצוֹת הָיוּ כְשֵׁרוֹת, אֶלָּא מִכָּאן הָיוּ מְבִיאִים. — *All lands are valid, but they would bring from these.*

All lands in Eretz Yisrael were halachically valid as sources for the grain of *menachos*, but these places produced the best grain and were therefore generally used (*Rav; Rashi*).[1]

1. Apparently, *Rashi* and *Rav* stipulate "in Eretz Yisrael" because this refers also to the *shtei halechem* which could not be brought from grain that grew outside of the Land, as

8 Michmas and Mezonichah are the preferred areas
2 for fine flour. Chafarayim in the valley is second to them. All lands are valid, but they would bring from these.

**2.** We do not bring either from a fertilized field, or from an irrigated field, or from a field of trees; but if one brought, it is valid. How does one do it? He plows it the first year,

### YAD AVRAHAM

## 2.

אֵין מְבִיאִין — *We do not bring*

The *menachos* of *omer* and *shtei halechem* are not brought from the following types of fields (*Rav; Rashi*).

Others contend that the restrictions of this mishnah apply to all *menachos* (*Tos.; Rambam, Isurei Mizbe'ach* 6:12; *Rashi* to *Pesachim* 11a ד״ה ושל בית העמקים).

לֹא מִבֵּית הַזְּבָלִים, — *either from a fertilized field,*

A field which must be fertilized is not acceptable as a source of grain for *menachos* because it may not have been sufficiently fertilized and its produce will then be inferior. Alternatively, the use of fertilizer, which is malodorous, adversely affects the taste of the produce (*Rav; Rashi*).

Another interpretation of בֵּית הַזְּבָלִים is *grain which grows in dung heaps* (*Rambam Comm.*).

וְלֹא מִבֵּית הַשְּׁלָחִים, — *or from an irrigated field,*

This refers to a field which requires an abundance of water and must therefore be irrigated. Such a field yields inferior produce (*Rav*).

וְלֹא מִבֵּית הָאִילָן; — *or from a field of trees;*

Grain which grows between the trees will generally be of inferior quality, because the trees drain the nutrients of the land (*Rav; Rashi*).

Others explain that the trees' shade impedes the growth of the grain (*Peirush*).

וְאִם הֵבִיא, כָּשֵׁר. — *but if one brought, it is valid.*

[If someone brings *menachos* from any of these fields, it is valid.]

כֵּיצַד הוּא עוֹשֶׂה? — *How does one do it?*

[How does one cultivate his field so that it should produce superior grain?]

נָרָהּ שָׁנָה רִאשׁוֹנָה, וּבַשְּׁנִיָּה זוֹרְעָהּ — *He plows it the first year, and in the second he plants it*

According to the *Gemara's* conclusion, this means that he plows the whole field the first year [so that there will be no wild growth to sap the soil's nutrients (*Tif. Yis.*)] but plants only half of it; the second year he again

stated in the beginning of the mishnah. (This passage does not seem to refer to the *omer*, which also had to be brought from the produce of Eretz Yisrael, because the *omer's* preferred area was the area closest to Jerusalem — see 10:2.) All other *menachos*, however, could be brought even from produce that grew outside of Eretz Yisrael, as stated in the beginning of the mishnah. See *Rambam Comm.*, who appears to interpret כָּל הָאֲרָצוֹת here as referring even to lands outside of Eretz Yisrael.

מנחות
ח/ג

וּבַשְּׁנִיָּה זוֹרְעָהּ קֹדֶם לַפֶּסַח שִׁבְעִים יוֹם, וְהִיא עוֹשָׂה סֹלֶת מְרֻבָּה. כֵּיצַד הוּא בוֹדֵק? הַגִּזְבָּר מַכְנִיס אֶת יָדוֹ לְתוֹכָהּ. עָלָה בָהּ אָבָק, פְּסוּלָה עַד שֶׁיְּנַפֶּנָּה. וְאִם הִתְלִיעָה, פְּסוּלָה.

[ג] **תְּקוֹעַ** אַלְפָא לַשֶּׁמֶן. אַבָּא שָׁאוּל אוֹמֵר: שְׁנִיָּה לָהּ רֶגֶב בְּעֵבֶר הַיַּרְדֵּן. כָּל הָאֲרָצוֹת הָיוּ כְשֵׁרוֹת, אֶלָּא מִכָּאן הָיוּ מְבִיאִין.

### ר׳ עובדיה מברטנורא

**ובשניה זורעה.** בגמרא (פה, ב) מסיק, דשנה ראשונה הוא ניר כולה וזורע חליה ומניח חליה ניר, וכן בשניה חורשה כולה וזורע החצי שלא זרע אשתקד, והחצי שזרע אשתקד מניחו ניר, וכן בכל שנה זורע ניר של אשתקד: **כיצד בודק.** הסולת אם מנופה כל צרכו אם לאו: **עלה בידו אבק.** קמח דק, וגרוע הוא: **עד שינפנה.** בנפה לעבור האבק דק שנשאר בה: **ואם התליעה.** הסלת או החטה, פסולה, והוא שהתליעה ברובה, וילפינן לה לקמן סוף פרקין (משנה ז) מדכתיב (במדבר כח, יט־כ) תמימים יהיו לכם ומנחתם, תמימים יהיו לכם ונסכיהם (שם שם, לא), שיהיו גם כן המנחות והנסכים תמימים: (ג) **תקועה.** עיר ששמה תקועה כדכתיב (שמואל־ב יד, ב) וישלח יואב תקועה: **אלפא לשמן.** השמן שלה ראשון ומובחר לשמנים, כאל״ף זו שהיא ראשונה לאותיות:

### יד אברהם

plows the whole field but plants only the half that lay fallow the previous year. He follows this alternating pattern every year, planting half one year and leaving that half fallow the next (*Rav*; see also *Rashi* and *Zevach Todah*).

קֹדֶם לַפֶּסַח שִׁבְעִים יוֹם, וְהִיא עוֹשָׂה סֹלֶת מְרֻבָּה. — *seventy days prior to Passover, and it produces fine flour in abundance.*

This planting is done seventy days prior to Passover, because at this time, the sun is sufficiently strong to generate the desired growth (*Peirush*).

כֵּיצַד הוּא בוֹדֵק? — *How does one check it?*

How does one examine the processed flour to see if it is sufficiently refined [to be used for *menachos*] (*Rav*)?

הַגִּזְבָּר מַכְנִיס אֶת יָדוֹ לְתוֹכָהּ. — *The treasurer inserts his hand into it.*

[The Temple treasurer, who is responsible for purchasing flour for the *menachos*, places his hand into the flour.]

עָלָה בָהּ אָבָק, פְּסוּלָה עַד שֶׁיְּנַפֶּנָּה. — *[If] dust comes up in it, it is unfit until he sifts it.*

If he withdraws his hand and finds in it tiny particles of inferior flour, he must sift the flour again to rid it of this flour dust (*Rav*).

וְאִם הִתְלִיעָה, פְּסוּלָה. — *If it becomes wormy, it is unfit.*

If the majority of the grain or flour becomes infested with worms, it is not valid for *menachos*, because *menachos* — like sacrificial animals — must be unblemished [see below mishnah 7] (*Rav* from *Gem.* 85b).

8 and in the second he plants it seventy days
3 prior to Passover, and it produces fine flour in abundance. How does one check it? The treasurer inserts his hand into it. [If] dust comes up in it, it is unfit until he sifts it. If it becomes wormy, it is unfit.

3. Tekoah is the preferred area for the oil. Abba Shaul says: Second to it is Regev beyond the Jordan. All lands are valid, but they would bring from these.

YAD AVRAHAM

The *Gemara* (ibid.) is uncertain whether each individual grain must be infested in its majority for it to be disqualified or if even a small degree of infestation in the major part of all the grain is sufficient to disqualify it. Because this doubt remains unresolved, the flour may not be used in either case (*Toras HaKodashim*).

Another interpretation of the *Gemara's* uncertainty is whether even a single grain which is mostly infested is enough to disqualify the rest, even when the majority of the crop is free of infestation (*Rambam, Hil. Isurei Mizbe'ach* 6:11).

## 3.

Having discussed which grains may be used for *menachos*, the chapter now deals with the grades of the oil and wine which may be used in Temple services.

.תְּקוֹעָה אַלְפָא לַשֶּׁמֶן — *Tekoah is the preferred area for the oil.*

Tekoah is a town in Eretz Yisrael[1] (*Rav;* see *II Samuel* 14:2) [that produced prime olive oil].

.אַבָּא שָׁאוּל אוֹמֵר: שְׁנִיָּה לָהּ רֶגֶב בְּעֵבֶר הַיַּרְדֵּן — *Abba Shaul says: Second to it is Regev beyond the Jordan.*

[The next best source of oil was the town of Regeb, which was situated on the eastern side of the Jordan River.]

Some identify Regev as the Biblical Argov [*Deut.* 3:4] (see *Aruch*).

.כָּל הָאֲרָצוֹת הָיוּ כְשֵׁרוֹת, אֶלָּא מִכָּאן הָיוּ מְבִיאִין — *All lands are valid, but they would bring from these.*

[Oil for *menachos* may be brought from anywhere, but the places cited were preferred due to the quality of their oil.]

1. In the text of the mishnah printed in the *Gemara* (85b), the word appears תְּקוֹעַ without the ה. According to *Rashash,* this version correctly reflects the proper name of the town as it appears elsewhere in *Tanach* (*Jeremiah* 6:1; *Amos* 1:1). In the verse which *Rav* cites (*II Samuel* 14:2), וַיִּשְׁלַח יוֹאָב תְּקוֹעָה, *and Joab sent to Tekoah,* the suffix ה is used in place of the prefix ל, *to,* and is not part of the name itself. See, however, *Shinnuyei Nuschaos,* who provides a justification for our version.

אֵין מְבִיאִין לֹא מִבֵּית הַזְּבָלִים, וְלֹא מִבֵּית הַשְּׁלָחִים, וְלֹא מִמַּה שֶׁנִּזְרַע בֵּינֵיהֶם; וְאִם הֵבִיא, כָּשֵׁר. אֵין מְבִיאִין אַנְפִּקָנוֹן, וְאִם הֵבִיא, פָּסוּל. אֵין מְבִיאִין מִן הַגַּרְגְּרִים שֶׁנִּשְׁרוּ בַמַּיִם, וְלֹא מִן הַכְּבוּשִׁים, וְלֹא מִן הַשְּׁלוּקִין; וְאִם הֵבִיא, פָּסוּל.

[ד] **שְׁלֹשָׁה** זֵיתִים, וּבָהֶן שְׁלֹשָׁה שְׁלֹשָׁה שְׁמָנִים. הַזַּיִת הָרִאשׁוֹן — מְגַרְגְּרוֹ בְּרֹאשׁ הַזַּיִת, וְכוֹתֵשׁ

**ר׳ עובדיה מברטנורא**

**אנפיקנון.** שמן העשוי מזיתים שלא הביאו שליש בשולן, והוא מר מאד: **שנשרו במים.** שהמים מקלקלים את השמן: (ד) **שלשה זיתים.** שלש פעמים בשנה מלקטים את הזיתים, ובהן שלש שמנים, בכל פעם יש שלשה מינים שמן: **הזית הראשון.** פעם ראשונה שמלקט: **מגרגרו בראש הזית.** מלקט גרגרים שהן בראש הזית, שהן מתבשלים תחלה לפי שהחמה זורחת עליהן ומבשלתן:

**יד אברהם**

אֵין מְבִיאִין לֹא מִבֵּית הַזְּבָלִים, וְלֹא מִבֵּית הַשְּׁלָחִים, — *We do not bring either from a fertilized field, or from an irrigated field,*

These fields produce an inferior grade of oil, as explained in the previous mishnah in regard to grain.

וְלֹא מִמַּה שֶׁנִּזְרַע בֵּינֵיהֶם; — *or from those [trees] between which vegetation grew;*

One should not use for *menachos* oil from olive trees which had anything planted between them (*Tif. Yis.*), because this vegetation has a detrimental effect on the olives and the quality of their oil (*Rashi*; *Tif. Yis.*).

וְאִם הֵבִיא, כָּשֵׁר. — *but if one brought, it is valid.*

[If oil from any of these fields was used for a *minchah*, it is valid.]

אֵין מְבִיאִין אַנְפִּקָנוֹן, וְאִם הֵבִיא, פָּסוּל. — *We do not bring from unripe olives, and if one did, it is invalid.*

This refers to oil from olives which did not attain one-third of their growth; such oil is very bitter (*Rav* from *Gem.* 86a) and cannot yet be legally defined as oil but rather as mere sap; therefore it is invalid if used (*Gem.* ibid.; *Tos.* ad loc.).

Other versions of the mishnah state *if one did, it is valid* (*Tos.* ibid.; *Rambam, Hil. Isurei Mizbe'ach* 6:14). [Accordingly, it is already considered oil at this stage.]

אֵין מְבִיאִין מִן הַגַּרְגְּרִים שֶׁנִּשְׁרוּ בַמַּיִם, — *We do not bring from oliveberries which were soaked in water,*

Olives which fall off the tree [prematurely] must be soaked [extensively] in water in order to extract their oil (*Tif. Yis.*). [This oil is unfit for *menachos*] because the water ruins the oil (*Rav*).

Some maintain that these are two distinct cases: גַּרְגְּרִים, *oliveberries* which fall from the tree, or שֶׁנִּשְׁרוּ בַמַּיִם, *olives soaked in water* (*Tos. Yom Tov*). [However, from

8
4 We do not bring either from a fertilized field, or from an irrigated field, or from those [trees] between which vegetation grew; but if one brought, it is valid. We do not bring from unripe olives, and if one did, it is invalid. We do not bring from oliveberries which were soaked in water, nor from the preserved, nor from the stewed; if one did, it is invalid.

**4.** There are three [categories of] olives, each with three oils. The first olive — he picks it from the top of the olive tree, and pounds

### YAD AVRAHAM

the wording of the *Peirush*, it is clear that he does not interpret the mishnah in this manner.]

וְלֹא מִן הַכְּבוּשִׁים, וְלֹא מִן הַשְּׁלוּקִין; — *nor from the preserved, nor from the stewed;*

The oil from preserved olives, i.e., olives soaked in vinegar (*Tif. Yis.*), or stewed olives is not acceptable for *menachos*.

Some interpret the mishnah to be referring to olives whose oil cannot be extracted without resorting to one of these three procedures, viz., extended soaking in water, soaking [in vinegar], or stewing (*Peirush*).

וְאִם הֵבִיא, פָּסוּל. — *if one did, it is invalid.*

[If one used any of these oils for *menachos*, it is invalid.]

4.

שְׁלֹשָׁה זֵיתִים, — *There are three [categories of] olives,*

Olives are picked from the trees at three different times during the year (*Rav; Rashi*).[1]

Others explain the mishnah to refer to the three different levels of the olive tree, which are harvested in different manners [but not necessarily at different times] (*Rambam, Hil. Isurei Mizbe'ach* 7:8).

וּבָהֶן שְׁלֹשָׁה שְׁלֹשָׁה שְׁמָנִים. — *each with three oils.*

Each of these three categories of olives produces three different grades of oil, so that there are a total of nine grades of oil (*Rav; Rambam, Hil. Isurei Mizbe'ach* 7:8).

הַזַּיִת הָרִאשׁוֹן – מְגַרְגְּרוֹ בְּרֹאשׁ הַזַּיִת, — *The first olive — he picks it from the top of the olive tree,*

The first time that the olives are

1. *Tosafos* (86a, s.v. שלשה) question this premise that olives were harvested three times a year, on the basis of the mishnah in *Peah* (1:5) which cites olives among the fruits from which *peah* is set aside — i.e., that a portion of the crop is left unpicked for the poor. As there is a principle that *peah* is taken only from those crops which are picked at one time (*Shabbos* 68a), it is thus difficult to accept this interpretation of our mishnah. *Tzon Kodashim*, however, suggests that the mishnah in *Peah* means to exclude only such crops as figs, which are picked at intervals a few at a time, but not olives, which were picked at three set times in large quantity.

מנחות ח/ד

וְנוֹתֵן לְתוֹךְ הַסַּל. רַבִּי יְהוּדָה אוֹמֵר: סְבִיבוֹת הַסַּל. זֶה רִאשׁוֹן. טָעַן בַּקּוֹרָה – רַבִּי יְהוּדָה אוֹמֵר: בָּאֲבָנִים – זֶה שֵׁנִי. חָזַר וְטָחַן וְטָעַן; זֶה שְׁלִישִׁי. הָרִאשׁוֹן לַמְּנוֹרָה וְהַשְּׁאָר לַמְּנָחוֹת. הַזַּיִת הַשֵּׁנִי – מְגַרְגְּרוֹ בְּרֹאשׁ הַגַּג וְכוֹתֵשׁ וְנוֹתֵן לְתוֹךְ הַסַּל. רַבִּי יְהוּדָה אוֹמֵר: סְבִיבוֹת הַסַּל. זֶה רִאשׁוֹן. טָעַן בַּקּוֹרָה – רַבִּי יְהוּדָה אוֹמֵר: בָּאֲבָנִים – זֶה שֵׁנִי. חָזַר וְטָחַן וְטָעַן; זֶה שְׁלִישִׁי. הָרִאשׁוֹן לַמְּנוֹרָה וְהַשְּׁאָר לַמְּנָחוֹת.

**ר׳ עובדיה מברטנורא**

**לתוך הסל.** ומסתנן ויוצא והכלי תחת הסל לקבל השמן: **רבי יהודה אומר סביבות דופני הסל.** נותן את [הזיתים], והשמן זב דרך הדפנות ונופל לשולי הסל ומשם מסתנן ויוצא ונמצא מזוקק, שהפסולת נשאר מדובק בדופני הסל, אבל לא יתנם בשולי הסל, מפני שמתערב בו שמן ושמרים ויוצאים ונמצא שמן עכור. והשמן הזב מאליו בלא שום טעינה נקרא שמן ראשון של הזית הראשון: **טען בקורה.** זיתים שבסל: **רבי יהודה אומר באבנים.** ולא בקורה, שהקורה כבדה ומוציאה את השמרים: **חזר** [וטוחן]. ברחים, את הזיתים שתחת הקורה, וטוען אחר כך הקורה: **הראשון למנורה.** דבעינן שמן זית זך: **והשאר כשר למנחות.** דלא כתיב בהו זך:

**יד אברהם**

picked (*Rav;* see above), those at the top of the tree are taken because they are the first to ripen, since they are most exposed to the sunlight (*Rav*). Alternatively, the mishnah is translated: *he allows them to fully ripen at the top of the tree* (*Rashi Peirush;* see *Gem.* 86a).

.וְכוֹתֵשׁ וְנוֹתֵן לְתוֹךְ הַסַּל — *and pounds and places [it] in the basket.*

The olives are pounded with a mortar (*Tif. Yis.*) and placed in a perforated basket. When in the basket, the oil that drips from the olives is strained through the basket's bottom and collected in a utensil which is placed under the basket (*Rav*).

.רַבִּי יְהוּדָה אוֹמֵר: סְבִיבוֹת הַסַּל — *R' Yehudah says: Around the basket.*

R' Yehudah contends that the olives should be placed around the [inner] walls of the basket so that the oil first drips down the sides of the basket and then strains through the bottom into the utensil beneath it. The oil is thus refined, because the sediment clings to the walls of the basket. He should not, however, place the olives in the bottom of the basket because the oil mixes with the sediment and becomes clouded (ibid.).

.זֶה רִאשׁוֹן — *This is the first.*

This oil which drips by itself from the olives is called the first oil of the olive (*Rav*) and it is the most superior (*Tif. Yis.*).

– טָעַן בַּקּוֹרָה — *He presses with the beam —*

A beam is then placed on the pounded olives [to press out the remaining oil] (*Tif. Yis.*).

– רַבִּי יְהוּדָה אוֹמֵר: בָּאֲבָנִים — *R' Yehudah says: With stones —*

R' Yehudah maintains that stones are used for this purpose, because a

8 and places [it] in the basket. R' Yehudah says: Around
4 the basket. This is the first. He presses with the beam — R' Yehudah says: With stones — this is the second. He again grinds and presses [them]; this is the third. The first is for the *menorah* and the rest is for *minchah*-offerings. The second olive — he picks it from the rooftop and pounds and places [it] in the basket. R' Yehudah says: Around the basket. This is the first. He presses with the beam — R' Yehudah says: With stones — this is the second. He again grinds and presses [them]; this is the third. The first is for the *menorah* and the rest is for *minchah*-offerings.

**YAD AVRAHAM**

beam is too heavy and would press out the sediments as well (*Rav*).

זֶה שֵׁנִי. — *this is the second.*

[This is the second grade of oil which is extracted from these olives.]

חָזַר וְטָחַן וְטָעַן; זֶה שְׁלִישִׁי. — *He again grinds and presses [them]; this is the third.*

The olives are next ground with a millstone and then pressed again with a beam [to produce the third grade of oil] (*Rav*).

הָרִאשׁוֹן לַמְּנוֹרָה — *The first is for the menorah*

Only the first grade of olive oil may be used for the menorah in the Temple, as the Torah (*Ex.* 27:20; *Lev.* 24:2) explicitly requires: שֶׁמֶן זַיִת זָךְ, *pure olive oil* (*Rav*).

וְהַשְּׁאָר לַמְּנָחוֹת. — *and the rest is for minchah-offerings.*

The remaining grades of oil are fit for *menachos*, for which the Torah does not specify "pure" (*Rav*).

הַזַּיִת הַשֵּׁנִי – מְגַרְגְּרוֹ בְּרֹאשׁ הַגַּג — *The second olive — he picks it from the rooftop*

The second group of olives to be picked when they ripen consists of those which are on the tree at the height of the rooftops (*Rav*).

Others interpret this passage of the mishnah to mean that the olives of the second harvest are laid out on the rooftops after they are picked in order to fully ripen (*Peirush*). *Rambam* (*Comm.; Isurei Mizbe'ach* 7:8) explains that the first category of olives consists of those which are hand-picked from the tops of trees when they are fully ripened. The olives of the second group are those which are picked in bulk, the ripe with the unripe, and laid out on the rooftops, where the ripe ones are then selected.

וְכוֹתֵשׁ וְנוֹתֵן לְתוֹךְ הַסַּל. רַבִּי יְהוּדָה אוֹמֵר: סְבִיבוֹת הַסַּל. זֶה רִאשׁוֹן. טָעַן בַּקּוֹרָה – רַבִּי יְהוּדָה אוֹמֵר: בָּאֲבָנִים – זֶה שֵׁנִי. חָזַר וְטָחַן וְטָעַן; זֶה שְׁלִישִׁי. הָרִאשׁוֹן לַמְּנוֹרָה וְהַשְּׁאָר לַמְּנָחוֹת. — *and pounds and places [it] in the basket. R' Yehudah says: Around the basket. This is the first. He presses with the beam — R' Yehudah says: With stones — this is the second. He again grinds and presses [them]; this is the third. The first is for the menorah and the rest is for minchah-offerings.*

[The same process used for the first category of olives is used for the

הַזַּיִת הַשְּׁלִישִׁי – עוֹטְנוֹ בְּתוֹךְ הַבַּיִת עַד שֶׁיִּלְקֶה וּמַעֲלֵהוּ וּמְנַגְּבוֹ בְּרֹאשׁ הַגַּג, וְכוֹתֵשׁ וְנוֹתֵן לְתוֹךְ הַסַּל. רַבִּי יְהוּדָה אוֹמֵר: סְבִיבוֹת הַסַּל. זֶה רִאשׁוֹן. טָעַן בַּקּוֹרָה – רַבִּי יְהוּדָה אוֹמֵר: בָּאֲבָנִים – זֶה שֵׁנִי. חָזַר וְטָחַן וְטָעַן; זֶה שְׁלִישִׁי. הָרִאשׁוֹן לַמְּנוֹרָה וְהַשְּׁאָר לַמְּנָחוֹת.

[ה] **הָרִאשׁוֹן** שֶׁבָּרִאשׁוֹן אֵין לְמַעְלָה מִמֶּנּוּ. הַשֵּׁנִי שֶׁבָּרִאשׁוֹן וְהָרִאשׁוֹן שֶׁבַּשֵּׁנִי שָׁוִין. הַשְּׁלִישִׁי שֶׁבָּרִאשׁוֹן,

### ר׳ עובדיה מברטנורא

**הזית השני.** פעם שניה כשמלקט את שנמצאים מבושלים עתה: **מגרגרן בראש הגג.** מלקט הגרגרין הסמוכים לגג, שזיתיהן היו סמוכים לגגותיהן, ואותן מתבשלים בשניה: **הראשון.** שיצא קודם טחינה, כשר למנורה: **הזית שלישי.** שמתלקט פעם שלישית, אין מתבשלים לעולם כל צרכן, שהן ענפים שתחת הגג שאין חמה מגעת בהם: **עוטנו.** לשון מעטן של זיתים, שהיא הגומא שמניחים בה הזיתים כדי שיתעפשו שם. ולשון מקרא הוא, עטיניו מלאו חלב (איוב כא, כד): **שילקה.** שיתעפש: **ומנגבו בראש הגג.** דמתוך שהוא צבור ומכונס במקום אחד ארבעה וחמשה ימים, זב מאליו מוהל שאינו יפה, לפיכך צריך לנגבו: (ה) **שוין.** לאו לכל מילי שוין, דהא בכולהו תנן הראשון למנורה והשאר למנחות, אלא שוין למנחות קאמר. ומשום דקיימא לן בכל מקום מבחר נדריך, שיביא מן המובחר, קא משמע לן השתא שהראשון שבשני והשני שבראשון שוין, שאם יש לו מנחה להביא ויש לו משניהם, מאיזה שירצה יביא, אבל אם יש לו משלישי שבראשון ומראשון שבשני, יביא מנחתו מראשון שבשני שהוא מובחר:

### יד אברהם

*takes it up and dries it atop the roof,*

Since the olives are packed together for several days, undesirable liquid oozes from them, and they must therefore be allowed to dry out (*Rav*).

וְכוֹתֵשׁ וְנוֹתֵן לְתוֹךְ הַסַּל. רַבִּי יְהוּדָה אוֹמֵר: סְבִיבוֹת הַסַּל. זֶה רִאשׁוֹן. טָעַן בַּקּוֹרָה – רַבִּי יְהוּדָה אוֹמֵר: בָּאֲבָנִים – זֶה שֵׁנִי. חָזַר וְטָחַן וְטָעַן; זֶה שְׁלִישִׁי. הָרִאשׁוֹן לַמְּנוֹרָה וְהַשְּׁאָר לַמְּנָחוֹת. — *and pounds and places [it] into the basket. R' Yehudah says: Around the basket. This is the first. He presses with the beam — R' Yehudah says: With stones — this is the second. He again grinds and presses [them]; this is the third. The first is for the menorah*

second to produce its three grades of oil. As in the case of the first category, only the first grade can be used for the *menorah*, whereas the two lower grades are fit only for *menachos*.]

הַזַּיִת הַשְּׁלִישִׁי – עוֹטְנוֹ בְּתוֹךְ הַבַּיִת עַד שֶׁיִּלְקֶה — *The third olive — he packs it inside the house until it decays*

The olives from the bottom of the tree never fully ripen, since the sun does not reach them. They are therefore taken inside the house and packed inside a cavity in which they become rotted [and soft] (*Rav*).

וּמַעֲלֵהוּ וּמְנַגְּבוֹ בְּרֹאשׁ הַגַּג, — *and he*

8 The third olive — he packs it inside the house until
5 it decays and he takes it up and dries it atop the roof, and pounds and places [it] into the basket. R' Yehudah says: Around the basket. This is the first. He presses with the beam — R' Yehudah says: With stones — this is the second. He again grinds and presses [them]; this is the third. The first is for the *menorah* and the rest is for *minchah*-offerings.

**5.** The first of the first is the most superior. The second of the first and the first of the second are equal. The third of the first, the

YAD AVRAHAM

*and the rest is for minchah-offerings.*

[Once again, the same process is employed to produce the three grades of oil, and their fitness for use is the same as that of the corresponding grade of the superior categories.]

5.

Although all of the grades of oil described in the previous mishnah are acceptable for *menachos,* there is nevertheless a principle of מִבְחַר נִדְרֵיכֶם, *the choice of your vows* (*Deut.* 12:11), which states that one should offer choice products for an offering. The mishnah therefore lists the order of preference of the aforementioned grades of oil for *minchah-offerings* (*Rav; Rambam, Hil. Isurei Mizbe'ach* 7:11).[1]

הָרִאשׁוֹן שֶׁבָּרִאשׁוֹן אֵין לְמַעְלָה מִמֶּנּוּ. — *The first of the first is the most superior* (lit., *there is none above it*).

[The first grade of oil from the first category of olives is the grade most preferable for use in the Temple, even for *menachos*.]

הַשֵּׁנִי שֶׁבָּרִאשׁוֹן וְהָרִאשׁוֹן שֶׁבַּשֵּׁנִי שָׁוִין. — *The second of the first and the first of the second are equal.*

[The second grade of oil from the first category of olives is equal in quality to the first grade from the second category of olives] and they are thus

1. *Rambam* (ibid.) expounds upon this theme with his famous comment: "One who desires to achieve merit for himself should subdue his [Evil] Inclination and generously bring his offering from the choicest quality possible. It is said in the Torah (*Gen.* 4:4): *And Abel, too, offered from the first of his flock and from their fattest, and HASHEM turned to Abel and to his gift.* The same applies to anything dedicated to the good God — that it should be from what is most beautiful and good: If one builds a House of Prayer, it should be more beautiful than his residence; when one feeds the hungry, he should feed them from the best and sweetest of his foods; when one clothes the naked, he should clothe them with his finest garments; when one consecrates something, he should consecrate the finest of his possessions. And so it is written (*Lev.* 3:16): *Every choice thing to HASHEM . . .*"

וְהַשֵּׁנִי שֶׁבַּשֵּׁנִי, וְהָרִאשׁוֹן שֶׁבַּשְּׁלִישִׁי שָׁוִין. הַשְּׁלִישִׁי שֶׁבַּשֵּׁנִי וְהַשֵּׁנִי שֶׁבַּשְּׁלִישִׁי שָׁוִין. הַשְּׁלִישִׁי שֶׁבַּשְּׁלִישִׁי אֵין לְמַטָּה מִמֶּנּוּ.

אַף הַמְּנָחוֹת הָיוּ בַדִּין שֶׁיִּטְעֲנוּ שֶׁמֶן זַיִת זָךְ; מָה אִם הַמְּנוֹרָה, שֶׁאֵינָהּ לַאֲכִילָה, טְעוּנָה שֶׁמֶן זַיִת זָךְ, הַמְּנָחוֹת, שֶׁהֵן לַאֲכִילָה, אֵינוֹ דִין שֶׁיִּטְעֲנוּ שֶׁמֶן זַיִת זָךְ? תַּלְמוּד לוֹמַר: ,,זָךְ כָּתִית לַמָּאוֹר" — וְלֹא זָךְ כָּתִית לַמְּנָחוֹת.

[ו] **וּמִנַּיִן** הָיוּ מְבִיאִין אֶת הַיַּיִן? קְרוּתִים וְהַטּוּלִים אַלְפָא לַיַּיִן. שְׁנִיָּה לָהֶן בֵּית רִמָּה וּבֵית לָבָן בָּהָר וּכְפַר סִגְנָה בַּבִּקְעָה. כָּל הָאֲרָצוֹת הָיוּ כְשֵׁרוֹת, אֶלָּא מִכָּאן הָיוּ מְבִיאִין.

**ר' עובדיה מברטנורא**

(ו) **קרותים והטולין.** שם מקומות הם:

**יד אברהם**

[Of all of the oils described in the previous mishnah, this is the least desirable.]

אַף הַמְּנָחוֹת הָיוּ בַדִּין שֶׁיִּטְעֲנוּ שֶׁמֶן זַיִת זָךְ; מָה אִם הַמְּנוֹרָה, שֶׁאֵינָהּ לַאֲכִילָה, טְעוּנָה שֶׁמֶן זַיִת זָךְ, הַמְּנָחוֹת, שֶׁהֵן לַאֲכִילָה, אֵינוֹ דִין שֶׁיִּטְעֲנוּ שֶׁמֶן זַיִת זָךְ? — *One could deduce that the minchah-offerings should also require pure olive oil; if the menorah, which is not for consumption, requires pure olive oil, surely the minchah-offerings, which are for consumption, should require pure olive oil.*

The consumption referred to here is that of the Altar (*Rashi*).

תַּלְמוּד לוֹמַר: ,,זָךְ כָּתִית לַמָּאוֹר" — וְלֹא זָךְ כָּתִית לַמְּנָחוֹת. — *Therefore, Scripture teaches* (Ex. 27:20): *"pure, beaten for the light" — but not pure, beaten for the minchah-offerings.*

equally acceptable for *menachos*. However, only the latter is acceptable for the menorah [as stated in the previous mishnah], because pure olive oil is required (*Rav*).

הַשְּׁלִישִׁי שֶׁבָּרִאשׁוֹן, וְהַשֵּׁנִי שֶׁבַּשֵּׁנִי, וְהָרִאשׁוֹן שֶׁבַּשְּׁלִישִׁי שָׁוִין. — *The third of the first, the second of the second, and the first of the third are equal.*

[These are equally acceptable for *menachos*, but only the last may be used for the menorah.]

הַשְּׁלִישִׁי שֶׁבַּשֵּׁנִי וְהַשֵּׁנִי שֶׁבַּשְּׁלִישִׁי שָׁוִין. — *The third of the second and the second of the third are equal.*

[These two grades are equally acceptable for *menachos*; however, neither is acceptable for the menorah.]

הַשְּׁלִישִׁי שֶׁבַּשְּׁלִישִׁי אֵין לְמַטָּה מִמֶּנּוּ. — *The third of the third is the most inferior (lit., there is none below it).*

8 second of the second, and the first of the third are equal.
6 The third of the second and the second of the third are equal. The third of the third is the most inferior.

One could deduce that the *minchah*-offerings should also require pure olive oil; if the menorah, which is not for consumption, requires pure olive oil, surely the *minchah*-offerings, which are for consumption, should require pure olive oil. Therefore, Scripture teaches: *pure, beaten for the light* — but not pure, beaten for the *minchah*-offerings.

**6.** And from where did they bring the wine? Kerusim and Hattulim are the preferred areas for wine. Second to them are Beth Rimah and Beth Lavan in the highland and Kefar Signah in the valley. All lands are valid, but they would bring from these.

### YAD AVRAHAM

To counter this deduction, Scripture stresses that the oil must be "pure" [i.e., oil that oozes naturally without being pressed] and "beaten" [i.e., as a result of mere crushing without being ground with a millstone] *for the light* [i.e., for the *menorah*] — but not for *menachos* (see *Gem.* 86b; *Rashi*, ad loc.). [Thus, the characteristics of being "pure" and "beaten," shared by the first grades of each of the three categories, are required only for the *menorah* but not for *menachos*.]

The *Gemara* (ibid.) offers an insight into this difference of requirements: [Hashem in His] Torah showed concern for the money of Israel and did not require the extra expense of using only the first grade of oil for *menachos* [which were numerous and thus would have required large amounts of this choicest oil — in contrast with the *menorah*, which required only three and a half *logs* of oil each day (*Rashi*)].

### 6.

וּמִנַּיִן הָיוּ מְבִיאִין אֶת הַיַּיִן? — *And from where did they bring the wine?*

[What was the preferred source of wine for the libations?]

It is unclear why, unlike the previous mishnayos, this mishnah prefaces its ensuing discussion with an outright question (*Meleches Shlomo*).

קְרוּתִים וְהַטּוּלִים אַלְפָא לַיַּיִן. שְׁנִיָּה לָהֶן בֵּית רִמָּה וּבֵית לָבָן בָּהָר וּכְפַר סִגְנָה בַּבִּקְעָה. כָּל הָאֲרָצוֹת הָיוּ כְשֵׁרוֹת, אֶלָּא מִכָּאן הָיוּ מְבִיאִין. — *Kerusim and Hattulim are the preferred areas for wine. Second to them are Beth Rimah and Beth Lavan in the highland and Kefar Signah in the valley. All lands are valid, but they would bring from these.*

[Although all lands are acceptable as a source of wine for the libations, these were the places which

מנחות
ח/ו

אֵין מְבִיאִין לֹא מִבֵּית הַזְּבָלִים, וְלֹא מִבֵּית הַשְּׁלָחִין, וְלֹא מִמַּה שֶּׁנִּזְרַע בֵּינֵיהֶן; וְאִם הֵבִיא, כָּשֵׁר. אֵין מְבִיאִין אַלְיַסְטוֹן, וְאִם הֵבִיא, כָּשֵׁר. אֵין מְבִיאִין יָשָׁן; דִּבְרֵי רַבִּי. וַחֲכָמִים מַכְשִׁירִין. אֵין מְבִיאִין לֹא מָתוֹק, וְלֹא מְעֻשָּׁן, וְלֹא מְבֻשָּׁל; וְאִם הֵבִיא, פָּסוּל. אֵין מְבִיאִין מִן הַדָּלִיּוֹת אֶלָּא מִן הָרוֹגְלִיּוֹת וּמִן הַכְּרָמִים הָעֲבוּדִים.

ר׳ עובדיה מברטנורא

**אליוסטן.** יין מתוק מחמת השמש, שתלו הענבים בשמש למתקן. שמש בלשון יון יוסטן: **יין ישן.** שעברו עליו שנים עשר חדש, עובר אדמימותו, והכתוב אומר (משלי כג, לא) אל תרא יין כי יתאדם, אלמא בשעת אדמימותו מובחר הוא: **לא מתוק.** כשהוא מתוק מחמת עצמו, דאילו מחמת שמש, הא תנא רישא אליוסטן אם הביא כשר. פירוש אחר, תירוש שלא עברו עליו ארבעים יום. וראשון עיקר: **מן הדליות.** מן הגפנים המודלות על גבי כלונסות וקנים גבוהים מן הארץ: **אלא מן הרגליות.** מגפנים ששוכבות על גבי קרקע בין רגלי בני האדם שאינן מודלות: **העבודים.** שנעבדו שתי פעמים

יד אברהם

tended to produce the most superior wines.]

אֵין מְבִיאִין לֹא מִבֵּית הַזְּבָלִים, וְלֹא מִבֵּית הַשְּׁלָחִין, וְלֹא מִמַּה שֶּׁנִּזְרַע בֵּינֵיהֶן; וְאִם הֵבִיא, כָּשֵׁר. — *We do not bring either from a fertilized field, or from an irrigated field, or from those [vines] between which vegetation grew; but if one brought, it is valid.*

[The products of these fields are considered inferior, as explained above in mishnah 3 in regard to olive trees. Therefore, it is preferable not to use wine produced by such fields for libations. Nevertheless, if such wines were used for libations, they are valid.]

אֵין מְבִיאִין אַלְיַסְטוֹן, וְאִם הֵבִיא, כָּשֵׁר. — *We do not bring from Elioston wine, but if one brought, it is valid.*

Elioston wine is wine from grapes which were hung out in the sun to sweeten (from the Greek word *helios* [sun]) (*Rav*). Elioston wine is very dark and is not considered to be a choice wine (*Aruch*). It is sweet and very weak (*Rashbam* to *Bava Basra* 97b). [This wine should preferably not be used for libations, but is not disqualified.]

אֵין מְבִיאִין יָשָׁן; דִּבְרֵי רַבִּי. — *We do not bring from old [wine]; [these are] the words of Rabbi.*

Wine which is over twelve months old loses its redness, and red wine is preferred because it is considered to be superior (*Rav* from *Gem.* 87a). However, even Rabbi (R' Yehudah HaNasi) agrees that the libation is valid if such wine was used (*Gem.* ibid.).

וַחֲכָמִים מַכְשִׁירִין. — *But the Sages declare [it] fit.*

According to the Sages, old wine is completely acceptable for libations and may be used without hesitation (*Likkutei Halachos*). This applies to wine up to two years old. After that point, it is no longer preferred but is acceptable if used, as long as its taste is intact (*Rambam, Hil. Isurei Mizbe'ach* 7:7).

8 We do not bring either from a fertilized field, or
6 from an irrigated field, or from those [vines] between which vegetation grew; but if one brought, it is valid. We do not bring from Elioston wine, but if one brought, it is valid. We do not bring from old [wine]; [these are] the words of Rabbi. But the Sages declare [it] fit. We do not bring either sweetened [wine], or smoked, or cooked; and if one brought, it is invalid. We do not bring from espaliers but only from trailing vines and from well-cultivated vineyards.

### YAD AVRAHAM

אֵין מְבִיאִין לֹא מָתוֹק, — *We do not bring either sweetened [wine],*

Wine which sweetened with the passage of time — as opposed to that sweetened by the sun, which was discussed above — may not be used for *menachos* [for the reason explained below, s.v. ואם] (*Rav; Rashi*).

*Rav* cites another interpretation that מָתוֹק refers to wine which is less than forty days old, but concludes in favor of the previous interpretation. Indeed, other commentators cite sources that wine need not be aged at all and even יַיִן מִגִּתּוֹ, *wine [fresh] from the press,* is also fit, after the fact, for libations (*Tos.; Tos. Yom Tov*).

וְלֹא מְעֻשָּׁן, — *or smoked,*

I.e., wine that is produced from grapes that are bitter and are smoked in order to sweeten them (*Peirush*). Alternatively, this refers to the unfavorable odor imparted to the wine by casks possessing a foul odor (*Tos. Yom Tov* from *Rambam Comm.*).

*Kaf Nachas* (cited by *Tos. Yom Tov*) interprets the mishnah to refer to wine stored in barrels that were smoked with sulfur when they were new. These smoked casks improve the wine's flavor. *Tos. Yom Tov* elaborates that since such wine is harmful to people's health, it is unfit for libations.

וְלֹא מְבֻשָּׁל; — *or cooked;*

[Neither may libations be brought from otherwise acceptable wine that was cooked.]

וְאִם הֵבִיא, פָּסוּל. — *and if one brought, it is invalid.*

[Libations brought from wine which was sweetened, smoked or cooked are invalid even after the fact.] Unlike sweetness caused by the sun, sweetness which develops by itself in wine is repulsive. Therefore, this latter type of wine is unfit for libations even after the fact (*Gem.* 87a).

אֵין מְבִיאִין מִן הַדָּלִיּוֹת אֶלָּא מִן הָרוֹגְלִיּוֹת — *We do not bring from espaliers but only from trailing vines*

Wine for libations should be produced only from vines which trail along the ground [רוֹגְלִיּוֹת is a derivate of רֶגֶל, *foot*, i.e., from those which grow among people's feet] because these grapes, closest to the ground and its nutrients, are the choicest fruits. However, the wine of grapes grown on espaliers should not be used for libations [since the vines being raised on trellises causes their fruits to be inferior] (*Rav; Tif. Yis.*).

וּמִן הַכְּרָמִים הָעֲבוּדִים. — *and from well-cultivated vineyards.*

[ז] **לֹא** הָיוּ כוֹנְסִים אוֹתוֹ בַּחֲצָבִים גְּדוֹלִים אֶלָּא בְחָבִיּוֹת קְטַנּוֹת, וְאֵינוֹ מְמַלֵּא אֶת הֶחָבִיּוֹת עַד פִּיהֶם כְּדֵי שֶׁיְּהֵא רֵיחוֹ נוֹדֵף. אֵינוֹ מֵבִיא לֹא מִפִּיהָ מִפְּנֵי הַקְּמָחִין, וְלֹא מִשּׁוּלֶיהָ מִפְּנֵי הַשְּׁמָרִים. אֶלָּא, מֵבִיא מִשְּׁלִישָׁהּ וּמֵאֶמְצָעָהּ. כֵּיצַד הוּא בוֹדֵק? הַגִּזְבָּר יוֹשֵׁב וְהַקָּנֶה בְּיָדוֹ. זָרַק אֶת הַגִּיד, וְהִקִּישׁ בַּקָּנֶה.

**ר׳ עובדיה מברטנורא**

בשנה, שחופרים סביבות הגפנים להפך בקרקע שבשרשיהן ועושין בהן גומות להשקותן, וזו היא עבודתן: (ז) **בחצבים גדולים.** שהכלים הגדולים פוגמים טעם היין: **כדי שיהא ריחו נודף.** כשהחבית מלאה, יוצא הריח לחוץ ואינו נודף: **קמחין.** כמין גרגרים דקים לבנים שטולים על פני היין דומין לקמח: **ומאמצעה.** משים ברזא באמצע החבית: **קנה.** אמת המדה שהיתה רגילה להיות ביד הגזבר: **זרק את הגיד והקיש בקנה.** כלומר כשזרק היין הגיד של שמרים, שמתחילים השמרים לצאת, הקיש הגזבר בקנה שבידו ודאהו שלא יכנס בכלי שיש בו היין. ורבותי פירשו הקיש בקנה שבידו לרמוז אל מושך היין מן החבית שיסתום החבית בברזא, ולא היה אומר לו סתום, לפי שהדבור קשה ליין. והכי מפרש ליה בגמרא (פז, א):

**יד אברהם**

The wine for libations must be produced by vineyards which are cultivated twice annually by digging around the roots of the vines and making holes around the stocks to enhance their aeration and irrigation (*Rav, Rambam Comm.* from *Gem.* 87a).

However, if libations were brought from wine produced from espaliers or uncultivated vines, the libations are valid (*Rambam, Hil. Isurei Mizbe'ach* 6:9).

## 7.

לֹא הָיוּ כוֹנְסִים אוֹתוֹ בַּחֲצָבִים גְּדוֹלִים אֶלָּא בְחָבִיּוֹת קְטַנּוֹת, — *They did not store it in large casks but rather in small barrels,*

The wine for libations was placed only in small barrels because the large casks impair the taste of the wine (*Rav*).

וְאֵינוֹ מְמַלֵּא אֶת הֶחָבִיּוֹת עַד פִּיהֶם כְּדֵי שֶׁיְּהֵא רֵיחוֹ נוֹדֵף. — *and one does not fill the barrel to its rim so that it should be aromatic.*

When the wine fills the barrel completely, the scent escapes from the barrel and the wine loses its fragrance; when there is room left at the top, the aroma is trapped and remains within the barrel (*Rav; Rashi*).

אֵינוֹ מֵבִיא לֹא מִפִּיהָ מִפְּנֵי הַקְּמָחִין, — *One does not bring from its mouth because of the mold,*

One should not use for libations the wine that is at the top of the barrel because of the small, white flour-like particles which form there (*Rav*).

8
7

7. They did not store it in large casks but rather in small barrels, and one does not fill the barrel to its rim so that it should be aromatic. One does not bring from its mouth because of the mold, nor from its bottom because of the sediment. Rather, one brings from the middle third and from its middle. How does he check? The treasurer sits with the reed in his hand. [When] it exuded the vein [of sediment], he struck with the reed.

YAD AVRAHAM

וְלֹא מִשּׁוּלֶיהָ מִפְּנֵי הַשְּׁמָרִים. — *nor from its bottom because of the sediment.*

[The wine at the bottom is also not desirable because of the sediment which settles there.]

אֶלָּא, מֵבִיא מִשְּׁלִישָׁהּ וּמֵאֶמְצָעָהּ. — *Rather, one brings from the middle third and from its middle.*

He places a spigot into the walls of the barrel in the middle of the middle third [and draws the wine from there] (*Rav* as explained by *Tos. Yom Tov*).

*Rambam* (*Hil. Isurei Mizbe'ach* 7:6) explains that the barrels were stacked three high; the mishnah here teaches that the wine for libations was drawn from the middle of the middle barrel (see *Lechem Mishneh* ad loc.).

כֵּיצַד הוּא בוֹדֵק? — *How does he check?*

[How did they monitor the wine coming out of the spigot to insure that it was not beginning to draw from the barrel's inferior wine (see *Rambam* ibid.; *Peirush; Rashash*)?]

הַגִּזְבָּר יוֹשֵׁב וְהַקָּנֶה בְּיָדוֹ. — *The treasurer sits with the reed in his hand.*

This is either a measuring stick, which the Temple treasurer would generally carry with him (*Rav*), or a cane, which the treasurer carried as a mark of distinction of his office (*Tif. Yis.*).

זָרַק אֶת הַגִּיד, וְהִקִּישׁ בַּקָּנֶה. — *[When] it exuded the vein [of sediment], he struck with the reed.*

When an issue of sediment[1] began to come from the barrel, the treasurer would tap the worker with his reed to indicate to him that he should close off the flow (*Rav; Rashi*). He would not simply tell this to the worker, because speaking in the vicinity of the wine has an adverse effect on its quality (*Rav* from *Gem.* 87a).[2]

Others interpret that the treasurer would hit the spigot with the reed and push it away to prevent the sediment from mixing with the wine being collected in the utensil underneath (*Rav; Rambam Comm.*).

1. Some commentators read הַגִּיר (instead of הַגִּיד) and render: *the whitish part* (*Peirush*; cf. *Rashi* ms).

2. According to *Tif. Yis.*, it is only considerable talking that has this adverse effect. However, they insured that there would be no considerable talking by refraining from any speech whatsoever.

מנחות ח/ז

רַבִּי יוֹסֵי בְּרַבִּי יְהוּדָה אוֹמֵר: יַיִן שֶׁעָלָה בוֹ קְמָחִין פָּסוּל, שֶׁנֶּאֱמַר: „תְּמִימִם יִהְיוּ לָכֶם וּמִנְחָתָם״; „תְּמִימִם יִהְיוּ לָכֶם וְנִסְכֵּיהֶם.״

— ר׳ עובדיה מברטנורא —

**רבי יוסי ברבי יהודה אומר יין שעלו בו קמחין** [פסול]. ואין הלכה כרבי יוסי ברבי יהודה. וכל הני דאמרינן במתניתין שהם פסולים, בין בסולת בין בשמן בין ביין, אם עבר והקדישן, מכין אותו מכות מרדות מדבריהם, כדין המקדיש בעל מום למזבח שהוא לוקה מן התורה, מדכתיב בבעל מום (ויקרא כב, כ) לא תקריבו, ואמרו בסיפרא, אין לא תקריבו אלא לא תקדישו. וכשם שהיו מביאים הסלת והיין והשמן ממקומות מובחרים ידועים כדתנן במתניתין, כך היו מביאים הקרבנות ממקומות ידועים, אילים ממואב, כבשים מחברון, עגלים משרון, גוזלות דהיינו תורים ובני יונה מהר המלך:

**יד אברהם**

רַבִּי יוֹסֵי בְּרַבִּי יְהוּדָה אוֹמֵר: יַיִן שֶׁעָלָה בוֹ קְמָחִין פָּסוּל, שֶׁנֶּאֱמַר: „תְּמִימִם יִהְיוּ לָכֶם — וּמִנְחָתָם״; „תְּמִימִם יִהְיוּ לָכֶם וְנִסְכֵּיהֶם.״ *R' Yose bar R' Yehudah says: Wine in which mold developed*[1] *is unfit, as it is stated (Num. 28:19-20,31): "Unblemished they shall be for you and their minchah-offerings"; "unblem-*

1. There is an apparent grammatical discrepancy in this phrase between the plural subject קְמָחִין and the singular verb form עָלָה. *Rambam Comm.* indeed has the singular קִמְחוֹן. Other editions of the mishnah have instead שֶׁיֵּשׁ בּוֹ קְמָחִין, *that has in it mold*.

8 R′ Yose bar R′ Yehudah says: Wine in which
7 mold developed is unfit, as it is stated (*Num.*
28:19-20, 31): *Unblemished they shall be for you and their minchah-offerings; unblemished they shall be for you and their libations.*

### YAD AVRAHAM

*ished they shall be for you and their libations.'*

[Verse 19 ends with the phrase תְּמִימִם יִהְיוּ לָכֶם, *unblemished they shall be for you,* and the following verse begins with the word וּמִנְחָתָם, *and their minchah-offerings.* Verse 31 concludes with the phrase תְּמִימִם יִהְיוּ לָכֶם וְנִסְכֵּיהֶם, *unblemished shall they be for you and their libations*. We can thereby derive that both *menachos* and libations must be unblemished, and anything considered the equivalent to a blemish in an animal sacrifice is not acceptable for these offerings. R′ Yose maintains that mold in the wine is tantamount to a blemish and is therefore invalid (see *Rambam Comm.*).

The halachah does not follow this view [that wine in which mold developed is unfit for libations] (*Rav; Rambam Comm.*).

If one consecrates for *menachos* or libations any of the flours, oils or wines cited in the mishnah as being unacceptable, it is an unresolved question in the *Gemara* (87a) whether one thereby violates the same Biblical law which prohibits consecrating a blemished animal for the Altar. Since this is an unresolved question, the Biblical penalty of lashes cannot be administered. Nevertheless, a Rabbinic penalty of lashes is administered (*Rav; Rambam Comm., Hil. Isurei Mizbe'ach* 6:3).

# פרק תשיעי
# Chapter Nine

[א] **שְׁתֵּי** מִדּוֹת שֶׁל יָבֵשׁ הָיוּ בַמִּקְדָּשׁ: עִשָּׂרוֹן וַחֲצִי עִשָּׂרוֹן. רַבִּי מֵאִיר אוֹמֵר: עִשָּׂרוֹן, עִשָּׂרוֹן, וַחֲצִי עִשָּׂרוֹן. עִשָּׂרוֹן מֶה הָיָה מְשַׁמֵּשׁ? שֶׁבּוֹ הָיָה מוֹדֵד לְכָל הַמְּנָחוֹת. לֹא הָיָה מוֹדֵד לֹא בְשֶׁל שְׁלֹשָׁה לַפָּר, וְלֹא בְשֶׁל שְׁנַיִם לָאַיִל; אֶלָּא מוֹדְדָן עֶשְׂרוֹנוֹת.

**ר׳ עובדיה מברטנורא**

**פרק תשיעי – שתי מדות. (א) שתי מדות.** עשרון עשרון וחצי עשרון. שתי מדות של עשרון היו, אחת מודדים אותה גדושה, שהיתה קטנה ולא היתה מחזקת כשהיא גדושה אלא עשרון, כשעור חברתה כשהיא מחוקה, דרבי מאיר גמר מקרא דכתיב (במדבר כח, כט) עשרון עשרון לכבש האחד, דשתי עשרונות היו שם, ואי שתיהן שוות, הויא לה מדה אחת, אלא אחת מחוקה ואחת גדושה, גדושה שבה היה מודד לכל המנחות, מחוקה שבה היה מודד לחביתי כהן גדול, וחכמים אומרים לא היה שם אלא עשרון אחד דכתיב (שם כט, ד) ועשרון אחד לכבש האחד, ואותו עשרון מחוק היה, ובו היו מודדים לכל המנחות. והלכה כחכמים: **לא בשל שלשה לפר.** למנחת נסכים של פר דכתיב ביה (שם כח, יב) ושלשה עשרונים לפר האחד, לא היו מודדין במדה אחת שתהא מחזקת שלשה עשרונים, שלא היתה שם מדה גדולה מעשרון: **אלא מודדן עשרונות.** כל עשרון עשרון בפני עצמו:

**יד אברהם**

## 1.

שְׁתֵּי מִדּוֹת שֶׁל יָבֵשׁ הָיוּ בַמִּקְדָּשׁ: — *There were two dry measures in the Temple:*

Dry measures of two different sizes were used in the Temple (*Tif. Yis.*) for measuring the flour of *menachos.*

עִשָּׂרוֹן וַחֲצִי עִשָּׂרוֹן. — *the issaron and the half-issaron.*

[I.e., a tenth and twentieth of an *ephah* (see mishnah 6:6, 7:1).]

In the view of *Targum Onkelos* to *Ex.* 25:29, as interpreted by *Ramban* (ibid.), there was also a two-*issaron* measure which was used for measuring the flour for the *lechem hapanim* (*Meleches Shlomo*).

רַבִּי מֵאִיר אוֹמֵר: עִשָּׂרוֹן, עִשָּׂרוֹן, וַחֲצִי עִשָּׂרוֹן. — *R' Meir says: An issaron, an issaron, and a half-issaron.*

R' Meir disagrees with the first *Tanna's* statement that there were only two dry measures in the Temple. In his view there were three: two separate measures for the *isssaron* and the one for half an *issaron*. The two *issaron* measures were different in the way they measured the *issaron*. One measured a full *issaron* when its contents were level. The other was an *issaron* when heaped. The one which measured a full *issaron* when level was used for the *minchas chavitin* of the *Kohen Gadol* (see 4:5). Since this offering was divided into halves (see below), using a heaped measure would likely result in some of it spilling when being divided. The other *issaron* measured an *issaron* when heaped and was used for all other *menachos.*

R' Meir derives his view from the

9
1

1. There were two dry measures in the Temple: the *issaron* and the half-*issaron*. R' Meir says: An *issaron*, an *issaron*, and a half-*issaron*. What was the function of the *issaron?* All *minchah*-offerings were measured in it. One did not measure with [one of] three [*essronos*] for the bull, nor with [one of] two [*essronos*] for the ram; rather, he measured them by the *issaron*. What was

YAD AVRAHAM

repetition of the phrase עִשָּׂרוֹן עִשָּׂרוֹן, *an issaron, an issaron,* which the Torah (*Num.* 28:29) uses to describe the *menachos*. The repetition indicates that there should be two distinct *issaron* measures (*Rav* from *Gem.* 87a).

The Sages, for their part, hold that only one measure, which contained an *issaron* when level,[1] was used. The extra word עִשָּׂרוֹן comes to add a half-*issaron* measure to be used as well (*Gem.* ibid.). The halachah follows the view of the Sages (*Rav; Rambam, Klei HaMikdash* 1:15; cf. *Zevach Todah*).

Curiously, *Rambam* makes no mention of whether the respective vessels measured their contents heaped or level. Apparently he holds that it would be valid either way (*Mishneh LaMelech* ad loc.; *Keren Orah*).

עִשָּׂרוֹן מֶה הָיָה מְשַׁמֵּשׁ? שֶׁבּוֹ הָיָה מוֹדֵד לְכָל הַמְּנָחוֹת. — *What was the function of the issaron? All minchah-offerings were measured in it.*

[All *menachos* require an *issaron* of flour or a multiple of an *issaron.*]

לֹא הָיָה מוֹדֵד לֹא בְשֶׁל שְׁלֹשָׁה לַפָּר, וְלֹא בְשֶׁל שְׁנַיִם לָאַיִל; — *One did not measure with [one of] three [essronos] for the bull, nor with [one of] two [essronos] for the ram;*

The Torah (*Num.* 28:12) requires a *minchah* of three *essronos* to be brought together with the sacrifice of a bull and one of two *essronos* to be brought together with a ram. Nevertheless, there were no measures in the Temple for these amounts (*Rav*).

אֶלָּא מוֹדְדָן עֶשְׂרוֹנוֹת. — *rather, he measured them by the issaron.*

The flour for those *menachos* was measured one *issaron* at a time (*Rav*).

1. It is not clear why it is that according to the Sages all the measures were level while according to R' Meir all the measures, with the exception of the one used for *chavitin*, were heaped. Apparently, it was preferable that the contents of the *issaron* measure be level so that they could be sanctified within the vessel. However, according to R' Meir, that Scripture teaches that there were two *issaron* measures, we are forced to distinguish between one *issaron* measure and the other. Therefore, he concludes that it is the *issaron* used for the *chavitin* that is level in order to avoid spillage, as explained above, whereas all other *menachos* were measured in a heaped fashion ( *Sfas Emes;* cf. *Keren Orah*).

חֲצִי עִשָּׂרוֹן מֶה הָיָה מְשַׁמֵּשׁ? שֶׁבּוֹ הָיָה מוֹדֵד חֲבִיתֵּי כֹּהֵן גָּדוֹל, מֶחֱצָה בַּבֹּקֶר וּמֶחֱצָה בֵּין הָעַרְבָּיִם.

[ב] **שֶׁבַע** מִדּוֹת שֶׁל לַח הָיוּ בַמִּקְדָּשׁ: הִין, וַחֲצִי הַהִין, וּשְׁלִישִׁית הַהִין, וּרְבִיעִית הַהִין; לֹג, וַחֲצִי לֹג, וּרְבִיעִית לֹג. רַבִּי אֱלִיעֶזֶר בַּר צָדוֹק אוֹמֵר: שְׁנָתוֹת הָיוּ בַהִין: עַד כָּאן לַפָּר; עַד כָּאן לָאַיִל; עַד כָּאן לַכֶּבֶשׂ.

### ר׳ עובדיה מברטנורא

**כי גרסינן, חצי עשרון מה היה משמש שבו היה מודד לחביתי כהן גדול** והכי פירושא, לחביתי כהן גדול מביא מביתו עשרון שלם, ומוצהו בחצי עשרון שבמקדש, ולא כל חצי עשרון בפני עצמו, ועושה מכל חצי עשרון שש חלות, שהן לשני חצאי עשרון שתים עשרה חלות, ואופה כולן ביחד, ואחר כך מחלק כל חלה לשנים, ומקריב שנים עשר חצאין בבקר, ושנים עשר חצאין בערב, וקודם שיקריב פותת אותן לפתין כזית, וכופל כל פתיתה לשנים ואינו מבדיל. אבל פתיתת כל שאר מנחות אף על פי שפתין שלהן כזית, כופל אותן לשנים ושנים לארבעה ומבדיל, כדתנן לעיל בפרק ו׳ (משנה ד): **(ב) שנתות היו בהין.** לא היה שם אלא הין, ובו היו סימנים מסמרות או פגימות: **עד כאן לפר.** חצי ההין: **עד כאן לאיל.** שלישית ההין: **ועד כאן לכבש.** רביעית ההין. ואין הלכה כרבי אליעזר:

### יד אברהם

חֲצִי עִשָּׂרוֹן מֶה הָיָה מְשַׁמֵּשׁ? שֶׁבּוֹ הָיָה מוֹדֵד חֲבִיתֵּי כֹּהֵן גָּדוֹל, — *What was the function of the half-issaron? The chavitin of the Kohen Gadol were measured in it,*

The *Kohen Gadol* is instructed to bring a *minchas chavitin* daily (*Lev.* 6:12ff). For this purpose, he brings a full *issaron* of flour and divides it into two halves, by placing the flour in consecrated half-*issaron* measures (*Rav; Rambam Comm., Hil. Maaseh HaKorbanos* 13:2).

מֶחֱצָה בַּבֹּקֶר וּמֶחֱצָה בֵּין הָעַרְבָּיִם. — *half in the morning and half in the afternoon.*

Each of the two halves of an *issaron* of flour was kneaded separately and made into six loaves. The twelve loaves were then baked together and divided into halves. Twelve of these halves were offered in the morning and twelve in the afternoon (ibid.).

The above is *Rambam's* view. Others contend that the division of the *chavitin* was done differently: Six *full* loaves were brought in the morning and the other six in the afternoon (*Ravad*, ad loc.; *Rashi*, 87b, s.v. במה מחלקה; see mishnah 4:5 and comm. ibid.).

According to this view, the *Kohen* has the choice of either baking six in the morning and six in the afternoon or else baking all of them in the morning and delaying the offering of the second group (*Mishneh LaMelech* ad loc.). Others submit that it is preferable for the baking to

9 the function of the half-*issaron?* The *chavitin* of
2 the *Kohen Gadol* were measured in it, half in the morning and half in the afternoon.

**2.** There were seven liquid measures in the Temple: a *hin,* a half of a *hin,* a third of a *hin,* and a fourth of a *hin;* a *log,* a half-*log,* and a quarter-*log.* R' Eliezer bar Tzadok says: There were notches in the *hin*: until here for the bull; until here for the ram; and until here for the lamb.

### YAD AVRAHAM

be done as close as possible to the offering, so that the second group of loaves were baked in the afternoon (*Mikdash David* 8:4).

## 2.

שֶׁבַע מִדּוֹת שֶׁל לַח הָיוּ בַמִּקְדָּשׁ: — *There were seven liquid measures in the Temple:*

[Measures of seven different volumes were utilized in the Temple for the measuring of liquid offerings such as oil and wine.]

The mishnah lists only those utensils used for measuring. There were, however, vessels of different sizes employed in the service of the *Beis HaMikdash*. For example, the vessels used to receive the blood were conceivably less than a *reviis*, although there is no mention of such a volume in the mishnah (*Igros Moshe, Orach Chaim* I, section on *Kodashim* 3).

הִין, — *a hin,*

A *hin* is the equivalent of twelve *logs* (*Gem.* 89a). Although no offering requires a measurement of a full *hin* (see below), the oil made in the Wilderness for anointing the *Kohanim* and the vessels of the Tabernacle — and later the Temple — amounted to a *hin* (*Gem.* 88a).

וַחֲצִי הַהִין, וּשְׁלִישִׁית הַהִין, וּרְבִיעִית הַהִין; לֹג, וַחֲצִי לֹג, וּרְבִיעִית לֹג. — *a half of a hin, a third of a hin, and a fourth of a hin; a log, a half-log, and a quarter-log.*

[The purpose for each of these measures will be explained in the following mishnah.]

רַבִּי אֱלִיעֶזֶר בַּר צָדוֹק אוֹמֵר: שְׁנָתוֹת הָיוּ בַהִין: עַד כָּאן לַפָּר; עַד כָּאן לָאַיִל; עַד כָּאן לַכֶּבֶשׂ. — *R' Eliezer bar Tzadok says: There were notches in the hin: until here for the bull; until here for the ram; and until here for the lamb.*

He contends that a *hin* was the only liquid measure used in the Temple. This *hin,* however, had notches on it to indicate when it was one-quarter full, a third full, and half full (*Rav; Rashi*), as well as for the measurements of *log,* half-*log,* and quarter-*log* (*Rashi Peirush*).

The above commentators apparently explain that according to R' Eliezer bar Tzadok there was only one liquid measure in the Temple — the *hin* — which was marked off to measure all of the seven liquid quantities. *Tosefta* (10:1), however, states that according to R' Eliezer bar Tzadok there were four measures rather than seven — one for the *hin* and its fractions, and one each for the *log,* the half-*log,*

רַבִּי שִׁמְעוֹן אוֹמֵר: לֹא הָיָה שָׁם הִין, וְכִי מֶה הָיָה הַהִין מְשַׁמֵּשׁ? אֶלָּא מִדָּה יְתֵרָה שֶׁל לֹג וּמֶחֱצָה הָיְתָה, שֶׁבָּהּ הָיָה מוֹדֵד לְמִנְחַת כֹּהֵן גָּדוֹל, לֹג וּמֶחֱצָה בַּבֹּקֶר וְלֹג וּמֶחֱצָה בֵּין הָעַרְבָּיִם.

[ג] **רְבִיעִית** מֶה הָיְתָה מְשַׁמֶּשֶׁת? רְבִיעִית מַיִם לַמְּצֹרָע וּרְבִיעִית שֶׁמֶן לַנָּזִיר.

### ר' עובדיה מברטנורא

**וכי מה היה ההין משמש.** שלא היה במקדש דבר שיהיה צריך להין שלם, שלעולם לא נצטרכו להין אלא בשמן המשחה בימי משה ואותו שמן עדיין הוא קיים ועומד, ואם כן לא היו צריכים להין: **אלא מדה יתירה.** היתה שם להשלים השבע מדות: **למנחת כהן גדול.** היו לה שלשה לוגין שמן, לוג ומחצה שחרית ולוג ומחצה בין הערביים: (ג) **רביעית מים למצורע.** דכתיב (ויקרא יד, ה) ושחט את הצפור האחת אל כלי חרש על מים חיים, למים שדם הצפור נראה בהם, ושיערו חכמים רביעית הלוג: **רביעית שמן לנזיר.** ללחם נזירות, ורביעית לא קדיש להיות כלי שרת משום רביעית מים של מצורע, דהא חוץ הוא, ולא משום לחם של נזיר, דאין לחם של נזיר קדוש אלא בשחיטת הזבח, אלא מפני שבה היה מודד לחביתי כהן גדול רביעית שמן לכל חלה וחלה, שהן שתים עשרה חלות ונסכיהן שלשה לוגין שמן:

### יד אברהם

and the quarter-*log* (*Tos.* 88a, s.v. שבע).

רַבִּי שִׁמְעוֹן אוֹמֵר: לֹא הָיָה שָׁם הִין, וְכִי מֶה הָיָה הַהִין מְשַׁמֵּשׁ? — *R' Shimon says: There was no hin there, for what function did the hin serve?*

The anointing oil measured by Moses remained intact throughout the times of the Temple, and thus, there was no further need for a vessel measuring a *hin* (*Rav;* see *Tos. Yom Tov*).

The Rabbis, however, maintain that once it was used it remained part of the Temple utensils, even though it was no longer needed (*Gem.* 88a).

אֶלָּא מִדָּה יְתֵרָה שֶׁל לֹג וּמֶחֱצָה הָיְתָה, — *Rather, there was a larger measure of a log and a half,*

As opposed to R' Eliezer bar Tzadok, R' Shimon shared a tradition with the first *Tanna* that there were a total of seven measures in the Temple. Since he dismisses the need for a measure of a *hin,* he is compelled to present an alternative for the seventh measure, that of a *log* and a half (*Gem.*).

שֶׁבָּהּ הָיָה מוֹדֵד לְמִנְחַת כֹּהֵן גָּדוֹל, לֹג וּמֶחֱצָה בַּבֹּקֶר וְלֹג וּמֶחֱצָה בֵּין הָעַרְבָּיִם. — *with which one would measure the minchah-offering of the Kohen Gadol, a log and a half in the morning and a log and a half in the afternoon.*

The *minchah* of the *Kohen Gadol* (*chavitin*) contained a total of three *log* of oil, one and a half for the morning offering and the same for that of the afternoon (*Rav*).

The Sages, however, contend that since this was needed only for this one offering, it could be measured with the half-*log* measure, and no separate utensil was necessary (*Gem.*; *Tos.*).

The halachah follows the view of the first *Tanna* (*Rambam, Hil. Klei HaMikdash* 1:17).

R′ Shimon says: There was no *hin* there, for what function did the *hin* serve? Rather, there was a larger measure of a *log* and a half, with which one would measure the *minchah*-offering of the *Kohen Gadol*, a *log* and a half in the morning and a *log* and a half in the afternoon.

3. What was the function of the quarter [-*log*]? A quarter [-*log*] of water for the *metzora* and a quarter [-*log*] of oil for the *nazir*.

YAD AVRAHAM

3.

The *Tanna* now goes on to enumerate and explain the use of all of the different measures listed in the previous mishnah, beginning with the smallest (*Tif. Yis.*).

רְבִיעִית מֶה הָיְתָה מְשַׁמֶּשֶׁת? — *What was the function of the quarter [-log]?*

The well-known term *reviis* — literally, a fourth — refers to a fourth of a *log*. It is used here in reference to the measuring vessel of that capacity (*Tif. Yis.*).

רְבִיעִית מַיִם לַמְּצֹרָע — *A quarter [-log] of water for the metzora*

The *taharah* (ritual purification) process for a *metzora* includes a ritual of taking two birds, one of which is to be slaughtered and the other to be set free. Concerning the slaughtered bird the Torah (*Lev.* 14:5) states: וְשָׁחַט אֶת הַצִּפּוֹר הָאֶחָת אֶל כְּלִי חֶרֶשׂ עַל מַיִם חַיִּים, — *and he shall slaughter the one bird into an earthen vessel upon spring water*, i.e., the blood of the slaughtered bird should fall into an earthenware vessel containing spring water. The Torah, however, does not specify how much water is to be in this vessel. The *Gemara* derives from the verse that the blood of the bird must be distinguishable in the water, i.e., that the water must be of a small enough volume that the blood does not become so diluted as to be indiscernible. The Rabbis estimated that the largest amount of water which still allows for the small amount of blood of a bird to be distinguishable is a *reviis* [quarter-*log*]. Hence, a *reviis* of water is required for the *taharah* process of the *metzora* (*Sotah* 16b, cited in brief by *Rav*; cf. *Rambam Comm.* and *Sfas Emes*).

וּרְבִיעִית שֶׁמֶן לַנָּזִיר. — *and a quarter [-log] of oil for the nazir.*

The amount of oil needed for the loaves of the *nazir* is a *reviis* (*Rav;* see 7:2). This amount was determined by an Oral Tradition given to Moses at Sinai (*Gem.* 89a).

The *Gemara* (88a,b) relates that R′ Yehudah HaNasi (Rabbi) was at a loss as to how to explain our mishnah. For although the uses described by the mishnah account for the function of these utensils in the Temple, they do not explain the need for their being consecrated vessels. Neither of these functions would require a *kli shareis* (consecrated vessel), since the water of the *metzora* was not brought into the Temple and the loaves of the *nazir* were consecrated

חֲצִי לֹג מֶה הָיָה מְשַׁמֵּשׁ? חֲצִי לֹג מַיִם לְסוֹטָה וַחֲצִי לֹג שֶׁמֶן לְתוֹדָה. וּבַלֹּג הָיָה מוֹדֵד לְכָל הַמְּנָחוֹת. אֲפִילוּ מִנְחָה שֶׁל שִׁשִּׁים עִשָּׂרוֹן, נוֹתֵן לָהּ שִׁשִּׁים לֹג. רַבִּי אֱלִיעֶזֶר בֶּן יַעֲקֹב אוֹמֵר: אֲפִילוּ מִנְחָה שֶׁל שִׁשִּׁים עִשָּׂרוֹן, אֵין לָהּ אֶלָּא לֻגָּהּ; שֶׁנֶּאֱמַר: „לְמִנְחָה וְלֹג שָׁמֶן.״ שִׁשָּׁה לַפָּר, אַרְבָּעָה לָאַיִל, שְׁלֹשָׁה לַכֶּבֶשׂ,

## ר׳ עובדיה מברטנורא

**חצי לוג מים לסוטה.** דכתיב (במדבר ה, יז) ולקח הכהן מים קדושים בכלי חרש, חצי לוג מים היה ממלא מן הכיור: **חצי לוג שמן לתודה.** הלכה למשה מסיני. וכן רביעית של נזיר. וחצי לוג נמי לאו משום חצי לוג מים של סוטה וחצי לוג שמן של תודה הוא דקדוש להיות כלי שרת, אלא מפני שבו מחלק חצי לוג שמן לכל נר ונר של מנורה: **אין לה אלא לוגה.** לוג אחד לכל ששים עשרון. ואין הלכה כרבי אליעזר בן יעקב: **ששה לוגים לפר.** דהיינו חצי ההין, כדכתיב (במדבר טו, ט) בלול בשמן חצי ההין. וארבעה לאיל, דהיינו שלישית ההין. ושלשה לכבש, דהיינו רביעית ההין, שההין שנים עשר לוגין:

## יד אברהם

only after his sacrifice had been slaughtered. Subsequently R' Yehudah HaNasi accepted R' Chiya's explanation that since this measure was also used to measure the oil for the *minchas chavitin* of the *Kohen Gadol*, a *reviis* for each loaf, it was required that it be sanctified (see *Sfas Emes*).

חֲצִי לֹג מֶה הָיָה מְשַׁמֵּשׁ? חֲצִי לֹג מַיִם לְסוֹטָה — *What was the function of the half-log? A half-log of water for a sotah*

A *sotah* is a suspected adulteress. [The exact procedure for establishing grounds for suspicion is outlined in *Sotah* Ch. 1, based on verses in the section in the Torah concerning *sotah* (*Numbers* Ch. 5).] As dictated by the Torah (ibid.), the *sotah* process (to determine her guilt or innocence) calls for giving the woman to drink a solution prepared by dissolving a specially written parchment (with the words from the Torah's section regarding the *sotah*) into water taken from the tank in the Temple (כִּיּוֹר) (*Numbers* 15:17). The mishnah (*Sotah* 2:2) states that the amount of water required to prepare this drink was half a *log* (*Rav*).

וַחֲצִי לֹג שֶׁמֶן לְתוֹדָה. — *and a half-log of oil for the todah-offering.*

[The oil used in the *minchah* of a *todah* also amounted to half a *log*.] Both these requirements are based on an Oral Tradition handed down to Moses at Sinai (*Rav* from *Gem.* 89a).

Here, too, neither of the functions cited by the mishnah account for the necessity to use sanctified measures. The water of the *sotah* is drawn from the special tank in the Temple known as the כִּיּוֹר, *kiyor*, and is thus already sanctified. Similarly, the *todah's* loaves are sanctified with the slaughter of the *todah* and thus need no prior sanctification. However, since the half-*log* measure is also used to fill the lamps of the *menorah*, which required half a *log* for each lamp — as stated below — it was

9 What was the function of the half-*log?* A half-*log* of
3 water for a *sotah* and a half-*log* of oil for the *todah*-offering. They measured all *minchah*-offerings with the *log*. Even for a *minchah*-offering of sixty *issaron*, one supplies for them sixty *log*. R' Eliezer ben Yaakov says: Even a *minchah*-offering of sixty *issaron* contains only its one *log*; as it is stated (*Lev.* 14:21): *for a minchah-offering, and a log of oil.* Six for the bull, four for the ram, three for the lamb,

**YAD AVRAHAM**

required to be a consecrated vessel[1] (*Rav* from *Gem.* 88b; cf. *Tos. Yom Tov*).

וּבַלֹּג הָיָה מוֹדֵד לְכָל הַמְּנָחוֹת. — *They measured all minchah-offerings with the log.*

[As derived by the *Gemara* (89a), the standard requirement of oil for a *minchah* is one *log.*]

אֲפִילוּ מִנְחָה שֶׁל שִׁשִּׁים עִשָּׂרוֹן, נוֹתֵן לָהּ שִׁשִּׁים לֹג. — *Even for a minchah-offering of sixty issaron, one supplies for them sixty log.*

The *Gemara* (89a) derives exegetically that any voluntary *minchah,* no matter what its volume of flour, was made with one *log* of oil for every *issaron* of flour. [Each *log* was measured separately in the measure of that size.]

The mishnah uses sixty *issaron* as an example because that is the largest quantity which can be mixed in one vessel (*Tif. Yis.;* see 12:4).

רַבִּי אֱלִיעֶזֶר בֶּן יַעֲקֹב אוֹמֵר: אֲפִילוּ מִנְחָה שֶׁל שִׁשִּׁים עִשָּׂרוֹן, אֵין לָהּ אֶלָּא לֻגָּהּ; שֶׁנֶּאֱמַר: „לְמִנְחָה וְלֹג שָׁמֶן.״ — *R' Eliezer ben Yaakov says: Even a minchah-offering of sixty issaron contains only its one log; as it is stated (Lev. 14:21): "for a minchah-offering, and a log of oil."*

He contends that the entire *minchah* requires only one *log* of oil, no matter what the quantity of flour, up to the maximum per vessel of sixty *issaron* (*Rav*). [This he deduces from the verse cited here, in which the Torah specifies a *log* of oil for a *minchah*, with no stipulation as to the quantity of flour involved.]

The halachah does not follow this view (*Rav; Rambam, Hil. Maaseh HaKorbanos* 2:8; cf. *Zevach Todah*).

שִׁשָּׁה לַפָּר, אַרְבָּעָה לָאַיִל, שְׁלֹשָׁה לַכֶּבֶשׂ, — *Six for the bull, four for the ram, three for the lamb,*

The half-*hin* measure cited in the previous mishnah was used for the *minchah* which accompanied the sacrifice of a bull (*minchas nesachim*), for which the Torah requires a half-*hin* — or six *log* — of oil to be added to its three *essronim* of flour (*Rav*). [Similarly, a *minchah* for the sacrifice of a ram requires a third of a *hin,* equaling four *log* for its two *essronim* of flour, and that of a lamb takes a fourth of a *hin,* three *log* for its *issaron*.]

1. It is not clear, though, why the oil for the *menorah* had to be sanctified [prior to placing it into the *menorah*] (*Tos.* 89a, s.v. חצי).

שְׁלֹשָׁה וּמֶחֱצָה לַמְּנוֹרָה; מֵחֲצִי לֹג לְכָל נֵר.

[ד] **מְעָרְבִין** נִסְכֵּי אֵילִים בְּנִסְכֵּי פָרִים, נִסְכֵּי כְבָשִׂים בְּנִסְכֵּי כְבָשִׂים, שֶׁל יָחִיד בְּשֶׁל צִבּוּר, שֶׁל יוֹם בְּשֶׁל אֶמֶשׁ.

### ר׳ עובדיה מברטנורא

**מחצי לוג לכל נר.** שצריך שיתן בה מדה שתהא דולקת והולכת מערב עד בקר, ושיערו חכמים חצי לוג שמן ללילי תקופת טבת הארוכים, וכן היה נותן בכל נר בכל לילה, ואם כבתה נפסלה אותה פתילה והשמן מלהדליק בהן עוד, אלא מסירן ונותן חצי לוג שמן אחר ופתילה חדשה ומדליק: (ד) **מערבין נסכי פרים.** מנחת נסכי פר במנחת נסכי איל, לפי שבלילת שתיהן שוה, שני לוגים לעשרון, דהא תנן לעיל (משנה ג) ששה לוגים לפר, וסלת הוי להו שלשה עשרונים כדכתיב (במדבר טו׳ ט) והקריב על בן הבקר מנחה סלת שלשה עשרונים בלול בשמן חצי ההין, דהיינו ששה לוגין, ולאיל ארבע לוגין, וסלת שני עשרונים לאיל: **נסכי כבשים.** שלשה לוגין לעשרון, דכתיב (שם ט, ד) עשרון אחד לכבש האחד וכתיב בלול בשמן כתית רביעית ההין, דהיינו שלשה לוגין: **ושל היום בשל אמש.** אם הביא אמש זבחו בלא נסכים, דקיימא לן אדם מביא זבחו היום ונסכיו מכאן ועד עשרה ימים. ואם היום הביא קרבן אחד ושני נסכים עמו אחד בשבילו ואחד בשביל של אמש, מערבין יחד אם הקרבנות שוין, שיהו שניהם כבשים או אילים [או פרים] או פר ואיל:

### יד אברהם

שְׁלֹשָׁה וּמֶחֱצָה לַמְּנוֹרָה; — *and three and a half for the menorah;*

[Each of the seven lamps of the *menorah* required half a *log* of oil every night for a total of three and a half-*logs*.] Although there was no measure this size in the Temple, the *Tanna* mentions it in connection with the required amounts of oil for the various offerings (*Shitah Mekubetzes*).

מֵחֲצִי לֹג לְכָל נֵר. — *[on the basis of] half a log for each lamp.*

[The total of three and a half *logs* for the *menorah* is due to that which each lamp requires half a *log* — and not due to some requirement involving the *menorah* as a whole.]

The Torah (*Ex.* 27:21) requires that the *menorah* burn the entire night, i.e., enough oil should be used to last from evening until morning. The Sages calculated that to maintain the flame through the long winter nights the amount of oil necessary is half a *log* [and thus this is the standard amount used every night] (*Rav* from *Gem.* 89a).

During the shorter nights of the year, they would use a thicker wick in order to use up the same amount of oil in less time (*Yerushalmi*, cited by *Tos.*; cf. *Rashi Peirush*).

## 4.

The following three mishnayos discuss the laws of the נְסָכִים, *libation offerings*, which accompany most animal sacrifices. The *nesachim* consist of two parts: a quantity of wine for libations, and a *minchah*-offering

9 and three and a half for the *menorah*; [on the
4 basis of] half a *log* for each lamp.

4. One may mix together the libation offerings of rams with those of bulls, the libation offerings of lambs with those of lambs, those of an individual with those of the community, [and] those of today with those of yesterday.

YAD AVRAHAM

(known as the *minchas nesachim*) which consisted of fine flour and oil (*Rambam, Maaseh HaKorbanos* 2:1).

As described in the Torah's section dealing with *nesachim* (*Numbers* 15:1ff), the amounts required for *nesachim* vary for each of the three types of animals that are brought as offerings — bulls, rams, and lambs. [Goats are included in the last category as well.] The following table gives the prescribed quantities of *nesachim* for each of these animals.

| | wine — יַיִן | oil — שֶׁמֶן | flour — סֹלֶת |
|---|---|---|---|
| **Bull — פָּר** | 6 *log* (1/2 *hin*) | 6 *log* (1/2 *hin*) | 3 *issaron* |
| **Ram — אַיִל** | 4 *log* (1/3 *hin*) | 4 *log* (1/3 *hin*) | 2 *issaron* |
| **Lamb — כֶּבֶשׂ** | 3 *log* (1/4 *hin*) | 3 *log* (1/4 *hin*) | 1 *issaron* |

מְעָרְבִין נִסְכֵּי אֵלִים בְּנִסְכֵּי פָרִים, — *One may mix together the libation offerings of rams with those of bulls,*

The *minchas nesachim* [which is also called simply *nesachim* (*Rambam Comm.*; see above, comm. to mishnah 2:4, s.v. הזבח)] of a bull may be mixed with those of the ram because their ratio of oil to flour is the same. Both call for two *logs* of oil for every *issaron* of flour. The *nesachim* for a bull consist of three *essronim* of flour and six *logs* of oil, while those for a ram are two *essronim* of flour and four *logs* of oil (*Rav*; see below).

נִסְכֵּי כְבָשִׂים בְּנִסְכֵּי כְבָשִׂים, — *the libation offerings of lambs with those of lambs,*

[Obviously, these contain the same ratio of flour to oil, as well as the same volume of wine.]

שֶׁל יָחִיד בְּשֶׁל צִבּוּר, — *those of an individual with those of the community,*

[Neither the ratio of oil to flour in a *minchah* nor the volume of wine required for the libation is affected by its owner status. It is the same whether it is an individual or communal offering.]

שֶׁל יוֹם בְּשֶׁל אֶמֶשׁ. — *[and] those of today with those of yesterday.*

As stated previously (see comm. to 2:4), one may bring a sacrifice on one day and its *nesachim* on a subsequent day. Accordingly, the *nesachim* of one day's sacrifices and that of another day's can both be valid on the same day and thus be mixed together (see *Rav*).

# אֲבָל אֵין מְעָרְבִין נִסְכֵּי כְבָשִׂים בְּנִסְכֵּי פָרִים וְאֵילִים.

ר' עובדיה מברטנורא

**אבל אין מערבים נסכי כבשים בנסכי פרים ואילים.** לפי שמנחת פר ואיל חריבה היא לגבי כבשים, ובולעת הימנה, ונמצאת של כבש חסרה וזו יתירה:

יד אברהם

אֲבָל אֵין מְעָרְבִין נִסְכֵּי כְבָשִׂים בְּנִסְכֵּי פָרִים וְאֵילִים. — *But one may not mix together the libation offerings of lambs with those of bulls and rams.*

As explained before, the *minchah* of *nesachim* for a bull and for a ram both consist of two *logs* of oil per *issaron* of flour. The *minchas nesachim* for a lamb, by contrast, calls for three *logs* of oil for one *issaron* of flour. Thus, the *minchah* for a bull and ram is less saturated with oil than that of a lamb. If the ingredients of the two *menachos* were to mix, the one which should have a smaller proportion of oil would absorb some of the other one's oil, thereby altering the prescribed ratio of each and invalidating them both (mishnah 1:3). Therefore, it is forbidden to mix them (*Rav*). [As the mishnah will explain below, the reference here is to a mixture of the ingredients of the two *menachos*, i.e., their oil and their flour. Once these have become mixed, the only way to prepare the two *menachos* would be to add all the flour and all the oil to one vessel and perform their required mixing [בְּלִילָה] as one. This would result in a dough made up of two and a half *logs* of oil per *issaron* — a blend insufficient for the lambs and too saturated for the bulls or rams. However, once the flour of each *minchah* has been properly mixed with its own oil, a mixture of the two doughs no longer invalidates, as stated in mishnah 3:2. This will be explained further below.]

We have explained the mishnah to this point in line with *Rav's* commentary. According to his interpretation, it is permitted to mix the ingredients of the *minchas nesachim* of a bull and a ram, since they are both subject to the same ratio of oil to flour. It is only forbidden in the case of the bull and lamb because they have different oil-to-flour ratios. However, as *Tos. Yom Tov* points out, this interpretation is consistent only with the initial position of the *Gemara* (89b). The *Gemara's* conclusion is that it is *not* permitted to mix the *minchas nesachim* of one offering with that of another even if they are both subject to the same ratio of oil to flour. This is derived from the verse: וְהִקְטִירוֹ, *and he shall burn it* [on the Altar] (*Lev.* 3:11), which indicates that things burnt on the Altar must each be offered separately, not mixed together with other sacrificial items. Accordingly, our mishnah which states that the *nesachim* may be mixed does not refer to the *minchah's* ingredients but to the wine of the libations. Technically, even the wine of libation (which is not burnt on the Altar[1] and is therefore not subject to the Biblical ban on mixing Altar items) is also Rabbinically prohibited from being mixed with wine from the *nesech* of

1. As noted several times previously, the wine is poured into a specially prepared bowl connected to the top of the Altar from which it runs down into a cavity beneath the Altar.

9 But one may not mix together the libation of-
4 ferings of lambs with those of bulls and rams.



another offering. This was enacted as a safeguard against confusing the wine of the *nesachim* with the *minchah* elements of the *nesachim*. This ban, however, applies only as long as the *menachos* themselves have not yet been offered on the Altar. Once they have, there is no longer a need to safeguard against their mixing with elements of another *minchah*, and it is therefore permitted to mix the wines of the respective libations. Thus, our mishnah, which permits the mixing of libations, is referring to the wine after the *menachos* have already been offered (*Tos. Yom Tov* and *Likkutei Halachos* from *Rashi* ad loc. and *Rambam, Temidin U'Mussafin* 10:17-20).

This is true for the wine of all *nesachim*, even those of lambs and bulls. Once their respective *menachos* have been offered on the Altar, the wines may be mixed before being poured on the Altar (ibid.). According to this interpretation, the mishnah's distinction between mixtures of bull and ram *nesachim* and those of bulls and lambs is in regard to the following: By the logic just given, it should follow that even if the *menachos* had not yet been offered, but had somehow become mixed together, it should now be permissible to deliberately mix the wine of their *nesachim* together as well. Since the *menachos* have in any case become mixed, there is no longer anything against which to safeguard!

This is in fact true in the case of the *nesachim* of the bulls and the rams. Although the Torah prohibits mixing two *menachos* so that each may be offered separately, should they become mixed they retain their sacrificial validity and are offered together (*Likkutei Halachos, Zevach Todah*). However, in the case of a mixture between the *menachos* of bulls (or rams) and those of lambs, the *menachos* are invalidated because of the shift of oil from the more oil-laden *minchah* to the less oil-laden one, as explained above. Consequently, new *menachos* will have to be brought for each and their wine components can therefore not be mixed unless these new *menachos* have been offered on the Altar (*Rashi ms* 89b, s.v. אמר אביי).

This is the distinction being made by our mishnah between mixtures of *nesachim* of the same proportions, such as those of bulls and rams, and mixtures between the *nesachim* of bulls and lambs, which are of different proportions. In the latter case, if their *minchah* ingredients became mixed, it is still (Rabbinically) forbidden to mix their wine components.

However, even with bulls and lambs, if the *menachos* had already been offered on the Altar [under valid conditions; see below], the wine for their libations could then be mixed, as explained above (*Zevach Todah* from *Tosefta* 10:1).

*Rambam* (*Temidin U'Mussafin* 10:18,19) contends that the mixing of the wine libations of lambs with those of rams or bulls is never permitted, even after the *menachos* have been offered. It is unclear how he resolves the statement of *Tosefta* cited above, which permits mixing the wine of lambs with that of rams and bulls, since he recognizes no instance in which this is acceptable (*Zevach Todah*).

מנחות
ט/ה

וְאִם בְּלָלָן אֵלּוּ בִּפְנֵי עַצְמָן וְאֵלּוּ בִּפְנֵי עַצְמָן וְנִתְעָרְבוּ, כְּשֵׁרִין; אִם עַד שֶׁלֹּא בָלַל, פָּסוּל. הַכֶּבֶשׂ הַבָּא עִם הָעֹמֶר, אַף עַל פִּי שֶׁמִּנְחָתוֹ כְּפוּלָה, לֹא הָיוּ נְסָכָיו כְּפוּלִין.

[ה] **כָּל** הַמִּדּוֹת שֶׁהָיוּ בַמִּקְדָּשׁ הָיוּ נִגְדָּשׁוֹת, חוּץ מִשֶּׁל כֹּהֵן גָּדוֹל, שֶׁהָיָה גוֹדְשָׁהּ לְתוֹכָהּ.

## ר׳ עובדיה מברטנורא

**ואם בללן.** שכבר הלכה מלות שמנן, כשרות, כרבנן דפליגי עליה דרבי יהודה בהקומץ רבה (כג, א) ואמרי חרב שנתערב בבלול יקרב: **ואם עד שלא בללן.** נתערבו, פסולות, דבעינן ראוי לבילה, וליכא, דחסרא לה של כבש ושל איל יתירה: **אף על פי שמנחתו כפולה.** כדכתיב באמור אל הכהנים (ויקרא כג, יג) ומנחתו שני עשרונים: (ה) **שהיה גודשה בתוכה.** כשהיה מחוק היה מחזיק כשאר עשרון גדוש. ומתניתין רבי מאיר היא דאמר בריש פרקין (משנה א) עשרון ועשרון היה במקדש אחד מחוק ואחד גדוש. ולית הלכתא כותיה:

## יד אברהם

וְאִם בְּלָלָן אֵלּוּ בִּפְנֵי עַצְמָן וְאֵלּוּ בִּפְנֵי עַצְמָן וְנִתְעָרְבוּ, כְּשֵׁרִין; — *If he combined [the ingredients of] each of them separately and they [then] mixed together, they are valid;*

[The mishnah now discusses the mixing of the *menachos* rather than the wine.][1] If the flour and oil of each *minchah* were first mixed together as they should be, and then the two *menachos* were placed together in the same vessel, they are valid. This is true even if one *minchah* is that of a lamb and the other that of a ram or bull (*Likkutei Halachos*). Once each *minchah* has been combined with its proper amount of oil, even if some of it should seep from one to the other, the *menachos* would no longer be invalidated.

Although this is actually the subject of a dispute between R' Yehudah and the Rabbis in mishnah 3:2 above, the mishnah here follows the view of the Rabbis there that such seepage does not invalidate (*Tos.* 89b, s.v. בללן; see comm. to mishnah 3:2, and *Chazon Ish* 29:3,15).

אִם עַד שֶׁלֹּא בָלַל, פָּסוּל. — *if before they were combined, they are invalid.*

If the oil of the two *menachos* become mixed, or their flour, before the flour and oil of each individual *minchah* are combined, both *menachos* are invalidated. This is because neither *minchah* is now capable of having its ingredients mixed in a proper manner, since the flour for the ram or bull will absorb some of the extra oil from the lamb and the ratios of both will thus be improperly altered (*Rav* from *Tos.* 89b, s.v. ואם).

It is clear from this that the mishnah invalidates only *menachos* of unequal ratios whose ingredients were mixed before each

1. *Rav* explained even the previous case to refer to a mixing of the *menachos*. According to his explanation the mishnah is now qualifying its previous ruling, making it clear that the above referred only to a mixing between the oil or flour of the two *menachos*, but not to the mixing of two properly blended *menachos*.

If he combined [the ingredients of] each of them separately and they [then] mixed together, they are valid; if before they were combined, they are invalid.

The lamb which comes with the *omer*-offering, although [the size of] its *minchah*-offering is doubled, its libations are not doubled.

**5.** All the measures which were in the Temple were heaped, except for that of the *Kohen Gadol*, which was heaped within.

YAD AVRAHAM

could be properly mixed with its own measure of oil. *Menachos* whose oil and flour are of equal proportions (such as those of rams and bulls) do not become invalidated even if their oil or flour become mixed before they are combined into proper *menachos*. In such a case it would be permissible to place all the oil and all the flour in one *kli shareis* and offer the entire mixture together (*Likkutei Halachos*), since their consistency is in any case destined to be the same (see *Chazon Ish* 29:3, 15, for an explanation of this). As noted above, the verse from which the *Gemara* derives that sacrifices should be offered separately means only to prohibit one from mixing them in the first place. Once they have become mixed, however, they may be offered even in their mixed state (*Tos. Yom Tov; Likkutei Halachos*). [This, however, is disputed by *Kesef Mishneh* to *Hil. Temidin U'Mussafin* 10:15; see *Likkutei Halachos*.]

הַכֶּבֶשׂ הַבָּא עִם הָעֹמֶר, — *The lamb which comes with the omer-offering,*

[The *minchah* of the *omer*, which is brought on the second day of Pesach, is accompanied by a lamb brought as an *olah-offering* (*Lev.* 23:12). The *nesachim* for this lamb are an exception to the general rule of *nesachim*: Instead of one *issaron* of flour, the Torah (ibid. v. 13) prescribes two.]

אַף עַל פִּי שֶׁמִּנְחָתוֹ כְּפוּלָה, לֹא הָיוּ נְסָכָיו כְּפוּלִין. — *although [the size of] its minchah-offering is doubled, its libations are not doubled.*

Although the amount of flour for this *minchas nesachim* is doubled, the oil and wine are not. Thus the amount of oil and wine used is the same as usual, three *logs* (*Tif. Yis.*), as derived exegetically (*Gem.* 89b).

5.

כָּל הַמִּדּוֹת שֶׁהָיוּ בַמִּקְדָּשׁ הָיוּ נִגְדָּשׁוֹת, — *All the measures which were in the Temple were heaped,*

As explained by the *Gemara* (90a), what our mishnah means is that all measurings in the Temple were performed in a heaped fashion — i.e., the utensil for measuring the *issaron* of flour for *menachos* was filled to the top and heaped above it (*Rashi ms*; see below). [The heap completed the *issaron*.]

חוּץ מִשֶּׁל כֹּהֵן גָּדוֹל, שֶׁהָיָה גוֹדְשָׁהּ לְתוֹכָהּ. — *except for that of the Kohen Gadol, which was heaped within.*

[The *minchas chavitin* of the *Kohen*

מִדּוֹת הַלַּח בֵּרוּצֵיהֶן קֹדֶשׁ, וּמִדּוֹת הַיָּבֵשׁ בֵּרוּצֵיהֶן חֹל. רַבִּי עֲקִיבָא אוֹמֵר: מִדּוֹת הַלַּח קֹדֶשׁ; לְפִיכָךְ בֵּרוּצֵיהֶן קֹדֶשׁ. וּמִדּוֹת הַיָּבֵשׁ חֹל; לְפִיכָךְ בֵּרוּצֵיהֶן חֹל. רַבִּי יוֹסֵי אוֹמֵר: לֹא מִשּׁוּם זֶה.

**ר׳ עובדיה מברטנורא**

**בירוציהן.** גודשן, דלא נמי איכא גודש פורתא: **מדות הלח בירוציהן קדש ומדות היבש בירוציהן חול.** בגמרא (צ, א) מפרש דהאי תנא סבר מדות הלח נמשחו בין מבפנים בין מבחוץ, הלכך שפת הכלי מקדשן לבירוצין, מדת היבש נמשחו מבפנים ולא נמשחו מבחוץ, הלכך בירוצין שאינן נוגעים מבפנים במקום משיחתן לא קדשי: **רבי עקיבא אומר מדת הלח קודש.** סבר מדות הלח נמשחו בין מבפנים בין מבחוץ: **מדות היבש חול.** דלא נמשחו כל עיקר. ומיהו מה שמודדים בהן קדוש קדושת הפה, וגברא למאי דצריך מקדש בפה, בירוצין לא מקדש להו דלא צריכי ליה: **רבי יוסי אומר לא משום זה.** רבי יוסי סבר אידי ואידי נמשחו מבפנים ולא נמשחו מבחוץ, והכא היינו טעמא, משום דלח נעכר, מה שבשולי הכלי כשמוסיפין עליו נעכר ומתערב ונבלל ועולה מלמעלה, ונמצא שכבר קדשו הבירוצין בתוך הכלי:

**יד אברהם**

*Gadol* was measured in a larger utensil, which measured a full *issaron* within it. Thus, its "heap," which in an ordinary measure would complete the *issaron*, was *heaped within.*] This follows the view of R' Meir (mishnah 1), who maintains that there were two *issaron* measures: one for all other measurings, which contained an *issaron* only when heaped, and one for the *chavitin*, which held the entire *issaron* within its walls (*Rav*).

The halachah does not follow R' Meir (*Rav; Rambam Comm.;* cf. *Tos. R' Akiva Eiger*).

מִדּוֹת הַלַּח בֵּרוּצֵיהֶן קֹדֶשׁ, — *The overflow of the liquid measures is sanctified,*

According to some commentators, the reference is to the liquids which overflow the tops of the measuring vessels. This spill is also sanctified although it does not remain within the consecrated vessel (*Rashi Peirush*). According to others, the mishnah refers to the crest of the full liquid-measuring vessel, which is the slight rise of the liquid contents over the rim of the vessel [created by surface tension]. Although, strictly speaking, this crest is beyond the confines of the vessel, the mishnah teaches that it is sanctified (*Rav; Rashi ms*).

According to the latter explanation, the mishnah's contrast of liquid measures to the dry measure means that the heaping of the dry measure, unlike the crest of the liquid measures, is not sanctified. This conclusion is apparently at variance with the statement made just previously that all dry measures were heaped, implying that the heaping *was* consecrated. Furthermore, the reasonings advanced by the *Gemara* for the difference between the dry and liquid measures (see below) do not apply if the subject of the discussion is the crest or the heaping (*Rashash*). For these reasons, the commentary will follow primarily the interpretation that the reference of the mishnah is to the overflow.

This *Tanna* contends that the liquid measures were consecrated with anointing oil from within and from

9 The overflow of the liquid measures is sanctified, but
5 the overflow of the dry measures is not sanctified. R' Akiva says: The liquid measures are consecrated; therefore their overflow is sanctified. The dry measures are not consecrated; therefore their overflow is not sanctified. R' Yose says: [It is] not for this reason.



without;[1] therefore, the outer surface of the vessel sanctifies the liquid which overflows (*Gem.* 90a).[2]

Actually, by Biblical law, a *kli shareis* does not sanctify the content without the intent of the owner to that effect. Accordingly, the overflow of the vessel should not be sanctified, as the owner had no intention to do so. Nevertheless, the Rabbis decreed that the overflow should be considered sanctified. This was due to their concern that people, who see it dealt with, otherwise might not realize that the overflow is not sanctified (because of lack of intent) and would thereby conclude that even things sanctified in a *kli shareis* may revert to *chullin* [unsanctified state] (*Gem.* ibid.).

וּמִדּוֹת הַיָּבֵשׁ בֵּרוּצֵיהֶן חֹל. — *but the overflow of the dry measures is not sanctified.*

The dry measures were sanctified only from within; therefore, their overflow does not become consecrated (*Rav* from *Gem.* ibid.).

רַבִּי עֲקִיבָא אוֹמֵר: מִדּוֹת הַלַּח קֹדֶשׁ; לְפִיכָךְ בֵּרוּצֵיהֶן קֹדֶשׁ. וּמִדּוֹת הַיָּבֵשׁ חֹל; לְפִיכָךְ בֵּרוּצֵיהֶן חֹל. — *R' Akiva says: The liquid measures are consecrated; therefore their overflow is sanctified. The dry measures are not consecrated; therefore their overflow is not sanctified.*

R' Akiva agrees with the first *Tanna* that the liquid measures were consecrated both from within and without, but contends that the dry measures were not consecrated at all. That which is placed within the measuring vessels is sanctified only by virtue of the owner's statement of consecration (קְדוּשַּׁת פֶּה, *oral sanctity*) [and only to the extent that such consecration is effective (see below, comm. to mishnah 12:1, and General Introduction to *Zevachim*)]. The intent of the owner, however, is to consecrate only as much of the flour as he needs for his *minchah*. Thus, the overflow, for which the owner has no sacrificial use, is not included in the consecration (*Rav* from *Gem.* ibid.).

רַבִּי יוֹסֵי אוֹמֵר: לֹא מִשּׁוּם זֶה. — *R' Yose says: [It is] not for this reason.*

It is not for this reason that there is a distinction between the liquid

1. Anointing oil was used to consecrate the vessels only in the days of Moses, when the *Mishkan* was first erected, while in subsequent generations new vessels are inaugurated into the Temple service through their first use [עֲבוֹדָתָן מְחַנְּכָתָן]. Nevertheless, the same rule applies even to the vessels of later generations. It stands to reason that the later consecration through use is effective only to the extent of the original consecration through anointing (*Zevach Todah*).

2. This seems to be the simple understanding of the *Gemara* (see *Rashi Peirush*). However, *Rav* (following *Rashi ms*) explains the word *outside* to refer to the upper surface of the vessel's rim.

אֶלָּא שֶׁהַלַּח נֶעְכָּר וְהַיָּבֵשׁ אֵינוֹ נֶעְכָּר.

[ו] **כָּל** קָרְבְּנוֹת הַצִּבּוּר וְהַיָּחִיד טְעוּנִין נְסָכִים, חוּץ מִן הַבְּכוֹר, וְהַמַּעֲשֵׂר, וְהַפֶּסַח, וְהַחַטָּאת, וְהָאָשָׁם. אֶלָּא שֶׁחַטָּאתוֹ שֶׁל מְצֹרָע וַאֲשָׁמוֹ טְעוּנִים נְסָכִים.

ר׳ עובדיה מברטנורא

**והיבש אינו נעבר.** אלא במקומו עומד, הלכך מה שבפנים קדוש ומה שבחוץ אינו קדוש: (ו) **חוץ מן הבכור והמעשר והפסח והחטאת והאשם.** משום דכתיב בפרשת נסכים (במדבר טו, ג) לפלא נדר או בנדבה, בא בנדר ובנדבה טעון נסכים, יצאו בכור ומעשר ופסח וחטאת ואשם שהן באים חובה לא לנדבה שאין טעונים נסכים. יכול אף חובות הבאות מחמת הרגל ברגל כגון עולות ראיה ושלמי חגיגה לא יהיו טעונות נסכים, תלמוד לומר (שם) או במועדיכם, כל הבא במועדיכם טעון נסכים. ושעירי חטאת שבאים חובה לרגל אין טעונים נסכים, דכתיב בפרשת נסכים (שם שם, ח) וכי תעשה בן בקר, בן בקר בכלל היה, בכלל ועשיתם אשה, דמשמע כל אשה טעון נסכים חוץ [מאשה] שמיעט, ולמה יצא, להקיש אליו, מה בן בקר מיוחד שבא בנדר ונדבה, אף כל בא בנדר ונדבה, יצאו שעירי הרגלים שהן באות חטאות, שאין חטאת בא בנדר ונדבה, שאין טעונות נסכים: **חטאתו ואשמו של מצורע טעונים נסכים.** לפי שאינן באים על חטא כשאר חטאות ואשמות. וחטאת נזיר אינה טעונה נסכים משום דנזיר חוטא הוא כדכתיב (במדבר ו, יא) מאשר חטא על הנפש, שציער עצמו מן היין:

יד אברהם

and dry measures in regard to the overflow. Unlike the previous two *Tannaim*, R' Yose holds that both the liquid and dry measures were consecrated only from within (*Rav*). [The difference between the dry and liquid measures must therefore be explained in a different manner, as follows.]

אֶלָּא שֶׁהַלַּח נֶעְכָּר וְהַיָּבֵשׁ אֵינוֹ נֶעְכָּר. — *Rather, [it is because] the liquid is displaced whereas the solid is not displaced.*

[R' Yose explains that the difference between liquid and dry measures is due to the respective physical properties of their contents.] When one liquid is poured into another liquid to the point of causing an overflow, the inflowing liquid enters the vessel and mixes with the liquid already in the vessel. Thus, that which overflows has already been sanctified in the vessel before leaving it. Dry contents, on the other hand, are added on top of that which is already within the vessel without mixing with it. Therefore, that which falls off the heaped top was never consecrated inside the utensil (*Tif. Yis.*).

## 6.

כָּל קָרְבְּנוֹת הַצִּבּוּר וְהַיָּחִיד טְעוּנִין נְסָכִים, — *All communal and individual sacrifices require libations offerings,*

All animal sacrifices except for those listed below must be accomplished by *nesachim* — the *minchah* and the wine libation. Bird offerings, however, are not included in the requirement of

9 Rather, [it is because] the liquid is displaced
6 whereas the solid is not displaced.

**6.** All communal and individual sacrifices require libation offerings, except for the *bechor*-offering, the *maaser*-offering, the *pesach*-offering, the *chatas-offering*, and the *asham-offering*. However, the *chatas-offering* of a *metzora* and his *asham-offering* do require libation offerings.

### YAD AVRAHAM

libations (*Tos. Yom Tov* from *Gem.* 90b).

חוּץ מִן הַבְּכוֹר, וְהַמַּעֲשֵׂר, וְהַפֶּסַח, וְהַחַטָּאת, וְהָאָשָׁם. — *except for the bechor-offering, the maaser-offering, the pesach-offering, the chatas-offering, and the asham-offering.*

The Torah's section dealing with *nesachim* uses the introductory phrase לְפַלֵּא נֶדֶר אוֹ בִנְדָבָה, *to utter a vow or a donation.* The *Gemara* (90b) derives from this that only those types of sacrifices which may be brought voluntarily [as a vow or a donation] require libations, but not those which are offered only in fulfillment of obligations. Thus, the *bechor* (male firstborn of cattle, goats, and sheep), the *maaser* (tithe of livestock), the *pesach*-offering and the *chatas* and *asham*, all of which are exclusively obligatory offerings, are excluded from the Torah's requirement for *nesachim*. The עוֹלַת רְאִיָּה (*pilgrimage olah*) and the שַׁלְמֵי חֲגִיגָה (*Festival shelamim*) brought by every individual in conjunction with the fulfillment of his Festival pilgrimage [עֲלִיָּה לָרֶגֶל] (see *Chagigah* 1:1), however, are accompanied by *nesachim*. Although these are obligatory, they require *nesachim* because they are of the *type* of offering also brought voluntarily (*Rav*). It goes without saying that the *mussaf* of Shabbos and of the Festivals, as well as the daily *tamid* — all of which are communal *olos* — are brought with *nesachim* stated explicitly in the Torah [*Numbers* ch. 28, 29) (*Rashi Peirush*).

אֶלָּא שֶׁחַטָּאתוֹ שֶׁל מְצֹרָע וַאֲשָׁמוֹ טְעוּנִים נְסָכִים. — *However, the chatas-offering of a metzora and his asham-offering do require libation offerings.*

The *taharah* (purification) process of the *metzora* included a *chatas* and an *asham* to be brought after the *tzaraas* (the skin disorder which was the physical symptom of the *tumah*) was healed (*Lev.* 15). The Torah specifies (ibid. v. 10) that these offerings be accompanied by a *minchah*, and the *Gemara* (loc. cit.) derives exegetically from another verse (*Num.* 15:5) that these *menachos* also required libations of wine.

A rationale why the Torah distinguishes between these and all other *chatas-* and *asham-offerings* is that these are occasioned by his condition and are not the atonement for a transgression [and are therefore not subject to the rules which generally govern the *chatas*] (*Rav; Rambam Comm.*).

[ז] **כָּל** קָרְבְּנוֹת הַצִּבּוּר אֵין בָּהֶם סְמִיכָה, חוּץ מִן הַפָּר הַבָּא עַל כָּל הַמִּצְוֹת וְשָׂעִיר הַמִּשְׁתַּלֵּחַ. רַבִּי שִׁמְעוֹן אוֹמֵר: אַף שְׂעִירֵי עֲבוֹדָה זָרָה.

**ר' עובדיה מברטנורא**

(ז) **פר הבא על כל המצות.** על אחת מכל המצות. כגון הורו בית דין שחלב מותר, וזהו פר העלם דבר של צבור שבמקרא, וסמיכה כתיבא ביה (ויקרא ד, טו) וסמכו זקני העדה את ידיהם על ראש הפר, ושלשה מזקני בית דין היו סומכין עליו: **ושעיר המשתלח.** לעזאזל, כתיב ביה (שם טז, כא) וסמך אהרן את שתי ידיו על ראש [השעיר החי]: **שעירי עבודה זרה.** דכתיב בפרשת שלח לך (במדבר טו, כב) וכי תשגו כו'. ואין הלכה כרבי שמעון:

**יד אברהם**

## 7.

The following mishnah deals with the law of *leaning* (*semichah*). This rite, which applies to animal offerings, calls for the owner of the sacrifice to place his hands and press his weight upon the sacrifice's head before it is slaughtered.

This rite was generally reserved for individual sacrifices, but according to an Oral Law transmitted to Moses at Sinai, there were two communal offerings that also required it. The mishnah now identifies these two offerings.

כָּל קָרְבְּנוֹת הַצִּבּוּר אֵין בָּהֶם סְמִיכָה, — *No communal offerings require leaning,*

[The Torah does not mandate *semichah* [leaning] for any communal offerings except those stated below.]

חוּץ מִן הַפָּר הַבָּא עַל כָּל הַמִּצְוֹת — *except the bull which comes for any of the commandments*

The Torah requires a special *chatas* for the inadvertent communal transgression of a prohibition which bears the penalty of *kares* (excision) for a willful violation. Usually referred to as the פַּר הֶעֱלֵם דָּבָר *[par he'elam davar]*, *bull for communal oversight*, it is referred to by our mishnah as the *bull which comes for any of the commandments*, after the phrase repeatedly used by the Torah (*Lev.* 4:2-13) to describe the inadvertent transgressions which occasion the special *chatas-offering*s for communal error (*Tos. Yom Tov*).

Specifically this refers to a situation whereby the majority of the community transgressed a *kares*-bearing prohibition of the Torah as a result of an erroneous permissive ruling issued by the Sanhedrin.[1] Although this offering is ostensibly a communal offering, it nonetheless requires *semichah*, as mandated explicitly by the Torah (ibid. v. 15). The *semichah* is performed by three members of the Sanhedrin (*Rav* from *Sanhedrin* 1:3; see *Yad Avraham* comm. to *Horayos* 2:2).

1. The laws of the *par he'elam davar* form the subject of the Tractate *Horayos*. See General Introduction to ArtScroll *Horayos* 1:1 for more details.

7. **N**o communal offerings require leaning, except the bull which comes for any of the commandments and the he-goat designated to be sent [to Azazel]. R' Shimon says: Even the he-goats for idolatry.

### YAD AVRAHAM

This is the view stated in the mishnah in Sanhedrin. However, the *Gemara* there (13b) ascribes this view to R' Shimon and cites a *Baraisa* which records the dissenting view of R' Yehudah to the effect that five judges must perform the *semichah.* There is disagreement among the authorities as to which is the prevailing view (see *Likkutei Halachos*).

וְשָׂעִיר הַמִּשְׁתַּלֵּחַ. — *and the he-goat designated to be sent [to Azazel].*

The Yom Kippur service in the Temple featured a pair of he-goats. By the drawing of lots one goat was designated for a sacrifice for *Hashem*, i.e., to be slaughtered in the Temple, and the other was designated to *Azazel*, i.e., to be thrown to its death from a cliff in the desert (see *Lev.* 16:21 and *Yoma* ch. 6). The he-goat to be sent to *Azazel* effects atonement for the sins of the community and as such should be exempt from *semichah*. However, here too the Torah explicitly mandates *semichah* by the *Kohen Gadol* (loc. cit.).

רַבִּי שִׁמְעוֹן אוֹמֵר: אַף שְׂעִירֵי עֲבוֹדָה זָרָה. — *R' Shimon says: Even the he-goats for idolatry.*

In the event that an erroneous permissible ruling by the Sanhedrin caused a communal transgression of the sin of idolatry, the *chatas-offering* is not a bull but a he-goat (*Num.* 15:24). This is called the *he-goat for avodah zarah*. In R' Shimon's view this offering too required *semichah* by the members of the Sanhedrin, although it atoned for the community at large.

R' Shimon disagrees with the first *Tanna* who counts the *he-goat for Azazel* as one of the two offerings designated by the Oral Tradition as exceptions to the rule exempting communal offerings from *semichah*. In his view, this tradition applies only to those offerings for which the *semichah* is performed by the owner of the sacrifice. The *semichah* for the he-goat designated to be sent to Azazel is performed by the *Kohanim*, despite the fact that it brings atonement for the rest of the Jewish nation. Therefore, R' Shimon argues, it must be a different sacrifice which is referred to by the Oral Tradition requiring *semichah* for two communal offerings. He derives exegetically that, in addition to the *par he'elam davar*, the other exception is the he-goat of idolatry.

The first *Tanna*, who is identified by the *Gemara* as R' Yehudah, contends that since *Kohanim* were also included in the atonement of the he-goat for Azazel, its *semichah* by them qualifies as one of the exceptions mandated by the Oral Tradition. He therefore disagrees with R' Shimon's requirement for *semichah* for the communal sin-offering for idolatry (*Gem.* 92a; *Tif. Yis.*).

The halachah follows the view of R' Yehudah (*Rav; Rambam, Hil. Maaseh HaKorbanos* 3:10).

מנחות ט/ח

כָּל קָרְבְּנוֹת הַיָּחִיד טְעוּנִים סְמִיכָה, חוּץ מִן הַבְּכוֹר, וְהַמַּעֲשֵׂר, וְהַפֶּסַח. וְהַיּוֹרֵשׁ סוֹמֵךְ, וּמֵבִיא נְסָכִים, וּמֵמִיר.

[ח] **הַכֹּל** סוֹמְכִין, חוּץ מֵחֵרֵשׁ, שׁוֹטֶה, וְקָטָן, סוּמָא, וְנָכְרִי, וְהָעֶבֶד, וְהַשָּׁלִיחַ,

ר׳ עובדיה מברטנורא

**כל קרבנות היחיד טעונים סמיכה.** דעיקר סמיכה בקרבן יחיד הוא דכתיבא (ויקרא ג, ב) וסמך ידו על ראש קרבנו: **היורש סומך.** אם התנדב אביו בקרבן עולה ושלמים ומת, בנו סומך עליו, ומביא נסכו של קרבן: **וממיר.** אם המירו בבהמה אחרת, תמורתו חלה עליה ושתיהן קדושות, כאילו המירה אביו: (ח) **חוץ מחרש שוטה וקטן.** לפי שאין להם דעת: **סומא.** דכתיב בפר העלם דבר של צבור (ויקרא ד, טו) וסמכו זקני העדה, והם סנהדרי גדולה, ובסנהדרין לא היה בהן סומא, כדמוכח במסכת סנהדרין (לו,ב), והוא הדין לכל שאר סמיכות שאין סומא יכול לסמוך: **ונכרי.** דכתיב (שם א, ב) דבר אל בני ישראל וגו׳, בני ישראל סומכין ואין הנכרים סומכין: **והעבד והשליח.** דכתיב (ויקרא א, ד) וסמך ידו, ולא יד עבדו ולא יד שלוחו:

יד אברהם

כָּל קָרְבְּנוֹת הַיָּחִיד טְעוּנִים סְמִיכָה, — *All offerings of individuals require leaning,*

The basic requirement for *semichah* is stated in regard to individual offerings (*Lev.* 3:2) (*Rav*). However, it applies only to animal sacrifices, not those of birds (*Tif. Yis.*).

חוּץ מִן הַבְּכוֹר, וְהַמַּעֲשֵׂר, וְהַפֶּסַח. — *except for the bechor-offering, the maaser-offering, and the pesach-offering.*

Since these do not require libations and *tenufah* (the waving of the breast and thigh parts) as do the other offerings of individuals, they cannot be derived from the latter to require *semichah* (*Gem.* 92b).

וְהַיּוֹרֵשׁ סוֹמֵךְ, — *An heir performs leaning,*

[As a rule, one who brings an offering not his own — e.g., one who acts as a proxy to bring an offering that belongs to someone else — does not perform *semichah* (*Gem.* 93a). Our mishnah teaches that this rule does not apply to an heir.]

If a person designated an *olah* or a *shelamim* and died before fulfilling his vow, his son, who inherits the sacrifice, performs *semichah* on it [as it is now considered his offering] (*Rav*).

This rule applies only to an *olah*- or *shelamim-offering*, as mentioned by *Rav*. However, if a person designated a *chatas*- or *asham-offering* and died before bringing it, the offering is not brought at all. See *Temurah* 3:3 (*Tos. Yom Tov*).

וּמֵבִיא נְסָכִים, — *and brings libations,*

[One who brings an offering he inherited from his father must also bring the appropriate *minchas nesachim.*]

Some maintain that this applies only if he inherited the *minchah* from his father as well (*Tos. Yom Tov*). Others contend that if his father left over only the animal for the offering, the son must provide the *minchas nesachim* from his own pocket (*Or Gadol*).

וּמֵמִיר. — *and makes a temurah exchange.*

As stated in the Torah (*Lev.* 27:10),

9 All offerings of individuals require leaning,
8 except for the *bechor*-offering, the *maaser*-offering, and the *pesach*-offering. An heir performs leaning, and brings libations, and makes a *temurah* exchange.

**8.** All must perform leaning, except for a deaf-mute, an imbecile, a minor, a blind man, a non-Jew, a slave, an agent, and a

### YAD AVRAHAM

in the event that one attempts to exchange a sacrifice by designating another in its place, both become sanctified, i.e., the original retains its status and the second one is also sanctified and must be offered as vowed (see comm. to mishnah 7:4, s.v. ותמורה). The power to consecrate the substitute animal through a *temurah* exchange is vested only in the owner of the offering (*Temurah* 1:1, *Zevachim* 6a). Our mishnah teaches that it applies to the heir as well; i.e., if an heir substitutes an animal for an offering designated by his father, both are sanctified (*Rav* from *Gemara* 93a).

## 8.

הַכֹּל סוֹמְכִין, חוּץ מֵחֵרֵשׁ, שׁוֹטֶה, וְקָטָן, — *All must perform leaning, except for a deaf-mute, an imbecile, a minor,*

[Anyone bringing one of the types of offering which requires *semichah* must carry out that requirement, with the exception of the following individuals.] A deaf-mute, imbecile, and minor are considered non-intelligent in regard to all matters of Jewish law [and are therefore excluded from the performance of this rite, as they are from all *mitzvos*] (*Rav* from *Gem.* 93a).

סוּמָא, — *a blind man,*

The exemption of a blind man from the *semichah* rite is derived from the exegetic comparison of the requirement for *semichah* by an individual to the Torah's requirement for *semichah* for the *par he'elam davar* performed by the Sanhedrin. Just as the *semichah* of the Sanhedrin does not include the blind — as the Sanhedrin members must be free of any physical defect (*Sanhedrin* 36b) — so too the general requirement for *semichah* does not include the blind (*Rav* from *Gem.* 93a).

It is unclear, though, why this source does not invalidate someone with *any* defect which disqualifies one for Sanhedrin rather than only blindness (*Tos.*).

וְנָכְרִי, — *a non-Jew,*

The passage in which the rite of *semichah* is mandated begins, דַּבֵּר אֶל בְּנֵי יִשְׂרָאֵל, *Speak to the Children of Israel* (*Lev.* 1:2), thereby excluding a non-Jew (*Rav* from *Gem.* 93a).

וְהָעֶבֶד, — *a slave,*

The Torah states (*Lev.* 1:4), וְסָמַךְ יָדוֹ, *and he shall lean his hand* — only *his* hand but not the hand of his slave (*Rav* from *Gem.* 93b).

Actually, there is a legal principle that יַד עֶבֶד כְּיַד רַבּוֹ, *the hand of a slave is [automatically] like the hand of his master.* However, that applies only when the act

# וְהָאִשָּׁה. וּסְמִיכָה שְׁיָרֵי מִצְוָה; עַל הָרֹאשׁ, בִּשְׁתֵּי יָדַיִם. וּבַמָּקוֹם שֶׁסּוֹמְכִין שׁוֹחֲטִין, וְתֵכֶף לִסְמִיכָה שְׁחִיטָה.

ר׳ עובדיה מברטנורא

**והאשה.** בני ישראל סומכין, ולא בנות ישראל סומכות: **וסמיכה שירי מצוה.** דאינה מעכבת כפרה. ומיהו מעלה עליו הכתוב כאילו לא כיפר: **בשתי ידים.** דכתיב בשעיר המשתלח (שם טז, כא) וסמך אהרן את שתי ידיו, זה בנה אב לכל הסמיכות שיהיו בשתי ידים: **ובמקום שסומכים שוחטים.** שאם סמך חוץ לעזרה, חוזר וסומך בעזרה במקום שחיטה: **ותכף לסמיכה שחיטה.** דכתיב (שם א, ד-ה) וסמך ושחט:

יד אברהם

involved is merely a means of effecting the desired result. In this case, however, it is the act itself which is required; i.e., the Torah requires the hands of the owner to be placed upon the animal's head. For this, the slave's hands are not acceptable (*Tif. Yis.*). [This would be similar to having the slave place *tefillin* upon his arm on behalf of his master, which clearly would not suffice for the master's obligation.]

וְהַשָּׁלִיחַ, — *an agent,*

[Despite the fact that the agent is a full-fledged Jew, he still may not perform the *semichah*. One cannot fulfill the *mitzvah* of *semichah* by proxy; it must be done by the owner himself.] This, too, is derived from the verse (ibid.): וְסָמַךְ יָדוֹ, *he shall lean his hand,* which emphasizes *his hand* but not the hand of a proxy (*Rav*).

The general principle that שְׁלוּחוֹ שֶׁל אָדָם כְּמוֹתוֹ, *a person's proxy is like himself*, does not apply to those *mitzvos* which involve the physical involvement of the obligated person. For example, one cannot assign a proxy to wear *tefillin* or sit in a *succah* on his behalf. According to one well-known explanation, the rationale behind this is that while the *action* of an agent is legally considered like that of the person he represents, his *person* is not. Thus, the *tefillin* placed on the agent's arm, for example, cannot be considered as a fulfillment of the *mitzvah* for anyone else (see *Tos. Rid, Kiddushin* 42a; *Ketzos HaChoshen* 182:1; *Lekach Tov* of *R' Yosef Engel* 1:5).

In light of the above discussion, some commentators question the necessity of the verse cited to exclude the proxy's *semichah*. Since the performance of *semichah* requires the physical action of the owner, it should go without saying that it cannot be performed through a proxy (*Chelkas Yoav; Choshen Mishpat* 4).

וְהָאִשָּׁה. — *and a woman.*

The verse cited above (s.v. ונכרי) specifies בְּנֵי יִשְׂרָאֵל, *the sons of Israel,* thereby excluding its daughters from this rite (*Rav* from *Gem.* 36a).

*Tosafos* (93a) question why this specific exclusion is necessary; women should be exempt from *semichah* under the general rule that women are exempt from all positive precepts that are time-related [מִצְוַת עֲשֵׂה שֶׁהַזְּמַן גְּרָמָא] (*Kiddushin* 1:1). *Semichah* is considered a time-related *mitzvah* because it is restricted to daytime, since it must immediately precede the *shechitah* (see following mishnah), which is invalid at night.

Some answer that since the verse is phrased וְסָמַךְ . . . וְשָׁחַט, *and he shall lean . . . and [then] slaughter*, we would suppose that *semichah* is compared to the *shechitah*. Just as the *shechitah* is valid if performed by a woman, so is the *semichah* (*Tos.* to *Kiddushin* 36a, s.v. הקבלות).

Others submit that the specific exclusion of women from *semichah* is to *prohibit* a woman from performing the *semichah*. Unlike other time-related *mitzvos*, which a woman may perform even though she is ex-

9
8

woman. Leaning is [considered] a remainder of the precept; [it is done] on the head, with two hands. In the place where the leaning is performed [the animal] is slaughtered, and the leaning immediately precedes the slaughtering.

YAD AVRAHAM

empt (e.g., hearing the *shofar* or taking the *lulav*), leaning's one's weight on a sacrificial animal where it is not mandated is a violation of the prohibition of עֲבוֹדָה בְּקָדָשִׁים, (personal) *use of consecrated objects*. Therefore, the *semichah* cannot be done unless mandatory (*Bircas HaZevach*).[1]

The exemption stated above applies to a woman who wishes to perform *semichah* on her own sacrifice. She is also disqualified from performing *semichah* on her husband's sacrifice, despite the fact that a woman and her husband are legally viewed as one unit. This is derived from the verse וְסָמַךְ יָדוֹ, *and he shall lean his hand*, cited earlier to preclude *semichah* by a slave or an agent. I.e., *semichah* must be performed by *his* hand and not anyone else's, including his wife (*Gem.* 93b).

Others contend that this is precisely the case of a woman being discussed in the mishnah, i.e., one who wishes to perform *semichah* for the offering of her husband, similar to the cases of agent and slave (*Tos. Yom Tov;* cf. *Zevach Todah*).

וּסְמִיכָה שְׁיָרֵי מִצְוָה; — *Leaning is [considered] a remainder of the precept;*

*Semichah* is considered the nonessential "remnant" of the offering in the sense that it is not critical to the basic atonement of the offering. Should one bring an offering and neglect to perform the rite of *semichah*, the sacrifice is valid (*Rav* from *Gem.* 93b). However, with the absence of *semichah* there is a degree of atonement lacking, inasmuch as the *mitzvah* was not performed in its entirety (ibid.; *Rashi ms*).

עַל הָרֹאשׁ, — *[it is done] on the head,*

[*Semichah* is performed by leaning one's full weight on the head of the animal, as stated explicitly in the passage.]

בִּשְׁתֵּי יָדַיִם. — *with two hands.*

Regarding the he-goat sent to Azazel of Yom Kippur, the Torah states clearly וְסָמַךְ אַהֲרֹן אֶת־שְׁתֵּי יָדוֹ . . ., *And Aaron shall lean his two hands* . . . This description is intended to describe the *semichah* for all sacrifices as well, and hence, we learn that *semichah* is performed with both hands (*Rav* from *Gem.* 93b).

וּבַמָּקוֹם שֶׁסּוֹמְכִין שׁוֹחֲטִין, — *In the place where the leaning is performed [the animal] is slaughtered,*

If one performed *semichah* outside the Temple Courtyard, where slaughtering for a sacrifice is not valid, he must redo it within the Courtyard (*Rav*).

וְתֵכֶף לִסְמִיכָה שְׁחִיטָה. — *and the leaning immediately precedes the slaughtering.*

This is stated as an explanation of the above principle. The reason the animal must be slaughtered in the place where *semichah* is performed is because the former must be done immediately

1. The last point, however, is apparently the subject of Tannaitic dispute. Some *Tannaim* hold that נָשִׁים סוֹמְכוֹת רְשׁוּת, *women performing semichah is a matter of choice*, i.e., women may perform the *semichah* if they so desire (see *Rosh Hashanah* 33a; *Chagigah* 16b, *Toras Kohanim, Vayikra* 2:2 and *Ravad* there).

[ט] **חֹמֶר** בַּסְּמִיכָה מִבַּתְּנוּפָה, וּבַתְּנוּפָה
מִבַּסְּמִיכָה. שֶׁאֶחָד מֵנִיף לְכָל
הַחֲבֵרִים, וְאֵין אֶחָד סוֹמֵךְ לְכָל הַחֲבֵרִים. וְחֹמֶר
בַּתְּנוּפָה, שֶׁהַתְּנוּפָה נוֹהֶגֶת בְּקָרְבְּנוֹת הַיָּחִיד
וּבְקָרְבְּנוֹת הַצִּבּוּר; בַּחַיִּים וּבַשְּׁחוּטִין; בְּדָבָר
שֶׁיֶּשׁ בּוֹ רוּחַ חַיִּים וּבְדָבָר שֶׁאֵין בּוֹ רוּחַ חַיִּים;
מַה שֶּׁאֵין כֵּן בַּסְּמִיכָה.

—— ר' עובדיה מברטנורא ——

(ט) **שאחד מניף לכל החברים.** שנתחברו להתנדב קרבן אחד. שכל קרבנות נדבה יכולים
להביא בשותפות, ואחד מניף על ידי כולן, אבל כולן יחד אין יכולין להניף דהויא חציצה בין ידו של
זה ולקרבן, וכהן שמניח ידו תחת יד הבעלים ומניף והויא יד בעלים חציצה, לא איכפת לן, דהא
עיקר תנופה בבעלים: **בקרבנות היחיד.** כגון חזה ושוק של שלמים: **ובקרבנות צבור.** כבשי
עצרת שטעונים תנופה חיים ושחוטים: **בדבר שיש בו רוח חיים.** קרבן בהמה: **ובדבר שאין
בו רוח חיים.** כגון לחמי תודה ונזיר:

**יד אברהם**

after the latter (*Gem.* 93b), as derived from the passage (*Lev.* 1:4,5) which mandates slaughtering immediately after *semichah* (*Rav*).

### 9.

The following mishnah compares the rite of *semichah*, just explained, to the rite of *tenufah*, discussed in chapter 5 (mishnah 6,7).

חֹמֶר בַּסְּמִיכָה מִבַּתְּנוּפָה, וּבַתְּנוּפָה מִבַּסְּמִיכָה.
— *There is stringency to [the rite of] leaning over [the rite of] waving, and stringency to [the rite of] waving over [the rite of] leaning.*

[I.e., each of these rites has an aspect of stringency that the other does not.]

שֶׁאֶחָד מֵנִיף לְכָל הַחֲבֵרִים, — *One may perform waving on behalf of all the fellow [owners]*

When a sacrifice is brought by a group of people in partnership, only one of them performs the *tenufah*.

The reason that only one of the owners performs the *tenufah* is that it is technically not possible to do otherwise. If all the members were to place their hands under the offering and wave it together, the *tenufah* would not be valid because the hand of the first person, which is directly underneath the offering, would constitute a חֲצִיצָה, interposition, between the offering and the hands of the other owners. On the other hand, having each member of the group perform *tenufah* successively (as it is done with *semichah*, see below) is ruled out by the Torah's use of the singular term תְּנוּפָה, which indicates that *tenufah* can be performed only once (*Rav* from *Gem.* 94a).

In light of the concept of חֲצִיצָה [*chatzitzah*], interposition, which invalidates a *tenufah* performed by two people at a time, the *Rishonim* pose the following question. Since the laws of *tenufah* requires the *Kohen* to place his hands under the owner's, why does the owner's hand not constitute a *chatzitzah* to the *Kohen's* hand?

**9.** There is stringency to [the rite of] leaning over [the rite of] waving, and stringency to [the rite of] waving over [the rite of] leaning. One may perform waving on behalf of all the fellow [owners] but one may not lean on behalf of all the fellow [owners]. The stringency of waving [is] that waving applies [both] to individual and communal offerings; while living and when slaughtered; with living matter and with non-living matter; which is not the case with leaning.

**YAD AVRAHAM**

One explanation is that actually the owner's part is the primary one in the *tenufah*, not the *Kohen's*. We are therefore not concerned that the *Kohen's* hand is not in direct contact with the offering (*Rav; Rashi*).

*Tosafos* explain that the *semichah* is performed in such a position that there is no interference of hands. The *Kohen's* hand is not directly beneath the owner's. Rather, the owner holds the edges and the *Kohen* places his hands underneath the object being raised (see *Tos.* to *Kiddushin* 36 and *Tos. Yom Tov* here for a third explanation).

וְאֵין אֶחָד סוֹמֵךְ לְכָל הַחֲבֵרִים. — *but one may not lean on behalf of all the fellow [owners].*

[If a group of people bring an offering in partnership, the *semichah* must be performed by all of them. This is because the Torah dictates that the rite of *semichah* be done for קָרְבָּנוֹ, *his offering* (*Lev.* 1:3), which indicates that each individual must perform the act of *semichah* on his own (*Gem.* 94a). Thus, each partner performs *semichah* separately (*Tos. Yom Tov* from *Rashi Peirush* 94a, s.v. תנופה; *Rambam, Maaseh HaKorbanos* 3:9).

וְחֹמֶר בַּתְּנוּפָה, שֶׁהַתְּנוּפָה נוֹהֶגֶת בְּקָרְבְּנוֹת הַיָּחִיד וּבְקָרְבְּנוֹת הַצִּבּוּר; — *The stringency of waving [is] that waving applies [both] to individual and communal offerings;*

The rite of *tenufah* is required for both offerings of individuals such as the breast and thigh parts of a *shelamim* (see above 5:6,7), and communal offerings, such as the two lambs brought on Shavuos (*Rav*).

בַּחַיִּים וּבִשְׁחוּטִין; — *while living and when slaughtered;*

*Tenufah* is sometimes performed even on live animals. This occurs with the כִּבְשֵׂי עֲצֶרֶת, *two lambs of Shavuos*. They are waved twice: once together with the *shtei halechem* when the lambs are still alive, and once when the chest and thigh parts are waved after the lambs have been slaughtered (see comm. to 5:7). Similarly, the breast and thigh parts of the slaughtered *shelamim* are waved.

בְּדָבָר שֶׁיֵּשׁ בּוֹ רוּחַ חַיִּים וּבְדָבָר שֶׁאֵין בּוֹ רוּחַ חַיִּים; — *with living matter and with non-living matter;*

The *tenufah* rite is performed with animals, as well as with inanimate offerings, such as the *shtei halechem* and the loaves of the *nazir* (*Rav;* see 5:4).

מַה שֶּׁאֵין כֵּן בַּסְּמִיכָה. — *which is not the case with leaning.*

[*Semichah* is performed only with the offerings of individuals, not communal offerings (with the exceptions stated above), and only to animals while they are still alive.]

# פרק עשירי

# Chapter Ten[1]

The following chapter deals with the particulars of the *mitzvah* of bringing the *omer*-offering. The Torah (*Lev.* 23:9ff) states: וַהֲבֵאתֶם אֶת עֹמֶר רֵאשִׁית... קְצִירְכֶם אֶל הַכֹּהֵן. וְהֵנִיף אֶת הָעֹמֶר לִפְנֵי ה׳ לִרְצֹנְכֶם; מִמָּחֳרַת הַשַּׁבָּת יְנִיפֶנּוּ הַכֹּהֵן, ... *and you are to bring an omer of the first of your reaping to the Kohen. And he shall wave the omer before* HASHEM *to your satisfaction; on the morrow of the Sabbath shall the Kohen wave it.*

The *omer* was a *minchah*-offering brought from barley. This is a *Halachah LeMoshe MiSinai* [a law taught by God to Moses, but not recorded in the Written Torah] (*Rambam, Hil. Temidin U'Mussafin* 7:11) and is indicated by the Torah's reference to the *omer* in *Lev.* 2:14 as אָבִיב, which elsewhere (*Ex.* 9:31) describes the ripening of barley (*Gem.* 68b; 84a). The Torah sets the date of the *omer* as *the morrow of the Sabbath.* According to tradition, this refers to the second day of Pesach, which is the morrow of [the first day of] the Pesach festival (which in this context is called the Sabbath; this point will be elaborated upon in mishnah 3). The reaping took place on the preceding night. There was a group of Jews called *Baytusim* [the followers of Baytus (Boethus)], who insisted that the date of the *omer* was literally *the morrow of the Sabbath,* i.e., Sunday. Thus, they claimed the *omer* was always brought on the first Sunday after Pesach. In order to counter this mistaken notion of the Baytusim and to firmly implant in their minds the true received tradition, the Sages ordained that the reaping of the *omer* on its proper date be accompanied with fanfare and special ceremonies, which will be discussed in the course of this chapter.

A function of the *omer* was to allow the use of the new crop of grain. Thus any grain that took root after the *omer* procedure was not allowed to be eaten until the following year when the *omer* was offered. This is called the prohibition of חָדָשׁ, *the new [grain of the five species].*

The first mishnah deals with the procedure of bringing the *omer* on the second day of Pesach when it falls on the Sabbath.

1. [In *Gemara* texts this chapter is the sixth rather than the tenth.]

מנחות י/א

**[א] רַבִּי** יִשְׁמָעֵאל אוֹמֵר: הָעֹמֶר הָיָה בָא בְּשַׁבָּת מִשָּׁלֹשׁ סְאִין, וּבְחֹל מֵחָמֵשׁ. וַחֲכָמִים אוֹמְרִים: אֶחָד בְּשַׁבָּת וְאֶחָד בְּחֹל, מִשָּׁלֹשׁ הָיָה בָא. רַבִּי חֲנִינָא סְגַן הַכֹּהֲנִים אוֹמֵר: בְּשַׁבָּת הָיָה נִקְצָר בְּיָחִיד, וּבְמַגָּל אַחַת, וּבְקֻפָּה אַחַת; וּבְחֹל בִּשְׁלֹשָׁה, וּבְשָׁלֹשׁ קֻפּוֹת, וּבְשָׁלֹשׁ מַגָּלוֹת.

**ר׳ עובדיה מברטנורא**

**פרק עשירי – רבי ישמעאל. (א) רבי ישמעאל אומר העומר היה בא בשבת.** כשחל ששה עשר בניסן להיות בשבת, העומר דוחה את השבת, שכל קרבן שזמנו קבוע דוחה את השבת ואת הטומאה. והיה העומר בא משלש סאין, שהיו קוצרין שלש סאין שעורין ומניפין אותן בנפה עד שמעמידין אותן על עשרון אחד מובחר: **ובחול.** אם חל ששה עשר בניסן להיות בחול, היו קוצרין אותו חמש סאין, דסבר רבי ישמעאל עשרון מובחר בלא טרחא שאינו מנפה אותו כל כך אתי מחמש, בטרחא כשמנפה אותו הרבה אתי משלש. בחול מייתינן מחמש, שכך משובח הדבר יותר שמניפין מכל סאה מעט אותו סלת דק היוצא ראשון שהוא מובחר, ומוציאין מחמש סאין עשרון. בשבת מביא שלש, מוטב שירבה במלאכה אחת שירקד שלש סאים פעמים הרבה, ואל ירבה במלאכות הרבה שיקצור ויברור ויטחון וירקד שני סאין יותר. ואין הלכה כרבי ישמעאל: **בשלשה בני אדם ובשלש קופות ובשלש מגלות.** לפרסם הדבר שקצירת העומר במוצאי חמשה עשר בניסן, מפני הצדוקים שהיו אומרים שאין העומר בא אלא באחד בשבת:

**יד אברהם**

## 1.

רַבִּי יִשְׁמָעֵאל אוֹמֵר: הָעֹמֶר הָיָה בָא בְּשַׁבָּת מִשָּׁלֹשׁ סְאִין, — *R' Yishmael says: The omer was brought on the Sabbath from three seah,*

Like any other offering which has a set time, the *omer* is brought even if its prescribed date occurs on the Sabbath. Moreover, the reaping itself also overrides the Sabbath (see mishnah 9 comm., s.v. ודוחה). However, in this case only that which is absolutely necessary for the offering to be brought may be done. Therefore, when the second day of Pesach fell on the Sabbath, only three *seah* [which equal one *ephah*] of barley were cut, since that is the minimum amount from which [with sufficient sifting] the required tenth of an *ephah* of fine flour can be extracted (*Rav*).

Although by reaping such a small amount of grain the refining process is necessarily increased because the flour must be sifted several times over in order to obtain the required amount, R' Yishmael holds that it is better to repeat one *melachah* (category of labor prohibited on the Sabbath) of sifting rather than to perform the multitude of *melachos* that reaping more grain would involve (*Gem.* 63b) — i.e., it is better to sift a smaller quantity of flour numerous times than to reap, select, grind, and winnow a larger quantity of grain (*Rav*).

The view of this mishnah that the reaping of the *omer* overrides the Sabbath is actually the subject of Tannaitic dispute. See below, mishnah 9 s.v. ודוחה.

וּבְחֹל מֵחָמֵשׁ. — *and on a weekday from five.*

**1.** R′ Yishmael says: The *omer* was brought on the Sabbath from three *seah*, and on a weekday from five. But the Sages say: Whether on the Sabbath or on a weekday, it came from three. R′ Chanina, the administrator of the *Kohanim*, says: On the Sabbath it was reaped by an individual, with one sickle, and in one basket; on a weekday by three, in three baskets, with three sickles.

**YAD AVRAHAM**

The required measure of fine flour is more readily extracted from five *seah* of grain than from three, and is of a finer quality. Therefore, on a weekday, when there is no *melachah* restriction involved, this was the quantity of grain which was reaped (*Rav* from *Gem.* 63b).

וַחֲכָמִים אוֹמְרִים: אֶחָד בְּשַׁבָּת וְאֶחָד בְּחֹל, מִשָּׁלֹשׁ הָיָה בָא. — *But the Sages say: Whether on the Sabbath or on a weekday, it came from three.*

The Sages hold that even on weekdays no more than three *seah* of grain were cut for the *omer*. [Even though it was preferable to process the necessary flour from five *seah*,] the lesser amount was reaped in order to minimize the burden upon the multitudes who stood and observed the reaping (see mishnah 3) and in order to expedite the readying of the flour for the offering and the subsequent permissibility of the new grain (*Tif. Yis.*).

The halachah follows this view (*Rav; Rambam, Hil. Temidin U'Mussafin* 7:11).

רַבִּי חֲנִינָא סְגַן הַכֹּהֲנִים אוֹמֵר: בְּשַׁבָּת הָיָה נִקְצָר בְּיָחִיד, וּבְמַגָּל אֶחָד, וּבְקֻפָּה אַחַת; וּבְחֹל בִּשְׁלֹשָׁה, וּבְשָׁלֹשׁ קֻפּוֹת, וּבְשָׁלֹשׁ מַגָּלוֹת. — *R′ Chanina, the administrator of the Kohanim,*[1] *says: On the Sabbath it was reaped by an individual, with one sickle, and in one basket; on a weekday by three, in three baskets,*[2] *with three sickles.*

As mentioned in the prefatory remarks, the Baytusim maintained that the *omer* was not offered on the second day of Pesach but rather on the first Sunday after Pesach. In order to clearly demonstrate the error of this view, it was ordained that the proceedings surrounding the *omer* be done on the proper date with much public fanfare. [Therefore, it was reaped by three people, each using a separate sickle, and each placing what he reaped in a separate basket] (*Rav*). However, on the Sabbath, the work was limited to the bare minimum necessary for the offering, in order to minimize desecration of the Sabbath (*Tif. Yis.*).

[Actually, this was not considered desecration of the Sabbath since all labor necessary for the *omer* is permitted. Nevertheless, R′ Chanina maintains that even the necessary labor was limited as much as possible.]

1. For a discussion regarding this title and the duties of its holder, see *Yad Avraham* to *Pesachim* 1:6.

2. In other editions, the order is: *with three sickles in three baskets*, which conforms to the sequence in the first part of the sentence (see *Shinnuyei Nuschaos*). Cf. *Tif. Yis.*

וַחֲכָמִים אוֹמְרִים: אֶחָד בְּשַׁבָּת וְאֶחָד בְּחֹל, בִּשְׁלֹשָׁה, וּבְשָׁלֹשׁ קֻפּוֹת, וּבְשָׁלֹשׁ מַגָּלוֹת.

[ב] **מִצְוַת** הָעֹמֶר לָבֹא מִן הַקָּרוֹב. לֹא בִכֵּר הַקָּרוֹב לִירוּשָׁלַיִם, מְבִיאִים אוֹתוֹ מִכָּל מָקוֹם. מַעֲשֶׂה שֶׁבָּא מִגַּגּוֹת צְרִיפִין, וּשְׁתֵּי הַלֶּחֶם מִבִּקְעַת עֵין סוֹכֵר.

[ג] **כֵּיצַד** הָיוּ עוֹשִׂים? שְׁלוּחֵי בֵית דִּין יוֹצְאִים מֵעֶרֶב יוֹם טוֹב וְעוֹשִׂים אוֹתוֹ כְּרִיכוֹת בִּמְחֻבָּר לַקַּרְקַע, כְּדֵי שֶׁיְּהֵא נוֹחַ לִקְצוֹר.

**ר׳ עובדיה מברטנורא**

(ב) **מצות העומר לבא מן הקרוב.** ממקום שקרוב לירושלים, לפי שאין מעבירין על המלות, הלכך כשיולא מירושלים לבקש עומר, אותה תבואה שמולא ראשונה נוטלה: **לא ביכר.** לא בשל כל לרכו: **מעשה שבא מגגות צריפין ועין סוכר.** רחוקים מירושלים הרבה, מפני שהחריבו הגייסות כל תבואות שסביבות ירושלים: (ג) **כריכות.** כורכים וקושרים ראשי שבולים מלא אגרוף:

**יד אברהם**

[The Sages contend that the necessity to demonstrate the error of the Baytusian view takes precedence over limiting the work on the Sabbath.] The halachah follows the view of the Sages (*Rambam*, loc. cit.).

וַחֲכָמִים אוֹמְרִים: אֶחָד בְּשַׁבָּת וְאֶחָד בְּחֹל, בִּשְׁלֹשָׁה, וּבְשָׁלֹשׁ קֻפּוֹת, וּבְשָׁלֹשׁ מַגָּלוֹת. — *But the Sages say: Whether on the Sabbath or on weekdays, [it was done] by three [people], with three baskets, and three sickles.*

## 2.

מִצְוַת הָעֹמֶר לָבֹא מִן הַקָּרוֹב. — *The mitzvah of the omer is that it come from the closest [fields].*

Ideally, the grain for the *omer* should be brought from the source of proper grain nearest to Jerusalem, because of the principle אֵין מַעֲבִירִין עַל הַמִּצְוֹת, *we do not pass over mitzvos* [i.e., a *mitzvah* should be performed as soon as the opportunity presents itself (see *Mechilta* to *Ex.* 12:17, cited by *Rashi* there; *Yoma* 33a, *Rashi* ad loc., s.v. אין מעבירין)]. Therefore, upon leaving Jerusalem to seek grain for the *omer*, it was necessary to select the first such grain that was encountered (*Rav* from *Gem.* 64b).

The *Gemara* also offers another explanation, based on the requirement that the grain for the *omer* must be soft and moist (see mishnah 9 and comm. s.v. מצותו לבא מן הלח). Therefore, it is necessary to bring from nearby so that the grains should not harden along the way (*Gem.* ibid.; *Rashi ms* ad loc.).

לֹא בִכֵּר הַקָּרוֹב לִירוּשָׁלַיִם, מְבִיאִים אוֹתוֹ מִכָּל מָקוֹם. — *If that which is closest to*

But the Sages say: Whether on the Sabbath or on weekdays, [it was done] by three [people], with three baskets, and three sickles.

**2.** The *mitzvah* of the *omer* is that it come from the closest [fields]. If that which is closest to Jerusalem did not ripen, we may bring it from any place. It once occurred that it came from Gaggoth Tzerifin, and the *shtei halechem* from the Ein Socher valley.

**3.** How did they do it? The court agents would go out on the eve of the Festival and make it into bundles while it was attached to the ground, so that it would be easier to reap.

YAD AVRAHAM

*Jerusalem did not ripen, we may bring it from any place.*

If the nearby grain was not fully ripened (*Rav*) [it may be passed over, and the *omer* can then be brought from any grain grown in *Eretz Yisrael*].

מַעֲשֶׂה שֶׁבָּא מִגַּגּוֹת צְרִיפִין, וּשְׁתֵּי הַלֶּחֶם מִבִּקְעַת עֵין סוֹכֵר. — *It once occurred that it came from Gaggoth Tzerifin, and the shtei halechem from the Ein Socher valley.*

The mishnah cites instances in which the barley for the *omer* and the wheat for the *shtei halechem* on Shavuos were brought from areas far from Jerusalem, because hostile armies had destroyed all the nearby crops[1] (*Rav*).

3.

כֵּיצַד הָיוּ עוֹשִׂים? — *How did they do it?*

[How did they reap the grain for the *omer?*]

שְׁלוּחֵי בֵית דִּין יוֹצְאִים מֵעֶרֶב יוֹם טוֹב וְעוֹשִׂים אוֹתוֹ כְּרִיכוֹת בִּמְחֻבָּר לַקַּרְקַע, כְּדֵי שֶׁיְּהֵא נוֹחַ לִקְצוֹר. — *The court agents would go out on the eve of the Festival and make it into bundles while it was attached to the ground, so that it would be easier to reap.*

On the day before Pesach, the agents of the court would go out to the field and tie together fistfuls of barley stalks at their tips (*Rav*) [in order to facilitate the reaping on the following evening].

1. During the Hasmonean period, there was a civil war during which Hyrkanos besieged Jerusalem, which was held by Aristobulus. At that time, the besieging troops destroyed the crops near Jerusalem and it became necessary to seek the *omer*-offering elsewhere (*Gem.* ibid.). See, however, *Tos.* (ad loc.), s.v. ועל, who cite other Rabbinic sources which attribute our mishnah's incident to a different case.

וְכָל הָעֲיָרוֹת הַסְּמוּכוֹת לְשָׁם מִתְכַּנְּסוֹת לְשָׁם כְּדֵי שֶׁיְּהֵא נִקְצָר בְּעֵסֶק גָּדוֹל. כֵּיוָן שֶׁחֲשֵׁכָה, אוֹמֵר לָהֶם: בָּא הַשֶּׁמֶשׁ? אוֹמְרִים: הֵין. בָּא הַשֶּׁמֶשׁ? אוֹמְרִים: הֵין. מַגָּל זוֹ? אוֹמְרִים: הֵין. מַגָּל זוֹ? אוֹמְרִים: הֵין. קֻפָּה זוֹ? אוֹמְרִים: הֵין. קֻפָּה זוֹ? אוֹמְרִים: הֵין. בְּשַׁבָּת, אוֹמֵר לָהֶם: שַׁבָּת זוֹ? אוֹמְרִים: הֵין. שַׁבָּת זוֹ? אוֹמְרִים: הֵין. אֶקְצֹר? וְהֵם אוֹמְרִים לוֹ: קְצֹר! אֶקְצֹר? וְהֵם אוֹמְרִים לוֹ: קְצֹר! שְׁלֹשָׁה פְעָמִים

**ר׳ עובדיה מברטנורא**

**מתכנסות לשם.** למוצאי יום טוב כשקוצרים אותו: **בדי שיהא נקצר בעסק גדול.** בקול המולה גדולה, שיכירו הצדוקים שבמוצאי יום טוב קוצרים אותו משום דאינהו לא מודו בהאי, כדלקמן: **אמר להן.** הקוצר, לבני העיירות העומדים עליו, בא השמש, ואמרו לו הין: **מגל זה.** כלומר, אקצור התבואה במגל זה: **קופה זו.** אכניס התבואה לתוך קופה זו: **שבת זו.** אקצור בשבת זו, ואמרו לו הין: **שלש פעמים.** שואל להן כל דבר ודבר:

**יד אברהם**

וְכָל הָעֲיָרוֹת הַסְּמוּכוֹת לְשָׁם מִתְכַּנְּסוֹת לְשָׁם — *All of the towns nearby would gather there*

At the close of the first day of Pesach, the inhabitants of all the nearby towns would assemble at the harvest site (*Rav*).

כְּדֵי שֶׁיְּהֵא נִקְצָר בְּעֵסֶק גָּדוֹל. — *so that it should be reaped with great ceremony.*

[The multitudes were assembled] so that the reaping of the *omer* should be accompanied by great commotion. This was done to make the Baytusim aware that it is indeed done on that night, unlike their misinterpretation that the *omer* is brought only on a Sunday (*Rav*).

The reaping took place at night because of the verse regarding the counting of the *omer* which states (*Lev.* 23:15): שֶׁבַע שַׁבָּתוֹת תְּמִימֹת תִּהְיֶינָה, *seven complete weeks they shall be,* indicating that the *counting* should begin immediately at nightfall of the first day so that the counted weeks should be complete. Since the Torah states elsewhere (*Deut.* 16:9) that the counting begins when the grain has been reaped, it is clear that the reaping must take place at night (*Rav* from *Gem.* 66a; see below s.v. מצותו לקצור).

כֵּיוָן שֶׁחֲשֵׁכָה, אוֹמֵר לָהֶם: בָּא הַשֶּׁמֶשׁ? אוֹמְרִים: הֵין. — *As soon as it became dark, he would say to them, "Has the sun set?" and they would say, "Yes."*

Each of the three men designated to do the reaping (*Tos. Yom Tov*) would ask the gathered masses if the sun had set, and they would answer affirmatively (*Rav*).

בָּא הַשֶּׁמֶשׁ? אוֹמְרִים: הֵין. — *"Has the*

10
3

All of the towns nearby would gather there so that it should be reaped with great ceremony. As soon as it became dark, he would say to them, "Has the sun set?" and they would say, "Yes." "Has the sun set?" and they would say, "Yes." "This sickle?" and they would say, "Yes." "This sickle?" and they would say, "Yes." "This basket?" and they would say, "Yes." "This basket?" and they would say, "Yes." On the Sabbath, he would say to them, "This Sabbath?" and they would say, "Yes." "This Sabbath?" and they would say, "Yes." "Shall I reap?" and they would say to him, "Reap!" "Shall I reap?" and they would say to him, "Reap!" Three times



*sun set?" and they would say, "Yes."*

[The exchange was repeated again — and then a third time as well — as explained below. The same was done with all the other exchanges enumerated below in the mishnah.]

מַגָּל זוֹ? אוֹמְרִים: הֵין. מַגָּל זוֹ? אוֹמְרִים: הֵין. — *"This sickle?" and they would say, "Yes." "This sickle?" and they would say, "Yes.'*

He then asks the assembled, "This sickle?" meaning, "Shall I use this sickle to cut the grain?" to which they would reply in the affirmative (*Rav*).

קֻפָּה זוֹ? אוֹמְרִים: הֵין. קֻפָּה זוֹ? אוֹמְרִים: הֵין. — *"This basket?" and they would say, "Yes." "This basket?" and they would say, "Yes."*

He would then ask, "This basket?" meaning, "Shall I place the grain in this harvesting basket?" to which they would reply in the affirmative.

בְּשַׁבָּת, אוֹמֵר לָהֶם: שַׁבָּת זוֹ? אוֹמְרִים: הֵין. שַׁבָּת זוֹ? אוֹמְרִים: הֵין. — *On the Sabbath, he would say to them, "This Sabbath?" and they would say, "Yes." "This Sabbath?" and they would say, "Yes."*

When the second day of Pesach fell on the Sabbath, he would ask the additional question, "This Sabbath?" meaning, "Shall I cut the grain on this Sabbath?" to which they would reply in the affirmative (*Rav*).

This mishnah, too, reflects the view that the reaping of the *omer* overrides the Sabbath — see below mishnah 9.

אֶקְצֹר? וְהֵם אוֹמְרִים לוֹ: קְצֹר! אֶקְצֹר? וְהֵם אוֹמְרִים לוֹ: קְצֹר! — *"Shall I reap?" and they would say to him, "Reap!" "Shall I reap?" and they would say to him, "Reap!"*

He then asks them if he should begin the reaping and they answer, "Reap" — rather than simply "yes" — in order to indicate that he should begin immediately (*Tos. Yom Tov; Tif. Yis.*).

עַל כָּל דָּבָר וְדָבָר, וְהֵם אוֹמְרִים לוֹ: הֵין, הֵין, הֵין. כָּל כָּךְ לָמָּה? מִפְּנֵי הַבַּיְתוֹסִים, שֶׁהָיוּ אוֹמְרִים אֵין קְצִירַת הָעֹמֶר בְּמוֹצָאֵי יוֹם טוֹב.

[ד] **קְצָרוּהוּ** וּנְתָנוּהוּ בַּקֻּפּוֹת, הֱבִיאוּהוּ לָעֲזָרָה. הָיוּ מְהַבְהֲבִין אוֹתוֹ בָּאוּר כְּדֵי לְקַיֵּם בּוֹ מִצְוַת קָלִי; דִּבְרֵי רַבִּי מֵאִיר. וַחֲכָמִים אוֹמְרִים: בְּקָנִים וּבִקְלִיחוֹת חוֹבְטִים אוֹתוֹ כְּדֵי שֶׁלֹּא יִתְמָעֵךְ.

### ר׳ עובדיה מברטנורא

**וכל כך.** שהיה שואל, למה: **מפני הצדוקים וביתוסים שהיו אומרים אין קצירת העומר במוצאי יום טוב.** אלא במוצאי שבת, דכתיב (ויקרא כג, טו) וספרתם לכם ממחרת השבת, ממחרת שבת בראשית משמע, ומסורת בידינו מאבותינו דהאי ממחרת השבת, היינו מחרת יום טוב ראשון של פסח בין שחל בחול בין בשבת, וכן מצינו בספר יהושע (ה, יא) ויאכלו מעבור הארץ ממחרת הפסח מצות וקלי, והרי נאמר בתורה (שם שם, יד) ולחם וקלי וכרמל לא תאכלו עד עצם היום הזה, ומאחר שתלה היתר החדש במחרת הפסח, הדבר ברור שמחרת הפסח הוא המתיר את החדש ובו קוצרים העומר בין שחל יום טוב ראשון של פסח בחול בין שחל להיות בשבת, ולפיכך הקוצרים מגביהין קולם כדי שישמעו הבייתוסים ולהוציא מלבן. וקוצרים העומר בלילה ולא ביום, דכתיב (ויקרא כג, טו) וספרתם לכם ממחרת השבת וגו׳ שבע שבתות תמימות תהיינה, ואי אפשר להיות תמימות אלא אם כן מתחיל למנות מתחלת הלילה, שהרי הלילה תחלת היום הוא, והרי הוא אומר (דברים טז, ט) מהחל חרמש בקמה תחל לספור, אלמא הקצירה בלילה הוא בשעה שמתחיל למנות: (ד) **מהבהבין אותו באור.** בעודו בשיבולין, כדי לקיים בו מצות קלי, כדכתיב (ויקרא ב, יד) אביב קלוי באש, ובמנחת העומר מיירי קרא: **וחכמים אומרים.** תחלה חובטים, ולא כדרך תבואה יבשה שחובטים אותו במקל, אלא קנים לחים, ובקולחת, בקלח של כרוב, כדי שלא יתמעך, ואחר כך מקיימין בו מצות קלי:

### יד אברהם

שְׁלֹשָׁה פְּעָמִים עַל כָּל דָּבָר וְדָבָר, וְהֵם אוֹמְרִים לוֹ: הֵין, הֵין, הֵין. — *Three times for each item, and they would say to him, "Yes, yes, yes."*

He asks each of the above questions three times (*Rav*) [and they answer in the affirmative to each of them].

כָּל כָּךְ לָמָּה? מִפְּנֵי הַבַּיְתוֹסִים, — *Why was all this necessary? Because of the Baytusim,*

These were a sect of Jews who began to reject the authenticity and interpretations of the Oral Torah and chose instead to accept only the apparent literal meaning of the Written Torah (see *Rambam Comm.* to *Avos* 1:3).

The Sadducees [צְדוֹקִים] were another sect that emerged at the same time and espoused a similar outlook. Eventually, these two sects became indistinguishable from each other (see *Tos. Yom Tov*).

שֶׁהָיוּ אוֹמְרִים אֵין קְצִירַת הָעֹמֶר בְּמוֹצָאֵי יוֹם טוֹב. — *who said that the omer is not reaped on motzaei Yom Tov.*

The Torah (*Lev.* 23:15), in discussing

for each item, and they would say to him, "Yes, yes, yes." Why was all this necessary? Because of the Baytusim, who said that the *omer* is not reaped on *motzaei Yom Tov*.

**4.** They would reap it and place it in baskets [and] bring it to the [Temple] Courtyard. They would toast it in fire in order to fulfill the *mitzvah* of toasting; [these are] the words of R' Meir. But the Sages say: They beat it with reeds and stalks so that it should not be crushed.

**YAD AVRAHAM**

the counting of the days following the *omer*-offering, states *and you shall count for yourselves from the morrow of the Sabbath.* The Oral Tradition explains this expression to mean the first day of Pesach, regardless of which day of the week it falls on. [The term Sabbath is used because of the obligation to cease from labor on that day.] The Baytusim and Sadducees, however, rejected the Oral Tradition and interpreted the Torah's expression *on the morrow of the Sabbath* to mean the morrow of the seventh day of the week, i.e., Sunday. The Sages therefore ordained that the reaping on the eve of the second day of Pesach be done with great fanfare to clearly demonstrate that this sectarian interpretation is erroneous (*Rav*).[1]

4.

קְצָרוּהוּ וּנְתָנוּהוּ בַּקֻּפּוֹת, הֱבִיאוּהוּ לָעֲזָרָה. הָיוּ מְהַבְהֲבִין אוֹתוֹ בָּאוּר כְּדֵי לְקַיֵּם בּוֹ מִצְוַת קָלִי; דִּבְרֵי רַבִּי מֵאִיר. — *They would reap it and place it in baskets [and] bring it to the [Temple] Courtyard. They would toast it in fire in order to fulfill the mitzvah of toasting; [these are] the words of R' Meir.*

The Torah (*Lev.* 2:14) states that the *minchas bikkurim* [i.e., the *omer*] should be brought אָבִיב קָלוּי בָּאֵשׁ גֶּרֶשׂ כַּרְמֶל, *when it is first ripe, toasted in fire, coarsely ground out of full ears of grain*. Therefore, the harvested barley had to be toasted before being offered as a *minchah* (*Rav*). R' Meir holds that true toasting is accomplished only when it is roasted directly in the fire without a utensil intervening. Therefore, it must be toasted while it is still in the stalks (*Rambam Comm.*).

וַחֲכָמִים אוֹמְרִים: בְּקָנִים וּבִקְלִיחוֹת חוֹבְטִים אוֹתוֹ כְּדֵי שֶׁלֹּא יִתְמָעֵךְ. — *But the Sages say: They beat it with reeds and stalks so that it should not be crushed.*

The Sages contend that the kernels

1. Ultimately, the strength of the traditional interpretation rests on its having been faithfully transmitted from generation to generation in an unbroken chain stretching back to Sinai (see *Rambam, Hil. Temidin U'Mussafin* 7:11). Nevertheless, many Scriptural supports have been adduced to corroborate this tradition — see *Gem.* 65a-66a; *Rambam* (loc. cit.); *Rav*; *HaMoadim BaHalachah* by R' S.Y. Zevin, *Shavuos*.

נְתָנוּהוּ לָאַבּוּב, וְאַבּוּב הָיָה מְנֻקָּב כְּדֵי שֶׁיְּהֵא הָאוּר שׁוֹלֵט בְּכֻלּוֹ. שְׁטָחוּהוּ בָּעֲזָרָה וְהָרוּחַ מְנַשֶּׁבֶת בּוֹ. נְתָנוּהוּ בְּרֵחַיִם שֶׁל גָּרוֹסוֹת וְהוֹצִיאוּ מִמֶּנּוּ עִשָּׂרוֹן, שֶׁהוּא מְנֻפֶּה מִשְּׁלֹשׁ עֶשְׂרֵה נָפָה. וְהַשְּׁאָר נִפְדֶּה וְנֶאֱכָל לְכָל אָדָם. וְחַיָּב בַּחַלָּה וּפָטוּר מִן הַמַּעַשְׂרוֹת. רַבִּי עֲקִיבָא מְחַיֵּב בַּחַלָּה וּבַמַּעַשְׂרוֹת.

### ר׳ עובדיה מברטנורא

**[נתנוהו לאבוב]**. דסבירא להו לרבנן שאם מהבהבים אותו באור ממש אין נקרא קלי, שאין נקרא קלי אלא על ידי דבר אחר דהיינו על ידי כלי, שנותנים אותו באבוב, והוא כלי של נחשת מנוקב שמוכרי קליות קולין בו. והלכה כחכמים: **ברחיים של גרוסות**. שאין טוחנות דק אלא עבה. שאם יטחנו יפה יעברו הסובין של קליפה בנפה עם הסלת. וגרוסות לשון גריסין של פול, ועל שם כן נקראת גרש כרמל: **וחייב בחלה**. דחיוב חלה היינו גלגול העסה, וגלגול עסה זו ביד הדיוט היא לאחר שנפדה: **ופטור מן המעשרות**. דמירוחו ביד הקדש הוא, ומירוח הקדש פוטר מן המעשרות: **רבי עקיבא מחייב**. האי קמח הנותר מעשרון של עומר, בחלה ובמעשרות, לפי שלא נתנו מעות הקדש אלא בצריך להם לעשרון לבד, אבל האחר לא קדש, הילכך לאו מירוח הקדש הוא, דהא לא קדוש. ואין הלכה כרבי עקיבא:

### יד אברהם

should be removed from the husks prior to the toasting. Since at that point the kernels are still soft and moist, they beat the husks with soft reeds and stalks — rather than with the normally used sticks — so that the kernels should not be crushed in the process (*Rav*). *Rambam Comm.* explains that the kernels are first removed from the husks, according to the Sages, because removing them after toasting is likely to crush and damage them since they will have already been softened by the toasting.

נְתָנוּהוּ לָאַבּוּב, וְאַבּוּב הָיָה מְנֻקָּב כְּדֵי שֶׁיְּהֵא הָאוּר שׁוֹלֵט בְּכֻלּוֹ. — *[Then] they would place it in a pipe, which was perforated so that the fire should prevail over all of it.*

The Sages maintain that the term קָלִי does not mean toasted directly over a fire, but rather toasted through a medium. Therefore it was necessary to use a utensil for the toasting. This utensil — a copper pipe — was perforated to allow the fire to affect all of the grain (*Rav*).

The halachah follows the view of the Sages (*Rav; Rambam, Hil. Temidin U'Mussafin* 7:12).

שְׁטָחוּהוּ בָּעֲזָרָה וְהָרוּחַ מְנַשֶּׁבֶת בּוֹ. — *They would spread it out in the Courtyard and the wind would blow on it.*

The toasted kernels were then spread out in the Temple Courtyard to dry out in the wind from any moisture that may have formed in the pipe during the toasting process (*Tif. Yis.*).

נְתָנוּהוּ בְּרֵחַיִם שֶׁל גָּרוֹסוֹת — *They would place it in a grist-mill*

The kernels were placed in a grist-mill, which grinds it coarsely, so that the pieces of the shell are still large enough that they will not pass through the sieve with the flour. Because of this

10
4

[Then] they would place it in a pipe, which was perforated so that the fire should prevail over all of it. They would spread it out in the Courtyard and the wind would blow on it. They would place it in a grist-mill and extract from it an *issaron*, which was sifted with thirteen sieves. The remainder is redeemed and may be eaten by anyone. It is subject to *challah* but exempt from *maaser*. R' Akiva declares it subject to *challah* and to *maaser*.

YAD AVRAHAM

grinding, the Torah refers to the *omer* as גֶּרֶשׂ כַּרְמֶל, *"coarsely ground* out of full ears of grain" (*Rav*).

וְהוֹצִיאוּ מִמֶּנּוּ עִשָּׂרוֹן, שֶׁהוּא מְנֻפֶּה מִשְּׁלֹשׁ עֶשְׂרֵה נָפָה. — *and extract from it an issaron, which was sifted with thirteen sieves.*

[They sifted the flour through thirteen sieves to produce the desired grade of flour, as explained above in 6:7.]

וְהַשְּׁאָר נִפְדֶּה וְנֶאֱכָל לְכָל אָדָם. — *The remainder is redeemed and may be eaten by anyone.*

[Since the grain was originally reaped for Temple use, it is all considered *hekdesh* — Temple property — and prohibited for private consumption. However, once the portion required for use in the Temple has been removed, the remainder may be redeemed and eaten anywhere by anyone.]

וְחַיָּב בַּחַלָּה — *It is subject to challah*

[As a rule, *hekdesh* property is exempt from *terumah* (the portion of produce separated for the *Kohen*), *maaser* (the various tithes that were then separated), and from *challah* (the portion of dough given to the *Kohen*). In our case, however, the dough made from the remainder of the grain is subject to the separation of *challah* despite the fact that the grain was initially *hekdesh*.] This is because the *challah* obligation takes effect at the time of גִּלְגּוּל עִיסָּה, *the making of the dough*, at which time the flour has already been redeemed and is *chullin* (*Rav*).

וּפָטוּר מִן הַמַּעַשְׂרוֹת. — *but exempt from maaser.*

Although the remaining grain is now *chullin*, the [*terumah* and] *maaser* portions that must generally be separated from produce grown in Eretz Yisrael are not separated from this grain. Unlike the *challah* obligation, which takes effect when the dough is made, the [*terumah* and] *maaser* obligations take effect when the winnowed pile of grain is smoothed, a process called מֵרוּחַ, *meruach* [see *Maasros* 1:6]. Since in our case the *meruach* [or its equivalent] occurred while the grain was still *hekdesh*, the grain never became subject to these obligations, and it remains exempt even when it is subsequently redeemed (*Rav*).

רַבִּי עֲקִיבָא מְחַיֵּב בַּחַלָּה וּבַמַּעַשְׂרוֹת. — *R' Akiva declares it subject to challah and to maaser.*

R' Akiva maintains that the remaining grain was never *hekdesh* in the first place. Since the original payment made from the Temple treasury to the owner of the field for his grain

בָּא לוֹ לָעִשָּׂרוֹן, וְנָתַן שַׁמְנוֹ וּלְבוֹנָתוֹ, יָצַק וּבָלַל, הֵנִיף וְהִגִּישׁ, וְקָמַץ וְהִקְטִיר; וְהַשְּׁאָר נֶאֱכָל לַכֹּהֲנִים.

[ה] **מִשֶּׁקָּרַב** הָעֹמֶר, יוֹצְאִין וּמוֹצְאִין שׁוּק יְרוּשָׁלַיִם שֶׁהוּא מָלֵא קֶמַח וְקָלִי, שֶׁלֹּא בִרְצוֹן חֲכָמִים; דִּבְרֵי רַבִּי מֵאִיר.

**ר׳ עובדיה מברטנורא**

**בא לו לעשרון.** נותן תחלה שמנו ולבונתו קודם נתינת הסלת: **יצק ובלל.** לאחר נתינת הסלת, כדרך כל המנחות שנותן שמן בכלי תחלה ואחר כך נותן סלת וחוזר ויוצק עליה שמן ובולל: **הניף והגיש.** דמנחת העומר טעונה הנפה והגשה, כדאמרינן בפרק כל המנחות (ה, ו): (ה) **שלא ברצון חכמים.** דגזרי שמא יאכל מן החדש כשקוצר קודם שיקריבו העומר, וזה שכבר הוא קמח, ודאי נקצר קודם העומר:

**יד אברהם**

was intended solely to procure the *issaron* for the *omer*, the remaining nine-tenths of the grain never became consecrated by this purchase. Thus, that part was not the property of *hekdesh* at the time of *meruach* and is fully subject to the [*terumah* and] *maaser* obligations of produce (*Rav*; see *Rambam Comm.*, ed. Kafich).

בָּא לוֹ לָעִשָּׂרוֹן, — *He approached the issaron,*

The following procedure took place on the morning of the sixteenth of Nissan (*Rashi*) but did not necessarily require the participation of a *Kohen*, as all steps of the *minchah* prior to *kemitzah* may be done by a non-*Kohen* as well (*Tif. Yis.*).

וְנָתַן שַׁמְנוֹ וּלְבוֹנָתוֹ, — *and put in its oil and frankincense;*

He put the oil and *levonah* in the vessel before adding the flour (*Rav; Rashi*).

יָצַק וּבָלַל, — *he [then] poured and mixed,*

After adding the flour, he poured more oil on top of it and mixed it all together, as is the procedure for all *menachos* (*Rav; Rashi ms;* see preface to 3:2).

In addition, a third measure of oil was poured on top of the mixture after it was mixed, as explained previously [in mishnah 6:3] (*Tos.* 67b, s.v. יצק). *Tos.* further maintain that the word יָצַק, *he poured,* indeed refers to this third pouring of oil, even though it precedes the word וּבָלַל, *and he mixed* (which, according to *Tos.*, encompasses both the second pouring of oil and its being mixed with the flour).

הֵנִיף וְהִגִּישׁ, — *waved and brought [it] near [to the Altar],*

The *minchas haomer* requires both procedures, as stated earlier [5:6] (*Rav*).

וְקָמַץ — *and performed kemitzah*

After moving the *levonah* to the side of the vessel, the *Kohen* performed *kemitzah* on the flour mixed with oil, as explained above in 1:2 (*Tos. Yom Tov*).

וְהִקְטִיר; — *and burnt [it] on the Altar;*

[After all of the aforementioned

10
5 He approached the *issaron*, and put in its oil and its frankincense; he [then] poured and mixed, waved and brought [it] near [to the Altar], and performed *kemitzah* and burnt [it] on the Altar; the remainder is eaten by the *Kohanim.*

**5.** After the *omer* was offered, they would go out and find the market place of Jerusalem full of flour and the flour of toasted grain, which was against the will of the Sages; [these are] the words of R' Meir.

YAD AVRAHAM

procedures were performed, the *kometz* that was removed was burnt on the Altar.]

It is unclear why the mishnah omits mention of the requirement to salt the offering [see above 3:2] (*Tos.*). Possibly, the mishnah is listing only those procedures which were particular to *menachos*, whereas salting is required for all offerings (*Tos. Yom Tov*; cf. *Mahariach*).

וְהַשְּׁאָר נֶאֱכָל לַכֹּהֲנִים. — *the remainder is eaten by the Kohanim.*

[The remainder of the flour *minchah* was eaten by the *Kohanim* in the Temple Courtyard, as is the case with all *menachos.*]

5.

מִשֶּׁקָּרַב הָעֹמֶר, יוֹצְאִין וּמוֹצְאִין שׁוּק יְרוּשָׁלַיִם שֶׁהוּא מָלֵא קֶמַח וְקָלִי, — *After the omer was offered, they would go out and find the market place of Jerusalem full of flour and the flour of toasted grain,*[1]

[After the offering of the *omer*, the market streets of Jerusalem would be filled with the new grain, which had been rendered permissible by that offering.]

שֶׁלֹּא בִרְצוֹן חֲכָמִים; דִּבְרֵי רַבִּי מֵאִיר. — *which was against the will of the Sages; [these are] the words of R' Meir.*

Since the markets were filled with flour produced from the new grain, which takes time to process, the new grain had to have been harvested before the *omer* was brought. The Rabbis disapproved of reaping new grain before the *omer* (which permitted consumption of the new grain) was brought, for fear that during his involvement in cutting the grain, a person might inadvertently eat some of it (*Rav*).

It is Biblically prohibited to reap the new grain before the *omer* is reaped [see below, *mishnayos* 7-8]. However, this prohibition does not apply to grain grown in certain types of fields (ibid.), or to plucking, rather than reaping, the grain (*Gem.* 68a; *Rashi*, s.v. מתוך). The Rabbinic disapproval mentioned here applies even to grains reaped in a Biblically permitted manner (*Tos. Yom Tov*).

1. Generally, קָלִי refers to the flour of toasted grain (see *Kereisos* 5a; *Rashi* to *Lev.* 23:14, *Shabbos* 155b s.v. קלי). However, it is apparently taken by some to refer to the toasted grain itself in this context (see *Rabbeinu Gershom* to 68a, s.v. דר׳ יהודה).

מנחות
י/ה

רַבִּי יְהוּדָה אוֹמֵר: בִּרְצוֹן חֲכָמִים הָיוּ עוֹשִׂים. מִשֶּׁקָּרַב הָעֹמֶר, הֻתַּר הֶחָדָשׁ מִיָּד. וְהָרְחוֹקִים מֻתָּרִים מֵחֲצוֹת הַיּוֹם וּלְהַלָּן. מִשֶּׁחָרַב בֵּית הַמִּקְדָּשׁ, הִתְקִין רַבָּן יוֹחָנָן בֶּן זַכַּאי שֶׁיְּהֵא יוֹם הָנֵף כֻּלּוֹ אָסוּר. אָמַר רַבִּי יְהוּדָה: וַהֲלֹא מִן הַתּוֹרָה הוּא אָסוּר, שֶׁנֶּאֱמַר: ,,עַד עֶצֶם הַיּוֹם הַזֶּה״?

ר׳ עובדיה מברטנורא

**רבי יהודה אומר ברצון חכמים.** דלא גזרו שמא יאכל כשקוצר. והלכה כרבי יהודה: **והרחוקים.** שאינן יודעים אם עדיין קרב העומר, מותרים מחצות היום ולהלן, כדקתני טעמא לקמן: **שיהא יום הנף.** יום ששה עשר בניסן שבו מניפין את העומר, כולו אסור לאכול בו חדש: **אמר רבי יהודה.** לתנא דמתניתין, וכי רבן יוחנן התקין, והלא מן התורה אסור בזמן שאין בית המקדש קיים, דתרי קראי כתיבי, כתוב אחד אומר (ויקרא כג, יד) עד עצם היום הזה, דמשמע דעצמו של יום כולו אסור, דעד ועד בכלל, וכתוב אחד אומר (שם) עד הביאכם את קרבן אלהיכם, דמשמע דלאחר קרבן העומר מותר, הא כיצד, כאן בזמן שבית המקדש קיים, כאן בזמן שאין בית המקדש קיים, אלמא בזמן שאין בית המקדש קיים שאין העומר קרב הוי יום הנף כולו אסור מן התורה, ומשני בגמרא (סח, ב) דהא דתנן התקין רבן יוחנן בן זכאי שיהא יום הנף כולו אסור, לא תימא התקין, אלא דרש והתקין, כלומר שדרש מקראות הללו ברבים והודיעם שכך הדין שיום הנף כולו אסור מן התורה משחרב בית המקדש. ואית דמפרשי בגמרא, שאין החדש אסור מן התורה ביום ששה עשר בניסן בזמן שאין מקדש אלא עד שיאיר פני המזרח שחרית ביום ששה עשר, דכתיב (שם) עד עצם היום הזה, עד ולא עד בכלל, והתקין רבן יוחנן בן זכאי שיהא יום הנף כולו אסור, משום מהרה יבנה בית המקדש ויאמרו אשתקד מי לא הוה אכלינן משהאיר המזרח, השתא נמי ניכול, והן אינן יודעים דבזמן המקדש אסור לאכול חדש עד שיקריב העומר, דכתיב (שם) עד הביאכם את קרבן אלהיכם, והכי פרשינן לה בפרק לולב הגזול (מסכת סוכה דף מא, א):

יד אברהם

רַבִּי יְהוּדָה אוֹמֵר: בִּרְצוֹן חֲכָמִים הָיוּ עוֹשִׂים. — *R' Yehudah says: [It was] in accordance with the will of the Sages [that] they did [it].*

R' Yehudah permits involvement with the new grain prior to the offering of the *omer*, because he does not fear that people will inadvertently eat from the new grain before the offering of the *omer* (*Rav*).

R' Yehudah holds (*Pesachim* 1:3) that one who has not searched for *chametz* prior to the point at which it becomes prohibited may not do so afterward because he may forget himself and eat from it upon discovering it. This would seem to be inconsistent with his opinion here, that we need not fear such a possibility. However, the two cases are not really comparable. Since a person is used to eating *chametz* before Pesach he is more likely to forget and eat it on Pesach. This is not true of the new grain which has been prohibited up to this point (*Gem.* 67b).

The halachah follows the view of R' Yehudah (*Rav; Rambam Comm.*).

מִשֶּׁקָּרַב הָעֹמֶר, הֻתַּר הֶחָדָשׁ מִיָּד. — *After the omer was offered, the new grain was permitted immediately.*

[In the times of the *Beis HaMikdash*, when the *omer*-offering was brought, it immediately rendered all new grain permissible for consumption.]

10
5 R' Yehudah says: [It was] in accordance with the will of the Sages [that] they did it.

After the *omer* was offered, the new grain was permitted immediately. Those who were distant were permitted from midday and onward. After the Temple was destroyed, Rabban Yochanan ben Zakkai instituted that the entire Day of Waving should be forbidden. Said R' Yehudah: Is it not Biblically forbidden, as it is stated (*Lev.* 23:14): *Until this very day?*

### YAD AVRAHAM

From the next part of the mishnah, which states that those who were distant were permitted to eat the new grain after midday, it is apparent that the *omer* was offered by midday. Accordingly, *Rambam's* statement (*Hil. Temidin U'Mussafin* 7:12) that the *kemitzah* of the *omer* was performed after the *mussaf* was offered cannot apparently be reconciled with *Rashi's* statement (*Pesachim* 58a, s.v. ר״ ישמעאל) that the *mussaf* was first offered at midday. According to *Rashi*, the *kemitzah* of the *omer* must have preceded the *mussaf*-offering (*Sfas Emes*).

וְהָרְחוֹקִים מֻתָּרִים מֵחֲצוֹת הַיּוֹם וּלְהַלָּן. — *Those who were distant were permitted from midday and onward.*

Those who were unable to ascertain the exact time that the *omer* was offered could assume that it had already been offered by midday — i.e., midday Jerusalem time (*Rambam Comm.*) — and eat from the new grain from that time on, as will be explained by the mishnah below (*Rav*).

מִשֶּׁחָרַב בֵּית הַמִּקְדָּשׁ, הִתְקִין רַבָּן יוֹחָנָן בֶּן זַכַּאי שֶׁיְּהֵא יוֹם הָנֵף כֻּלּוֹ אָסוּר. — *After the Temple was destroyed, Rabban Yochanan ben Zakkai instituted that the entire Day of Waving should be forbidden.*

Following the destruction of the Temple and the consequent cessation of the *omer*-offering, Rabban Yochanan ben Zakkai instituted the practice that the new grain should be prohibited until after the entire day of the sixteenth of Nissan — the day on which the *omer* had been waved when the Temple was standing — had passed (*Rav*). [The reason for this institution is explained in the commentary to the next section.]

אָמַר רַבִּי יְהוּדָה: וַהֲלֹא מִן הַתּוֹרָה הוּא אָסוּר, שֶׁנֶּאֱמַר: „עַד עֶצֶם הַיּוֹם הַזֶּה״? — *Said R' Yehudah: Is it not Biblically forbidden, as it is stated (Lev.* 23:14): *"Until this very day"?*

Although when the *omer* is brought the new grain is permitted immediately, when it is not brought it remains prohibited by Torah law, in R' Yehudah's view, until the end of the sixteenth day. R' Yehudah bases his opinion on the resolution of two seemingly contradictory statements in the Torah. On one hand, the Torah (*Lev.* 23:14) states: וְלֶחֶם וְקָלִי וְכַרְמֶל לֹא תֹאכְלוּ עַד עֶצֶם הַיּוֹם הַזֶּה, *the bread and flour [from new grain] you shall not eat "until this very day,"* indicating that new grain may not be eaten until after the sixteenth day (interpreting עַד, *until*, as *until and including*). On the other hand, the Torah immediately adds:

מִפְּנֵי מָה הָרְחוֹקִים מֻתָּרִים מֵחֲצוֹת הַיּוֹם וּלְהַלָּן? מִפְּנֵי שֶׁהֵן יוֹדְעִין שֶׁאֵין בֵּית דִּין מִתְעַצְּלִין בּוֹ.

[ו] **הָעֹמֶר** הָיָה מַתִּיר בַּמְּדִינָה, וּשְׁתֵּי

**ר' עובדיה מברטנורא**

**(ו) העומר היה מתיר במדינה.** לאכול החדש בכל המקומות:

**יד אברהם**

עַד הֲבִיאֲכֶם אֶת קָרְבַּן אֱלֹהֵיכֶם, *until you bring the offering of your God*, which clearly permits the new grain upon the bringing of the *omer*. R' Yehudah explains that both statements are true: When the [Temple is standing and the] *omer* is offered, it is the *omer* which permits new grain; when there is no *omer*-offering, the new grain may not be eaten until the entire sixteenth day of Nissan has passed. R' Yehudah challenges the previous mishnah's statement[1] that it was Rabban Yochanan ben Zakkai who instituted this rule, maintaining instead that it is a Biblically mandated practice. R' Yochanan ben Zakkai, however, interprets the verse cited by R' Yehudah differently. The phrase עַד עֶצֶם הַיּוֹם הַזֶּה, *until this very day*, means until daybreak [i.e., sunrise (*Rashi* 68a, s.v. האיר; cf. *Sfas Emes* ad loc.)] of the sixteenth day rather than the end (עַד, *until*, being explained to mean *until but not including*). Thus, whereas the *omer*-offering permits the new grain in Temple times, when there is no Temple the new grain is Biblically permitted at daybreak of the sixteenth day. Nevertheless, Rabban Yochanan ben Zakkai feared that people accustomed to eating the new grain on the morning of the sixteenth would continue to do so even after the Temple is rebuilt, not realizing that one must then wait until the *omer* is brought. Thus the possibility that מְהֵרָה יִבָּנֶה בֵּית הַמִּקְדָּשׁ, *the Temple will be speedily rebuilt*, caused him to ordain that for the whole of the sixteenth day it is prohibited to eat the new grain (*Rav* from *Gem.* 68b).

This concern could have apparently been addressed by prohibiting the new crop on the sixteenth day until noon (the time by which the *omer* service was invariably completed, as stated in this mishnah). Nevertheless, R' Yochanan ben Zakkai forbade it the *entire* day because of the possibility that the Temple would be rebuilt on the eve of the sixteenth, making the *omer*-offering immediately incumbent. The various preparations of the barley for the *omer* would only then begin and extend into the afternoon, thus delaying offering of the *omer* until late in the day (*Gem., Rosh Hashanah* 30a; see *Yad Avraham* to *Rosh Hashanah* 4:3).

The *Gemara* (66b) also provides an alternative explanation for R' Yochanan ben Zakkai's view, according to which he actually agrees with R' Yehudah's contention that in the absence of the *omer* the new grain is Biblically prohibited for the entire day. Accordingly, the term הִתְקִין רַבָּן יוֹחָנָן בֶּן זַכַּאי, *Rabban Yochanan ben Zakkai instituted*, does not mean that he *legislated*

1. R' Yehudah's remarks are not addressed to R' Yochanan ben Zakkai himself, who lived several generations prior to R' Yehudah (see *Rashi* to *Rosh Hashanah* 30b, s.v. בשיטת).

Why are those who are distant permitted from midday and onward? Because they know that the court does not procrastinate with it.

**6.** The *omer*-offering rendered [the new grain] permissible in the Provinces, and the *shtei*



this rule but rather that he saw to it that this Biblical rule, which had just become applicable with the Temple's destruction, should be established in practice (*Rav* from *Gem.* 68b; *Rambam Comm.*; *Rashi* to *Rosh Hashanah* 30b, s.v. דרש והתקין). R' Yehudah, however, misunderstood the mishnah to mean that R' Yochanan ben Zakkai legislated a Rabbinic prohibition, and therefore expressed his opinion as a rejoinder (*Gem.* 68b).

מִפְּנֵי מָה הָרְחוֹקִים מֻתָּרִים מֵחֲצוֹת הַיּוֹם וּלְהַלָּן? — *Why are those who are distant permitted from midday and onward?*

[The mishnah now explains the ruling stated above, that those who are not present in the vicinity of Jerusalem may assume that the new grain has become permitted by midday.] This question applies according to all opinions, as even R' Yehudah agrees that when the Temple was standing the new grain became permitted with the offering of the *omer*, as explained above (*Rashi ms*).

מִפְּנֵי שֶׁהֵן יוֹדְעִין שֶׁאֵין בֵּית דִּין מִתְעַצְּלִין בּוֹ. — *Because they know that the court does not procrastinate with it.*

[The people can justifiably rely on the energy and diligence of the court to see to it that the *omer* is offered as quickly as possible.]

Despite the court's diligence in seeing to it that the *omer*-offering should be completed with dispatch, it was entirely possible that some disqualification would happen to the offering and force a delay in the offering well past midday. True, the mishnah in *Avos* 5:5 states that the phenomenon that no disqualification ever happened to the *omer* was one of the miracles that occurred in the Temple; nevertheless, in light of the principle that we do not act based on miraculous expectations, how were people permitted to assume that the *omer* had been successfully offered by midday without mishap? This must be because of the principle, הוֹלְכִין אַחַר הָרוֹב, *one follows the majority*, and in the majority of instances the *omer* is brought without mishap (*Sfas Emes*).

## 6.

As stated in the previous mishnah, no new grain may be eaten prior to the offering of the *minchas haomer* on the second day of Passover. However, before new grain could be used for an offering in the Temple, the *shtei halechem*, the two loaves of Shavuos, needed to be brought. This mishnah cites these principles and distinguishes between the two.

הָעֹמֶר הָיָה מַתִּיר בַּמְּדִינָה, — *The omer-offering rendered [the new grain] permissible in the Provinces,*

With the offering of the *omer*, it became permissible to eat from the new grain of that year in all places (*Rav*).

הַלֶּחֶם בַּמִּקְדָּשׁ. אֵין מְבִיאִין מְנָחוֹת, וּבִכּוּרִים, וּמִנְחַת בְּהֵמָה קֹדֶם לָעֹמֶר; וְאִם הֵבִיא, פָּסוּל. קֹדֶם לִשְׁתֵּי הַלֶּחֶם לֹא יָבִיא; וְאִם הֵבִיא, כָּשֵׁר.

**ר׳ עובדיה מברטנורא**

**ושתי הלחם במקדש.** שקודם שתי הלחם אין מביאין מנחה מתבואה חדשה, דכתיב בשתי הלחם (במדבר כח, כו) מנחה חדשה, שתהא חדשה לכל המנחות: **ומנחת בהמה.** מנחת נסכים של בהמה: **ואם הביא.** קודם לעומר, פסול, שלא הותר החדש מכללו אפילו אצל ההדיוט. אבל קודם שתי הלחם לא יביא ואם הביא כשר, שכבר הותר מכללו אצל ההדיוט:

**יד אברהם**

וּשְׁתֵּי הַלֶּחֶם בַּמִּקְדָּשׁ. — *and the shtei halechem [did so] in the Temple.*

The offering of the *shtei halechem* from the new wheat crop on Shavuos made it permissible to bring *menachos* from the new crops of grain. Before the *shtei halechem*, however, a *minchah*-offering [other than the *omer*-offering from barley] could not be brought from the new grain (*Rav*).

The Torah (*Num.* 28:26) refers to the *shtei halechem* brought on Shavuos as מִנְחָה חֲדָשָׁה, *the new minchah.* From this we see that it is to be the first *minchah* brought from the new grain of that year (*Rav* from *Gem.* 84b).

אֵין מְבִיאִין מְנָחוֹת, — *We do not bring minchah-offerings,*

Before the *omer* is brought, new grain may not be used for a *minchah*-offering.

This applies even to the barley of the מִנְחַת קְנָאוֹת, *jealousy minchah* of a *sotah,* which cannot be brought from the new barley crop before the *shtei halechem* are offered (*Tos. Yom Tov* from *Gem.* 84b).

וּבִכּוּרִים, — *or bikkurim,*

*Bikkurim* [first-fruits] are those first fruits separated from the seven species [wheat, barley, grapes, figs, pomegranates, olives, and dates (*Deut.* 8:8)] and brought to the Temple (see *Deut.* 26:1-11). They are then given to the *Kohen* and have a status similar to *terumah*. The mishnah here teaches that *bikkurim* may not be brought from the new crops prior to the *omer*-offering (see *Tos. Yom Tov*).

וּמִנְחַת בְּהֵמָה קֹדֶם לָעֹמֶר; — *or the minchah-offering of an animal prior to the omer-offering;*

One may also not use the new grain for the *menachos* of libations which accompany animal offerings (*Rav; Tif. Yis.*). Some interpret this to refer to the wine of the libations as well; it, too, may not be brought from the new grapes before the *omer* (see *Tos. Yom Tov; Rashash*).

וְאִם הֵבִיא, פָּסוּל. — *and if one brought, it is invalid.*

If any of these offerings were brought from new grain prior to the *omer*-offering, they are not valid. At this point, the new grain is still prohibited for ordinary consumption. Now, the prophet refers to Temple sacrifices as coming מִמַּשְׁקֵה יִשְׂרָאֵל, *from Israel's meals* (*Ezek.* 45:15), i.e.,

*halechem* [did so] in the Temple. We do not bring *minchah-offerings*, or *bikkurim*, or the *minchah*-offering of an animal prior to the *omer*-offering; and if one brought, it is invalid. Prior to the *shtei halechem* one may not bring; but if he brought, it is valid.



foods permitted for a Jew's consumption. Since the new grains are prohibited for eating prior to the *omer*-offering, offerings brought from them are invalid (*Tos.* 68b, s.v. לא; see *Gem.* 5a).

Others, however, explain that even non-grain offerings from the new crop are invalid prior to the *omer*-offering, even though they are permitted for ordinary consumption (see *Tos. Yom Tov*; see below, footnote 1).

קֹדֶם לִשְׁתֵּי הַלֶּחֶם לֹא יָבִיא; — *Prior to the shtei halechem one may not bring;*

[Even though the new grain becomes permitted for ordinary consumption with the offering of the *omer*, it may still not be used for Temple offerings until after the *shtei halechem* are brought from the new wheat crop on Shavuos.]

וְאִם הֵבִיא, כָּשֵׁר. — *but if he brought, it is valid.*

[If one transgresses and brings any of these offerings from the new grain between the offering of the *omer* and that of the *shtei halechem*, it is valid.] This is not comparable to bringing an offering from the new grain before the *omer*. Before the *omer*, new grains are prohibited even for ordinary consumption and thus any offering from them is invalid. A *minchah* brought from new grain before the *shtei halechem*, however, is valid after the fact because the grain is already fit for ordinary consumption (*Gem.* 68b; *Tos.*).

Libations from new wine are valid even prior to the *omer* because the prohibition of חָדָשׁ, *new grain*, applies to grain, not fruit. Thus, they are similar to new grain brought prior to the *shtei halechem*, which are valid because they are permitted for private use. Nevertheless, there is a prohibition to bring libations from new wine before the *omer*, just as it is prohibited to offer new grain before the *shtei halechem* (*Zevach Todah*).[1]

## 7.

Pursuant to the mishnah's discussion of the laws of *chadash* — the new grain which is prohibited before the *omer* — the *Tanna* cites a mishnah which deals in part with these laws. This same mishnah is found in *Challah* (1:1).

1. *Rambam* (*Hil. Isurei Mizbe'ach* 5:9) seems to include libations in his listing of new offerings that are invalid if brought before the *omer*. However, many commentators interpret this to refer to the *minchah* of libations rather than to the libations themselves, as would appear from his phrasing of this ruling in *Temidin U'Mussafin* 7:17 (*Birchas HaZevach; Zevach Todah*; cf. *Tos. Yom Tov*).

[ז] **הַחִטִּים,** וְהַשְּׂעֹרִים, וְהַכֻּסְּמִין, וְשִׁבֹּלֶת שׁוּעָל, וְהַשִּׁיפוֹן חַיָּבִין בְּחַלָּה וּמִצְטָרְפִים זֶה עִם זֶה. וַאֲסוּרִים בֶּחָדָשׁ מִלִּפְנֵי הַפֶּסַח וּמִלִּקְצֹר מִלִּפְנֵי הָעֹמֶר.

ר׳ עובדיה מברטנורא

(ז) **ומצטרפין זה עם זה.** להשלים שיעור העיסה החייבת בחלה. ולא שילטרפו כולן יחד, דמין בשאינו מינו אין מלטרף, אלא החטין מלטרפין עם הכוסמין בלבד מפני שהן מינן, והשעורים מלטרפין עם הכל חוץ מן החיטים. ואף על גב דכוסמין מין חטין הן, לאו מין חטין דוקא, אלא מין שעורים ואף מין חטים, ומלטרפין עם החטים והשעורים. ומיהו בירושלמי משמע דאם נלושו יחד מלטרפין, אפילו מין בשאינו מינו, אבל אם לא נלושו יחד אלא שאחר כך היו נושכות העסות זו בזו, מין במינו מלטרפין, שלא במינו אין מלטרפין: **ואסורים בחדש.** כדכתיב (ויקרא כג, יד) ולחם וקלי וכרמל לא תאכלו עד עלם היום הזה, וגמרינן לחם לחם מפסח, מה להלן מחמשת המינים אף כאן מחמשת המינים: **ומלקצור מלפני הפסח.** שאסור לקלור מאחד מחמשת המינים קודם קלירת העומר, דכתיב בעומר (שם שם, י) ראשית קלירכם, שתהא תחלה לכל הקלירים, ואתיא ראשית ראשית מחלה, כתיב התם (במדבר טו, כ) ראשית עריסותיכם, וכתיב הכא ראשית קלירכם, מה להלן מחמשת המינים אף כאן מחמשת המינים:

יד אברהם

הַחִטִּים, וְהַשְּׂעֹרִים, וְהַכֻּסְּמִין, וְשִׁבֹּלֶת שׁוּעָל, וְהַשִּׁיפוֹן חַיָּבִין בְּחַלָּה — *Wheat, barley, spelt, oats, and rye are subject to challah*

When one kneads a dough from one of these five species of grain, a portion of the dough [called *challah*] must be separated and given to the *Kohen* [see *Num.* 15:17-21]. The Torah (ibid.) obligates the separation of challah "when you eat from the *bread* of the Land." Just as the term "bread" in the context of *matzah* ["the *bread* of affliction" (*Deut.* 16:3)] refers specifically to unleavened bread made from one of these five species (which alone can achieve halachically defined leavening), so too does the term "bread" in the context of *challah* refer specifically to that made from one of these five species (*Rav* to *Challah* 1:1; *Gem.* 70b).

וּמִצְטָרְפִים זֶה עִם זֶה. — *and combine with one another.*

A minimum quantity of flour [the volume of 43 1/5 eggs] must be used in order for the obligation of *challah* to apply [see *Challah* 2:6]. This minimum quantity can consist of a combination of flour from the various species of grain.

The implication of the mishnah here is that any combination of these species suffices to create the obligation of *challah*. However, another mishnah (*Challah* 4:1-2) teaches that even among these five species of grain, different species combine for the obligation of *challah* only if they are similar species but not if they are dissimilar. [The two main categories are wheat and barley, which this mishnah rules are dissimilar and cannot be combined. Spelt is similar to and combines with either wheat or barley; oats and rye are similar to and combine with barley only (ibid.; *Tos.* 70a-b, s.v. תנא).]

Some explain that the second mishnah actually qualifies the first; the first

7. **W**heat, barley, spelt, oats, and rye are subject to *challah* and combine with one another. They are forbidden [to be eaten] as *chadash* before Pesach and from being reaped before the *omer.*

YAD AVRAHAM

mishnah does not mean that *all* species combine with one another, but only that those of similar kinds combine (see *Rav; Rashi msc.* 70a, s.v. כסומין; *Tos.* loc. cit.).

However, *Yerushalmi* (*Challah* 1:1) explains that the two *mishnayos* refer to different types of combining. The first mishnah (cited here) refers to one dough that is kneaded from different flours, in which case all grains can combine, even those which are considered dissimilar. The second mishnah, on the other hand, refers to a case in which the doughs of the respective flours were kneaded separately but later attached to one another; then the requirement of similarity applies, and wheat can combine only with spelt while barley can combine with everything except wheat [as explained above] (*Rav; Tos.*).

וַאֲסוּרִים בֶּחָדָשׁ מִלִּפְנֵי הַפֶּסַח — *They are forbidden [to be eaten] as chadash before Pesach*[1]

None of these five grains may be eaten as *chadash* [new crop] before the *omer* is brought, as stated in the Torah (*Lev.* 23:14): "the *bread* ... [from new grain] you shall not eat until this very day" [see above, mishnah 5, s.v. אמר רבי יהודה]. Just as the term "bread" used in the context of *matzah* refers specifically to that made from these five species [see above, s.v. החטים], so too does the prohibition of *chadash* refer specifically to these five species of grain (*Rav* from *Gem.* 70b).

וּמִלִּקְצֹר מִלִּפְנֵי הָעֹמֶר. — *and from being reaped before the omer.*

In addition to the prohibition of eating new grain before the *omer*, there is also a prohibition against reaping the new grain before the *omer* is cut. This is derived from the Torah's reference to the *omer* as רֵאשִׁית קְצִירְכֶם, *the first of your reaping* (*Lev.* 23:10), thereby prohibiting the reaping of any new grain prior to that of the *omer*. As the word רֵאשִׁית is also used in the context of *challah*, which is called רֵאשִׁית עֲרִסֹתֵכֶם, *the first of your dough* (*Num.* 15:20), it can be exegetically derived that the prohibition against reaping before the *omer* applies to the five grains from which *challah* is taken (*Rav* from *Gem.* 70b).

The *Gemara* (68a) states that the prohibition against reaping before the *omer* applies only to one who reaps with a sickle; to pluck by hand is permitted.

In other versions of the mishnah, the words "Pesach" and "*omer*" are transposed, resulting in the reading: *They are forbidden [to be eaten] as chadash "before the omer" and from being reaped "before Pesach"* (see *Tos. Yom Tov* to *Challah* 1:1). Our version [*forbidden as chadash before Pesach*] seems problematic because it can mislead one to deduce that *chadash* is permitted once Pesach arrives, which is not true since *chadash* is prohibited until the *omer*, which is offered on the second day of Pesach. However, a similar objection

1. Other versions read: *before the omer*; this is discussed in commentary to the following section.

וְאִם הִשְׁרִישׁוּ קֹדֶם לָעֹמֶר, הָעֹמֶר מַתִּירָן; וְאִם לָאו, אֲסוּרִים, עַד שֶׁיָּבֹא עֹמֶר הַבָּא.

[ח] **קוֹצְרִים** בֵּית הַשְּׁלָחִים שֶׁבָּעֲמָקִים,

ר׳ עובדיה מברטנורא

**ואם השרישו.** אחד מחמשת המינים הללו קודם קצירת העומר: **העומר מתירן.** ומותר לקצרן אחר קצירת העומר, דכתיב (שמות כג, טז) אשר תזרע בשדה, משעה שנזרע ונשרש בשדה: **ואם לאו.** שלא השרישו אלא לאחר קצירת העומר: **אסורים עד שיבא העומר הבא.** של שנה הבאה: **(ח) קוצרים בית השלחים שבעמקים.** שתבואתן רעה ואין מביאין עומר משם, ותניא, כתוב אחד אומר (ויקרא כג, י) וקצרתם את קצירה והבאתם את עומר, דמשמע דיכול לקצור קודם הבאת

יד אברהם

the new crop is offered in the Temple" (*Tos. Yom Tov*). Others explain it to mean "before the leftovers of the *pesach*-offering are burnt," which is done on the sixteenth by day (*Rash Sirilio* cited by *Meleches Shlomo* to *Challah* 1:1).] According to the version that prohibits *chadash* "before the *omer*," the prohibition against eating *chadash* remains in force in times of the Temple until the *omer* is offered.

וְאִם הִשְׁרִישׁוּ קֹדֶם לָעֹמֶר, הָעֹמֶר מַתִּירָן; — *If they took root before the omer, the omer renders them permissible;*

Whatever grain takes root before the reaping of the *omer*[2] ceases to be *chadash* with the *omer* procedure, even though this grain will not grow or be harvested until well after Pesach. It can then be reaped and eaten at any time (*Rambam Comm.* ed. Kafich).

This is alluded to in the Torah's reference to Shavuos as the time of בִּכּוּרֵי מַעֲשֶׂיךָ אֲשֶׁר תִּזְרַע בַּשָּׂדֶה, *the first of*

cannot be raised according to the second version [*forbidden from being reaped before Pesach*]. In this case no one will deduce that it is permitted to reap *chadash* on the first day of Pesach, because reaping is one of the *melachos* which are prohibited on *Yom Tov*. One will deduce only that it is permitted to reap *chadash* after the close of *Yom Tov* on the eve of the sixteenth; this is indeed the case, as the reaping of the *omer* on that night invariably takes place before anyone else has a chance to do so (*Tos. Yom Tov* loc. cit.; see *Rashi* 70b, s.v. אלא, *Tos.* s.v. מאי). *Yerushalmi* to *Challah* 1:1 (cited by *Tos. Yom Tov* loc. cit.), however, cites both versions of the first part of the mishnah, viz., *they are forbidden as chadash before Pesach*, and *they are forbidden as chadash before the omer*, and explains that they reflect different views. According to the version that prohibits *chadash* "before Pesach," the prohibition against eating *chadash* ceases at daybreak of the sixteenth.[1] [Accordingly, "before Pesach" means "before that day of Pesach on which

1. Although the *prohibition* against *chadash* ceases then, according to this view, one may still not eat *chadash* until the *omer* is brought later that day. It is questionable whether this interim restriction is Biblical [carrying only the force of a positive precept rather than that of a prohibition] or merely Rabbinic (ibid.; cf. *Gem.* 68a, *Tos.* ad loc. s.v. והא, 5b s.v. האיר).

2. Actually, it is a subject of dispute in the *Gemara* (70b; *Yerushalmi, Challah* 1:1) whether the grain must take root before the reaping of the *omer*, or whether it is sufficient that it take root before the offering of the *omer*. *Rambam Comm.* (followed by *Rav*) rules that it must take root before the reaping of the *omer*. However, in *Hil. Maachalos Asuros* 10:4, he seems to rule that it is sufficient that it take root before the offering of the *omer* (*Kesef Mishneh* ad loc.; see, however, *Rashash* to this mishnah).

10
8

If they took root before the *omer*, the *omer* renders them permissible; if not, they are forbidden until the following *omer*.

**8.** We may reap the irrigated fields in the valleys,



*your work that you plant in the field* (*Ex.* 23:16), i.e., when the *shtei halechem* are offered. This offering lifts the prohibition against offering new grain in the Temple. The Torah thus indicates that the *shtei halechem* permit for offering any grain *that you plant in the field*, i.e., that has taken root in the ground. As the *shtei halechem* render permitted for Temple use only grains that the *omer* has already rendered permitted for ordinary consumption, this verse necessarily refers to taking root before the *omer*, not before Shavuos (*Gem.* 71a; *Rashi* ad loc.).

וְאִם לָאו, אֲסוּרִים, עַד שֶׁיָּבֹא עֹמֶר הַבָּא. — *if not, they are forbidden until the following omer.*

Whatever grain did not take root before the reaping of this year's *omer* does not become permissible to reap until the reaping of the grain for the *omer* of the coming year (*Rav; Rambam Comm.*). Similarly, whatever grain takes root after this year's *omer* cannot be eaten until after the *omer* of the coming year (*Rambam, Maachalos Asuros* 10:4; see *Rashash* to this mishnah).[1]

[As regards the applicability of the laws of *chadash* outside of Eretz Yisrael, see Appendix II: *Chadash*.]

## 8.

As stated in the previous mishnah, there is a prohibition against reaping the new crop of grain before the *omer*. There are, however, exceptions to this prohibition. These exceptions are the subject of the following two mishnayos.

קוֹצְרִים בֵּית הַשְּׁלָחִים שֶׁבָּעֲמָקִים, — *We may reap the irrigated fields in the valleys,*

The prohibition against reaping the new grain crop prior to the *omer* does not apply to reaping areas that produce grain of inferior quality which is not used for the *omer*-offering. This exception can be derived in the following manner. The Torah states

1. According to some authorities, the amount of time necessary for grain to take root is subject to the same Tannaitic dispute regarding the planting of trees in *Sheviis* 2:6 [see *Yad Avraham* comm. there] (*Nekudas HaKesef, Yoreh Deah* 293:1; *Turei Even* to *Rosh Hashanah* 10b, s.v. כל הרכבה). Others maintain that as regards grain, a three-day period is universally accepted as sufficient for the grain to take root (see *Yad Avraham* loc. cit.).

However, such legal time periods are generally considered to run until nightfall of the final day [and do not represent complete twenty-four-hour periods]. Accordingly, it should be impossible for grain to be legally considered to have taken root between the cutting of the grain for the *omer* and its offering, which were both performed on the same day! *Turei Even* (loc. cit.) considers several solutions to this problem, among them the assertion that these time periods represent only general legal assumptions, but plants may in fact be observed to take root sooner. See also *Tos. R' Akiva Eiger* here.

מנחות
י/ח

# אֲבָל לֹא גוֹדְשִׁין. אַנְשֵׁי יְרִיחוֹ קוֹצְרִין בִּרְצוֹן חֲכָמִים וְגוֹדְשִׁין שֶׁלֹּא בִרְצוֹן חֲכָמִים, וְלֹא מִחוּ בְיָדָם חֲכָמִים. קוֹצֵר לַשַּׁחַת וּמַאֲכִיל לַבְּהֵמָה. אָמַר רַבִּי יְהוּדָה: אֵימָתַי? בִּזְמַן שֶׁהִתְחִיל עַד שֶׁלֹּא

**ר׳ עובדיה מברטנורא**

העומר, וכתוב אחר אומר (שם) ראשית קצירכם, דמשמע שתהא ראשית לכל הקצירות, הא כיצד, ממקום שאתה יכול להביא העומר אי אתה קוצר קודם לעומר, ממקום שאי אתה מביא, כגון בית השלחים ובית העמקים שאין מביאין עומר מהן לפי שהן רעות, אתה קוצר מהן קודם לעומר: **אבל לא גודשין.** לעשותן גדיש, דכמה דאפשר לשנויי משנינן: **אנשי יריחו.** בית השלחין הוו להו: **קוצר לשחת.** מותר לקצור לשחת קודם לעומר ומאכיל לבהמתו: **אימתי בזמן שהתחיל.** לקצרה לצורך בהמתו עד שלא הביאה שליש אחרון של גמר בשולה, קוצר אף לאחר שהביאה שליש:

**יד אברהם**

(*Lev.* 23:10): ... כִּי תָבֹאוּ אֶל הָאָרֶץ וּקְצַרְתֶּם אֶת קְצִירָהּ, וַהֲבֵאתֶם אֶת עֹמֶר רֵאשִׁית קְצִירְכֶם אֶל הַכֹּהֵן, *when you come into the land ... and you will reap its harvest, then you shall bring the omer of the first of your harvest to the Kohen*. The first part of the verse implies that the obligation of *omer* applies *after* you begin the harvest; thus it is permitted to harvest grain before the *omer*. On the other hand, the second part of the verse, which calls the *omer* "the *first* of your harvest," teaches that no grain may be harvested before the *omer*. The Oral Tradition teaches the following resolution: Those areas from which the *omer* may be brought may not be reaped before the *omer*; those areas from which the *omer* may not be brought may be reaped before the *omer* (*Gem.* 71a; *Rambam Comm.*; *Rav*). Irrigated fields in the valleys produce grain [of such inferior quality] that the *omer* is invalid if brought from it. Therefore, the prohibition to harvest such grain fields before the *omer* does not apply (*Tos. Yom Tov* from *Tos.* 68a, s.v. קוצרים).[1] Alternatively, the grain of irrigated fields in the valleys is fit expost facto for the *omer*, just like the grain of any irrigated field mentioned above in 8:2. Accordingly, the exception to the Biblical prohibition against reaping before the *omer* applies even to those areas enumerated above in 8:2, whose grains are merely not *preferred* for the *omer* but which are acceptable expost facto. Nevertheless, the Rabbis prohibited reaping those grains before the *omer* [so that one not come to eat that grain before the *omer* — see below, s.v. אבל לא גודשין]. However, in the case of irrigated fields in valleys, the Rabbis allowed the Biblical permit to stand, because the grain of these fields is especially susceptible to damage if not harvested early (*Tos.* loc. cit.).

Other mishnah texts read: קוֹצְרִים בֵּית הַשְּׁלָחִים וְשֶׁבָּעֲמָקִים, *We may reap irrigated fields or those in the valleys*. According to

1. However, an objection to this explanation could be raised that if the grain of this new category of בֵּית הַשְּׁלָחִים שֶׁבָּעֲמָקִים, *irrigated fields in the valleys*, is unfit for the *omer* even expost facto, then why was this not specifically mentioned by the mishnah in 8:2 where such disqualifications are discussed, or anyplace else in the mishnah (ibid.)?

but we may not stack. The people of Jericho reaped with the approval of the Sages and stacked against the Sages' wishes, but the Sages did not issue a protest against them. One may reap unripe grain and feed it to animals. Said R' Yehudah: When? When he began before it

YAD AVRAHAM

this version as well, it is Biblically permitted to harvest before the *omer* the areas whose grain is merely not preferred for the *omer*, which are enumerated above in 8:2. Nevertheless, the Rabbis prohibited the harvesting of those areas except for irrigated fields or fields in valleys, whose grain would spoil if not harvested early. What remains difficult according to this explanation is why the category of "fields in valleys" was omitted from the mishnah's list in 8:2 of fields whose grain is not preferred for the *omer* but acceptable expost facto (ibid.).

.אֲבָל לֹא גוֹדְשִׁין — *but we may not stack.*

It is not permitted to stack the harvested grain in organized piles prior to the reaping of the *omer*, because the stacking is not necessary to forestall damage to the grain. The Sages prohibited unnecessary involvement in processing the grain so that one should not come to eat it before the *omer* is offered (*Rashi, Pesachim* 56a, s.v. וגודשין); it is therefore required that the normal manner of harvesting be varied as much as possible (*Rav*).

This mishnah, which teaches that unnecessary processing of the *chadash* crop before the *omer* is prohibited, does not conflict with the view of R' Yehudah in mishnah 5 that the Sages approved of the full processing of *chadash* before the *omer* [as evidenced by the fact that they approved of the streets of Jerusalem being filled with new flour immediately after the *omer* was offered]. In the case of mishnah 5, the Sages made a special exception to their ban in order to provide for the needs of the people who traveled to Jerusalem for the Festivals (*Tos.* 68a, s.v. אבל). Alternatively, it was permitted in that case in order to beautify the streets of Jerusalem with produce, which is the equivalent of the need to forestall a loss (*Shitah Mekubetzes* to 71b #1).

אַנְשֵׁי יְרִיחוֹ קוֹצְרִין בִּרְצוֹן חֲכָמִים וְגוֹדְשִׁין שֶׁלֹּא בִרְצוֹן חֲכָמִים, וְלֹא מִחוּ בְיָדָם חֲכָמִים. — *The people of Jericho reaped with the approval of the Sages and stacked against the Sages' wishes, but the Sages did not issue a protest against them.*

The people of Jericho owned irrigated fields (*Rav*) [and thus were permitted to harvest their grain before the *omer*. However, they exceeded the limits dictated by the Sages and went as far as to stack the grain prior to the reaping of the *omer*. Nevertheless, the Rabbis did not see fit to pursue the issue and reprimand them].

.קוֹצֵר לְשַׁחַת וּמַאֲכִיל לַבְּהֵמָה — *One may reap unripe grain and feed it to animals.*

It is permitted to reap unripe grain before the reaping of the *omer* in order to feed it to animals as fodder (*Rav*) because harvesting unripe grain for animal feed is not halachically classified as קְצִירָה, *reaping* (*Gem.* 71b; see *Tos.* ad loc., s.v. אימור).

.אָמַר רַבִּי יְהוּדָה: אֵימָתַי? בִּזְמַן שֶׁהִתְחִיל עַד שֶׁלֹּא הֵבִיאָה שְׁלִישׁ — *Said R' Yehudah: When? When he began before it reached a third.*

If one began to reap his grain before

מנחות י/ט

הֲבִיאָה שְׁלִישׁ. רַבִּי שִׁמְעוֹן אוֹמֵר: אַף יִקְצֹר וְיַאֲכִיל אַף מִשֶּׁהֵבִיאָה שְׁלִישׁ.

[ט] **קוֹצְרִין** מִפְּנֵי הַנְּטִיעוֹת, מִפְּנֵי בֵית הָאֵבֶל, מִפְּנֵי בִטּוּל בֵּית הַמִּדְרָשׁ. לֹא

**ר׳ עובדיה מברטנורא**

**רבי שמעון אומר אף יקצור ויאכיל.** יתחיל לקצור ומאכיל לבהמתו משהביאה שליש, דכל לשחת לאו קציר הוא. והלכה כרבי יהודה, שבא לפרש דבריו של תנא קמא: **(ט) קוצרים.** קודם לעומר. **מפני הנטיעות.** שלא יפסידו, לפי שאותה תבואה אינה ראויה לעומר, כדאמרינן בפרק כל הקרבנות (פרק ח משנה ב) אין מביאין לא משדה בית השלחים ולא משדה אילן, ולעיל (משנה ח) אמרינן ממקום שאי אתה מביא אתה קוצר. פירוש אחר, מפני הנטיעות משום כלאים, לפי שפעמים אדם זורע תבואה ואין שם נטיעות, ולאחר זמן עולות שם נטיעות ביניהן מאיליהן, וצריך לקצור הזרעים משום כלאים: **ומפני בית האבל.** שאין להם מקום פנוי לישב לברך ברכת רחבה שאומרים בבית האבל: **ומפני בית המדרש.** שאין מקום לתלמידים לישב. וטעמא דכל הני, משום דקציר מצוה נינהו, והכתוב אומר (ויקרא כג, י) ראשית קצירכם, שיהיה העומר ראשית לקצירכם של רשות ולא ראשית לקציר של מצוה:

**יד אברהם**

רַבִּי שִׁמְעוֹן אוֹמֵר: אַף יִקְצֹר וְיַאֲכִיל אַף מִשֶּׁהֵבִיאָה שְׁלִישׁ. — *R' Shimon says: He may reap and feed [it] even after it has reached a third.*

According to R' Shimon, cutting any unripe grain [for fodder] is not considered reaping [and is therefore not in the category of reaping prohibited prior to the *omer*]. Therefore, he may begin reaping even after the grain has reached a third (*Rav*).

The halachah follows the view of R' Yehudah, who is not disagreeing with the *Tanna Kamma* but merely elaborating upon his view (*Rav; Rambam Comm.*).

it reached the last third of its growth, he may continue to do so even after it reaches that point (*Rav; Rambam Comm.*). Others interpret this to refer to the first third of its growth (see *Meleches Shlomo; Rashash*). Once the grain has reached that point he may no longer begin reaping, but he may continue to reap if he began beforehand.

Although the grain is by then already fit for human consumption and thus subject to the prohibition of *chadash* prior to the *omer*, it may be fed to animals because *chadash* is prohibited only for eating, not for benefit (*Pesachim* 23a; *Tos.* ad loc., s.v. קוצר; *Tos.* 71b, s.v. אימור).

## 9.

קוֹצְרִין מִפְּנֵי הַנְּטִיעוֹת, — *We may reap for the benefit of the saplings,*

It is permitted to reap prior to the reaping of the *omer* grain which grows among the saplings, in order to prevent the damage to the saplings which will result if the grain is left there too long. Since the grain which grows is of inferior quality and not preferred for the *omer* [see 8:2], there is no Biblical prohibition against harvesting it before the *omer* [see

reached a third. R' Shimon says: He may reap and feed [it] even after it has reached a third.

**9.** We may reap for the benefit of the saplings, for a place of mourning, [and] in order to [avoid] a cessation of study. He may not

### YAD AVRAHAM

mishnah 8]. In this case, the Rabbis did not enact a prohibition against harvesting it to safeguard against one coming to eat it, because such an enactment would cause damage to the saplings (*Rav; Rashi*).

Alternatively, the mishnah is referring to a situation in which one planted grain in an area in which there were no saplings visible, but saplings subsequently grew there. The mixed planting in such a case would constitute *kilayim* — the prohibited planting of different species in the same place — and the grain must therefore be removed (ibid.; see *Rambam, Hil. Kilayim* 1:6, and *Ravad, Kesef Mishneh, Radbaz*, ad loc.). Such reaping is considered a reaping for *mitzvah* purposes, which is not included in the Biblical prohibition of reaping before the *omer* [see below, s.v. מפני בטול] (*Rashi* 72a, s.v. מ״ט).

**מִפְּנֵי בֵית הָאֵבֶל,** — *for a place*[1] *of mourning,*

The first meal served to a mourner [see *Moed Katan* 27b] was arranged in a broad, open area, where the mourner's blessing would be recited[2] (*Rashi* to *Kesubos* 8b, s.v. ברחבה). If there is no suitable area available with enough space to accommodate the number of people in attendance, it is permitted to reap a grain field to make the necessary room even before the *omer* has been cut [for reasons that will be explained below] (*Rav; Rashi*).

**מִפְּנֵי בִטּוּל בֵּית הַמִּדְרָשׁ.** — *[and] in order to [avoid] a cessation of study.*[3]

If there is not sufficient place for those who are studying Torah to sit, it is permitted to reap grain prior to the *omer* to make room for them (*Rav*).

The reason for the exceptions in the latter two cases is that the prohibition against reaping before the *omer* is implied by the Torah's reference to the *omer* as רֵאשִׁית קְצִירְכֶם, *the first of your harvests* (*Lev.* 23:10); the phrase "*your* harvests" indicates that it is harvesting for private benefit which may not precede that of the *omer*, but that which is done for the sake of a *mitzvah* is not included in the prohibition (*Rav* from *Gem.* 72a).

1. The word בַּיִת, which usually means "house," is sometimes used in the sense of "place" or "area" (*Tif. Yis.*) or "assemblage" or "entourage" (*Tos. Yom Tov*).

2. This blessing is known as בִּרְכַּת אֲבֵלִים, *mourners' blessing*, or בִּרְכַּת רְחָבָה, *blessing [recited in] the broad area* (*Megillah* 23b). Its formulation was subject to various customs (see *Tur, Yoreh Deah* 376) and it is no longer the custom to recite it (ibid.).

3. בֵּית הַמִּדְרָשׁ literally means *the House of Study*. Many mishnah texts, however, do not contain the word בֵּית here, and read simply: מִפְּנֵי בִטּוּל הַמִּדְרָשׁ (see *Tos. Yom Tov; Shinnuyei Nuschaos*).

יַעֲשֶׂה אוֹתָן כְּרִיכוֹת; אֲבָל מַנִּיחָן צְבָתִים. מִצְוַת הָעֹמֶר לָבֹא מִן הַקָּמָה; לֹא מָצָא, יָבִיא מִן הָעֳמָרִים. מִצְוָתוֹ לָבֹא מִן הַלַּח; לֹא מָצָא, יָבִיא מִן הַיָּבֵשׁ. מִצְוָתוֹ לִקְצוֹר בַּלַּיְלָה; נִקְצַר בַּיּוֹם, כָּשֵׁר. וְדוֹחֶה אֶת הַשַּׁבָּת.

**ר׳ עובדיה מברטנורא**

**כריכות.** אלומות קשורות: **צבתים.** אגודות בלא קשור. פירוש אחר, כריכות אלומות גדולות, צבתים אגודות קטנות: **מן הקמה.** שיהא קוצר לשמו: **לא מצא.** שכבר נקצר הכל: **מן הלח.** דכתיב (ויקרא ב, יד) כרמל, רך ומל: **לקצור בלילה.** כדילפינן בריש פרקין (משנה ג) מדכתיב (דברים טז, ט) מהחל חרמש בקמה תחל לספור, משעה שאתה מונה אתה קוצר, והספירה צריכה להיות בלילה דכתיב (ויקרא כג, טו) שבע שבתות תמימות:

**יד אברהם**

לֹא יַעֲשֶׂה אוֹתָן כְּרִיכוֹת; — *He may not make them into bundles;*

[I.e., even in situations in which the reaping is permitted before the *omer*, he may nonetheless not perform the reaping in its ordinary manner.] He may not tie the cut grain into bundles (*Rav; Rashi; Rambam Comm.*), which is the usual procedure when preparing the grain for threshing (*Tif. Yis.*).

אֲבָל מַנִּיחָן צְבָתִים. — *rather, he leaves them in heaps.*

He must leave them instead in the form of untied piles (*Tif. Yis.*). This restriction was enacted in order to minimize as much as possible one's involvement with the harvesting process prior to the *omer*-offering (*Gem.* 72a) [so that one not come to inadvertently eat from the still forbidden grain]. Since harvesting even in this fashion is sufficient to clear the fields for the purposes of Torah study or the place of mourning, further involvement with the grain was prohibited.

Alternatively, the mishnah means that he may not tie them into large bundles but rather into small sheaves (*Rav* citing יֵשׁ מְפָרְשִׁים). The rationale for this is that although sheaving in this fashion is more time consuming, the constant interruptionof tying small bundles will serve as a reminder not to eat the grain (*Tif. Yis., Boaz*). *Tos.* (72a s.v. כריכות), however, reject this interpretation on the basis of the *Gemara* in *Bava Metzia* 22b which indicates clearly that כְּרִיכוֹת refers to *small* bundles.

מִצְוַת הָעֹמֶר לָבֹא מִן הַקָּמָה; — *The commandment of the omer is that it should come from standing grain;*

In order to properly fulfill the *mitzvah* of *omer*, the *omer* should be brought from standing grain, i.e., the grain should be reaped specifically for the *omer*-offering (*Rav*). This is indicated in the verse (*Deut.* 16:9) which stipulates that the counting of the *omer* begins מֵהָחֵל חֶרְמֵשׁ בַּקָּמָה, *from when the sickle begins [to reap] amidst the standing grain* (*Rashi* to 72a).

לֹא מָצָא, יָבִיא מִן הָעֳמָרִים. — *if he did not find, he may bring from the sheaves.*

If all the grain was already harvested without specific *omer* designation, the *omer* may be brought from already harvested grain (*Rav*).

10 make them into bundles; rather, he leaves them in
9 heaps. The commandment of the *omer* is that it should come from standing grain; if he did not find, he may bring from the sheaves. Its commandment is that it come from the fresh; if he did not find, he may bring from the dry. Its commandment is that it be reaped by night; if it is reaped by day it is valid. And it overrides the Sabbath.

### YAD AVRAHAM

מִצְוָתוֹ לָבֹא מִן הַלַּח; לֹא מָצָא, יָבִיא מִן הַיָּבֵשׁ. — *Its commandment is that it come from the fresh; if he did not find, he may bring from the dry.*

In order to properly fulfill the *mitzvah*, grain used for the *omer* should be fresh and moist. This is indicated by the Torah's reference to the *omer* grain as כַּרְמֶל (*Lev.* 2:14), a word which the *Gemara* (66b) interprets as denoting רַךְ וּמָל, *tender and easy to be shelled*, i.e., fresh grain (*Rav*). However, if such grain is unavailable, the *omer* may be brought from grain that has already dried out.

מִצְוָתוֹ לִקְצוֹר בַּלַּיְלָה; — *Its commandment is that it be reaped by night;*

The Torah describes the counting of the *omer* as beginning from the time of the reaping of the grain for the *omer* [see above, s.v. מצות]. Since the Torah requires שֶׁבַע שַׁבָּתוֹת תְּמִימֹת, *seven full weeks* (*Lev.* 23:15), it is necessary to begin the counting on the eve of the first of the forty-nine days. Therefore, it is evident that the reaping of the *omer* should also take place at that time (*Rav* from *Gem.* 66a).

נִקְצַר בַּיּוֹם, כָּשֵׁר. — *if it is reaped by day, it is valid.*

[However, if the *omer* was not reaped on the night of the sixteenth, it may be reaped the following day.]

The *Gemara* (72a) explains that our mishnah's ruling is actually the subject of Tannaitic dispute. R' Elazar ben R' Shimon (cited in a *Baraisa*) contends that the *omer* is invalid if the grain is not reaped on that night. His view is reflected in the mishnah in *Megillah* (2:6) which lists the reaping of the *omer* as one of the procedures whose time is at night, and concludes: זֶה הַכְּלָל: דָּבָר שֶׁמִּצְוָתוֹ בַּיּוֹם כָּשֵׁר כָּל הַיּוֹם; דָּבָר שֶׁמִּצְוָתוֹ בַּלַּיְלָה כָּשֵׁר כָּל הַלַּיְלָה, *This is the general rule: Any procedure which is to be done by day may be performed throughout the day; any procedure which is to be done at night may be performed throughout the night*. The mishnah's comparison of the two time periods suggests that just as a *mitzvah* which is to be done during the day (e.g., *shofar, lulav*) cannot be done at night, so too a *mitzvah* which is performed at night (such as cutting the *omer*) cannot be done by day. Our mishnah's statement to the contrary reflects the view of Rabbi (R' Yehudah HaNasi) who disagrees with R' Elazar ben R' Shimon. Some authorities rule in accordance with the mishnah in *Megillah* that the *omer* may not be reaped by day (*Tos.* 72a, s.v. הא). *Rambam* (*Hil. Temidin U'Mussafin* 7:7), however, rules in accordance with our mishnah, that if the *omer* was reaped by day, it is valid.

וְדוֹחֶה אֶת הַשַּׁבָּת. — *And it overrides the Sabbath.*

The offering of the *omer* [which involves *melachah* that is prohibited on the Sabbath] is performed even if the

second day of Pesach is the Sabbath. [In this regard, the *omer* is no different from any other sacrifice that must be brought at a specific time, whose offering is performed even when that time coincides with the Sabbath.] However, the reaping of the *omer* [which, according to our mishnah, is valid even when done before Pesach — see below] does not have this dispensation and it may not be done on the Sabbath (*Tos. Yom Tov* from *Gem.* 72b).

The flow of the mishnah would certainly seem to indicate that it is the *reaping* of the *omer* which is under discussion, not the *offering* of the *omer* as stated above. However, in view of the *Tanna's* previously stated opinion that the reaping can, if necessary, be done during the day, we are forced to conclude that the reaping does not override the Sabbath. This is because of the general principle that only those *mitzvos* which *must* be performed on that day (e.g., *milah*) override the Sabbath. A *mitzvah* which can be performed (even as a last resort) at another time cannot override the Sabbath (*Shabbos* 19:1). Since in our *Tanna's* view, the *omer* is valid if reaped by day, the Torah's assignment of a specific time for the *omer's* reaping [i.e., the night of the sixteenth — see above, s.v. מצותו לקצור] is not essential to the *omer's* validity, and it is valid if cut before *Yom Tov* as well. Therefore, reaping the *omer*, according to our *Tanna*, cannot override the Sabbath. Rather, when the sixteenth of Nissan falls on the Sabbath, the *omer* must be reaped before *Yom Tov* (see *Gem.* 72a; *Rashi*, s.v. ואי ס״ד).

The statement in the first mishnah of this chapter that the *omer* is reaped on the Sabbath is thus in accord with the opinion of R' Eliezer ben R' Shimon cited above, that the *omer* is invalid if not reaped on the night of the sixteenth. Reaping the *omer* thus has a specific time mandated by the Torah, and must be performed even if that time coincides with the Sabbath (*Gem.* 72b).

There is considerable discussion in Rabbinic literature concerning reconciling *Rambam's* ruling (*Hil. Temidin U'Mussafin* 7:6) that the reaping of the *omer* overrides the Sabbath with his ruling (ibid. 7) that the *omer* which was reaped during the day is valid. According to the *Gemara* cited above, these two positions are in conflict, for if the *omer* can be reaped by day it cannot override the Sabbath.

One possible resolution is suggested by *Or Sameach* (ad loc.), who asserts that *Yerushalmi* (*Megillah* 2:9) reconciles our mishnah with that of *Megillah* 2:6 [see above, s.v. נקצר] in a manner different from that of our *Gemara*: The fact that the ideal *mitzvah* is fulfilled when the *omer* is reaped by night is sufficient basis for it to be permitted on the Sabbath, despite the fact that it is valid as a last resort if done at another time [cf. *Gemara* 72a-b]. *Or Sameach* suggests that *Rambam* follows *Yerushalmi's* resolution, which is more compatible with the simple reading of the mishnah, and there is thus no contradiction between *Rambam's* ruling that the *omer* may be reaped on the Sabbath and that in which he validates the *omer* even if it was reaped by day (cf. *Lechem Mishneh* ad loc.; *Tif. Yis.*; *Zevach Todah*).

# פרק אחד עשר
# Chapter Eleven

[א] **שְׁתֵּי** הַלֶּחֶם נִלּוֹשׁוֹת אַחַת אַחַת וְנֶאֱפוֹת אַחַת אַחַת. לֶחֶם הַפָּנִים נִלּוֹשׁ אֶחָד אֶחָד וְנֶאֱפֶה שְׁנַיִם שְׁנַיִם. וּבְטְפוּס הָיָה עוֹשֶׂה אוֹתָן, וּכְשֶׁהוּא רָדָן, נוֹתְנָן בִּטְפוּס, כְּדֵי שֶׁלֹּא יִתְקַלְקְלוּ.

**ר׳ עובדיה מברטנורא**

**פרק אחד עשר – שתי הלחם** (א) **שתי הלחם** [כו׳] **לחם הפנים נילוש אחד אחד.** דכתיב ביה (ויקרא כד, ה) שני עשרונים יהיה החלה האחת, מלמד שנלושות אחת אחת. ומנין שאפייתן שתים שתים, תלמוד לומר (שם שם, ו) ושמת אותם, שימה ראשונה שאתה עושה מהם דהיינו בתנור תהא בלשון אותם, דמשמע שהיה נותן שנים בשני דפוסים יחד בתנור. יכול אף שתי הלחם כן, תלמוד לומר ושמת אותם, שהיה לו לומר ושמתם, מה תלמוד לומר ושמת אותם, אותם אתה נותן שנים שנים בתנור, ואין אתה נותן שתי הלחם שנים שנים אלא אחד אחד: **ובטפוס.** כמו דפוס, פורמ״א בלע״ז, כמין תיבה שנטל כסויה ושתי דפנותיה זו כנגד זו, כך הלחם היו לו שתי דפנות ושולים רחבים ומתקן הבצק בתוך הדפוס שיהא עשוי כעין הדפוס: **וכשהוא רודה.** אותן מן התנור: **נותנן בדפוס. כדי שלא יתקלקלו.** וישברו. נמצא שלשה דפוסים הן, אחד כשהיא בצק, ואחד היה לה בתנור כשהיא נאפית, ואחד כשהוא רדה מן התנור נותנה בדפוס כדי שלא תתקלקל:

**יד אברהם**

## 1.

This chapter deals with the preparation and arrangement of the שְׁתֵּי הַלֶּחֶם, *two loaves* of Shavuos, and the loaves of the לֶחֶם הַפָּנִים, *lechem hapanim*, the twelve loaves placed each week on the golden *shulchan* which stands in the Holy.

שְׁתֵּי הַלֶּחֶם — *The shtei halechem*

On the Festival of Shavuos, a communal offering of bread is brought. The two loaves of this offering are known as the *shtei halechem* [literally, *two breads*]. In a departure from other flour offerings, these are baked as leavened bread and are therefore חָמֵץ, *chametz*. These are not offered on the Altar; indeed no *chametz* offering is ever permitted on the Altar (*Lev.* 2:11). Rather, they are accompanied by two communal *shelamim* lambs [כִּבְשֵׂי עֲצֶרֶת], as well as two bulls, a he-goat, and seven lambs, all of them *olah-offering*s (see *Lev.* 23:17-19). The two loaves are waved together with the two *shelamim* lambs, and upon the completion of the offering of the lambs, the breads are eaten by the *Kohanim* (see above, mishnah 4:3).

נִלּוֹשׁוֹת אַחַת אַחַת וְנֶאֱפוֹת אַחַת אַחַת. — *are kneaded one by one and baked one by one.*

Each loaf is made from an *issaron* of fine flour. The *shtei halechem* cannot be made together in one dough but must each be kneaded separately. Similarly, they must each be baked separately in the oven. This is derived from Biblical exegesis (*Rav* from *Gem.* 94a).

The mishnah discusses the *shtei halechem* prior to the *lechem hapanim* (see below) despite the fact that the latter appears first in the Torah, because its laws are simpler and dealt with more quickly (*Likkutei Halachos*).

11
1 **1.** The *shtei halechem* are kneaded one by one and baked one by one. The *lechem hapanim* are kneaded one by one but are baked two by two. One would make them in a mold, and when he removed them, he placed them in a mold so that they should not be damaged.

### YAD AVRAHAM

לֶחֶם הַפָּנִים — *The lechem hapanim*

[These are the twelve loaves placed each Shabbos on the *shulchan* (table) in the קֹדֶשׁ, *Holy*, of the Temple Sanctuary. They remain there throughout the week and are removed the following Shabbos, when they are replaced by new breads. The breads are accompanied on the *shulchan* by two spoonfuls of *levonah*; when the breads are removed, their *levonah* is taken and burnt on the Altar in the Courtyard, and the *lechem hapanim* is then eaten by the *Kohanim*. These breads were not *chametz* (*see mishnah* 5:1).]

As has been previously noted, the term לֶחֶם, *bread*, is used by the Torah and the Mishnah to refer to both leavened and unleavened (*matzah*) loaves.

נִלוֹשׁ אֶחָד אֶחָד וְנֶאֱפֶה שְׁנַיִם שְׁנַיִם. — *are kneaded one by one but are baked two by two.*

The twelve loaves of the *lechem hapanim* — each consisting of two *essronim* of flour — must each be kneaded separately, but they are baked in the oven in pairs, as derived from Scripture (*Rav* from *Gem.* ibid.).

וּבִטְפוּס הָיָה עוֹשֶׂה אוֹתָן, — *One would make them in a mold,*

The dough is prepared for baking in a special mold, with sides but no top, in order to give the loaves the desired shape (*Rav*; see below, mishnah 5).

וּכְשֶׁהוּא רָדָן, נוֹתְנָן בִּטְפוּס, כְּדֵי שֶׁלֹּא יִתְקַלְקְלוּ. — *and when he removed them, he placed them in a mold so that they should not be damaged.*

When the *Kohen* baking the bread would remove it from the oven, he would place it in a mold again, so that it would not be vulnerable to being broken (*Rav*). A separate mold was used, rather than the mold in which it had been prepared, because the loaf would expand in baking and would no longer fit into the original mold (*Gem.* 94a).

The *Gemara* (ibid.) states that in addition to the two molds described in the mishnah, there was another within the oven itself in which the breads baked.

This follows the interpretation of *Rav*, *Rashi*, and *Rambam* in his *Commentary*. *Tosafos* (94a, s.v. ובדפוס) consider the possibility that the bread was shaped around the molds, rather than within them, and then placed in the oven still wrapped around the mold. [As mishnah 5 will explain, the *lechem hapanim* were U shaped; see below.] The basis for this is that it would otherwise not be possible for them to expand in the oven. However, *Rambam* deals with this point and explains that the loaves were baked in the oven in a mold until they filled the space of the mold — i.e., the mold in the oven was larger than the first one and left room for the bread's expansion. *Tos. Yom Tov* infers from *Rav's* wording that the loaf was first prepared within a mold but was then removed from there and baked around the mold in the oven.

[ב] **אֶחָד** שְׁתֵּי הַלֶּחֶם וְאֶחָד לֶחֶם הַפָּנִים, לִישָׁתָן וַעֲרִיכָתָן בַּחוּץ, וַאֲפִיָּתָן בִּפְנִים; וְאֵינָן דּוֹחוֹת אֶת הַשַּׁבָּת.

**ר' עובדיה מברטנורא**

(ב) **לישתן ועריכתן בחוץ ואפייתן בפנים.** לא אתברירא טעמא דהא מלתא בגמרא אמאי לישתן ועריכתן בחוץ ואפייתן בפנים: **ואינן דוחות את השבת.** אפייתן:

**יד אברהם**

## 2.

אֶחָד שְׁתֵּי הַלֶּחֶם וְאֶחָד לֶחֶם הַפָּנִים, לִישָׁתָן וַעֲרִיכָתָן בַּחוּץ, — *Both the shtei halechem and the lechem hapanim are kneaded and shaped outside [the Temple Courtyard],*

[The *shtei halechem* (two loaves of Shavuos) and the weekly *lechem hapanim* may both be kneaded into a dough and shaped into their proper forms outside the Temple Courtyard. At this stage of their preparation they are not yet sanctified as offerings and there is therefore no reason to insist on their remaining within the Courtyard.]

This follows the view of R' Akiva in mishnah 9:5 that the utensils used in the Temple as dry measures, such as the *issaron*, were not consecrated as *klei shareis* (see comm. there). Therefore, the flour measured out in them for making the *shtei halechem* and the *lechem hapanim* was not sanctified by being placed in a *kli shareis*, and it may thus be removed from the Temple Courtyard (*Gem.* 95b). According to those who maintain that the dry measures were consecrated, the flour would become sanctified in them and would then be subject to the disqualification of יוֹצֵא, *removal from the permitted confines*. It could then not be kneaded outside the Courtyard (*Rashi*).

*Tosafos* (95b, s.v. לִישָׁתוֹ) dispute this and contend that sanctification in a *kli shareis* is not sufficient to render a substance subject to the disqualification of removal from its confines.[1] Nonetheless, it is considered unbecoming to take out from the Courtyard something already sanctified as an offering. Therefore, if the dry measures were consecrated, the mishnah would have required the kneading to take place in the Courtyard.

וַאֲפִיָּתָן בִּפְנִים; — *and are baked within [it];*

1. This dispute between *Rashi* and *Tosafos* is not limited to the *shtei halechem* and *lechem hapanim* of our mishnah, but relates to all *menachos*. In *Tosafos'* view, sanctification in a *kli shareis* prior to the beginning of the *avodah* renders the substance subject only to the disqualifications of לִינָה, *being left overnight*, and טֻמְאָה, *tumah contamination* (*Me'ilah* 2:8), but it is not until the *avodah* actually begins (with *kemitzah* in the case of a *minchah*) that the substance becomes subject to the disqualification of יוֹצֵא , *removal from its permitted confines* (see *Tos.* 9a, s.v. ריש לקיש ; and *Zevachim* 20b, s.v. יציאה ). [Although *Tosafos* suggest that *menachos* that have no *avodah* to permit them because they are burnt in their entirety on the Altar do become subject to the disqualification of *removal* as soon as they are sanctified in a *kli shareis* (ibid.), this would not apply to the *lechem hapanim* and *shtei halechem*. These two offerings have an *avodah* to permit them — the *shtei halechem*, the slaughter of the two *shelamim* lambs (see above, mishnah 7:3), and the *lechem hapanim*, the burning of the spoonfuls of *levonah*.]

11
2

**2.** Both the *shtei halechem* and the *lechem hapanim* are kneaded and shaped outside [the Temple Courtyard], and are baked within [it]; and they do not override the Sabbath.

YAD AVRAHAM

They must be baked within the Courtyard because the oven in which offering loaves are baked is consecrated and the loaves therefore become sanctified in the oven (*Gem.* ibid.).

Actually, it would still be possible to bake outside the Temple by using an oven that does not belong to the Temple. What the *Gemara* means is that since the oven is consecrated and has the power to sanctify, the bread is supposed to be sanctified at that point by being baked in a consecrated oven. Since *klei shareis* can sanctify only inside the Courtyard (*Zevachim* 9:7), the loaves must be baked inside (*Mishneh LaMelech* to *Temidin U'Mussafin* 5:7; see *Me'ilah* 2:7). Similarly, according to the opinion that the utensils used as dry measures are consecrated, it is a *mitzvah* to use consecrated measuring utensils in order to sanctify the flour immediately (*Chazon Ish* 24:10).

The *Gemara* (95b) points out that this seems inconsistent with the mishnah's previous ruling that utensils used for dry substances were not consecrated. The *Gemara* concludes that a distinction must be drawn between the measures, which were not consecrated, and the ovens, which were consecrated.

*Rambam* (*Hil. Temidin U'Mussafin 5:7*) rules in accordance with this mishnah, that the loaves may be kneaded outside the Courtyard. However, he also rules (*Klei HaMikdash* 1:19) that the dry measures were consecrated, which our *Gemara* states is incompatible with the first ruling. However, *Rambam* (*Comm.*, followed by *Rav*) says explicitly that the reason for the mishnah's distinction between kneading and baking is unknown. It is apparent that *Rambam* did not have in his version of this *Gemara* the conclusion that the dry measures were not consecrated and that a distinction is to be drawn between the measures and the ovens. According to *Rambam's* version of the text, the *Gemara* leaves unresolved the reason for the mishnah's distinction between making the dough and baking it. Apparently, the *Gemara* did not wish to assume that this anonymous mishnah is incompatible with the view of the *Tanna Kamma* of mishnah 9:5 who holds that the dry measures were not consecrated. Accordingly, *Rambam* follows the ruling of our mishnah and permits making the dough outside the Courtyard even though he accepts the view of the *Tanna Kamma* of mishnah 9:5 that the dry measures were consecrated (*Tos. Yom Tov*). [Even according to our texts, the *Gemara* prefaces its explanation with the word "perhaps." *Rambam* may have taken this as an indication that the *Gemara* is not really satisfied with this solution but offers it merely in response to the questioner's statement there that the problem is compelling (*Meleches Shlomo, Mahariach*).]

.וְאֵינָן דּוֹחוֹת אֶת הַשַּׁבָּת — *and they do not override the Sabbath.*

I.e., these loaves may not be baked on Shabbos (*Rav*) [because of the *melachah* involved].

The requirement to offer the Sabbath and Festival offerings does override the prohibition of doing *melachah* (forbidden labor) on the Sabbath for those aspects of the offering which cannot be done before the Sabbath. Since the mishnah prohibits baking them on the Sabbath, it is evident that the mishnah is of the opinion that

רַבִּי יְהוּדָה אוֹמֵר: כָּל מַעֲשֵׂיהֶם בִּפְנִים. רַבִּי שִׁמְעוֹן אוֹמֵר: לְעוֹלָם הֱוֵי רָגִיל לוֹמַר שְׁתֵּי הַלֶּחֶם וְלֶחֶם הַפָּנִים כְּשֵׁרוֹת בָּעֲזָרָה וּכְשֵׁרוֹת בְּבֵית פָּאגֵי.

[ג] **חֲבִתֵּי** כֹּהֵן גָּדוֹל, לִישָׁתָן וַעֲרִיכָתָן וַאֲפִיָּתָן

**ר' עובדיה מברטנורא**

**וכשרות בבית פאגי.** רמב"ם אומר שהוא מקום סמוך להר הבית מחוץ, ששם היו אופים המנחות, מלשון פת בג המלך. ואין הלכה אלא כדברי תנא קמא: (ג) **חביתי כהן גדול לישתן ועריכתן בפנים.** לדברי הכל, שאותו חצי עשרון שחולק בו עשרונו של כהן גדול נמשח ונתקדש ומקדש את המנחה:

**יד אברהם**

these loaves can be baked on Friday and then be used the next day. This, however, is inconsistent with the mishnah's previous ruling that the loaves are sanctified in the oven as soon as they are baked. Once something is sanctified, it is disqualified by being left overnight and it cannot be used the next day (*Gemara* 95a).[1] It must therefore be assumed that these two rulings were authored by two different *Tannaim* who are in dispute over this matter (*Tos.* 95b, s.v. אלא). According to the *Tanna* who holds the view that the oven was consecrated, the *shtei halechem* [and *lechem hapanim*] were indeed baked on Shabbos (*Tos.* to *Me'ilah* 8a, s.v. קרמו פניה; cited by *Tos. Yom Tov* ibid. 2:6).

As noted above, *Rambam* rules that these breads must be baked in the Courtyard. Nevertheless, he rules (*Temidin U'Mussafin* 5:10) that their baking does not override the Shabbos, and that they must therefore be baked before Shabbos. Although the *Gemara* points out that these two rulings are inconsistent with each other, *Rambam's* view is that since the *Gemara* does not resolve the inconsistency, nor does it explicitly say that the two rulings are the opinions of two different *Tannaim*, both rulings must be accepted as halachah, despite our inability to explain the matter (*Tos. Yom Tov*). These rulings may have been a tradition received by the Sages, possibly even an oral halachah received by Moses at Sinai, and they are therefore incontestable despite their apparent inconsistency (*Sfas Emes*).

Some suggest that this means that the oven in the Temple only partially consecrates the *lechem hapanim* [and *shtei halechem*], so that while it is necessary to bake them inside, they are not yet sanctified to the extent of being disqualified by being left overnight (*Lechem Mishneh* ibid:7). As *Chazon Ish* (24:10) explains this, the oven sanctifies the breads only to the extent of making them susceptible to disqualification by *tumah*, but they do not become subject to the disqualification of being left overnight until they are placed on the *shulchan* (in the case of the *lechem hapanim*).[2] Nevertheless, there is an obligation to bake them inside the Courtyard in a consecrated oven so that they at least

1. In the case of the *lechem hapanim*, the disqualification is only if they are held overnight before being arranged on the *shulchan*, where they remain for an entire week.

2. According to this explanation, the *shtei halechem* would become subject to the disqualification of being left overnight only when the כִּבְשֵׂי עֲצֶרֶת, *Shavuos lambs offering*, are slaughtered.

R' Yehudah says: All their procedures are [performed] within [the Courtyard]. R' Shimon says: Always be accustomed to say that the *shtei halechem* and the *lechem hapanim* are valid [both] in the Courtyard and in Beis Paggi.

**3.** The *chavitin* of the *Kohen Gadol* are kneaded, shaped, and baked within [the Courtyard];

YAD AVRAHAM

become sanctified in regard to *tumah*. Since they do not become sanctified in respect to the disqualification of being left overnight, they can be baked before the Sabbath, and their baking therefore does not override the Sabbath even according to the opinion that the oven is sanctified.

.רַבִּי יְהוּדָה אוֹמֵר: כָּל מַעֲשֵׂיהֶם בִּפְנִים — *R' Yehudah says: All their procedures are [performed] within [the Courtyard].*

R' Yehudah had a tradition from his teachers that both the dry measures and the oven sanctify their contents, so that they cannot be removed from the Courtyard (*Tos.Yom Tov* from *Gem. 96a*; *Rashi*). [Thus, all of the procedures discussed above must be done within the Courtyard.]

רַבִּי שִׁמְעוֹן אוֹמֵר: לְעוֹלָם הֱוֵי רָגִיל לוֹמַר שְׁתֵּי הַלֶּחֶם וְלֶחֶם הַפָּנִים כְּשֵׁרוֹת בָּעֲזָרָה וּכְשֵׁרוֹת בְּבֵית פָּאגִי. — *R' Shimon says: Always be accustomed to say that the shtei halechem and the lechem hapanim are valid [both] in the Courtyard and in Beis Paggi.*

[R' Shimon contends that neither the measures nor the oven sanctify, and it is therefore permissible to make the dough as well as bake it outside the Courtyard in the Beis Paggi.]

Beis Paggi was an area outside the Temple Mount in which they used to bake the *menachos* (*Rav; Rambam Comm.;* see comm. to 7:3). The baking is not restricted to this one place, but may actually take place anywhere in the city (*Rashi*).

R' Shimon's view is based on a tradition he received from his teacher and not on Scriptural exegesis (*Gem.* 96a). For this reason he would exhort others to accustom themselves to it, so that it not be forgotten (*Tif. Yis.*).

3.

,חֲבִתֵּי כֹהֵן גָּדוֹל — *The chavitin of the Kohen Gadol*

This refers to the twelve loaves of the *minchas chavitin* which the *Kohen Gadol* brought as an offering every day, half in the morning and half in the evening (see 4:5).

;לִישָׁתָן וַעֲרִיכָתָן וַאֲפִיָּתָן בִּפְנִים — *are kneaded, shaped, and baked within [the Courtyard];*

This *minchah* was prepared within the Temple Courtyard, because all agree that the half-*issaron* measure which was used for measuring this offering (see 9:1) was consecrated (*Rav; Rashi*). Although some *Tannaim* in the previous mishnah maintain that the general *issaron* measure was not consecrated [for which reason they allowed the *lechem hapanim* to be

בִּפְנִים; וְדוֹחוֹת אֶת הַשַּׁבָּת. טְחוּנָן וְהֶרְקֵדָן אֵינָן דּוֹחוֹת אֶת הַשַּׁבָּת. כְּלָל אָמַר רַבִּי עֲקִיבָא: כָּל מְלָאכָה שֶׁאֶפְשָׁר לָהּ לֵעָשׂוֹת מֵעֶרֶב שַׁבָּת, אֵינָהּ דּוֹחָה אֶת הַשַּׁבָּת; וְשֶׁאִי אֶפְשָׁר לָהּ לֵעָשׂוֹת מֵעֶרֶב שַׁבָּת, דּוֹחָה אֶת הַשַּׁבָּת.

[ד] **כָּל** הַמְּנָחוֹת יֵשׁ בָּהֶן מַעֲשֵׂה כְלִי בִּפְנִים, וְאֵין בָּהֶן מַעֲשֵׂה כְלִי בַּחוּץ.

ר׳ עובדיה מברטנורא

**ודוחות את השבת.** לפי שאי אפשר לעשות לישתו ועריכתו ואפייתו מאתמול, דכיון דמקדשה בכלי מפסלה בלינה: (ד) **יש בהן מעשה כלי בפנים.** במלאכתן שנעשה בהן בפנים טעונים כלי, לאפוקי על גבי טבלא, ובמלאכתן שנעשית בחוץ, כגון לישתו ועריכתו של לחם הפנים, אינו טעון כלי:

יד אברהם

kneaded outside the Courtyard], this is because the *issaron* must be used by everyone bringing a *minchah*, and there is concern that someone may then take [the flour] out of the Courtyard. The half-*issaron*, however, is used exclusively by the *Kohen Gadol* who can be relied upon to act properly (*Rashi* 96a, s.v. חביתי).

*Tosafos* dispute the logic of this distinction and contend (in one approach) that if the full *issaron* was not consecrated neither was the half-*issaron*. However, even if the measures for dry substances are not consecrated (and the flour is therefore not sanctified), the *chavitin* can still not be kneaded in unconsecrated vessels. This is because the *chavitin* are made with oil, and the oil must first be measured in a liquid measure to insure that the proper amount is used. Liquid measures were certainly consecrated according to all opinions (see mishnah 9:5); consequently, the oil added to the *chavitin* is sanctified oil. Since it would be inappropriate to take sanctified matter and put it in an unconsecrated vessel, the dough had to be made in a consecrated utensil within the Courtyard.[1] *Lechem hapanim* and *shtei halechem*, however, contain no oil. Therefore, if the vessels used to measure their flour were not consecrated, there is no reason to require the preparation of their dough in a consecrated vessel. Thus, they can be kneaded outside the Courtyard as well.

Accordingly, this distinction is not limited to the *minchas chavitin* but applies to any *minchah* which is made with oil. The mishnah cites this offering specifically because it contrasts with the *shtei halechem* and *lechem hapanim* in regard to both this law and issue of overriding the Sabbath (*Tos.* 95b, s.v. ומאי).

וְדוֹחוֹת אֶת הַשַּׁבָּת. — *and they override the Sabbath.*

The *chavitin* of Shabbos are baked on Shabbos (*Rav*). [Since the dough has been sanctified in a *kli shareis* during its kneading, if it were baked on Friday, it would become invalidated by

1. The *Gemara* (75a) cites a *Baraisa* in which there is a dispute whether the oil is added before or after the dough is made. Even according to the latter opinion, the addition of the oil takes place in the same vessel in which the dough is prepared. Thus, the vessel must be a consecrated one (*Tos.*).

and they override the Sabbath. Their grinding and sifting do not override the Sabbath. R' Akiva stated a rule: Any labor which can be done prior to the Sabbath does not override the Sabbath; whereas one which cannot be done prior to the Sabbath overrides the Sabbath.

**4.** All *minchah*-offerings are processed in a vessel [if prepared] within [the Courtyard], and are processed without a vessel [if prepared] outside [the Courtyard].



virtue of being left overnight, as the mishnah explains below. Therefore, unlike the *shtei halechem* and *lechem hapanim*, there is no alternative to baking the *chavitin* on Shabbos.]

טְחוּנָן וְהַרְקָדָן אֵינָן דּוֹחוֹת אֶת הַשַּׁבָּת. — *Their grinding and sifting do not override the Sabbath.*

[The grinding and sifting of the flour for the *chavitin* of Shabbos may not be done on that day. Since the flour does not become sanctified during these processes, they can be done before Shabbos without adversely affecting the validity of the offering. Consequently, these *melachos* (see *Shabbos* 7:2) do not override the Sabbath.]

כְּלָל אָמַר רַבִּי עֲקִיבָא: כָּל מְלָאכָה שֶׁאֶפְשָׁר לָהּ לֵעָשׂוֹת מֵעֶרֶב שַׁבָּת, אֵינָהּ דּוֹחָה אֶת הַשַּׁבָּת; וְשֶׁאִי אֶפְשָׁר לָהּ לֵעָשׂוֹת מֵעֶרֶב שַׁבָּת, דּוֹחָה אֶת הַשַּׁבָּת. — *R' Akiva stated a rule: Any labor which can be done prior to the Sabbath does not override the Sabbath; whereas one which cannot be done prior to the Sabbath overrides the Sabbath.*

[Since the Torah explicitly requires the offering of sacrifices on the Sabbath, it is clear that the obligation to bring these offerings — when necessary — overrides the prohibition of doing *melachah* on Shabbos. However, this exception to the *melachah* prohibition is implicit only for those activities which must be performed on Shabbos, not for those which can be done just as well before Shabbos.]

This rule is also stated in mishnayos elsewhere (*Shabbos* 19:1; *Pesachim* 6:2). The reason for this repetition is that it is appropriate in discussing each of these topics to establish when they override the Sabbath prohibitions (*Tos. Yom Tov*).

### 4.

כָּל הַמְּנָחוֹת יֵשׁ בָּהֶן מַעֲשֵׂה כְלִי בִּפְנִים, וְאֵין בָּהֶן מַעֲשֵׂה כְלִי בַּחוּץ. — *All minchah-offerings are processed in a vessel [if prepared] within [the Courtyard], and are processed without a vessel [if prepared] outside [the Courtyard].*

Any portion of a *minchah's* preparation which must be done within the Temple Courtyard — such as the baking of the *lechem hapanim* — must be done in a *kli shareis*, as derived by the *Gemara* (96a). That which may be done outside the Courtyard — e.g., the kneading and shaping of the *lechem*

מנחות
יא/ד

כֵּיצַד? שְׁתֵּי הַלֶּחֶם, אָרְכָּן שִׁבְעָה, וְרָחְבָּן אַרְבָּעָה, וְקַרְנוֹתֵיהֶן אַרְבַּע אֶצְבָּעוֹת. לֶחֶם הַפָּנִים, אָרְכּוֹ עֲשָׂרָה, וְרָחְבּוֹ חֲמִשָּׁה, וְקַרְנוֹתָיו שֶׁבַע אֶצְבָּעוֹת. רַבִּי יְהוּדָה אוֹמֵר: שֶׁלֹּא תִטְעֶה; זד״ד יה״ז. בֶּן זוֹמָא אוֹמֵר: „וְנָתַתָּ עַל הַשֻּׁלְחָן לֶחֶם פָּנִים לְפָנַי תָּמִיד״ — שֶׁיְּהֵא לוֹ פָּנִים.

**ר׳ עובדיה מברטנורא**

**וקרנותיהן.** שהוא מדביק בצק לכל דופן כמין קרנים, ואורך הקרן יוצא ארבע אצבעות: **רבי יהודה אומר שלא תטעה.** בין שתי הלחם ללחם הפנים בין בשיעור אורך ורוחב בין בשיעור הקרנות, בשתי הלחם ארכו שבעה ורחבו ארבעה וקרנותיו אצבעות, וסימנך זד״ד, ולחם הפנים ארכו עשרה ורחבו חמשה וקרנותיו שבע אצבעות, וסימנך יה״ז. ודרכו של רבי יהודה לתת סימנים, כמו דצ״ך עד״ש באח״ב: **שיהא לו פנים.** דפנות, [שיהא לו פינים זויות] והן הן הקרנים: (ה)

**יד אברהם**

*hapanim* — may be done on any surface, even a board (*Rav; Rambam Comm.*).

According to this interpretation, the mishnah's distinction refers primarily to the *lechem hapanim* and *shtei halechem* discussed in mishnahs 1 and 2 [since other *menachos* must have even their kneading done in the Courtyard] (*Rambam Comm.; Tos. Yom Tov*).

*Rashi* (96a, s.v. מעשה) understands this segment of the mishnah to refer to *menachos* other than the *lechem hapanim, shtei halechem,* and *chavitin* discussed to this point. The mishnah states that the rule for these other *menachos* is that all their work — kneading, shaping, and baking — is done within the Courtyard in a *kli shareis*.

*Tosafos* (95b, s.v. ומאי קושיא) follow *Rashi* in explaining this part of the mishnah to refer to *menachos* other than those discussed to this point. However, they explain that the mishnah is in fact making two statements in connection with *menachos* in general — that the main part of their work is done in the Courtyard in a *kli shareis* but that the part of their preparation which may be done outside — namely, the grinding and sifting — is done in a non-sacred vessel.

?כֵּיצַד — *How so?*

The mishnah now refers back to the statement made in mishnah 1, that the *lechem hapanim* (and *shtei halechem*) were baked in molds (*Rambam Comm.* cited by *Tos. Yom Tov*). [The mishnah describes the unusual shape of these breads which necessitated the use of these molds.]

*R' Yosef Kafich,* in his notes to his edition of *Rambam's Comm.,* records that *Rambam* later revised his text of the mishnah to delete this word. This accords with the version of the mishnah found in the *Gemara* in which the word כֵּיצַד, *how so,* does not appear.

שְׁתֵּי הַלֶּחֶם, אָרְכָּן שִׁבְעָה, וְרָחְבָּן אַרְבָּעָה, וְקַרְנוֹתֵיהֶן אַרְבַּע אֶצְבָּעוֹת. — *The length of [each of] the shtei halechem [is] seven [handbreadths], and its width four [handbreadths], and its horns four fingers.*

[The dough is shaped into loaves which — when baked — are seven טְפָחִים, *handbreadths,* long and four wide.] An additional clump of dough was attached to the top of each corner; these "horns" were four fingerbreadths high (*Rav; Rashi*).

*Rambam* (*Hil. Temidin U'Mussafin*

11
4

How so? The length of [each of] the *shtei halechem* [is] seven [handbreadths], and its width four [handbreadths], and its horns four fingers. The length of the *lechem hapanim* [is] ten [handbreadths], its width five, and its horns are seven fingers. R' Yehudah says: In order that you should not err; ZaDaD YaHaZ. Ben Zoma says: *And you shall place upon the Table lechem panim before Me always* (*Ex.* 25:30) — that it should have faces.

**YAD AVRAHAM**

8:10) states that the thickness of each of the loaves was four fingerbreadths. Apparently, his interpretation of the mishnah is that this statement does not refer to "horns" but to the thickness of the entire loaf (*Kesef Mishneh* ad loc.). [In fact, in his *Comm., Rambam* says so explicitly. Presumably, then, the term קְרָנוֹת is taken to mean *corners* rather than horns.]

Others dispute this explanation of *Rambam's* view. *Tiferes Yisrael* (in his intro. to *Seder Kodashim* 2:51) calculates that the amount of dough used for these *menachos* could not possibly be made into loaves that size, and therefore contends that *Rambam* is discussing only the thickness of the loaves at their corners (cf. *Aruch HaShulchan HeAsid* 110:25; 118:16).

לֶחֶם הַפָּנִים, אָרְכּוֹ עֲשָׂרָה, וְרָחְבּוֹ חֲמִשָּׁה, וְקַרְנוֹתָיו שֶׁבַע אֶצְבָּעוֹת. — *The length of the lechem hapanim [is] ten [handbreadths], its width five, and its horns are seven fingers.*

[The loaves of the *lechem hapanim* are ten handbreadths long and five wide, with horns of seven fingerbreadths jutting at the corners.]

Here, too, *Rambam* (*Temidin U'Mussafin* 5:9) explains the קְרָנַיִם to refer to the thickness of the loaves (see commentary above).[1]

See also *Ralbag* cited by *Kesef Mishneh* (ibid.) for a completely novel explanation.

רַבִּי יְהוּדָה אוֹמֵר: שֶׁלֹּא תִטְעֶה; זד״ד יה״ז. — *R' Yehudah says: In order that you should not err; ZaDaD YaHaZ.*

R' Yehudah offers a mnemonic to help remember the cited proportions of the two *menachos*. The dimensions of the *shtei halechem* loaves were *zayin* (numerical value seven) — handbreadths long, *dalet* — four wide, and *dalet* — four fingerbreadths for the horns. The *lechem hapanim* breads were *yud* — ten handbreadths long, *hei* — five wide, and *zayin* — seven fingerbreadths for the horns (*Rav;* see *Tif. Yis.*). [R' Yehudah was known for offering these mnemonic devices, as is well known from the Haggadah, in which he offers his famous mnemonic for the ten plagues: דצ״ך עד״ש באח״ב.]

בֶּן זוֹמָא אוֹמֵר: ,,וְנָתַתָּ עַל הַשֻּׁלְחָן לֶחֶם פָּנִים לְפָנַי תָּמִיד״ — שֶׁיְּהֵא לוֹ פָּנִים. — *Ben Zoma says: "And you shall place upon the Table lechem panim before Me always" (Ex.* 25:30*) — that it should have faces.*

Ben Zoma cites the Biblical source for the unusual shape of the *lechem hapanim* (*Tos. Yom Tov*). He interprets

1. However, the *Gemara (Pesachim* 37a) seems to say that the *lechem hapanim* were one handbreadth thick *(Minchas Chinuch, mitzvah* 97; *Rashash*).

[ה] **הַשֻּׁלְחָן** אָרְכּוֹ עֲשָׂרָה וְרָחְבּוֹ חֲמִשָּׁה; לֶחֶם הַפָּנִים אָרְכּוֹ עֲשָׂרָה וְרָחְבּוֹ חֲמִשָּׁה. נוֹתֵן אָרְכּוֹ כְּנֶגֶד רָחְבּוֹ שֶׁל שֻׁלְחָן וְכוֹפֵל טְפָחַיִם וּמֶחֱצָה מִכָּאן וּטְפָחַיִם וּמֶחֱצָה מִכָּאן.

### ר׳ עובדיה מברטנורא

**ארכו עשרה ורחבו חמשה.** כדכתיב (שמות כה, כג) אמתים ארכו ואמה רחבו. רבי יהודה לטעמיה דאמר של כלים בת חמשה טפחים היא: **נותן ארכו.** של לחם הפנים כנגד רחבו של שלחן: **וכופל.** הלחם, טפחיים ומחצה למעלה בגובה מכאן ומכאן, והן הן הקרנות, ונמצאו זקופות

### יד אברהם

the word פָּנִים [*panim*] to mean that the breads should have both walled sides (see mishnah 2) and corners [i.e., horns facing out from the loaves] (*Rav; Rashi*). The word פָּנִים, literally, *faces,* indicates that the loaf must have parts that face each other, thus necessitating opposing walls (which will be described in mishnah 5). It can also be read as פִּנִּים, which would mean *corners.* This is taken as a reference to the "horns" that jut out from each corner (*Tos. Yom Tov*).

*Rambam* interprets this to mean that it should have many faces — i.e., the six surfaces of the *lechem hapanim* loaves. [Since each loaf was folded up on both sides, as described below, the three inner surfaces are thus added to the three outer surfaces of the loaves. As noted above, *Rambam* omits any mention of horns on the loaves.]

## 5.

The following mishnah deals with the dimensions of the *shulchan* in the Temple and the arrangement of the *lechem hapanim* upon it. The Torah (*Exodus* 25:23) states that the *shulchan* was two אַמּוֹת, *cubits,* long and one cubit wide. However, there is a dispute between R' Yehudah and R' Meir (*Keilim* 17:10) whether the cubit measurement used for the Temple's vessels [אַמַּת כֵּלִים] was five handbreadths long or six. Thus, the actual size of the *shulchan* is in dispute.

הַשֻּׁלְחָן אָרְכּוֹ עֲשָׂרָה וְרָחְבּוֹ חֲמִשָּׁה; — *The shulchan [is] ten [handbreadths] long and five wide;*

The Torah (*Ex.* 25:23) describes the *shulchan* (table) in the Tabernacle as being two cubits long and one cubit wide. According to this first *Tanna* (R' Yehudah), this adds up to a length of ten handbreadths and a width of five. Although a cubit is generally six handbreadths long, the cubits of the Temple vessels are reckoned as five handbreadths long (*Rav, Rashi* from *Gem.* 97a, *Keilim* 17:10). This he derives from a verse in *Ezekiel* (43:13), as explained by the *Gemara* (97a).

לֶחֶם הַפָּנִים אָרְכּוֹ עֲשָׂרָה וְרָחְבּוֹ חֲמִשָּׁה. נוֹתֵן אָרְכּוֹ כְּנֶגֶד רָחְבּוֹ שֶׁל שֻׁלְחָן — *the lechem hapanim [is] ten [handbreadths] long and five wide. One would place its length along the width of the shulchan*

As stated above (mishnah 4), the *lechem hapanim* are also ten handbreadths long and five wide. In arranging the loaves on the table, the *Kohen* would lay the long side of the breads across the width of the *shulchan* (*Rav*). [Since the *shulchan* was only five handbreadths wide, however, this would result in an overlap of two-and-a-half handbreadths on each side. Therefore ...]

5. The *shulchan* [is] ten [handbreadths] long and five wide; the *lechem hapanim* is ten [handbreadths] long and five wide. One would place its length along the width of the *shulchan* and fold [it] two-and-a-half handbreadths on each side.

YAD AVRAHAM

וְכוֹפֵל טְפָחַיִם וּמֶחֱצָה מִכָּאן וּטְפָחַיִם וּמֶחֱצָה מִכָּאן. — *and fold [it] two-and-a-half handbreadths on each side.*

The breads were folded up at each end to a height of two-and-a-half handbreadths (*Rav*).

Although the mishnah's text indicates that this was done as it was placed on the

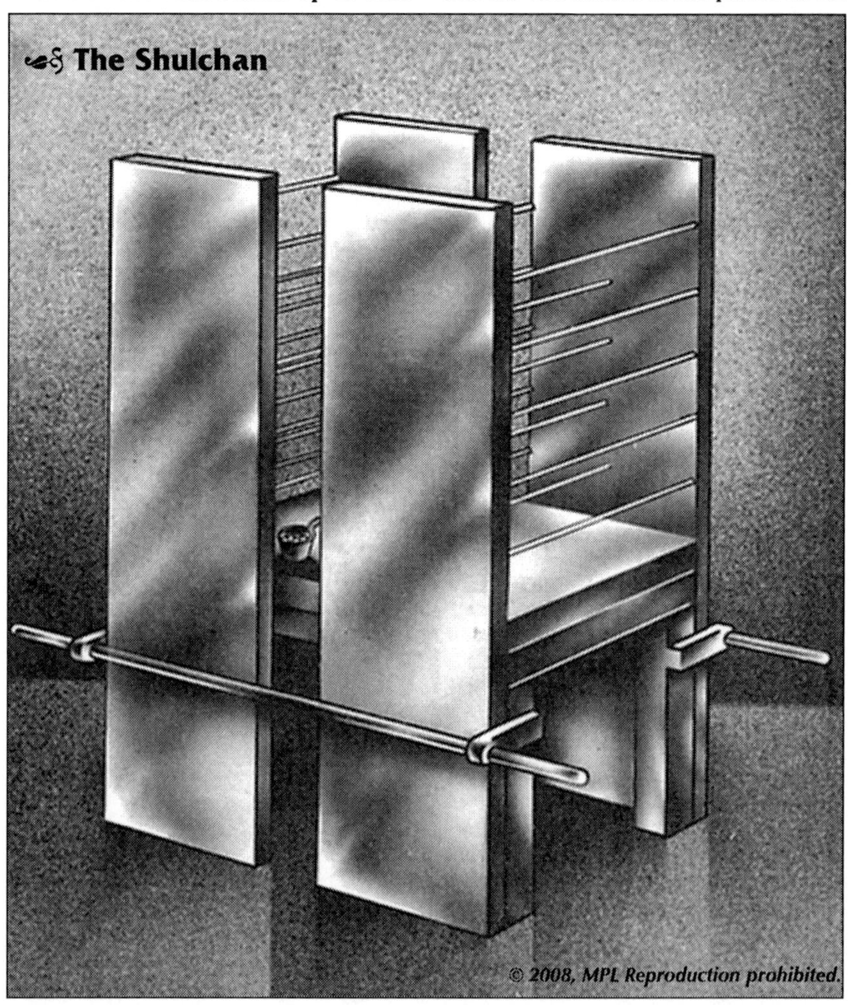

נִמְצָא אָרְכּוֹ מְמַלֵּא כָּל רָחְבּוֹ שֶׁל שֻׁלְחָן; דִּבְרֵי רַבִּי יְהוּדָה. רַבִּי מֵאִיר אוֹמֵר: הַשֻּׁלְחָן אָרְכּוֹ שְׁנֵים עָשָׂר וְרָחְבּוֹ שִׁשָּׁה; לֶחֶם הַפָּנִים אָרְכּוֹ עֲשָׂרָה וְרָחְבּוֹ חֲמִשָּׁה. נוֹתֵן אָרְכּוֹ כְּנֶגֶד רָחְבּוֹ שֶׁל שֻׁלְחָן וְכוֹפֵל טְפָחַיִם מִכָּאן וּטְפָחַיִם מִכָּאן וּטְפָחַיִם רֶוַח בָּאֶמְצַע, כְּדֵי שֶׁתְּהֵא הָרוּחַ מְנַשֶּׁבֶת בֵּינֵיהֶן.

### ר' עובדיה מברטנורא

בשוה לשפת השלחן: **ונמצא ארכו ממלא רחבו של שלחן.** ורחבו מחזיק חצי אורך של שלחן, וכשהיה מסדר אחר אצלו, נמצא שלחן כולו מלא: **ארכו שנים עשר.** רבי מאיר לטעמיה דאמר כל אמה בת ששה טפחים, חוץ ממזבח הזהב וקרן מזבח החיצון והסובב והיסוד. והלכה כרבי מאיר: **לחם הפנים ארכו עשרה.** בהא מודה רבי מאיר: **וטפחיים ריוח באמצע.** בין שני הסדרים, דרחב הלחם לא הוי אלא חמשה, שני הסדרים מחזיקין עשרה בשלחן לארכו, פשו להו טפחיים ריוח בין סדר לסדר, שתהא רוח מנשבת בהם שלא יתעפשו:

### יד אברהם

a maximum width of five handbreadths according to R' Yehudah, and six according to R' Meir. In addition, both the front and back of the folded bread were pinched together to complete the shape of a hull, and the horns were folded into the interior of the hull *(Rashi;* cf. *Tos.)* However, many technical details of this view are unclear (see *Sfas Emes* and others).

*Rambam* (*Hil. Temidin U'Mussafin* 5:9) rules in accordance with the view of R' Chanina (see *Kesef Mishneh, Lechem Mishneh* ibid.). *Rashi* in his comm. to *Chumash* (*Ex.* 25:29) also explains the structure of the *lechem hapanim* in this manner.

נִמְצָא אָרְכּוֹ מְמַלֵּא כָּל רָחְבּוֹ שֶׁל שֻׁלְחָן; דִּבְרֵי רַבִּי יְהוּדָה. — *Thus, its length fills the entire width of the shulchan; [these are] the words of R' Yehudah.*

[When the loaf, whose length was ten handbreadths, was folded up at each end to a height of two-and-a-half, this left a surface length of five handbreadths, the exact width of the table.] Its width of five handbreadths filled exactly half the length of the *shulchan,* it seems that this was actually done when the dough was shaped, and that the breads were baked into this shape through the use of the molds mentioned in mishnah 1 (*Meleches Shlomo,* see *Ramban's* and *Rashi's* Comm. to *Ex.* 25:29,30 cited in support; see also *Rashi* to 94a, s.v. ועדיין היא בצק; *Tif. Yis.*).

However, *Rambam* in *Hil. Temidin U'Mussafin* 5:9 seems to say that they were folded after being placed on the *shulchan.* This required the dough to be prepared in an extraordinary fashion, to allow the finished bread to be bent without breaking; see *Rambam Comm.* to *Yoma* 3:12).

The *Gemara* (94b) cites a dispute concerning the shape of the *lechem hapanim.* R' Chanina maintains that they were shaped like an open box with two sides missing — i.e., with a flat surface and two sides jutting straight up (*Rashi* ibid.) as described above. R' Yochanan contends, however, that they were shaped like the hull of a ship — with a flat surface (keel) of one fingerbreadth in the center and two sides sloping outward and upward from there to a height of two handbreadths and

11
5 Thus, its length fills the entire width of the *shulchan*; [these are] the words of R' Yehudah. R' Meir says: The *shulchan* [is] twelve long and six wide; the *lechem hapanim* [is] ten long and five wide. He would place its length along the width of the *shulchan* and fold two handbreadths from each side and [leave] two handbreadths space in between so that the air should flow between them.

YAD AVRAHAM

table, thus leaving room for the two parallel rows of loaves with no space in between (*Rav*).

רַבִּי מֵאִיר אוֹמֵר: הַשֻּׁלְחָן אָרְכּוֹ שְׁנֵים עָשָׂר וְרָחְבּוֹ שִׁשָּׁה; לֶחֶם הַפָּנִים אָרְכּוֹ עֲשָׂרָה וְרָחְבּוֹ חֲמִשָּׁה. נוֹתֵן אָרְכּוֹ כְּנֶגֶד רָחְבּוֹ שֶׁל שֻׁלְחָן וְכוֹפֵל טְפָחַיִם מִכָּאן וּטְפָחַיִם מִכָּאן — *R' Meir says: The shulchan [is] twelve long and six wide; the lechem hapanim [is] ten long and five wide. He would place its length along the width of the shulchan and fold two handbreadths from each side*

R' Meir is true to his opinion that the cubits used in the Temple were six

handbreadths long, with the exception of those used for the Altars (*Rav*). [Thus, the loaves, which all agree are ten handbreadths (*Rashi*), extend beyond the width of the *shulchan* only four handbreadths, thereby requiring folds of only two handbreadths on each end.]

The halachah concerning the length of the *shulchan* follows R' Meir (*Rav; Rambam, Beis HaBechirah* 3:12).

וּטְפָחַיִם רֶוַח בָּאֶמְצַע, כְּדֵי שֶׁתְּהֵא הָרוּחַ מְנַשֶּׁבֶת בֵּינֵיהֶן. — *and [leave] two handbreadths space in between so that the air should flow between them.*

The combined width of the two racks of loaves is ten handbreadths, leaving a space of two handbreadths between them to allow air to flow there and prevent spoilage (*Rav*). Although the *Gemara* (96b) states that the loaves of the *lechem hapanim* would miraculously remain fresh from the time they were placed on the *shulchan* until a week later when they were removed, they did not rely upon miracles [any more than necessary] and did as much as possible to keep them from becoming moldy (*Tif. Yis.*).

מנחות
יא/ו

אַבָּא שָׁאוּל אוֹמֵר: שָׁם הָיוּ נוֹתְנִין שְׁנֵי בְזִיכֵי לְבוֹנָה שֶׁל לֶחֶם הַפָּנִים. אָמְרוּ לוֹ: וַהֲלֹא כְבָר נֶאֱמַר: „וְנָתַתָּ עַל הַמַּעֲרֶכֶת לְבֹנָה זַכָּה״? אָמַר לָהֶן: וַהֲלֹא כְבָר נֶאֱמַר: „וְעָלָיו מַטֵּה מְנַשֶּׁה״?

[ו] **אַרְבָּעָה** סְנִיפִין שֶׁל זָהָב הָיוּ שָׁם, מְפֻצָּלִין מֵרָאשֵׁיהֶן, שֶׁהָיוּ סוֹמְכִים בָּהֶן, שְׁנַיִם לְסֵדֶר זֶה וּשְׁנַיִם לְסֵדֶר זֶה.

### ר׳ עובדיה מברטנורא

**אבא שאול אומר שם.** באותו ריוח שבין סדר לסדר נותנים הבזיכים: **והלא כבר נאמר ונתת על המערכת.** ועל, ממש משמע: **ועליו מטה מנשה.** והיינו סמוך, הכא נמי על סמוך. והלכה כאבא שאול: (ו) **מפוצלין.** לתת ראשי קנים באותן פצולים. וכמנין הקנים כך מנין הפצולים: **ארבעה עשר לסדר זה.** שש חלות שהיו בסדר המערכת, לארבעה מהן לכל אחת שלשה קנים, הרי שנים עשר קנים, והעליונה אינה צריכה אלא שנים לפי שאין עליה משאוי, הרי ארבעה עשר. החלה התחתונה אינה צריכה כל עיקר, לפי שמונחת על טהרו של שלחן:

### יד אברהם

אַבָּא שָׁאוּל אוֹמֵר: שָׁם הָיוּ נוֹתְנִין שְׁנֵי בְזִיכֵי לְבוֹנָה שֶׁל לֶחֶם הַפָּנִים. — *Abba Shaul says: There they would place the two spoons of frankincense of the lechem hapanim.*

[He concurs with the view of R' Meir that a space is left between the two racks of bread] but contends that its purpose is to leave place for the two spoons filled with *levonah* which must accompany the bread (*Rav*).

אָמְרוּ לוֹ: וַהֲלֹא כְבָר נֶאֱמַר: „וְנָתַתָּ עַל הַמַּעֲרֶכֶת לְבֹנָה זַכָּה״? — *They said to him: Does it not already say (Lev. 24:7): "And you shall place on the rack pure frankincense"?*

The word עַל, *on*, indicates that the dishes of frankincense were placed atop the racks of bread and not between them (*Rav*).

אָמַר לָהֶן: וַהֲלֹא כְבָר נֶאֱמַר: „וְעָלָיו מַטֵּה מְנַשֶּׁה״? — *Said he to them: Does it not already say (Num. 2:20): "And upon him the tribe of Menasheh"?*

[In describing the encampment of the Jewish nation in the Wilderness, the Torah uses the phrase וְעָלָיו, *and upon him*, to describe the position of the tribe of Menasheh as next to the tribe of Ephraim.] Just as the word עָלָיו in this context obviously means *next to* or *nearby* rather than on top of, so too the word עַל in regard to the frankincense means *next to* rather than on top of (*Rav*).

There is a dispute among the authorities whether the halachah follows the view of Abba Shaul (*Rav; Rambam, Beis HaBechirah* 3:14) or that of the Rabbis who dispute him (*Semag;* see *Zevach Todah*).

Abba Shaul says: There they would place the two spoons of frankincense of the *lechem hapanim.* They said to him: Does it not already say (*Lev.* 24:7): *And you shall place on the rack pure frankincense*? Said he to them: Does it not already say (*Num.* 2:20): *And upon him the tribe of Menasheh*?

**6.** There were four props of gold there, branched at their tops, which supported them, two for each arrangement. [There were]

### YAD AVRAHAM

## 6.

The following mishnah continues to give a description of the *shulchan* and the arrangement of the *lechem hapanim*.

The Torah's (*Ex.* 25:29) description of the accessories to the *shulchan* states: וְעָשִׂיתָ קְעָרֹתָיו וְכַפֹּתָיו וּקְשׂוֹתָיו וּמְנַקִּיֹּתָיו אֲשֶׁר יֻסַּךְ בָּהֵן, *And you shall make its molds; its dishes; its beams; and its rods, with which to cover them.*

This is explained by *Gem.* (97a) item by item, as follows:

קְעָרֹתָיו — *its molds* [in which the breads are fashioned and baked (*Rashi*)];

כַּפֹּתָיו — *its spoons* [the two bowls which contained the *levonah*];

קְשׂוֹתָיו — *its props* [which support the breads and keep them from breaking (*Rashi*); from the root קָשֶׁה — *hard* or *firm* (*Tos. Yom Tov*)];

מְנַקִּיֹּתָיו — *its rods* [half pipes which formed the racks, as it were, on which the *lechem* were stacked. Using half pipes allowed for the circulation of air to keep the breads mold-free; hence, the term מְנַקִּיֹּתָיו from the root-word נָקִי, *clean*, or mold-free (*Rashi*)].

אַרְבָּעָה סְנִיפִין שֶׁל זָהָב הָיוּ שָׁם, — *There were four props of gold there,*

Four [beamlike] props stood on the ground alongside the *shulchan* (*Tif. Yis.*).

מֻפְצָלִין מֵרָאשֵׁיהֶן, — *branched at their tops,*

Along the portion of the beams which rose above the *shulchan*, there were extensions that protruded over the table [to support the rods, as described below] (*Tif. Yis.*).

*Rashash* conjectures that the rods were not supported by extensions from the beams. Rather, the beams had holes into which the rods were inserted. On one side the hole went completely through the prop so that the rods could be removed and inserted without removing the breads.

שֶׁהָיוּ סוֹמְכִים בָּהֶן, שְׁנַיִם לְסֵדֶר זֶה וּשְׁנַיִם לְסֵדֶר זֶה. — *which supported them, two for each arrangement.*

One pair of props was placed on one side of the *shulchan* and another on the opposite side, directly facing the other two across the length of the table. The rods which supported the layers of loaves were supported in turn by these props, each rod resting on the protrusions jutting out from the two opposing props (*Tif. Yis.*).

# וְעֶשְׂרִים וּשְׁמוֹנָה קָנִים, כַּחֲצִי קָנֶה חָלוּל; אַרְבָּעָה עָשָׂר לְסֵדֶר זֶה, וְאַרְבָּעָה עָשָׂר לְסֵדֶר זֶה. לֹא סִדּוּר קָנִים וְלֹא נְטִילָתָן דּוֹחֶה אֶת הַשַּׁבָּת. אֶלָּא נִכְנָס מֵעֶרֶב שַׁבָּת וְשׁוֹמְטָן, וְנוֹתְנָן לְאָרְכּוֹ שֶׁל שֻׁלְחָן.

# כָּל הַכֵּלִים שֶׁהָיוּ בַמִּקְדָּשׁ, אָרְכָּן לְאָרְכּוֹ שֶׁל בַּיִת.

**ר׳ עובדיה מברטנורא**

**לא סדור קנים.** במערכה החדשה: **ולא נטילתן.** מעל הישנה, דוחה שבת: **נכנס מערב שבת ושומטן.** מבין כל לחם ולחם, ומניחם לארכו של שלחן, ולמחר מסדר הלחם, ולמוצאי שבת נותן הקנים בין כל לחם כמשפטן: **ארכן לארכו של בית.** ממזרח למערב היו מונחין בארכן, חוץ מן הארון שארכו לרחבו של בית, שהבדים שבארון היו בולטים ודוחקין בפרוכת ודומין כשני דדי אשה, שנאמר (במלכים-א ח, ח) ויאריכו הבדים ויראו, והבדים לרחבו של ארון היו מונחים, דאילו לארכו של ארון היו בדים, לא היה בין בד לבד אלא שיעור רוחב הארון דהיינו אמתא ופלגא, ותרי גברי הנושאים בשני בדים את הארון שניס מכאן ושניס מכאן לא הוו מצי ליכנס בין בד לבד, אלא ודאי לרחבו נתונים, והם היו ממזרח למערב שהרי היו דוחקים בפרוכת, נמצא ארכו של ארון לרחבו של בית:

**יד אברהם**

וְעֶשְׂרִים וּשְׁמוֹנָה קָנִים, כַּחֲצִי קָנֶה חָלוּל; — *[There were] twenty-eight rods, [each] like half a hollow reed;*

The loaves were supported by a total of twenty-eight rods, each of which was semicircular, rather than circular, to allow for more air to flow among the loaves (*Rambam, Temidin U'Mussafin* 5:14).

אַרְבָּעָה עָשָׂר לְסֵדֶר זֶה, וְאַרְבָּעָה עָשָׂר לְסֵדֶר זֶה. — *fourteen for one arrangement and fourteen for the other arrangement.*

The *lechem hapanim* were arranged on the *shulchan* vertically, with six loaves stacked one above the other in two columns, or vertical racks. The bottom loaf rested directly on the *shulchan* and needed no other support. The top loaf required only two rods to support it, since it carried only its own weight. The other four loaves required three rods each upon which to rest. Thus, a total of fourteen rods was required for each row (*Rav* from *Gem.* 97a).

לֹא סִדּוּר קָנִים וְלֹא נְטִילָתָן דּוֹחֶה אֶת הַשַּׁבָּת. — *Neither the arrangement of the rods nor their removal overrides the Sabbath.*

The act of arranging or removing the rods from among the loaves is Rabbinically prohibited on the Sabbath because of its resemblance to *building* and *dismantling* — two of the prohibited labors on the Sabbath (*Rashi* to 97a, s.v. אמאי לא דחי שבת).

The usual rule that אֵין שְׁבוּת בַּמִּקְדָּשׁ, *Rabbinical edicts concerning the Sabbath do not apply in the Temple* [see *Eruvin* 10:11ff], does not apply here because of the resemblance of the arranging of the rods to a Torah *melachah* (*Rashi* ibid.).

Alternatively, *Tos.* (ad loc.) suggest that

twenty-eight rods, [each] like half a hollow reed; fourteen for one arrangement and fourteen for the other arrangement. Neither the arrangement of the rods nor their removal overrides the Sabbath. Rather, he would enter on the eve of the Sabbath and remove them, and place them along the length of the Table.

All the utensils which were in the Temple [were placed with] their length [parallel] to the length of the Temple.

**YAD AVRAHAM**

arranging and removing the rods falls within the constraints of טִלְטוּל, *moving objects*, since arranging the rods is considered a non-essential action and therefore prohibited according to some *Amoraim* (see *Shabbos* 123b-124a; *Rashba* there). *Tos. Yom Tov* points out that, elsewhere, *Tosafos* suggest that the rods may be considered *muktzeh*, as something designated only for the fulfillment of a *mitzvah* is not defined as a functional utensil (see *Tos., Succah* 42b, s.v. טלטול). This restriction, then, constitutes an exception to the rule that Rabbinic edicts of the Sabbath do not apply in the Temple. Such exceptions appear elsewhere, as well [see *Eruvin* 10:12] (*Tos.* loc. cit.).

Ordinarily, all labors which are necessary to the proper functioning of the Temple are permitted on the Sabbath. However, this is true only if there is no alternative, as explained above (mishnah 3). Since the delay of the insertion of the rods for one day is not likely to cause the loaves to spoil, this act is thus forbidden (*Gem.* ibid.).

אֶלָּא נִכְנָס מֵעֶרֶב שַׁבָּת וְשׁוֹמְטָן, — *Rather, he would enter on the eve of the Sabbath and remove them,*

The *Kohen* would enter on Friday and remove the rods from beneath the loaves and put them down. After Shabbos, they would be replaced beneath the new loaves which had been arranged on Shabbos (*Rav*).

וְנוֹתְנָן לְאָרְכּוֹ שֶׁל שֻׁלְחָן. — *and place them along the length of the table.*

Upon removing the rods, he would place them on the floor along the length of the *shulchan*, as there was no room for them on the *shulchan* itself (*Tos.;* cf. *Tos. Yom Tov*).

כָּל הַכֵּלִים שֶׁהָיוּ בַמִּקְדָּשׁ, אָרְכָּן לְאָרְכּוֹ שֶׁל בַּיִת. — *All the utensils which were in the Temple [were placed with] their length [parallel] to the length of the Temple.*

All of the accessories of the Temple [e.g., the *shulchan*, the *menorah*, etc.) were placed east to west, so that their length ran parallel to the length of the Temple itself. The exception to this was the Ark, which was placed in the Holy of Holies with its length running north to south, as derived by the *Gemara* (*Rav*).

The *Gemara* (98b) cites a *Baraisa* which records a dispute among the *Tannaim* in this matter. Rabbi holds the view of our mishnah, but R' Elazar bar R' Shimon contends that the *menorah* and the *shulchan* were positioned from north to south, perpendicular to the length of the Temple.

*Rambam* rules (*Beis HaBechirah* 3:12)

[ז] **שְׁנֵי** שֻׁלְחָנוֹת הָיוּ בָאוּלָם מִבִּפְנִים עַל פֶּתַח הַבַּיִת, אֶחָד שֶׁל שַׁיִשׁ וְאֶחָד שֶׁל זָהָב. עַל שֶׁל שַׁיִשׁ נוֹתְנִים לֶחֶם הַפָּנִים בִּכְנִיסָתוֹ, וְעַל שֶׁל זָהָב בִּיצִיאָתוֹ, שֶׁמַּעֲלִין בַּקֹּדֶשׁ וְלֹא מוֹרִידִין.

**ר' עובדיה מברטנורא**

(ז) **על פתח הבית.** אלא פתח ההיכל בכניסתן. ולא היו מניחים שם אלא להראות שמעלין בקודש, דעכשיו מניחין על של שיש, ומיד נושאין להיכל ומסדרן על של זהב של משה: **ועל של זהב ביציאתו.** עד שיוקטרו בזיכים, כדקתני לקמן במתניתין:

**יד אברהם**

that the *menorah's* position was from north to south, but other vessels, such as the *shulchan*, were positioned east to west. Others rule according to Rabbi completely and maintain that the *menorah*, too, stood lengthwise from east to west (see *Tos. Yom Tov; Likkutei Halachos; Zevach Todah*).[1]

## 7.

שְׁנֵי שֻׁלְחָנוֹת הָיוּ בָאוּלָם מִבִּפְנִים — *There were two tables within the Antechamber*

[The outer chamber of the Temple (known as either the הֵיכָל, *Heichal*, or the קוֹדֶשׁ, *Holy*) was fronted by a large Antechamber called the אוּלָם, *Ulam*. In the interior of this Antechamber there were two tables, one upon which the *lechem hapanim* breads were placed prior to their arrangement on the *shulchan* in the Holy, and a second one upon which they were placed after their removal, as explained below.]

עַל פֶּתַח הַבַּיִת, אֶחָד שֶׁל שַׁיִשׁ וְאֶחָד שֶׁל זָהָב. — *at the entrance to the Temple building, one of marble and one of gold.*

[The Temple Courtyard surrounds a building which houses the Holy and the Holy of Holies. The *Ulam* is the antechamber of this building, opening from it onto the Courtyard.]

They were placed there near the entrance of the Temple building to allow for a view of the transfer of the *lechem hapanim* from the marble table in the *Ulam* to the *shulchan* of gold in the Temple building (*Rav, Rashi*).

עַל שֶׁל שַׁיִשׁ נוֹתְנִים לֶחֶם הַפָּנִים בִּכְנִיסָתוֹ, — *They would place the lechem hapanim upon the one of marble when it was brought in,*

1. A ramification of this dispute is reflected in the following area of practical halachah.

In recording the custom to kindle Chanukah lights in the synagogue, *Shulchan Aruch* (*Orach Chaim* 571:8) notes that the *menorah* should be placed along the southern wall and *Rama* adds that it should be positioned from east to west. Commentaries explain that this is because the synagogue's *menorah* is intended to resemble the *menorah* of the Temple, which according to many authorities was placed in this manner (*Turei Zahav* ad loc.). *Magen Avraham* (ibid.) cites a custom to place the *menorah* from north to south, in accordance with the view of *Rambam* that this was the position of the Temple's *menorah*.

7. There were two tables within the Antechamber at the entrance to the Temple building, one of marble and one of gold. They would place the *lechem hapanim* upon the one of marble when it was brought in, and upon the one of gold when it was taken out, because we ascend in holiness but do not descend.

YAD AVRAHAM

Before they were brought into the Holy to be placed on the *shulchan*, the breads were momentarily placed on the marble table. The contrast between the marble of the table in the *Ulam* and the gold of the *shulchan* of the Temple's interior serves to demonstrate the principle of מַעֲלִין בַּקּוֹדֶשׁ, *we ascend in holiness* (*Rav; Rashi*). [I.e., that all procedures should flow from a state of lesser holiness to one of greater holiness, not vice versa.]

[Although gold is not intrinsically more holy than marble, its greater value makes it a more fitting substance with which to show honor to *Hashem* and the Temple in which we serve Him. Thus moving the breads from a marble table to the golden *shulchan* is to move up in the Divine service.]

Some question the choice of marble for the table on which the incoming breads are placed, since it would be more befitting the dignity of the Temple to use a silver table.[1] The principle of ascending in holiness could be demonstrated just as well by the transfer of the breads from a silver table to the golden *shulchan* (*Tos. Tom Tov* citing *Tamid* 31b; *Roth* and *Rav* in their commentaries to *Shekalim* 6:4; see *Sfas Emes*).

Another reason given for the choice of marble for this table is its cooling properties. The breads are placed on this table while still warm from baking. Leaving them on the marble table allows the breads to cool off until their arrangement (*Tos. Yom Tov*).

Thus it is probable that the breads were placed there for the extended period from their baking until the arrangement, rather than just momentarily before the arrangement as would be indicated by the reasoning of *Rashi* and *Rav* (*Sfas Emes*).

וְעַל שֶׁל זָהָב בִּיצִיאָתוֹ, שֶׁמַּעֲלִין בַּקֹּדֶשׁ וְלֹא מוֹרִידִין. — *and upon the one of gold when it was taken out, because we ascend in holiness but do not descend.*

After removing the bread from the *shulchan*, it is placed on the golden table at the entrance of the *Ulam* until the spoonfuls of *levonah* are burnt on the Altar [at which time the breads became permissible for consumption to the *Kohanim*] (*Rav*). [Since the *shulchan* inside the Temple upon which they had been sitting was of gold, subsequently placing them on a table made from anything less would constitute a descending level of holiness.]

1. There are texts of the mishnah which do indeed read אֶחָד שֶׁל כֶּסֶף, *one of silver*, indicating that the breads were placed on a silver table rather than on one of marble (*Tos.* 99b). All of our texts indicate, however, that the table was of marble. (See ArtScroll *Shekalim* 6:4 and *Yad Avraham* comm. there.)

וְאֶחָד שֶׁל זָהָב מִבִּפְנִים שֶׁעָלָיו לֶחֶם הַפָּנִים תָּמִיד. אַרְבָּעָה כֹהֲנִים נִכְנָסִין, שְׁנַיִם בְּיָדָם שְׁנֵי סְדָרִים, וּשְׁנַיִם בְּיָדָם שְׁנֵי בְזִיכִים. וְאַרְבָּעָה מַקְדִּימִין לִפְנֵיהֶם, שְׁנַיִם לִטּוֹל שְׁנֵי סְדָרִים, וּשְׁנַיִם לִטּוֹל שְׁנֵי בְזִיכִים. הַמַּכְנִיסִים עוֹמְדִים בַּצָּפוֹן וּפְנֵיהֶם לַדָּרוֹם, הַמּוֹצִיאִין עוֹמְדִים בַּדָּרוֹם וּפְנֵיהֶם לַצָּפוֹן. אֵלּוּ מוֹשְׁכִין וְאֵלּוּ מַנִּיחִין, וְטִפְחוֹ שֶׁל זֶה כְּנֶגֶד טִפְחוֹ שֶׁל זֶה; שֶׁנֶּאֱמַר: ,,לְפָנַי תָּמִיד.'' רַבִּי יוֹסֵי אוֹמֵר: אֲפִילוּ אֵלּוּ נוֹטְלִין וְאֵלּוּ מַנִּיחִין, אַף זוֹ הָיְתָה ,,תָּמִיד.''

### ר' עובדיה מברטנורא

**המכניסים עומדים בצפון.** דהכי עדיף טפי דלותן שמסדרים העבודה יהיו בצפון: **אלו מושכין.** ועד שלא יגביהו מן השלחן אלו מניחין: **אפילו אלו נוטלין.** ואלו עלמן מניחין אחר שנטלו: **אף זו היתה תמיד.** דסבר רבי יוסי דאין תמיד אלא שלא ילין שלחן לילה אחד בלא לחם:

### יד אברהם

וְאֶחָד שֶׁל זָהָב מִבִּפְנִים — *There was one of gold within*

[The *shulchan* of the Temple was identical to that of the *Mishkan* (Sanctuary) in the times of Moses: wood covered by gold (*Ex.* 23,24).]

שֶׁעָלָיו לֶחֶם הַפָּנִים תָּמִיד. — *upon which the lechem hapanim stood constantly.*

[The Torah requires that the *lechem hapanim* be on the *shulchan* constantly, as it says (ibid. 25:30): וְנָתַתָּ עַל הַשֻּׁלְחָן לֶחֶם פָּנִים לְפָנַי תָּמִיד, *and you shall place lechem hapanim on the table before Me constantly.*]

אַרְבָּעָה כֹהֲנִים נִכְנָסִין, — *Four Kohanim enter,*

Each Shabbos [four *Kohanim* enter the Temple to perform the service of the *lechem hapanim*] (*Tif. Yis.*).

שְׁנַיִם בְּיָדָם שְׁנֵי סְדָרִים, וּשְׁנַיִם בְּיָדָם שְׁנֵי בְזִיכִים. — *two with the two arrangements in their hands, and two with the two spoons in their hands.*

[These *Kohanim* bring in the *lechem hapanim* arrangement for the new week. Two of them bear the stacks of bread, and two carry the spoons of frankincense.]

וְאַרְבָּעָה מַקְדִּימִין לִפְנֵיהֶם, שְׁנַיִם לִטּוֹל שְׁנֵי סְדָרִים, וּשְׁנַיִם לִטּוֹל שְׁנֵי בְזִיכִים. — *Four [others] precede them, two to take away the two arrangements, and two to take away the two spoons.*

[Before the four *Kohanim* could place the new arrangements on the *shulchan*, four other *Kohanim* had to carry out the previous week's loaves and spoons of *levonah*. This, too, is performed by four *Kohanim* — two for the bread and two for the *levonah*.]

הַמַּכְנִיסִים עוֹמְדִים בַּצָּפוֹן וּפְנֵיהֶם לַדָּרוֹם, — *Those who are bringing in stand to the north facing south,*

Arranging the new breads is considered a more sanctified service than removing the old ones. It is therefore appropriate that those who come to arrange the new breads stand on the

11 There was one of gold within upon which the
7 *lechem hapanim* stood constantly. Four *Kohanim* enter, two with the two arrangements in their hands, and two with the two spoons in their hands. Four [others] precede them, two to take away the two arrangements, and two to take away the two spoons. Those who are bringing in stand to the north facing south, [while] those who are taking out stand to the south facing north. These withdraw and these place down, with the handbreadth of this one filling the handbreadth of this one; as it is stated (*Ex.* 25:30): *before me constantly.* R' Yose says: Even if these take away and these place down, this too is *constantly.*

### YAD AVRAHAM

north side [of the *shulchan*] to perform this service, because this side is considered more sanctified (*Rashi; Rav*). This is evidenced from that which the קָדְשֵׁי קָדָשִׁים, *most-holy offerings,* must be slaughtered in the northern portion of the Temple Courtyard [see *Zevachim* 6:1] (*Tos. Yom Tov* from *Rashi*).

הַמּוֹצִיאִין עוֹמְדִים בַּדָּרוֹם וּפְנֵיהֶם לְצָפוֹן. — *[while] those who are taking out stand to the south facing north.*

[As explained below, the two groups of *Kohanim* synchronized their service and therefore needed to stand facing each other.]

אֵלּוּ מוֹשְׁכִין וְאֵלּוּ מַנִּיחִין, — *These withdraw and these place down,*

The *Kohanim* standing to the south of the *shulchan* gradually pull the breads of the previous week off the *shulchan*, while those standing to the north place the new breads upon it, as the old ones are removed (*Rav; Rashi*).

וְטִפְחוֹ שֶׁל זֶה כְּנֶגֶד טִפְחוֹ שֶׁל זֶה; — *with the handbreadth of this one filling the handbreadth of this one;*

[As each handbreadth of space on the *shulchan* was cleared from the previous week's loaves, it was filled immediately with those for the new week.]

שֶׁנֶּאֱמַר: „לְפָנַי תָּמִיד.״ — *as it is stated (Ex. 25:30): "before me constantly."*

Since the Torah dictates that there always be *lechem hapanim* on the *shulchan*, it is necessary to refrain from removing the old arrangement until it can be replaced immediately by the new one (*Tif. Yis.*).

רַבִּי יוֹסֵי אוֹמֵר: אֲפִילוּ אֵלּוּ נוֹטְלִין וְאֵלּוּ מַנִּיחִין, אַף זוֹ הָיְתָה „תָּמִיד.״ — *R' Yose says: Even if these take away and these place down, this too is "constantly."*

According to R' Yose, the word תָּמִיד, *constantly,* does not mean that the *shulchan* cannot remain empty for even a moment. It means simply that it cannot remain empty overnight (*Rav; Rashi*). [Thus, there is no need to place down the new bread on the

יָצְאוּ וְנָתְנוּ עַל הַשֻּׁלְחָן שֶׁל זָהָב שֶׁהָיָה בָאוּלָם. הִקְטִירוּ הַבְּזִיכִין, וְהַחַלּוֹת מִתְחַלְּקוֹת לַכֹּהֲנִים. חָל יוֹם הַכִּפּוּרִים לִהְיוֹת בְּשַׁבָּת, הַחַלּוֹת מִתְחַלְּקוֹת לָעֶרֶב. חָל לִהְיוֹת עֶרֶב שַׁבָּת, שְׂעִיר שֶׁל יוֹם הַכִּפֻּרִים נֶאֱכָל לָעֶרֶב.

ר' עובדיה מברטנורא

**והחלות מתחלקות לכהנים.** משמר היוצא חולק עם משמר הנכנס: **חל יום הכיפורים להיות בשבת.** שדין לחם הפנים לאכלו באותו שבת שנוטלים אותו מעל השלחן, ועכשיו אין יכולים לאכלו מפני התענית: **החלות מתחלקות לערב.** ואין ממתינים לחלקו למחר מפני שנפסל בלינה לאחר זמנו שנסתלק: **השעיר.** של מוסף שהוא חטאת ונאכל לכהנים: **נאכל לערב.** בלילי שבת, שזמנו ליום ולילה עד חצות, ואף על פי שאין יכולים לבשלו בשבת ולא ביום הכיפורים:

יד אברהם

*shulchan* as the other bread is being removed. As long as it is done during that day it is sufficient.]

R' Yose's view is reflected in the mishnah in *Megillah* (2:6) that states: *This is the rule: Any rite, which is to be done by day, may be performed throughout the day.* The *Gemara* (ibid. 21a) interprets this generalization to mean that the arrangement of the new bread is valid at any time during the day, even after the removal of the old bread. Since the mishnah in *Megillah* is presented anonymously, some rule in accord with R' Yose (*Ritva* ad loc.). *Rambam* (*Temidin U'Mussafin* 8:5), however, rules like the majority opinion of the first *Tanna* in our mishnah, apparently because this is the primary source of the laws of the *lechem hapanim* (*Tos. Yom Tov*).

יָצְאוּ וְנָתְנוּ עַל הַשֻּׁלְחָן שֶׁל זָהָב שֶׁהָיָה בָאוּלָם. — *They went out and placed [them] upon the golden table which was in the Antechamber.*

[The previous week's loaves and spoonfuls of *levonah* were removed and placed on the golden table which stood in the *Ulam* near the entrance.]

הִקְטִירוּ הַבְּזִיכִין, — *They burned the spoonfuls [on the Altar],*

The *levonah* was then taken and burned on the Altar, thereby rendering the loaves permissible to the *Kohanim* for consumption.

וְהַחַלּוֹת מִתְחַלְּקוֹת לַכֹּהֲנִים. — *and the loaves were divided among the Kohanim.*

The responsibility for administering the service of the Temple was divided among the *Kohanim* on a rotation basis, consisting of a cycle of twenty-four מִשְׁמָרוֹת, *watches*, each serving for a single week. The watches were changed on the Sabbath. On that day the service was shared by both watches: The outgoing *Kohanim* offered the *tamid* of the morning and the *mussaf-offering*, and the incoming watch offered the *levonah* of the previous week's *lechem hapanim* (*Succah* 56b; see *Yad Avraham* comm. to *Succah* 5:8).

The loaves of the *lechem hapanim* are divided equally between the incoming and outgoing watches of *Kohanim* (*Rav*).

חָל יוֹם הַכִּפּוּרִים לִהְיוֹת בְּשַׁבָּת, הַחַלּוֹת מִתְחַלְּקוֹת לָעֶרֶב. — *If Yom Kippur falls on the Sabbath, the loaves are distributed at evening.*

Ordinarily, the loaves are eaten on

11
7 They went out and placed [them] upon the golden table which was in the Antechamber. They burned the spoonfuls [on the Altar], and the loaves were divided among the *Kohanim*. If Yom Kippur falls on the Sabbath, the loaves are distributed at evening. [If] it falls on Friday, the he-goat of Yom Kippur is eaten at evening.



the Shabbos in which they are removed from the table. When Yom Kippur comes out on Shabbos, however, the loaves can obviously not be eaten on that day, since it is a fast day. They may also not be left until the following day, because they would become invalidated by the reason of לִינָה, *being left overnight*. Therefore, they must be eaten by the *Kohanim* on the evening following Yom Kippur (*Rav*).

Although the *lechem hapanim* are not subject to the invalidation of being left overnight for the seven days that they are on the *shulchan*, once their time on the *shulchan* passes, they become subject to this invalidation (see below, mishnah 8 s.v. כיצד יעשה, and s.v. שאפילו היא על השולחן ימים רבים).

The breads are first distributed at night, not after they are removed from the *shulchan* on Yom Kippur. This is done either because it is better not to handle food items on the fast day or simply because such unnecessary efforts on the festival are to be avoided (*Sfas Emes*).

חָל לִהְיוֹת עֶרֶב שַׁבָּת, — *[If] it falls on Friday* (lit., *the eve of the Sabbath*),

In the fixed calendar in use today, the calendar has been so arranged that Yom Kippur can never fall on either Friday or Sunday (or Tuesday, for that matter) (*Succah* 54b). However, it is apparent that when the calendar was determined by the testimony of witnesses (see General Introduction to ArtScroll *Rosh Hashanah*), Yom Kippur could fall on any day (*Rambam Comm.*; cf. *Tos. Yom Tov*).[1]

שְׂעִיר שֶׁל יוֹם הַכִּפֻּרִים נֶאֱכָל לָעֶרֶב. — *the he-goat of Yom Kippur is eaten at evening.*

The only item of the Yom Kippur service which was eaten was the goat of the *mussaf* of Yom Kippur (*Rambam Comm.*). This must be eaten by the *Kohanim* within a day and night of its sacrifice — i.e., by midnight of the eve following Yom Kippur. It was therefore eaten on the eve of the Sabbath which followed Yom Kippur (*Rav*). [This is actually true regardless of which day Yom Kippur falls out. However, when it falls out on Friday, there is a further difficulty attached to its consumption, since the meat cannot be cooked that night because of the Sabbath prohibition on cooking.]

1. *Rambam's* emphasis of this point is an implied rejection of the view expounded by *R' Saadya Gaon* and *Rabbeinu Chananel* (*Shabbos* 115a) that the origin of the restrictions built into the calendar is an Oral Law transmitted to Moses at Sinai (see also *Rambam Comm.* to *Rosh Hashanah* 2:7 at greater length). According to this latter view, it must be concluded that our mishnah — which clearly states that Yom Kippur and Shabbos can follow each other — is not accepted as halachah (*Rabbeinu Chananel* loc. cit.; see *R' Y. Kafich's* notes to *Rambam Comm.* here, note 33).

הַבַּבְלִיִּים אוֹכְלִין אוֹתוֹ כְּשֶׁהוּא חַי, מִפְּנֵי שֶׁדַּעְתָּן יָפָה.

[ח] **סִדֵּר** אֶת הַלֶּחֶם בְּשַׁבָּת וְאֶת הַבְּזִיכִים לְאַחַר שַׁבָּת, וְהִקְטִיר אֶת הַבְּזִיכִים בְּשַׁבָּת, פְּסוּלָה; וְאֵין חַיָּבִין עֲלֵיהֶן מִשּׁוּם פִּגּוּל, נוֹתָר, וְטָמֵא. סִדֵּר אֶת הַלֶּחֶם

### ר' עובדיה מברטנורא

**הבבליים.** כהנים שעלו מבבל. ובגמרא (ק, א) מפרש דלא בבליים היו אלא אלכסנדריים היו, ועל שם ששונאים תלמידי חכמים שבארץ ישראל את הבבליים, קראו לאלכסנדריים שעושים מעשה רעבתנות בבליים: **היו אוכלין אותו חי.** כשחל יום הכיפורים להיות בערב שבת: **מפני שדעתן יפה.** ואינן קצים לאכול הבשר כשהוא חי: (ח) **ואת הבזיכים לאחר שבת.** ודינן היה לסדרן בשבת בשעת עריכת הלחם: **והקטיר את הבזיכים בשבת פסולה.** דמחוסר זמן הוא, שלא היה על השלחן אלא ששה ימים. והכא אי אפשר לתקן ולומר יניחנו עד שבת הבאה, דכיון דלחם נסדר כדינו בשבת, קדשו שלחן ושוב אינו יכול לשהותו אלא עד שבת ראשונה דמפסיל בלינה: **ואין חייבין עליהם משום פגול.** אם הקטירן על מנת לאכול הלחם למחר, אינו פגול, שלא קרב המתיר כמצותו:

### יד אברהם

הַבַּבְלִיִּים אוֹכְלִין אוֹתוֹ כְּשֶׁהוּא חַי, מִפְּנֵי שֶׁדַּעְתָּן יָפָה. — *The Babylonians eat it raw, because they are not fastidious.*

As one may cook neither on the Sabbath nor on Yom Kippur, under these circumstances it is only possible to eat this sacrifice raw. It was therefore given to *Kohanim* from Babylon, who were not particularly fastidious and were able to eat raw meat (*Yom Tov*).

According to the *Gemara* (100a) these *Kohanim* were actually Alexandrians, not Babylonians. However, the Sages of Eretz Yisrael disliked the Babylonians — because they did not return to Eretz Yisrael with Ezra the Scribe (*Tos.*). Therefore, the term *Babylonians* was used as a pejorative for people who ate raw meat in barbaric fashion.[1]

In this instance eating raw meat was done for the sake of performing a *mitzvah*, but these people were nonetheless regarded as gluttons because they would eat like this throughout the year (*Tos.*).

Eating raw meat that is unsalted is forbidden according to many authorities (see *Rambam* and *Ravad, Maachalos Assuros* 6:12). Apparently then, this raw meat was salted before it was eaten. Although salting meat on the Sabbath is prohibited by Rabbinical law (see *Shabbos* 108b and *Tos.* ibid. 75b s.v. אין), under these circumstances the Rabbis waived this restriction.

However, the halachah is that one may eat raw meat without salting it first, as long as all veins have been removed and the meat is thoroughly rinsed (*Yoreh Deah* 67:2).

1. *R' Yitzchak Isaac HaLevi* notes that it is out of character for the mishnah to refer to people by pejorative cognomens. He cites the testimony of Josephus Flavius that there were groups of Jewish brigands and mercenaries from Babylonia who had settled in and about Alexandria. It is to these uncouth and half-wild Babylonian "Alexandrians" and their descendants that the old-line Alexandrians — and thus the Mishnah — referred to as *Babylonians* (*Doros HaRishonim* Part I, Vol. 3, pp. 115-117).

The Babylonians eat it raw, because they are not fastidious.

**8.** [If] one arranged the bread on the Sabbath and the spoonfuls [of frankincense] after the Sabbath, and burnt the spoonfuls on the Sabbath, it is invalid; and one is not liable on their account for *piggul*, *nossar*, or *tamei*. [If] he arranged the loaves

### YAD AVRAHAM

## 8.

As explained above, the service for the *lechem hapanim* requires that the loaves and spoons of *levonah* be placed on the *shulchan* on the Sabbath and be removed the following Sabbath. The *levonah* is offered on the Altar during that Sabbath day and the loaves are then eaten by the *Kohanim* (*Rambam Comm.*). This mishnah discusses the law in situations in which this procedure is not followed correctly.

סִדֵּר אֶת הַלֶּחֶם בְּשַׁבָּת וְאֶת הַבָּזִיכִים לְאַחַר שַׁבָּת, — *[If] one arranged the bread on the Sabbath and the spoonfuls [of frankincense] after the Sabbath,*

[He properly arranged the *lechem* on the *shulchan* on Shabbos but did not place the spoonfuls of *levonah* with them until after Shabbos.]

וְהִקְטִיר אֶת הַבָּזִיכִים בְּשַׁבָּת, — *and burnt the spoonfuls on the Sabbath,*

He burnt the *levonah* on the Altar on the following Shabbos (*Rambam, Hil. Temidin U'Mussafin* 5:12).

פְּסוּלָה; — *it is invalid;*

Since the *levonah* was not on the *shulchan* for the required seven days prior to being burned on the Altar, it is the equivalent to a sacrifice which is offered prior to its time, which is invalid (*Rav*).

וְאֵין חַיָּבִין עֲלֵיהֶן מִשּׁוּם פִּגּוּל, — *and one is not liable on their account for piggul,*

The *lechem hapanim* which has not been arranged in the proper time cannot become *piggul* [even if the *Kohen* burnt its *levonah* with the intention of eating its breads beyond the allotted time (see mishnah 1:3)]. Only an offering which otherwise meets its requirements can become *piggul* (*Rav;* see mishnah 1:4). [Therefore, although the *lechem hapanim* is in any case invalid, there is no penalty of *kares* attached to its consumption.]

נוֹתָר, — *nossar,*

The prohibition against נוֹתָר [*nossar*], *an offering left over past its allotted time* — which bears a penalty of *kares* — applies only to an offering which would otherwise be permissible to eat. Thus, it does not apply to *lechem hapanim* not arranged in its proper time, which is invalid immediately (*Rav*).

וְטָמֵא. — *or tamei.*

Ordinarily, one who eats from sanctified food while he is in a state of *tumah* is punished by *kares*. However, this prohibition, too, applies only to an offering which is permitted for consumption. [These loaves, which are prohibited to everyone, are thus

וְאֶת הַבָּזִיכִין בְּשַׁבָּת, וְהִקְטִיר אֶת הַבָּזִיכִין לְאַחַר שַׁבָּת, פָּסוּל; וְאֵין חַיָּבִין עֲלֵיהֶן מִשּׁוּם פִּגּוּל, וְנוֹתָר, וְטָמֵא. סִדֵּר אֶת הַלֶּחֶם וְאֶת הַבָּזִיכִין לְאַחַר שַׁבָּת, וְהִקְטִיר אֶת הַבָּזִיכִין בְּשַׁבָּת, פָּסוּל. כֵּיצַד יַעֲשֶׂה? יַנִּיחֶנָּה לְשַׁבָּת הַבָּאָה, שֶׁאֲפִילוּ הִיא עַל הַשֻּׁלְחָן יָמִים רַבִּים אֵין בְּכָךְ כְּלוּם.

ר' עובדיה מברטנורא

**ולא משום נותר.** שאין נותר חל על הלחם, שהרי אין ראוי לאכילה: **וטמא.** האוכלו בטומאת הגוף אינו בכרת, כדאמרינן בהקומץ [דף כה, ב] הניתר לטהורים חייבים עליו משום טומאה, וזה לא ניתר לטהורים מעולם, דבזיכים הוו מתירים דידיה ולא קרבו כהלכתן: **יניחנו לשבת הבאה.** ויעמוד שבועיים על השלחן, דכיון דלא נסדר בשבת, אין שלחן מקדש עד שתגיע שבת, ומאותו שבת יכול להשהותן שבעת ימים: **שאפילו היה על השלחן ימים רבים.** קודם השבת, אין בכך כלום, שאין השלחן מקדשו עד השבת, הלכך לא מיפסל בלינה לאחר השבת:

יד אברהם

rules that in this case [in which the *lechem hapanim* was arranged properly but the *levonah* was burnt at the wrong time] the prohibitions of *piggul, nossar*, and *tamei* do take effect. Apparently, his version to the mishnah read וְחַיָּבִין עֲלֵיהֶם מִשּׁוּם פִּגּוּל וכו', *and one is liable on their account for piggul*, etc.

The reasoning behind this ruling is that as long as the *lechem* and *levonah* were placed on the *shulchan* in accordance with the law, they achieve the basic level of sanctity which leaves them to be susceptible to the invalidations which apply to otherwise valid offerings (*Kesef Mishneh* ad loc.; cf. *Tos. Yom Tov*).

סִדֵּר אֶת הַלֶּחֶם וְאֶת הַבָּזִיכִין לְאַחַר שַׁבָּת, וְהִקְטִיר אֶת הַבָּזִיכִין בְּשַׁבָּת, פָּסוּל. — *[If] he arranged the loaves and the spoonfuls [of frankincense] after the Sabbath and burnt the spoonfuls on the Sabbath, it is invalid.*

[If he arranged them on the *shulchan* during the week and burnt the *levonah* on the Altar on that Shabbos, it is invalid, since the *lechem* was not on the *shulchan* from one Shabbos to the next.]

exempted from the transgression created by the state of *tumah*] (*Rav* from *Gem.* 25b).

סִדֵּר אֶת הַלֶּחֶם וְאֶת הַבָּזִיכִין בְּשַׁבָּת, וְהִקְטִיר אֶת הַבָּזִיכִין לְאַחַר שַׁבָּת, — *[If] he arranged the loaves and the spoonfuls [of frankincense] on the Sabbath, and burnt the spoonfuls after the Sabbath,*

He placed the *lechem* and the *levonah* on the *shulchan* on Shabbos as required, but did not wait until the following Shabbos to burn the *levonah* on the Altar. Rather, he burned it on the Sunday following its arrangement (*Rabbeinu Gershom*).

פָּסוּל; וְאֵין חַיָּבִין עֲלֵיהֶן מִשּׁוּם פִּגּוּל, וְנוֹתָר, וְטָמֵא. — *it is invalid; and one is not liable on their account for piggul, nossar, or tamei.*

[Since the *levonah* was offered earlier than its proper time, the offering is invalidated, with the same ramifications as those stated in the previous case.]

*Rambam* (*Temidin U'Mussafin* 5:14)

11 and the spoonfuls [of frankincense] on the Sab-
8 bath, and burnt the spoonfuls after the Sabbath, it is invalid; and one is not liable on their account for *piggul, nossar,* or *tamei*. [If] he arranged the loaves and the spoonfuls [of frankincense] after the Sabbath and burnt the spoonfuls on the Sabbath, it is invalid. What should he do? He should leave it there until the next Sabbath, for even if it is on the *shulchan* many days it is of no consequence.

## YAD AVRAHAM

כֵּיצַד יַעֲשֶׂה? יַנִּיחֶנָּה לְשַׁבָּת הַבָּאָה, — *What should he do? He should leave it there until the next Sabbath,*

He must leave the *lechem* and the *levonah* on the *shulchan* until the following Shabbos, thereby allowing them to remain there from one Shabbos to the next (*Rav*). Generally, after remaining on the *shulchan* beyond the required seven days, they would become invalidated as נוֹתָר, *being left overnight*. However, in this instance, in which they were initially not placed on the *shulchan* properly, their placement there has no validity and they are not thereby consecrated. Therefore, they do not become invalidated by virtue of being left over after seven days have passed (*Gem.* 100a).

In the first case of the mishnah, in which merely the *levonah* was arranged after Shabbos, the mishnah does not mention the corrective measure of waiting till the next Shabbos to burn them on the Altar. This is because in that case the loaves were placed on the *shulchan* on Shabbos as required. The proper arrangement of the *lechem* — even without the *levonah* — is sufficient to render them susceptible to the invalidation of *nossar*, and thus if they remain on the *shulchan* beyond the allotted seven days they become invalidated (*Rav; Rashi*).

שֶׁאֲפִילוּ הִיא עַל הַשֻּׁלְחָן יָמִים רַבִּים אֵין בְּכָךְ כְּלוּם. — *for even if it is on the shulchan many days it is of no consequence.*

The fact that the *lechem* and the *levonah* were on the *shulchan* for an extended period before their proper time [from Sunday till Shabbos] has no effect on their status. Only their placement there on Shabbos consecrates them for their offering and renders them susceptible to the invalidation of לִינָה, *remaining overnight* beyond their allotted time (*Rav; Rashi*).

*Rambam* (*Temidin U'Mussafin*), in citing the mishnah's law, states that *even if the loaves and levonah remain on the shulchan for many weeks it is of no consequence*. The use of the phrase *many weeks* (instead of *many days*, as it appears in our mishnah) indicates that even if it remained there for longer than from one Shabbos to the next it does not become invalidated. This is contrary to the implication of our *Gemara* that after one full week the invalidation of לִינָה, *being left overnight*, applies. [Apparently *Rambam* follows the implication of the *Gemara* elsewhere (*Zevachim* 87a) that as long as the loaves remain on the *shulchan* they are not susceptible to that invalidation (*Lechem Mishneh* loc. cit.).]

מנחות
יא/ט

[ט] **שְׁתֵּי** הַלֶּחֶם נֶאֱכָלוֹת אֵין פָּחוּת מִשְּׁנַיִם וְלֹא יָתֵר עַל שְׁלֹשָׁה. כֵּיצַד? נֶאֱפוֹת מֵעֶרֶב יוֹם טוֹב וְנֶאֱכָלוֹת בְּיוֹם טוֹב, לִשְׁנַיִם. חָל יוֹם טוֹב לִהְיוֹת אַחַר הַשַּׁבָּת, נֶאֱכָלוֹת לִשְׁלֹשָׁה.

לֶחֶם הַפָּנִים נֶאֱכָל אֵין פָּחוּת מִתִּשְׁעָה וְלֹא יָתֵר עַל אַחַד עָשָׂר. כֵּיצַד? נֶאֱפֶה בְּעֶרֶב שַׁבָּת וְנֶאֱכָל בְּשַׁבָּת, לְתִשְׁעָה. חָל יוֹם טוֹב לִהְיוֹת עֶרֶב שַׁבָּת, נֶאֱכָל לַעֲשָׂרָה. שְׁנֵי יָמִים טוֹבִים שֶׁל רֹאשׁ הַשָּׁנָה, נֶאֱכָל לְאַחַד עָשָׂר.

**ר׳ עובדיה מברטנורא**

(ט) **אין פחות משנים.** משני ימים משנאפו: **נאכל לשלשה.** שאופים בערב שבת, לפי שאין אפייתן דוחה לא שבת ולא יום טוב: **לתשעה.** בשבת שניה, שהוא תשיעי לאפייתו: **לעשרה.** שנאפו בחמישי בשבת: **שני ימים טובים של ראש השנה.** קודם לשבת, נאפה ברביעי ונאכל בשבת שניה, הרי לאחד עשר. ואם תאמר, הרי שנים עשר ניהו, דהא אותה שבת הוי יום הכיפורים ואין הלחם נאכל עד למוצאי שבת, הא לא קשיא, דלענין אכילת קדשים הלילה הולך אחר היום שעבר, הלכך מקרי אחד עשר:

**יד אברהם**

## 9.

As noted earlier (mishnah 2), the baking of the *shtei halechem* and the *lechem hapanim* does not supersede the Sabbath prohibition, and these must therefore be baked prior to the Sabbath. This mishnah teaches that it is forbidden to bake them on *Yom Tov* as well.

שְׁתֵּי הַלֶּחֶם נֶאֱכָלוֹת אֵין פָּחוּת מִשְּׁנַיִם — *The shtei halechem are eaten no earlier than two [days]* (lit., *no less than two days*)

The *shtei halechem* are never eaten earlier than on the second day after they are baked (*Rav; Tif. Yis.;* cf. *Tos. Yom Tov*).

וְלֹא יָתֵר עַל שְׁלֹשָׁה. — *and no later than three [days]* (lit., *and no more than three*).

[I.e., on occasion, the *shtei halechem* are not eaten until the third day from their baking, as will be explained, but it can never be more than that. After three days from their baking they have the status of an offering left past its allotted time and are prohibited.]

כֵּיצַד? — *How so?*

[What determines whether they are eaten on the second day or on the third?]

נֶאֱפוֹת מֵעֶרֶב יוֹם טוֹב וְנֶאֱכָלוֹת בְּיוֹם טוֹב, לִשְׁנַיִם. — *[If] they are baked on the eve of the Festival and eaten on the Festival, that is two.*

[Under normal circumstances, the loaves are baked on the day before Shavuos and eaten on the day of the Festival. Thus, they are eaten on the second day from their baking.]

חָל יוֹם טוֹב לִהְיוֹת אַחַר הַשַּׁבָּת, נֶאֱכָלוֹת לִשְׁלֹשָׁה. — *[If] the Festival falls on Sunday, they are eaten on the third* (lit., *for three*).

**9.** The *shtei halechem* are eaten no earlier than two [days] and no later than three [days]. How so? [If] they are baked on the eve of the Festival and eaten on the Festival, that is two. [If] the Festival falls on Sunday, they are eaten on the third.

The *lechem hapanim* are eaten no earlier than nine [days] and no later than eleven [days]. How so? [If] they are baked on Friday and eaten on the Sabbath, that is nine [days]. [If] a Festival falls on Friday, it is eaten on the tenth [day]. [If] the two days of Rosh Hashanah, it is eaten on the eleventh [day].

### YAD AVRAHAM

If Shavuos is on a Sunday, the loaves must be baked on the preceding Friday (*Tif. Yis.*). Thus, there is a three-day lapse from the baking to the eating.

לֶחֶם הַפָּנִים נֶאֱכָל אֵין פָּחוּת מִתִּשְׁעָה וְלֹא יָתֵר עַל אַחַד עָשָׂר. — *The lechem hapanim are eaten no earlier than nine [days] and no later than eleven [days].*

[The earliest the *lechem hapanim* may be eaten is on the ninth day from the day they are baked, and the latest, when circumstances warrant it, is on the eleventh.]

Under certain circumstances, the period from the baking till the eating can last as long as thirteen days, as described in the previous mishnah. Our mishnah's rule, however, refers to normal situations in which there were no irregularities with the *avodah* of the *lechem hapanim* or the *levonah* (*Tif. Yis.*).

כֵּיצַד? — *How so?*

[The mishnah now explains the circumstances which affect the number of days that elapse before the *lechem hapanim* is eaten.]

נֶאֱפֶה בְּעֶרֶב שַׁבָּת וְנֶאֱכָל בְּשַׁבָּת, לְתִשְׁעָה. — *[If] they are baked on Friday and eaten on the Sabbath, that is nine [days].*

[These are the normal circumstances in which the *lechem hapanim* are baked on Friday and placed in the Temple on Shabbos, to be removed and eaten on the following Shabbos (see mishnah 8). Thus, the consumption takes place on the ninth day after their baking.]

חָל יוֹם טוֹב לִהְיוֹת עֶרֶב שַׁבָּת, נֶאֱכָל לַעֲשָׂרָה. — *[If] a Festival falls on Friday, it is eaten on the tenth [day].*

[If the day before Shabbos is a *Yom Tov*, on which the *lechem hapanim* may not be baked, the breads must be baked on Thursday. Thus, when they are eaten the following Shabbos, it is the tenth day from their baking.]

שְׁנֵי יָמִים טוֹבִים שֶׁל רֹאשׁ הַשָּׁנָה, נֶאֱכָל לְאַחַד עָשָׂר. — *[If] the two days of Rosh Hashanah, it is eaten on the eleventh [day].*

[Of all the Festivals, Rosh Hashanah is the only one which extends for two days even in Eretz Yisrael (see *Beitzah* 5a). Therefore, only Rosh Hashanah could advance the baking of the *lechem hapanim* for two days — i.e., if Rosh Hashanah comes out on Thursday and Friday, the *lechem hapanim*

# וְאֵינוֹ דוֹחֶה לֹא אֶת הַשַּׁבָּת וְלֹא אֶת יוֹם טוֹב. רַבָּן שִׁמְעוֹן בֶּן גַּמְלִיאֵל אוֹמֵר מִשּׁוּם רַבִּי שִׁמְעוֹן בֶּן הַסְּגַן: דּוֹחֶה אֶת יוֹם טוֹב וְאֵינוֹ דוֹחֶה אֶת יוֹם צוֹם.

### ר׳ עובדיה מברטנורא

**ואינו דוחה לא את השבת ולא את יום טוב.** לפי שאין אופים ומבשלים ביום טוב אלא מה שאוכל באותו היום בלבד: **רבן שמעון בן גמליאל אומר וכו׳.** ואין הלכה כרבן שמעון בן גמליאל:

### יד אברהם

must be baked on Wednesday. In such a case, the *lechem hapanim* is not eaten until the eleventh day from baking.]

One may well ask that if Rosh Hashanah is on Thursday and Friday, the following Shabbos is Yom Kippur, and the loaves cannot be eaten until the night after the fast, which is actually the eve of the twelfth day from baking! The explanation, however, is that in dealing with offerings in the Temple, the night is viewed as the extension of the day which precedes it, not the beginning of the one that follows it. Thus, the night after Yom Kippur is therefore still considered the eleventh day from baking (*Rav; Rashi*).

*Tosafos* submit that *Rashi's* question is not really a problem. In the times when the calendar was determined by eyewitness testimony, the only situation that called for a two-day Rosh Hashanah was one in which the witnesses appeared after the afternoon *tamid*, thereby requiring *beis din* to declare the first and second day as Rosh Hashanah [see *Beitzah* 5a for a fuller discussion]. In such an event, the true day of Rosh Hashanah was the *second;* the remainder of the first was conducted as a Festival only to prevent any error in subsequent years. Thus, when Rosh Hashanah is Thursday and Friday, as far as the calendar reckoning is concerned the first day of Tishrei is Friday and Yom Kippur is Sunday. Accordingly, in such a situation, the *lechem hapanim* would be eaten on Shabbos, eleven days after it was baked.

**וְאֵינוֹ דוֹחֶה לֹא אֶת הַשַּׁבָּת וְלֹא אֶת יוֹם**

11
9

It does not override either the Sabbath or the Festival. Rabban Shimon ben Gamliel says in the name of R′ Shimon the son of the administrator: It overrides the Festival but it does not override the day of the fast.



טוֹב. — *It does not override either the Sabbath or the Festival.*

Baking on *Yom Tov* is permitted only when it is for the needs of the day, but since these breads will not be eaten until one week later, their baking is prohibited (*Rav* from *Pesachim* 47a).

The *shtei halechem*, too, may not be baked on *Yom Tov* although they are eaten on that day, because the Torah permits labor only for the food purposes of an individual, not for items which are for the Temple service (even if they are ultimately eaten). This is derived from the verse (*Ex.* 12:16): אַךְ אֲשֶׁר יֵאָכֵל לְכָל נֶפֶשׁ, הוּא לְבַדּוֹ יֵעָשֶׂה לָכֶם, *Only that which is eaten by any person, that alone may be made for you*, which is interpreted as לָכֶם, וְלֹא לְגָבוֹהַּ, *for you* [i.e., for your personal needs], *but not for the sake of Heaven* (*Gemara* ibid.).

רַבָּן שִׁמְעוֹן בֶּן גַּמְלִיאֵל אוֹמֵר מִשּׁוּם רַבִּי שִׁמְעוֹן בֶּן הַסְּגַן: דּוֹחֶה אֶת יוֹם טוֹב — *Rabban Shimon ben Gamliel says in the name of R′ Shimon the son of the administrator: It overrides the Festival*

[If Friday is a *Yom Tov* the *shtei halechem* may be baked.] In his opinion the word לָכֶם, *for you*, excludes only the needs of a non-Jew but not those of the Temple (*Tif. Yis.* from *Gemara* ibid.).

וְאֵינוֹ דוֹחֶה אֶת יוֹם צוֹם. — *but it does not override the day of the fast.*

If Yom Kippur falls out on Friday, however, the *lechem hapanim* may not be baked then (*Rashi*) [as Yom Kippur has the same stringency as Shabbos regarding which labors are permitted].

The halachah follows the view of the first *Tanna* (*Rav; Rambam, Temidin U′Mussafin* 5:10).

# ◆ פרק שנים עשר ◆
# Chapter Twelve

# [א] הַמְּנָחוֹת וְהַנְּסָכִים שֶׁנִּטְמְאוּ – עַד שֶׁלֹּא קִדְּשָׁן בִּכְלִי, יֵשׁ לָהֶם פִּדְיוֹן; מִשֶּׁקִּדְּשׁוּ בִּכְלִי, אֵין לָהֶם פִּדְיוֹן.

ר׳ עובדיה מברטנורא

**פרק שנים עשר – המנחות והנסכים. (א) המנחות והנסכים. עד שלא קדשו בכלי.** אינן קדושים קדושת הגוף, אלא קדושת דמים, שצריך לפדותן והדמים קדושים. ודוקא כשנטמאו יש להן פדיון אם לא קדשו בכלי, אבל לא נטמאו אף על פי שלא קדשו בכלי אין פודים אותן:

**יד אברהם**

## 1.

A person consecrating an object may do so for two purposes: to donate the value of the object to the Temple treasury, or to sanctify the object to serve as an offering. The level of sanctity attained by the object depends on the type of consecration. Where the consecration has been made to the Temple treasury, the object becomes the property of the Temple treasury and acquires קְדוּשַּׁת בֶּדֶק הַבַּיִת, *treasury sanctity* [literally, *sanctified for the repair of the House*]. At this level, it possesses קְדוּשַּׁת דָּמִים, *monetary sanctity* — i.e., sanctity for its value, not for its essence.[1] Thus, it may be redeemed by the original owner or be sold by the treasury to obtain funds. The money obtained in payment assumes the sanctity previously inherent in the object, and the object reverts to *chullin* [non-holy] status.[2]

Objects fit for the Altar which have been consecrated to serve as offerings — such as [unblemished] bulls, lambs, goats, flour, wine or oil — attain קְדוּשַּׁת הַגּוּף, *physical sanctity*, and these can no longer be sold or redeemed. In the case of an animal offering, should the animal become blemished and thereby unfit to serve as an offering, redemption is once again feasible, as derived by the *Gemara*

1. Although all objects consecrated to the Temple treasury possess only monetary sanctity, the two terms — קְדוּשַּׁת בֶּדֶק הַבַּיִת, *treasury sanctity*, and קְדוּשַּׁת דָּמִים, *monetary sanctity* — are not identical. A person may consecrate money or other objects to pay for the purchase of sacrifices. The money or objects in this case acquire *monetary sanctity* but they are not the property of the Temple treasury. Rather, they remain under the donor's personal supervision and he must use them to purchase the designated offerings [or sell them to obtain the money with which to purchase the designated offerings]. Similarly, if an animal set aside as an offering becomes blemished, and thus unfit for offering, its sanctity level drops from קְדוּשַּׁת הַגּוּף, *physical sanctity*, to קְדוּשַּׁת דָּמִים, *monetary sanctity*. Here too, the animal is sold and the money is used to purchase a replacement sacrifice.

2. An unblemished animal which is consecrated to the Temple treasury for its worth [מַתְפִּיס תְּמִימִים לְבֶדֶק הַבַּיִת], and thus possesses only monetary sanctity and not physical sanctity, can be redeemed but only for the purpose of serving as an offering; that is, it can be sold by the treasurer only to a buyer who will use it for a sacrifice. In this manner, the Temple's treasury obtains its funds while the animal remains to be used as a sacrifice. In the words of the *Tosefta*: "If unblemished animals are assigned to the Temple treasury, they may not be redeemed except for [use on] the Altar. For whatever is fit for the Altar does not leave the province of the Altar ever" [i.e., once it has become "fit" for the Altar by being assigned to the Temple, it no longer leaves the Temple] (*Tosefta Temurah* 1:6, cited by *Gem.* here 101a).

1. Minchah-offerings and libation offerings which became contaminated with *tumah* — before they were sanctified in a vessel they can be redeemed; once they were sanctified in a vessel, they cannot be redeemed.

### YAD AVRAHAM

(101a). [The money obtained from the redemption then goes for the purchase of a replacement offering, while the redeemed animal reverts to *chullin* status.[1] However, once an animal is slaughtered it can never again be redeemed even if the offering becomes invalidated (*Rashi* 101a). In such a case, the carcass must be burned in the בֵּית הַשְּׂרֵפָה, *the place of burning* [for disqualified offerings].

The following mishnah will define the rule of redemption for *menachos* and other non-animal offerings.

הַמְּנָחוֹת וְהַנְּסָכִים שֶׁנִּטְמְאוּ – עַד שֶׁלֹּא קִדְּשָׁן בִּכְלִי, יֵשׁ לָהֶם פִּדְיוֹן; — *Minchah-offerings and libation offerings which became contaminated with tumah — before they were sanctified in a vessel they can be redeemed;*

Flour which was orally designated for a *minchah*, or wine which was orally designated for *nesachim* [libations] (*Tif. Yis.*), [but was not yet consecrated by being placed in a *kli shareis*] has only קְדוּשַּׁת דָּמִים, *monetary sanctity* (see prefatory note), and not קְדוּשַּׁת הַגּוּף, *physical sanctity*. Therefore, if the *minchah* or wine becomes *tamei* and can no longer be offered on the Altar, it can be redeemed. The redemption money becomes sanctified (*Rav; Rashi*) [and must be used to purchase new flour or wine for the offering].

The mishnah states the law of redemption for flour and wine that have become *tamei* and thus unfit for offering. The *Gemara* records a dispute of *Amoraim* whether uncontaminated flour and wine may also be redeemed. In the opinion of Shmuel, these may be redeemed, since they possess only monetary sanctity until they are consecrated by placement in a *kli shareis*. In the opinion of Rav Kahana and R' Elazar they may only be redeemed if they have become *tamei* and thus disqualified (*Gem.* 100b, 101a). This is based on the general rule that "whatever has become fit for the Altar [by being consecrated] does not leave the province of the Altar" (*Tos. Yom Tov* from *Gem.* 101a; see fn. above). The one exception to this is the sinner's *minchah* (see 1:1), concerning which the *Gemara* (ibid.) derives exegetically that it can be redeemed even if it has not been contaminated. The halachah follows this latter view (*Rambam, Hil. Isurei Mizbe'ach* 6:5).

מִשֶּׁקְּדָשׁוּ בִּכְלִי, אֵין לָהֶם פִּדְיוֹן. — *once they were sanctified in a vessel, they cannot be redeemed.*

Once the flour is placed in a *kli shareis* in the Temple [even before *kemitzah*] it acquires קְדוּשַּׁת הַגּוּף, *physical sanctity*, and can no longer be redeemed (*Rav*). Although even an animal offering which possesses physical sanctity can be redeemed if it acquires a blemish [and thereby loses its fitness for offering] — and

1. However, it does not entirely revert to *chullin* status. Even after redemption, the animal may only be used for meat but not for work, wool (if it is a sheep), or milk (*Sifri* to *Deut.* 12:15; *Bechoros* 2:3, 15a; see *Rambam, Hil. Me'ilah* 1:9).

הָעוֹפוֹת, וְהָעֵצִים, וְהַלְּבוֹנָה, וּכְלֵי שָׁרֵת אֵין לָהֶם פִּדְיוֹן, שֶׁלֹּא נֶאֱמַר אֶלָּא בְהֵמָה.

**[ב] הָאוֹמֵר:** „הֲרֵי עָלַי בְּמַחֲבַת,״ וְהֵבִיא בְמַרְחֶשֶׁת; „בְּמַרְחֶשֶׁת,״

**ר׳ עובדיה מברטנורא**

**העופות והעצים והלבונה [וכלי שרת] שנטמאו אין להם פדיון.** שלא נאמר פדיון בקדושת הגוף אלא בבהמה בעלת מום, דכתיב (ויקרא כז, יא) ואם כל בהמה טמאה, אשר לא יקריבו ממנה קרבן לה׳, והעריך הכהן אותה וכו׳, ובבעלי מומים שיפדו הכתוב מדבר, דאי בבהמה טמאה ממש, כשהוא אומר (שם שם, כז) ואם בבהמה הטמאה ופדה בערכך, הרי בהמה טמאה אמורה. ואשמועינן במתניתין דאף על גב דאשכחן בקדוש קדושת הגוף ונפל ביה מומא דמפריק, העופות והעצים והלבונה וכלי שרת דקדשי קדושת הגוף ונטמאו לא מפרקי:

**יד אברהם**

*minchah*-flour and *nesech*-wine which have become *tamei* are somewhat analogous to this — the level of sanctity attained by being sanctified in a *kli shareis* is more than simple physical sanctity and precludes the possibility of redemption (*Gem.* 100b). Nowhere do we find a substance sanctified in a *kli shareis* remaining eligible for redemption (*Gem.* 101a), even an animal offering. Once the animal has been slaughtered and thereby sanctified by the knife, it can no longer be redeemed even if it is subsequently disqualified (*Rashi* 101a, s.v. דמכלי שרת).

הָעוֹפוֹת, — *Birds,*

This refers to a bird which was designated for a sacrifice and then became blemished;[1] as the mishnah states below, the bird can not be redeemed despite its disqualification. However, if it was already blemished at the time it was sanctified, it can be redeemed (*Tos.* 100b, s.v. העופות; see *Rashash*).

If a bird becomes *tamei* after its slaughter, it can also not be redeemed (*Tos. Yom Tov*).

וְהָעֵצִים, וְהַלְּבוֹנָה, — *wood, frankincense,*

The wood used for burning on the Altar, as well as *levonah*, are neither utensils [כֵּלִים] nor edible foods [אוֹכְלִים]. Thus, they are not subject to *tumah*-contamination, since susceptibility to *tumah* is restricted to the above-mentioned categories. Since they never become *tamei*, they cannot be redeemed even if they have been in contact with a *tumah*-transmitting object (*Gem.* 101a).

Even Shmuel, who rules that flour and wine may be redeemed even if they are not *tamei* (see above, s.v. יש להן פדיון), agrees in the case of wood and *levonah* that they may not be redeemed as long as they remain fit for the Altar. This is due to the fact that these items, in the form fit for the Altar, are not that readily available, and we therefore do not allow them to be redeemed as long as they are fit (*Gem.* 101a).

Actually, wood and *levonah* can also become *tamei* once they have been sanctified

1. In contrast to an animal, a bird does not become disqualified by a blemish unless it loses a limb. A withered limb (or organ), such as a paralyzed wing or a blind eye, constitutes a loss of limb even though it has not actually been severed (*Zevachim* 7:5).

12
2

Birds, wood, frankincense, and sacred vessels cannot be redeemed, for it only says an animal.

**2.** [If] one says, "I take upon myself [to bring a *minchah*-offering] in a *machavas*," and he brought [it] in a *marcheshes*; [or he said,] "in a *marcheshes*," and he

## YAD AVRAHAM

by a *kli shareis*, such as the Temple ax which is used to cut them to size (in the case of the wood), or the bowl in which the *levonah* is placed. Although they are still not foods, the principle of חִבַּת הַקּוֹדֶשׁ מַכְשַׁרְתָּן, *the esteem in which holy things are held renders them susceptible*, causes them to be treated as the equivalent of foods and therefore susceptible to *tumah* (*Gem.* ibid.). [However, the mishnah does not refer to such a case, because once they have been sanctified by a *kli shareis*, it goes without saying that they cannot be redeemed, as explained above in the case of flour and wine (s.v. משקדשו).][1]

וּכְלֵי שָׁרֵת — *and sacred vessels*

The *kli shareis* themselves cannot be redeemed even if they become *tamei*, because they can be rendered *tahor* again by being immersed in a *mikveh* (ibid.). Thus, *tumah* never disqualifies them beyond reclaim.

אֵין לָהֶם פִּדְיוֹן, — *cannot be redeemed,*

[All of these cannot be redeemed for the reasons stated above. The reason why birds cannot be redeemed is stated presently by the mishnah itself.]

שֶׁלֹּא נֶאֱמַר אֶלָּא בְּהֵמָה. — *for it only says an animal.*

The verse in the Torah from which the redemption of a blemished sacrifice is derived (*Lev.* 27:11) refers explicitly to *an animal* (*Rav* from *Gem.*). Thus, redemption of a blemished bird is excluded. This point of the mishnah refers only to the exclusion from redemption of a blemished bird. The other things excluded by this mishnah are for the reasons given above (*Zevach Todah*).

## 2.

הָאוֹמֵר: ,,הֲרֵי עָלַי בְּמַחֲבַת,״ וְהֵבִיא בְּמַרְחֶשֶׁת; ,,בְּמַרְחֶשֶׁת,״ וְהֵבִיא בְּמַחֲבַת — מַה שֶּׁהֵבִיא הֵבִיא, וִידֵי חוֹבָתוֹ לֹא יָצָא. — *[If] one says, "I take upon myself [to bring a minchah-offering] in a machavas," and he brought [it] in a marcheshes; [or he said,] "in a marcheshes," and he brought [it] in a machavas — what he has brought he has brought, but he has not fulfilled his obligation.*

1. *Rashi* seems to have understood the *Gemara* to mean that wood and *levonah* become susceptible to *tumah* only once they have been sanctified by a *kli shareis*. *Tosafos* (101a, s.v. אע״ג) take issue with this and assert that even before sanctification they are susceptible to *tumah*, albeit only on a Rabbinical level, due to the principle of *the esteem accorded to holy things renders them susceptible to tumah*. Nevertheless, because this *tumah* is not consistent with the regular rules of *tumah* — which apply only to food or utensils — the wood is viewed in regard to the rule of redemption like something which cannot become contaminated. Once they have been sanctified by a *kli shareis* they are susceptible to *tumah* even on a Biblical level (see further, *Sfas Emes*; see also *Zevachim* 4:5 and comm. there).

## וְהֵבִיא בְמַחֲבַת — מַה שֶׁהֵבִיא הֵבִיא, וִידֵי חוֹבָתוֹ לֹא יָצָא. „זוֹ לְהָבִיא בְמַחֲבַת," וְהֵבִיא בְמַרְחֶשֶׁת; „בְּמַרְחֶשֶׁת," וְהֵבִיא בְמַחֲבַת — הֲרֵי זוֹ פְּסוּלָה.

### ר' עובדיה מברטנורא

(ב) **מה שהביא הביא.** דאמרינן לא לשם נדרו הביאה, אלא נדבה אחרת היא זו: **זו להביא במחבת.** שהיתה עשרון סלת מונחת לפניו, ואמר, זו להביא במחבת וכו': **הרי זו פסולה.** דקבעה לכלי שהזכיר בה ואין יכול לשנותה לכלי אחר:

### יד אברהם

There are two similar types of voluntary *menachos*, both of which are fried. The *machavas* is made on a griddle and thus bakes as a drier cake. The *marcheshes* is made in a pan and is thus spongier (see mishnah 5:8).

[If someone vowed to bring one of these offerings and he instead brought the other, he has not fulfilled his vow, as the two are not interchangeable. Although the *machavas* and *marcheshes* both consist of the same ingredients, the declaration of an obligation to offer one type of *minchah* obligates him to bring specifically that type of *minchah*. Should he offer the other type of *minchah* in fulfillment of this obligation, he has not fulfilled it (see *Gem.* 3a).]

However, the offering itself is valid, because we interpret his actions to mean that he is donating an additional offering besides the one which he previously vowed to bring (*Rav*).

[*Rav's* statement implies that if the *minchah* was in fact intended to fulfill the vow, the *minchah* itself is invalid. The intention to offer the flour in a prescribed manner, coupled with a sanctification of the flour in a *kli shareis*, sanctifies it to be valid as only that sort of *minchah*. For example, if one intends a *minchah* to be of the *marcheshes* type, and he places it in a *kli shareis* to sanctify it for that purpose, it becomes designated and remains fixed as a *minchas marcheshes* (see below, s.v. זו להביא במרחשת). If it is later prepared and offered as a *machavas*, it is invalidated (*Zevach Todah*; see below). This is not comparable to the case of a *marcheshes* offered with the intent that it be a *machavas* regarding which the mishnah (1:1; see comm. there) rules that it is valid. That case refers to a *minchah* which was designated to be a *marcheshes* and actually offered in that manner; the *intent* that it serve in lieu of a *machavas* cannot per se invalidate the *minchah*. Our mishnah, however, discusses a *minchah*-offering *prepared* in a manner which deviates from its designated purpose, and rules that such a deviation does invalidate.]

„זוֹ לְהָבִיא בְמַחֲבַת," וְהֵבִיא בְמַרְחֶשֶׁת; „בְּמַרְחֶשֶׁת," וְהֵבִיא בְמַחֲבַת — *[If he said,] "This is to be brought in a machavas," and he brought [it] in a marcheshes; [or he said,] "in a marcheshes," and he brought [it] in a machavas —*

[Instead of a general vow specifying his obligation, he designated a particular *issaron* of flour as a *minchah* of one type and then brought it in a vessel befitting another type of *minchah*.]

הֲרֵי זוֹ פְּסוּלָה. — *it is invalid.*

Since he designated this flour to be offered as a *minchah* in a particular

12
2

brought [it] in a *machavas* — what he has brought he has brought, but he has not fulfilled his obligation. [If he said,] "This is to be brought in a *machavas*," and he brought [it] in a *marcheshes*; [or he said,] "in a *marcheshes*," and he brought [it] in a *machavas* — it is invalid.

YAD AVRAHAM

type of vessel [and sanctified it as such in a *kli shareis*], he cannot change and bring it in another type of vessel [which causes it to be categorized as a different type of offering]. If he does, it is invalid and may not be offered upon the Altar (*Rav; Rashi*).

[In the previous case, in which the vow did not refer to any specific *issaron* of flour but to a general obligation, the *minchah* brought for a different designation can be construed as being a new donation; therefore the *minchah* remains valid while the vow remains unfulfilled. In this last case, however, the vow refers to a specific *issaron* of flour; thus, if it cannot be valid as the *minchah* of the vow, it cannot be valid at all.]

As noted above, the disqualifications of this mishnah apply even if the *minchah* was not actually processed and offered, but merely placed in a *kli shareis* and brought to be offered (see *Gem.* 102b; *Zevach Todah; Chazon Ish* 29:18). Therefore, even if he should now fry it according to the method stipulated in his vow, it would still be invalid.

Actually, it seems from the *Gemara* that placing the *minchah* in the *machavas* or *marcheshes* does not constitute a bona fide sanctification, and does not per se render the *minchah* fit for offering (*Gem.* 102b).[1] Hence, one should be allowed to remove the *minchah* from that vessel and prepare it in the type of vessel he specified in his vow (*Rashi*). Nevertheless, the vessel does confer a degree of sanctification. The *minchah* is now categorized as an offering and is susceptible to those disqualifications which pertain only to offerings, i.e., it is now subject to the disqualifications arising out of *tumah* and being left overnight [לִינָה] (*Gem.* 102b). [Consequently, the lesser degree of sanctification designates and fixes the *minchah* permanently as the type of *minchah* fitting for that vessel and precludes that *minchah* being offered in a different manner. Since this sanctification contradicts the oral designation of this *minchah*, the *minchah* is invalid.]

The ruling of this mishnah applies only if his specification that the flour be for a certain type of *minchah* was made at the time of his original vow to bring an offering. However, if the original vow was merely to bring a *minchah* and he did not specify the type intended until later (see mishnah 13:1), the flour which he brings to fulfill that vow does not become invalidated if he then uses it for the other type of *minchah*. This is derived by the *Gemara* exegetically from the Torah (*Gem.* 103a as interpreted by *Rashi*). The principle established by this is that since the person's original vow was a general one, and the later designation of an *issaron* serves merely to orally consecrate flour for the fulfillment

1. The *Gemara* does not indicate why placing it in the vessel is not a bona fide sanctification in our case. *Mikdash David* (3:3, p. 22) conjectures that bona fide sanctification is accomplished only when an offering is placed in a vessel fitting for it. In our case the *minchah* was placed in a vessel fit for the *minchah* type specified by oral designation.

„הֲרֵי עָלַי שְׁנֵי עֶשְׂרוֹנִים לְהָבִיא בִּכְלִי אֶחָד," וְהֵבִיא בִשְׁנֵי כֵלִים; „בִּשְׁנֵי כֵלִים," וְהֵבִיא בִכְלִי אֶחָד — מַה שֶּׁהֵבִיא הֵבִיא, וִידֵי חוֹבָתוֹ לֹא יָצָא. „אֵלּוּ לְהָבִיא בִכְלִי אֶחָד," וְהֵבִיא בִשְׁנֵי כֵלִים; „בִּשְׁנֵי כֵלִים," וְהֵבִיא בִכְלִי אֶחָד — הֲרֵי אֵלּוּ פְּסוּלִין.

**ר' עובדיה מברטנורא**

**אלו להביא בכלי אחד.** אלו שהיו מונחים לפניו: **הרי אלו פסולים.** דהיכא דנדר בכלי אחד והביא בשני כלים מפריש ממנה שני קומצים, והוא לא נדר אלא קומץ אחד, ועוד, שמנחה חסרה היא בכל כלי וכלי. והיכא דנדר בשני כלים והביא בכלי אחד, הויא מנחה יתירה ומיעט בקומצין, שהוא בירר לה שתי קמיצות ולא קמץ אלא אחד:

**יד אברהם**

differently. If he designated it for a *minchah* without specifying which type and subsequently placed it into either a *machavas* or a *marcheshes* and then switched it to the other type of vessel, the placement into the first vessel is not considered tantamount to specifying that the flour be for that type of *minchah*. The offering is therefore valid (*Zevach Todah*).[1]

„הֲרֵי עָלַי שְׁנֵי עֶשְׂרוֹנִים לְהָבִיא בִּכְלִי אֶחָד," וְהֵבִיא בִשְׁנֵי כֵלִים; — *"I take upon myself to bring two essronim in one vessel," and he brought [them] in two vessels;*

[Although there is a fixed minimum amount for a *minchah*-offering (see above 3:5 and mishnah 3 below), one may vow to bring any multiple of an *issaron*. He may then offer each *issaron* as a separate *minchah*, or offer the entire amount as one *minchah*. However, sixty *issaron* is the maximum amount which may be brought as one *minchah* (see mishnah 4).]

In the present case, despite his vow of the vow, it cannot consecrate that flour to any more specific purpose than called for by the original vow. Therefore, even though at the consecration of the flour he designates it to be a *machavas* (for example), this designation is not binding. The person is not authorized at this point to change or add to his original vow with an oral declaration, and since his original declaration could be fulfilled with any type of *minchah*, the flour takes on only that general designation (*Chazon Ish* 29:20).

However, placing the *minchah* in a *kli shareis* afterward does determine the type of *minchah* it will be, even in the case of a general vow. This can be inferred from the ruling stated earlier that a *kli shareis* has the power to sanctify and fix a *minchah* even when the sanctification contradicts the previous, oral vow, although the vessel's sanctification thereby serves only to disqualify the *minchah* (ibid.; see *Sfas Emes*; cf. *Even HaAzel* to *Maaseh HaKorbanos* 17:3).

*Rambam* (*Maaseh HaKorbanos* 17:3) seems to interpret this *Gemara* somewhat

1. The ruling attributed to *Rambam* is difficult to reconcile with the earlier stated rule that a *shareis* vessel *does* fix and determine a *minchah* into a specific mode. *Chazon Ish* (loc. cit.) construes *Rambam* to mean only that he subsequently *declared* to put the *minchah* into a *machavas* or *marcheshes*. Hence *Rambam's* view is in accord with *Rashi*.

12 "I take upon myself to bring two *essronim* in
2 one vessel," and he brought [them] in two vessels; [or he said,] "in two vessels," and brought [them] in one vessel — what he has brought he has brought, but he has not fulfilled his obligation. [If he said,] "These are to be brought in one vessel," and he brought [them] in two vessels; [or he said,] "in two vessels," and he brought [them] in one vessel — they are invalid.



to bring both *essronim* in one vessel (as a single *minchah*), he brought each *issaron* in a separate vessel (i.e., each as a separate *minchah*).

,,בִּשְׁנֵי כֵלִים,״ וְהֵבִיא בִכְלִי אֶחָד – מַה שֶּׁהֵבִיא הֵבִיא, וִידֵי חוֹבָתוֹ לֹא יָצָא. — *[or he said,] "in two vessels," and brought [them] in one vessel — what he has brought he has brought, but he has not fulfilled his obligation.*

[Or, he vowed to bring two *essronim* each in a separate vessel (i.e., as two *menachos*), but later brought them both in a single vessel (as one *minchah*). Since he did not designate any specific container of flour when making his vow, that which he brought in a manner different from what he vowed is understood to be a separate offering, which is valid in its own right. However, his original vow must still be fulfilled.]

Further on (13:8) the mishnah states that if one vowed to bring a small offering he can discharge his obligation by bringing a big one. It follows from this that if one vowed to bring a *minchah* consisting of one *issaron* he discharges his obligation by bringing a *minchah* of two *essronim*. Hence, in the case in which he vowed to bring two *essronim* in two vessels, there is no reason why bringing a *minchah* of two *essronim* in one vessel should not at least be counted as a discharge of half the obligation, and it should be considered as if he had brought at least one of the two *menachos*. Accordingly, we must assume that the ruling of the mishnah means that he has not *fully* discharged his obligation and must bring yet another *minchah* of one *issaron* (*Sfas Emes*).

,,אֵלּוּ לְהָבִיא בִכְלִי אֶחָד,״ וְהֵבִיא בִשְׁנֵי כֵלִים; ,,בִּשְׁנֵי כֵלִים,״ וְהֵבִיא בִכְלִי אֶחָד – הֲרֵי אֵלּוּ פְּסוּלִין. — *[If he said,] "These are to be brought in one vessel," and he brought [them] in two vessels; [or he said,] "in two vessels," and he brought [them] in one vessel — they are invalid.*

If he designated a specific volume of flour as a single *minchah* of two *essronim*, and he then brought that flour in two separate vessels as two separate *menachos* of one *issaron* each, or vice versa, they are both invalid.

The reason for this is that one *minchah* of two *essronim* requires only one *kemitzah*, whereas two *menachos* require a separate *kemitzah* for each one. Therefore, in offering it in one vessel instead of two, or two instead of one, he is offering the *minchah* in a manner which deviates from his vow in a basic fashion. In addition, when he vowed to bring a single *minchah* of two *essronim* and then offered them

מנחות
יב/ב

„הֲרֵי עָלַי שְׁנֵי עֶשְׂרוֹנִים לְהָבִיא בִכְלִי אֶחָד,” וְהֵבִיא בִשְׁנֵי כֵלִים; אָמְרוּ לוֹ: „בִּכְלִי אֶחָד נָדַרְתָּ” — הִקְרִיבָן בִּכְלִי אֶחָד, כְּשֵׁרִים; וּבִשְׁנֵי כֵלִים, פְּסוּלִין. „הֲרֵי עָלַי שְׁנֵי עֶשְׂרוֹנִים לְהָבִיא בִשְׁנֵי כֵלִים,” וְהֵבִיא בִכְלִי אֶחָד; אָמְרוּ לוֹ: „בִּשְׁנֵי כֵלִים נָדַרְתָּ” — הִקְרִיבָן בִּשְׁנֵי כֵלִים, כְּשֵׁרִים.

ר' עובדיה מברטנורא

**אמרו לו בכלי אחד נדרת.** ולא חש לדבריהם והקריבה בשני כלים, פסולים, ואף על גב דלא אמר אלו להביא בכלי אחד, משום דהשתא ליכא למימר לשום נדבה אחרת אייתי לה, דכיון דאמרי ליה בכלי אחד נדרת הוה ליה למימר להו אנא משום נדר אחרינא מייתינא לה:

יד אברהם

[Although he had previously placed them in two *klei shareis*, since he transferred them to a single *kli shareis* as soon as he was informed of his error, his offering is valid and he thereby fulfills his vow.]

Earlier in this mishnah we learned that when a *minchah* is brought in a manner which contradicts the terms of the vow, once it has been placed in a *kli shareis* it becomes sanctified for the vessel's designation (rather than the vow's) and it can no longer be restored to its proper state (see above, s.v. האומר and הרי זו פסולה, in connection with the *machavas* and the *marcheshes*). The mishnah makes the point here that the disqualification which is occasioned by placing the *minchah's* flour in the *kli shareis* in a way which contradicts its oral consecration is limited to instances in which the act of placing the *minchah* in the *kli shareis* is deliberate — i.e., the person realizes the contradiction and nevertheless proceeds to place it in the wrong vessel with the intent of deviating from his oral declaration. If, however, it becomes clear that there was no deliberate intent to alter the

as two *menachos*, the volume of flour in each vessel is less than the amount this *minchah* calls for, and a *minchah* which is less than its required amount is not valid (*Rav; Rashi;* see 3:5). In the opposite case, in which he changed the offering from two vessels to one, he thereby reduces the required two *kemitzahs* to only one, and it too is therefore invalid (ibid.). See below, s.v. נתנן בכלי אחד.

„הֲרֵי עָלַי שְׁנֵי עֶשְׂרוֹנִים לְהָבִיא בִכְלִי אֶחָד,” וְהֵבִיא בִשְׁנֵי כֵלִים; אָמְרוּ לוֹ: „בִּכְלִי אֶחָד נָדַרְתָּ” — *[If he said,] "I take upon myself to bring two essronim in one vessel," and he brought [them] in two vessels; [and] they said to him, "You vowed [to bring them] in one vessel"* —

[Someone vowed to bring a *minchah* of two *essronim* in one vessel and then placed the flour in two vessels, as in the case above. In this instance, however, after he had placed it in two vessels, he was reminded by others that he had vowed to bring it in one vessel and he therefore transferred it all into one vessel.]

הִקְרִיבָן בִּכְלִי אֶחָד, כְּשֵׁרִים; — *[if] he brought them in one vessel, they are valid;*

12 [If he said,] "I take upon myself to bring two
2 *essronim* in one vessel," and he brought [them] in two vessels; [and] they said to him, "You vowed [to bring them] in one vessel" — [if] he brought them in one vessel, they are valid; in two vessels, they are invalid. [If he said,] "I take upon myself to bring two *essronim* in two vessels," and he brought [them] in one vessel; [and] they said to him, "You vowed [to bring them] in two vessels" — [if] he brought them in two vessels, they are valid.



*minchah*, no disqualification results from the faulty sanctification, because a sanctification in error is not effective. Therefore, if his improper conduct was pointed out to him and the person immediately abandoned his faulty course of action and commenced to offer the *minchah* in the manner prescribed by his oral declaration, the *minchah* remains valid (*Zevach Todah*).

Accordingly, the same would be true in the case of the *machavas/marcheshes* reversal: If he was told that he was making a mistake and responded by shifting the flour to its proper vessel, the *minchah* would be valid (*Zevach Todah*).

[However, the mishnah seems to imply that deliberate intent to deviate is assumed unless there is definite evidence to the contrary. Thus, in the previous case, in which the person specified, "These are to be brought in one vessel..." the *mishnah* disqualifies the *minchah* for being placed in two vessels, without raising the question of error at all (cf. *Chazon Ish* 29:19).]

**וּבִשְׁנֵי כֵלִים, פְּסוּלִין.** — *in two vessels, they are invalid.*

If he continued to bring the flour in two separate vessels despite the protestations of onlookers, it is invalid. Since he did not respond to them by stating that this is meant for a separate offering, it is understood that he means to bring it in fulfillment of his vow. Therefore, the fact that it does not coincide with the specifications of his vow invalidates it (*Rav; Rashi*).

[As explained above, the validity of the *minchah* in such a case rests upon the assumption that the *minchah* offered in a manner departing from the original vow was not meant to be a fulfillment of the vow. The person's lack of response to the correction indicates that he indeed intends the *minchah* as fulfillment of the vow but wishes to offer it in a manner differing from his original vow. Consequently the *minchah* is disqualified.]

**,,הֲרֵי עָלַי שְׁנֵי עֶשְׂרוֹנִים לְהָבִיא בִשְׁנֵי כֵלִים,״ וְהֵבִיא בִכְלִי אֶחָד; אָמְרוּ לוֹ: ,,בִּשְׁנֵי כֵלִים נָדַרְתָּ״ – הִקְרִיבָן בִּשְׁנֵי כֵלִים, כְּשֵׁרִים.** — *[If he said,] "I take upon myself to bring two essronim in two vessels," and he brought [them] in one vessel; [and] they said to him, "You vowed [to bring them] in two vessels" — [if] he brought them in two vessels, they are valid.*

[In this instance, he placed the two *essronim* into one vessel and then transferred the flour to two separate

# נִתָּנָן בִּכְלִי אֶחָד, כִּשְׁתֵּי מְנָחוֹת שֶׁנִּתְעָרְבוּ.

# [ג] "הֲרֵי עָלַי מִנְחָה מִן הַשְּׂעוֹרִין," יָבִיא

ר' עובדיה מברטנורא

**כשתי מנחות שנתערבו.** [דאמרינן] בפרק הקומץ (ג, ג), אם יכול לקמוץ מזו בפני עצמה ומזו בפני עצמה, כשרות, ואם לאו, פסולות. והא דקתני לעיל אלו להביא בשני כלים והביא בכלי אחד פסולות, מיירי כגון דלא יכול לקמוץ מכל אחת בפני עצמה: (ג) **הרי עלי מנחה מן השעורים יביא מן החטים.** שאין מנחת נדבה באה אלא מן החטים, וכגון שאמר אילו הייתי יודע שאין מביאים מנחה מן השעורים לא הייתי נודר אלא מן החטים, אבל אם אמר לא הייתי נודר כלום, אינו חייב כלום:

יד אברהם

vessels in accordance with his vow, due to the protest of the onlookers. As in the case above, this is an acceptable fulfillment of his vow.]

נִתָּנָן בִּכְלִי אֶחָד, כִּשְׁתֵּי מְנָחוֹת שֶׁנִּתְעָרְבוּ. — *[If] he placed them in one vessel, [it is] like two minchah-offerings which were mixed together.*

If he ignored the warning and offered the two *essronim* in one vessel, it is tantamount to mixing two separate *menachos* together and offering them. In that case, the mishnah (3:3) states that if they are sufficiently distinguishable one from the other to allow for *kemitzah* to be performed separately with each of them, it is acceptable; but if they are completely mixed and this cannot be done, they are invalid (*Rav; Rashi*).

According to this ruling, the mishnah's statement earlier, that if he brought it in one vessel instead of two it is invalid, refers to a case in which *kemitzah* could not be performed with each one separately (ibid.).

Others contend that the mishnah here is discussing a case in which he immediately placed the two *essronim* into two separate vessels as soon as he was informed that he had vowed to bring them in two vessels. Only later did he transfer them back to one vessel. Thus, it corresponds completely to the case in the third chapter (*Tos.*). [Since he initially demonstrated that the consecration in one vessel was erroneous (and re-consecrated the flour correctly as two *menachos* in two vessels), the subsequent placing of both of them into one vessel is viewed as merely mixing together two separate *menachos* in one vessel, and they are not disqualified per se.] According to this view if he initially ignored the warning, and did not remove the *minchah* flour from the vessel and thereby expressed his consent to the faulty sanctification, it is sanctified as one *minchah* and is thereby invalidated (*Zevach Todah*).

## 3.

"הֲרֵי עָלַי מִנְחָה מִן הַשְּׂעוֹרִין," יָבִיא מִן הַחִטִּים. — *[If he said,] "I take upon myself [to bring] a minchah-offering from barley," he must bring one from wheat.*

The Torah does not provide for a voluntary *minchah*-offering from barley flour (*Rav*). The only personal offering that is ever brought from barley flour is the מִנְחַת קְנָאוֹת, *jealousy minchah* (see mishnah 1:1), but this is only brought by a *sotah* as a required offering, never as a voluntary one (*Rashi* 103a, s.v. בשעורין). A personal vow can only take effect in regard to wheat flour, and he must

[If] he placed them in one vessel, [it is] like two *minchah*-offerings which were mixed together.

**3.** [If he said,] "I take upon myself [to bring] a *minchah*-offering from barley," he must bring

YAD AVRAHAM

therefore bring a *minchah* from wheat flour (*Rav*).

The reason his vow obligates him to bring any *minchah* at all is that it is very possible that this person's primary intention was to bring a *minchah*, but he mistakenly assumed that he had an option of offering a barley *minchah* and he therefore chose to vow that type. Had he known, however, that this option was not open to him he would have accepted upon himself a wheat *minchah*, since his primary concern in uttering this vow is to obligate himself to offer an acceptable *minchah*, not specifically a barley one (*Tos. Yom Tov* from *Tos.* 102b-103a, s.v. הא מני; *Rabbeinu Gershom* 103a, s.v. אפילו תימא בה).[1] However, since it is not certain that this was his intention, the obligation to bring a wheat *minchah* applies only if upon being asked, he states that had he known that there is no such thing as a voluntary *minchah*-offering from barley he would have vowed instead to bring one from wheat. If he asserts, however, that had he known he would not have vowed to bring any *minchah*-offering whatsoever, he is exempt from any obligation (*Rav* from *Gem.* 103a).

Accordingly, the *Gemara* (103a) states that the mishnah's ruling applies only to a person who vows to bring a "*minchah* from barley" but not to one who vows to bring "a *minchah* from lentils" (or some other substance). Since there are in fact two types of *menachos* which are made from barley flour — viz., the jealousy *minchah* of the *sotah* and the *omer minchah* — it is possible to assume that he thought he could offer a voluntary barley *minchah* as well. However, everyone knows that a *minchah* cannot be made from lentils; thus, one who vowed to bring a *minchah* from lentils clearly never intended to offer an acceptable *minchah*. Therefore, even if he later protests that he was mistaken, his vow does not stand (*Rashi; Tos. R' Akiva*).[2]

1. *Kesef Mishneh* (*Maaseh HaKorbanos* 17:9) cites the commentary of *Ri Benveniste* who explains that his declaration taking upon himself to bring מִנְחָה מִן הַשְּׂעוֹרִין, *a minchah of barley*, can be seen as essentially a two-part statement: (1) a vow to bring a *minchah;* (2) a qualification that barley flour be used. If the latter statement was meant to be as binding as the former, then his vow is null because the Torah does not empower a person to volunteer a barley *minchah*. However, if it was meant merely as a preference and not as a binding stipulation, then since it is impossible to fulfill it as stated, it is discounted. The result of this is that the first part of the statement — the vow to bring a *minchah* — takes effect without the qualification he attached to it and obligates him to bring a proper (wheat) *minchah* [since he does not wish for his stipulation to undermine his vow]. What he really meant is determined by asking him what he would have said had he known the halachah, as explained by the *Gemara*.

2. [It is axiomatic that a vow cannot take effect unless it has been verbalized; mere intent is insufficient to establish a legal obligation. A subsequent clarification of the vow is effective only if the spoken words can be assumed to bear that meaning. Where it seems

מִן הַחִטִּים. „קֶמַח," יָבִיא סֹלֶת; „בְּלֹא שֶׁמֶן וּלְבוֹנָה," יָבִיא עִמָּהּ שֶׁמֶן וּלְבוֹנָה; „חֲצִי עִשָּׂרוֹן," יָבִיא עִשָּׂרוֹן שָׁלֵם. „עִשָּׂרוֹן וּמֶחֱצָה," יָבִיא שְׁנַיִם. רַבִּי שִׁמְעוֹן פּוֹטֵר, שֶׁלֹּא הִתְנַדֵּב כְּדֶרֶךְ הַמִּתְנַדְּבִים.

[ד] **מִתְנַדֵּב** אָדָם מִנְחָה שֶׁל שִׁשִּׁים עִשָּׂרוֹן וּמֵבִיא בִּכְלִי אֶחָד.

ר' עובדיה מברטנורא

**יביא סלת.** דכתיב (ויקרא ב, א) סלת יהיה קרבנו: **רבי שמעון פוטר.** רבי שמעון סבר בגמר דבריו אדם נתפס, והואיל וגמר דבריו שלא כדין המנחה, אינו חייב כלום. ואין הלכה כרבי שמעון:

יד אברהם

The *Gemara* cites the view of Zeiri (103b) that this applies only if he says הֲרֵי עָלַי מִנְחָה מִן שְׂעוֹרִים, *"I will bring a minchah from barley."* However, if he says מִנְחַת שְׂעוֹרִים, *a minchah of barley* [in the possessive form],[1] there is no vow for a *minchah* whatsoever unless it is of barley — and a barley *minchah* cannot be volunteered. According to *Rambam* (*Hil. Maaseh HaKorbanos* 17:9), this qualification is the halachah. Others contend that Zeiri's statement was made only according to a view in the *Gemara* which is not accepted as halachah, and therefore it too is not halachah (*Ravad*, ad loc.; *Rashi* to *Gem.* 103b; see *Chazon Ish* 42:30).

„קֶמַח," יָבִיא סֹלֶת; — *[If he said,] "coarse flour," he must bring fine flour;*

A voluntary *minchah* must always be brought from סֹלֶת, *fine flour*, as stated explicitly in the Torah (*Lev.* 2:1).

„בְּלֹא שֶׁמֶן וּלְבוֹנָה," יָבִיא עִמָּהּ שֶׁמֶן וּלְבוֹנָה; — *"without oil and frankincense," he must bring it with oil and frankincense;*

A voluntary *minchah* is never offered without oil and *levonah* (see 5:3).

„חֲצִי עִשָּׂרוֹן," יָבִיא עִשָּׂרוֹן שָׁלֵם. — *"half an issaron," he must bring an issaron;*

The *Gemara* (89a) derives exegetically that a *minchah* must contain a minimum of an *issaron* — one-tenth of an *ephah* of flour.

„עִשָּׂרוֹן וּמֶחֱצָה," יָבִיא שְׁנַיִם. — *"an issaron and a half," he must bring two.*

[If he vowed to bring an *issaron*

clear that the words were not intended to mean this, the vow is null (regardless of what was intended). This issue is discussed at greater length in the *Yad Avraham* comm. to *Nazir* 1:1, s.v. האומר אהא.]

1. [This distinction is especially plausible according to the explanation of *Ri Benveniste* cited in the earlier footnote. Since the obligation for a wheat *minchah* takes effect only because his declaration is viewed as essentially two separate statements, where the use of the possessive form strongly indicates that only a single combined statement is intended, no obligation can take effect regardless of his subsequent interpretation of his words.]

one from wheat. [If he said,] "coarse flour," he must bring fine flour; "without oil and frankincense," he must bring it with oil and frankincense; "half an *issaron*," he must bring an *issaron*; "an *issaron* and a half," he must bring two. R' Shimon exempts [him] because he did not donate in the manner of those who donate.

**4.** A person may donate a *minchah*-offering of sixty *issaron* and bring [it] in one vessel.

YAD AVRAHAM

and a half for his *minchah*, he must bring two *essronim*. A *minchah* can be brought only in multiples of an *issaron*.[1]]

רַבִּי שִׁמְעוֹן פּוֹטֵר, שֶׁלֹּא הִתְנַדֵּב כְּדֶרֶךְ הַמִּתְנַדְּבִים. — *R' Shimon exempts [him] because he did not donate in the manner of those who donate.*

He maintains that a person's words are interpreted primarily by their conclusion and since he concludes his vow with a non-binding specification, the entire vow does not take effect (*Rav* from *Gem.* 103b).

## 4.

The standard volume of flour used in a *minchah* is one *issaron*. Along with that *issaron*, a *log* of oil must be included in the offering (mishnah 9:3). As noted there, a *minchah* may also be offered consisting of more than one *issaron*. However, in such a case there is a dispute among *Tannaim* (ibid.) whether one *log* is required for each *issaron*, or whether, as is the view of R' Elazar ben Yaakov, one *log* suffices for the entire offering. The following mishnah discusses the upper limits of a *minchah*-offering.

מִתְנַדֵּב אָדָם מִנְחָה שֶׁל שִׁשִּׁים עִשָּׂרוֹן וּמֵבִיא בִּכְלִי אֶחָד. — *A person may donate a minchah-offering of sixty issaron and bring [it] in one vessel.*

[A person may obligate himself to bring a *minchah* consisting of up to sixty times the standard volume of one *issaron*, place the entire quantity of flour into one utensil, and offer it as a single *minchah*.]

1. According to the view of Zeiri cited above, this ruling is puzzling. Since his mention of a *minchah* is fulfilled by bringing the first *issaron*, the half that he mentioned afterward should be viewed as if he had vowed to bring it without mentioning the word *minchah* and it should be non-binding. Accordingly, the *Gemara* concludes that the mishnah is discussing a situation in which he said, "I vow to bring a *minchah* which is half an *issaron* plus an *issaron*." Since he mentioned the half first, it is included in the connotation of the word *minchah* and is thus binding. *Rambam's* ruling in this matter, however, presents difficulties. See *Kesef Mishneh* and *Lechem Mishneh* to *Maaseh HaKorbanos* 17:10.

אִם אָמַר: „הֲרֵי עָלַי שִׁשִּׁים וְאֶחָד,״ מֵבִיא שִׁשִּׁים בִּכְלִי אֶחָד, וְאֶחָד בִּכְלִי אֶחָד. שֶׁכֵּן צִבּוּר מֵבִיא בְּיוֹם טוֹב הָרִאשׁוֹן שֶׁל חָג שֶׁחָל לִהְיוֹת בַּשַּׁבָּת שִׁשִּׁים וְאֶחָד; דַּיּוֹ לַיָּחִיד שֶׁיְּהֵא פָּחוּת מִן הַצִּבּוּר אֶחָד. אָמַר רַבִּי שִׁמְעוֹן: וַהֲלֹא אֵלּוּ לַפָּרִים וְאֵלּוּ לַכְּבָשִׂים — וְאֵינָם נִבְלָלִים זֶה עִם זֶה!

### ר׳ עובדיה מברטנורא

(ד) **שכן צבור מביאים וכו׳.** שלשה עשרונים לפר, לשלשה עשר פרים הם תשעה ושלשים עשרונים, ועשרון לכבש, לארבעה עשר כבשים הם ארבע עשר עשרונים, ושני עשרונים לאיל, לשני האילים הם ארבע עשרונים, הרי חמשים ושבעה, ולשני תמידים שנים, ולשני כבשי מוסף שבת שנים, הרי ששים ואחד. ואמר להם רבי שמעון, וכי כל אותן של אותו יום בכלי אחד היו, והלא אלו לפרים ואלו לאילים ולכבשים, ואי מערב להו מפסיל, שמנחת פרים בלילתן עבה, שני לוגים לעשרון, חצי ההין לשלשה עשרונים, ומנחת כבשים בלילתן רכה, רביעית ההין לעשרון דהיינו שלשה לוגים, והן בולעות זו מזו, ונמצאת זו חסרה וזו יתירה, אלא מפני מה אין מביא יחיד ששים ואחד עשרונים בכלי אחד, דעד ששים יכול להבלל בלוג אחד. והאי תנא סבר לה כרבי אליעזר בן יעקב דאמר בפרק שתי מדות (ט,ג) אפילו מנחה של ששים עשרונים אין לה אלא לוג, ואף על פי שלא נבללה כולה, כיון שראויה להבלל אין הבלילה מעכבת, דהכי קיימא לן דכל הראוי לבילה אין בילה מעכבת בו, וכל שאינו ראוי לבילה בילה מעכבת בו:

### יד אברהם

אִם אָמַר: „הֲרֵי עָלַי שִׁשִּׁים וְאֶחָד,״ מֵבִיא שִׁשִּׁים בִּכְלִי אֶחָד, וְאֶחָד בִּכְלִי אֶחָד. — *If he said, "I take upon myself [to bring] sixty-one [issaron]," he brings sixty in one vessel and one in another.*

[If he obligated himself to bring a *minchah* consisting of sixty-one *issaron*, he may not bring the entire *minchah* in one vessel, but must divide it up into two vessels (and two *menachos*). One vessel he fills with sixty, and the other *issaron* is offered separately.]

שֶׁכֵּן צִבּוּר מֵבִיא בְּיוֹם טוֹב הָרִאשׁוֹן שֶׁל חָג שֶׁחָל לִהְיוֹת בַּשַּׁבָּת שִׁשִּׁים וְאֶחָד; — *For similarly the congregation brings sixty-one on the first day of Succos which falls on the Sabbath;*

There are thirteen bulls which are offered on the first day of Succos as part of the *mussaf-offering*. Each of these is accompanied by a *minchas nesachim* of three *essronim*, so that the sum total of *menachos* for all the bulls is thirty-nine *essronim*. There are also fourteen lambs in the *mussaf*, each requiring one *issaron* for its *minchah*, yielding another fourteen *issaron*. In addition, the two rams of the *mussaf* each require two *essronim*, and the two *tamid* sacrifices also require an *issaron* each. Should the first day of Succos occur on Shabbos, there is a further requirement of two lambs for the Sabbath *mussaf* each of which also comes accompanied by a *minchas nesachim* of one *issaron*. Thus, the number of *essronim* needed for the communal *minchas nesachim* of that day is sixty-one (*Rav*).

[There is no requirement (even according to this first *Tanna*) to offer all the *menachos*

**12**
**4** If he said, "I take upon myself [to bring] sixty-one [*issaron*]," he brings sixty in one vessel and one in another. For similarly the congregation brings sixty-one on the first day of Succos which falls on the Sabbath; it is sufficient for the individual that he be one less than the congregation. Said R' Shimon: But aren't these for the bulls and these for the lambs — and they may not be mixed with one another!

**YAD AVRAHAM**

of the communal offerings of one day together in one vessel. On the contrary, even he agrees that they are generally not offered together. However, the assumption is made by him that they *may* be offered in one vessel, and this assumption is the basis for the analogy made to establish the maximum allowable amount for one *minchah* (see below).]

דַּיּוֹ לַיָּחִיד שֶׁיְּהֵא פָּחוּת מִן הַצִּבּוּר אֶחָד. — *it is sufficient for the individual that he be one less than the congregation.*

Since the offerings of the congregation are generally more than those of an individual (*Tif. Yis.*), it is legitimate to assume that in this too, the maximum volume for the *minchah* of an individual is less than that of the congregation. Therefore, no more than sixty *issaron* may be brought in an individual's single *minchah*-offering.

אָמַר רַבִּי שִׁמְעוֹן: וַהֲלֹא אֵלּוּ לַפָּרִים וְאֵלּוּ לַכְּבָשִׂים — וְאֵינָם נִבְלָלִים זֶה עִם זֶה! — *Said R' Shimon: But aren't these for the bulls and these for the lambs — and they may not be mixed with one another!*

R' Shimon contends that the offerings of Succos cannot serve as a model for the quantity of flour which can be brought in one vessel because the offerings of the first day of Succos include both bulls and lambs. Since the ratio of flour to oil for the *menachos* of these offerings differ, they cannot be mixed together, as we learned above, because the *minchah* for the bulls would absorb some of the oil from that of the lambs and thereby invalidate both of them (see mishnah 9:4). Accordingly, it is clear that these *menachos* were brought in separate vessels (*Rav*; cf. *Tos. R' Akiva*).

[The first *Tanna's* opinion may be based on the fact that there are circumstances under which all sixty-one *issaron* can be brought in one vessel, in spite of the problem of different consistencies. As we learned in mishnah 9:4, if *menachos* of different oil consistencies were mixed together in one vessel *after* having been mixed with their respective amounts of oil, they are valid. Although it is not permitted to mix them in the first place, [or even those of two bulls, for that matter,] the fact remains that if they become mixed, they are still valid and are offered in one vessel. Since a communal offering this size is at least theoretically possible, the *Tanna Kamma* is of the opinion that it can be used as a guideline to establish the upper limit of an individual's *minchah*-offering (*Sfas Emes*).

However, the *Tosefta* (12:3) has R' Shimon quoting the first *Tanna's* response to R' Shimon as follows: They (the Sages represented by the first *Tanna*) said to me, "If not [i.e., if our argument is faulty], you expound ...', indicating that the *Tanna Kamma* accepted R' Shimon's argument. However, this may be only because the

אֶלָּא עַד שִׁשִּׁים יְכוֹלִים לְהִבָּלֵל. אָמְרוּ לוֹ: שִׁשִּׁים נִבְלָלִים, וְשִׁשִּׁים וְאֶחָד אֵין נִבְלָלִים? אָמַר לָהֶן: כָּל מִדּוֹת חֲכָמִים כֵּן; בְּאַרְבָּעִים סְאָה הוּא טוֹבֵל, בְּאַרְבָּעִים סְאָה חָסֵר קֻרְטוֹב אֵינוֹ יָכוֹל לִטְבּוֹל בָּהֶן.

ר׳ עובדיה מברטנורא

**ששים ואחד אין נבללים.** בתמיה: **קרטוב.** רביעית של רביעית הלוג:

יד אברהם

*Rav* and *Rashi* state that this mishnah follows the view of R' Eliezer ben Yaakov (see preface), that one *log* of oil suffices for any *minchah* no matter what the quantity of flour. Accordingly, if there are more than sixty *issaron* of flour, they cannot be fully mixed with so small an amount of oil. According to this view, the mishnah is not accepted as halachah, since we do not follow the ruling of R' Eliezer ben Yaakov (*Tos. Yom Tov*). However, *Rashi* elsewhere (18b, s.v. ששים ואחד) states that this reasoning is valid even according to the opposing view, that one *log* of oil is required for each *issaron* of flour in the *minchah*, because beyond a certain volume it is too unwieldy to mix it even if the ratio of flour to oil allows for it. *Rambam* apparently follows this view as well, as he rules in accordance with R' Shimon's view (*Hil. Maaseh HaKorbanos* 17:6), yet decides (ibid. 8:2) against the opinion of R' Eliezer ben Yaakov (*Tos. Yom Tov*).

אָמְרוּ לוֹ: שִׁשִּׁים נִבְלָלִים, וְשִׁשִּׁים וְאֶחָד אֵין נִבְלָלִים? — *They said to him: "Sixty can be mixed and sixty-one cannot be mixed?"*

[Can it be that the addition of just one more *issaron* to a vessel already containing sixty makes the difference between being mixable and unmixable?]

אָמַר לָהֶן: כָּל מִדּוֹת חֲכָמִים כֵּן; — *He said to them: All measurements of the Sages are thus;*

manner in which *menachos* of different consistencies may be offered in one vessel is surely not the regular and ideal method of offering, so that one cannot assume that all the communal *menachos* of one day would be offered in one vessel.]

אֶלָּא עַד שִׁשִּׁים יְכוֹלִים לְהִבָּלֵל. — *Rather, until sixty they can be mixed.*

[R' Shimon concurs with the previous ruling that the maximum volume of a *minchah* in one vessel is sixty *issaron*, but he offers a different explanation for the reason.] The greatest quantity of flour which can be properly mixed with oil in one vessel is sixty *issaron*; more becomes too unwieldy. Therefore, only a *minchah* up to sixty *issaron* is valid.

Although the rule is that a *minchah* is valid even if it was not mixed (as long as its oil was added; see comm. to mishnah 3:2, s.v. לא בלל), that is only if it was possible to mix it but it was not done. This is the well-known rule of כָּל הָרָאוּי לְבִילָה אֵין בִּילָה מְעַכַּבְתּוֹ, *Whatever is fit to be mixed is not disqualified by not being mixed.* However, a *minchah* which is not capable of being properly mixed is invalid (*Rav* from *Gem.* 103b), because the fact that the Torah mandates its mixing indicates that the *minchah* discussed by the Torah is at least one which can be mixed (*Rashbam* to *Bava Basra* 81b).

12 Rather, until sixty they can be mixed. They said to
4 him: "Sixty can be mixed and sixty-one cannot be
mixed?" He said to them: All measurements of the Sages are thus; in forty *seah* one can immerse, [but] in forty *seah* less one *kortov* he cannot immerse.

### YAD AVRAHAM

[Any measure specified by the Sages is open to question in this fashion, since the small difference between the acceptable amount and the unacceptable is never likely to make a total difference in the capacity of any entity to fulfill its function. Nevertheless, some point must be set, and these measurements were defined as the decisive borderline in halachah.]

בְּאַרְבָּעִים סְאָה הוּא טוֹבֵל, בְּאַרְבָּעִים סְאָה חָסֵר קָרְטוֹב אֵינוֹ יָכוֹל לִטְבּוֹל בָּהֶן. — *in forty seah one can immerse, [but] in forty seah less one kortov he cannot immerse.*

[This is R' Shimon's illustration of his point. The halachah is that a *mikveh*, within which one immerses to purify himself from *tumah* contamination, must contain forty *seah* of water to effect purification. If that measure falls short by the slightest amount, the *mikveh* is no longer valid and cannot be used for purification until it is filled to the prescribed amount.

Now the basis for the forty-*seah* minimum is the verse in reference to purification in a *mikveh* (*Lev.* 15:16): *... and he shall bathe in the water all of his body*. The phrase *all of his body* is construed as modifying the words *in the water* (i.e., the *mikveh*) [probably because these words follow immediately after the word *bathe* instead of after *all of his body*, as usual]. Thus the verse is understood as saying *he shall bathe in the water*, i.e., a body of water equal in measure to all of his body. The space occupied by an average person is taken to be 1x1x3 cubits which equals forty *seah* (*Pesachim* 109a,b). Here too one could argue that a *kortov* was insignificant and should not render the volume of the *mikveh* unfit to accommodate a person. Nevertheless a *mikveh* which has one *kortov* less than the minimum is not valid. So too is it in regard to a *minchah*; even slightly more than sixty *issaron* is not considered properly mixable, and it may therefore not be brought in one vessel.]

*Rav* states that a *kortov* equals one-sixteenth of a *log*. This seems to contradict the *Gemara* (*Bava Basra* 90) which states explicitly that it is one sixty-fourth of a *log* (*Tos. Yom Tov*). However, other versions to the *Tosefta* cited there in the *Gemara* state one-sixteenth, as cited by *Rav* (*Tos. Chadashim*).[1]

The *mikveh* is invalidated if there is even one drop of water less than forty *seah*. The mishnah mentions a *kortov* only because it was the smallest measure in use (*Tos.* to *Rosh Hashanah* 13a, s.v. חסר).

1. *Rav's* statement here was probably based on *Rambam's Comm.* as found in the usual versions, which states that the *kortov* is two-eighths (i.e., one-quarter) of a *reviis*, or one-sixteenth of a *log*. However, in the [more correct] Eretz Yisrael version (see also Kafich ed.) the statement reads one-half eighth (i.e., one-sixteenth) of a *reviis*, which equals one sixty-fourth *log* (*Tos. Yom Tov*).

אֵין מִתְנַדְּבִים לֹג, שְׁנַיִם, וַחֲמִשָּׁה; אֲבָל מִתְנַדְּבִים שְׁלֹשָׁה, וְאַרְבָּעָה, וְשִׁשָּׁה, וּמִשִּׁשָּׁה וּלְמַעְלָה.

[ה] **מִתְנַדְּבִים** יַיִן, וְאֵין מִתְנַדְּבִים שֶׁמֶן; דִּבְרֵי רַבִּי עֲקִיבָא. רַבִּי טַרְפוֹן אוֹמֵר: מִתְנַדְּבִין שֶׁמֶן. אָמַר רַבִּי טַרְפוֹן:

**ר׳ עובדיה מברטנורא**

**אין מתנדבים לוג.** יין לנסכים, שלא מלינו מנחת נסכים של לוג אחד ולא של שנים ולא של חמשה, אבל מתנדבים שלשה לוגים, דחזו לכבש, וארבעה דחזו לאיל, וששה לוגים שהוא חלי ההין דחזו לפר, ומששה ולמעלה מתנדבים, דשבעה חזו שלשה מינייהו לכבש וארבעה לאיל, ושמנה חזו לשני אילים, ותשעה חזו לכבש ופר, עשרה חזו לאיל ופר, אחד עשר חזו לשני אילים ולכבש, וכן לעולם: (ה) **מתנדבים יין.** בלא סלת ושמן, ומנסכו לשיתין בפני עלמו: **ואין מתנדבים שמן.** בלא סלת ויין: **מתנדבין שמן.** וקומלו ומקטיר הקומץ ושירים נאכלים:

**יד אברהם**

אֵין מִתְנַדְּבִים לֹג, שְׁנַיִם, וַחֲמִשָּׁה; אֲבָל מִתְנַדְּבִים שְׁלֹשָׁה, וְאַרְבָּעָה, וְשִׁשָּׁה, וּמִשִּׁשָּׁה וּלְמַעְלָה — *One cannot donate a log, two [lugin], or five; but he can donate three, four, or six, and from six and up.*

If one donates wine for a libation offering he must donate a quantity of wine for whose validity there is a basis in Torah law. Therefore, he can donate three *lugin,* which is the amount which accompanies the offering of a lamb; four *lugin,* which is the amount for a ram; and six *lugin,* which is the amount for a bull (see *Numbers* 15:1-10). One, two, and five *lugin,* however, are not mandated by the Torah to accompany any offering, and so have no basis for validity as an offering. Beyond six, any number of *lugin* is valid, because it can always be divided into the amounts cited above, which are mandated by Torah law (*Rav*).

This mishnah seems to contradict the previous one, in which it was stated that if someone vows to offer half an *issaron* as a *minchah*, he must bring a full *issaron.* From this mishnah, on the other hand, it appears that one who vows to bring a wine offering which is smaller than the acceptable minimum does not become obligated by that vow whatsoever (*Tos.* 104a, s.v. אין מתנדבין). It is possible, however, that the mishnah here means only to state that an offering of wine cannot be brought in these amounts; but just as in the case of the previous mishnah, if he states that he would have made the vow for more had he known that it was required, the vow takes effect for the greater amount (*Tos. Yom Tov*). However, *Rambam* (*Maaseh HaKorbanos* 17:14) clearly understands the mishnah to mean that if he vowed less than three *lugin,* he is not obligated to bring anything, and as a result he rules that if one vowed to bring a libation consisting of only one or two *lugin,* he is exempt from bringing anything; the vow is null (*Tos. Yom Tov*).

*Tosafos* suggest that the mishnah refers to a case in which he consecrated specific *lugin* of wine which were before him as his offering (rather than vowing a certain number of unspecified *lugin*). In such a case it goes without saying that this cannot impose a general obligation for the proper complement of *lugin.*

One cannot donate a *log*, two [*lugin*], or five; but he can donate three, four, or six, and from six and up.

**5.** One can donate wine, but one cannot donate oil; [these are] the words of R' Akiva. R' Tarfon says: One can donate oil. Said R' Tarfon:



The *Gemara* (104a) ponders the question whether a vow to bring a certain number of *lugin* as a libation (without specification as to how many vessels be used to contain the wine) is assumed to be a categorical vow to bring the entire amount in one unit, or whether no such assumption can be made, and the libations may be split and offered in more than one unit (see there for the cases in which it is advantageous to assume the latter position). *Rambam* (*Maaseh HaKorbanos* 17:14) rules that one must always bring the entire vowed sum as one offering.

## 5.

Almost all *menachos* include oil along with the flour. In addition, the *minchas nesachim* which accompanies animal sacrifices (see preface to 2:4) also includes an offering of wine which is poured into the bowls at the top of the southwestern corner of the Altar (see *Succah* 4:9, *Zevachim* 6:6). This mishnah discusses whether one may offer either a libation of wine or an offering of oil on its own, without the accompanying *minchah* of flour.

מִתְנַדְּבִים יַיִן, — *One can donate wine,*

The *Gemara* (104a) derives exegetically that one can donate an offering which consists solely of wine to be poured into the bowls atop the southwestern corner of the Altar from where it drains to the cavity (*shissin*) below the Altar (*Rav*).[1]

וְאֵין מִתְנַדְּבִים שֶׁמֶן; דִּבְרֵי רַבִּי עֲקִיבָא. — *but one cannot donate oil; [these are] the words of R' Akiva.*

Oil cannot be offered on its own without flour [to make it a *minchah*] (*Rav*).

רַבִּי טַרְפוֹן אוֹמֵר: מִתְנַדְּבִין שֶׁמֶן. — *R' Tarfon says: One can donate oil.*

[The Torah does provide for an oil offering.] According to R' Tarfon, the procedure for such an offering is to remove a *kometz* from the oil offering and burn it upon the Altar, as with every *minchah*; the remainder is then distributed to the *Kohanim* for consumption (*Rav* from *Zevachim* 91b). It is of course obvious that the *kometz* is not separated as with a *minchah*, i.e., the *Kohen* does not fill his fist with oil. Rather, he pours off a volume of

1. The *Amora* Shmuel is of the opinion that a donation of wine is also sprinkled over the Altar fires (*Zevachim* 91b). *Rav* follows the view of other *Amoraim* (loc. cit.), which are accepted as halachah by *Rambam* (*Maaseh HaKorbanos* 16:14), that a donated wine libation is treated in the same fashion as an obligatory libation. Curiously, in his comm. to *Zevachim* (10:8), *Rav* explains the disposition of a wine donation according to Shmuel's view (*Tos. Yom Tov* to 6:2; see further, *Yad Avraham* comm. to *Zevachim* 10:8).

מַה מָּצִינוּ בַּיַּיִן שֶׁבָּא חוֹבָה וּבָא נְדָבָה, אַף הַשֶּׁמֶן בָּא חוֹבָה וּבָא נְדָבָה. אָמַר לוֹ רַבִּי עֲקִיבָא: לֹא. אִם אָמַרְתָּ בַּיַּיִן, שֶׁכֵּן הוּא קָרֵב חוֹבָתוֹ בִּפְנֵי עַצְמוֹ. תֹּאמַר בַּשֶּׁמֶן, שֶׁאֵינוֹ קָרֵב חוֹבָתוֹ בִּפְנֵי עַצְמוֹ?

אֵין שְׁנַיִם מִתְנַדְּבִים עִשָּׂרוֹן אֶחָד, אֲבָל מִתְנַדְּבִים עוֹלָה וּשְׁלָמִים, וּבָעוֹף, אֲפִילוּ פְרִידָה אַחַת.

### ר׳ עובדיה מברטנורא

**שכן הוא קרב חובתו בפני עצמו.** עם חובתו הוא קרב בפני עצמו. אף על פי שהוא בא חובה עם המנחה אינו מעכב המנחה: **תאמר בשמן כו׳.** דכיון דלא אשכחא ליה דליתי בכלי בפני עצמו, השתא נמי לא ליתי: **אפילו פרידה אחת.** תור אחד, או בן יונה אחד, מתנדבים בין שנים. והלכה שמתנדבים יין ושמן בפני עצמן. ומתנדבים מנחת נסכים בין נסכי פר בין נסכי איל וכבש. וכל הקרבנות באים בנדבה בשותפות, חוץ מן המנחה לפי שנאמר בה נפש, דכתיב (ויקרא ב, א) ונפש כי תקריב קרבן מנחה:

### יד אברהם

oil equivalent to a *kometz* into a vessel and burns the oil upon the Altar (*Tos. Yom Tov*).[1]

The *Gemara* (*Zevachim* 91b) explains that R' Tarfon's ruling exegetically is based on the otherwise superfluous word *minchah* which appears in the verse concerning the *minchah*-offering (*Lev.* 2:1). This is taken to allude to an offering of oil alone. The *Gemara* concludes from this that the offering of oil is similar to a *minchah* and requires [the equivalent of] *kemitzah*, the burning of that amount, and the consumption of the remainder by the *Kohanim*.

אָמַר רַבִּי טַרְפוֹן: מַה מָּצִינוּ בַּיַּיִן שֶׁבָּא חוֹבָה וּבָא נְדָבָה, אַף הַשֶּׁמֶן בָּא חוֹבָה וּבָא נְדָבָה. — *Said R' Tarfon: Just as we find concerning wine that it comes as an obligation or as a donation, so too, oil comes as an obligation or as a donation.*

[There is no reason to differentiate between wine and oil; just as the former can be brought on its own for a donation, so can the latter.]

This statement is difficult to comprehend in the light of the *Gemara* cited above. If R' Tarfon's principle can be derived from the word *minchah* in the Torah, why is it necessary to compare oil to wine (*Tos.* to *Zevachim* 91b)? However, he may have found it necessary to provide some basis for the assumption that the extra word is meant specifically to include oil, since there is no inherent indication to that effect (*Korban Aharon*, cited by *Meleches Shlomo*). [On the other hand, just the analogy to wine would not teach us that an oil donation requires *kemitzah*, which is the

1. From *Tosafos*, though (74b, s.v. קומצו), it seems that the *kometz* is separated from oil with the fist — in the same manner as is done with a *minchah* (see also *Mikdash David* 11:2).

Just as we find concerning wine that it comes as an obligation or as a donation, so too, oil comes as an obligation or as a donation. R' Akiva said to him: No. If this is said of wine, it is because it is brought as an obligation on its own. Can you say [the same] of oil which is not brought as an obligation on its own?

Two [people] cannot donate one *issaron,* but they can donate an *olah-offering* and a *shelamim-offering*, and with a bird, even a single bird.

## YAD AVRAHAM

lesson implicit in the verse's inclusion of the oil donation in the word *minchah.*]

אָמַר לוֹ רַבִּי עֲקִיבָא: לֹא. אִם אָמַרְתָּ בַּיַּיִן, שֶׁכֵּן הוּא קָרֵב חוֹבָתוֹ בִּפְנֵי עַצְמוֹ. תֹּאמַר בַּשֶּׁמֶן, שֶׁאֵינוֹ קָרֵב חוֹבָתוֹ בִּפְנֵי עַצְמוֹ? — *R' Akiva said to him: No. If this is said of wine* (lit., *if you stated with wine*), *it is because it is brought as an obligation on its own. Can you say [the same] of oil which is not brought as an obligation on its own?*

[R' Akiva disputes the validity of R' Tarfon's analogy between wine and oil and contends that the two are not comparable.] When one brings a *minchas nesachim*, the offering of the wine is not essential to the validity of the *minchah* [i.e., the *minchah* is valid even if the libation is not brought], thus indicating that the libation is viewed as an independent portion of the entire offering (see 4:1). This is not the case with oil, which must be included in the *minchah* for it to have any validity (*Rav*).

Others interpret that wine can be brought as its own voluntary offering because it is offered separately when brought for an obligation as well, since the *minchah* is burned on the Altar while the wine is poured into the bowls and through the pipes leading to the *shissin* beneath the Altar. Oil, however, is brought together with the flour, and there is thus no basis to validate it as an independent offering (*Rashi*). Although the ritual for a *metzora* includes the sprinkling of oil toward the Holy of Holies, it does not constitute an offering upon the Altar (*Tif. Yis.*).

אֵין שְׁנַיִם מִתְנַדְּבִים עִשָּׂרוֹן אֶחָד, — *Two [people] cannot donate one issaron,*

Two people cannot share in offering a *minchah* consisting of one *issaron* of flour, as derived from the verse (*Lev.* 2:1): *A soul which shall offer a minchah* — i.e., a single soul (*Gem.* 104b).

Although the mishnah states the unacceptability of a jointly owned *minchah* for a *minchah* of one *issaron*, the same is true for any *minchah* (see *Gem.* 104b; *Rambam, Maaseh HaKorbanos* 14:2).

אֲבָל מִתְנַדְּבִים עוֹלָה וּשְׁלָמִים, וּבָעוֹף, אֲפִילוּ פְּרִידָה אַחַת. — *but they can donate an olah-offering and a shelamim-offering, and with a bird, even a single bird.*

Animal sacrifices are not limited in this manner, and two people can join to donate an offering of one animal or bird (*Rav*).

# פרק שלשה עשר
# Chapter Thirteen

[א] „הֲרֵי עָלַי עִשָּׂרוֹן" — יָבִיא אֶחָד; „עֶשְׂרוֹנִים" — יָבִיא שְׁנַיִם. „פֵּרַשְׁתִּי, וְאֵינִי יוֹדֵעַ מַה פֵּרַשְׁתִּי" — יָבִיא שִׁשִּׁים עִשָּׂרוֹן. „הֲרֵי עָלַי מִנְחָה" — יָבִיא אֵיזוֹ שֶׁיִּרְצֶה.

ר' עובדיה מברטנורא

**פרק שלשה עשר – הרי עלי עשרון. (א) הרי עלי עשרון. פירשתי.** כמה עשרונים אביא, ואיני יודע כמה אמרתי, יביא ששים עשרונים, דאי בליר מהכי נדר, לא איכפת ליה, דמתנה ואומר מה שפירשתי יהא לנדרי והשאר יהא לנדבה, ובטפי מהכי ליכא לספוקי, דאין מנחה אחת יתירה מששים עשרון: **הרי עלי מנחה.** האומר הרי עלי מנחה סתם, יביא איזה שירצה, מחמש מנחות:

יד אברהם

## 1.

This chapter deals with vows one makes for different types of sacrifices in which he does not specify the particulars of his vow or else does not recall those specifics. In the case in which he did not specify the terms of his vow, he is only obligated to bring the smallest amount implied by the terms of his vow. Since his words do not indicate a willingness to bring more than the minimum, the vow cannot obligate more. However, in the case in which he is in doubt about what amount he specified, he must bring whatever may possibly have been specified, in order to insure his fulfillment of his vow.

„הֲרֵי עָלַי עִשָּׂרוֹן" — יָבִיא אֶחָד; — *[If one said,] "I take upon myself [to bring] an issaron" — he brings one;*

[If someone vowed to offer an *issaron* of flour for a *minchah*, he need bring only one such measure.] Although this is obvious, the mishnah states it as a preface to the following ruling (*Gem.* 104b).

[It should be pointed out, however, that this is not as obvious in Hebrew usage as it would appear in our translation of it. The Hebrew does not necessarily carry the implied article *an* which we have inserted. The word *issaron* is a unit name, and the use of the term without specifying the number of units is not as strong an indication that only one unit is meant.]

„עֶשְׂרוֹנִים" — יָבִיא שְׁנַיִם. — *[if he said,] "essronim" — he brings two.*

If he vowed to bring *essronim* — the plural form of *issaron* — without specifying how many such measures, he need bring only two, because that is the minimal plural measure (*Gem.* ibid.). [Thus, the language of his vow cannot be conclusively shown to refer to any larger number.]

„פֵּרַשְׁתִּי, וְאֵינִי יוֹדֵעַ מַה פֵּרַשְׁתִּי" — יָבִיא שִׁשִּׁים עִשָּׂרוֹן. — *[If he said,] "I specified, but I do not know what I specified" — he must bring sixty issaron.*

If he specified an amount of flour in his vow but when it comes to fulfilling it he does not recall what he specified, he must bring a *minchah* consisting of sixty *issaron* of flour. This is because sixty *issaron* is the largest *minchah* which can be brought in one

13 1. [[If one said,] "I take upon myself [to bring] an
1 *issaron*" — he brings one; [if he said,] "*essronim*" — he brings two. [If he said,] "I specified, but I do not know what I specified" — he must bring sixty *issaron*.

[If he said,] "I take upon myself [to bring] a *minchah*-offering" — he may bring whichever he wishes.

**YAD AVRAHAM**

vessel (as explained in mishnah 12:4).[1] However, since the vow might actually have been for less than this, he stipulates that whatever is not included in the obligation incurred by the vow is being brought as a voluntary offering (*Rav*).

*Rav* and *Rashi's* commentary is based on the assumption that the fulfillment of the vow is accomplished only with the amount specified in the vow. Any amount above the specified one is considered a separate, donated *minchah*. The *Gemara* (106a,b) deals with this explanation but notes that it causes several problems. First, it is questionable whether one may bring two such *menachos* together in one vessel. Furthermore, if they are two *menachos*, two *kematzin* have to be separated and burnt; but if they are really only one, it is forbidden to burn the second *kometz* on the Altar, since it is really the remainder of a *minchah*, not a *kometz*. The *Gemara* discusses these and other connected problems and concludes that this explanation can be maintained only by assuming that the mishnah follows the view of R' Eliezer (*Zevachim* 8:4) that the non-Altar parts of an offering can be burnt on the Altar by "viewing them as wood." [Thus, in this case he would stipulate that if the second *kometz* is really a *kometz* (of a second *minchah*), let it be burnt as an offering; if it is in reality the remainder of a *minchah*, it should be burnt "as wood" (i.e., not as an offering; see comm. to *Zevachim* 8:4 for a fuller explanation of this principle). Various other stipulations would also be required, to circumvent other such problems.]

The *Gemara's* last explanation of this mishnah is R' Ashi's who argues that the *Tanna* of our mishnah follows the view of the Sages (mishnah 8) that one can fulfill his vow for a small offering even by bringing a larger one of that kind (e.g., if one vowed a lamb he fulfills his vow even by bringing a sheep). Thus, in the case of a *minchah*, one can fulfill his vow by bringing a greater number of *issarons* than originally specified in the vow, and the offering is viewed as a single big offering brought in fulfillment of the vow. According to this view it is not necessary to stipulate that whatever is above the original specification be a donative offering (*Zevach Todah*, *Tosafos Chadashim*; cf. *Sfas Emes*, *Rashash*; see comm. to mishnah 2, s.v. רבי אומר).

„הֲרֵי עָלַי מִנְחָה" — יָבִיא אֵיזוֹ שֶׁיִּרְצֶה. — *[If he said,] "I take upon myself [to bring] a minchah-offering" — he may bring whichever he wishes.*

The Torah specifies five types of *menachos* which can be brought voluntarily: the *minchah* of *soless* (fine flour), the *machavas*, *marcheshes*, *challos*, and *rekikin* (see *Lev.* 2; above mishnah 3:2, 5:8, 5:9). If someone vowed to bring a *minchah* without specifying which of the five types he

1. Since it is nowhere stated that he remembers vowing to bring everything in one vessel, why is his obligation limited to the maximum that can be brought in one vessel? *Sfas Emes* suggests that it is because people generally do not make vows larger than this.

רַבִּי יְהוּדָה אוֹמֵר: יָבִיא מִנְחַת הַסֹּלֶת, שֶׁהִיא מְיֻחֶדֶת שֶׁבַּמְּנָחוֹת.

[ב] **„מִנְחָה"**, „מִין הַמִּנְחָה" — יָבִיא אַחַת. „מְנָחוֹת, מִין הַמְּנָחוֹת" — יָבִיא שְׁתַּיִם. „פֵּרַשְׁתִּי, וְאֵינִי יוֹדֵעַ מַה פֵּרַשְׁתִּי" — יָבִיא חֲמִשְׁתָּן. „פֵּרַשְׁתִּי מִנְחָה שֶׁל עֶשְׂרוֹנִים, וְאֵינִי יוֹדֵעַ מַה פֵּרַשְׁתִּי" — יָבִיא מִנְחָה שֶׁל שִׁשִּׁים עִשָּׂרוֹן. רַבִּי אוֹמֵר:

### ר' עובדיה מברטנורא

**מיוחדת.** שנקראת מנחה סתם ואין לה שם לווי. וכל שאר מנחות יש להם שם לווי, מנחת מחבת, מנחת מרחשת, מנחת מאפה. ואין הלכה כרבי יהודה: (ב) **מנחה מין המנחה.** האומר הרי עלי מנחה, או מין מנחה, יביא אחת מן המנחות האמורות בפרשה: **מנחות.** עלי, או שאומר מין מנחות עלי, יביא שתי מנחות ממין אחד: **פירשתי.** מיני מנחות שאביא, ואיני יודע כמה מינים הם שנדרתי להביא, מביא חמשתן, מנחת סלת, מנחת מרחשת, מנחת מחבת, מנחת מאפה תנור והיא באה שני מינים, חלות ורקיקין: **פירשתי.** מנחה של עשרונים בכלי אחד, ואיני יודע כמה עשרונים קבעתי בה: **יביא ששים עשרון.** דטפי מהכי ליכא לספוקי, ואי בציר מהכי נדר לא איכפת לן, דמתנה ואומר כמה שפירשתי יהא לנדרי והשאר יהא לנדבה: **רבי אומר.** כיון דאמר מנחה דמשמע חדא, אלמא בכלי אחד קבעה, ואם יביא ששים בכלי אחד, שמא בציר מהכי נדר והוי מנחה יתירה, דאית ליה לרבי דקביעותא דמנא מלתא היא, הלכך יביא ששים מנחות מאחת ועד ששים, חדא של עשרון אחד, וחדא של שנים, וחדא של שלשה, וחדא של ארבע, עד ששים, שנמצא מביא בין הכל אלף שמונה מאות ושלשים עשרון, דודאי חדא מינייהו נדר, ואינך נדבה. ואין הלכה כרבי:

### יד אברהם

The only offering referred to in the Torah as a *minchah* without any adjective attached to it is the *minchas soless* — the *minchah* of fine flour. Therefore, one who vows to bring a *minchah* without further specifying which type is understood to refer to that type (*Rav* from *Gem.* 105a).

*Rambam* (*Maaseh HaKorbanos* 17:5) rules in accordance with the view of the first *Tanna*, whereas *Semag* maintains that the halachah follows the opinion of R' Yehudah (see *Zevach Todah*).

had in mind, he may bring any of them (*Rav; Rashi*). However, he may not bring a *minchas nesachim* (of libations), despite the fact that this too may be offered voluntarily (see 12:5), because it can be assumed that he means one of the *menachos* which are generally brought voluntarily and not as an accompaniment for an animal sacrifice (*Tos.* 104b, s.v. הרי).

רַבִּי יְהוּדָה אוֹמֵר: יָבִיא מִנְחַת הַסֹּלֶת, שֶׁהִיא מְיֻחֶדֶת שֶׁבַּמְּנָחוֹת. — *R' Yehudah says: He must bring the minchah of fine flour, for that is the principal minchah-offering.*

13 R′ Yehudah says: He must bring the *minchah* of fine
2 flour, for that is the principal *minchah*-offering.

**2.** [If he said, "I take upon myself to bring] a *minchah*-offering," [or] "a kind of *minchah*-offering" — he brings one. [If he said,] "*minchah*-offerings," [or] "a kind of *minchah*-offerings" — he brings two. [If he said,] "I specified, but I do not know what I specified" — he must bring all five of them. [If he said,] "I specified a *minchah*-offering of *issarons* but I do not know what I specified" — he must bring a *minchah*-offering of sixty *issaron*. Rebbi says:

YAD AVRAHAM

## 2.

„מִנְחָה״, „מִין הַמִּנְחָה״ – יָבִיא אַחַת. — *[If he said, "I take upon myself to bring] a minchah-offering," [or] "a kind of minchah-offering" — he brings one.*

If someone vowed to bring a *minchah* or that he would bring a type of *minchah* [without specifying which type], he must bring one of the five *menachos* cited above (*Rav*).

„מְנָחוֹת, מִין הַמְּנָחוֹת״ – יָבִיא שְׁתַּיִם. — *[If he said,] "minchah-offerings," [or] "a kind of minchah-offerings" — he brings two.*

If he refers to *menachos* in the plural form [even if he says *a kind* (singular) of *menachos*], he is understood to mean two *menachos* from one type (*Rav; Rashi*).

*Kesef Mishneh* (*Maaseh HaKorbanos* 17:5) states that only in the latter case is he limited to two of the same kind; in the first case, in which he simply vowed to bring *menachos*, they may be of different types as well. It is possible that *Rav* and *Rashi* also mean only the latter case in making this statement (*Zevach Todah*).

„פֵּרַשְׁתִּי, וְאֵינִי יוֹדֵעַ מַה פֵּרַשְׁתִּי״ – יָבִיא חֲמִשְׁתָּן. — *[If he said,] "I specified, but I do not know what I specified" — he must bring all five of them.*

If he remembers that he had specified one of the types of *menachos* in his vow, but does not recall which he specified, he must bring one of each of them to be certain that he has fulfilled his vow (*Rav*).

„פֵּרַשְׁתִּי מִנְחָה שֶׁל עֶשְׂרוֹנִים, וְאֵינִי יוֹדֵעַ מַה פֵּרַשְׁתִּי״ – יָבִיא מִנְחָה שֶׁל שִׁשִּׁים עִשָּׂרוֹן. — *[If he said,] "I specified a minchah-offering of issarons but I do not know what I specified" — he must bring a minchah-offering of sixty issaron.*

If he recalls having vowed to bring a *minchah* of a specific number of *issaron* in one vessel but does not remember the measure stated, he must bring a *minchah* of sixty *issaron*, since that is the largest measure which can be brought in one vessel. He must also stipulate that whatever exceeds his original vow should be a voluntary offering [as explained in mishnah 1] (*Rav*).

In this case, too, *Rav* follows one of the *Gemara's* first explanations; according to

יָבִיא מְנָחוֹת שֶׁל עֶשְׂרוֹנִים מֵאֶחָד וְעַד שִׁשִּׁים.

[ג] „הֲרֵי עָלַי עֵצִים" — לֹא יִפְחֹת מִשְּׁנֵי גְזָרִין. „לְבוֹנָה" — לֹא יִפְחֹת מִקֹּמֶץ.

ר' עובדיה מברטנורא

(ג) **לא יפחות משני גזירים.** שתי בקעיות גדולות, דמיעוט עלים שנים:

יד אברהם

account for the possibility that there are two *menachos* here, two *kematzin* have to be separated and burnt on the Altar. However, if there is really only one *minchah*, the second *kometz* is really not a *kometz* but part of the remainder of the one *minchah*. Accordingly, it is subject to the prohibition on burning the non-Altar parts of sacrifices [see above 3:3, s.v. לא יקטיר] (*Gem.* 106a,b).]

Offering sixty *issaron* each in a separate vessel is also not a remedy (both according to Rebbi and the first *Tanna*). Since the person says that he vowed *a* (singular) *minchah*, [it is assumed, or at least feared, that he used the phrase *a minchah* in making the vow, and] he thereby obligated himself to offer the specified amount as one *minchah* (*Rav; Rashi* to *Gem.* 106a). Therefore, he must bring sixty different offerings, one of each of the measures ranging from one *issaron* to sixty, equaling a total of 1830 *issaron*[1] (*Rav* from *Gem.* 106a).

The *Gemara* (106b) cites, among others, R' Ashi's view that the basis for this dispute is that the first *Tanna* considers a larger offering acceptable in fulfillment of a vow for a smaller one, while Rebbi disagrees (see mishnah 8).

R' Ashi's conclusion (see below) this is not necessary, because a larger offering is considered a legitimate fulfillment of a vow to bring a smaller one (*Tos. Chadashim*).

רַבִּי אוֹמֵר: יָבִיא מְנָחוֹת שֶׁל עֶשְׂרוֹנִים מֵאֶחָד וְעַד שִׁשִּׁים. — *Rebbi says: He must bring [all] minchah-offerings from one to sixty issaron.*

[Rebbi (R' Yehudah HaNasi) holds that if one vowed to bring a *minchah* of one *issaron* he does not fulfill his vow by offering one that is larger than that (see mishnah 8; *Gemara* 106b). Consequently, if he brings a *minchah* of sixty *issaron* to fulfill his vow — the greatest quantity allowable for one *minchah* (see 12:4) — only the amount actually specified in the vow can be counted toward the fulfillment of the vow. Thus if the vow was actually for less than sixty *issaron*, the difference must either be left *chullin* (unconsecrated) or consecrated as a donation [נְדָבָה]. Neither of these two options is acceptable to Rebbi. The *chullin* option is not viable because one may not offer up *chullin* on the Altar. The donation option is also not open for a variety of reasons. One is that in the opinion of Rebbi one may not offer a donated *minchah* in the same vessel with a vowed *minchah*. A second is that to

1. This total can be calculated simply by adding the smallest and largest numbers in the series (61) and multiplying that sum by one half of the amount of numbers in the series, which in this case is thirty (*Tos.* 106a, s.v. שהן). [This is the well-known method for calculating the sum of an arithmetic series.]

He must bring [all] *minchah*-offerings from one to sixty *issaron*.

**3.** [If he said,] "I take upon myself [to bring pieces of] wood" — he may not bring less than two logs. "Frankincense" — he may not bring less than a *kometz*.

### YAD AVRAHAM

The previous mishnah presented a case in which a person vowed to bring a specified amount of *issarons* but forgot the exact amount. The mishnah there rules that he must bring sixty *issaron*, but does not record that Rebbi dissents. The *Gemara* (104b) makes note of this difficulty and records the resolutions offered by two *Amoraim*. Chizkiah maintains that Rebbi disagrees in mishnah 1 as well, and rules that here too the person must bring sixty *menachos* for a total of 1830 *issaron*. R' Yochanan, however, argues that mishnah 1 discussed a case in which the person remembers that the language he used provided for the vowed *minchah* to be offered either in one vessel or more than one. Hence in the case of mishnah 1, Rebbi concurs that one discharges his obligation with offering sixty *issaron*. However, according to Rebbi, each of the sixty *issaron* will have to be brought in a separate vessel (see *Rashi* there). [Obviously there is no substantive difference of opinion among the *Amoraim*. They merely disagree about the circumstances of the case in mishnah 1.]

### 3.

„הֲרֵי עָלַי עֵצִים" — *[If he said,] "I take upon myself [to bring pieces of] wood"* —

[The *Gemara* (106b) derives exegetically that one can consecrate wood to be used for the Altar, and a vow to that effect is binding.]

לֹא יִפְחֹת מִשְּׁנֵי גְזָרִין. — *he may not bring less than two logs.*

He must bring two large logs of wood, because the minimum amount of plural units of wood is two (*Rav*). Consequently, if one used the singular form עֵץ, *wood*, he need not bring more than one log (*Tos.* from *Yerushalmi Shekalim* 6:6).

The size of the logs is defined more exactly by *Rambam* (*Maaseh HaKorbanos* 16:13, *Isurei Mizbe'ach* 7:3): Each log is one cubit square and has the thickness of a (standard) stick used to level off a *se'ah* measure of wheat (see *Yerushalmi* to *Shekalim* 6:6, *Gem. Zevachim* 62b).

„לְבוֹנָה" — לֹא יִפְחֹת מִקֹּמֶץ. — *"Frankincense" — he may not bring less than a kometz.*

*Levonah* (frankincense), too, is derived by the *Gemara* to be acceptable as a voluntary offering (106b). [If he makes such a vow he must bring at least a *kometz* of *levonah*.]

A *minchah*, too, requires a *kometz* of *levonah*. However, the *Gemara* (11a,b) establishes that there is a dispute among the *Tannaim* whether the minimal measure of *levonah* necessary to validate a *minchah* after the fact (i.e., if some *levonah* was lost) is also a full *kometz*, or whether the *minchah* remains valid if even only one or two grains are burnt [although one is initially required to consecrate a *kometz*] (see comm. to 1:3, s.v. חיסר לבונתה). There is a further dispute in the *Gemara* (there) whether that same disagreement applies to *levonah* brought as an independent offering or whether such *levonah* must measure at least a *kometz* at the time of burning

חֲמִשָּׁה קְמָצִים הֵן: הָאוֹמֵר: „הֲרֵי עָלַי לְבוֹנָה" – לֹא יִפְחֹת מִקֹּמֶץ. הַמִּתְנַדֵּב מִנְחָה יָבִיא עִמָּהּ קֹמֶץ לְבוֹנָה; הַמַּעֲלֶה אֶת הַקֹּמֶץ בַּחוּץ – חַיָּב; וּשְׁנֵי בְזִיכִין טְעוּנִין שְׁנֵי קְמָצִים.

[ד] „הֲרֵי עָלַי זָהָב" – לֹא יִפְחֹת מִדִּינַר זָהָב.

ר' עובדיה מברטנורא

**והמעלה את הקומץ בחוץ חייב.** כרת, דהעלאה היא. ובהאי כללא הוי נמי המעלה קומץ בפנים דהקטרה מעלייתא היא, הלכך חשיב חמשה קומצים ותו לא, ולא חשיב להאי דהמעלה קומץ בפנים לקומץ שני: **ושני בזיכים.** של לחם הפנים: (ד) **לא יפחות מדינר זהב.** והוא שיאמר מטבע של זהב, דאי לא, דלמא נסכא דדהבא קאמר, דהיינו חתיכה של זהב:

יד אברהם

*levonah*, it is valid [according to the view of R' Yehudah (*Gem.* 11b) which is accepted as halachah; see comm. to mishnah 1:3].

As noted in the comm. there (s.v. חסר לבונתה), *Rav*, and it would seem *Rambam* as well, is of the opinion that even if he transgressed and only placed two grains of *levonah* on the *minchah* in the first place, the *minchah* is still valid. In their opinion, the *kometz* requirement is the proper procedure but not essential to the *minchah's* validity (*Sfas Emes*).

הַמַּעֲלֶה אֶת הַקֹּמֶץ בַּחוּץ – חַיָּב; — *one who offers up a kometz outside [the Temple Courtyard] is liable;*

[The Torah dictates the penalty of *kares* for one who brings a Temple offering outside the Courtyard (*Deut.* 17:4; see *Zevachim* Ch. 13). In this context the term הַמַּעֲלֶה, *one who offers up*, refers to burning upon an Altar.]

[The mishnah now refers to the *kometz* (of flour) of a *minchah* (not of *levonah*),] and it teaches that one is liable to the punishment of *kares* for offering it outside the Temple Courtyard only if he offers the entire *kometz* (*Rav, Rashi*).

It follows from this that the amount according to all Tannaitic opinions (*Tos. Yom Tov*). *Rambam* (*Hil. Pesulei HaMukdashin* 11:17) rules that for a *levonah* offering a *kometz* is always required (*Rashash* to 11b; *Kesef Mishneh* ad loc.).

*Yerushalmi* (*Shekalim* 6:4) records a dispute in regard to whose hand is used to measure the *kometz* of *levonah* — that of the owner or that of the *Kohen* who offers it on the Altar (*Tos. Yom Tov*).

חֲמִשָּׁה קְמָצִים הֵן: — *There are five kematzin:*

[The measure of a *kometz* (plural, *kematzin*) applies in five instances.]

הָאוֹמֵר: „הֲרֵי עָלַי לְבוֹנָה" – לֹא יִפְחֹת מִקֹּמֶץ. — *[If] one said, "I take upon myself [to bring] frankincense" — he may not bring less than a kometz.*

[As explained above.]

הַמִּתְנַדֵּב מִנְחָה יָבִיא עִמָּהּ קֹמֶץ לְבוֹנָה; — *One who donates a minchah-offering must bring with it a kometz of frankincense;*

The *Gemara* (106b) derives exegetically that the amount of *levonah* which must accompany any *minchah* is a *kometz*. Nevertheless, if some of the *levonah* was lost and the *minchah* was brought with only two grains of

13
4

There are five *kematzin*: [If] one said, "I take upon myself [to bring] frankincense" — he may not bring less than a *kometz*. One who donates a *minchah*-offering must bring with it a *kometz* of frankincense; one who offers up a *kometz* outside [the Temple Courtyard] is liable; and the two spoonfuls require two *kematzin*.

**4.** [If one said,] "I take upon myself [to bring] gold" — he may not bring less than a dinar of gold.

**YAD AVRAHAM**

needed to validate a *minchah*-offering on the Temple Altar is also a full *kometz* [since there is liability for burning outside the Temple only a substance which would have been valid as an offering inside the Temple]. Accordingly, this listing includes with itself the sixth instance of *kometz* not listed explicitly in this mishnah — the *kometz* necessary to validate a *minchah*-offering (*Rav, Rashi*).

The ruling stated here, that there is no liability for offering less than a full *kometz* outside the Temple, is actually the subject of a dispute in *Zevachim* (13:4) between the Sages and R' Elazar, with the former maintaining that one is liable even if he offers only a *kezayis* of the *minchah's kometz* outside the Temple, whereas R' Elazar contends that the entire *kometz* must be offered outside to incur *kares*. Thus, our mishnah would seem to follow the minority view of R' Elazar.

However, it is possible that the mishnah does not refer to the *kometz* of the *minchah*, but to the two spoonfuls of *levonah* — which amounts to two *kematzin* — which are offered upon the Altar as an adjunct of the *lechem hapanim*. According to this explanation the point is not that a *kometz* is *necessary* to incur *kares*, but rather that it is sufficient (actually even a *kezayis* is sufficient). The mishnah hereby counters another view of R' Elazar (ibid. 13:6), that if one offers the *levonah* of the *lechem hapanim* outside, he is liable only if he offered both *kematzin*. If this interpretation is accepted, the mishnah does not discuss the law regarding the *kometz* of the *minchah* at all (*Tos.* 106b, s.v. המעלה).

**וּשְׁנֵי בְזִיכִין טְעוּנִין שְׁנֵי קְמָצִים.** — *and the two spoonfuls require two kematzin.*

The two spoonfuls of *levonah* which are placed alongside the *lechem hapanim* on the *shulchan* in the Temple (see 11:5) require a *kometz* of *levonah* in each of them, as derived exegetically in *Toras Kohanim* (*Tos. Yom Tov*).

4.

**„הֲרֵי עָלַי זָהָב" — לֹא יִפְחוֹת מִדִּינַר זָהָב.** — *[If one said,] "I take upon myself [to bring] gold" — he may not bring less than a dinar of gold.*

If someone vows to donate gold to the Temple, he is assumed to have meant the treasury (*Rambam Comm.*). [He must bring a minimum of one gold dinar, which is the equivalent of twenty-five silver dinars.]

This applies only if he specified a gold coin, i.e., he said, "I take upon myself [to bring] a gold coin"; otherwise, he may have meant a piece of gold metal (*Rav* from *Gem.* 107a). *Yerushalmi* (*Shekalim* 6:4) rules that

„כֶּסֶף" — לֹא יִפְחֹת מִדִּינַר כֶּסֶף. „נְחֹשֶׁת" — לֹא יִפְחֹת מִמָּעָה כֶּסֶף. „פֵּרַשְׁתִּי, וְאֵינִי יוֹדֵעַ מַה פֵּרַשְׁתִּי" — הוּא מֵבִיא עַד שֶׁיֹּאמַר: „לֹא לְכָךְ נִתְכַּוַּנְתִּי."

[ה] **„הֲרֵי** עָלַי יַיִן" — לֹא יִפְחֹת מִשְּׁלֹשָׁה לֻגִּין. „שֶׁמֶן" — לֹא יִפְחֹת מִלֹּג.

ר' עובדיה מברטנורא

**נחושת לא יפחות ממעה כסף.** שיביא נחושת ששוה מעה כסף: **פירשתי.** כך וכך זהב, ואיני יודע כמה פירשתי, יביא כל כך עד שידע בעצמו שמעולם לא נתכוין לכל כך: (ה) **הרי עלי יין.** לנסכים, לא יפחות משלשה לוגין, שהן פחותים שבנסכים, רביעית ההין לכבש תלתא לוגין הוו, שהין שנים עשר לוגין: **שמן לא יפחות מלוג.** שהפחות שבמנחה עשרון סלת, והיא טעונה לוג שמן:

יד אברהם

in such a case it is sufficient to give enough gold to make a gold hook (*Tos.* 107a s.v. ודילמא נסבא). Others maintain that in such a case he must bring as much gold as he considers possible to have been included in his original intention (*Rambam, Hil. Arachin* 2:10).

The *Gemara* (107a) further explains that the mishnah speaks of a vow made in a place where gold coins smaller than a dinar are not in currency. Where such coins are in use, one is obligated to give only the smallest coin in currency (see *Tos.* s.v. ודילמא).

„כֶּסֶף" — לֹא יִפְחֹת מִדִּינַר כֶּסֶף. — *"Silver" — he may not bring less than a dinar of silver.*

If he vows to donate silver, he is assumed to have meant at least a silver dinar, and he must bring that amount (to the Temple treasury). However, this applies only in a place where silver *perutos* [small coins] are not prevalent (see *Sfas Emes*). If they are, he need not donate more than that amount. [As explained in the preface to mishnah 1, where the language of his vow is open to different meanings, the obligation takes effect only for the least of them.]

Moreover, the mishnah speaks of a case in which he pledged "a silver coin." If he did not specify "coin," he can discharge his vow by bringing a piece of silver [as explained above] (*Gem.* 107a).

The silver dinar weighed as much as 96 barley grains, approximately 4.8 grams or 15 troy ounces. However, there is a question whether the gold dinar, which was valued at 25 silver dinars (*Bava Metzia* 44b), was the same weight as the silver dinar. *Rabbeinu Tam* (*Tos.* to *Bechoros* 50a, s.v. דמודבנא) supposes that it weighed about twice as much as the silver dinar. Thus, weight for weight it was worth only twelve times as much as silver.

„נְחֹשֶׁת" — לֹא יִפְחֹת מִמָּעָה כֶּסֶף. — *"Copper" — he may not bring less than [the equivalent of] a maah of silver.*

If he vowed to donate copper, he must bring enough to equal in value a *maah* — one-sixth of a dinar — of silver (*Rav*).

[In this case one cannot give a copper *maah*, since the *maah* was universally made

"Silver" — he may not bring less than a dinar of silver. "Copper" — he may not bring less than [the equivalent of] a *maah* of silver. "I specified, but I do not know what I specified" — he must bring until he [can] say, "I did not intend this.'

**5.** [If he said,] "I take upon myself [to bring] wine" — he may not bring less than three *lugin*. "Oil" — he may not bring less than a *log*.

**YAD AVRAHAM**

of silver, hence the vow must have meant to give copper equivalent to a silver *maah*. *Rav's* and *Rashi's* language infers that in this case there is no obligation to give coins; rather, one may give copper metal worth a silver *maah*. This is no doubt also due to the reason given above — there is not a copper coin worth a *maah*. Thus, in spite of the fact that the person specified a coin of copper, this is construed to mean *copper* worth as much as the smallest *silver coin*.]

If the person said, "I obligate myself to give copper" [without referring to a coin], it is sufficient to give a piece of copper big enough to make a small copper hook (*Gem.* 107a).

*Tosafos* (*Shabbos* 90a, s.v. לא) wonder why a vow concerning a copper coin is not assumed to mean the smallest copper coin — a *perutah* (*Tos. R' Akiva*).

„פֵּרַשְׁתִּי, וְאֵינִי יוֹדֵעַ מַה פֵּרַשְׁתִּי" — הוּא מֵבִיא עַד שֶׁיֹּאמַר: לֹא לְכָךְ נִתְכַּוַּנְתִּי." — "*I specified, but I do not know what I specified" — he must bring until he [can] say, "I did not intend this.'*

If he remembers having specified a measure of any of these coins, but does not recall the specification, he must bring as much as is conceivable to him that he may have vowed to donate (*Rav*).

## 5.

In mishnah 12:5 we learned that one may offer a voluntary *nesech* (libation) of wine apart from any *minchas nesachim*. There is also a dispute whether oil, too, may be offered by itself as a voluntary offering. The following mishnah follows the view of R' Tarfon that oil may be donated as a voluntary offering.

„הֲרֵי עָלַי יַיִן" — לֹא יִפְחֹת מִשְּׁלֹשָׁה לֻגִּין. — *[If he said,] "I take upon myself [to bring] wine" — he may not bring less than three lugin.*

If someone vowed to offer a voluntary *nesech* of wine without specifying the amount of wine involved, he must bring a minimum of three *logs*. This is the smallest measure of wine sanctioned as a libation by the Torah, inasmuch the offering of a lamb requires an accompanying wine *nesech* of one-fourth of a *hin*, which equals three *lugin* (*Rav*).

The *Gemara* (107a) derives from Scriptural exegesis that one may donate a wine libation, and that it may be as large as the vower wishes, but not less than the smallest required libation — three *lugin*.

„שֶׁמֶן" — לֹא יִפְחֹת מִלֹּג. — *"Oil" — he may not bring less than a log.*

If he vowed to bring an offering of

רַבִּי אוֹמֵר: שְׁלֹשָׁה לֻגִּין. „פֵּרַשְׁתִּי, וְאֵינִי יוֹדֵעַ מַה פֵּרַשְׁתִּי" — יָבִיא כְיוֹם הַמְרֻבֶּה.

[ו] „**הֲרֵי** עָלַי עוֹלָה" — יָבִיא כֶבֶשׂ. רַבִּי

ר' עובדיה מברטנורא

**רבי אומר שלשה לוגין.** כפחות שבמנחת נסכים, עשרון לכבש בלול ברביעית ההין שמן. ואין הלכה כרבי: **ביום מרובה.** כיום טוב ראשון של חג הסוכות כשחל להיות בשבת, שאותו היום מרובה בנסכים לקרבנות של חובת היום מכל שאר ימות השנה, דהוו שלשה עשר פרים וארבעה עשר כבשים וארבעה מוספים, שנים מוסף דשבת ושנים מוסף דחג, ואילים שנים ושעיר אחד. והנסכים הצריכים לכולם, מאה וארבעים לוג:

יד אברהם

oil, he must bring at least one *log*, since that is the smallest amount of oil required for the smallest possible *minchah* — one *issaron* of flour (*Rav*). The vow of oil is compared to the oil in a *minchah* although it differs from it in essence. The oil of a *minchah* is mixed with the flour, while the oil of this vow is offered by itself. As noted above, this mishnah accepts the view of R' Tarfon (above mishnah 12:5) that one may vow to offer oil upon the Altar by itself (*Rashi*).

רַבִּי אוֹמֵר: שְׁלֹשָׁה לֻגִּין. — *Rebbi says: Three lugin.*

He contends that the minimum measure for a donation of oil is three *logs*, since that is the smallest measure of oil brought for a *minchas nesachim* — to accompany with the offering of a lamb.

The *Gemara* (107a) explains the disagreement as follows: The Scriptural provision for donations of oil is based on the seemingly superfluous word קָרְבַּן, *offering*, which appears in the context of the donated *minchah* (*Lev.* 2:1; see comm. above to 12:5). The *Tanna Kamma's* view is that since this oil offering is derived from wording stated in connection with a voluntary *minchah*, it is preferable to compare the oil donation to the oil in the *minchah*. [This is the exegetical principle known as דוּן מִינָּהּ וּמִינָּהּ, *derive from it and* (*according to*) *it*.] Accordingly, the minimum amount of oil for an oil donation is one *log*. Rebbi, however, maintains that in spite of the source for the oil donation, it is preferable to compare it to other donations which are offered by themselves, such as the wine donation. [This perspective of the exegetical principle is referred to as דוּן מִינָּהּ וְאוֹקֵי בְּאַתְרֵיהּ, *derive from it but place it in its context*.] (See the *Gemara* for another explanation of the dispute.)

The halachah follows the view of the first *Tanna*, that only one *log* is required (*Rav; Rambam, Maaseh HaKorbanos* 17:15).

„פֵּרַשְׁתִּי, וְאֵינִי יוֹדֵעַ מַה פֵּרַשְׁתִּי" — יָבִיא כְּיוֹם הַמְרֻבֶּה. — *"I specified, but I do not know what I specified" — he must bring like [the amount brought] on the day with the greatest [requirement].*

If someone vowed to bring an offering of wine or oil, but does not recall what quantity he vowed, he must bring an offering equal to the total of wine or oil brought on the first day of

Rebbi says: Three *lugin*. "I specified, but I do not know what I specified" — he must bring like [the amount brought] on the day with the greatest [requirement].

**6.** [If one said,] "I take upon myself [to bring] an *olah*" — he brings a lamb. R'

## YAD AVRAHAM

Succos which falls on Shabbos. This is the day on which the greatest amount of both wine and oil for the *nesachim* are brought. The offerings brought on that day which require oil for the *minchas nesachim* and wine for the libations include thirteen bulls, fourteen lambs, and two rams for the Festival *mussaf-offerings*, two lambs for the Shabbos *mussaf*, and two lambs for the daily *tamid*. The thirteen bulls require six *lugin* of wine and oil each, totaling seventy-eight *lugin* of oil and seventy-eight of wine. The lambs require three *lugin* apiece, totaling another fifty-four *lugin* of each. The two rams each require four *lugin* of oil and wine, adding another eight *lugin* of oil and eight of wine. In all, then, the total quantity of wine brought on that day is one hundred and forty *lugin*, and the same for oil (*Rav; Tos. Yom Tov*). Thus, this person too must bring a hundred and forty *lugin* of either oil or wine to discharge his uncertain obligation.

*Sfas Emes* questions why this amount should serve as the yardstick.[1]

## 6.

„הֲרֵי עָלַי עוֹלָה" — יָבִיא כֶבֶשׂ. — *[If one said,] "I take upon myself [to bring] an olah" — he brings a lamb.*

The *Gemara* explains that this *Tanna* lived in a place where people referred only to the animal *olah-offering* as an (unmodified) *olah-offering*. When a bird *olah* was meant, they specified a "bird *olah*." Therefore, one who vows to bring an *olah*, without giving any explanation of his intent, is understood to be referring to that of an animal, of which the smallest possible example is a lamb (*Rav, Rambam* from *Gem.* 107b).

Although animals for sacrifices were generally purchased in Jerusalem where they were offered, the owner of the sacrifice is nevertheless understood to have the standards of his hometown in mind when making his vow (*Tos.* 107a, s.v. ר״ אלעזר בן עזריה).

Alternatively, this *Tanna* lived in a place in which lambs were less expensive than birds and therefore that was the minimal fulfillment of his vow (*Gem.* 107b as understood by *Rashi*; see *Zevach Todah*).

1. [Perhaps the answer is that there is a general presumption that a person would not ordinarily donate an offering larger than one which appears in the Temple service. Therefore, unless there is an indication to the contrary, his vow is assumed not to have exceeded the maximum amount of oil or wine ever brought at one time as a required Temple offering. (A similar idea is suggested by *Sfas Emes* to resolve a similar problem in the comm. to mishnah 1, s.v. יביא ששים עשרון.)]

אֶלְעָזָר בֶּן עֲזַרְיָה אוֹמֵר: אוֹ תוֹר אוֹ בֶן יוֹנָה. „פֵּרַשְׁתִּי מִן הַבָּקָר וְאֵינִי יוֹדֵעַ מַה פֵּרַשְׁתִּי" — יָבִיא פַּר וְעֵגֶל. „מִן הַבְּהֵמָה, וְאֵינִי יוֹדֵעַ מַה פֵּרַשְׁתִּי" — יָבִיא פַּר וְעֵגֶל, אַיִל, גְּדִי וְטָלֶה. „פֵּרַשְׁתִּי, וְאֵינִי יוֹדֵעַ מַה פֵּרַשְׁתִּי" — מוֹסִיף עֲלֵיהֶם תּוֹר וּבֶן יוֹנָה.

## ר' עובדיה מברטנורא

(ו) **הרי עלי עולה יביא כבש. רבי אלעזר בן עזריה אומר או תור או בן יונה.** באתריה דתנא קמא לא היו קורים עולה סתם אלא לעולת בהמה, ופחותה שבעולת בהמה הוא כבש, הלכך יביא כבש, ובאתריה דרבי אלעזר בן עזריה היו קורים עולה סתם גם לעולת העוף, הלכך יביא תור או בן יונה, ומר כי אתריה ומר כי אתריה: **יביא פר ועגל.** זכרים ולא נקבות, דעולה ליכא לספוקי אלא בזכרים, ומתניתין רבי היא דאמר לקמן (משנה ח) המתנדב קטן והביא גדול לא יצא, אבל רבנן פליגי עליה ואמרי המתנדב קטן והביא גדול יצא, דיש בכלל מרובה מועט. והלכה כחכמים: **פירשתי.** אחד מקרבנות הבהמה ואיני יודע מאיזה מהן פירשתי, יביא מכל מיני בהמה הזכרים גדולים וקטנים, דהיינו פר ועגל איל ושעיר וגדי וטלה: **פירשתי.** את המין ואיני יודע מה פירשתי, אם מין בהמה או מין עוף:

## יד אברהם

78b; *Rambam, Maaseh HaKorbanos* 16:7).

„פֵּרַשְׁתִּי מִן הַבָּקָר וְאֵינִי יוֹדֵעַ מַה פֵּרַשְׁתִּי" — יָבִיא פַּר וְעֵגֶל. — *"I specified from cattle but I do not know what I specified" — he must bring a bull and a calf.*

If someone specified that he was going to bring an *olah* from a specific animal category but he does not recall what animal in that category he specified, he must bring at least one of any animal which could possibly be included in his vow. Since an *olah* may be brought only from male animals (*Lev.* 1:3,10), the possibilities are limited to an adult bull and a calf (*Rav*).

A calf is defined as a male of the cattle species in its first year (*Tif. Yis.*). A פַּר, *bull*, is defined as a male of the cattle species in its second and third years (*Rambam, Maaseh HaKorbanos* 1:11,14).[1]

רַבִּי אֶלְעָזָר בֶּן עֲזַרְיָה אוֹמֵר: אוֹ תוֹר אוֹ בֶן יוֹנָה. — *R' Elazar ben Azariah says: Either a pigeon or a young dove.*

R' Elazar ben Azariah lived in an area where the *olah* of a bird was also referred to simply as an *olah*, with any adjective. Since the vow can be plausibly construed to refer to a bird, such an offering also constitutes a fulfillment of his vow (*Rav* from *Gem.* 107b; cf. *Rashi*). Thus, there is no real dispute between the *Tanna Kamma* and R' Elazar ben Azariah (*Gem.* 107b).

The ruling of the mishnah applies even if he first designated an ox for the fulfillment of his vow and it was later stolen. [Since the designation of an ox for the fulfillment of his vow does not redefine the essence of the vow itself (see comm. to mishnah 12:2, s.v. הרי זו פסולה),] he may still exercise his right to offer a lamb or bird to fulfill his vow (*Bava Kamma*

1. *Rambam* does not clarify the status of a bull older than three years. Some maintain that a bull of this age is invalid as an offering (at least on a Rabbinic level), whereas others hold

13
6

Elazar ben Azariah says: Either a pigeon or a young dove. "I specified from cattle but I do not know what I specified" — he must bring a bull and a calf. "From animals, but I do not know what I specified" — he must bring a bull and a calf, a ram, a kid, and a lamb. "I specified, but I do not know what I specified" — he adds to them a pigeon and a young dove.

**YAD AVRAHAM**

This segment of the mishnah, which states that one must bring an animal from each category, follows the view of Rebbi (below, mishnah 8), that one does not discharge a vow by bringing a larger animal (of the same species) than that which was specified in the vow. According to the Sages' view in that mishnah, one does discharge his vow in this manner; thus, even if his vow had specified a calf he would discharge his obligation with a bull. Consequently, in the case now under consideration, it would suffice for him to bring just an adult bull (*Rav* from *Gem.* 107b).

„מִן הַבְּהֵמָה, וְאֵינִי יוֹדֵעַ מַה פֵּרַשְׁתִּי" — יָבִיא פַּר וְעֵגֶל, אַיִל, גְּדִי וְטָלֶה. — *"From animals, but I do not know what I specified" — he must bring a bull and a calf, a ram, a kid, and a lamb.*

If he remembers only that he specified an animal [and not a bird], he must bring all of the animals cited, since any one of them may have been the one he specified. In this case, too, since the vow concerned an *olah*, only male animals are included (*Rav*).

A male sheep in its second year (beginning with the fourteenth month from birth) is referred to as a ram; in its first year, it is called a lamb. The same distinction applies to a goat and a kid (*Tif. Yis.*).

The mishnah does not mention that he must bring an (adult) goat; goats and kids, too, constitute separate categories, as stated in mishnah 7 (*Tos. Yom Tov*). However, *Rav* does list a goat in his roster of animals which must be offered. *Tosafos* (107a, s.v. פרשתי) note that some versions of the mishnah delete the word וְשָׂעִיר, *and a goat* (as do our versions), but that the word should be part of the text [it is in the mishnah text printed with the Talmud].

„פֵּרַשְׁתִּי, וְאֵינִי יוֹדֵעַ מַה פֵּרַשְׁתִּי" — מוֹסִיף עֲלֵיהֶם תּוֹר וּבֶן יוֹנָה. — *"I specified, but I do not know what I specified" — he adds to them a pigeon and a young dove.*

[If he has no recollection whatsoever as to the animal specified, he must bring all of the possibilities listed above — as well as a dove and a pigeon, the two varieties of birds which may also be brought as an *olah*.]

As noted previously, this mishnah follows the view of Rebbi, who maintains (mishnah 8) that one who vows

that although it is not proper to offer such an older animal, it is nevertheless a valid offering expost facto (see *Mishneh LaMelech, Isurei Mizbe'ach* 2:6; *Aruch HaShulchan HeAsid* 52:25, 63:16).

Some contend that in the first month of the second year (i.e., the thirteenth month), the animal is in an intermediary state, and is classified neither as a calf nor as a bull (*Aruch HaShulchan HeAsid* 63:23; *Tif. Yis.* in *Chomer BaKodesh* 2:6; cf. *Tif. Yaakov*).

[ז] „הֲרֵי עָלַי תּוֹדָה וּשְׁלָמִים" — יָבִיא כֶבֶשׂ. „פֵּרַשְׁתִּי מִן הַבָּקָר, וְאֵינִי יוֹדֵעַ מַה פֵּרַשְׁתִּי" — יָבִיא פַר וּפָרָה, עֵגֶל וְעֶגְלָה. „מִן הַבְּהֵמָה, וְאֵינִי יוֹדֵעַ מַה פֵּרַשְׁתִּי" — יָבִיא פַר וּפָרָה, עֵגֶל וְעֶגְלָה, אַיִל וְרָחֵל, גְּדִי וּגְדִיָּה, שָׂעִיר וּשְׂעִירָה, טָלֶה וְטַלְיָה.

[ח] „הֲרֵי עָלַי שׁוֹר" — יָבִיא הוּא וּנְסָכָיו

**ר׳ עובדיה מברטנורא**

(ז) **תודה ושלמים.** תודה או שלמים: **יביא כבש.** פחות שבתודה ושלמים: **יביא פר ופרה.** דתודה ושלמים איכא לספוקי בזכרים ונקבות: **ורחל.** נקבה בת שתי שנים: **גדי.** בן שנה מן העזים: **שעיר.** עזים בן שתי שנים: **טלה.** כבש בן שנתו: (ח) **יביא הוא ונסכיו במנה.** כך נתפרש דינו בתורה שבעל פה, שיהא ערך השור עם נסכיו מנה:

**יד אברהם**

to bring a smaller offering cannot fulfill that vow with a larger one. Therefore, each of the animals listed must be brought. According to the Sages, however, only a bull need be offered, since the offering of a larger animal is considered a legitimate fulfillment of a vow to bring a smaller one in their view (*Rav* from *Gem.* 187b). Hence, if he vowed to bring his offering from cattle but does not remember if he specified a calf or a bull, he fulfills his vow by bringing only a bull. Similarly, if he vowed to bring an offering from the sheep species, he need bring only a ram, and if the vow concerned the goat species, he need bring only an adult goat. If he remembered specifying the type of animal but does not remember even which species he mentioned, he need bring only a bull, a ram, and adult goat (*Rambam, Maaseh HaKorbanos* 16:9).

## 7.

This mishnah follows the pattern of the previous one and is also in accordance with the view of Rebbi cited above.

„הֲרֵי עָלַי תּוֹדָה וּשְׁלָמִים" — יָבִיא כֶבֶשׂ. — *"I take upon myself [to bring] a todah-offering" or "a shelamim-offering" — he brings a lamb.*

If someone vowed to bring a *todah* or a *shelamim*, without specifying the nature of that offering, he need only bring a lamb in its first year (*Tif. Yis.*). This is the smallest possible offering for these sacrifices (*Rav*).

Although the mishnah mentions that he bring a כֶּבֶשׂ which is a male lamb (the term for a female lamb is כִּבְשָׂה), this is not meant to exclude females. He may discharge this vow with either a male or a female (*Meleches Shlomo*).

„פֵּרַשְׁתִּי מִן הַבָּקָר, וְאֵינִי יוֹדֵעַ מַה פֵּרַשְׁתִּי" — יָבִיא פַר וּפָרָה, עֵגֶל וְעֶגְלָה. — *"I specified from cattle, but I do not know what I specified" — he must bring a*

**7.** 'I take upon myself [to bring] a *todah* offering" or "a *shelamim-offering*" — he brings a lamb. 'I specified from cattle, but I do not know what I specified" — he must bring a bull and a cow, and a male calf and a female calf. "From animals, but I do not know what I specified" — he must bring a bull and a cow, a male calf and a female calf, a ram and a ewe, a male kid and a female kid, a male goat and a female goat, a male lamb and a female lamb.

**8.** [If he said,] "I take upon myself [to bring] an ox" — he must bring it and its libation offering



*bull and a cow, and a male calf and a female calf.*

If he remembers having specified cattle, he must offer all of these possibilities, which include both male and female (*Rav*) [since for these offerings both male and female animals are valid].

„מִן הַבְּהֵמָה, וְאֵינִי יוֹדֵעַ מַה פֵּרַשְׁתִּי" – יָבִיא פַּר וּפָרָה, עֵגֶל וְעֶגְלָה, אַיִל וְרָחֵל, גְּדִי וּגְדִיָּה, שָׂעִיר וּשְׂעִירָה, טָלֶה וְטַלְיָה. — *"From animals, but I do not know what I specified" — he must bring a bull and a cow, a male calf and a female calf, a ram and a ewe, a male kid and a female kid, a male goat and a female goat, a male lamb and a female lamb.*

[If he recalls having specified a beast but does not remember which, he must bring every one of the animals which are valid for these offerings.] The distinction between adult and young in all of these categories is the difference between an animal in its second year and one in its first (*Rav*).

[As noted above, this ruling follows the view of Rebbi. According to the halachically accepted view of the Sages, it suffices to bring just a bull and a cow, a ram and ewe, and an adult male goat and female goat (*Rambam, Maaseh HaKorbanos* 16:10).]

## 8.

„הֲרֵי עָלַי שׁוֹר" – יָבִיא הוּא וּנְסָכָיו בְּמָנֶה. — *[If he said,] "I take upon myself [to bring] an ox" — he must bring it and its libation offering for a maneh.*

[One who vows to bring an ox for an offering must bring one whose value, together with that of its libations — i.e., the *minchas nesachim* and the wine libation itself which accompany the sacrifice (*Tos. Yom Tov*) — equals one hundred *dinar* in value.] This is in accordance with the dictates of the Oral Law transmitted down through the generations (*Rav; Rashi*).

Others contend that the amounts cited in this mishnah are the median value of these animals [and thus the assumed value intended unless otherwise specified] (*Rambam Comm.; Maaseh HaKorbanos* 16:4).

בְּמָנֶה. „עֵגֶל" — יָבִיא הוּא וּנְסָכָיו בְּחָמֵשׁ; „אַיִל" — יָבִיא הוּא וּנְסָכָיו בִּשְׁתַּיִם; „כֶּבֶשׂ" — יָבִיא הוּא וּנְסָכָיו בְּסֶלַע.

„שׁוֹר בְּמָנֶה" — יָבִיא בְמָנֶה חוּץ מִנְּסָכָיו. „עֵגֶל בְּחָמֵשׁ" — יָבִיא בְחָמֵשׁ חוּץ מִנְּסָכָיו. „אַיִל בִּשְׁתַּיִם" — יָבִיא בִשְׁתַּיִם חוּץ מִנְּסָכָיו. „כֶּבֶשׂ בְּסֶלַע" — יָבִיא בְסֶלַע חוּץ מִנְּסָכָיו.

„שׁוֹר בְּמָנֶה" — וְהֵבִיא שְׁנַיִם בְּמָנֶה, לֹא יָצָא; אֲפִילוּ זֶה בְּמָנֶה חָסֵר דִּינָר וְזֶה בְּמָנֶה חָסֵר דִּינָר. „שָׁחוֹר" — וְהֵבִיא לָבָן; „לָבָן" — וְהֵבִיא שָׁחוֹר; „גָּדוֹל" — וְהֵבִיא קָטָן, לֹא יָצָא. „קָטָן" — וְהֵבִיא גָדוֹל, יָצָא. רַבִּי אוֹמֵר: לֹא יָצָא.

**ר' עובדיה מברטנורא**

**עגל יביא הוא ונסכיו בחמש.** סלעים: **אמר הרי עלי שור במנה.** יביאנו במנה חוץ מנסכיו שהרי כך קבעו: **שור במנה והביא שנים במנה לא יצא.** שהרי קבע שור במנה: **קטן והביא גדול יצא רבי אומר לא יצא.** משום הכי תנא פלוגתא דרבי ורבנן הכא בסיפא, לפרושי דרישא

**יד אברהם**

„עֵגֶל" — יָבִיא הוּא וּנְסָכָיו בְּחָמֵשׁ; „אַיִל" — יָבִיא הוּא וּנְסָכָיו בִּשְׁתַּיִם; „כֶּבֶשׂ" — יָבִיא הוּא וּנְסָכָיו בְּסֶלַע. — *"A calf" — he must bring it and its libation offering for five; "a ram" — he must bring it and its libation offering for two; "a lamb" — he must bring it and its libation offering for a selah.*

If he vowed to bring a calf, he must bring an offering whose total value, including its libations, is five *selahs* (*Rav*) — i.e., twenty dinars. [For a ram he must bring a combined offering two *selahs* in value, and for a lamb, one *selah*. These sums are based on the same reasoning as that of the ox.]

„שׁוֹר בְּמָנֶה" — יָבִיא בְמָנֶה חוּץ מִנְּסָכָיו. „עֵגֶל בְּחָמֵשׁ" — יָבִיא בְחָמֵשׁ חוּץ מִנְּסָכָיו. „אַיִל בִּשְׁתַּיִם" — יָבִיא בִשְׁתַּיִם חוּץ מִנְּסָכָיו. „כֶּבֶשׂ בְּסֶלַע" — יָבִיא בְסֶלַע חוּץ מִנְּסָכָיו. — *[If he said,] "An ox for a maneh" — he must bring it for a maneh besides its libation offering. "A calf for five" — he must bring it for five besides its libation offering. "A ram for two" — he must bring it for two besides its libation offering. "A lamb for a selah" — he must bring it for a selah besides its libation offering.*

If he specifies in his vow to bring an ox worth a *maneh*, that value can no longer include the *nesachim* as well (*Rav*). [The same applies to any of the other animals cited.]

„שׁוֹר בְּמָנֶה" — וְהֵבִיא שְׁנַיִם בְּמָנֶה, לֹא יָצָא; אֲפִילוּ זֶה בְּמָנֶה חָסֵר דִּינָר וְזֶה בְּמָנֶה חָסֵר דִּינָר. — *[If he said,] "An ox for a maneh" — and he brought two for a maneh, he has not fulfilled his obligation; even if each is for a maneh less a dinar.*

If he specified that he would bring an ox worth a *maneh*, he cannot discharge his obligation by bringing a *maneh's*

13 for a *maneh*. "A calf" — he must bring it and its
8 libation offering for five; "a ram" — he must bring it and its libation offering for two; "a lamb" — he must bring it and its libation offering for a *selah*.

[If he said,] "An ox for a *maneh*" — he must bring it for a *maneh* besides its libation offering. "A calf for five" — he must bring it for five besides its libation offering. "A ram for two" — he must bring it for two besides its libation offering. "A lamb for a *selah*" — he must bring it for a *selah* besides its libation offering.

[If he said,] "An ox for a *maneh*" — and he brought two for a *maneh*, he has not fulfilled his obligation; even if each is for a *maneh* less a dinar. "Black" — and he brought a white [one]; [or] "white" — and he brought a black [one]; "large" — and he brought a small [one], he has not fulfilled his obligation. "Small" — and he brought a large [one], he has fulfilled his obligation. Rebbi says: He has not fulfilled his obligation.

### YAD AVRAHAM

worth of oxen, because his vow specified one ox of that value (*Rav*).

„שָׁחוֹר" – וְהֵבִיא לָבָן; „לָבָן" – וְהֵבִיא שָׁחוֹר; — *"Black" — and he brought a white [one]; [or] "white" — and he brought a black [one];*

[If he specified a black ox and brought a white one, or vice versa, he does not thereby fulfill his obligation. We understand his specification of color to be essential to the vow,] because the color of the ox may affect its function [and is therefore considered a vital factor] (*Tos.*; 107b, s.v. שחור see *Nazir* 31b).

„גָּדוֹל" – וְהֵבִיא קָטָן, לֹא יָצָא. — *"large" — and he brought a small [one], he has not fulfilled his obligation.*

[If he specified a large animal and brought a small one, he has also not lived up to the requirements of his vow.]

„קָטָן" – וְהֵבִיא גָּדוֹל, יָצָא. — *"Small" — and he brought a large [one], he has fulfilled his obligation.*

If he vows to bring a smaller animal and offers a larger one instead, the Rabbis [i.e., the first *Tanna*, whose identity is not cited in order to grant him the authority of a majority view] maintain that he has fulfilled his vow (*Rav*).

[Obviously, this refers only to a big and small animal of the species which was specified. If one, however, specified to bring an animal from a small species, he does not fulfill his vow by bringing one from a bigger species. Consequently, according to the first *Tanna*, if one vowed to bring a calf, his vow can be fulfilled with a bull. But he cannot discharge his vow to bring a lamb with a bull or adult goat (see *Rambam, Maaseh HaKorbanos* 16:1).

רַבִּי אוֹמֵר: לֹא יָצָא. — *Rebbi says: He has not fulfilled his obligation.*

[Rebbi contends that a vow to bring

[ט] „**שׁוֹר** זֶה עוֹלָה," וְנִסְתָּאֵב, אִם רָצָה יָבִיא בְדָמָיו שְׁנַיִם. „שְׁנֵי שְׁוָרִים אֵלּוּ עוֹלָה," וְנִסְתָּאֲבוּ, אִם רָצָה יָבִיא בִדְמֵיהֶם אֶחָד. רַבִּי אוֹסֵר.

**ר' עובדיה מברטנורא**

לאו דברי הכל היא אלא רבי היא ולא רבנן. ואין הלכה כרבי: (ט) **ונסתאב.** שנפל בו מום. דבעל מום אקרי טמא כדכתיב (ויקרא כז, יא) ואם כל בהמה טמאה אשר לא יקריבו ממנה קרבן לה', ובבעלי מומין שיפדו הכתוב מדבר, כדפרשינן בפרקין דלעיל (פרק יב משנה א): **אם רצה יביא בדמיו שנים.** ולא דמי לרישא דאמרינן שור במנה והביא שנים במנה לא יצא, דהתם דאמר הרי עלי שור במנה חייב עד שיביאנו, אבל הכא בשור זה ונסתאב שאני, דכיון דאמר שור זה אקריב עולה ונסתאב, אזל ליה נדריה, דתו לא מצי לקיומיה: **רבי אוסר.** לכתחלה, אבל אם הביא יצא, דכיון דאמר זה, אינו חייב באחריותו. ואין הלכה כרבי:

**יד אברהם**

The halachah follows the view of the first *Tanna* (*Rav; Rambam, Maaseh HaKorbanos* 16:1).

a small animal cannot be discharged by offering a larger one, and he must still bring the one specified in his vow.]

## 9.

As explained earlier (12:1), if someone consecrates an animal for a sacrifice and it subsequently becomes invalidated by virtue of a blemish, he must redeem it and bring another with the money. This mishnah discusses the legitimacy of using that money for a different type of animal or a different number of animals.

„שׁוֹר זֶה עוֹלָה," וְנִסְתָּאֵב, — *[If he said,] "This ox shall be an olah-offering," and it became blemished,*

The ox he designated for an offering became blemished, and he therefore redeemed it. The mishnah uses the term וְנִסְתָּאֵב — which is literally rendered *it became unclean* — because the Torah (*Lev.* 27:11) refers to a blemished animal as having become unclean (*Rav*).

אִם רָצָה יָבִיא בְדָמָיו שְׁנַיִם. — *if he wishes he may bring two for its money.*

[He may use that money to purchase two smaller oxen and offer them as sacrifices.]

The mishnah speaks here of a case in which his vow referred to a specific animal ["*This* ox shall be an *olah*"], not to a general personal obligation ["I take upon myself to bring an *olah*"]. Since this type of vow [known as נְדָבָה (*nedavah*) *donated offering*] is formulated in terms of the consecration of a specific animal, the vower's liability is limited to offering this particular animal; if it is lost or stolen, he has no further obligation whatsoever (see comm. at end of mishnah 7:4). Therefore, if it becomes blemished and unfit for offering, he has no personal obligation to replace it with a similar animal. The only obligation which remains is to use the redemption money — which has now assumed the animal's sanctity (in this mishnah's case,

13
9

9. [If he said,] "This ox shall be an *olah-offering*," and it became blemished, if he wishes he may bring two for its money. "These two oxen shall be an *olah-offering*," and they became blemished, if he wishes he may bring one with their money. Rebbi prohibits [it].

YAD AVRAHAM

*olah* sanctity) — to purchase other animals which will in turn assume the sanctity present in the money (i.e., *olah* sanctity). But there is nothing here which would require that the money be spent on the same number of animals or the same-size ones. Consequently, he may use the money to purchase even a greater number of smaller animals.

The previous mishnah, however, dealt with cases in which the vow was made in terms of a personal obligation to bring a certain type of offering. [This is known as נֶדֶר (*neder*), *personal vow*.] Since the vow referred to his personal obligation and not any specific animal, as long as he does not bring exactly what he vowed to bring, he has not fulfilled his vow. For this reason, the previous mishnah ruled that if he vowed to bring one ox for a *maneh*, he may not divide the value among two; offering two oxen worth a *maneh* together does not fulfill the terms of the original vow to bring a single ox worth that amount (*Rav* from *Gem.* 108b).

"שְׁנֵי שְׁוָרִים אֵלּוּ עוֹלָה," וְנִסְתָּאֲבוּ, אִם רָצָה יָבִיא בִדְמֵיהֶם אֶחָד. — *"These two oxen shall be an olah-offering," and they became blemished, if he wishes he may bring one with their money.*

[The same ruling as stated above applies in the reverse situation, and he may bring one larger ox for the money with which he redeemed two smaller ones that became blemished.]

רַבִּי אוֹסֵר. — *Rebbi prohibits [it].*

Although Rebbi agrees that if one made the exchange it is valid, he nevertheless prohibits doing so in the first place — i.e., replacing the two smaller animals with a single larger one.

[This is a Rabbinic prohibition based, presumably, on the resemblance of this case to the case of a personal obligation to offer two oxen. As explained above, in that type of vow the substitution does not discharge the vow. As a safeguard, therefore, Rebbi decrees that a declaration stated in the form of a *nedavah* — "This ... shall be ..." — should be treated, at least initially (לְכַתְּחִילָּה), as the equivalent of a *neder* vow — one formulated as "... I take upon myself ..."] Since a *neder* to bring two animals could surely not be discharged by bringing one large animal, even one equivalent in price to the two (*Rashi* to *Gem.* 108b), Rebbi forbids substituting one large animal for the two disqualified ones even in the case of a *nedavah* vow (*Rav* from *Gem.* 108b).

[However, Rebbi agrees that from a strictly Biblical perspective there is no personal obligation to buy the same-size animal. Consequently, he agrees that if the person did replace the specified smaller offerings with a single larger one, the replacement is valid

„אַיִל זֶה עוֹלָה,״ וְנִסְתָּאֵב, אִם רָצָה יָבִיא בְדָמָיו כֶּבֶשׂ. „כֶּבֶשׂ זֶה עוֹלָה,״ וְנִסְתָּאֵב, אִם רָצָה יָבִיא בְדָמָיו אַיִל. רַבִּי אוֹסֵר.

הָאוֹמֵר: „אֶחָד מִכְּבָשַׂי הֶקְדֵּשׁ,״ „וְאֶחָד מִשְּׁוָרַי הֶקְדֵּשׁ״ — הָיוּ לוֹ שְׁנַיִם, הַגָּדוֹל שֶׁבָּהֶן הֶקְדֵּשׁ; שְׁלֹשָׁה, הַבֵּינוֹנִי שֶׁבָּהֶן הֶקְדֵּשׁ.

ר׳ עובדיה מברטנורא

**הבינוני שבהן הקדש.** אף הבינוני שבהן הקדש, דכי יש לו שנים, הגדול הקדש, שהמקדיש בעין יפה מקדיש ומסתמא מוטב שבהן הקדיש דכתיב (דברים יב, יא) מבחר נדריכם, וכי יש לו שלשה, חוששין אף לבינוני, דלא ידעינן אהי מינייהו חל ההקדש, אי אגדול דהוי עין יפה, אי אבינוני דהוי עין יפה לגבי קטן, הלכך תרוייהו אסירי, מיהו לא קרב למזבח אלא חד מינייהו. והיכי עביד דלשתרי חד מינייהו, ממתין לבינוני עד שיומם, ומחלל אותו בגדול, דממה נפשך, אי אבינוני חל ולא אגדול, הרי נפל בו מום וחללו, ואי אגדול חל מעיקרא, נמצא בינוני חולין מעיקרא:

יד אברהם

and there is no further obligation to bring two smaller offerings.] [1]

Rebbi's reasoning applies equally to the first case of the mishnah and prohibits two smaller animals from being brought in place of the bigger animal initially consecrated. As explained in mishnah 8, it is Rebbi's view that one does not fulfill a vow by bringing a larger animal than the one he specified. Hence, if one vowed to bring a large animal, he cannot discharge the vow by bringing two smaller ones (even though two small animals would be considered a "big" offering in comparison to the single animal of equal worth; see *Rashi* to *Gem.* 108b). Consequently, Rebbi surely disagrees with the *Tanna Kamma's* ruling in the first case as well and prohibits replacing a large blemished offering with two smaller ones (*Tos. Yom Tov* from *Gem.* 108b).

„אַיִל זֶה עוֹלָה,״ וְנִסְתָּאֵב, אִם רָצָה יָבִיא בְדָמָיו כֶּבֶשׂ. „כֶּבֶשׂ זֶה עוֹלָה,״ וְנִסְתָּאֵב, אִם רָצָה יָבִיא בְדָמָיו עוֹלָה. רַבִּי אוֹסֵר. — *"This ram shall be an olah-offering," and it became blemished, if he wishes he may bring a lamb with the money. "This lamb shall be an olah-offering," and it became blemished, if he wishes he may bring a ram with its money. Rebbi prohibits [it].*

[The same reasoning explained above in regard to replacing a single animal with two smaller ones, or vice versa, applies to the exchange of one type of animal for another, as long as they are of equal value.] The same would apply to an ox exchanged for another animal; the mishnah specifies ram and lamb because it would be unlikely to find another animal to equal an ox in value (*Tif. Yis.*).

הָאוֹמֵר: „אֶחָד מִכְּבָשַׂי הֶקְדֵּשׁ,״ „וְאֶחָד מִשְּׁוָרַי הֶקְדֵּשׁ״ — הָיוּ לוֹ שְׁנַיִם, הַגָּדוֹל שֶׁבָּהֶן הֶקְדֵּשׁ; — *If one said, "One of my lambs shall be consecrated," [or] "one of my oxen shall be consecrated" — [if] he had two, the larger of them is consecrated.*

1. Expost facto in this context seemingly refers to the consecration of the animals chosen to be offered in lieu of the disqualified offerings. Even if the offering has not yet been slaughtered there will be no further obligation upon the owner of the original offering.

'This ram shall be an *olah-offering*," and it became blemished, if he wishes he may bring a lamb with the money. "This lamb shall be an *olah-offering*," and it became blemished, if he wishes he may bring a ram with its money. Rebbi prohibits [it].

If one said, "One of my lambs shall be consecrated," [or] "one of my oxen shall be consecrated" — [if] he had two, the larger of them is consecrated. [If he had] three, the middle one of them is consecrated.

**YAD AVRAHAM**

When someone donates an offering the assumption is that he does so generously. Therefore, if his vow does not specify which of two animals should be consecrated, it is assumed that he intended the larger one (*Gem.* 108b).

[The concept that a person is assumed to donate generously refers only to animals of the same species and age category. When there is a question as to which category, species, or amount was meant, the first seven mishnayos of this chapter have already established the principle that the person is obligated to bring only the least expensive offering.]

.שְׁלֹשָׁה, הַבֵּינוֹנִי שֶׁבָּהֶן הֶקְדֵּשׁ — *[If he had] three, the middle one of them is consecrated.*

If he owned three animals and declared that one be consecrated, the middle one is also consecrated [in addition to the largest]. This consecration, however, is not a definite one, but only a possible one — i.e., there is a doubt whether the one he meant to consecrate is the middle one or the largest one. Accordingly, both animals must be treated as possibly consecrated. The reason for this is that it is uncertain in such a case whether his generosity extends only to offering better than his smallest or whether it extends even to his largest.

However, in this case it is not necessary for him to offer both, because there is a possibility of resolving this situation in the following manner with just one offering. He should allow both animals to graze until the middle one becomes blemished. If that occurs, he may then redeem it with the larger one and thereby permit the smaller one. The reason for this is that if the middle one was the one really consecrated, the larger one was *not* holy and it can therefore be used to redeem the blemished middle one. This redemption relieves the middle one of its sanctity and transfers it to the large one. On the other hand, if the large one was the one originally consecrated, the middle one was *never* holy and does not really need redemption. Thus, regardless of the truth of the original situation, once the middle one becomes blemished and the large one is used to redeem it, the large one is now the only consecrated animal and the middle one is now *chullin*. The large one is therefore offered as a sacrifice, and the middle one becomes permitted for use. However, since only a blemished offering may be redeemed, until the middle one becomes blemished, both oxen are prohibited for private benefit, due to the doubt as

# „פֵּרַשְׁתִּי, וְאֵינִי יוֹדֵעַ מַה פֵּרַשְׁתִּי," אוֹ שֶׁאָמַר: „אָמַר לִי אַבָּא, וְאֵינִי יוֹדֵעַ מָה" — הַגָּדוֹל שֶׁבָּהֶן הֶקְדֵּשׁ.

**ר' עובדיה מברטנורא**

**פירשתי.** איזה מהן ולא ידעתי איזה הוא: **או שאמר לי אבא.** בשעת מיתתו, אחד משורי הפרשתי להקדש ואיני יודע על איזה מהן אמר לי: **הגדול שבהן הקדש.** דהיכא דאמר פירשתי ליכא ספיקא דודאי הגדול פירש:

**יד אברהם**

to which one is consecrated (*Rav* from *Gem.* 108b).

If the larger one becomes blemished, the same method can be employed; in this case, however, additional money will have to be added to the redemption to cover the excess value of the larger ox over the medium one (*Tos. Yom Tov*).

Normally, it would be prohibited to delay the offering of a vowed sacrifice in this manner. However, in this case, there is no viable alternative, since to offer the one which was not consecrated would be prohibited, and he is not obligated to offer a second animal in order to facilitate the offering of the first one (*Tif. Yis.*).

„פֵּרַשְׁתִּי, וְאֵינִי יוֹדֵעַ מַה פֵּרַשְׁתִּי," אוֹ שֶׁאָמַר: „אָמַר לִי אַבָּא, וְאֵינִי יוֹדֵעַ מָה" — הַגָּדוֹל שֶׁבָּהֶן הֶקְדֵּשׁ. — *[If he said,] "I specified, but I do not know which I specified," or he said, "My father told me, but I do not know which" — the largest of them is consecrated.*

If he remembers having specified one of the animals, or his father had made the vow and specified one of them, and he does not know which was specified, it is assumed that he specified the largest — since the verse (*Deut.* 12:11) uses the phrase *the best of your vows* (*Rav*).

Only where the consecration was unspecified, as in the previous case where he said merely, *"One of my oxen shall be consecrated,"* is there uncertainty whether the middle one was also included in the consecration. Where there was specification we can assume that the biggest one was singled out for explicit mention (*Aruch HaShulchan HeAsid* 94:26; cf. *Tif. Yis.*).

This ruling is puzzling. Why is there more reason to assume that the person who specified would choose a better animal than the person who did not specify would have chosen?

*Sfas Emes* conjectures that by saying, "*one* of my oxen," and not clearly identifying the best one, the person gives some slight indication that perhaps he did not mean the very best one. The principle that one who consecrates does so generously can only be used to show that he did not mean the worst, but not that he meant the very best, as explained above. Since the language of his vow does not conclusively demonstrate an intention to offer the very best one, it cannot obligate him to do so.

In this latter case, however, he did specify but he no longer remembers what he specified. Since it is certainly proper to donate the choicest animal, and there is no indication to the contrary, the assumption may be made that this is indeed the one that was consecrated.

[However, *Rambam's* paraphrase of this mishnah (*Maaseh HaKorbanos* 16:9) indicates that he understood this ruling as referring to a *neder* vow taking on a personal obligation to bring an offering ["I take upon myself to bring . . ."], and not a *nedavah* one involving an actual consecration.

13
9 [If he said,] "I specified, but I do not know which I specified," or he said, "My father told me, but I do not know which" — the largest of them is consecrated.

### YAD AVRAHAM

The mishnah's ruling establishes that the vow is definitely fulfilled by bringing the biggest animal; thus it reflects the view of the Sages (mishnah 8) that if one vowed to bring a small animal but brought a big one instead, he has discharged his vow. Therefore, it may be that in a case in which the consecration of a specific animal did take place, and it is not known now which animal, the middle one is also in doubt.]

## 10.

Before the great *Kohen Gadol* Shimon HaTzaddik[1] died, he dictated that his younger son, Chonyo (Onias), should succeed him as *Kohen Gadol*. Chonyo deferred to his elder brother, Shimmi, and allowed him to assume that position, but subsequently became jealous and regretted his decision. At that point, Chonyo instructed his brother [who was apparently ignorant] to wear some pieces of women's clothing with his priestly vestments when he began to perform the *avodah* of the *Kohen Gadol*. When Shimmi complied, Chonyo went to the other *Kohanim* and informed them that Shimmi had promised a woman to wear some of her clothing when he performed the *avodah* and was now fulfilling that pledge. Shimmi defended his actions and explained what had transpired, and the *Kohanim* sought to kill Chonyo for his misdeed. Chonyo escaped to Alexandria, where he erected a temple and offered sacrifices. This became known as the *Temple of Chonyo*; it lasted approximately two hundred years[2] (*Rav* from *Gem.* 109b).

The *Gemara* (109b) records a Tannaitic dispute whether the Temple of Chonyo was dedicated to the service of *Hashem* or idolatry. R' Meir states that it was idolatrous, while R' Yehudah maintains that it was not.[3] Nevertheless,

1. Shimon HaTzaddik was one of the last of the אַנְשֵׁי כְּנֶסֶת הַגְּדוֹלָה, *Men of the Great Assembly*, the Great Sanhedrin which flourished in the early years of the Second Temple, among whom were the last of the prophets. This body was responsible for strengthening Jewish life and practice in the beginning of the Second Temple era (see *Pirkei Avos* 1:1-2). He served as *Kohen Gadol* for forty years (*Gem.* 109b). It is assumed that he died c. 3490 (see *Doros HaRishonim* vol. 1, pp. 196-7).

2. The figure "two hundred years" appears only in the prevalent translations of *Rambam Comm.*; the more authoritative Kafich edition reads "hundreds of years." The Jewish historian Josephus Flavius, who was an eyewitness to the Destruction of the Holy Temple in Jerusalem, reports that the Temple in Alexandria was destroyed shortly after the destruction of the Holy Temple (c. 3833; Ch. 13 *Wars* 8:10:2). This would mean that it stood throughout most of the Second Temple period, close to four hundred years.

3. There is a dispute among the commentators as to the nature of the sacrifices which were brought in the Temple of Chonyo according to this opinion. Some say that Chonyo taught the non-Jews of Alexandria to sacrifice to God, but Jews did not themselves bring offerings there, due to the prohibition to sacrifice to the Almighty outside the Temple in Jerusalem (*Tos.*). *Rambam* (*Comm.*) states that Chonyo did transgress this interdiction by offering sacrifices himself. Furthermore, he influenced the Coptic population (see Kafich

[י] „הֲרֵי עָלַי עוֹלָה,” יַקְרִיבֶנָּה בַּמִּקְדָּשׁ, וְאִם הִקְרִיבָהּ בְּבֵית חוֹנְיוֹ לֹא יָצָא. „שֶׁאַקְרִיבֶנָּה בְּבֵית חוֹנְיוֹ,” יַקְרִיבֶנָּה בַּמִּקְדָּשׁ, וְאִם הִקְרִיבָהּ בְּבֵית חוֹנְיוֹ יָצָא. רַבִּי שִׁמְעוֹן אוֹמֵר: אֵין זוֹ עוֹלָה.

„הֲרֵינִי נָזִיר,” יְגַלַּח בַּמִּקְדָּשׁ, וְאִם גִּלַּח בְּבֵית חוֹנְיוֹ לֹא יָצָא. „שֶׁאֲגַלַּח בְּבֵית חוֹנְיוֹ,”

**ר' עובדיה מברטנורא**

(י) **בית חוניו.** בית המקדש שבנה חוניו בנו של שמעון הצדיק באלכסנדריא של מצרים, שכשמת שמעון הצדיק אמר להם, חוניו בני ישמש תחתי, מפני שהיה בקי ורגיל בעבודה יותר משמעי אחיו, ולא קבל עליו חוניו להיות כהן גדול לפי שהיה שמעי אחיו גדול ממנו שתי שנים ומחצה, ונתמנה שמעי כהן גדול תחת אביו, לימים נתקנא חוניו בשמעי אחיו, אמר לו בא ואלמדך סדר עבודה, הלבישו כתונת בד דקה שלובשות הנשים על בשרן ועליה אזור צר קטן והעמידו אצל המזבח, יצא ואמר לאחיו הכהנים ראו מה נדר זה וקיים לאהובתו, אותו היום שאתמנה לכהן גדול אלבש כתונת שליכי ואחגור באזור שליכי, בקשו אחיו הכהנים להרגו, סח להם כל המאורע, בקשו להרוג את חוניו, רץ מפניהם לבית המלך, ועדיין כל הרואה אותו אומר זה הוא, הלך לו לאלכסנדריא של מצרים שהיו בה רבבות מישראל, ועשה שם מקדש ובנה מזבח והעלה עליו לשם ה', ועל אותו מזבח נתנבא ישעיה [יט, יט] ביום ההוא יהיה מזבח לה' בתוך ארץ מצרים, ועמד הבית ההוא קרוב למאתים שנה ונקרא בית חוניו על שמו, והכל מודים שהקרבנות שהיו קרבים שם אינן קרבן, לפיכך מי שאמר הרי עלי עולה והקריבה שם, לא יצא ידי נדרו: **שאקריבנה בבית חוניו.** נעשה כאומר הרי עלי עולה על מנת שאהרגנה ולא אתחייב באחריותה, הלכך אם הקריבה בבית חוניו יצא ידי נדרו אבל חייב כרת משום שוחט בחוץ, שהרי קרא עליה שם עולה: **רבי שמעון אומר אין זו עולה.** והרי היא חולין גמורים, שאין שם הקדש חל עליה כלל כשאמר שאקריבנה בבית חוניו. ואין הלכה כרבי שמעון: **ואם גלח בבית חוניו לא יצא.** אלא יחזור ויגלח במקדש בירושלים, ושם יביא קרבנותיו:

**יד אברהם**

even R' Yehudah agrees that it was forbidden to offer a sacrifice there, since once the Temple was built in Jerusalem, it became permanently forbidden to offer sacrifices outside it (*Tos.* 109b, s.v. והעלה, based on *Zevachim* 14:8).

„הֲרֵי עָלַי עוֹלָה,” יַקְרִיבֶנָּה בַּמִּקְדָּשׁ, וְאִם הִקְרִיבָהּ בְּבֵית חוֹנְיוֹ לֹא יָצָא. — *[If one said,] "I take upon myself [to bring] an olah-offering," he must offer it in the Holy Temple, and if he offered it in the Temple of Chonyo he has not fulfilled his obligation.*

If someone vowed to bring an *olah*, it is understood that he means to offer it in the Holy Temple in Jerusalem, since an offering is valid only there. Therefore, if he offered it

ed.) of Egypt to offer sacrifices to *Hashem*, thereby fulfilling *Isaiah's* prophecy (*Isaiah* 19:19): *On that day there will be an Altar to HASHEM in the land of Egypt* . . . [However, in general, the Jewish population of Alexandria did not sacrifice there even according to this view.] See also *Tif. Yis.*.

**10.** [If one said,] "I take upon myself [to bring] an *olah*-offering," he must offer it in the Holy Temple, and if he offered it in the Temple of Chonyo he has not fulfilled his obligation. "That I shall offer it in the Temple of Chonyo," he should offer it in the Holy Temple, but if he offered it in the Temple of Chonyo he has fulfilled his obligation. R' Shimon says: This is not an *olah*-offering.

[If one said,] "I am a *nazir*," he must shave in the Holy Temple, and if he shaved in the Temple of Chonyo he has not fulfilled his obligation. "That I shall shave in the Temple of Chonyo,"

YAD AVRAHAM

in the Temple of Chonyo he has not fulfilled his vow (*Rav*). In addition, having designated it as an *olah*, he is liable to *kares* for having brought an offering outside the Temple (*Tif. Yis. from Zevachim* 13:1).

„שֶׁאַקְרִיבֶנָּה בְּבֵית חוֹנְיוֹ," יַקְרִיבֶנָּה בַּמִּקְדָּשׁ, וְאִם הִקְרִיבָהּ בְּבֵית חוֹנְיוֹ יָצָא. — *"That I shall offer it in the Temple of Chonyo," he should offer it in the Holy Temple, but if he offered it in the Temple of Chonyo he has fulfilled his obligation.*

If he specified that he intends to offer his *olah* in the Temple in Alexandria, it is tantamount to vowing to bring an *olah* with the stipulation that he have the right to kill it without being responsible to replace it. If he wishes to fulfill his vow correctly, he must offer the sacrifice in the Temple in Jerusalem (*Zevach Todah*) [since it was legitimately designated as a sacrifice to *Hashem*]. However, if he actually offers it in the Temple of Chonyo, he is no longer bound by his vow [since offering it there is tantamount to killing it wantonly]. Nevertheless, he is liable to *kares* for having brought an offering outside the Temple (*Rav* from *Gem.* 109a).

רַבִּי שִׁמְעוֹן אוֹמֵר: אֵין זוֹ עוֹלָה. — *R' Shimon says: This is not an olah-offering.*

R' Shimon maintains that when one stipulates in his vow that the offering may be offered in the Temple of Chonyo [he has negated the vow, and] an animal consecrated in this manner does not assume any sanctity whatsoever (*Rav*).

The halachah does not follow the view of R' Shimon (*Rav; Rambam, Maaseh HaKorbanos* 14:7).

„הֲרֵינִי נָזִיר," יְגַלַּח בַּמִּקְדָּשׁ, וְאִם גִּלַּח בְּבֵית חוֹנְיוֹ לֹא יָצָא. — *[If one said,] "I am a nazir," he must shave in the Holy Temple, and if he shaved in the Temple of Chonyo he has not fulfilled his obligation.*

[A *nazir* is someone who takes upon himself a vow which requires him to abstain from wine and grape products, from cutting his hair, and from coming into contact with the dead. Taking this vow does not involve listing the various abstentions; rather, by stating, "I am a *nazir*," a

# יְגַלַּח בַּמִּקְדָּשׁ, וְאִם גִּלַּח בְּבֵית חוֹנְיוֹ יָצָא. רַבִּי שִׁמְעוֹן אוֹמֵר: אֵין זֶה נָזִיר.

# הַכֹּהֲנִים שֶׁשִּׁמְּשׁוּ בְּבֵית חוֹנְיוֹ לֹא יְשַׁמְּשׁוּ

### ר׳ עובדיה מברטנורא

**שאגלח בבית חוניו אם גלח בבית חוניו יצא.** דהאי גברא שנדר בנזיר כדי שיגלח בבית חוניו, לנטורי נפשיה נתכוין, ומפני שהיה קרוב לבית חוניו ורחוק מארץ ישראל, אמר אי סגיא בבית חוניו טרחנא, טפי לא מצינא לאנטורי, ולא חל שם נזירות עליו, אבל נעשה כמי שנשבע שלא לשתות יין עד זמן פלוני: **רבי שמעון אומר.** אינו נזיר כלל ומותר לשתות יין. ואין הלכה כרבי שמעון:

### יד אברהם

legal state (called *nezirus*) is created in which the person automatically becomes subject to all the restrictions and requirements set forth by the Torah for a *nazir*.] Among these is the requirement that when he completes his *nazir* vow — generally after thirty days — he must shave his hair at the entrance to the Temple and burn it on the fire over which he cooks the meat of the *shelamim* he must bring (*Num.* 6:17). If he shaved and burned his hair in the Temple of Chonyo, he has not fulfilled this requirement and he must repeat the process in the Temple in Jerusalem (*Rav*).

**,,שֶׁאֲגַלַּח בְּבֵית חוֹנְיוֹ," יְגַלַּח בַּמִּקְדָּשׁ, וְאִם גִּלַּח בְּבֵית חוֹנְיוֹ יָצָא.** — *"That I shall shave in the Temple of Chonyo," he should shave in the Holy Temple, but if he shaved in the Temple of Chonyo he has fulfilled his obligation.*

If he stipulated at the time of his vow that upon its completion he be permitted to shave his hair in the Temple of Chonyo, he has no further obligation should he do so.

The *Gemara* states that this applies only to one who lived closer to Alexandria than to Jerusalem. The intent behind his stipulation is understood to be that he wishes to undergo the restrictions of the *nazir* but is not willing to be bound to travel the greater distance to Jerusalem in order to bring the necessary offerings (*Rav* from *Gem*. 109a). Therefore, his vow is construed to be a general vow to abstain from certain things but not really a vow of *nezirus*. As such, its fulfillment is not ruled by the procedure set forth in the Torah for the completion of a *nazir's* vow. Accordingly, the fulfillment of the vow depends exclusively upon the stipulation made by the vower. Since he expressed his desire to shave his hair in the Temple of Chonyo, his vow is considered fulfilled once he does so (*Rav*; see *Tif. Yis.*).

It follows from this that the mishnah's statement that his shaving take place in Jerusalem means only that if he wishes to do so he may, and he is not required to shave in the Temple of Chonyo. Although shaving in Jerusalem involves bringing the associated offerings of the concluding *nazir*, this would not constitute bringing a non-consecrated offering in the Temple [which is prohibited], because if he actually does bring it to Jerusalem he thereby indicates that his intention from the very beginning was for a true vow of *nezirus* (*Zevach Todah*).

The mishnah states in *Nazir* (4:2) that if someone vows to be a *nazir* but stipulates that he be permitted to drink wine, the vow takes effect and the stipulation is null,

13
10

he should shave in the Holy Temple, but if he shaved in the Temple of Chonyo he has fulfilled his obligation. R' Shimon says: This is not a *nazir*.

The *Kohanim* who served in the Temple of Chonyo may not serve in the Holy Temple in



because a stipulation to transgress the laws of the Torah has no validity. In this case, however, he thought that it is permissible to bring the offering in the Temple of Chonyo; his stipulation is thus not meant to transgress Torah law and it therefore takes effect (*Tos.* to *Kesubos* 56a).

Above, it was explained that the vow to offer an *olah* in the Temple of Chonyo is construed as a true *olah* vow, albeit with a stipulation that he not be responsible to replace it if he kills it. The *nazir* vow cannot be interpreted in this manner. If it were, we would have to view the person as a bona fide *nazir*, and understand his stipulation to shave his hair in the Temple of Chonyo — ostensibly an invalid act — as a condition that he not be required to undergo the procedure prescribed by the Torah for completing his term of *nezirus*. This would obviously be an invalid stipulation, since one cannot impose a condition which would circumvent Torah law (*Tos. Yom Tov* from *Gem.* 109a). [Since his vow can not be valid in any other way, we construe it to mean a general vow to abstain from things prohibited to a *nazir*, but not an actual acceptance of the state of *nezirus.*]

.רַבִּי שִׁמְעוֹן אוֹמֵר: אֵין זֶה נָזִיר — *R' Shimon says: This is not a nazir.*

R' Shimon contends that such a vow has no legitimacy, and the vower does not even become obligated to comply with the restrictions of a *nazir* (*Rav*).

The halachah follows the view of the *Tanna Kamma* (*Rav; Rambam* loc. cit.).

הַכֹּהֲנִים שֶׁשִּׁמְּשׁוּ בְּבֵית חוֹנְיוֹ לֹא יְשַׁמְּשׁוּ בַּמִּקְדָּשׁ בִּירוּשָׁלַיִם, — *The Kohanim who served in the Temple of Chonyo may not serve in the Holy Temple in Jerusalem,*

[Once a *Kohen* has desecrated his sanctity by serving in the Temple of Chonyo, he may no longer perform the *avodah* in the Temple.]

This restriction applies only if he performed *avodos* which are restricted to *Kohanim*. If he merely slaughtered sacrifices in Alexandria, he is not thereby disqualified from fulfilling his function in the Temple, because the actual slaughtering of a sacrifice is a service that can be performed even by a *non-Kohen* (*Gem.* 109a).

The *Gemara* cites a dispute concerning this matter. R' Sheshes contends that the distinction between slaughter and other *avodos* applies only to one who transgressed the prohibition against serving in the Temple of Chonyo inadvertently [i.e., without realizing it was prohibited]. In such a case he is disqualified only from performing those rites which are restricted to *Kohanim*. However, if he did so purposely, he is disqualified even if he only slaughtered sacrifices there. R' Nachman maintains that one who transgresses inadvertently is never disqualified from serving in the Temple. Only one who does so intentionally is disqualified, and even then only if he did the actual service of *Kohanim*. The halachah follows the view of R' Sheshes (*Rambam, Hil. Bias Mikdash* 9:13).

בַּמִּקְדָּשׁ בִּירוּשָׁלַיִם, וְאֵין צָרִיךְ לוֹמַר לְדָבָר אַחֵר, שֶׁנֶּאֱמַר: „אַךְ לֹא יַעֲלוּ כֹּהֲנֵי הַבָּמוֹת עַל מִזְבַּח ה׳ בִּירוּשָׁלָיִם, כִּי אִם אָכְלוּ מַצּוֹת בְּתוֹךְ אֲחֵיהֶם.״ הֲרֵי הֵם כְּבַעֲלֵי מוּמִין: חוֹלְקִין וְאוֹכְלִין, אֲבָל לֹא מַקְרִיבִין.

[יא] **נֶאֱמַר** בְּעוֹלַת הַבְּהֵמָה: „אִשֵּׁה רֵיחַ נִיחוֹחַ,״ וּבְעוֹלַת הָעוֹף: „אִשֵּׁה רֵיחַ נִיחוֹחַ,״ וּבַמִּנְחָה: „אִשֵּׁה רֵיחַ נִיחוֹחַ.״ לְלַמֵּד שֶׁאֶחָד הַמַּרְבֶּה וְאֶחָד הַמַּמְעִיט, וּבִלְבַד שֶׁיְּכַוֵּן אָדָם אֶת דַּעְתּוֹ לַשָּׁמַיִם.

### ר׳ עובדיה מברטנורא

**ואין צריך לומר לדבר אחר.** אם שמשו לעבודה זרה שלא ישמשו עוד בירושלים: **והרי הן כבעלי מומין.** שחולקים ואוכלים בקדשים:

### יד אברהם

וְאֵין צָרִיךְ לוֹמַר לְדָבָר אַחֵר, — *and certainly if [they served] another thing,*

Certainly if a *Kohen* performed services for idolatry he is thereby disqualified from subsequently serving in the Temple (*Rav*).

The mishnah here indicates that it follows the view of R' Yehudah (cited in the preface) that the Temple of Chonyo was erected to serve *Hashem;* therefore, serving there is not as grave an offense as serving idols. According to R' Meir, however, it was built for idolatry [and serving there is thus the same as any other idol worship] (*Gem.* 109b).

The mishnah refers to idolatry as *another thing* to hint that even if his intention was for another purpose — i.e., his service of the false god was inadvertent — he may no longer serve in the Temple. This is in accordance with the view of R' Sheshes cited above (*Shoshanim LeDavid* cited in margin of Mishnah ed. Vilna).

שֶׁנֶּאֱמַר: „אַךְ לֹא יַעֲלוּ כֹּהֲנֵי הַבָּמוֹת עַל מִזְבַּח ה׳ בִּירוּשָׁלָיִם, כִּי אִם אָכְלוּ מַצּוֹת בְּתוֹךְ אֲחֵיהֶם.״ — *as it is stated (II Kings 23:9): "But the Kohanim of the bamah places would not be allowed to come up to the Altar of HASHEM in Jerusalem; however, they ate matzah among their brothers."*

[Those *Kohanim* who had performed sacrificial service on the *bamos* — the illegal private altars — were disqualified from serving in the Temple, but could nevertheless eat from the consecrated foods along with the other *Kohanim*.]

הֲרֵי הֵם כְּבַעֲלֵי מוּמִין: חוֹלְקִין וְאוֹכְלִין, אֲבָל לֹא מַקְרִיבִין. — *They are like those who are blemished: They share and eat, but do not offer.*

Those who served idolatry are considered similar to *Kohanim* who have physical defects which render them

Jerusalem, and certainly if [they served] another thing, as it is stated (*II Kings* 23:9): *But the Kohanim of the bamah places would not be allowed to come up to the Altar of* HASHEM *in Jerusalem; however, they ate matzah among their brothers.* They are like those who are blemished: They share and eat, but do not offer.

**11.** It is said regarding the animal *olah* (*Lev.* 1:9): *a fire-offering, a pleasing aroma*, and regarding the bird *olah* (*Lev.* 1:17): *a fire-offering, a pleasing aroma,* and regarding the *minchah*-offering (*Lev.* 2:2): *a fire-offering, a pleasing aroma*. This teaches that [there is no difference] between the one who offers much and the one who offers little, as long as he directs his mind to Heaven.

YAD AVRAHAM

disqualified for service in the Temple. These *Kohanim* are nevertheless permitted to partake of the food from the offerings together with the other *Kohanim* (*Rav* from *Zevachim* 12:1).

However, in our times a *Kohen* who served idolatry and then repented is not disqualified from the rites of *Kehunah* — i.e., the priestly benediction and being honored with the first portion when reading the Torah (*Tos.* citing *Rashi*; see *Orach Chaim* 128:37).

11.

נֶאֱמַר בְּעוֹלַת הַבְּהֵמָה: „אִשֵּׁה רֵיחַ נִיחוֹחַ״, — *It is said regarding the animal olah* (*Lev.* 1:9): *"a fire-offering, a pleasing aroma,"*

The Torah describes the animal *olah*-offering as *a fire-offering, a pleasing aroma,* i.e., it is, so to speak, pleasing to God that He commanded and His will was fulfilled (*Rashi* ad loc.; see *Zevachim* 4:6 and *Yad Avraham* comm. there).

וּבְעוֹלַת הָעוֹף: „אִשֵּׁה רֵיחַ נִיחוֹחַ,״ וּבַמִּנְחָה: „אִשֵּׁה רֵיחַ נִיחוֹחַ.״ — *and regarding the bird olah* (*Lev.* 1:17): *"a fire-offering, a pleasing aroma," and regarding the minchah-offering* (*Lev.* 2:2): *"a fire-offering, a pleasing aroma."*

[The Torah describes the less expensive bird *olah*, and the least expensive *minchah*-offering (made of flour), in the same terms that it uses to describe the most expensive animal *olah* — *a fire-offering, a pleasing aroma.*]

לְלַמֵּד שֶׁאֶחָד הַמַּרְבֶּה וְאֶחָד הַמַּמְעִיט, וּבִלְבַד שֶׁיְּכַוֵּן אָדָם אֶת דַּעְתּוֹ לַשָּׁמַיִם. — *This teaches that [there is no difference] between the one who offers much and the one who offers little, as long as he directs his mind to Heaven.*

[In other texts, as well as in the

many places that this mishnah is cited in the *Gemara*, the reading is וּבִלְבַד שֶׁיְּכַוֵּן לִבּוֹ לַשָּׁמַיִם, *as long as one directs his heart to Heaven.*]

The Torah is teaching us that the reward of one who serves God with a small gift is just as great as the reward of one who serves Him with a large gift (see *Rashi*, *Berachos* 17a s.v. שנינו), as long as his heart is directed to Heaven [i.e., that it is his sincere intent to serve God to the best of his ability].

Similarly, the *Gemara* (104b) points out that in contrast to the more expensive animal sacrifices that the Torah describes as being offered by אָדָם, *a person* (*Lev.* 1:2), the inexpensive *minchah*-offering is described as being offered by נֶפֶשׁ, *a soul* (*Lev.* 2:1). That is because a *minchah* is usually offered by a poor person, who cannot afford anything more expensive. Therefore, God accepts the poor man's meager gift and considers it as if he has offered up his very soul.

This mishnah does not mean that the monetary value of one's offering or the degree of one's service is of no consequence. Rather, the mishnah is teaching that the value of one's service cannot be measured in absolute terms but is relative to his circumstances. A poor man who strains himself to scrape together a meager offering is as beloved before God as the wealthy man who expends vast fortunes in His service. The same applies for all areas of Torah and *mitzvos*. It is the effort and devotion that counts (see *Tos. Yom Tov* to *Avos* 2:16).

Even if the wealthy man's intent in his extensive service is also sincere and devout, God values the sincere efforts of the poor man who can do no more just as much (*Magen Avraham* 1:6; see also *Taz* there).

# סליק מסכת מנחות

# Appendix I: Techeiles

Twice daily in *Krias Shema*, a Jew recites the *mitzvah* to use a strand of wool dyed with *techeiles* on his *tzitzis*. *Techeiles* is a blue dye produced from the "blood" [i.e., an inky secretion] of a (Mediterranean) sea creature called *chalazon*. However, as is well known, the *mitzvah* of *techeiles* is not practiced nowadays.

It is not clear exactly when Jews stopped fulfilling this *mitzvah*, but there is a consensus that *techeiles* was available during the entire Talmudic era (4260/500 C.E.).

R' Achai Gaon, who lived approximately two and a half centuries after the Talmudic era, does not discuss *techeiles* when he presents *Hilchos Tzitzis* in his *She'iltos D'Rav Achai Gaon*, thereby implying that the *mitzvah* was no longer performed in his days. The obvious reason for the discontinuance of this *mitzvah* was the non-availability of the *techeiles* dye. *Rif* (*Halachos Ketanos*, *Hil. Tzitzis*) remarks: ... וְהָאִידְנָא דְּלֵית לָן תְּכֵלֶת, *And nowadays when we have no techeiles* ... Various reasons have been advanced for the non-availability of the *techeiles*. Some conjecture that the severe persecution of Jewish religious practices in the Byzantine Empire, which ruled Eretz Yisrael and the entire Mediterranean region — the habitat of the *chalazon* — for several centuries, caused the identity of the *chalazon* and the art of producing *techeiles* dye from it to be forgotten. Others add that the Jewish population of Eretz Yisrael dwindled dramatically after the Arab occupation of Eretz Yisrael, and with the passage of time the art of catching the *chalazon* and producing the *techeiles* from its blood — which required special expertise, as stated in *Menachos* (42b, *Rambam Tzitzis* 2:4) — was forgotten. An additional factor was the substitution of other blue dyes for use in the garments of the nobility, thus drastically reducing the theretofore widespread availability of the *techeiles* dye, which had now become limited in use to the *mitzvah* of *tzitzis* alone. Others argue that the *chalazon* was "hidden" by Divine intervention, and point out that the *Midrash* (*Midrash Rabbah* and *Tanchuma* to *Numbers* 15) uses the term נִגְנַז, *was hidden*, in regard to the disappearance of the *techeiles*.

For more than thirteen centuries after the Talmudic era, there is no evidence that any attempt was made to re-establish the use of the *techeiles* dye. Approximately one hundred years ago, however, the renowned *gaon* and chassidic Rebbe, R' Gershon Henoch Leiner, better known as the Radziner Rebbe (author of the encyclopedic *Sidrei Taharos* on the Mishnah *Seder Taharos*), undertook to investigate the feasibility of identifying and finding the *chalazon*, and extracting and producing the *techeiles* dye. He printed his findings in a small work called *Maamar Sefunei Temunei Chol* (Warsaw 5647). In this work he concluded that the *chalazon* had not been "hidden" by Divine decree, and proceeded to piece together a composite description of the *chalazon*

and the color of the *techeiles* dye. He then set out for Italy and spent the better part of a year at the world-famous aquarium in Naples in order to study the various Mediterranean sea creatures housed there in surroundings simulating their respective native habitats. He found there that the cuttlefish (*Sepia Officinialis*) fitted, with some modification, the description he had developed in *Sefunei Temunei Chol*. He returned to Poland with a substantial amount of this creature's "blood," and published his new findings in *Maamar Pessil Techeiles* (Warsaw 5648). He then set about devising a method to produce a *techeiles* dye from the "blood" and the procedure for dyeing *tzitzis* from it. By the beginning of the year 5650, the procedure was already well established and the Rebbe began to produce *techeiles* for the public's use. As a result (in the Rebbe's words): "With G-d's help, many thousands of Jews use *techeiles* in their *tzitzis*."

The response to the Radziner Rebbe's bold innovation was mixed. While thousands accepted the *techeiles*, the leading halachic authorities of the age were cautious and ambivalent. None of the leading sages of the age endorsed the *techeiles* explicitly; the revered *gaon* R' Yehoshua of Kutna wrote a response outlining his cautious and carefully worded reservations about the matter, and expressed his opinion that it was not advisable to accept the Radziner Rebbe's *techeiles*. He did, however, qualify his comments with the statement that he could not aver with certitude that the new dye was not the true *techeiles*, and added that the Rebbe's innovation was possibly a harbinger of the messianic age (*She'eilos U'Teshuvos Yeshuos Malko, Orach Chaim* §2). Neither did any of the leading chassidic rebbes of the generation endorse the *techeiles*; of all the chassidic circles, only the Breslover chassidim accepted the *techeiles*. However, some authorities, notably the famed *posek* R' Shalom Mordechai Schwadron (*Maharsham*) of Brezan, secretly used *techeiles* in a *tallis kattan* worn beneath their garments. In fact, the *Maharsham* left instruction in his will that he be buried with the *tallis kattan* which had *techeiles*.

Many rank-and-file scholars made known to the Rebbe their reservations about the *techeiles*. R' Gershon Henoch wrote another work, *Ein HaTecheles* (printed posthumously, Warsaw 5651), in which he responded vigorously to the criticisms addressed to him. R' Hillel Moshe Meshl Gelbstein of Jerusalem published a sharp rejection of the Rebbe's *techeiles* in a pamphlet entitled *Pessil Techeiles* (printed together with *Or LaYesharim*, Jerusalem 5651; later in his *Mishkanos LaAvir Yaakov* v. 2, Jerusalem 5654). See also *Aruch HaShulchan, Orach Chaim* 8:12. For a thorough understanding of the problems associated with the "Radziner *techeiles*," see the Rebbe's three works on the subject. Recently R' Menachem Burstein has written a thorough and exhaustive study of this subject entitled *HaTecheiles* (*Jerusalem* 5748).

# Appendix II: Chadash

Recent years have seen a renewed popular interest in observing the laws of *chadash* in the Diaspora. Yet, for many centuries, it has been the widespread custom of the Diaspora's Jews to rely on various permits which assert that these laws do not apply to their situation. The following aims to provide a very brief survey of some of the issues involved.

The Mishnah (*Kiddushin* 1:9) records a difference of opinion among the *Tannaim*. The *Tanna Kamma* holds that *chadash* does not differ from any of the other *mitzvos* which "depend on land" (e.g., *terumah* and *maaser*). Just as all *mitzvos* in this category apply only to Eretz Yisrael but not "outside of the Land," so too does *chadash* not apply to grain grown outside of Eretz Yisrael. R' Eliezer, however, maintains that *chadash* is an exception to the rule and that it does indeed apply to grain grown outside of Eretz Yisrael. Elsewhere (*Orlah* 3:9), however, the Mishnah records R' Eliezer's view anonymously. Because of this anonymous statetment (*stam mishnah*), virtually all of the *Poskim* (see *Rif; Rambam, Maachalos Asuros* 10:2; *Rosh; Shulchan Aruch, Orach Chaim* 489:10, *Yoreh Deah* 293:3) accept R' Eliezer's opinion as the halachah. However, it seems that even in the days of the *Rishonim*, the prohibition of *chadash* was not widely observed in the Diaspora, at least not in Germany and France. The *Poskim* advance many reasons for this lenient practice in regard to *chadash*. Some of the main points are briefly summarized here:

1) One is permitted to assume that any given grain has taken root before Pesach, and that the *chadash* prohibition has therefore already been lifted. There are two halachic reasons for making this assumption: a) Most grain is planted before the day of the *omer*. b) There exists a multiple doubt (סְפֵק סְפֵיקָא) regarding the applicability of *chadash* to any grain, since the grain may in fact be from the previous year's crop; and even if it is from the new crop, it may have been planted (and have taken root) before the *omer* (see *Mordechai* to *Kiddushin* #501, *Teshuvos HaRosh* 2:1, *Tur, Yoreh Deah* 293, *Rama* in *Shulchan Aruch*, there).

2) It may be that *chadash* is not applicable to grain grown in a non-Jew's field (at any rate, if his field is outside Eretz Yisrael) (*Bach* to *Yoreh Deah* 293; cf. *Tos.* to *Kiddushin* 36b, s.v. כל).

3) The prohibition against *chadash* outside of Eretz Yisrael may be Rabbinical in origin (see *Menachos* 68b). Therefore, the prohibition could be considered comparable to the Rabbinic obligation to separate *terumah* and *maasros* which applied during the era of the *Tannaim* and *Amoraim* only in the lands near Eretz Yisrael, but not to the more distant lands (*R' Baruch* cited in *Teshuvos HaRosh* 2:1; in regard to *terumah*, see *Tos.* to *Kiddushin* 36b s.v. כל).

For a further discussion of this point see *Magen Avraham* 489:9 and *Beur HaGra, Yoreh Deah* 293:2; see also *Aruch HaShulchan, Yoreh Deah* 293:1-21. The question of *chadash* outside of Eretz Yisrael is also discussed at great length by *Pnei Yehoshua* in an appendix to his novellae on *Kiddushin*, *Shaagas Aryeh HaChadash*, and R' Aryeh Leib Tzuntz in *Shein Chadash* (printed together with his *Magen HaElef*).

# Glossary

**altar:** any raised platform made for the purpose of burning offerings.

**Altar, golden:** see **Altar, inner**.

**Altar, incense:** see **Altar, inner.**

**Altar, inner:** a 1x1x1-cubit gold-covered Altar which stands in the Holy. It is used for the daily incense service, and for the blood applications of **inner chataos**.

**Altar, outer:** the big Altar, 32x32x10 cubits, built of stone, which stands in the Temple Courtyard. This is the Altar on which the blood of all offerings (except **inner chataos**) is applied, on which all **libations** are poured, and on which the burning of the **emurin** of all offerings and the **limbs** of **olah**-offerings takes place.

**aninus:** the state of being an **onein**.

**Antechamber:** a high chamber which fronted the Temple edifice.

**asham:** *guilt-offering*; an offering brought to atone for a group of specific sins and for the purification of a **metzora** (see *Zevachim* 5:5).

**av hatumah:** an object possessing a degree of **tumah** sufficient to contaminate a person or utensil. Usually an *av hatumah* is one of the persons or substances which are the ultimate sources of *tumah*, such as **neveilah, metzora**, et al.

**avodah** [pl., **avodos**]**:** the sacrificial service or any facet of it.

**bamah:** private altar built outside the Temple. During certain periods of history these were permitted (see *Zevachim* 14:4-8).

**Baraisa:** statement of the **Tannaim** not included in the Mishnah.

**base:** a steplike ledge which circled the **outer Altar** at ground level, one cubit high and one cubit wide. The remainder of the blood of all offerings was poured out upon the base, from where it drained into a channel and flowed out of the **Courtyard**.

**bechor:** (a) firstborn male; (b) firstborn offering. The firstborn of cattle, sheep, and goats is automatically consecrated to be an offering (see *Zevachim* 5:8).

**bikkurim:** the first-fruit offering (see 10:6).

**blood avodos:** those **avodos** in an animal or bird offering performed with its blood. They consist of **shechitah, kabbalah, holachah**, and **zerikah**.

**chadash:** the prohibition of the year's new crop of grain prior to the offering of the **omer** (10:7).

**chalal:** a **Kohen** whose genealogy has been tainted by descent from a union not permitted to **Kohanim**.

**challah** [pl., **challos**]**:** (a) one of the two types of oven-baked **minchah**-offerings (see mishnah 5:9). (b) the portion which is removed from a bread dough and given to a *Kohen*. The dough must be made from flour equal in volume to at least 43.2 eggs — one **issaron**.

**chametz:** leavened bread; in contrast to **matzah.**

**chatas** [pl., **chataos**]: *sin-offering*; an offering generally brought in atonement for the inadvertent transgression of a **kares**-bearing sin. There are two types of *chatas* — inner and outer. The **inner chatas'** blood is applied to areas of the **Sanctuary** and the **inner Altar**, while the blood of the **outer chatas** is applied to the **outer Altar**.

**chullin:** any substance which has not been consecrated.

**conveying:** see **holachah.**

**Courtyard:** see **Temple Courtyard**.

**Curtain:** the curtain [פָּרֹכֶת, *paroches*] which in the Second Temple separated the **Holy** from the **Holy of Holies.**

**emurin:** the parts separated from every animal offering for burning upon the Altar. The *emurin* are comprised mainly of the hard fats, kidneys, and part of the liver.

**ephah:** a Biblical dry measure (see comm. 7:1); see **issaron**.

**essronim, essronos:** plural of **issaron.**

**Gemara:** the section of the Talmud that explains the Mishnah.

**gezeirah shavah:** one of the thirteen hermeneutic rules of Biblical exegesis, which allows halachic analogies to be drawn between different laws, based on identical or similar terms stated in the respective Biblical passages dealing with them. Only terms which are designated for this purpose by the Oral Tradition can serve as the basis for a *gezeirah shavah*.

**gidim:** veins, arteries, or sinews.

**hagalah:** purging a vessel of the absorption in its walls by boiling water in it, or scalding it with boiling water, as required.

**hagashah:** the rite of bringing a *minchah*-offering near to the southwest corner of the Altar before beginning its **avodah** (see 5:5).

**halachah:** (a) a Torah law; (b) in cases of dispute, the position accepted as definitive by the later authorities and followed in practice; (c) the body of Jewish law.

**hekdesh:** a thing consecrated either to the Temple treasury or as an offering.

**hin:** a Biblical liquid measure, equal to twelve **log.**

**holachah:** conveying sacrificial materials to the Altar. This is one of the **avodos**, viz., conveying the blood of an animal offering to the Altar for **zerikah**, or the **kometz** or **emurin** for burning on the Altar.

**Holy:** the Temple edifice is divided into two chambers. The anterior chamber is the Holy, and contains the **shulchan**, **inner Altar,** and **menorah.**

**Holy of Holies:** the inner chamber of the Temple edifice. During most of the First Temple era, it contained the Holy Ark; later it was empty of any utensil. Even the **Kohen Gadol** is prohibited from entering it except on Yom Kippur.

**Holy Temple:** see **Temple.**

**horns of the Altar:** the cubelike protuberances which crown the four corners of both the outer and inner Altars.

**inner chatas:** a **chatas**-offering whose blood is applied in the **Holy** and/or **Holy of Holies.**

**issaron** [pl., **essronim, essronos**]**:** a tenth of an **ephah**; the minimum amount of flour for any **minchah.** It is equal to the volume of 43.2 eggs.

**jealousy minchah:** *minchah* brought as part of the ritual of testing a **sotah** [suspected adulteress] (see comm. 1:1).

**kabbalah:** receiving of the blood; after the animal is slaughtered, the blood is received into a **kli shareis** as it gushes forth from the incision in the animal's neck.

**kal vachomer:** One of thirteen hermeneutic principles, reasoning from a minor premise to a major one; see comm. to *Zevachim* 7:6.

**kares:** Divinely imposed premature death; the penalty decreed by the Torah for certain classes of transgression.

**kav:** a Mishnaic measure (see 7:1).

**kemitzah:** the **avodah** of removing the required amount of flour (or baked substance) from a **minchah** for burning on the Altar.

**ketores:** incense offering burnt each day on the **inner Altar**.

**kezayis:** an olive's volume, lit., *as an olive*. The minimum volume of food for which one is liable for punishment, or to bring an offering in atonement, for violation of a commandment which concerns eating. Also the minimum volume of food with which one fulfills a positive commandment which involves eating; and the minimum amount for which **piggul** takes effect.

**kli shareis** [pl., **klei shareis**]**:** vessel sanctified for use in the Temple service. These have the ability to sanctify substances placed in them.

**kodashim kalim:** *offerings of lesser holiness* — one of the two classifications of sacrificial offerings; these are not subject to the stringencies applied to **kodshei kodashim**.

**kodesh:** (a) any consecrated object; (b) the anterior chamber of the Temple — the Holy; (c) offering parts designated for eating.

**kodshei kodashim:** *most holy offerings* — one of the two classifications of sacrificial offerings; this classification means that these offerings are subject to certain restrictions beyond those which apply to **kodashim kalim**; see *Zevachim* 5:1-5.

**Kohen** [pl., **Kohanim**]**:** a member of the priestly family descended in the male line from Aaron. The *Kohen* is bound by special laws of sanctity decreed by the Torah, as well as accorded the special priestly duties and privileges associated with the Temple.

**Kohen Gadol:** the **Kohen** appointed to serve in the Temple as High Priest. The sanctity laws and priestly duties and privileges accorded him exceed those of an ordinary *Kohen.*

**kometz** [pl., **kematzin**]**:** the amount of flour (or baked substance) which is removed from the *minchah* during the **avodah** of **kemitzah** to be burnt upon the Altar (see 1:2). This is the amount which fits into the cavity formed by the three middle fingers of the *Kohen's* right hand when he folds them over the palm of his hand; see comm. to 1:2.

**lechem hapanim:** [*show bread*] the twelve loaves that the Torah states should be placed on the **shulchan** each Sabbath, where they remain for the entire week. They are baked in a special shape (11:4), and are accompanied on the *shulchan* by **two spoonfuls** of **levonah.**

**levonah:** frankincense; this is placed on top of most *minchah*-offerings and is burnt on the Altar together with its **kometz.** It is also the companion on the **shulchan** of the **lechem hapanim** and is burnt on the Altar each week after being replaced. It is also the substance used for the **ketores** offering, and it may also be brought as an independent offering (13:3).

**libation:** see **nesachim.**

**libation minchah-offering:** see **minchas nesachim.**

**limbs:** referring generally to the limbs of an **olah**-offering. The *olah* is dismembered and its limbs burnt upon the Altar.

**maaser:** (a) tithe of the crop; (b) the tithe-offering. Every year, a tenth of all the new offspring of cattle, sheep, and goats is set aside to be offered in sacrifice (see *Zevachim* 5:8).

**maaser ani:** see **maaser sheni.**

**maaser rishon** [*first tithe*]**:** the tithe which must be taken from the crops of Eretz Yisrael and given to a *Levi.*

**maaser sheni** [second tithe]**:** the tithe taken from the produce of Eretz Yisrael in the first, second, fourth, and fifth years of each seven-year **shemittah** cycle. It must be brought to Jerusalem and eaten there, or else redeemed for money which is then taken to Jerusalem and used to buy food to eat there. In the third and sixth years of the cycle it is replaced by **maaser ani,** the tithe given to the poor.

**machavas:** (a) a griddle used for preparing the **minchas machavas;** (b) the *minchas machavas.*

**marcheshes:** (a) a pan used to prepare the **minchas marcheshes;** (b) the *minchas marcheshes.*

**matir:** (a) an action or **avodah** which renders another substance permissible for consumption or burning upon the Altar; e.g., the act of burning the **kometz** renders the **remainder** of the **minchah** permissible for consumption; the act of **zerikah** renders the meat permissible for eating and the **emurin** for burning upon the Altar (see 4:2); (b) the substance used to render others permissible; e.g., the *kometz* of flour is the *matir* of the remainder; the blood of the offering is the *matir* for the meat and *emurin* (see 4:3).

**matzah:** unleavened bread; any loaf made from dough that has not been allowed to ferment or rise. In the context of **menachos,** it does not necessarily refer to the crackerlike substance known by that name today.

**me'ilah:** unlawful appropriation or use of sacred property or offerings.

**melikah:** the method of slaughter employed for bird offerings. The **Kohen** uses his sharpened thumbnail to cut through the back of the bird's neck.

**menachos:** the plural of **minchah.**

**menorah:** the seven-branched candelabrum which stands in the **Holy**; lighted each day.

**merikah:** a special type of purging (in boiling water) required of utensils in which sacrificial meat was cooked (*Zevachim* 11:17).

**metzora:** a person afflicted with certain skin conditions and discolorations described in *Lev.* Ch. 13. He is thereby rendered **tamei** and upon healing must undergo the purification process outlined in *Lev.* Ch. 14 and bring offerings.

**mikveh:** a body of standing water which is qualified to purify persons immersing themselves in it of their **tumah** contamination. The water may not be drawn but must be gathered by natural means, and it must consist of at least forty **seah** [1 *seah* = appr. 4.5 gal.].

**milluim:** initiation-offerings offered at the time of the erection of the **Mishkan**.

**minchah** [pl., **menachos**]: an offering of flour, generally consisting of fine wheat flour, oil, and frankincense. In certain forms, it is fried or baked before being offered.

**minchah of fine flour:** see **minchas soless.**

**minchas machavas:** one of the two types of fried *minchah*-offerings; it is fried in oil on a flat griddle and is drier than its counterpart, the **minchas marcheshes** (5:8).

**minchas marcheshes:** the other of the two types of fried *minchah*-offerings; it is fried in oil in a pan and therefore has a spongier consistency than the **minchas machavas.**

**minchas nesachim:** a *minchah* which accompanies an animal **olah-** or **shelamim-**offering, as part of a complement consisting of the *minchah* and a wine libation (**nesachim**).

**minchas soless:** a type of *minchah* which is not baked before its **avodah**, but whose **kometz** is removed while it is still flour; also known as the **minchah of fine flour.**

**Mishkan:** the Tabernacle which served as the portable Temple in the Wilderness.

**mitzvah:** a Biblical or Rabbinic precept.

**most holy offerings:** see **kodshei kodashim**.

**nazir:** a person who has bound himself with a vow not to drink wine or eat grapes, cut his hair, or contaminate himself with corpse **tumah**. The period of **nezirus** is concluded by bringing a complement of offerings.

**nazir tamei:** a **nazir** who has been contaminated with corpse **tumah**. He must purify himself, bring offerings, and begin again his period of **nezirus**.

**nedavah:** a donation; a vow which consecrates a specific object to be an offering; see **neder** and comm. to 13:9.

**neder:** a vow; in this volume it refers specifically to a vow obligating a person to bring any kind of offering, without assigning the specific animal, flour, wine, etc., to be used to fulfill this vow; see comm. to 13:9.

**nesachim** [sing., **nesech**]: a libation; wine poured upon the Altar as an offering. There is also a water libation on Succos.

**neveilah:** an animal which has died without benefit of a valid **shechitah**.

**nezirus:** the state of being a **nazir**.

**non-Kohen:** any person not of the seed of Aaron.

**nossar:** the meat or sacrificial parts of an offering which were *left over* beyond the time prescribed for them. These must be burned and they are forbidden for consumption on penalty of **kares**.

**offerings of lesser holiness:** see **kodashim kalim**.

**olah** [*burnt-offering*]: an animal or bird offering which is burnt in its entirety on the Altar, with no part being eaten.

**omer:** the barley *minchah*-offering which is brought on the sixteenth day of Nissan to permit the consumption of the year's new crop of grain (see Ch. 10).

**onein:** a person in a state of mourning on the day of the demise of a close relative; he may not eat of offerings, and if he is a **Kohen**, may not perform the **avodah** (see 2:1).

**par he'elem davar:** the communal **chatas** offered by the Sanhedrin for an erroneous ruling on their part to permit something which is forbidden on penalty of **kares**. It is offered only when the majority of Israel acted on that ruling and thereby transgressed; see *Horayos*. It is an **inner chatas**.

**paroches:** see **Curtain.**

**pesach:** the offering brought on the afternoon of the fourteenth of Nissan; every individual must have a share in one of these offerings. It is eaten at the Seder meal with *matzah* and *maror*.

**piggul:** lit., *abomination*; an offering during whose **avodah** the intention was expressed to eat of it after the time allotted to it (see prefatory section in comm. to mishnah 1:3).

**receiving:** see **kabbalah**

**rekikin:** one of the two types of oven-baked *minchah*-offerings (see mishnah 5:9).

**remainder:** the part of the **minchah** which remains after the **kometz** has been removed. It is eaten by the **Kohanim** once the *kometz* has been burnt on the Altar.

**revuchah**: one of the varieties of breads that accompanies a **todah** and a **nazir's** offering. Its dough is scalded in hot water (see comm. 7:1).

**Rosh Chodesh:** the first day of the Jewish month.

**sacrificial parts:** see **emurin**.

**Sanctuary:** a term applied to the entire Temple edifice, consisting of the **Holy, Holy of Holies,** and **Antechamber.**

**seah:** a Mishnaic measure; 6 **kav**.

**semichah:** the rite of leaning upon the head of an offering prior to its slaughter (5:7).

**shechitah:** the method prescribed by the Torah for killing an animal. It consists of cutting through most of the esophagus and windpipe from the front of the neck with a sharp knife. In regard to animal offerings, it is the first **avodah.**

**shelamim:** *peace-offering*; an offering of lesser holiness, generally brought by an individual on a voluntary basis. Its **emurin** are offered on the Altar, and its meat is eaten by the owner of the offering [and his guests]. See *Zevachim* 5:7.

**shelamim lambs:** the two lambs offered on Shavuos as a communal **shelamim**-offering. These accompanied the **shtei halechem** (2:2, 4:3).

**shemittah:** the Sabbatical year, occurring every seventh year, during which the land of Eretz Yisrael may not be cultivated. Various restrictions also apply to any produce which grows wild; see Tractate *Sheviis.*

**shtei halechem:** the two special loaves brought on Shavuos from the year's new crop of grain. These were accompanied by the two **communal shelamim**.

**shulchan:** the golden table for the *lechem hapanim* which is situated in the **Holy**.

**sinner's minchah:** a *minchah*-offering brought by an impoverished sinner for certain transgressions in lieu of a **chatas** (see comm. 1:1).

**slaughtering:** see **shechitah**

**sotah:** an adulteress or suspected adulteress.

**taharah:** the state of ritual purity, the absence of **tumah** contamination.

**tahor:** a person or object which is in a state of **taharah**.

**tamei:** an object which has been contaminated by **tumah**.

**tamid:** the **daily offering.** Every day two lambs are offered in the Temple, one in the morning and the other in the afternoon.

**Tanna Kamma:** the anonymous first opinion of a mishnah. It is generally assumed to reflect the majority view.

**Tanna** [pl., **Tannaim**]: a Sage quoted in the Mishnah or in other works of that period (e.g., **Baraisa**).

**Temple:** the Beis HaMikdash built in Jerusalem by Solomon for the sacrificial service to *Hashem*.

**Temple Courtyard:** the unroofed Courtyard that surrounds the Temple edifice. All sacrifices are made within the Courtyard, and even the eaten portions of many

offerings may not be removed from there.

**tenufah:** the rite of waving which certain offerings require (see 5:5).

**tereifah:** an animal possessing one of a well-defined group of life-threatening body defects. The defect renders it prohibited for consumption even if slaughtered properly. It is therefore also invalid as an offering.

**terumah:** portion of the crop of Eretz Yisrael which must be separated and given to a **Kohen**. Upon separation it attains a state of sanctity which prohibits its being eaten by a non-*Kohen* or a *Kohen* in a state of **tumah.**

**tevel:** the produce of Eretz Yisael prior to the separation of its **terumah** and **maaser** portions.

**tevul yom:** lit., *one who has immersed today.* A person who has purified himself from **tumah** by immersion in a **mikveh** retains a vestige of his prior *tumah* for the remainder of the day (see 1:2).

**throwing the blood:** see **zerikah.**

**todah:** a type of **shelamim**-offering brought as an expression of thanksgiving. It is accompanied by four varieties of loaves (7:1; see *Zevachim* 5:6).

**tumah:** a legally defined state of contamination [or impurity] inherent in certain people [e.g., a *niddah* (menstruant)] or objects [e.g., a corpse] that under specific conditions can be transmitted to other people or objects. Those in a state of *tumah* are restricted from contact and certain other forms of interactions with sanctified or holy things by a series of intricate and complex laws.

**todah breads:** the four varieties of bread that accompany a **todah**-offering. These are **challos, rekikin, revuchah,** and **chametz.**

**Tosefta:** additional statements of **Tannaim** not recorded in the Mishnah, but later collected and edited by R' Chiya and R' Oshaya; see **Baraisa.**

**two lambs:** see **shelamim lambs.**

**two loaves:** see **shtei halechem.**

**two spoonfuls:** of **levonah**; these accompany the **lechem hapanim.**

**Ulam:** see **Antechamber.**

**zav:** a man who has become **tamei** because of a specific type of seminal emission (see 14:3). If three emissions were experienced, the person must bring offerings.

**zavah:** a woman experiencing an irregular menstruation very closely after her regular cycle. If the menstruation lasts for three consecutive days she must bring offerings.

**zerikah:** throwing or applying the blood of an animal offering to the **Altar.**

This volume is part of
THE ARTSCROLL SERIES®
an ongoing project of
translations, commentaries and expositions
on Scripture, Mishnah, Talmud, Halachah,
liturgy, history, the classic Rabbinic writings,
biographies and thought.

For a brochure of current publications
visit your local Hebrew bookseller
or contact the publisher:

Mesorah Publications, ltd
4401 Second Avenue
Brooklyn, New York 11232
(718) 921-9000
www.artscroll.com

MW01097304